Music and Soviet Power
1917

Marina Frolova-Walker
& Jonathan Walker

THE BOYDELL PRESS

© Marina Frolova-Walker and Jonathan Walker 2012

All Rights Reserved. Except as permitted under current legislation no part of this work may be photocopied, stored in a retrieval system, published, performed in public, adapted, broadcast, transmitted, recorded or reproduced in any form or by any means, without the prior permission of the copyright owner

The right of Marina Frolova-Walker and Jonathan Walker to be identified as the author of this work has been asserted in accordance with sections 77 and 78 of the Copyright, Designs and Patents Act 1988

First published 2012
The Boydell Press, Woodbridge
Paperback edition 2017

ISBN 978 1 84383 703 9 hardback
ISBN 978 1 78327 193 1 paperback

The Boydell Press is an imprint of Boydell & Brewer Ltd
PO Box 9, Woodbridge, Suffolk IP12 3DF, UK
and of Boydell & Brewer Inc.
668 Mt Hope Avenue, Rochester, NY 14620–2731, USA
website: www.boydellandbrewer.com

A CIP catalogue record for this book is available
from the British Library

The publisher has no responsibility for the continued existence or accuracy of URLs for external or third-party internet websites referred to in this book, and does not guarantee that any content on such websites is, or will remain, accurate or appropriate

This publication is printed on acid-free paper

Designed and typeset in Myriad Pro and Warnock Pro by
David Roberts, Pershore, Worcestershire

Printed and bound by TJ International Ltd, Cornwall

Music and Soviet Power
1917–1932

To Alla, Edna, and John

Contents

Preface *ix*
Acknowledgements *xx*
Note on transliteration *xx*
Chronology of Political and Musical Events *xxi*

October 1917–18 Out of Chaos 1

N. Petrov Opera and Its New Audience 13
B. Krasin The Tasks of the Music Section [of Moscow Proletkult] 15
Igor Glebov A Lull 19
'R.' Art and the Proletariat 21

1919 Depression and Fever 23

※ Declaration of the Music Section [of Narkompros] 29
Ant. Dianov Musical Responses 32
Vyacheslav Ivanov On Wagner 34

1920 Bureaucracy on the Rise 37

Andrey Levinson *Petrushka* at the Academy Opera and Ballet Theatre 46
Victor Serge Chaliapin in the Soviet 50

1921 Should I stay or should I go? 54

N. Strelnikov *The Christmas Tree* at the Mikhailovsky Theatre 61
Anatoliy Kankarovich Eyes and Wings: Under the Impression of Scriabin Concerts at the Philharmonia 63
M. Zagorsky Impressions [On Isadora Duncan] 65

1922 Just Like the Old Days? 67

L. Sabaneyev The Revolutionary Years in Music 75
Arseny Avraamov The Symphony of Sirens, and The Baku Experiment 81

1923 The Birth of ASM and RAPM 85

※ On the Romantic *R.S.F.S.R.*: A Conversation with the Composer Ya. Polferov 93
※ The Association of Proletarian Musicians (Composers, Teachers, and Performers) 95
A. Sergeyev A Musical Cul-de-Sac 97

1924 **ASM in the Ascendant** 100

A. Sergeyev Those on the Other Side 113
'Communist' Diatribes 116
※ A Statement by a Group of Moscow State Conservatoire Professors 118
N. Malkov *The Struggle for the Commune*, or The Exploded Bomb 120
Igor Glebov Composers! Keep up! 124
※ Ideological Platform of the Russian Association of Proletarian Musicians 128

1925 **Equilibrium** 132

N. Malkov *For Red Petrograd* 143
V. Blyum Foxtrot: The Dance and the Music 147
Igor Glebov Sergey Prokofiev's Third Concerto 150

1926 **Guests from the West** 155

Viktor Belyayev 'Production' Music: on Kastalsky's *Village Symphony* 167
The Double-Faced Janus 170
Nikolai Malko Jazz-Band in Moscow 173
※ A Letter from Komsomol Members in the Conservatoire to Cmrd A. V. Lunacharsky and Cmrd A. V. Lunacharsky's Response 175

1927 **Celebrations** 179

※ The 'Left' Wing of Contemporary Music 188
'Sadko' *The Red Poppy* at the Bolshoi 193

1928 **At the Crossroads** 197

A. Lunacharsky At *Der Sprung über den Schatten* 208
N. Vygodsky *The Path of October* 210
I. Sollertinsky *Johnny* at the State Maly Opera House 214

1929 ***Velikiy perelom* – The Great Turning Point** 217

A. Weprik Bartók and the Problem of Folk Music 233
Boris Filippov The Third Musical Olympiad in Leningrad 238
Yu. Keldysh The Ballet *Steps of Steel* and its Composer, Prokofiev 243
D. Zhitomirsky *The Nose* – an Opera by D. Shostakovich 253

	1930	**RAPM's Glorious Year?** 261
	'Uriel'	Can a Phone Call Be Sung? Notes on *The Wind from the North* 271
	N. Malko	Letter to the Editors [of *Proletarian Musician*] 275
	L. Lebedinsky	Our Mass Music [excerpts] 277

1931 RAPM's Fortunes Turning 284

    ※ A Kiev Newspaper on Shostakovich's Ballet [*The Golden Age*] 296

N. Vygodsky Heavenly 'Idyll', or Fascism in Priestly Garb 298

'Terzetto' Under a Proletarian Veil 302

Kl. Korchmaryov Music for the film *Alone* 308

A. Davidenko How I Worked on the Song 'They Wanted to Beat Us' 310

1932 The Rules Change 314

    ※ On the Restructuring of Literary and Artistic Organisations. Resolution of the Central Committee of the VKP(b) of 23 April 1932 324

    ※ On the Music Front 326

D. Kabalevsky A Symphony of Struggle: On Myaskovsky's Twelfth Symphony 328

D. Shostakovich A Tragedy-Satire [*Lady Macbeth of the Mtsensk District*] 331

M. Grinberg The Opera and the Composer [*Lady Macbeth of the Mtsensk District*] 332

Igor Glebov Music of the 'Third Estate' [On the Ballet *The Flames of Paris*] 335

Vl. Derzhanovsky In the Carriage (Sergei Prokofiev: Marking His Arrival in the Soviet Union) 339

Key to Acronyms and Institutional Bodies 341
Glossary of Names 345
Bibliography 381
Index 391

Preface

Mr Scogan, a character from Aldous Huxley's *Crome Yellow*, doubted that people could ever get away from themselves entirely, as if they were to embark forever on a 'complete holiday', claiming that they 'never succeed in getting farther than Southend'. Gombaud, his interlocutor, disagreed:

> '… personally I found the war quite as thorough a holiday from all the ordinary decencies and sanities, all the common emotions and preoccupations, as I ever want to have.'
>
> 'Yes', Mr Scogan thoughtfully agreed. 'Yes, the war was certainly something of a holiday. It was a step beyond Southend, it was Weston-super-Mare; it was almost Ilfracombe.'

For the Russians, 'the war' – World War I – was only the beginning. After two revolutions, they withdrew from that war, only to be faced with invasion from fourteen hostile nations together with a civil war much protracted by funding from the same nations. An enforced holiday from normal life turned into a protracted voyage that took them ever further from their pre-Revolutionary selves. To use an expression from the poet Osip Mandelshtam, people were 'knocked out of their biographies like billiard balls out of pockets'. For some, a metaphoric holiday trip turned into real exile: abroad, as émigrés, they often sought to reconstitute the past, with little success. Those who stayed in the country, also longed to return to something, at least to a semblance of stable life, with reassuring routines. Yet by 1924, when that degree of normality had returned for the music intelligentsia at the centre of our narrative, their social position, professional status, and outlook were all undergoing a process of radical change. Knowingly or unknowingly, willingly or unwillingly, they began to weave themselves into the fabric of the emerging Soviet system, and there they remained, whatever the vagaries of Soviet cultural policy. By 1932, when the term 'Socialist Realism' was first coined and a comprehensive aesthetic doctrine began to take shape, most musicians were ready not only to tolerate it, but to embrace it. Most of the institutions, aesthetic attitudes and everyday practices that we now recognise as typically Socialist Realist were already in place. Musical life in 1932 once again seemed 'normal', but this normality was far from the normality of 1913 or even of 1924.

It is the higher aim of this book to trace the transformation of pre-Revolutionary Russian music culture into Soviet music culture over the space of fifteen years, constantly weighing up cultural continuity and change. The main source material presented in this volume is music criticism – which in this period is a particularly lively and exciting field, and, more often than not, a battlefield of competing aesthetic and ideological programmes. Leafing through the yellowed pages of numerous music periodicals of the 1920s, some with the lifespan of a mayfly, we were struck by how much light even mundane reviews threw on the general state of culture and how helpful they were in unravelling its extremely complex and ever-changing patterns. The idea for this book was thus born out of a desire to share these riches with Anglophone readers. It was clear that a selection of translated reviews and manifestos would require much commentary, and indeed, a substantial portion of this material would otherwise be opaque or even downright misleading. In the preparation of this commentary, we soon realised that the colourful and intense public musical life reflected in these articles is only half the story, since there were private strands equally deserving of attention and well preserved in the archives. Accordingly, we decided to devote a substantial portion of the commentary to the private accounts of early Soviet musical life, turning to a different kind of primary source: the protagonists' letters, diaries and memoirs, most of which have so far been unavailable to Western readers, or which have remained altogether forgotten. Much as this task had to be limited due to considerations of space, time, or availability of materials, we believe that this private dimension is an essential addition to our understanding of the period.

It seems fair to say that the 1920s still remain an under-researched and often misunderstood period in Soviet music history, although the situation has greatly improved in recent years, both in Russia and in the West. Russian scholars such as Inna Barsova, Levon Hakobian, Svetlana Savenko, Viktor Varunts, Ekaterina Vlasova, Marina Lobanova and Olesya Bobrik should take much credit for the great advances that have made in the field. The German scholars Dorothea Redepenning and Detlef Gojowy have also made a notable contribution. In the Anglophone world, historians rather than musicologists have led the way: Neil Edmunds' book on the 'proletarian' composers, for all its limitations, was a pioneering effort, while Amy Nelson's more recent *Music for the Revolution* is simply invaluable.

Working on this period, we have turned on many occasions to the scholarship of Sheila Fitzpatrick, and have found her articles and books on Soviet culture in the 1920s indispensable. Many other recent Western publications by historians and Slavists, listed in the Bibliography, have guided our inquiry or confirmed that we were on the right path. But we are just as indebted to Soviet-era publications of letters and other documents, some of them humble and obscure volumes (the collection of Alexander Davidenko's letters could hardly have been much in demand); even so, they proved extremely useful, although our work among the original documents allowed us to restore occasional cuts.

The volume is organised chronologically, year-by-year, since this ordering of the material allows readers to follow the complex chains of events and the rapid changes in the musical and ideological landscape, which could otherwise seem hopelessly confusing. We decided to follow the natural variation between 'lean' years short on music publications, and other years that offered an abundance of material, such as 1924 and 1929 (economic and political conditions, of course, affected both the nature and quantity of published discourse on music). Of necessity, we restricted ourselves largely to events in the two capitals, Moscow and Petrograd/Leningrad, since the bulk of publications were issued there, but we have ranged further afield to take in other events of importance. We have also chosen to focus on the music of Russian/Soviet 'high culture', discussing popular music and politicised genres where they impinged on the former. This approach took advantage of the richest sources of documentary material, and best allowed a coherent narrative to emerge within the space of a monograph this size, but we certainly have no wish to present this as the only possible focus.

Even with our chosen focus in mind, we still had to settle on a particular route through a wide range of sources, and at times this inevitably reflected personal interests and tastes: opera is one noticeable strand, contacts with the West another; we also felt that many readers would be anxious to follow the first Soviet successes of Sergei Prokofiev and Dmitry Shostakovich. But even given these arbitrary aspects to the choice of material for translation, the introductions provide readers with an overview of each year that draws from our knowledge of an extensive range of sources beyond the documents presented in full or at length. Readability was also a crucial consideration: much Soviet writing of the period is jargon-filled and paid for by the word, with results that are sometimes barely digestible; and in order not to bore readers, we had to present a higher proportion of more lucid and engaging material than any random cross-section could have produced. Where the commentary is embroidered with personal accounts, our choice naturally draws most heavily from the more prolific diarists and correspondents whose archives are well preserved, in particular Prokofiev, Nikolai Myaskovsky and Boris Asafyev, but also the lesser known Vladimir Derzhanovsky, whose accounts proved especially enlightening (and often amusing). These were all major players on the 'contemporary music' side of early Soviet musical life. But we also tried to give voice to those on the other side, the more politically driven musicians who exerted considerable influence at times during the period covered here, such as Davidenko and Lev Shulgin. Beyond the composers, performers and critics, we also introduce others who belonged to the various state and independent institutions that played a role in Soviet musical life, from government ministers down to functionaries in bodies such as the Artworkers' Union and the state music publishing house. Some of these characters in the narrative have been much harder to flesh out, as their extant archives are thin, but the challenge they posed had a special fascination for us. Not unlike Senhor José, the protagonist of José Saramago's novel *All the Names*, who develops an obsession for the life story of one ordinary individual after spotting a misfiled archival record card, we attempted to piece together scenes from these obscure lives.

Although we have sought to be as accurate as possible in reproducing and quoting from the sources, our approach to translation was not to aim at a word-for-word correspondence, which tends to produce results that are at best wooden and unidiomatic, and at worst incomprehensible. Our intention was to preserve the meaning and also the tone of what was said, and to make it as readable as it was in the original (or at times, in the most convoluted texts, to improve readability slightly). We were heartened to see this issue discussed passionately in a review that compared the new (and much more literalistic) English translation of one celebrated Russian novel with the first English version, much to the advantage of the earlier translators.[1] The method of the first translators was to read a whole page of text, and then render it into English from memory, since arriving at an idiomatic and lively translation demanded a certain distance from the lexical and grammatical details of the Russian text. Only afterwards was the result rechecked with the original to ensure accuracy. The recent translation, by contrast, remains very close to the surface features of the original Russian text, resulting in English sentences that are strangely out of focus, and with phrases here and there that

---

[1] Ann Pasternak Slater, 'Words Apart', *The Saturday Guardian*, 6 Nov 2010, Review section, 20.

could only be understood by a Russian speaker through back-translation. We cannot claim to rival the feats of memory achieved by the earlier translators of that novel, but we certainly position ourselves towards that end of the spectrum, taking as our unit of translation the whole sentence (and occasionally more than one), rather than single clauses or individual words.

We also decided to avoid locutions that would tend to exoticise the subject matter for readers: Anatoly Lunacharsky, therefore, is named according to his role, as the government minister placed in charge of education and the arts, rather than as 'the Narkom' or 'the Commissar for Enlightenment', which have a bizarre ring in English that is lacking when such names appear in Russian texts. We followed this policy so that readers would not have to negotiate an obstacle course of the imagination in order to see the familiar as such; this also means that those aspects of early Soviet life that were genuinely remote from our societies today are set in relief, instead of being submerged in a general cloud of exoticism. The one exception is 'automobile' instead of 'car': when, for example, Sollertinsky's review of Krenek's *Johnny Spielt Auf* refers several times to 'automobiles', these were an exciting feature of 'life of the modern city', as Sollertinsky says. For the contemporary Soviet reader, these machines were exotic, whereas today 'cars' have been a routine part of life for several generations. We have, of course, retained customary acronyms where these were widely used and where they allow readers to keep track of particular organisations. In a few instances, when there was a degree of arbitrary variation in name that did not reflect any difference in the organisation concerned, we made the name uniform throughout the text, hence the consistent use of 'RAPM', instead of the occasional variants 'APM' and 'VAPM'.

※ ※ ※ ※ ※

Even though the book, due to its fragmentary and chronicle-like nature, does not lend itself easily to summarisation, we would like at this point to present its brief overview, drawing the readers' attention to the documents and narrative strands that we consider most important.

The fifteen years within the book's remit we divide into three periods: 1917–22, 1923–8, and 1929–32, dominated by the Civil War, NEP and the First Five Year Plan respectively, each phase stamping its different character on musical life. The first period is that of the lean years, when little was published on music and critics devoted much of their writing to complaints about what was lacking in musical life: few new works were being written and still fewer performed; there had been almost no musical contact with the West since before the First World War (which made Russian composers feel provincial); and among established composers, there was little or no interest in reflecting revolution and war in their works, let alone the notion of a future socialist society. In 1922, several critics, and even Lunacharsky, the Minister of Education, looked back over the musical landscape of the past five years, drawing uniformly gloomy conclusions. In short, there had been an explosion of talent and innovation in the visual arts and theatre, whereas music – in the concert hall and opera house at least – seemed to be in much the same state as it was before the Revolution. This was perhaps not so surprising: for all their achievements and undoubted abilities, Myaskovsky and Glière were not capable of becoming the musical counterparts of Malevich or Meyerhold; unlike the two composers, the latter already had a reputation for radical innovation prior to the Revolution, and they hitched their art and public personas to the Revolution in various ways. Stravinsky was their equal, but he had emigrated long before the Revolution, to which he was in any case hostile; Rachmaninov emigrated for good in 1917, while Prokofiev was not to return until his first tour of 1927.

The apparent barrenness of these first five years has led many histories of Soviet music to compress them out of existence. But a very different impression is gained as soon as the scope of music is extended beyond the confines of composition alone, since, to a surprising degree, music-making continued and at times even flourished during these years of privation under war and trade embargo. There was, of course, Proletkult, which for a time became a genuine mass movement democratising music education, with its legacy of work-place choirs and ensembles, many of which survived for decades. But even high-culture music was able to continue apace, and the centre of musical activity on this level was the opera house: it seems startling, given the circumstances, but on the night of 24 April 1919, for example, a Muscovite could choose between *Die Walküre*, *The Queen of Spades*, *Hansel and Gretel* and Napravnik's *Dubrovsky*. On 14 November of the same year, *Die Walküre* was still running, even though the temperature was freezing both outside and inside the theatre. Opera in such conditions was highly impractical: it was labour-intensive and very costly to maintain at a time of great hardship, and also seemed socially out of place, but the very fact that even the unlikeliest of high-culture institutions was able to survive ensured that others – the conservatoires, orchestras, and so forth – would not continually have to justify their existence. Another pillar of musical culture that withstood the upheavals was the institution of music publishing, which was fortunate to fall into the capable hands of Pavel Lamm and his circle, including the most influential of his composer friends, Myaskovsky. Despite bitter fights around the state music publishing house, due to the powerful role it played within the music world, Myaskovsky managed to remain within this institution for most of his life.

There was also much that was new: some of the institutions and projects of these years carry a distinct War-Communism flavour, and that flavour is, surprisingly perhaps, the taste of unlimited funding from the state. In the pre-NEP years, the Narkompros budget was huge, and at times spent with remarkable profligacy: take, for example, the creation of the Petrograd Philharmonic, complete with the ultra-rapid renovation of a beautiful but derelict building, new carpets and chandeliers (see the Introduction to 1921). Or consider the cellist Victor Kubatsky, who was sent to travel thousands of miles around the country in his personal train carriage to stop precious musical instruments being spirited abroad under the fog of war; the result was a state collection of instruments that survives to the present day, and which, among other things, enabled Kubatsky to set up his own ensemble, the appropriately named Stradivari Quartet.

Even Proletkult drew its funding from the Narkompros tap, until 1920, when the organisation lost its high degree of autonomy due mainly to Lenin's suspicions about its wide appeal and the nature of its policies. For Proletkult, the tap was now turned off, but elements of its programme for the arts survived through other organisations, including RAPM, Rabis (the art-workers' union) and indeed the wider trade-union network, which helped support the workplace ensembles.

Around the few stable institutions was a sea of other activities typical of the early Soviet period: performers travelled from one concert to another, from clubs to army garrisons, often under the banner of Proletkult, while musicologists, critics and some composers assembled livelihoods from peripatetic lecturing (Proletkult again) and scraps of journalism. Many of the latter also served on an 'artistic council' or 'music section' of this or that body, thereby taking their first step towards integration into the Soviet system. The process was not as fast or as all-embracing as it could have been, not only because of anti-Soviet sentiments across a large swathe of the intelligentsia, but also because a reversal in the Civil War was still a serious possibility until 1921, and many had an eye on their prospects if the Soviet dispensation was suddenly swept away. In July 1918, the music critic and editor Vladimir Derzhanovsky wrote a striking letter to his critic friend Boris Asafyev, appealing to the latter to issue a call to Russian musicians (we quote from the letter in the introduction to one of Asafyev's subsequent articles, *A Lull*). In the letter, Derzhanovsky, among other things, explained why he thought musicians must participate in the new institutions that had the power to shape the musical world. Whether musicians were sympathetic, indifferent or hostile to the new power was not the issue, Derzhanovsky argued. Participation was for the sake of music.

In Derzhanovsky's case, he viewed this participation as a means to the advancement of new music – he was well aware of the flourishing Futurist groupings in the other arts. But we can extend the same reasoning across the whole of the musical world: it mattered little that Lenin happened to value symphony orchestras if the players all emigrated or starved from a lack of work. To ensure that there was continuity in the music world through the privations and chaos of the Civil War period, musicians did indeed begin to work for the new Soviet institutions. The work offered a wage too, of course, and bare survival was often the paramount consideration in these years; but it also resulted from a desire to be of use to their art, which could not survive off the grumbling of would-be internal exiles.

In 1923, at the beginning of our second period, the economic situation was improving, patterns of life became more stable, and most of the intelligentsia who had remained in the country had found employment either within the state system, or within the small but functioning private sector. As NEP increasingly reshaped everyday life, popular commercial music enjoyed mass consumption, to the consternation of the music intelligentsia, much of which would have supported a counter-offensive by the state, which was equally disapproving – but the state now lacked the means, and in any case generally submitted to the logic of compromises entailed by NEP. But the state also lacked the funds for the sometimes-extravagant projects it had been able to support earlier. The Petrograd Philharmonic fell on harder times, while Persimfans, the conductorless orchestra, flourished. While in literature, this ensemble is usually presented as an iconic revolutionary institution, 'a utopia in miniature, a model workshop for the communist future' (Stites),[2] it could, with at least equal accuracy be described in other ways: it was a novelty act,

---

[2] Richard Stites, *Revolutionary Dreams: Utopian Vision and Experimental Life in the Russian Revolution* (New York and Oxford: Oxford University Press, 1989), 136.

a 'joint-stock' company, a cottage industry run from a small apartment with little or no state subsidy – in short, a typical NEP enterprise.

1923 also marks the birth of two associations, ASM (the Association for Contemporary Music) and RAPM (the Russian Association of Proletarian Musicians), which have usually served as polar opposites for most accounts of 1920s' musical life. This opposition is to some extent a false one, used more as a historiographical narrative convenience than as an accurate representation of the situation. ASM and RAPM had such different constituencies that in slightly different circumstances their paths need seldom have crossed: ASM was preoccupied with making propaganda for new music to a very select elite audience (a large proportion of their concerts were by invitation only). RAPM, on the contrary, devoted its attention to the proletarian mass audience, which it aimed to turn away from NEP popular music to something more ideologically edifying. With such distinct remits, in principle ASM and RAPM could have co-existed peacefully. The problem, however, was that neither was commercially viable, and so they both ended up competing for the same government funds and indeed for the same seat of institutional power, namely the Music Section of the State Publishers (Muzsektor Gosizdata); and it was the struggle to gain control of the latter institution that brought them into direct ideological confrontation (see 1924). Another of RAPM's campaigns was fought within Moscow Conservatoire, in an attempt to turn this elite hothouse for virtuosos into a factory for mass-music cadres, but this, strictly speaking, had little to do with the activities of ASM.

While RAPM still lacked both funds and institutional power, ASM seemed well placed to flourish under NEP, preserving pre-Revolutionary musicians' circles, developing its international contacts and serving a narrow educated elite. There were no stylistic prohibitions, and even thoroughgoing modernists were generally left untroubled to go about their business (the main constraints were commercial rather than political). At the level of individuals, no significant problem is visible, but if we zoom out and consider instead the public image of music as a whole, then the picture is quite different. The other arts had taken a more Soviet direction already, with novels, plays, films, paintings and sculptures on Soviet themes. Music, by contrast, seemed to be falling behind: there was elite new music, there were performances of classic operas and concert works attracting a larger audience, and finally, there was commercial music with a mass audience, but in none of these areas was there any significant work on Soviet themes. Admittedly, there had been some attempts to add revolutionary elements to opera plots (or sometimes merely to enhance revolutionary elements already present), with action set in recent Soviet history, or at the time of previous uprisings, such as the Paris Commune. There was also a repertoire of simple song-settings of Soviet poems, and some composers were now aiming at larger-scale works: Soviet cantatas, or Soviet versions of Beethoven's Ninth. It was no longer enough to continue along pre-Revolutionary lines. Nor was there any more mileage in the kind of argument that Roslavets and some others had offered to their critics, namely that social revolution entailed a revolutionizing of compositional technique – a path that was later dismissed as 'formalism' (although this became a blanket term of musicianly abuse at times). Increasingly, ASM musicians felt that they were being left behind, forming an *arrière-garde* and leaving a leadership role open to others, including RAPM.

This anxiety lies behind another prescient letter from Derzhanovsky to Asafyev,[3] in which Derzhanovsky imagines how musical leadership could be wrested back (we quote from it at length in the Introduction to 1924). It would be necessary, he argues, for prominent ASM composers, such as Myaskovsky, to start writing music on revolutionary themes. But crucially, he says, this must not take the form of mere hackwork that was obviously distinct from the composer's serious manner; rather, the composers should enter imaginatively into the task and create works that satisfied their normal artistic standards. Myaskovsky, he guesses, would actually 'love to write a revolutionary cantata, a symphony, an opera or something else in some as-yet-unknown form, except it has to be monumental, and justified in terms of his creative path, so that it would be a step forward for him too, or at least a step sideways'. He imagines himself and Asafyev acting as 'nannies' to composers who might at first be reluctant, putting the seeds of the new subject matter into their heads and helping them to cultivate their ideas. There was even a well-known model for this in Russian music's recent past, namely the relationship between the composers of The Five and their intellectual mentor, Stasov. In good Stasovian manner, adapted to Soviet circumstances, Derzhanovsky wanted to shape ASM's composers into an organised faction that would court Lunacharsky, thereby (he hoped) gaining at least enough power in the music world to obtain sinecure positions that would guarantee them a secure livelihood and ensure that their work was performed widely. An ambitious task, certainly, but Derzhanovsky reckoned that the first step – persuading the composers to reform – would be the most difficult part. He conceded that this was likely to happen gradually: a series of smooth modulations proceeding through pivot chords, as he put it. He proposed to Asafyev, accordingly, that they should assign the composers tasks that would take them step-by-step towards the winning formula for Soviet success.

Derzhanovsky's vision was indeed realised: Myaskovsky, by a process of smooth modulations, did eventually become a leading Soviet composer, while still retaining his status (at least inside the Soviet Union) as a serious symphonist. Many others around him did likewise, organizing for themselves a convenient network of 'sinecure' jobs and financial benefits. Likewise, they did indeed take advice from their musicologist nannies on which way the ideological wind was blowing, and how this should affect their work. But what Derzhanovsky had unwittingly described is, in fact, the state of the musical world in the years after 1932, under Socialist Realism. In 1924, Myaskovsky and his friends were not remotely prepared to move in this direction. The younger and more flexible Shostakovich was the one who showed the way with his Second Symphony (*To October*) of 1927, which became an important landmark on the path high-culture music took towards Sovietisation. This work (among others) demonstrates that even in the NEP years, when RAPM's influence was still negligible, the forging of Soviet music culture was already taking place. The Second Symphony should also direct us to the source of the commission, namely Shulgin of the agitprop department at

---

[3] Letter from Derzhanovsky to Asafyev of 5 Dec. 1924, RGALI, fond 2658 (Asafyev), op. 2, ye. kh. 45, l. 5.

Muzsektor, who was also the head of the association ORKiMD (the Association of Revolutionary Composers and Music Workers). In our account of the events, we attempt to shed more light on this organisation, which was bound to remain in the shadows for as long as narratives of the period followed the ASM–RAPM dichotomy. ORKiMD's more centrist ideological stance, and the power it gained through the Muzsektor connection, allowed it to act as a major player between 1925 and 1929.

We also show that there were other acute conflicts in the musical world that had nothing to do with the divisions between ASM and RAPM. One such conflict, for example, emerged in the wake of the premiere of the 'original' *Boris Godunov*, which pitted Asafyev against the powerful clan that had been formed by Rimsky-Korsakov's family and followers. To gain the upper hand, Asafyev availed himself freely of Soviet-style rhetoric, presenting the original *Boris* as an opera about the rising masses, and he did not hesitate to seek the backing of Soviet officials for his position.

In the final period covered by the book, 1929–32, NEP culture gives way to the more astringent atmosphere of the first Five Year Plan. The ASM–RAPM opposition is now only kept alive by RAPM's continuing attacks on an empty name: ASM was effectively defunct from mid 1929, its members demoralised by the loss of their journal, their state subsidies and their foreign connections. But although RAPM was now the most powerful force in the music world, it never achieved unchallenged domination, and in the end, it was abruptly shut down by order of Stalin in April 1932. Our goal in the introductory essays to each of these years was to present a more detailed picture that differs in important respects from the standard one. It is true that RAPM's power was considerable in most musical institutions in the relatively short span between the spring of 1930 and the autumn of 1931 – about half the time of their supposed period of dominance. We also show that the fight against RAPM never ceased. At no time was RAPM placed entirely beyond criticism: there was Meyerhold and his mockery, there were the 'foxtrot composers' who defiantly continued to sell their wares, and there was the Conservatoire professor, Mikhail Gnesin, who stood his ground against the destructive reorganisation of his institution. These and plenty of others were not prepared to take RAPM's bullying lying down.

But all this resistance was possible because of the tacit understanding that RAPM did not represent the Party. RAPM's members were also Party members, but collectively, they never won the Party's full support. Sometimes the Party gave them encouragement, sometimes it merely tolerated them, and at other times it reined them in or restricted their field of operation (notably, the Bolshoi was off limits for RAPM). These 'proletarians' served Stalin's interests well for a time, when he sought to discipline the intelligentsia, beginning with engineers, but spreading the campaign to all sectors of the sciences and arts. RAPM placed the music intelligentsia in conditions of dogmatic unfreedom, inducing them to speak the militaristic officialese, and showed them how their livelihood was directly dependent on those who were now in control (which was no longer Lunacharsky and others of like mind). When the excess pressure was taken off in April 1932, Soviet composers experienced it as freedom, barely noticing the fact that they were now all writing commissioned pieces on Soviet themes. This brings to mind a fable that is well known in Russia. A peasant family wanted relief from the cramped squalor of their small house, packed with both humans and animals. They went to the village sage, who bizarrely told them to bring a goat into the house. Adding a goat to all the other inhabitants made life in the house still more unbearable, and it was not long before the family returned to the sage. 'Now take the goat out', he told them. The family breathed a sigh of relief: now the house felt spacious. For Soviet musicians, RAPM was the extra goat in the house: with RAPM gone, they accepted tighter government control of music as a relief.

Was RAPM's domination inevitable? In general terms, yes, since proletarian organisations in the other arts experienced a similar elevation. But perhaps RAPM's temporary success would have been weaker and shorter if it were not for the role of one man, Platon Kerzhentsev, who held office in the Party's Agitprop section, but also happened to take a strong interest in music (and opera in particular). Most important, he was hostile to Lunacharsky, both as an individual and as the representative of a broad and tolerant Soviet approach to the arts. Kerzhentsev was adept as a puppet master in effecting the shift of power in the music world from the Lunacharskyites of Narkompros to an array of hardliners operating through a number of institutions and organisations, including RAPM. Outside of the present narrative, he came to historical prominence in 1936 as the powerful Chairman of the Committee for Arts Affairs, when he played a leading role in the debacle over Shostakovich's *Lady Macbeth*.[4] In 1929, however, he waged war on the music front at a time when Stalin's attention was entirely absorbed by economic matters and internal Party struggles. Without Kerzhentsev, music could have stayed in the shadows away from 'class struggle' a little longer.

One of our goals in creating this book, as already mentioned, was to bring to life, dramatise and humanise a period that often suffers from the desiccating force of unpalatable officialese and unpronounceable acronyms. What do we learn from looking into the human dimension of the power struggles around music? One of the most striking things for us was the profound scepticism and often cynicism in the intelligentsia's attitudes to the Sovietizing of their lives and careers. We can only smile now, remembering the mythology of 'totalitarianism' and its ability to gain absolute control over minds, which for decades compelled Western commentators to debate earnestly whether Shostakovich sincerely believed in Communism and to wonder at what point, if any, he stopped believing in it. The sources we have had at our disposal make such a question seem completely irrelevant. The question of becoming a Soviet composer, or 'music worker', was a matter of accepting the inevitable, sometimes with pain and regret, sometimes in an opportunistic quest for power and personal benefit, sometimes in an attempt to make genuine sense of the new dogmas, but most often simply as a matter of learning how to cope with the new language and to speak it convincingly. This is the case equally for the older generation of Myaskovsky, Derzhanovsky, Asafyev, and also for Shostakovich and his contemporaries.

If we sometimes find it hard to sympathise with some of ORKiMD's theories and – harder still – with RAPM's behaviour, we find, by contrast, that even

---

[4] See Leonid Maksimenkov, *Sumbur vmesto muziki: Stalinskaya kul'turnaya revolyutsiya, 1936–1938* (Moscow: Yuridicheskaya kniga, 1997).

when they play the game with cynicism, this was in the zealous pursuit of higher principles that they sincerely believed in. When we read Davidenko's personal letters or the transcripts of ORKiMD meetings, we do not find a mismatch between private and public attitudes and beliefs: these were people who believed that their programme for the future of Soviet music was morally right, and not merely a lever for personal gain. By contrast, when we read the 1920s correspondence of Myaskovsky, Derzhanovsky, Asafyev, we see instead that they are only attempting to fit in with the Soviet system, to carve out a niche for themselves and to outwit their persecutors. Even so, their efforts to make the best of the hand they had been dealt brought about a slow, but irreversible change of perspective: what was unthinkable at the beginning of the twenties was often quite acceptable a decade later. Hence Derzhanovsky's joyful report to Prokofiev, when the April Resolution of 1932 finally swept RAPM away: his letter is full of official clichés, as if he is talking to one of the functionaries set to head the future Union of Composers, rather than to an émigré of fourteen years' standing. Or a year earlier, Myaskovsky, now a member of a RAPM satellite for fellow travellers, discussing collectivisation with his former student, the RAPM member Marian Koval. Beneath these surface details, Derzhanovsky, Myaskovsky and Asafyev understood that their true cause – progressive new music – was incompatible with providing art for 'the people'. The music they fought for was for the relative few who not only had the will, but also the time and opportunities. Their cause was a lost one, but they salvaged what they could from defeat.

As our narrative approaches its end, in 1932, we see the main forces of Soviet music for the next two decades lining up. The Union of Composers has been officially created, at least on paper, and its journal, in which composers and critics will speak with one voice, is already in print. Two major Soviet composers have undergone a substantial reform in their compositional styles: Myaskovsky has stepped on the 'correct path' with his Twelfth Symphony (known as 'The Collective Farm'), while Shostakovich has tempered the modernism of *The Nose* in his new opera, *Lady Macbeth of Mtsensk* (although in a few years that would also cease to be sufficient). A third figure, Prokofiev, not yet a Soviet composer, has already had a chance to taste both Soviet fame and infamy, but undeterred, is eyeing the field and weighing his options. All of them have made many little steps towards the acceptance of what had once seemed unacceptable.

Acknowledgements

The research for this book was carried out unobtrusively for many years, but it was thanks to the Research Leave Grant from the Arts and Humanities Research Council awarded to Marina Frolova-Walker in 2007–8 that it was able to take shape as a focused project. We are much obliged to Michael Middeke, the commissioning editor of this book, for placing his trust in the project and offering unwavering support throughout.

The material was collected from many archives and libraries whose helpful staff we would like to thank, in particular the Russian State Archive for Literature and Art (RGALI) and the Manuscript Department of the Glinka Museum, as well of the Russian State Library (the music section and the newspaper section especially), the Historical Library and the Library of the Composers' Union in Moscow, the Serge Prokofiev Archive in London, the British Library and the Cambridge University Library. Sincere gratitude is due to the many colleagues and friends who supported this work by supplying guidance and advice, answering questions and procuring rare books and scores: Olga Digonskaya, David Fanning, Laurel Fay, Simon Franklin, Hubertus Jahn, Olga Khvoina, Veronica Kiss, Victoria Lyubitskaya, Fiona McKnight, Simon Morrison, Vladimir Orlov, Roger Parker, Daniil Petrov, Svetlana Savenko, Richard Taruskin, Elena Tchougounova, and Ekaterina Tsareva. Special thanks is due to Patrick Zuk for reading through the manuscript in its final stages and for his valuable advice. We are also grateful to David Roberts for work on the proofs that went well beyond the call of duty, and to Simon Loxley for his very stylish cover design. Marina Frolova-Walker would also like to thank The Music Faculty at the University of Cambridge, Clare College Cambridge, and Cambridge Committee for Russian and East European Studies for providing her with a stimulating research environment. We are full of gratitude to the tireless and loving grandparents of our son Alex, Alla Krylova and Edna and John Walker, who put in endless hours of babysitting and thus allowed us to bring the project to completion. It is to them that this book is dedicated.

Note on transliteration

The system of transliteration we have adopted is based on that used in the *New Grove Dictionary of Music and Musicians* (second edition, London, 2001, vol. 1, xxi), and has been widely used by Anglophone music scholars. The sole exception is the use of the standard English-language rendering of familiar names (e.g. Myaskovsky, Glière, Asafyev) within the main text of the book. In the notes, however, where Russian sources are cited, the same names are spelled in accordance with the transliteration system used in *Grove* (e.g. Myaskovskiy, Gliyer, Asaf'yev).

Chronology of Political and Musical Events

Politics	Music and the Arts
1917	
	Sept: Proletkult created
Oct 25 (Nov 7): October Revolution (old calendar) ends period of 'dual control', replacing Provisional Government with Bolshevik/Left-SR coalition reflecting current elected majorities in the Soviets	
Oct 26 (Nov 8): Second All-Russian Congress of Soviets passes decrees on withdrawal from the War and on radical land reform	
Oct 29: Government bans counter-revolutionary press	
	Dec: Rachmaninov leaves Russia
1918	
Jan 5–6: Constituent Assembly meets; refuses to call new elections reflecting SR split; locked out and disbanded	Jan: MUZO formed in Petrograd; Lourié appointed
Mar 3: Treaty of Brest-Litovsk cedes Ukraine and other Western territories to Germany as price for withdrawal from War.	Mar 3: Blok's *The Twelve* published
Mar 10: Soviet government moves to Moscow.	
May 26: Czech Legions being evacuated eastwards refuse disarmament, leading to first hostilities of 'Civil War'	May 29: Prokofiev leaves Russia
	June 1: MUZO opens in Moscow
	June 12: Decree nationalising Moscow and Petrograd Conservatoires (thus granting them state funding)
	August 1: First Proletkult Conference issues appeal against 'Gypsy music'
Aug 30: Assassination attempt leaves Lenin seriously wounded	
Sept 23: Counter-revolutionary Russian government-in-waiting set up in Ufa	
	Nov 7: Premiere of Mayakovsky's *Mystery-Bouffe*, directed by Meyerhold, marking first anniversary of October Revolution

Politics	Music and the Arts
Nov 18: Former admiral Kolchak becomes dictator of Ufa government	
	Dec: Opening of Choral Academy (Moscow Academy is former Synodal School; Petrograd Academy is former Court Cappella)
	Dec 9: Nationalisation of pre-Revolutionary publishing houses

1919

Politics	Music and the Arts
Mar 2–6: Founding Congress of Comintern, with delegates from 34 Communist Parties spanning four continents	
Mar 21–Aug 6: Hungarian Soviet Republic (first socialist republic to be established outside former Russian Empire)	
Oct: Yudenich's White Army advances on lightly defended Petrograd; defeated by Red Army reinforcements arriving by rail	
	Nov: State Collection of Musical Instruments founded; expropriation prevents valuable instruments being sold abroad

1920

Politics	Music and the Arts
Jan 16: Allied Supreme Council issues communiqué revoking blockade of Soviet Union and allowing trade; diplomatic recognition not granted	Mayakovsky's *150,000,000* published (anonymously)
Apr 24: Polish advance into Ukraine	
May: Soviet Trade Delegation opens talks in London for potential thaw in Anglo-Soviet relations	
Jul 19-Aug 7: 2nd Congress of Comintern, setting 21 conditions for affiliation, including support for anti-colonial liberation movements	
Oct: Polish–Soviet War ends	1 Oct: Rebikov dies in Yalta
	20 Nov: Premiere of *Petrushka* in Petrograd
	Dec: Proletkult subordinated to Narkompros and publicly censured (for political rather than artistic activities)

Chronology of Political and Musical Events

Politics	Music and the Arts
1921	
Mar 2–17: Kronstadt rebellion	
Mar 16: Anglo–Soviet Trade Agreement signed	
Mar 18–31: German Communist Party's calls for general strike and uprising fail and Party made illegal	
Mar 21: NEP declared at 10th Party Congress	
June 22–July 12: 3rd Congress of Comintern prepares member parties for uprisings and civil wars considered imminent, but also draws lessons from German debacle in March	June 12: Inauguration of Petrograd Philharmonia
July 13: Gorky alerts world to impending famine after crop failure following 6½ years of war; famine extends from Ukraine to Tatarstan, affecting next 2 years; international relief effort	
	Aug 7: Death of Blok
	Sept 7: Music History Section of Russian Arts History Institute founded (first Soviet musicological institution)
	Oct 5: Lev Termen (Theremin) demonstrates his electrical instrument at state conference on electrification of Russia
	Nov 7: Isadora Duncan dances at Bolshoi
	Late 1921: Medtner leaves Russia
1922	
	Jan 12: Lenin proposes closure of Bolshoi Theatre, but loses argument to Lunacharsky
	Feb 13: Persimfans gives first concert
Apr 3: Stalin appointed to new post of Party General Secretary by 11th Party Congress	Early 1922: Reorganisation of Narkompros results in disappearance of dedicated sections for music and other arts
Apr 16: Treaty of Rapallo establishing close diplomatic and trade relations between Soviet Union and Germany	
	June 6: Glavlit created
	Nov 7: Avraamov's 'Symphony of Sirens' performed in Baku

Politics	Music and the Arts
	Dec 3: Reopening of renovated Philharmonia building in Petrograd
December 30: Creation of USSR, comprising Russian, Ukrainian, Transcaucasian and Belarussian republics	Dec: Oskar Fried first foreign conductor to perform in Russia since outbreak of First World War

1923

Politics	Music and the Arts
	Feb 9: Glavrepertkom created
	April: First issue of *Towards New Shores*
	June: RAPM founded
Oct 15: Declaration of the 46, prominent Party members protesting at lack of democracy within the Party; formed basis for Left Opposition	Sept–Oct: Music Exhibitions at Mezhkniga
Oct 23: Communist uprising in Hamburg left isolated through communication failures and defeated; emergence of 'Socialism in One Country' policy in Soviet discourse	
	Nov 29: ASM formally founded

1924

Politics	Music and the Arts
Jan 21: Death of Lenin; Nadezhda Krupskaya sends his Testament (calling for demotion of Stalin) to Central Committee; document suppressed by Stalin, Zinoviev and Kamenev	Jan 12: Red Professors' Fraction founded at Moscow Conservatoire
Feb 18: Stalin, Zinoviev and Kamenev denounce Trotsky and his Left Opposition at 13th Party Congress	Feb: Changes at Moscow Conservatoire; resignation of Goldenweiser as Director
	May–June: 'Purge' at Moscow Conservatoire
	May 4: Premiere of Myaskovsky's Sixth Symphony (Moscow)
	June 6: Premiere of *Salome* at former Mariinsky
	Oct 29: Premiere of Deshevov's ballet *Red Whirlwind* in Leningrad
Nov 26: Mongolian People's Republic declared; ruling party joins Comintern	
Dec 1: Failure of Communist coup attempt (with Comintern support) in Estonia	

Chronology of Political and Musical Events xxv

Politics	Music and the Arts
	1925
Jan 6: Trotsky forced to relinquish charge of Ministry of Military and Naval affairs in favour of his deputy, Mikhail Frunze	
	Apr 24: Premiere of Gladkovsky's and Prussak's opera *For Red Petrograd*, first opera on Soviet subject
	Early May: Grechaninov leaves Russia
	May 9: Premiere of Schreker's *Der Ferne Klang* at former Mariinsky
June 18: Party Resolution on Literature	
	July 21: Politburo resolves to allow Prokofiev and Stravinsky to visit USSR
Oct 31: Death of Frunze during operation; Stalin under suspicion in some quarters; military now placed under charge of Stalin loyalist, Kliment Voroshilov	
Dec 1: Signing of Locarno Treaties normalises relations between Germany and Western powers, causing anxieties about renewed war in Soviet Union	
Dec 23: Under leadership of Stalin and Bukharin, New Opposition of Zinoviev and Kamenev defeated at 14th Party Congress	Dec 21: Eisenstein's *Battleship Potemkin* released
	1926
	Feb 18: Russian premiere *of Love for Three Oranges* in Leningrad
	May 12: Premiere of Shostakovich's First Symphony
Oct 23: Trotsky expelled from Politburo	
	1927
	Jan: Prokofiev comes to USSR for concert tour
Apr: Chiang Kai-Shek ruptures friendly relations with Soviet Union, leading massacres of Chinese Communist Party members; seen as major Comintern failure	
May 26: British government revokes trade agreement with Soviet Union and breaks off diplomatic relations	May 21: Russian premiere of Krenek's *Der Sprung über den Schatten*

Politics	Music and the Arts
	June 13: Russian premiere of Berg's opera *Wozzeck*
	June 14: Premiere of Glière's ballet *The Red Poppy*
Nov 12: Trotsky and Zinoviev expelled from Party	Nov 5: Premiere of Shostakovich's Second Symphony, *To October*
Dec 2: United Opposition members expelled from Party at 15th Party Congress	Dec 4: ASM's concert for 10th anniversary of Revolution
Dec 14: Chiang Kai-Shek breaks off diplomatic relations with Soviet Union	Dec 14: Release of Pudovkin's film *The End of St Petersburg*, commissioned for 10th anniversary celebrations of October Revolution
	Dec 18: Premiere of Prokoll's *Path of October*

1928

	Feb 16: Premiere of original *Boris Godunov* at former Mariinsky
	Apr 13: Glaviskusstvo created
May 18: Shakhty Trial begins (engineers charged with sabotage), placing intelligentsia in general under suspicion.	
Oct. 1: Official beginning of First Five-Year Plan and consequently end of NEP	
	Nov 16: *Pravda* article criticises Moscow Conservatoire

1929

	Jan 8: Release of Dziga Vertov's avant-garde film *Man with a Movie Camera*
	June 14–16: First All-Russian Conference of Music Workers
	Sept 12: Lunacharsky resigns as Minister of Arts, Sciences and Education; replaced by Bubnov
	Oct: Raskolnikov appointed as Head of Glaviskusstvo
Nov 5: Restoration of Anglo-Soviet diplomatic relations	
Nov 17: Central Committee resolution on collectivisation of agriculture; Bukharin, opposed to the policy, expelled from Politburo	

Politics	Music and the Arts
	Dec 9: Meyerhold's production of Gogol's *The Government Inspector*
Dec 27: Stalin declares intent to eliminate 'kulaks' as a class; initiates policy of mass deportations of peasants	

1930

	Feb: 'Purge' at Glaviskusstvo
Mar 2: *Pravda* publishes Stalin's article 'Dizzy with Success', signalling in veiled terms temporary relaxation of agricultural collectivisation policy, due to peasant resistance	
Apr 25: System of 'corrective labour camps' (GULags) established	Apr 14: Mayakovsky's suicide
	May 10: Politburo places Bolshoi under aegis of TsIK (effectively preserving it from RAPM interference)
Nov 25–Dec 7: Trial of 'Industrial Party' (group of engineers and economists allegedly plotting coup on behalf of foreign powers); death sentences commuted to prison terms	

1931

	Feb 2: Moscow Conservatoire renamed Felix Kon Higher Music School
June 23: Stalin's speech 'New Conditions – New Tasks' signals thaw in relations with intelligentsia	
Nov 7: Chinese Soviet Republic declared in Northern China	

1932

	Mar: Mosolov's letter to Stalin
	Apr 23: Party Resolution dissolving RAPP, RAPM, and other cultural organisations
	June 1: Premiere of Myaskovsky's Twelfth Symphony
Autumn 1932: Poor harvest causes mass famine, exacerbated by collectivisation policies	Nov 6 or 7: Premiere of Asafyev's ballet *The Flames of Paris*
Dec 31: First Five-Year Plan declared complete	

October 1917–1918
Out of Chaos

We shall begin with two stories of the October Revolution, as recalled by Russian musicians then at the peak of their careers. The first was provided by Fyodor Chaliapin, who was on stage as King Philip II in a performance of *Don Carlos* at the moment when a great thunderclap threw singers and audience alike into disarray. As all present later understood, this was the shot fired by the battleship Aurora, the designated signal for the insurrection to begin. Reliving the moment, Chaliapin reports:

> From the cathedral steps. I see that my people have lost their nerve. The third and fourth shots, one after another. My square began to empty. Choir members and extras started moving towards the wings and, forgetting about the heretics, began to discuss which way they should run. The Spanish king, Philip II, had much trouble persuading his timid subjects that there was nowhere to run, since it was quite impossible to determine where the shells might fall. After a minute, several people came in from outside the theatre, and told us that the shells are flying in the opposite direction and we have nothing to fear. We remained on stage and the action continued. The audience also stayed put, not knowing where to run either and deciding to remain in their seats. [...] By the end of the performance, the guns had fallen silent [...][1]

A second, contrasting account comes from the diary of the pianist, Alexander Goldenweiser, who happened to live next to the headquarters of the Moscow Garrison, where the Bolsheviks met with protracted resistance. In Petrograd, as we saw, the takeover proceeded so smoothly and swiftly that there was no need even to halt the performance of an opera, but in Moscow, the process was difficult and bloody. Having spent the previous night in the basement, sheltering from shelling that damaged his building, Goldenweiser describes the first morning of peace:

> A quiet grey morning, intoxicating fresh air; on the right, trenches, planks of wood, sacks, rags, and on the left, a gas streetlamp burning out of control. Some have already come out onto the street. They all look as if they have risen from the dead ... [...] The two [warring] sides begin to engage in peaceful conversation. The people pluck up their courage, and the street becomes livelier [...] Someone started cursing the Bolsheviks. Bitterly, a soldier standing nearby issued a sharp reprimand ... The usual thing started: You've drunk enough of our blood ... [...] That first good minute of benevolence has passed. I immediately felt that the sea of mutual hatred was overflowing, and that this was only the beginning.[2]

---

[1] Quoted from *Letopis' zhizni i tvorchestva F. I. Shalyapina*, ed. by Yu. Kotlyarov and V. Garmash, vol. 2 (Leningrad: Muzïka, 1985), 123.

[2] Diary entry of 24 July 1918, in A. B. Gol'denveyzer, *Dnevnik: tetradi vtoraya-shestaya* (Moscow: Tortuga, 1997), 25.

Both accounts are symbols of the times in their own way. The first stands for the continuity of culture through political upheaval: indeed the Mariinsky Opera continued in existence throughout the Soviet period, and still plays *Don Carlos* today, nearly a century later. The second is couched in terms of rupture and sees only darkness ahead. These two views neatly summarise the poles of Russian historical discourse in the post-Soviet period, swinging between the Yeltsin era's repudiation of everything from Lenin to Gorbachev, combined with a sentimental reverence for Tsarism, and the Putin era's attempts to arrive at a more inclusive narrative of Russian history that absorbs the Soviet period into its grand synthesis. Both rupture and continuity have their place in any attempt at a scholarly account of the period, and neither will be given undue favour here.

Chaliapin and Goldenweiser also serve as symbols of the sometimes astonishing reversals in personal fortune that litter Soviet history. Chaliapin became a leading celebrity of the Civil War period, a People's Artist of the Republic, and yet he was an émigré after 1921. Goldenweiser, for all his initial hostility, remained as a professor at Moscow Conservatoire until his death in 1961, picking up a Stalin Prize, two orders of Lenin and other prestigious awards, and also rising to a lofty position in Soviet arts administration.

The earliest cultural communications after the October Revolution seem to inhabit a rarefied atmosphere, in which quite routine events are coloured by a sense that history was being played out at the grandest level:

> The artistes of the Mikhailovsky Theatre's French troupe have decided to give a farewell festive performance for the revolutionary people. They will present Daudet's drama *L'Arlésienne* [title garbled in original] with music and a chorus by Bizet, the composer of the opera *Carmen*. The performance will be free, and tickets will be given to People's Commissar Lunacharsky for distribution. Because the play will run in French, a Russian summary will be read out beforehand. The date of the performance is still to be announced.[3]

There is something quite touching here: the French troupe, which formerly served the Francophone court and aristocracy, understood that it had no future in the new Russia, but instead of slinking away, it decided to finish with a blaze of confidence, addressing its new audience for the first and last time. Such farewell notices sit alongside appeals from the Revolutionary Government for artists to help create a new culture:

> We ask all comrade artists, musicians, writers and performers who want to join us in the work of bringing the masses closer to art in all of its manifestations […] to come to the office of the Commissar for People's Enlightenment in the Winter Palace.[4]

Anatoly Lunacharsky was appointed head of Narkompros (the People's

---

[3] *Izvestiya Soveta Krestyanskikh, rabochikh i soldatskikh deputatov*, no. 7 (11 Jan. 1918), 4. The Mikhailovsky Theatre would eventually be reborn as the Maly Opera.

[4] *Literaturnaya zhizn' Rossii 1920-kh godov: Sobïtiya. Otzivï sovremennikov. Bibliografiya*, ed. by A. Yu. Galushkin, vol. 1, pt 1 (Moscow: IMLI RAN, 2006), 62.

Commissariat of Enlightenment) on the third day of the Bolshevik Revolution, 27 October 1917. On 2 November, after less than a week at his post, he offered his resignation in protest at the great damage wrought upon the Kremlin buildings in the course of fighting between pro- and anti-Bolshevik forces in Moscow:

> It is impossible to remain at my post when I am left without power. This is why I am resigning. But I beg you, comrades, to give me your support and assistance. Guard the beauties of our land for yourselves and for our successors. Act as the guardians of the people's property.[5]

According to Lunacharsky himself, Lenin called him in and deployed his own rhetorical powers:

> How can you care so much about this or that old building, no matter how fine it may be, when what is at stake now is to throw open the doors to a social structure that can create beauties far in excess of anything they could dream of in the past?[6]

But Lunacharsky hints that harsher words were also spoken to him. Raising himself up from this initial despair, Lunacharsky launched himself into feverish activity directed towards the preservation of Russia's cultural patrimony while most of his comrades had their minds on other things: he safeguarded buildings, institutions, and collections of musical instruments, but above all, he wanted to preserve the country's culture-bearers. He was ideal for the role, with a foot effectively in both worlds. A Bolshevik of long-standing and seniority, he was also a keen theatregoer, an occasional arts critic and a playwright; he was cultured and eloquent: the benign face of the new regime for many of the old intelligentsia. His popular weekly reports on cultural affairs were crowded events, and if one sceptical witness is to be credited, Lunacharsky was prone to 'hysterics' and his efforts to ingratiate himself with his audience were 'beyond restraint'.[7] More sober summaries of these talks can be found in print, as in his appeal to artists of the state theatres (12 December 1917):

> Dear citizens
>
> You know very well how important it is to regulate the relationship between the artists and workers of the state theatre on the one hand and the state itself on the other.
>
> It is perhaps unnecessary to say that the new power does not require workers in any sphere to adopt any particular political credo, and even less so in the sphere of art. You are free citizens, free artists, and no one is violating your freedom.
>
> But there is a new master in the country: the working people. The working people cannot support state theatres until they are sure that these

---

[5] *Literaturnaya zhizn' Rossii 1920-kh godov*, 55.

[6] Lunacharsky, 'Lenin i literaturovedeniye', quoted in V. I. Lenin, *O literature i iskusstve*, ed. by N. I. Krutikova (Moscow: Khudozhestvennaya literatura, 1979), 674.

[7] A description by N. Yakubovich, quoted in *Literaturnaya zhizn' Rossii 1920-kh godov*, 60.

do not exist for the entertainment of the rich, but for the satisfaction of the great cultural needs of the working population. Democracy – the public – should make an agreement with the artists. Such an agreement is entirely possible.[8]

One of Lunacharsky's most pressing tasks was to establish personal contact with the creative leadership of the Bolshoi and the Mariinsky Opera Houses, whose administrative apparatus had been already disbanded. The Bolshoi's programme had been suspended for a fortnight, but when the company resumed activity on 21 November 1917, the leaders of the Moscow Soviet, who had been elected earlier in the autumn, took up their seats in the royal box. Aware that the audience (or at least those in the more expensive seats) were no supporters of the Revolution, their appearance in the royal box was no doubt intended as a signal that even opera houses now fell under the rule of the producing classes. Their reception was more hostile than they could have expected, since the militia had to intervene to protect them. Well-heeled members of the audience rose and began to pelt the leaders of the Soviet with whatever objects came to hand. The Bolshoi's royal box, it must be said, makes its occupants very accessible as targets. The militia took advantage of the theatre's design, and locked the doors to the boxes so that they could make arrests later at their leisure.[9] In Petrograd, the royal box at the Mariinsky was at the centre of a different row: in the closing days of 1917, the manager of the theatre, Alexander Siloti, presented the keys of the box to some of the more right-wing delegates to the Constituent Assembly, while the choir and some other members of the company staged an anti-Bolshevik protest. Their efforts won them a swift rebuke: Siloti was confined under guard to his splendid apartment for two weeks, while the choir was sacked.[10] Members of the Revolutionary Government and their foreign guests were then able to enjoy performances from the royal box in relative peace.

Russia's two main opera houses (much like their counterparts around the world) had never served as pure temples to culture: social hierarchy was clearly demarcated, and the power of the land had made its presence felt. Both these functions continued as before in the period after the October Revolution, but the occupants of the better seats were put on notice, and as they were gradually deprived of the sources of their wealth (namely, the work of others), the appearance and composition of the audience changed. The Bolshoi, Mariinsky and other former Imperial Theatres were now declared State Theatres, but after the initial squabbling had subsided, the change proved little more than nominal: the direction of the theatres remained, in practice, independent of the Soviets and the government, which had more pressing matters to attend to. The Bolshoi troupe, noticing the strength of its position, even passed a resolution expressing its contempt for the Revolutionary Government:

---

[8] 'Artistam gosudarstvennïkh teatrov', 12 Nov. 1917. Repr. in A. V. Lunacharskiy, *O muzïke i muzïkal'nom teatre* (Moscow: Muzïka, 1981), vol. 1, 286.

[9] RGALI, fond 1933 (Malinovskaya), op. 2, ye. kh. 12, ll. 8–9.

[10] See A. V. Lunacharsky, *O muzïke i muzïkal'nom teatre* (Moscow: Muzïka, 1981), vol. 1, 287–8.

The activity of the theatre as an institution serving the eternal mission of art and artistic culture must continue irrespective of political coups and changes in the state power. It must be resumed as soon as technically possible, and as soon as elementary civil liberties are reinstated, such as freedom of conscience and press, inviolability of person and dwelling. Considering ourselves part of the great democracy, and deeply grieving for the fraternal blood that was spilt, we speak out against the savage vandalism, which did not spare the old, sacred places of the Russian people, those monuments to art and artistic culture. The State Moscow Bolshoi Theatre as an autonomous artistic institution does not recognise any right of interference in its internal and artistic life on the part of powers that have not arisen from within the theatre and have not been elected by it.[11]

The apparent autonomy of the Bolshoi was maintained under the careful leadership of Elena Malinovskaya, who was appointed the director of the former Imperial Theatres by Lunacharsky shortly after the Revolution (after administrative restructuring, she became the director of the Bolshoi alone from 1920 to 1924 and again from 1930 to 1935). She was soon accepted for the cultured and colourful individual she was and, according to the conductor Emil Kuper,[12] won great respect from the troupe. She was also the wife of Pavel Malinovsky, a distinguished architect and a Bolshevik, who after the Revolution became responsible for the preservation of historic buildings in Moscow. Out of all the Bolshevik wives (so to speak) who chose to work in the field of culture, she played perhaps the most notable and independent role in this transitional period (even if we include Lenin's own wife, Nadezhda Krupskaya, who had previously been more prominent in her own right). In the early days of her directorship, as she found her way, Malinovskaya ruled with a very light touch, while the glory of presiding over the Bolshoi assembly fell to the Bolshoi's own knight in shining armour, Leonid Sobinov, the company's acclaimed Lohengrin.

While the Bolshoi assembly saw itself as a saviour of culture, a bulwark against the passing vicissitudes of political change, the government's concern was merely that work in the theatres continued as normal; the motivation, at this juncture, mattered little. The troupe liked to imagine that it was soldiering on against the odds; the government, from its point of view, saw co-operation, and both sides were thus content.

If Malinovskaya was a successful appointment for Lunacharsky, others were more problematic. Few had good words for Arthur Lourié, who became head of MUZO (Narkompros's *Muzikal'niy otdel*, or Music Section, which functioned in Petrograd from January 1918, and in Moscow from July). This appointment was indeed quite random: Lourié and his artist friend Nikolai Punin, both still in their twenties, had walked into Lunacharsky's deserted ministry seeking permission to hold a concert at the Winter Palace; by the time they left the building, they had both been appointed to positions of some seniority in the ministry, heading the sections for their respective

[11] Ibid.
[12] Emil Kuper, 'Nezakonchennaya avtobiografiya muzkal'noy kar'yeri', GTsMMK, fond 334 (Kuper), ye. kh. 1, 131 and 134.

arts.¹³ This sequence of events was not quite as bizarre as it might at first seem. Most of the Russian intelligentsia was hostile to the Revolutionary Government at this stage; even Maxim Gorky, who had been sympathetic to the October Revolution, was now voicing discontent in his *Untimely Thoughts*. Talented young artists making friendly approaches to the culture ministry on their own initiative would have been able to count on a warm reception from Lunacharsky. A self-selecting aspect was at work, moreover: Lourié and Punin considered themselves to be Futurists, a loose grouping that saw the upheaval as a great opportunity: cultural life, shaken loose from its old foundations, could be pushed in any direction, given the right ideas and sufficient effort. Although Lunacharsky had no personal bias in favour of Futurism and artistic iconoclasm, this was the camp that was initially most friendly towards the Bolsheviks. Seen in this context, it was hardly surprising that he found himself working alongside David Shterenberg as head of IZO (the Fine Arts Section) and Vsevolod Meyerhold as head of TEO (the Theatre Section). He also clearly staked the future of revolutionary literature on Vladimir Mayakovsky: on 23 May 1918 he even delivered a lecture on the Futurist poet's works (Mayakovsky had joined the Bolsheviks at an early age, but ever his own man, he was seen yawning contemptuously in the front row).¹⁴

And yet Lourié's appointment still remains a curious affair. In spite of the controversies they provoked, Shterenberg, Meyerhold and Mayakovsky were widely recognised as major artists, and they commanded substantial followings. Lourié, by contrast, was isolated as a composer, and, facing resentment from most musicians, he did very little to promote any new music other than his own, which he published copiously, even when paper was very scarce. He was best known for his most experimental works, such as *Forms in the Air* for piano (which anticipated avant-garde scores of the fifties and sixties, such as Stockhausen's Piano Piece XI), but he was not generally considered to be a composer of real talent. As Nadezhda Bryusova recalled, no one greeted Lourié's high jinks with any enthusiasm, but neither did he provoke outrage for the most part; he was simply ignored.¹⁵ His only claim to any wider renown came from his 'melodeclamation' *'Nash marsh'* (Our March), a setting of a popular poem by Mayakovsky. While this piece is often cited as the earliest example of Soviet agitational music, its categorisation is moot: it could be located more easily in the Futurist camp than the communist. The briefest glance at the score shows that, whatever Lourié had in mind, his piece was certainly not well suited to stir up the masses, even if it was hardly avant-gardist either. Here we have a 'march' in triple time, with key signatures unfriendly to worker-musicians (D♭ major and F♯ major), and patches of Debussian pentatonic writing. Lourié's dedication was a long shout-out to all his Futurist friends: Bruni, Miturich (who produced the cubist-style cover page), Punin, Tatlin, Khlebnikov, Mayakovsky, Arens, Poletaev, and Petlikov. The work's ambiguities stem in part

---

¹³ Sheila Fitzpatrick, *The Commissariat of Enlightenment: Soviet Organization of Education and the Arts under Lunacharsky, October 1917–1921* (Cambridge: Cambridge University Press, 1970), 122.

¹⁴ *Literaturnaya zhizn' Rossii 1920-kh godov*, 194.

¹⁵ N. Bryusova, 'Pervïye godï posle Oktryabrya', draft typescript/manuscript, RGALI, fond 2009 (Bryusova), op. 1, ye. kh. 148, l. 26.

from the Mayakovsky poem itself, which was widely known to have irritated Lenin, who renamed it 'Their March'.[16] In 1918, Lourié was invited to the unveiling of a new monument to Marx, and 'Our March' had been chosen to accompany the ceremony. Lourié decided his prestige demanded that he place himself at the centre of attention, and turned up in a large red-draped car (perhaps he hoped to catch the attention of Zinoviev, who was presiding).[17] Later, after he had abandoned his post and defected to the West, Lourié found there was a price to pay for the official Soviet use of 'Our March', and he was kept at arm's length by his fellow émigrés.

MUZO could claim much of the credit for routine concert organising, and especially for widening the social base of the audience. Lunacharsky, however, was personally involved in all crucial decisions on music. After he had ensured that the major opera houses faced a stable future, he turned his attention to the conservatoires, offering them state funding in return for their co-operation. In July, the deal went ahead, and Narkompros took on the financial burden of the conservatoires through nationalisation; additionally, students were no longer required to pay fees.[18] This was followed swiftly by a decree abolishing entrance exams for all higher schools in an attempt to democratise the intake, but although the conservatoires were originally included within the scope of the decree, Lunacharsky had them exempted.[19] This step was not decisive, however, and the struggle to maintain the character of the conservatoires continued for several years. Various religious institutions that had been maintained by the Tsarist state were, of course, closed down; but even so, the new government chose to preserve the choirs that had flourished within these institutions. Accordingly, the former Moscow Synodal School and the Petersburg Court Cappella were amalgamated into a new Choral Academy in December 1918, and established composers of church music, led by Alexander Kastalsky, were expected to help construct a revolutionary choral repertoire.

The Cheka decree of 5 November, against the plunder of the artistic patrimony, included another act of rationalisation and preservation, in this case, of valuable musical instruments. A young cellist from the Bolshoi orchestra, Viktor Kubatsky, later took credit for directing Lunacharsky's attention to the flow of such instruments out of the country, and told some colourful stories about the expropriations designed to prevent further losses. An elderly Count Zubov, for example, was confronted in his own home by Kubatsky, accompanied by several Cheka officers; the count asked them how the instruments were going to be used, then requested a moment to change into his full military regalia in order to enact an ad hoc, but solemn ritual, transferring his four Stradivaris into the hands of

[16] Anatoliy Mariyengof, 'Moy vek, moi druz'ya i podrugi', in *Moy vek, moi druz'ya I podrugi: vospominaniya Mariyengofa, Shershenevicha, Gruzinova*, ed. by S. V. Shumikhin and K. S. Yur'yeva (Moscow: Moskovskiy rabochiy, 1990), 96.

[17] I. Nest'yev, 'Iz istorii russkogo muzïkal'nogo avangarda', *Sovetskaya muzïka* (1991), no. 1, 75–87, esp. 81.

[18] L. A. Barenboym et al. (eds), *Iz istorii sovetskogo muzykal'nogo obrazovaniya: sbornik materialov i dokumentov, 1917–1927* (Leningrad: Muzïka, 1969), 15.

[19] Ibid., 31.

the state.[20] The search spread out from the two capitals to the provinces and sea ports, and the resulting State Collection of Musical Instruments grew in size and importance, eventually becoming one of the world's greatest. In 1920, Kubatsky made a trip to the Crimea in a dedicated railway carriage, and, to ensure the efficacy of his mission there, he was granted a car, a lorry, armed guards and a pass for free and unrestricted access. Allegations of personal gain from this trip were made against Kubatsky a few years later, and these almost derailed his application to join the Party. Lunacharsky's help was enlisted, and he attested that Kubatsky 'was a trusted friend of the Communists, unafraid of being compromised a thousand times in the eyes of the philistines because of his energetic work under the direction and with the closest involvement of the VChK organs'.[21]

If Kubatsky refrained from making any material gains from his work, he certainly benefited musically through the establishment of the Stradivari Quartet, which played instruments from the State Collection from 1919 onwards; the Quartet consisted of Karpilovsky, Pakelman, Bakaleynikov and Kubatsky himself. Lunacharsky acted as a powerful patron for the Quartet, which was frequently invited to play at his private soirées for other discerning listeners drawn from the Bolshevik elite and foreign guests. This touch of exquisite artistry, in the midst of a war-torn country, no doubt earned Russia some international prestige.

Lunacharsky's guiding hand was evident again in the programmes of special festive concerts marking the introduction of new Red days into the calendar. The grand civic festivals of the French Revolution featured almost obsessively in his writings during this period, and he saw them as a model for Soviet musical life in particular (although it should be noted that concerts with revolutionary themes had already appeared soon after the Revolution of February 1917). On May Day 1918, Lunacharsky himself gave a pre-concert lecture on Mozart's Requiem, which was to be performed in memory of the fallen in the Revolution. The concert took place in a highly symbolic venue: the Armorial Hall in the Winter Palace, a venue for state ceremonies in Tsarist times. On 7 November, in the same place, the audience was able to hear several new pieces on revolutionary themes, including Lourié's 'Our March'. There was also a revolutionary hymn composed by the great bass Chaliapin, but this piece was even less Soviet in character, having been written in the wake of the February Revolution, and submitted for consideration as the new Russian national anthem (it had been rejected by Alexander Glazunov and Nikolai Tcherepnin, who found it too dilettantish).[22] But at least both these offerings had been written as celebrations of revolution, whereas Igor Stravinsky, whose *Firebird* Suite was also included, was openly opposed to the new Russia, although his story of the Firebird helping to bring about the downfall of the evil king, Kashchei, was open to revolutionary interpretation.

The festive concerts in Moscow conducted by Emil Kuper (6, 7 November)

---

[20] Vyacheslav Smirnov, 'Dostoyanie respubliki', http://www.versiasovsek.ru/material.php?3475, accessed 22 June 2010.

[21] Letter from Lunacharsky to Comrade Kiselyov, Chairman of the Committee on Registration of Party Members (summer 1921), GTsMMK, fond 336 (Kubatsky), ye. kh. 461.

[22] *Letopis' zhizni i tvorchestva F. I. Shalyapina*, vol. 2, 117.

included Scriabin's *Prometheus*, with a purpose-built translucent set by Aristarkh Lentulov, illuminated in an attempt to follow Scriabin's instructions. Beethoven's Ninth, Rimsky-Korsakov's *Maid of Pskov* (the Veche scene) and Glazunov's *Stepan Razin* also had suitably revolutionary or liberatory associations. Kuper tells us that since the tickets to these concerts were not sold, but distributed among thousands of workers, he ran his Scriabin–Beethoven programme ten times until all of his vast audience had been able to hear it.[23] The opera houses also presented repertoire that could be interpreted as revolutionary. The former Zimin Opera in Moscow, now nationalised and renamed after the MSRD (the Moscow Soviet of Workers' Deputies), played *Fidelio* and *The Golden Cockerel* during the first anniversary celebrations, while the Mariinsky ran *Fenella* (*La muette de Portici*). Still, these programmes were all backward looking, with only a smattering of the new, and they look decidedly conservative beside the most striking of the theatrical offerings that marked the anniversary, namely the premiere of Mayakovsky's scandalous revolutionary play *Mystery Bouffe*, in a riotous production by Meyerhold. This was art that had been unthinkable under the Tsar, and the comparison only shows how far music lagged behind.

While Narkompros, the state ministry, organised cultural reform on the national level, smaller-scale cultural reorganisation was carried out by a separate organisation that belonged neither to Party nor state: this was Proletkult (Proletarian Organisations for Cultural Enlightenment), which had been created before the October Revolution. While its central committee was allowed to meet in the Narkompros building, it exercised a high degree of autonomy in the first years after the Revolution. Its founder and leader was Alexander Bogdanov, a colourful and charismatic figure who had been a Bolshevik until, almost a decade earlier, his philosophical treatise *Empiriomonism* received a long and crushing rebuttal from Lenin (the main charge against Bogdanov's treatise was idealism, although much the same could be said of Lenin's reply). Bogdanov also wrote science fiction, formulated an early version of systems theory and eventually met his end during one of his own experiments in rejuvenation through blood transfusion. For Proletkult specifically, he developed a theory of proletarian culture and set in motion a movement that, at its peak, established workers' clubs and other artistic circles all over the country, with a membership of up to half a million people. Invoking the Marxist premise that a new cultural superstructure will follow in the wake of each new economic base, he drew the personal conclusion that the proletariat would create its own distinctive culture, instead of assimilating the 'bourgeois' culture that already existed ('culture' here is meant in the broadest sense, to include science and technology). Proletkult aimed to speed up the process, attempting to raise the cultural level of workers so that they could produce the expected proletarian culture themselves. Accordingly, when a Proletkult-based journal, *Proletarian Culture*, appeared, the work of proletarian poets was to be found among its pages already. Among the performing arts, amateur dramatics and choral singing flourished. In effect, the progressive members of the intelligentsia would aid the working class to render the entire intelligentsia obsolete. Proletkult had its own publishing houses in the capital and

---

[23] Kuper, 135.

in the provinces, and, among many other projects, it printed the first agitational music: unpretentious and utilitarian. Nikolai Kochetov's *'Gimn-Marsh'* (March-Hymn or March-Anthem) appeared in 1918 or 1919, incongruously bearing a dainty Art Nouveau-style floral design on its title page. The slogan 'Proletarians of All Lands, Unite!' was discreetly incorporated into the pattern. This was the humble prototype for the tens of thousands of agitational works that appeared in the Soviet Union over the succeeding years.

Proletkult's first national forum, held in September 1918, made Narkompros look like the junior partner in the relationship. Nadezhda Bryusova, who was present as a mass-music-education worker, recalled in the 1940s the mood of 'exhilaration' even before the event had begun, and the excitement generated by Bogdanov's ideas (although she chose her words carefully in her memoirs, this passage was still deemed unpublishable).[24] Bogdanov was not able to attend, but he was represented by Pyotr Lebedev-Polyansky, who articulated Bogdanov's vision of the future culture under socialism: 'The proletariat is destined to create its own literature and poetry, which will be distinct in essence from those of the bourgeois past'.[25] Proletkult's task was to assist and accelerate this process. Lenin did not attend, but sent a greeting.

The Resolution passed at the forum declared that 'Music is the purest reflection of our inner spiritual life, the most powerful force organising the will and feelings of the masses, and a great force for the reconstruction [*peresozdaniye*] of humankind. As such, it must form an integral part of proletarian culture.'[26] Amidst all the heady rhetoric, there was a sour note that gave a hint of the future, namely Boris Krasin's attack on the highly popular 'gypsy music' genre, which he deemed unhealthy for the proletariat.[27] In the twenties, once the world-changing aspirations had begun to look out of place, much musical campaigning would revolve around the idea that communist intellectuals knew what was best for the proletariat, and that it should be weaned off its taste for 'gypsy' and other popular music.

Proletkult's family relations with Narkompros (family relations in every sense, since Bogdanov was Lunacharsky's brother-in-law), were strained from as early as the spring of 1918. Narkompros proposed to absorb Proletkult within its administrative structure in April, but the move was contentious, and was voted down by the left SRs (the majority of the Socialist Revolutionary Party, which was initially in coalition with the Bolsheviks). And so this huge, lively cultural mass movement was allowed to continue growing outside the boundaries of the state and the Bolshevik Party, with the 'idealist' Bogdanov at its head. Lenin was to become increasingly uneasy over Proletkult's independence (we shall see how this played out in the chapter on 1920).

1918 subjected the Russian intelligentsia to a series of shocks: the convocation and then dissolution of the Constituent Assembly, the execution of Nicholas II and his family, and, after an assassination attempt on Lenin, a wave of arrests

[24] Bryusova, 27.
[25] Ibid.
[26] Ibid., 24.
[27] *Literaturnaya zhizn' Rossii 1920-kh godov*, 115.

and executions on a scattershot basis. The Civil War, which began in May, placed doubts in the minds even of those who wanted to co-operate with the new power, since the odds were stacked high in favour of the other side, which was backed militarily and financially by fourteen states, representing much of the world's wealth. War-time rations were introduced in June, on a class basis, designed to favour the army, producers of food and essential workers. The intelligentsia found themselves at the bottom of the scale, alongside priests, capitalists, and (curiously) doctors.[28] But if there was no carrot, there was no stick either, since Lunacharsky echoed the artists' own demands that art should be separate from the state, and expanding on this, added that it should remain free from all regimentation.[29]

Even so, 1918 also saw the emergence of one institution that proved very durable in Soviet cultural life, namely the open competition organised by the state for revolutionary artworks. In the spring, the first such competition was announced, calling upon poets and composers to provide 'texts for a new, original and revolutionary proletarian anthem and new proletarian choral and solo songs, with prizes of 300, 200 and 100 roubles.' The music journalist Yevgeny Braudo, who later became a well-established *Pravda* correspondent, was not impressed; in an article entitled 'A hymn written to order' he wrote:

> In the very fact that such a competition has been announced [...] there is at the very least a simplistic understanding of the psychology of artistic creation [...] the state power offers a certain reward for artists, and that is enough to make them create for its glorification [...][30]

Then again, perhaps Braudo had a simplistic understanding of the psychology of artistic commission.

While those who flocked to Proletkult clearly found the situation invigorating and inspiring, many or most professional musicians, like much of the intelligentsia, were disorientated and often outraged, and suddenly had to worry about procuring enough bread and firewood for the first time in their lives. But these musicians also gradually attempted to fit into the new system that was slowly coalescing, and they even participated in shaping it, as their initial hostility to the new dispensation began to dissipate over time and through habit. The pianist Goldenweiser, as we saw earlier, recalled his presentiments of doom after the Bolsheviks triumphed in the October Revolution. But this recollection was committed to paper in July 1918, when the routines of daily life – some old, some new – were uppermost in his thoughts. After his account of the Revolution, he switches to the present day:

---

[28] Ibid., 217.

[29] Lunacharsky's overtures to the existing Union of Art Workers (*Soyuz deyateley iskusstv*), headed by the Symbolist poet Fyodor Sologub, were initially rejected: Sologub insisted that 'we must keep art and state separate'. A few months later, Lunacharsky was to be found canvassing the same idea, comparing the independent status of art to that of the church. *Literaturnaya zhizn' Rossii 1920-kh godov*, 60 and 159.

[30] Yevg. Braudo, 'Gimn po zakazu', *Vecherniye vedomosti*, 22 Apr. 1918, quoted in *Literaturnaya zhizn' Rossii 1920-kh godov*, 166.

I am busy with public activities (The Music Council). There is much hustle and bustle here, much work needed for this or that reason, but there is no satisfaction or joy in that. Often a bad taste in the mouth ... Yet it is impossible to push the work aside (or is it because I don't know how?).[31]

This could have been written in 1928, 1938 or 1948. Goldenweiser, a deeply religious Tolstoyan, initially resented every moment he had to spend under 'the Bolshevik tyranny'. But if even he could be transformed into a Soviet functionary in a matter of months, then most other members of the intelligentsia could do likewise, and with still less difficulty.

[31] Gol'denveyzer, 26.

N. Petrov, 'Opera i noviy zritel'' [Opera and Its New Audience], *Artist-muzïkant*, no. 2 (1918), 5.

The author begins his article by discussing the need to monitor the reactions of workers and peasants, as they start to attend theatre productions for the first time. He then addresses method, and the place of questionnaires and statistics in the task.

N. Petrov
Opera and Its New Audience

[...]
We have not made use of questionnaires so far, and have not even drawn them up as yet (this we consider to be an extremely difficult task, with a bearing on the destiny of our native art), and so, in parallel with such statistical methods, we will also need to introduce a method that can throw some light on the matter and flesh out the results with concrete details: namely, the method of the individual approach to spectators, where we hold conversations with those in the seats around us at the theatre. But this must be nothing more than a conversation, the kind of talk from which we can expect sincere, simple, unpretentious responses, and answers that would be true, not false. The moment it resembles official questioning, or a reporter's interview, the soul of your interlocutor will be closed up under seven seals, and instead of a sincere expression of heartfelt opinion, you will only see a pose, a bureaucratic formal reply [*otpiska*], and the material will be devoid of all value.

As a person directly interested in the standing of music and music-theatrical performance for the new audiences, I have started up conversations with people sitting next to me in the opera stalls. They have always been workers – skilled workers.

At the first performance of *Boris Godunov*, I was sitting next to a worker in a white shirt, who was no longer young and had a large beard.

He was late, having missed the two scenes of the Prologue, and only arrived for the beginning of Act 1; he took his seat just at the moment when the orchestra started to play again.

Without paying attention to the orchestra, my neighbour addressed me with a question: 'Comrade, can you tell me what's already been shown?' I replied that now, during the music, I couldn't do this, but that I would tell him later. He did not believe me and probably took offence. These negotiations took up the nine bars of the orchestral introduction, and then Pimen began: 'One more tale, the last one'. My neighbour, who had been indifferent to the raising of the curtain, the bright stage set and the actors who were then revealed (and it was all this that should have been gripping the spectators' attention), fell silent at once, and then sat throughout the whole scene with a happy – I would even say blissful – expression on his face, prompting aloud Pushkin's words, which he knew by heart, and restoring the cuts that Musorgsky had made.

This man, who [had acquired the attitudes of] a typical *intelligent*, was intoxicated by literature's sweet poison; he was completely in thrall to the power of the word, and for him, the other arts did not exist, since he did not notice any colours or movements, and did not hear the music.

Music, painting, and acting passed him by. He was mistaken in coming to the opera. I fled from him in the first interval.

On Tuesday, at another performance of *Boris*, I was sitting next to a worker again; he turned out to be a metalworker from one of the largest of the Moscow factories.

This worker, by contrast, was mainly responsive to the music. For him, the performance started not with the raising of the curtain, but with the first note, that first C♯ in the *cor anglais* and bassoon, at the opening of the opera's wonderful orchestral prelude.

To my question (which I must confess was sly) whether he found it unnatural that the characters sang instead of talking, he replied categorically, as if stating an inviolable truth, that 'there is nothing unnatural about this', that the music allows us (I can't quite remember how he expressed it) to feel the soul and the emotions of the characters, that 'the spectator becomes more sympathetic' to them thanks to the music, and finally, that the music allows us to gain a sense of 'the historical, the life of past times'. The tone painting of the orchestral accompaniment in the same Pimen scene ('He writes, he calmly writes') did not escape him. When I asked him about the scenery and the costumes, he said with conviction that they are 'very interesting' but once again started talking about the music: 'the music follows [the action] precisely'.

This is what a metalworker from the Dobrov and Nabholz factory said to me.

Music was singing in his soul.

B. Krasin, 'Zadachi muzïkal'nogo otdela' [The Tasks of the Music Section], *Gorn*, no. 1 (1918), 58–61.

This is Boris Krasin's report on the activities of the Music Section of Moscow Proletkult, delivered at the First All-Russian Conference of the Organisations of Proletarian Cultural Enlightenment. Some aspects of the Proletkult programme, such as the fight against 'restaurant music' or the encouragement of choral singing, were later taken up again by RAPM. But the expectation that the workers themselves would some day become composers – even en masse – is unique to Proletkult. It is also notable that the meeting considered some music to be pernicious in itself, irrespective of any lyrics attached to it: music that was 'vulgar' and 'bourgeois' could not be redeemed by a revolutionary text.

B. Krasin

The Tasks of the Music Section
[of Moscow Proletkult]

The Music Section sets itself the following tasks in its activities first, it is necessary to provide a lead in the decisive struggle against all the anti-artistic music that has found favour with the masses: namely, restaurant music (i.e. the so-called 'gypsy romances'), vulgar songs, dances, marches, and similar surrogates for real music. All this music reflects the degradations of bourgeois society, which has poured it into the mouths of the people like a poison. All this music was published and distributed in millions of copies across the whole vast territory of Russia: this musical vulgarity could be heard in the furthest corners of the country, on the open stage, on the boulevards, in the taverns, in the villages, and on the streets of the cities. Millions of peasants and workers were recruited into the army, and there the brass trumpets and the drums forcibly blew this bourgeois poison into their ears. Various entrepreneurs made vast quantities of gramophone records and, sending these out to 'everyone, everyone, everyone', they spread the infection to the furthest corners of Russia.

By giving lectures, and performing models that show what true art music is, we will fight this evil.

To wash away this poison, to kill the 'musical body of capitalism', so to speak – this is our task; and we expect to succeed, since the innate artistic taste and creativity of the workers and peasants is already being awakened. We foresee another attack of musical vulgarity in disguise: many composers who used to pander to bourgeois and philistine tastes, will take the character of the present times into account and attempt to clothe their vulgar works in revolutionary garb; they will try to peddle their goods in the guise of revolutionary marches, anthems and songs; but this provocation will also meet with a deserved rebuff.

Our second task is to help the proletariat to master, as far as possible, all of humanity's truly artistic musical heritage.

The revival of the art of folk song is, in our opinion, one of the most important and urgent tasks.

This kind of song is a colossal treasure and an almost unique example of the mighty collective creative work that capitalism tried to take away from the people, and which should, by right, be restored to its creators.

We consider ourselves obliged to help the people win back their musical offspring, and as far as we can tell, the proletariat itself also wants the same thing – this is its will. The musical native tongue of folk song will be the first language of the creative proletariat.

If there is a French *Internationale*, there will be a Russian one too, and it will be sung by all the peoples of the world.

Folk song, of course, is not our dogma and final goal, since it was created in different times and with a different consciousness, but even so, it almost always gave expression to a longing for future freedom, or a joyful striving towards it. This is why only folk song, which is comprehensible to the people, can be the starting point for the new musical creation of the proletariat. New forms will, of course, emerge; new sounds and rhythms, the rhythms of the cities, of war and revolutions will make themselves heard in the new song, and the freedom for which it had been longing will now be glorified.

Here we approach the main goal of the Music Section's activities, and all the above-mentioned tasks are to some extent only the means that lead up to this.

The main goal is to support and help reveal the new musical creativity of the proletariat.

We must help them master the techniques of musical creativity; we must help the future proletarian artists, performers and creators to find their way, and this means both collective and individual manifestations.

Today, it is impossible to tell what kind of creative work this will be, and it is impossible to say what methods will be used. It is possible, and even very probable, that we ourselves will have much to learn. This kind of work can benefit from experience.

Our work is laboratory work, and we are not afraid to make mistakes, for the mighty creativity of the free proletariat will discover the correct path in the end.

Although the work of the Music Section only began quite recently, some matters have already been dealt with.

Report on the work of the Section

In our opinion, the best and shortest path towards the above-mentioned goals is choral singing, which will also assume additional importance as an organising and unifying force, as artistic work directed towards a harmonious collective consciousness. This is why the Music Section has paid particular attention to this aspect of the work by creating a Section for Choral Studios at the outset, which began organising proletarian choral studios by district at the Soviets of deputies, the working clubs and the trade unions. These studios accept all workers interested in music and singing free of charge; here they can quench their musical thirst from the pure wellsprings of the great folk-song heritage, cleansing themselves of the poison with which the capitalist city had polluted them.

In the studios, they learn folk and revolutionary songs, study musical literacy, and attend talks about music.

In the near future, our studios will see the introduction of a course in music appreciation, lectures on music with musical illustrations, and, lastly, a course in the composition of choral songs.

The participants at the studios are all normally divided into groups according to their level of musical proficiency; those completely lacking in experience are admitted at first as listeners, but not participants in the singing.

※ ※ ※ ※ ※

Igor' Glebov, 'Zatish'ye' [A Lull], *Zhizn' iskusstva*, no. 48 (28 Dec. 1918), 1–2.

Towards the end of 1918, Boris Asafyev (under the pseudonym of Igor Glebov) wrote several essays for the Petrograd arts newspaper Zhizn' iskusstva *(Artistic Life), with repeated laments over the silence and passivity of Russian composers. He had been encouraged to write just such articles by his Moscow friend Vladimir Derzhanovsky, who saw the current period of disorder as an opportunity for new music. In his letter to Asafyev during the summer, Derzhanovsky said that he was dismayed to see this opportunity squandered because of the wait-and-see attitudes of his fellow 'music workers', while the greater daring displayed in the other arts had led to a flourishing of modernism. Derzhanovsky was planning to revive his pre-revolutionary journal* Muzïka, *and to publish his own appeal to Moscow's composers there. Aware that the journal might not last in the current circumstances, Derzhanovsky told Asafyev he was determined to persevere:*

> When there is the opportunity, even for a brief moment, to leave behind all our desiccating idleness, the useless grumbling, and outrageous inaction, how can we, the workers of Russia's youthful musical culture, fail to grasp this opportunity? For us, Bolshevism, Menshevism, or Kadetism [...] do not and cannot exist, and the only thing that does and should exist for us is Russian music, the national music culture, the demands and needs of youthful artistry, which was treated badly under the [previous] 'order', and which will be treated even worse when the hoped-for order is restored, but which *for the moment* at least, is given an opportunity to set out its compositions and all its efforts in the conditions it deserves. [...]
>
> I ardently call upon you to work. And not just on the journal, but on everything that MUZO is feverishly attempting to start up. If you know anyone who cares about music, call them to work. Reassure the timid: those who work in Narkompros (and this is the place where all living pedagogical forces have gathered) risk nothing – their work is little connected with politics and goes completely under the well-known principles of workers' schools [adult education], which weren't invented by the Bolsheviks; those who work for MUZO have still less to fear; finally, if anyone is still afraid, it is the work that matters, not title pages – even if they have to remain in hiding [*v pokhoronkakh*], they can still work. This is especially true for the journal, where articles can, of course, be left unsigned.[32]

The 'fears' that he wanted Asafyev to address, were fears that any collaboration with the Bolsheviks would lead to career setbacks or persecution in the event of a White victory in the Civil War. In the end, though, Derzhanovsky was unable to bring his journal back into print, and had to wait until 1923 to grasp the next opportunity. In 1918, it fell to Asafyev to make the call to composers.

---

[32] Derzhanovsky's letter to Asafyev of 24 July 1918, RGALI, fond 2658 (Asafyev), op. 2, ye. kh. 43, ll. 37–8.

Igor Glebov
A Lull

Modern Russian music has been pushed into a corner. Who and what is to blame for this, no one knows. Is it the apathy and inertia of the musicians themselves, or the unpredictability of events, or simply a kind of spiritual laziness papered over with excuses about fatigue and exhaustion? Most probably it is the last, arising from that characteristic of the Russian nation: the inability to settle down to things. Spiritual values can be nurtured only by nations that thirst for life, that desire to sow memories of themselves and to live on through their offspring; spiritual values cannot be nurtured by those who live only for the present. We Russians are inclined to discard and waste our creative ideas, thinking nothing of their fate, failing to embody them in *things*, never striving to see our immortality in their safety [i.e. when the ideas have been embodied for posterity]. We have the mentality of people who are used to spread out their thoughts in boundless space, a mentality inherited from nomads and nourished by the fluidity and immortality of our plains, fields and steppes. Whether in the sphere of material comforts, in the domestic sphere or in the sphere of spiritual values, we still have the same relationship to life: the Russian peasant would never think of paving the road or constructing a firm bridge over a stream, choosing instead to cover the muddy track with straw or crossing the stream on the first plank that comes to hand; likewise, a Russian member of the intelligentsia is unable to sustain intensive work for the protection of culture, for the protection of the spiritual values that he himself brought into being, and instead of struggling in unity with others, he prefers to withdraw from his business and mope, grumbling and growling away to himself. It is typical of Russian musicians to reject creative work entirely if they do not meet with a response in their milieu, or to lock themselves into a narrow circle of purely personal experiences, into so-called art for oneself, as if they lack any desire to make it known publicly. As a result, ideas exhaust themselves with no influence from their environment, neither injecting life into it nor drawing life from it. This is how things have been since Glinka, who imagined that his passive withdrawal from his art would somehow hurt people; the composer had his own weighty reasons to be angry with Russian society, which he considered unworthy to receive his works, and so he expended his artistic forces on impotent grumbling. Outside a small circle, of course, there was really no one who gave a damn whether Glinka composed his music or not! Such a relationship between the milieu and the creators of culture reflects painfully on the destiny of Russian music. It would seem that musical thought, gripped in a vice, sharpened and enflamed by hunger, could be fired up by itself and fire up the will to self-expression. Alas, no! This does not seem to be taking place, and we know, even, of some talented people who sit in corners withdrawn into themselves, searching for oblivion in their art: there is no possibility to incite them to struggle, to struggle for the right to show their conceptions to the world around them. Their creative work speaks of their languishing. Of course, there is no support around them: performers are content with the old things they learnt long ago, and so it is hard to blame composers when they complain about their fate. There is a demand for performers, who all hurry to collect as many jobs as possible, so that they can scratch out a living. They have no time to cultivate an interest in the destiny of the art of music, or in the further development of their own gifts. Of course, in chasing after the next loaf of bread, their artistic side is not in evidence, but what can we do if life demands of people a stronger will and greater spiritual fortitude than they actually possess!

Publishers have always been indifferent or mean in supporting Russian music, and even the great patronage of [Mitrofan] Belyayev,[33] when it fell into the hands of musicians themselves, was stifled by censorship. The prospect of a state publishing house still lies in the future. The conservatoire has succeeded in conserving itself so well that it has come to a complete standstill. The goals of concert life are in opposition to the interests of modern musicians and modern music, and the conductors are also a problem, since they are indifferent or untalented. Thus one obstacle breeds another, external reasons are woven together with the fading and extinction of the spirit, and there is no strength left to tear through this tormented languishing. Is there no way for composers to come together and take from life what they are owed?!

---

[33] Mitrofan Petrovich Belyayev (1836–1904) was a wealthy industrialist and patron of Russian music. He estalished the famous Belyayev Circle, which included Rimsky-Korsakov and Glazunov among its members, and set up a successful music-publishing business, M. P. Belaieff of Leipzig. Not to be confused with Viktor Belyayev, the musicologist, who features prominently elsewhere in the present volume.

R., 'Iskusstvo i proletariat' [Art and the Proletariat], *Zhizn' iskusstva*, no. 50 (31 Dec. 1918)

> This report contains many of the ideas that would resurface in 1932, at the end of our period, such as the concept of an artistic union and a preference for art rooted in tradition. While there were many other possible routes that post-Revolutionary culture could have taken, these particular elements were present in Soviet artistic discourse from the outset.

'R.'
Art and the Proletariat

A series of discussions on the topic 'Art and the proletariat' has just concluded. It was held in the Palace of Labour, and organised by the Petrograd Soviet of Trade Unions.

The final discussion, taking place on 29 December, once again attracted a large audience that was dominated by the painters, as before.

This final discussion was of a more political nature.

The opponents of Futurism levelled a number of accusations against the representatives of leftist art, in terms that were sometimes harsh.

The spokesmen for the leftist artistic camp gave replies that were equally harsh towards the old art.

The last word was given to Cmrd. Tsïperovich, who also debated with participants in the discussion, although mainly with the defenders of the Futurist tendency in art.

The discussion ended with a reading of the theses that had been proposed by Cmrd. Tsïperovich.[34]

These were met with applause, and won the assent of most in the audience.

The theses were as follows:

The highest form of socialist production is art. The highest form of socialist life is beauty. Only the masses can be the true creators of socialist life, but the working class considers artists, poets, musicians and actors to be capable of giving expression to its will towards socialist beauty.

The proletariat is striving towards new, mass forms of art and towards new socialist content for art. But in doing so, it takes its material from the art of the past. The proletariat will arrive at the new socialist art only through schooling in the best work of the greatest artists, which it has not had access to until now. It decidedly rejects adventurism in new endeavours, and demands that these should present a socialist conclusion drawn from

---

[34] Most likely Grigoriy Vladimirovich Tsïperovich (1871–1932). A revolutionary from his early years, he was arrested and exiled. He only joined the Communist Party in 1919. At this point, he was one of the leaders of the Petrograd Trade Unions.

all the premises humanity has created, rather than a simple rejection and destruction of existing culture.

The proletariat, which is used to creating things in an organised fashion, believes that the creators of beauty – painters, actors, musicians – will join its family as an organised mass.

But keeping in mind the peculiarities of art and its creators, the proletariat thinks it necessary to facilitate the organisation of artists and actors by refraining from any demand that the artists should form strict and complete organisations; this should help them in every way to bring about unity, both amongst themselves, and also between themselves and the working class.

For this reason, the Petrograd Soviet of Trade Unions is inviting the newly created union of artists and actors to join the Soviet as an autonomous section via the department of culture and education.

Through this union, we can, in practice, realise the task of serving industry through the work of creators of art. [a misprint in the original has rendered the meaning of this sentence unclear] It will also provide a firm basis for the distribution of creative forces across the production unions, with the goal of raising production to the level of art.

Given all that has been said, the Soviet of Unions invites artists, musicians, poets, sculptors, and actors to come together into one close family, to organise a union of the arts with urgency, and to join the ranks of the proletariat for the purpose of working together in the name of socialism, in the name of universal equality, and in the name of universal beauty.

1919
Depression and Fever

The Music Section of Narkompros (MUZO) continued in its attempts to organise the country's disparate and chaotic musical activities, and to direct these towards the needs (as it perceived them) of the working classes. In June, to minimise the duplication and confusion that was rife among the many fledgling organisations, Lunacharsky approved a statute that pronounced MUZO to be the sole body responsible for managing and unifying musical activities across the Soviet Republic. The statute's insistent language evinces a degree of desperation in the face of anarchy: 'the resolutions of the Music Section are obligatory for all citizens, organisations and institutions of RSFSR without exception'.[1] MUZO created a register of all existing choirs and orchestras in Moscow,[2] and was soon able to offer the services of its own two choirs and a string quartet.[3] It opened a People's Music School that was free to anyone with an ear for music, with Bryusova adding prestige to its teaching staff. In order to prevent their disappearance, many valuable pre-Revolutionary cultural institutions were nationalised and renamed, while most of the old personnel continued work much as normal. Even Sergei Zimin, the owner of the Private Opera (Moscow's second opera house), was retained in the salaried position of theatre manager. The many music shops and publishers were also nationalised, but again there was a desire to avoid disruption where possible: like Zimin, the prominent publisher Boris Jurgenson was retained as manager of the new state-run enterprise.

The theatre season of 1918–19 proceeded under the most testing conditions. The scarcity of food sometimes led to performers fainting from hunger. Indeed, many of the performances were paid for in food or tobacco. Actresses who had formerly relied on servants now had see to their own cooking, laundering and childcare. In the ballet companies, malnutrition among the male dancers so weakened them that they could no longer lift their female partners. Many artists fell ill, and the death rate was correspondingly higher. The papers reported the suicide of several prominent figures.[4] Although there was a drive to stockpile fuel for the following season, the winter of 1919–20 proved to be no less difficult. On 14 November, Kuper conducted *Die Walküre* at the Mariinsky in an unheated auditorium where the temperature had fallen to freezing point. Artists needed to hold down more than one job in order to survive, causing members of the Mariinsky orchestra to neglect their duties. At one point in the season, the absence of more than a third (or, by another account, half) of the string players almost led to the cancellation of a performance; the conductor Grzegorz Fitelberg was eventually persuaded to perform with only three out of twelve cellos in the pit.

[1] 'Muzïkal'nïy otdel', *Zhizn' iskusstva*, no. 162 (13 June 1919), 3.

[2] S. R. Stepanova, *Muzïkal'naya zhizn' Moskvï v pervïye godï posle Oktyabrya: Khronika, dokumentï, materialï* (Moscow: Sovetskiy kompozitor, 1972), 123.

[3] Stepanova, 123–4.

[4] I. S. Rozenberg, 'Tyazhyolïy sezon', *Biryuch Petrogradskikh gosudarstvennïkh teatrov* (June–Aug. 1919), 172–6.

The absentees were sacked, but the rest of the orchestra went on strike in protest, and for two weeks operas were performed to piano accompaniment, which evidently did not daunt the audience, since the opening of a new production of *Carmen* was sold out.[5] In October, Lunacharsky passed a special resolution forbidding the closure of theatres for lack of fuel; if a concession was needed, they were allowed to cut the number of performances each week. In December, the former Mariinsky took advantage of this, and cancelled all Wednesday and Friday performances.[6]

In Petrograd, the theatres only closed for a fortnight, when the front line had nearly advanced upon the city, reaching the Pulkovo heights. At that stage, it seemed very likely that the city would be taken by White forces under General Yudenich; the city was declared under siege, and the population mobilised. But the Red Army managed to push the offensive away from the city, and the state theatres were able to hold solemn reopening nights on the second anniversary of the Revolution (7 November new style): the Mariinsky performed Rimsky-Korsakov's *The Maid of Pskov*, in which 'several revolutionary episodes' were remarked upon,[7] while the GosBOT played *Die Meistersinger*, which was now presented as an opera about workers and for workers. A concert held on the same day featured Berlioz's Triumphal Symphony (the title given in the listings), a performance of the ubiquitous *Internationale* in an arrangement by a former composer of liturgical music, Alexander Arkhangelsky, and in a new addition to the repertoire, various songs of the French Revolution were unearthed, translated and arranged on MUZO's initiative (these included the *Carmagnole* and *Ça ira*, which, it was claimed, were previously unknown in Russia).[8] It seemed nothing could quench the love affair between the theatres and their public: when an 11 pm curfew was imposed, the theatres simply moved their starting time to 6 pm; when the tram services had to be severely curtailed, the public was prepared to trudge through the dark and snowy city streets.

Despite the hardships, the Mariinsky managed to mount some new productions, beginning with Rimsky-Korsakov's *Kashchei the Immortal* (early 1919). Complaining about the 'soulless' production and 'revolting' performance in a letter, the critic and music scholar Viktor Belyayev was convinced that '*Kashchei* is deemed worthy now because it was first staged in 1905 and thus acquired the reputation of being a "revolutionary" opera'.[9] Other new productions, Wagner's *Tannhäuser* and Serov's *Power of the Fiend* (directed by Chaliapin) could boast no such revolutionary credentials. The opera-going public was largely the same

---

[5] *Zhizn' iskusstva*, no. 302 (26 Nov. 1919); also 'Nebrezhnost' orkestrantov', *Krasnaya gazeta*, no. 272 (27 Nov. 1919), 4; also 'Dirizhyor bez orkestra', *Krasnaya gazeta*, no. 278 (4 Dec. 1919), 4.

[6] Stepanova, 172.

[7] A.A-v, 'K oktyabr'skim torzhestvam', *Krasnaya gazeta*, no. 224 (4 Oct. 1919), 4.

[8] N.R., 'K godovshchine Oktyabr'skoy revolyutsii', *Krasnaya gazeta*, no. 221 (1 Oct. 1919), 4; 'Teatrï i zrelishcha k dnyu Oktyabr'skoy godovshchinï', *Krasnaya gazeta*, no. 254 (5 Nov. 1919), 4.

[9] Letter from Belyayev to Myaskovsky of 5 Feb. 1919, RGALI, f. 2040 (Myaskovsky), op. 1, ye. kh. 102, l. 8.

as before the Revolution, but from the autumn of 1919 the system that allowed subscribers to reserve a family box for the season was abolished.

In Moscow, the Bolshoi offered a programme of standard repertoire, with Russian classics such as *The Queen of Spades, Ruslan and Lyudmila, Sadko,* and *The Tsar's Bride,* together with Western favourites including *La Traviata, Aida, Samson and Dalila,* and *Romeo and Juliet.* The spring premiere was *Die Walküre.* But the Bolshoi now had a close rival in the former Zimin Opera, renamed The Theatre of the Soviets of Workers' Deputees (Teatr SRD). The repertoire was again quite standard, with the exception of Sergei Taneyev's *Oresteia.* The third Moscow opera house, under the unpronounceable name 'Studiya KhPSRO',[10] hosted Fyodor Komissarzhevsky's experimental productions; this theatre is better known under its later name, The New Opera (Novaya Opera). The Bolshoi Theatre also managed to open a second stage, an opera studio placed under the direction Konstantin Stanislavsky.

The Operetta Theatre opened in Moscow in the autumn of 1919; among the operettas it presented was Kálmán's *Der Kleine König* (known in Russia as *Mateo*) with a thoroughly reworked libretto under the name 'The Revolutionary' (*Revolyutsionerka*). Nevertheless, the authorities doubted whether such frothy entertainment was appropriate for the times, and since every open theatre meant an extravagant consumption of heat and electricity in a period of extreme scarcity, it was hardly surprising that in December a resolution was passed to close the Operetta.

'A sea of concerts – large, small, chamber, symphonic, historical … What is going on? Is this really prompted by a powerful need, some elemental thirst for music, or does this wild array of programmes (the majority graced by the same artists, reshuffled in various permutations) scream only of "dire necessity"?' – enquired one critic.[11] He was correct: singers and instrumentalists indeed performed as often as they could out of 'dire necessity', staving off starvation; but it was also true that the entertainment they provided met a genuine hunger on the part of audiences, who needed moments of beauty and reassurance to fortify them for their daily hardships and worries.

Symphonic concerts were dominated by Sergei Koussevitzky, who appeared not only as conductor, but also played the solo part in his own Concerto for Double Bass, reminding his audiences that his nickname 'the Chaliapin of the double bass' was well deserved. He was accompanied by the young conductor Nikolai Golovanov, then at the very beginning of his illustrious career. Sacred music was by no means out of bounds: one of Koussevitzky's concerts featured the premiere of Alexander Grechaninov's *Demestvennaya Liturgiya* (Domestic Liturgy), performed alongside sacred pieces by J. S. Bach.

In spite of this plethora of concerts, 'new music' was conspicuous by its absence. Understandably, musicians performing to stay alive were not keen to take risks with their repertoire. Three piano recitals in Moscow, all falling in February, were a notable exception: Alexander Borovsky played Prokofiev's Second and

---

[10] *Studiya khudozhestvenno-prosvetitel'skikh rabochikh organizatsiy* (Theatre Workshop of the Workers' Organisations for Artistic Education).

[11] A.Ts., 'Kontsertï Kusevitskogo', *Vestnik teatra*, no. 13 (19–21 Mar. 1919), 9.

Third Sonatas, the *Visions fugitives* and the *Sarcasms*; Mark Meychik played Scriabin's Third and Fifth Sonatas; and Goldenweiser played Scriabin's Ninth and Tenth, together with some of the preludes. The two Scriabin recitals were given a further splash of colour with introductory lectures by the celebrated Symbolist poets, Vyacheslav Ivanov and Yuri Baltrušaitis, both Scriabin fanatics. There was another, large-scale attempt to present new music, mostly by young unknowns, in a series of 'musical exhibitions'. Three of these 'exhibitions' were mounted by the Moscow Conservatoire, but by all accounts they provided little pleasure (and the composers mostly sank back into obscurity). Pavel Lamm, for example, jotted down the following disparaging comments in his programme booklet for the Second Musical Exhibition (11 May, Conservatoire Chamber Hall):

Ye. Kashperova-Levshina (very poor, in the Russian style)
A. Miller (rubbish)
V. Nebolsin (uninteresting)
A. Dianov (no, not the right thing!)
A. Dzegelyonok (boring and indifferent; silly)
Ye. Pavlov (rubbish)
A. Shaposhnikov (à la Debussy and not so bad)
A. Parusnikov (immeasurable boredom)[12]

The concert calendar shows the old and new rubbing shoulders: the traditional Easter break was still observed, while the death of the prominent Bolshevik, Yakov Sverdlov, led to the cancellation of all entertainments on 18 March.

Moscow's composers organised themselves into a trade union, electing Nikolai Roslavets as chair, but this was only one of a series of powerless and short-lived organisations that failed to make an impact on the lives of musicians. Another such body was the Association for Contemporary Music (ASM) at MUZO, the first, abortive, attempt to create such an organisation. (The more prominent organisation of the 1920s was not continuous with its 1919 namesake, and was only launched five years later.) The membership of the 1919 incarnation of ASM included Lourié, Nikolai Roslavets, Nikolai Myaskovsky, Nikolai Medtner, Alexander Gedike, Anatoly Aleksandrov, Alexander Krein and Grigory Krein, together with the conductor Golovanov, who at that point also fancied himself as a composer (Myaskovsky became a founder member of the later ASM, while others, such as Medtner and Lourié, had left Russia by that stage).

Organising aspects of musical life was one thing, but composition was quite another, and these composers generally felt under no obligation – political or aesthetic – to change their style or choice of genres to fit the times. For the most part the idea was not even entertained. A striking exception was Alexander Kastalsky, the director of the prestigious Moscow Synodal Choir, and of its secularised successor, The People's Choral Academy. He made a significant

[12] Evgeny Pavlov belonged to Yesenin's circle of Imaginists, and was the author of this group's Musical Manifesto (1921). Adrian Grigoryevich Shaposhnikov (1887–1967) studied under Glazunov. From 1918 to 1936, he worked as an engineer and only composed sporadically. In 1937, he moved to Ashkhabad and reinvented himself as a national composer of Turkmenistan. For Nebolsin, Dianov, and Dzegelyonok see Glossary.

contribution to the new adult music-education programmes, and fulfilled several Narkompros commissions: he reharmonised and arranged the *Internationale* for different ensembles, and wrote music to the poem *Sten'ka Razin* by Vasily Kamensky for an orchestra of woodwind and domras (a balalaika-type instrument). He also composed a larger-scale work entitled *Festivals of the People* [*Narodnïye prazdnovaniya*] 'at the insistence of A. S. Lourié'.[13] While most prominent musicians played no part in public debates on the political direction of the arts, Kastalsky again was the exception:

> at a public gathering in the Palace of Arts, I delivered a paper on a topic 'The most urgent tasks of proletarian art'. After I'd finished, Balmont launched into a eulogy of 'art for art's sake', and suffered a well-deserved fiasco.[14]

Behind all of this feverish activity, the artistic intelligentsia suffered from confusion, depression, and a crisis of purpose. Some characteristic comments on these matters can be found in the private correspondence of Belyayev, who was one of several figures attempting to re-establish various collapsed musical institutions:

> We are all either consumed by ceaseless activity, or else we retreat into ourselves, in order to find an interior equilibrium that will allow us to stand firm in all the confusion about us. I must say that life gives us a schooling that we could never have dreamed of or guessed at.[15]

Writing to Myaskovsky, Belyayev urges him to visit their mutual friend, the music critic and scholar Boris Asafyev, who, in his words, 'is consumed with anxiety [*izvelsya chelovek strashno*]. The Revolution interrupted his work as a writer, which is what he was born to do; now it's back to the old ways of earning money through quite excessive labour, everything down to the composition of incidental music or bureaucratic work at the Music Section [MUZO], in terrible psychological conditions.'[16] The maintenance of various pre-Revolutionary activities now acquired a nostalgic, escapist air, an attempt to hold on to scraps of old life. Lamm's famous music circle kept meeting even when there was no food or drink to serve at the table; one of its regulars, Sergei Popov, who was mobilised into the army, enquired:

---

[13] Letter from Kastalsky to Asafyev of 1 Sept. 1919, RGALI, f. 2658 (Asafyev), op. 1, ye. kh. 581, l. 35.

[14] Ibid. The official report from the meeting confirms Kastalsky's account: 'Citizen Kastalsky pointed out that we had to take Russian folk art into account in the building of proletarian culture [...] K. D. Balmont's speech was met with stormy protests, and only the threat [...] that the meeting would be closed [...] enabled him to say a few words to the effect that for him, art could not be divided into the bourgeois and the proletarian [...]' *Literaturnaya zhizn' Rossii 1920-kh godov: Sobïtiya. Otzïvï sovremennikov. Bibliografiya*, ed. by A. Yu. Galushkin (Moscow: IMLI RAN, 2006), vol. 1, part 1, 377.

[15] Letter from Belyayev to Myaskovsky of 22 Jan. 1919, RGALI, f. 2040 (Myaskovsky), op. 1, ye. kh. 102, l. 5.

[16] Letter from Belyayev to Myaskovsky of 5 Feb. 1919, ibid., l. 8v.

Do you still hold musical soirées or any kind of gatherings? I have always attended them with great pleasure: your place is so comfortable and welcoming, and in our conversations about the arts, we used to become totally oblivious to the hard life around us.[17]

---

[17] Letter from Popov to Lamm of 9 Oct. 1919, RGALI, f. 2743 (Lamm), op. 1, ye. kh. 176, l. 6.

※ ※ ※ ※ ※

'Deklaratsiya Muzïkal'nogo otdela NKP' [Declaration of the NKP Music Section], *Lad*, vol. 1 (Peterburg: Izdaniye muzïkal'nogo otdela N.K.P., 1919), 2–5.

This extraordinary document combines stylistic elements from Symbolist poetry with ideas on adult music education drawn from Proletkult. The author, Arthur Lourié, headed the music section at Narkompros, but his artistic mentor was the leading Symbolist poet, Alexander Blok. In April 1918, Blok wrote in his diary: 'A meeting with Lourié – he is supportive of my musical inclinations. A (future) declaration of the Music Department on the spirit of music'. Lourié characterised their relationship in these words: 'Together with Blok and under his tutelage, I listened to the music of the Revolution'.[18]

Declaration of the Music Section [of Narkompros]

The Music Section holds that the natural destiny of music is to bring about a bright renewal in ordering the lives of the peoples. From time immemorial, music was a rebellious, burning element and a creative, constructive force. Possessing the energy of rhythm and word (sound), music embodies a spiritual, thermal will to live: man exists only when he inhabits the state of music. Perceived always as true actuality (self-consciousness) and conceptualised always as the greatest kind of abstraction (estrangement), music is the world of the highest reality. Some are able to hear the rhythm of the cosmos – the movement of the stars, while others cannot even perceive the primary elements of music, and so exist outside living folk song. If the paths of living folk song lead to cognition of the movement of the stars and the rhythm of the universe, then existence in the spirit of music alone is a sun-filled world of joy. To those who do not perceive the primary elements of music, as perfectly revealed in the speech of living folk song, music does not exist, even if they accept it in its formal-schematic state as a result of long experience of musical-professional specialisation (the history of music). Inside the world cataclysm, when all humanity is being renewed and the very foundations of existence, the forms of the state and everyday life are transformed, music – drawing the universal collectivity of the people into the cycle of its organic processes – its births, flowerings and extinctions – invisibly rules over all the forms into which life is poured, seeking out the borders and destroying them. Only theatre in its best periods – tragedy and liturgy – participated in the action of music, for music is the eternal force of action, whereas theatre existed and established itself as theatre only when it rose to its greatest heights in the collective consciousness of the people; its decline led to catastrophe. Other varieties of art, having stifled the

---

[18] This connection to Blok is first mentioned in I. Nest'yev, 'Iz istorii russkogo muzïkal'nogo avangarda', *Sovetskaya muzïka* (1991), no. 1, 75–87 (80), and the quotations are also taken from this source.

music that sounds within them, exist only in the processes of individual perception and cognition. In these heroic times, the spirit of music reveals itself in the seething rhythms of the world uprising: avenging, casting into oblivion and melting the layers of dead formations, which have been erected by cowering humanity in its deafness, stubbornly and blindly fettering the life-giving force of music. Having failed to detect the spirit of music in the formal configurations of academic music, and recognising the complete futility of efforts expended within the methods of the current system of music education and realisation [i.e. performance], arising from the severance of the other arts' connections with their musical natures, the Music Section DECLARES that from now on music is free from all existing false canons and rules of musical scholastics, in all its manifestations, both in the creative sphere and in the sphere of music pedagogy. It affirms that cultivated music, as a reflection of the spirit of music, is subordinate to the laws of nature alone, with regard both to individual and collective sensual cognition and embodiment. The Music Section ANNOUNCES that it has found paths towards collective self-affirmation in everyday life through a holistic manner of perception, forming a counterweight to that habitual tendency towards faceless schematicism and individual outbursts, which are the lifebelts of clichéd and philistine artistry today. A general music education leads to the mastering of the pure natural materials of music through immediate experience. Instead of adopting the mechanical givens of rational suggestion, which rest on an endless repetition of learnt material, it allows connection and interpenetration between the personal gift of embodiment and the perceiving milieu. Freely mastering the material (the organic technique of embodiment), a sensitive mind and cognising heart transubstantiate that which is close to all, that which is familiar and stable – into an eternal striving for the immutable and desirable, through the affirmation of Love. In the sphere of visible actuality, the Music Section CREATES foundations for the complete involvement of the masses in their active self-realisation by means of the state-led construction of musical culture, arming these masses, the spirit of music hidden deep within them, with knowledge and experience. The reform of specialised (professional) education is announced today, in accordance with the tempo of the times, as a complete split from the milieu of the former *Kulturträgern* of sound and from the sphere of 'sound-making', and as a return instead to the free forms of the people's artistic creativity. The State Musical University[19] unites all the vital forces of the country, preserving the integrity and unity of the cause, and embracing all the tasks that the artistic will sets for perception, and realisation [i.e. performance] and embodiment [i.e. composition]. Understanding adult education as its means of contact with the mass audience, the Music Section DECLARES extra-curricular artistic education the foundation stone for all the work of construction for musical culture undertaken by associations for teaching, scholarship and public enlightenment. All concert activity, as a demonstration of music, will take place through large and small model collectives (orchestral or chamber ensembles) and through choral societies. Regenerating play and festivities, musical life organises

---

[19] The State Musical University (*Gosudarstvenniy muzikal'niy univesitet*) was a projected integrated system of music education running from beginner to tertiary level. It was never fully realised.

the street, imbuing it with the uplifting spirit of song. The other aspects of the Music Section's activities (teaching and scholarship – schools, courses, lectures; the publishing house; distribution and production) serve as an adjunct to the main goal, namely, the work of adult education. The Music Section BELIEVES that the landmarks established here will serve as directives to all who set out on the paths of music, remembering the spirit of music in the uplifting character of song.

Chairman of the Collegium of the Music Section, Arthur Lourié.
Members of the Collegium, B. V. Asafyev, S. S. Mitusov,[20]
A. P. Vaulin, V. L. Pastukhov
Petrograd, March 1919

---

[20] Stepan Stepanovich Mitusov (1878–1942) was a pianist and music teacher, and a friend of Rimsky-Korsakov and Stravinsky (he wrote the libretto for the latter's opera *The Nightingale*). At this juncture, he was responsible for concert organisation in MUZO.

※ ※ ※ ※ ※

Ant. Dianov, 'Muzïkal'nïye otkliki' [Musical Responses], *Gorn*, nos. 2–3, 106.

This article provides us with an example of a common complaint of the first decade after the Revolution, namely that serious composers were failing to take up Soviet themes in their music. This omission was suddenly made good in 1927, when a large batch of symphonic works was produced for the tenth anniversary of the Revolution (among them Shostakovich's Second Symphony, 'To October').

Ant. Dianov

Musical Responses

At the moment of the revolutionary uprising of the world proletariat, at the moment of a titanic struggle, of victory and our striving towards new possibilities for the social construction of life, people are thirsting for ardent words of appeal, for magnificent and jubilant songs of victory. And at this moment, out of the huge number of diverse revolutionary musical works that are being published, that are being consumed by the Russian proletariat quickly and greedily, a good half of these are unsuccessful, and at times utterly pitiful attempts to express in song the feelings born from the overturning of life now taking place.

It is so frustrating, after looking carefully through works published and not yet published, to find a poverty of musical thought, a lack of taste, or plain illiteracy.

Those who work in the Music Department of Moscow Proletkult have to meet the creators of these 'revolutionary' works, and must accept from them their fabricated marches, anthems, etc., with requests to have them performed as soon as possible; and all of these composers are either modest dilettanti, who are mistaken about their musical gifts, or cunning salesmen, who wish to use their talents to compose in a restaurant style, so that they can quickly become known to the masses and receive a solid return from them.

At this moment, I have in my hands a number of works published by Petrograd Proletkult. I will list these:

1) 'In Memory of Karl Marx', words by Yasinsky, music by Ozolin
2) 'The First of May' anthem, words by V. Kirillov, music by Ozolin
3) 'The Workers' Palace' (dedicated to the choir of Petrograd Proletkult), words by Pomorsky, music by Ozolin
4) The anthem 'Peace of the Peoples', by Bankovsky.[21]

---

[21] Yan Ozolin, or Jānis Ozoliņš, of Latvian origin, made many arrangements of revolutionary songs and also composed his own (in 1931, he published a collection of these, with Latvian texts). He is not to be confused with a more prominent composer of the same name who lived from 1908 to 1981 and also composed choral works. The identity of the Bankovsky mentioned here is uncertain, but the most likely candidate is Grigory Bankovsky (Ban'kovskiy), an Orthodox priest who

I will repeat that all these works have been published by Petrograd Proletkult, and we can only wonder what criteria the musicians of Petrograd Proletkult used when they offered the people such fruits for adding to the wreath of Proletarian Culture. Neither Ozolin nor Bankovsky can be called composers, since their music shows not a single spark of inspiration; somehow everything remains dull, uninteresting and pointless; the empty impoverished little themes, which at times remind us of something from the past, were equally empty and tasteless. We won't even mention technique – they don't have any.

Now this begs a question: where are the composers who have all the gifts sufficient for musical creation? Perhaps the moment of creative inspiration has not yet come, or perhaps they are already writing, and a work will appear imminently, a work that will glitter with the sparks of the revolutionary mood. The poets have already begun to sing with strength and ardour (Gastev, Kirillov, Yesenin),[22] but music is silent. In the end, this is understandable. Music is the most fragile, the most delicate and immaterial of all the arts. And this is why it can be born only after feelings have been poured into life in a more material way. Let us remember that when naturalism in painting and literature was already dying, it was still blossoming in music. After the appearance of mystical philosophical theories and a great many theosophists, mystics and spiritualists, music also began to display various abstract and mystical philosophical thoughts and moods. I think also that music is the final conclusion to everything that comes before, a synthesis of all those ideas and feelings of men that are hard to grasp, ineffable. Therefore we hope that the time will come, and musicians will emerge, most probably from the depths of the revolutionary proletariat, which will by then have realised its own power. Bright and inspired songs songs full of goodness will flow from its heart like a broad free river, and the Russian proletariat will create its own workers' *Marseillaise*, its ardent hymns of Freedom, its victorious sounds of joyful festivities and triumphal processions.

---

had published some church music shortly before the revolution (if this is correct, he was only one of many defectors from the Church to the Revolution). Alexander Pomorsky and Vladimir Kirilov are better-known figures, both earning their literary reputations as "proletarian poets" in the 20s. The poet and critic, Ieronim Yasinsky (1850–1931), began his extraordinary career in the 1870s as a narodnik supporter, but later transformed himself into a liberal, then an anti-rationalist conservative, and finally, at the age of 70, he joined the Communist Party.

[22] Aleksey Kapitonovich Gastev (1882–1939, misspelled in the original as Gostev) and Vladimir Timofeyevich Kirillov (1890–1937) were both revolutionary activists and poster boys of Proletkult poetry, and both perished in the Purges. See Glossary entry for Yesenin.

※ ※ ※ ※ ※

Vyacheslav Ivanov, 'O Vagnere' [On Wagner], *Vestnik teatra*, nos. 31–2 (9–15 June 1919), 8–9.

Vyacheslav Ivanov, a Symbolist poet who for many years had gathered likeminded artists at his residence ('The Tower'), now co-operated with the Soviet Government, as did fellow Symbolists such as Alexander Blok and Valery Bryusov. Ivanov, indeed, went further, and took up a post in the Theatre Department (TEO) of Narkompros. This speech, given at a high-profile conference on extramural education, makes a tidy connection between the ideas of Symbolism (those of sobornost' *– a sense of spiritual community) and communism, and along the way validates Wagner, the Symbolists' idol, by placing him between the two composers who were recognised as 'revolutionary' at the time, namely Beethoven and Scriabin.*

Vyacheslav Ivanov
On Wagner

[Speech to the members of the Congress for Further Education at the Moscow Bolshoi Theatre, prior to a performance of *Die Walküre*, 17 May 1919]

Three musical geniuses are especially dear and close to us, all standing on the threshold: Beethoven, Wagner and Scriabin. They are connected to each other through common strivings and by a continuous line. Wagner considered himself a follower of Beethoven's cause, and the one who fulfilled Beethoven's behests. When the biblical Elijah ascended to the heavens in a flaming, thunderous chariot, he threw off his cloak into the hands of his pupil, Elisha, who together with the cloak inherited the gift of prophecy from his teacher. Wagner felt he was Elisha to Beethoven's Elijah. And Scriabin, who was blindly unresponsive towards Beethoven's music, saw Wagner as his predecessor. But perhaps all three will only prove to be the forerunners of a kind of art that would, for the first time, fulfil their greatest hopes entirely and with utter simplicity; for the first time, this would be an art in the grand style that will merge the masses into one single spiritual body, creating a united spirit within them. This future art for all the people could not be realised until now, because it requires a culture that differs from the previous culture, whose layers its shoots had to fight their way through: it will not tolerate the culture of the separate and the lonely, but wants a culture united by a shared grand idea, by a common will.

In Beethoven's music, according to Wagner, the deepest self-consciousness of the human spirit found its dynamic and immediately comprehensible language: this was his first deed. The second was to raise the image of the hero through music, revealing the beauty of the human will in all its astonishing magnificence. And the third of Beethoven's deeds was the inauguration of an assembled [*sobornïy*] choral element as something supreme in the building of a new life. In his Ninth Symphony, through a mighty appeal to a universal dance of freedom and joy, he assembles the whole of humanity into one single family, which has for the first time found its true historical form in a union of equals and in a communion of high inspiration.

The same strivings can be seen in Scriabin's creations. For him too, music is an expression of the foundations of the human spirit, and in it he nurtures the idea of the heroic sacrifice for the whole, for everyone; he, too, assembles people into a single chorus which actively changes all life to its very fundamentals. Some universal conflagration – he imagined – must turn the whole world to ashes and transfigure the face of the earth. But death halted his irrepressible creative flight, and he did not have the time to leave us a finished work, which he imagined as a choral enactment of that universal shift.

Nietzsche was right about the birth of tragedy from the spirit of music, and this was confirmed before our eyes by Scriabin's example: the elemental music that possessed him and pushed him inexorably towards the form of an act. The many-voiced instrumental symphony sought its ultimate incarnation in the living word and the movement of the assembled [*sobornoye*] multitude. The Mysterium, whose idea could be called otherworldly, remained beyond the threshold of realisability and realisation, although the composer of genius viewed his every new work as a preparatory achievement on the way to this supreme, single goal: the distant Mysterium was akin to a magnetic pole in his creative life. But the Preparatory Act was already underway: we have its complete poetic text and for some parts, we have sketches, still vague, of its grandiose musical contours. The Preparatory Act, according to the composer's strict instructions, was not to be performed before a passive gathering of mere spectators. Those present, every one of them, were to be clad in festive garments and were required to participate in the performance of the sacred drama by singing in the choruses or marching in the solemn processions. The *sobornost'* had to be realised in art, and art had to be transformed into life's events. That is how Scriabin expressed this most profound idea of our times.

Wagner stands chronologically between Beethoven and Scriabin, and serves as an intermediary link in the golden chain of these artistic quests. He clothes the heroic element in superhuman images and in the destinies of mythical heroes embodied on the stage; to him, myth is a tool for revealing in images the deepest insights into the meaning of life, into the tragic mystery of existence. But in the world epic that Wagner unfolds before us, we see only unique heroes; there is no room there for the multitude of the people, and the many-mouthed voice of the live chorus does not sound there, unlike Beethoven's Ninth Symphony and Scriabin's *Prometheus* – 'a poem of fire'. Nevertheless, Wagner's music dramas were conceived as universal 'festive acts'. The assembled voice of humanity is hidden in the orchestra's harmonies: from the mighty, stormy, sonorous sea of instrumental music, in which, according to the composer's conception, the will of the world seeks its expression, the colourful mirage of the stage emerges like the golden cloud of a prophetic dream, like a magic mirror, revealing life in its hidden essence as it presents itself to clairvoyant contemplation. In the sonorities of the wordless instrumental chorus, according to the composer's ideas, the assembled will of all humanity sounds, and, merging with the soul of the symphony, we ourselves summon and create that vision of the transformed human being in the images of the gods and heroes who move before us, as if we cast our reflections into some supra-worldly space.

No, there is no liberated, self-conscious humanity, at least in the *Ring of the Nibelungs*: it is only in the process of being created there. Wotan himself, the supreme god of this primeval universe, is a wise god and a creator, but not omniscient, not omnipotent, not eternal; he longs for a free human being who knows no fear. We are present at his birth: before us are Siegmund and Sieglinde, a brother and sister who innocently fell in love with each other, not knowing who the other was, and who are punished for their sinful love; Siegmund has to die, but Sieglinde is saved in order to give life to Siegfried. The sun hero will perish like the sun, and will take with him the whole of Valhalla, the whole world of the first gods; but on the ruins of Valhalla, the new humanity will rise … A lofty prophecy, but we now await different acts, not acts of promise, but acts of fulfilment, acts of choral multitudes, a many-mouthed human voice and a real, rather than magical and symbolic human heroism. We await these, and we will, I know, live to see them.

1920

Bureaucracy on the Rise

Musical life here is organised by anyone and everyone. There are no less than four main institutions: MUZO (the Music Section of Narkompros), MONO (the Moscow Department of People's Education), Proletkult and the Academy Theatres. But to this we must add TEO (the Theatre Section of Narkompros), which is also in charge of music, and all the military institutions, all the clubs, and many others. [...] A terrible hostility and competition can be noticed among them, and this is very much at odds with the goals of the Soviet power. We think that the overlaps could be forgiven, if it were not for the mutual hatred and the desire of each organisation to monopolise music for its own benefit.[1]

Thus wrote a weary Leonid Sabaneyev, commenting on an emerging pattern in the organisation of Soviet musical life – a pattern that was never eradicated even under Stalinist centralisation in the 1930s. The desire for more efficient organisation and more thorough control in fact led to a proliferation of institutions with overlapping remits and ill-defined relationships, all competing for the same tranche of government funds. In November of 1920, for example, a new organisation was created to 'unify all work in political education and agitation', namely Glavpolitprosvet, which served as a Political Education section within Narkompros. The arts sections that already existed (MUZO, TEO, IZO, LITO, FOTO-KINO and others) were supposed to retain the degree of autonomy they already enjoyed, except in their propaganda and education work, where they were now subordinate to Glavpolitprosvet. At the same time, there were still private theatres and concert organisations in existence, which further duplicated the functions of the state bodies.[2]

An interesting example of the possible overlaps between a private enterprise and a state body arose with Koussevitzky's concerts during this period. A given programme was presented first in Koussevitzky's own subscription series, and then usually repeated several days later in a state concert series organised by MUZO. While programme and performers were identical, with no heating in either auditorium, the subscription concerts were always full, even though the tickets were generally sold at much higher prices, while the audience at the MUZO concerts was very sparse.[3] MUZO had clearly miscalculated the situation badly. Koussevitzky's public was evidently satisfied to hear a given programme once, and there was no separate audience prepared to attend at MUZO's lower prices (or at any rate, MUZO's publicity failed to attract any such audience). The failure of MUZO's Koussevitzky concerts also tells us that Koussevitzky's regular

---

[1] L. Sabaneyev, 'Ocherednïye zadachi muzikal'nogo stroitel'stva', *Vestnik rabotnikov iskusstv*, nos 2–3 (Nov.–Dec. 1920), 16–20.

[2] M. Miklashevskiy, 'O parallelizme', *Khudozhestvennaya zhizn'*, no. 3 (March–Apr. 1920), 35–6.

[3] 'Vnimaniyu MUZO', *Vestnik teatra*, no. 55 (2–7 March 1920), 13.

audience was happy to pay more than MUZO's ticket prices for the sake of the greater social prestige that adhered to the Koussevitzky subscription series. The concerts included an enterprising Scriabin cycle to mark the fifth anniversary of the composer's death, which imaginatively included readings by the Symbolist poets Balmont and Baltrušaitis between the pieces.

Koussevitzky showed a great willingness to work with the new regime, and not just by doubling up in MUZO's series. He conducted one of the most prominent concerts of the year for Paris Commune Day, 18 March 1920. This was a characteristic early-Soviet rally-concert ('*kontsert-miting*'), with speeches from Lunacharsky and Karl Radek and a musical programme to match: the *Internationale* in a new harmonisation and orchestration by Kastalsky, the funeral march from Beethoven's *Eroica*, and the entire Ninth Symphony. The invited audience consisted largely of communist-cell members from Moscow's Soviet institutions.[4] The state rewarded Koussevitzky's loyalty by sending him on a working trip to London, Paris, Brussels and Berlin, so that he could find out for himself what was new and worthwhile in music there. At the same time, it was hoped that he could help restore cultural contacts that had been broken off during the Civil War because of European embargoes on trade with the Soviet Union.[5] These embargoes were lifted in February 1920, leading to hopes that Soviet cultural life could become part of the wider European scene. Lourié, in an interview, was evidently elated at the prospects:

> I am talking about our participation in the coming renewal of Russian life with the removal of the embargo and the restoration of trade relations with Europe. Of all fields of enterprise, the musical-instrument industry was particularly choked by this embargo [...] The stocks of musical instruments and accessories are exhausted. Production has declined and is now barely even functioning. [...] there is a dearth of strings that must be remedied [...] European cultural life has achieved a lot during the time we have been forcibly separated from it, and we will immediately import into Russia the best creations of French, English, and other composers and will make them accessible to the broad masses of the population here. Our educational institutions have many vacant chairs, and we will invite fresh pedagogical forces from Europe to fill these.[6]

Lourié's joy was premature, however, and the continuing hardships in the wake of the Civil War would delay the beginning of trade negotiations on music until the end of the following year.

In the meantime, Soviet music suffered an unexpected blow. Koussevitzky failed to return from his European trip. In response, the state nationalised his enormous music library. The iconoclastic opera director, Komissarzhevsky, seemed to be doing likewise, although he obscured matters by sending regular missives to the Soviet press detailing his progress abroad, while saying nothing about when he

---

[4] 'Internatsional v novoy garmonizatsii', *Vestnik teatra*, no. 57 (16–21 March 1920), 13.

[5] 'V Yevropu za muzïkoy', *Vestnik teatra*, no. 63 (4–9 May 1920), 14.

[6] 'Muzïka i blokada (Beseda s A. S. Lur'ye)', *Vestnik teatra*, no. 54 (24–29 Feb. 1920), 13.

might return. With the borders still closed (war with Poland continued for most of the year), the only legal way for musicians to leave the country was to petition the government for a business trip or concert tour abroad, or to complain of health problems that required convalescence in the balmy climes of Italy or at a German spa resort. Lunacharsky readily granted permission, while the Foreign Ministry just as readily vetoed his decisions. Several literary celebrities, including Fyodor Sologub, Andrey Bely and Vyacheslav Ivanov, had repeatedly petitioned for an exit visa with no success. One cultural asset Lunacharsky very much wanted to keep was Chaliapin, who was content to remain in Russia for the time being. He seemed insulated from common privations, and was rumoured to earn enormous quantities of food through his concerts.

Thanks to stoical troupes and their under-rewarded support staff, the opera houses were still able to run performances almost every day. Audiences still gathered in strength, even though severe shortages of fuel meant that the auditoriums were generally unheated. In Moscow, the Bolshoi's somewhat restricted repertoire was centred around the Russian classics (Glinka's *Ruslan*, Borodin's *Prince Igor*, Tchaikovsky's *Queen of Spades*, and four Rimsky-Korsakov works: *Sadko*, *The Tsar's Bride*, *Saltan*, and *The Golden Cockerel*). Only three Western operas played at the Bolshoi that year: *The Barber of Seville*, *Lakmé*, and *Aida*. When the Bolshoi troupe requested permission to close the 1919/20 season early, due to exhaustion after a difficult winter, Lunacharsky remonstrated. His letter to the theatre demonstrates that the work of the Bolshoi troupe was now of great importance for garnering international prestige. Moscow was about to receive numerous foreign delegates to the second Comintern Congress, and Lunacharsky had earmarked the Bolshoi production of *Prince Igor*, under Golovanov, as the ideal entertainment for his guests and as a showcase for Russian culture. An early close to the season would have spoilt his plans.[7]

Less importance was attached to the former Zimin Opera, now renamed the Malaya Opera ('Small' Opera), and its April programme was suspended while deliberations on its future took place. One possibility was that the progressive director, Iosif Lapitsky, famous for his Music Drama Theatre in Petrograd would be invited to take over the Malaya. In the end, it was decided that it would best serve as a second, smaller stage to the Bolshoi, a kind of Opéra Comique, with a repertoire of popular favourites. During the current season, it was running *La Bohème*, *The Demon*, *Boris Godunov*, *Eugene Onegin*, *The Queen of Spades* and *The Barber of Seville*; only *Lohengrin* stood out as more ambitious and somewhat outside the mainstream for Russian opera. After the closure was lifted, the Malaya Opera returned undaunted, with a new production of *Faust* (under the title of *Margarita*). Lapitsky was still brought to Moscow, not for the Malaya Opera, but for his own Music Drama Theatre, to be run along similar lines to his former company of the same name in Petrograd. The Malaya Opera, however, did not survive the cold season and was closed. In December 1920, the government decided that fuel shortages rendered the remaining private theatres an unconscionable luxury, and

---

[7] See Lunacharsky's letter to the executive of the Council of Ministers of 29 April 1920, in A. V. Lunacharskiy, *O muzike i muzikal'nom teatre*, vol. 1 (Moscow: Muzïka, 1981), 309–10.

so they were officially closed down. As it happened, this was a very short-lived measure, since the advent of the New Economic Policy in the following spring allowed the private theatres to open again.

In Petrograd, the former Mariinsky was slightly more adventurous in its repertoire than the Bolshoi: the hit of the 1920/21 season was a new production of Serov's *Power of the Fiend* (with sets by Boris Kustodiev), with Chaliapin in one of his most famous roles. As the amusing but sinister folk entertainer Yeryomka, Chaliapin was 'frightening ... revealing the whole shame of a Russian drunkard in his unstoppable rush to the abyss of baseness', according to Asafyev.[8] The Mariinsky ballet made a great impact with its Russian premiere of *Petrushka*, since the ailing ballet companies were otherwise merely repeating stale productions of *Swan Lake*, *Le corsaire* and *Raymonda* and a handful of other pieces from their core repertoire. These productions were noticeably shopworn by now, as various theatrical materials were depleted by requisitioning: *Sadko*, the season's opener, for example, suffered from motley sets that originated from productions of different operas.[9]

But the biggest and most memorable show of the year was not to be found inside the walls of any theatre. A one-off performance of a vast production entitled *The Taking of the Winter Palace* took place in the former Palace Square (renamed Uritsky Square), as the centrepiece of the celebrations marking the third anniversary of the October Revolution. On 8 November, at 10 p.m., a crowd of between six and ten thousand spectators turned up to watch the performance, which took place against the imposing Main Headquarters' Arch (although, strictly speaking, the events depicted took place on the opposite side of the square). Two platforms dominated the scene, one White (with a throne in an assembly hall), the other Red (with factories). A bridge allowed the performers to pass from one to the other. The director of the event was stationed on his own platform, which was attached to the Alexander column in the centre of the square. A call to attention was issued by a cannon, followed by eight trumpeters sounded a fanfare. The now attentive audience was able to hear Litolff's *Robespierre* overture arranged for military band – selected for its political appropriateness, in the face of derision from some critics. The action began with Kerensky and his ministers, who were musically represented by the *Marseillaise* arranged as a polonaise (intended, no doubt, to imply that they were merely posing as revolutionaries), while the Provisional Government's Moscow assembly was accompanied by Glinka's 'Glory' chorus from *A Life for the Tsar*, with the usual ringing of church bells. The battle scenes were made vivid by the use of real gunfire, together with cannon shots from the Aurora battleship itself (which had fired the signal for the Revolution three years earlier). The moment of victory was marked by the *Internationale*, and the night sky was suddenly illuminated by fireworks.[10] The critics mentioned that from the vantage point of many in the crowd, the spectacle was rather confused.

For concerts, Moscow led the way, thanks above all to the Bolshoi, which was now a major cultural force once again. The Bolshoi orchestra played regular

[8] Igor' Glebov, 'Vrazh'ya sila', *Zhizn' iskusstva*, no. 595 (29 Oct. 1920), 1.
[9] V.G., 'Ocherednoy, no ne noviy', *Krasnaya gazeta*, no. 209 (19 Sept. 1920), 4.
[10] N. Shubskiy, 'Na ploshchadi Uritskogo', *Vestnik teatra*, no. 75 (30 Nov. 1920), 4–5.

Sunday matinees in the main auditorium, including an ambitious Richard Strauss cycle under the baton of Fitelberg (with pre-concert lectures by the ever-enthusiastic Lunacharsky). The former royal foyer was reshaped into the new 700-seat Beethoven Hall, primarily intended for chamber concerts, but large enough to hold an orchestra when required. The Stradivari Quartet, which also had connections to the Bolshoi, now gave concerts on a weekly basis, and in the autumn, it was promoted from a smaller hall to the Conservatoire's Grand Hall. By the end of the year, the quartet had given more than 100 concerts – totalling almost one concert for every week of its existence up to this point.[11] Together with the pianist Isay Dobroveyn, they entertained Lenin on his fiftieth birthday.

This rich musical life scattered some crumbs of comfort and pleasure after six years of almost continuous warfare had created extreme scarcity in every corner of material existence. Understandably, this was not a time when the public was seeking out the shock of the new. Living Russian composers had difficulties making their music heard in this environment, but Myaskovsky fared better than most, and 1920 saw the premiere of his Fifth Symphony in the summer series at the Hermitage Garden in Moscow.[12] Admittedly, this was a relatively easy-going work for Myaskovsky, hardly more demanding than a Glazunov symphony, but it was striking nevertheless that a composer still in his thirties could enjoy a symphonic premiere at this juncture.

Like many of his friends and associates, Myaskovsky became a part of Soviet cultural administration at an early stage, working for MUZO while still holding a desk job as an officer in the Soviet Navy. (In 1921, he secured a post at MUZO.) While it is likely that such work had its benefits for composers, the benefits remained intangible – it is unknown when a supportive word in the corridors of power was uttered, or when it was even needed. Belyayev, as Myaskovsky's leading supporter in Petrograd, organised a concert of the composer's chamber works on 18 April at the assembly of the 'House of the Arts' (the Dom iskusstv), an elite literary and artistic association. Myaskovsky's Cello Sonata and various songs attracted a prestigious audience including Lourié, Asafyev, the artists Konstantin Somov and Albert Benois, and even Myaskovsky's former composition teacher Ivan Kryzhanovsky.[13] Another Petrograd concert took place on 19 June (the Cello Sonata and songs once again, together with the Second Quartet). This time Belyayev failed to recognise anyone in the audience:

> There were quite a lot of people, but no one that I knew. All the pieces without exception and each movement of the quartet were successful,

---

[11] L.S., '"Moskovskaya" muzïka', *Vestnik rabotnikov iskusstv*, nos 2–3 (Nov.–Dec. 1920), 63–4.

[12] S. R. Stepanova, *Muzïkal'naya zhizn' Moskvï v pervïye gody posle Oktyabrya* (Moscow: Sovetskiy kompozitor, 1972), 205.

[13] Letter from Belyayev to Myaskovsky of 17 Apr. 1920, RGALI, f. 2040 (Myaskovsky), op. 1, ye. kh. 102, l. 11. Konstantin Andreyevich Somov (1869–1939) was a *Mir iskusstva* artist who left Russia in 1923. Albert Benois (Benua, 1852–1936) was an architect and watercolourist; his brother was the more prominent Alexander Benois (see fn. 24 below).

always being welcomed with applause. The performers, on the contrary, were met with silence, since they were unknown to the audience.[14]

Yet these were rare moments of affirmation for Russian composers and critics, who generally felt disorientated and marginalised in their new environment. Some of them nurtured hopes for a reversal of the Revolution, but as these began to fade, a sense of fatigue and depression began to set in. Those whose thoughts did not stretch to emigration, allowed themselves the occasional bitter word, like Sergei Popov: 'Are we really destined to perish in this foulness and baseness, without a ray of hope?'[15] Even the most active participants in the new fabric of musical life, like Belyayev, were becoming weary and now looked to the past with nostalgia:

> For the past two or three years, I was expending my energies on thoughtless activity – activity for the sake of the moment, for its own sake and for the people. [...] Sometimes I long for a life of peace and quiet, for freedom from the hard labour of today that I carry out with never a rest or break. I long to keep fit by playing sports or by doing some hunting. [...] My usual state is prostration, procrastination up to the very last moment, and a feeling of the greatest depression in the face of failure [...][16]

Belyayev summed up the feelings of one who was involved in feverish bureaucratic activity, participating in many of the new ventures (one of which was the Music History Faculty at the State Institute for the History of the Arts – the first musicological institution in Russia), and yet feeling that his efforts were largely wasted and that real power lay elsewhere, out of reach. Somehow, creative musicians found themselves to be 'passive onlookers', as Bryusova described them. As they looked on, the times were changing. Even while the government persisted with declarations of non-interference in the business of the arts, artists began looking to the government as the sole patron in reality. As the paper crisis reached its height, the State Publishing House became a monopoly by default. A chasm opened between Soviet court writers like Demyan Bedny, who occupied an apartment within the Kremlin Wall, and most others, who were no longer able to have their work published. Characteristically, some of these, like Yesenin and his Imaginists group, lobbied the government for support, inaugurating the tradition of desperate artists' letters addressed to the leadership.[17]

The end of 1920 would seem the most suitable place to recount the story of Lenin's struggle against Proletkult. While various twists in the story took place over the following years, the pivotal events occurred at this juncture. From the outset, Lenin was extremely suspicious of this organisation. In the years following the

[14] Letter from Belyayev to Myaskovsky of 23 June 1920, ibid., l. 20.

[15] Postcard from Popov to Lamm of 8 Apr. 1920, RGALI, f. 2743 (Lamm), op. 1, ye. kh. 176, l. 13.

[16] Letter from Belyayev to Myaskovsky of 28 Nov. 1920, RGALI, f. 2040 (Myaskovsky), op. 1, ye. kh. 102, l. 30–1.

[17] *Literaturnaya zhizn' Rossii 1920-kh godov: Sobïtiya. Otzïvï sovremennikov. Bibliografiya*, ed. by A. Yu. Galushkin (Moscow: IMLI RAN, 2006), vol. 1, pt 1, 525–6.

failed revolution of 1905, Lenin's leadership of the Bolsheviks had been challenged by Alexander Bogdanov. On the brink of defeat, Lenin transformed the situation by destroying Bogdanov's reputation as a philosopher among the Bolsheviks, arguing that his theories led to a fundamentally un-Marxist idealism. Bogdanov had left the Bolsheviks and led a rival group for a while (which included Lunacharsky); no reconciliation had taken place since. During 1917, Bogdanov had helped to found Proletkult, had sat on its central committee, and had acted as its principal theorist. He had also been an outspoken left-wing critic of the Bolsheviks in the period following the October Revolution. All of these developments alerted Lenin to Proletkult's potential for troublemaking. However much Lenin disapproved of and ridiculed the scorched-earth cultural outlook of Bogdanov and his sympathisers within Proletkult, the main danger did not reside there. Proletkult was not merely an artistic organisation, but an autonomous mass workers' organisation that ran its own political wing. Especially with Bogdanov at the helm, Lenin could see the makings of a serious political opposition here.

In 1919, Lenin had already pointed out that so-called 'proletarian culture' did not stem from workers, but was invented for them by members of the intelligentsia that used to serve the old ruling class. What was needed, Lenin argued, was 'not the invention of a new Prolet-culture, but rather the development of the best models, traditions, and results of the existing culture from a Marxist point of view and the development of the conditions of proletarian life and struggle in the era of its dictatorship' (from a draft resolution debated at Proletkult's first all-Russian congress in 1920).[18] Lunacharsky's reminiscences cast light on the broader implications of 'proletarian culture' for Lenin:

> Vladimir Ilyich had a great fear of one apparently logical conclusion: if existence determines consciousness, then bourgeois ideology was determined by bourgeois life and so down with the whole bourgeois heritage! Consequently, we would need to throw away all technology. It is absolutely clear that a major error is rooted here. The bourgeois life contained a great many problems that confront us too, and either these have been solved by the bourgeoisie more or less satisfactorily, or else we simply haven't any better solution for the time being. Vladimir Ilyich was very much afraid that we would forget this, that we would throw away the valuable component of the bourgeois heritage, and start to invent our own. It was from this perspective that he harboured a fear of Proletkult too.[19]

As a fervent believer in scientific progress, Lenin feared the 'democratisation of science', foreseeing the risk of developments like the later elevation of Trofim Lysenko, and accordingly, he sought to protect university professors from the attacks of over-zealous Party cells. As he put it in one colourful phrase recalled by Lunacharsky, 'We absolutely need the scholars; the cells ought to be flogged senseless'.

---

[18] Lenin's draft resolution of 9 Oct. 1920, in V. I. Lenin, *O literature i iskusstve*, ed. by N. I. Krutikova (Moscow: Khudozhestvennaya literatura, 1979), 445.

[19] Lunacharsky, speaking at a meeting of the Press Section of the Central Committee on 9 May 1924, in Lenin, 673.

But while the general issue of 'proletarian culture' could continue as a staple topic of debate in the press, the particular matter of Proletkult's autonomy had to be resolved urgently, especially after August, when Proletkult took the first steps towards establishing its own international network. Lenin intervened personally in the organisation of the First Proletkult Congress in 1920 instead of trying to act through Lunacharsky (who hardly fitted the purpose), and demanded that Proletkult accept subordination to Narkompros. Lenin's concern was not over Proletkult's ability to act autonomously in the sphere of the arts. Proletkult also had its scientific and political sections, and autonomy in these areas he saw as the real threat: in the sciences, he was concerned about the potential damage if doctrines of 'proletarian science' took hold, and in politics, organised political activity outside of Party and state institutions was no longer considered legitimate.[20] Proletkult was weakened as a result, and a change of leadership followed, but its troubles were not yet over. The following year, at the Second Congress, a political grouping of self-styled 'collectivists' distributed an anti-NEP manifesto, attacking state policy from the left. This was the last straw for Lenin, and Proletkult's days as a political force in its own right were swiftly brought to an end: its publications were closed down, and a Politburo resolution called for the organisation to rid itself of harmful bourgeois elements (as the Politburo saw them). As it happens, Proletkult was not able to withstand the operation of market forces under NEP, and without financial support from the state, it could no longer sustain its many activities. The organisation began to fall apart. In 1922, the new leader of Proletkult, Valerian Pletnev, engaged in one more political skirmish (to raise the profile of the forthcoming Third Congress), and still had enough prestige to have his essay published in *Pravda*. Lenin preserved his thoughts in the form of marginal notes that were passed on to Yakov Yakovlev, deputy head of Agitprop, as the basis for a public reply. Some of the shorter notes will give the flavour of Lenin's marginalia. Pletnev: 'The task of building proletarian culture can be solved only by the forces of the proletariat itself, by the scholars, artists, engineers, and the like who come from its midst.' Lenin: 'Utter falsehood'. Pletnev: 'The proletarian artist will be at the same time an artist and a worker'. Lenin: 'Nonsense'. Yakovlev's reply was oddly eclectic, taking shots from both the left and right. The ensuing flurry of polemics proved that the notion of 'proletarian culture' had not been squashed, even after Proletkult ceased to play any significant role in Soviet society (it continued, nominally, until 1932). 'Proletarian culture' had a clear appeal to those who wanted a reassuringly simple and schematic Marxism, in distinction to Lenin's compromises with the market and his acceptance of 'bourgeois' science. For them, the Revolution had broken sharply with the past to bring about a new economic base, and this entailed a new superstructure that broke just as sharply

---

[20] *Literaturnaya zhizn' Rossii 1920-kh godov*, 657. The Party CC on 10 November 1920 entrusted to the Politburo the final version of the resolution 'on the forms of merging Proletkult with Narkompros, to make it clear that the Proletkult work in the area of scientific and political education is merged with the work of Narkompros and local education departments [*gubnarobrazï*]. As for the artistic sphere (music, theatre, fine arts, literature), Proletkult work remains autonomous, and the leading role of Narkompros is preserved only for fighting obviously bourgeois deviations'.

with the past. We shall pick up this thread again in 1923 (with RAPM Mark 1), in 1925 (with ORKiMD), and in the period 1929–31 (with RAPM Mark 2).

The blow Lenin dealt to Proletkult's ambitions entailed the denigration of Futurism as a by-product. Lenin had made a swipe at Futurists on several occasions previously, but the most open statement on this iconoclastic trend appeared in the Party letter 'On Proletkults' which was published in *Pravda* on 1 December 1920 (it was drafted by Zinoviev with participation of Lenin, Stalin, and others, but failed to win the support of some important figures, like Bukharin):

> Proletkult emerged before the October Revolution. It was declared an 'independent' workers' organisation, independent of the ministry of people's education in Kerensky's time. The October Revolution changed the perspective. The Proletkults remained 'independent', but now they were 'independent' from Soviet power. For this and several other reasons, petit-bourgeois elements – elements socially alien to us – flooded Proletkult and virtually hijacked its leadership. At times, Proletkult affairs fell into the hands of Futurists, decadents, followers of idealist philosophy hostile to Marxism, and various failures from the ranks of bourgeois journalists and philosophers.
>
> Under the guise of 'proletarian culture' the workers are offered bourgeois views in philosophy (Machism). In the arts, workers have been injected with inane and perverse tastes.[21]

Proletkult acted swiftly. In order to strengthen their position on the struggle for the organisation's continued existence, the Futurists were jettisoned. The leadership issued a resolution prohibiting Proletkult groups from using the services of any 'persons who present themselves as Futurists and ComFuturists in art, as leaders, instructors, specialists, or lecturers'.[22]

And yet the Futurists had until very recently been feted by the state that now repudiated them. They had been pushed to the forefront of Soviet culture at various state celebrations, receiving state endorsement in full view of the public. Now they had been demoted to the same level as any other artistic faction, free to continue creating their art, but without the support of the state. Members of the old artistic intelligentsia were unperturbed by Futurism's earlier successes, or by its sudden demotion. In the NEP marketplace it became just another artistic trend. Perhaps only Lenin took Futurism at its word: that all past culture should be destroyed or forgotten. This, he forcibly demonstrated, would never be the attitude of the Soviet state, for as long as he had any say in the matter.

---

[21] Lenin, 586.

[22] *Literaturnaya zhizn' Rossii 1920-kh godov*, 682.

※ ※ ※ ※ ※

Andrey Levinson, '"Petrushka" (Akademicheskiy teatr operï i baleta)' [*Petrushka* at the Academy Opera and Ballet Theatre), *Zhizn' iskusstva*, no. 616–18 (26–8 Nov. 1920), 2–3.

This is one of the last Russian essays written by the prominent ballet critic Andrey (André) Levinson before he emigrated to Berlin (and later to Paris).

Andrey Levinson
Petrushka at the Academy Opera and Ballet Theatre

The paths of national art are truly inscrutable: they have only now led *Petrushka* to its native stage after nine years of its existence, and even then by the roundabout route of the Paris Grand Opera where it first saw the light of day, and then the Champs-Élysées Theatre where its success was confirmed.

Petrushka was born and grew up in voluntary emigration, which characterised the whole enterprise of that great initiator and businessman Diaghilev, who was a little bit of a hoaxer, too. This enterprise was his own idea, and it represented Russia before the face of a bemused Europe in an original, sharp, and arbitrary way, while Russia itself could only judge the matter on the basis of rumour.

Finally on Saturday 20 November, the old Petersburger Petrushka puppet, a staple of our childhood, jerked to life before its own native audience – although, prior to that, there had been attempts to trail off the motley rags of his musical clothing and to display these by themselves. And what happened? During the concert performance of Igor Stravinsky's score, the theatrical flesh and blood of the 'comic scenes' was missing; the sleeves of the white coat swung empty, and the hat fell onto the shoulders for the lack of Petrushka's wooden head underneath it.

And indeed, this wonderful theatrical story cannot be separated out into layers of scenery, action and music.

The astounding impression it makes is all bound together.

Its bare action, the double existence of puppets come alive, is schematic, and one might nearly say negligible; the music taken on its own is a mosaic – superficial, like a musically-organised noise – but the combination of the two elements is unforgettable. And this time, too, from the moment when the Shrovetide din welled up from the depths of the orchestra until the moment when the curtain went down for the last time, the spectators were astonished and captivated completely (and that curtain was a night sky with flying devils as if conjured up by the superstitious nightmare of a painter's apprentice).

Comparing my new impressions with the observations I had jotted down in Paris, I would hardly change anything in my notes. The scenery remained roughly the same; there are variations in the cut and colour of the costumes, while the dances and the pantomime choreographed by Leontyev are in many respects a facsimile of Fokine's original.²³ And the very fabric of the events on stage, what the English call the 'story' of the play, unfolds in the same way.

The conductor tapped his baton on the music stand and as soon as he raised it, the auditorium was filled with the discordant and boisterous hum of the folk fair, the whooping and stamping of rowdy dancing, the shrill calls of the theatre-booth owner, the rustling of the streaming crowd, the tinkling of the bells on the buffoon's cap, the clatter of wooden rattles – a chaos of sounds, into which is poured a jingling and stuttering, the murmur of a decrepit barrel-organ, and this, in turn, is overpowered by the drunken roar of the accordion, and then by tin sounds of the flute solo (almost ugly by contrast, sharp and piercing like needles), which a mysterious Oriental wizard and magician, dressed in a long coat and high hat, uses to attract his audience.

The magic pipe gradually brings the festive bustle to a halt: the annoying booth owner falls silent, the street dancer rolls up her threadbare rug, the curtain on the booth is pulled, and three puppets are revealed: the black-faced moor in a green, richly embroidered jacket; a ballerina puppet in a short skirt exposing violet pantaloons, lengthened by lace frills, and with graceful legs shod in traditional ballet shoes; and finally, Petrushka himself. The puppets flounder rhythmically, stuck to their iron stands, until the magic wand summons them to step forward and continue their dance among the crowd, which gawps in amazement. The Moor tries to embrace the Ballerina, but Petrushka wields a cudgel, which he has inherited from his Italian brother, Harlequin. He strikes the cunning Moor on the neck, but the Moor chases after him with a curved cardboard sword, and, in the midst of the general merriment, Petrushka flees. The curtain falls momentarily at the end of the scene and is raised again to reveal the inside of the booth. Alone with his own thoughts but under the watchful eye of the magician, whose image stands out against the black background of the paper wall, Petrushka reveals by desperate gesticulation the hidden torments of his soul, enslaved within the buffoonish image of a puppet, and his shy and jealous love for the Ballerina. Here she appears in the doorframe, but instead of a passionate confession, the puppet-like body of Petrushka writhes around in a comic and ugly fit, and the Ballerina turns away from him with contempt and horror.

Meanwhile, amidst the rugs and cushions of an Oriental tent, and against the background of an exotic tapestry with palm trees, lions and snakes, the Moor neglects to take a well-deserved rest, because there is another activity he wants to pursue, with a passion: he tries to crack the shell of a coconut and, after turning it every possible way and blunting his sword on it, he prostrates himself on his belly, and worships the coconut like a god. The Ballerina slips into the tent with a brass trumpet in her hands; putting the sonorous instrument to her mouth and moving her long fingers, she begins to dance; the Moor has already forgotten about the mysterious nut when the unexpected arrival of the desperate Petrushka interrupts

[23] Leonid Sergeyevich Leontyev (1885–1942) was a dancer and choreographer at the Mariinsky from 1903 to 1922. Michel Fokine (or Mikhail Mikhaylovich Fokin, 1880–1942) also began his career at the Mariinsky, and produced several innovative ballets there that caught the attention of Diaghilev, who then invited Fokine to work for his troupe in 1909. *Petrushka* became one of his most celebrated creations.

his flirting – but again Petrushka has to flee from the curved sword. The Ballerina seeks salvation in the strong arms of her black-faced rescuer.

On the meadow, in the meantime, the festive smoke is rising, while 'nursemaids' in folk dress and headgear float about, moving their arms and waving their hands, coachmen in blue shirts stamp their heels heavily, lively grooms rush by in a squatting dance, the masqueraders with their frightening faces mingle with the crowd, and ladies accompanied by stately officers in helmets and fops in fur-coats, peer squeamishly through their eye-glasses at the rough entertainments of the simple folk.

Suddenly the curtain of the tent is pulled aside, and Petrushka appears, pursued by the victorious Moor, the sword glistening; Petrushka falls to the ground lifeless, sliced in two. Worried by the convincing realism of the spectacle, the crowd calls the policeman with a halberd, who drags off the puppet-master by the collar, but he, laughing, displays the two halves of Petrushka's wooden head. The people disperse and the booth-owner, relieved, drags the remains of the irksome puppet back into his tent; but he stops in his tracks, astonished at the appearance of Petrushka's double on the balustrade of the roof, and he flees in horror. Separated from its puppet body, the live soul of Petrushka mourns the death of its earthly shell.

Such are the 'comic scenes' of Benois,[24] a Russian Harlequinade against the background of St Petersburg saturnalia. The picturesque setting is full of verisimilitude and fantastic suggestion. The chorus of this puppet tragicomedy is the festive crowd of the Nicolaian era. Under the cover of scrupulous documentary accuracy pulses the wholeness of saturated, full-blooded everyday life. Extremely detailed treatment of movement, a multitude of episodes, multifarious asymmetric gestures against a labyrinth of musical themes – together these form a unity of stage rhythm. Every dance motive that emerges from the orchestra is sharpened into a musical grotesque, and is answered by the dancing woodcut on stage, with comically emphasised accents and broken movement – a *parody* of dancing. The puppets' acting itself unfolds in the closest contact with the musical text, reproducing its every rhythmic impulse in movement. And the very movement of every puppet is limited by the angular and soulless motions of its mechanism. A dramatic impression is created by the restriction of the enslaved souls by the pitiful gestures imposed on them, set against their vain attempts to break out into the wide expanse of expressive and free movement.

This drama was strongly felt by Leontyev, playing Petrushka. He represented automatism and was completely filled by the music. There was also a great intensity in Petrushka's attempts to spread his soul beyond its comic shell. We did not witness the characteristics of that genius in plasticity, that hidden grace that never deserted Nijinsky[25] in his Petrushka. But in Leontyev, both as an

---

[24] Alexander Benois (Aleksandr Nikolayevich Benua, 1870–1960) was a painter, art scholar and critic, and one of the founders of the *Mir iskusstva* group. The scenario for *Petrushka* was his original idea.

[25] Vaslav Nijinsky (1889–1950) was Diaghilev's star dancer, who took male dancing to new heights of virtuosity. *Petrushka* was one of his most celebrated and innovatory roles.

actor and as a director, there was the rational and triumphant will of a sensitive artist. He conquered the absolute unprecedentedness of Benois' and Stravinsky's work.

Ye. M. Lyukom, as the Ballerina, did not make me forget Karsavina's doll-like face with its eerily empty eyes.[26] But the whole performance of these 'scenes' is surprisingly well worked out and disciplined. It shows what great efforts can be made in our ballets if there is a directing will and the gravitational pull of lofty goals.

Of course, Benois' work is not a ballet. The master himself knows that, hence the subtitle of 'comic scenes'. Many spectators are ready to hold this against him. I myself am one of those whose criticism has nurtured such a purism of judgement. In ballet proper, the musical fabric only clothes the symmetrical forms of self-sufficient dance. Bodily movement rules over musical rhythm.

But *Petrushka* is a pantomime with music, where every movement is penetrated and suggested by sound. This blending of these two elements, these two dynamics, gives rise to its effect. The simple restoration of picturesque and everyday memories of our past (the St Petersburg of the 1840s, unexpectedly resurrected in our own times) would not have been able to turn the performance of *Petrushka* into the most intense and outstanding hour of theatrical life we have seen in the capital over recent years.

---

[26] Elena Mikhaylovna Lyukom (1891–1968) was a soloist at the Mariinsky who had also danced for Diaghilev; Tamara Platonovna Karsavina (1885–1978) was a prima ballerina at the Mariinsky until Diaghilev invited her to join his troupe in 1909.

※ ※ ※ ※ ※

Viktor Serzh, 'Shalyapin v Sovete' [Chaliapin in the Soviet], *Teatr i muzika*, no. 32 (18 Sept. 1923), 1032–3. Reprinted from *Clarté*, no. 41 (Aug. 1923).

The author of this essay was born to Russian revolutionaries who had fled to Brussels to evade the reach of the Tsar. Victor Serge (known in Russia as Kibalchich), journalist, novelist, translator and a political activist from an early age, wanted to experience Revolutionary Russia for himself in spite of the Civil War. He arrived in 1919, and by the time of the 1920 New Year concert described in this article, he was already working for the Soviet government (under Zinoviev) and for the Comintern. The article itself was published three years later in the review Clarté, *published by the prominent French communist writer Henri Barbusse. At the time, Serge's work for the Comintern had taken him back to Western Europe for two years. He returned to Russia in 1925, and became a supporter of the United Opposition, which led to his arrest in 1928. He was released after two months, thanks to international pressure, but in 1933 he was sentenced to exile in Siberia, where he spent three years before international pressure once again brought about his release, via the first Congress of Writers. He was allowed to leave Russia at this point, although his wife was kept behind to serve out her 25 years of Siberian exile. Serge's many books of fiction and non-fiction document his experiences, and he continued to campaign on the anti-Stalinist left until his death in Mexico, in 1947.*

After several years as a celebrity in the poverty of war-ravaged Russia, Chaliapin was one of several celebrated artists who went on tour but failed to return in 1921 (the article, restricted to events of 1920, does not mention this). His former official honorific 'People's Artist' was belatedly withdrawn six years later.

Victor Serge
Chaliapin in the Soviet

During the present Revolution, Russian theatres have served and continue to serve the people's movement much better than they do here in France. Democratic assemblies used to meet in Petrograd's Alexandrine Theatre even during Kerensky's rule, and on the most solemn occasions, the Moscow Soviet still meets in the Bolshoi Theatre. I remember one New Year's night I spent at the Mariinsky Theatre in Petersburg – a night when I witnessed a dazzling people's celebration.

Along every street adjoining Theatre Square, endless crowds hurried to the theatre, which was illuminated with large swinging lights that gave the red banners a blood-like glow. And beyond the theatre, everything was darkness, with hardly a gleam from the snow, the sky dense and grey, as were the vague silhouettes of the houses. From our gloomy dwellings, we ran over to this brightly lit corner; for at the time, during a minus-25 degree frost, there was neither fuel nor light to be had; we were without water, without the most basic conveniences, feeding on coarse rye cakes, with meagre rations of black bread, and drinking ersatz tea with saccharine. The blockade was total, and not a single European paper reached us.

The new year was beginning, the third after the Revolution, the year 1920. The elections to the Soviet had just ended, and the celebratory meeting in the Mariinsky was just about to begin.

On the invitations, the order of the evening was inscribed as follows: 1. Election to the Presidium; 2. Speeches from Zinoviev and Kalinin,[27] and afterwards, a whole programme of entertainment, which ended with an eloquent promise: 'tea will be offered to all those present'. How distant all of this was from those solemn assemblies in which societies of the old world froze in their traditional rituals. It takes a bold revolutionary people to put out of mind the fact that there is only one step from the sublime to the ridiculous.

The theatre is full. Here are workers, soldiers, Soviet civil servants – a grey crowd in which there are no elegant outfits to be seen; women from the simple people, simply dressed, leather jackets, grey army coats, the short haircuts of the communists. The Emperor's box is full of women workers; under the glitter of the light-blue and gilded chandeliers, the magnificent décor has been preserved from the times when the old regime's aristocrats gathered here together with princesses, high-society ladies and courtesans. When you look at these people, so noisy and merry, you realise immediately that they are the victors, while those others are dead, utterly dead.

A long red table stands centre stage. Zinoviev, Zorin,[28] and Kalinin, the Chairman of the Executive Committee of the Soviets, all step out onto the stage and take their seats to unanimous cheers and applause from the crowd. There is a special ovation for Kalinin. He is greeted as an old peasant, fresh from the plough, who became head of the People's Government. After the speeches, there is a meeting of the new Executive Committee, and then the stage is approached by a man in a soldier's uniform, who announces that the Red Army has taken Yekaterinoslav. This New Year celebration needed a victory, for we live only when we prevail over those who want to destroy us. And we did prevail ...

And then on the stage there are ballerinas in white and pink tutus, they flit about, light and glittering – this is such a feast for the eyes, especially for famished, exhausted people who are destined to face further great hardships. The best numbers are encored. Here is one of them, with almost tragic import: from the depths of the hall, four shabby street musicians emerge, vagrants, like those we saw under the old regime, except back then they were in the grimy yards of the capital city. Two homeless women sing with cracked voices, accompanying themselves on fiddle and pipe. And they dance, parodying the elegant dances the rich invented for their own pleasures.

---

[27] Mikhail Ivanovich Kalinin (1875–1946) was one of the few Bolsheviks from a peasant background. At this point, he headed the Central Executive Committee of the Party, he was also re-elected Chairman of the Presidium at every Congress of Soviets. For Zinoviev, see Glossary.

[28] Sergey Semyonovich Zorin (Gomberg) (1891–1937) was at this point Secretary of the Petrograd Party Committee, and Zinoviev's assistant.

You blush inadvertently when you look at them, bitterness rises up from the heart, and you think to yourself 'What is this for? Why such a revolting sight here?' But perhaps the whole spectacle was not without reason. After what we have just seen, but before the singing of the *Internationale*, Kalinin says: 'You can see the kind of art which they kept for themselves, and the kind they left for us.'

Suddenly the crowd explodes with an ecstatic 'Bravo!' – and before us is Chaliapin. Faultlessly attired in a chic suit with white tie and patent leather shoes, he approaches the edge of the stage, to stand inches from his audience. The public is thrilled and applauding. Chaliapin is a great favourite, the crowd adores him, because he is the only great *artiste* who has remained loyal to the people. He could be continuing his glittering career in Monte Carlo or somewhere else – money, entertainment, everything would have been at his disposal. But he chose to remain in starving Petrograd. And this is proof of his genuine attachment. Because, whatever the evil tongues say, the handsome fees, the sacks of flour, the comfort he has preserved in his home – none of these alleged advantages can outweigh the general suffering [that he shares with everyone else].

And now he rules here. Chaliapin is a wonderfully impressive figure. He is tall, broad-shouldered, with agile movements, white-faced, his radiant grey eyes burning into you. He bows with ease, with a special magnificence. He knows the power he holds over the crowd, a power that undoubtedly arises from his talents. He is loved and proud of it, and that is perhaps what ties him to Red Petrograd.

Having formerly experienced the enthusiasm of elegant ladies in décolleté, various high-society types and drunks from the gentlemens' clubs, he drinks in the powerful and healthy atmosphere of this hall, and is now intoxicated by the sincere delight he finds there. Chaliapin is present, he is a member of the Soviet, and for the past six months he has been a representative of Russian theatre and opera.

Chaliapin sings painstakingly, and only goes full tilt in a few passages. But his manner, diction and expression are all marked by the highest mastery. Chaliapin is instantly recognisable on the stage.

Having sung several numbers, the great *artiste* was about to leave the stage when someone began shouting, 'Dubinushka! Dubinushka!' [The Cudgel!] A brief and friendly exchange ensued between a smiling Chaliapin and his anonymous interlocutors, whom he addressed as 'comrades'. And we heard the *Dubinushka*: an irremediable melancholy, patience when no end is in sight, and finally protest – everything poured out in his marvellous singing. After each verse Chaliapin summoned the crowd to rise with a broad gesture, and he conducted it as they sang along. And in the last verse, when he finally sang about the terrible cudgel falling on the backs of the rich and the Tsar, the hall trembled, united in pleasure.

In order to make our enjoyment of the evening absolutely complete, the Soviet arranged for little bags to be distributed to all present, in which we found a few sweets, a piece of bread and some cheese.

That was truly a rare feast.

It is nearly one o'clock in the morning. The *Internationale* can still be heard on the stairs of the theatre and in the streets. A black night. A biting frost. Several automobiles drive up, and there is a voice: 'Former Schlüsselburgers over here!'

[i.e. former inmates of the Tsarist Schlüsselburg prison]. And the Schlüsselburgers are driven away. Now it is their turn to ride.

You walk along the dark streets, sinking into the snow at every step. And this black night sets you thinking about the Revolution's astonishing contrasts.

During this evening I've passed in the theatre, it seems I've learned to love the Revolution and understand it better – all on New Year's Eve.

1921
Should I stay or should I go?

1921 was a pivotal year for the Russian intelligentsia. The most startling event was the death of the eminent poet, Alexander Blok, which came to be regarded within the intelligentsia as a symbol that cultural continuity was now a forlorn hope. Before Blok died, he had petitioned the government for permission to emigrate in order to undergo much-needed medical treatment abroad. The permission was granted, but too late to save him, and he died shortly afterwards, still in Moscow. A few weeks before his death, he left a poignant note in his diary, which saw flashes of beauty amidst the dreariness:

> In Moscow, many members of the intelligentsia – musicians, doctors and others – are cruelly being ejected from their own apartments. Moscow is worse than last year, but are a lot of people around, some managing to look very well ... The street is noisy, the cars speed about, it's warm (although not for me), everything is in bloom (the apple trees, lilacs, dandelions, primulas), and we have thunderstorms and showers.[1]

These sentiments were all the more striking because Blok had greeted the October Revolution with enthusiasm, setting to work on one of his greatest, and certainly his most controversial poem, *The Twelve*, which he published in 1918. Although his present-day reputation is partly based on this work, it lost him much of his existing following, while its mysticism repelled most of the potential support he might have won from senior Bolsheviks. Lunacharsky voiced a sense of personal guilt when he heard the news of the poet's death – he had previously accepted all applications by cultural figures for travel abroad, but material conditions had sunk so low by this juncture that a haemorrhage of talent had resulted. The international embargo against trade with Soviet Russia, and seven years of war (counting from 1914, under the Tsar), had so ravaged the economy that moving abroad could mean the difference between survival and death from malnutrition or hypothermia (the material situation eventually changed for the better in Russia, and life abroad proved grim for many Russian artists, but that is another story). Whatever their former enthusiasms for the new Russia, or their acts of solidarity with the Russian people, artists were understandably failing to return. Out of 19 prominent figures who left with a Narkompros permit, only five had returned. When it came to the turn of the 'People's Artist' Chaliapin, his 'temporary' exit in May 1921 was granted on the obviously unenforceable condition that he must return – in the event, he too remained abroad. In desperation, Narkompros attempted to impose a *krugovaya poruka* system (circle of trust), under which no new applicants could be granted leave until the previous set had returned. Still, one by one, the luminaries of Russian culture jumped ship, including the poets

---

[1] Mikhail Vostrïshev, *Moskva stalinskaya: Bol'shaya illyustrirovannaya letopis'* (Moscow: Algoritm, 2008), 117. Blok is most likely referring to the policy of turning larger apartments into collections of studios with shared kitchen and bathroom, the original owner keeping one room to himself.

Andrey Bely and Alexei Remizov, the writer Ilya Ehrenburg and the choreographer Alexander Gorsky.

With the defeat of the Kronstadt uprising in March 1921, the Bosheviks were evidently here to stay (if Kronstadt had held out until the thaw, Western navies would have been able to take Petrograd and relaunch the war). The poet Mikhail Kuzmin noted in his diary simply: 'It's all over. Back to Soviet drudgery' [*opyat' sovetskaya lyamka*]. While this was an unwelcome outcome for Kuzmin and many members of the intelligentsia, the coming of peace had its rewards: 'Many are content with the calm, the theatres, the removal of the state of siege.'[2] As it happened, the end of this state of siege was about to bring changes that would give further comforts to Kuzmin's 'many'.

In March 1921, the Tenth Congress of the Party adopted the New Economic Policy (NEP), which reintroduced the marketplace within the economy. In May, the previous nationalisation of small enterprises was reversed, and immediately, a 'bacchanalia' of small trade, as many called it, began, sparking off a period of racing hyperinflation. Mikhail Bulgakov wrote:

> In Moscow, people are only counting in millions and hundreds of thousands. Black bread is 4,600 a pound, white bread 14,000. And the prices are still rising all the time! The shops are full, but what can you buy? The theatres are full too, but yesterday, as I was passing near the Bolshoi [...] there were touts selling tickets at 75-, 100- and 150-thousand roubles. You can find everything in Moscow: footwear, textiles, meat, caviar, tinned food, various delicacies – everything! Cafés are opening, springing up like mushrooms! There's a seething ocean of speculation.[3]

While Moscow was suddenly transformed by the new department stores and cabarets (including the famous Neriday, 'Don't Weep'), the provinces were affected by famine. Appeals were issued to the creative intelligentsia: 'Onto the stage, actor! To the pen, writer! To the brush, artist! Explain through your art the necessity of fighting famine!' Kastalsky created perhaps the most prominent response:

> I recently cooked up an appeal addressed 'To our brothers abroad' [*K zarubezhnïm brat'yam*], for (choral) bass accompanied by the humming of a wordless choir [...] The text is mine (Russian translated into English, French and other languages), approved by Lunacharsky and the like. The subject matter takes hunger as its theme, together with the idea that Russia has, in its time, given a lot of help to others.[4]

Many Soviet artists heeded the appeals, their works used to raise much needed funds. Material relief began to arrive, most prominently from the American business magnates Herbert Hoover and Armand Hammer. Gorky founded and

---

[2] The diary of Kuzmin, quoted in *Literaturnaya zhizn' Rossii 1920-kh godov: Sobïtiya. Otzïvï sovremennikov. Bibliografiya*, ed. by A. Yu. Galushkin (Moscow: IMLI RAN, 2006), vol. 1, pt 2, 37.

[3] From Bulgakov's letter to his mother of 17 Nov. 1921, quoted in Vostrïshev, 122.

[4] Letter from Kastalsky to Asafyev of 12 Aug. 1921, RGALI, f. 2658 (Asafyev) op. 1, ye. kh. 581, l. 37v.

headed a committee to seek more foreign aid for the famished. Accordingly, he travelled abroad to conduct negotiations, but then added to the Soviet government's embarrassment by resettling in Italy (where he had formerly lived in exile during the last years of the Tsar).

For most of the intelligentsia, the new luxuries were enticing, but unaffordable (they were for the NEPmen – the newly enriched business class). Food and fuel remained their first concern. Belyayev, in his correspondence, voices his anxieties over the possible loss of his 'academic' ration (Moscow and Petrograd each had an allocation of only six to seven hundred of these), and records that he spent three days during summer breaking up a boat for firewood.[5] The wood evidently amounted to little, since Belyayev's letters became more desperate even before the onset of winter:

> It's already cold here. The chimney on the roof has collapsed. There's no heat, for want of firewood. The last possessions have been sold off.[6]

Typically for many intellectuals of the time, Belyayev managed to make ends meet by holding down three jobs (at the Petrograd Conservatoire, with the Petrograd Professional Education authority, and at the Philharmonia), but even then, hyperinflation kept him firmly on the breadline.[7]

There was a difficult transitional period in the first weeks after NEP had been declared, when state funding began to disappear, but private enterprise was still too sporadic to take up the breach. At this stage, the relationship between the state, the artistic institutions and the cultural workers were in considerable flux and the positions of individuals could be precarious.

While NEP would inevitably cause state funding and organisation of the arts to recede as private enterprise advanced, there was still a further skirmish over Futurism to be played out – perhaps the full implications of NEP were not always apparent in advance. Lunacharsky now faced criticism from Lenin's wife, Krupskaya, who wanted the arts to come under her wing at Glavpolitprosvet (even though NEP would make this increasingly irrelevant):

> Narkompros's task was to make art a kind of resonator, amplifying all that is communist, all that is collective, cheerful and beautiful [...] I fear that Narkompros has not succeeded in turning art into a mighty weapon for the fostering of communist feelings [...] It was the Futurists who came to prominence with particular vigour, but they debase art, and bring back the worst elements of old [despite their claims].[8]

---

[5] Letter from Belyayev to Myaskovsky of 12 Sept. 1921, RGALI, f. 2040 (Myaskovsky), op. 1, ye. kh. 103, l. 18, and his letter to Lamm of 10 July 1921, RGALI, f. 2743 (Lamm), op. 1, ye. kh. 84, l. 1.

[6] Letter from Belyayev to Myaskovsky of 10 Oct. 1921, RGALI, f. 2040, op. 1, ye. kh. 103, l. 21.

[7] Letter from Belyayev to Myaskovsky of 4 Nov. 1921, RGALI, ibid., l. 22v.

[8] Krupskaya's article 'Glavpolitprosvet i iskusstvo' was published in *Pravda* on 13 Feb. 1921, quoted from *Literaturnaya zhizn' Rossii 1920-kh godov: Sobïtiya. Otzïvï sovremennikov. Bibliografiya*, ed. by A. Yu. Galushkin (Moscow: IMLI RAN, 2006), vol. 1, pt 2, 28–9.

Lunacharsky, feeling that he was now implicitly being cast as a proponent of Futurism, tried to defend himself:

> Personally I think that the path that runs from the art of the past towards proletarian and socialist art does not pass through Futurism [...] To my mind, the proletariat and the peasantry will undoubtedly gain much more from works created in the best eras of the past that are full of human content, that are deeply ideological [in a positive sense] and deeply meaningful, than from art that declares in advance that it is contentless, purely formalist, and goes as far as to advocate absolute plotlessness. [...] In general [however], while giving no privileges to the new art, we shouldn't start persecuting it [...][9]

But persecution was exactly what ensued on this occasion. Noticing that Mayakovsky's new poem, *150,000,000*, had been awarded an exceptionally generous print run of 5,000 copies (generous in view of the paper shortage), Lenin read it for himself and was predictably outraged that so much paper had been dedicated to such an uncompromisingly Futurist piece. Bypassing Lunacharsky, he sent a letter instead to Mikhail Pokrovsky, Lunacharsky's deputy: 'I very strongly request your assistance in the fight against Futurism'. The request was carried down the ranks, and an opportunity sought. On 6 May a 'disciplinary comradely court' pronounced a judgement against the Mayakovsky–Meyerhold production of *Mystery Bouffe*.[10] This materialised in a *Pravda* article under a pointed headline 'Enough of all this Mayakovsky nonsense [*Mayakovshchina*]', and the production was duly banned, over the protests of the beleaguered Lunacharsky.[11]

The main trend, nevertheless, was towards minimal state intervention in musical life, not always as a matter of deliberate policy, but sometimes simply because failing state institutions no longer had to be rescued. At the beginning of the year, Lourié resigned from an ailing MUZO and was replaced by Boris Krasin, the brother of the much more prominent Leonid Krasin, who held top ministerial and diplomatic positions in the Soviet government (earning Boris the nickname *Narkombrat* – 'Narkombrother'). Sabaneyev described him as 'a very sweet and responsible person, not at all a Communist, and not especially bright'.[12] Krasin, whose previous experience was in Proletkult, struggled to turn MUZO around, but it had failed by the autumn, threatening to drag the state music publishing house down with it. Krasin was then reappointed head of Gosfil (State Philharmonia), a concert organisation designed to fit the new economic dispensation better. Profitability now became much more important, and concert programmes immediately had to be given a bias towards the popular. Remaining in the concert business over the next few years, Krasin became known as a manager who consistently favoured box-office takings over more adventurous programming.

---

[9] Lunacharsky's response 'Nashi zadachi v oblasti khudozhestvennoy zhizni: Glavpolitprosvet i iskusstvo' was published in *Krasnaya nov'*, no. 1, quoted from *Literaturnaya zhizn' Rossii 1920-kh godov*, vol. 1, pt 2, 29.

[10] *Literaturnaya zhizn' Rossii 1920-kh godov*, 76 and 125.

[11] *Literaturnaya zhizn' Rossii 1920-kh godov*, 135.

[12] L. L. Sabaneyev, *Vospominaniya o Rossii* (Moscow: Klassika–XXI, 2005), 187.

While Krasin was still at MUZO, Lunacharsky managed to secure another important appointment: Boleslav Yavorsky was called up from Kiev to head the music section of Glavprofobr (the Professional Education authority) – in simpler terms, this placed him in charge of the conservatoires. Yavorsky was an unusual figure. On the one hand, he had favoured Proletkult-type mass music education, and, together with Bryusova, he had organised a People's Conservatoire in Moscow prior to the Revolution. On the other hand, he was no less at home at the elite end of musical life, as a composer of complex music, and as a formidable music theorist – the author of a densely argued work on modality. His partner, Sergei Protopopov, with whom he shared quarters, also faced in both directions: he worked as a choral conductor in mass music-making projects, but at the same time, he strove to embody Yavorsky's theories in his ambitious compositions. When Yavorsky was called to Moscow from his previous post in Kiev, Krasin warned him that some of the Moscow professors would be wary of him because of their general dislike of state interference. He advised Yavorsky to move slowly and cautiously with any reforms:

> I think that institutions like the Conservatoire and former Imperial Theatres are impossible to reform through revolutionary methods because they are colossally inert: anything so complex and awkward would break from a sharp impact, or else break the thing that struck it. Only a very strong but steady force can set them moving or make them speed up.[13]

Yavorsky, it seems, heeded this advice, conducting himself diplomatically, and serving as a non-partisan arbiter of factional disputes in the conservatoires. He enjoyed a similar reputation in the post he took up in 1922, as head of GUS (the State Scholarly Council). He soon became Lunacharsky's right hand, and his ghostwriter on issues of professional education.

One undeniable success story of 1921 was the work of the newly created 'Philharmonia' in Petrograd, using the name of the defunct pre-Revolutionary institution. Initiated by Kuper, who was Russia's leading conductor during these years of hardship, the Philharmonia brought 'all academic, performing and support collectives into a single united musical collective, a single ideologically coherent institution', as Kuper later put it.[14] A high level of state support was granted to establish the organisation. The beautiful Philharmonia building housing Petrograd's celebrated concert hall was run down, after having served as a hospital during the First World War, but extensive renovation work began immediately, and on 12 June, Kuper was able to conduct the Philharmonia's inaugural concert. As he recounted in his memoirs:

> Petrograd, in the summer of 1921, witnessed a phenomenon without precedent in world music-history: during the three summer months in the half-empty city, and still [effectively] before War Communism had

[13] Letter from Krasin to Yavorsky of 17 Apr. 1921, publ. in *B. Yavorskiy: Stat'yi, vospominaniya, perepiska*, ed. by I. S. Rabinovich (Moscow: Sovetskiy kompozitor, 1972), 315.

[14] Kuper's memoirs, 'Nezakonchennaya avtobiografiya muzïkal'noy kar'yerï', GTsMMK, fond 334 (Kuper), ye. kh. 1, list 148.

come to an end, the Philharmonia held 54 symphony concerts, all sold out.[15]

During these concerts the orchestra played 32 different programmes, conducted by Kuper himself, or by Nikolai Malko, Glazunov, and Sergei Lyapunov, sharing the platform with celebrity soloists such as the singer Ivan Yershov, and the pianists Vladimir Sofronitsky and Mariya Yudina. Kuper's favourite warhorse, Beethoven's Ninth Symphony, was played with massed choirs, bringing the number of performers involved to 500. Some new music was played too, with Petrograd composers Vladimir Shcherbachov and Anatoly Kankarovich conducting their own works. In the autumn, the building work continued, heating was installed, and the orchestra then presented an equally successful winter season. NEP eventually caught up with the new venture, however, and on 1 July 1922 it was taken off the state payroll and taxed at 10% in line with all other spectacles and entertainments, which curtailed its activities somewhat. Yet this child of War Communism survived, and became the most distinguished of all Russian orchestras.

Another extravagant initiative emerged from the immediate pre-NEP period: a State Institute for Music Scholarship (GIMN), located in Moscow. Musicologists in Petrograd also organised themselves into a section at GIII (State Institute for Arts History), but never had the luxury of a completely independent institution. The specialist bias of GIMN towards the science of music, acoustics and aural perception, as promoted by its director Nikolai Garbuzov, no doubt assisted the institute's claim on state funds, since science and technology in general fitted better with the state's priorities. On 5 October 1921, Lev Termen (who became known as Theremin) demonstrated his new electrical musical instrument at the conference held to mark Lenin's electrification plan, and the invention made a great impression.[16] A few months later Lenin himself wished to see him, and Theremin not only performed in his presence but even managed to give him a lesson:

> I took his hands from behind and assisted him. He began to play 'Skylark' [a Glinka song]. He had a very good ear, and he sensed where he had to move his hands to obtain the sound, lowering or raising them as needed. By the middle of the piece, I thought that he could make the hand movements by himself. So I withdrew my hands, and he completed the whole thing independently, by himself, with great success, followed by much applause. He was delighted that he could play the instrument by himself.[17]

The composer Nikolai Kochetov was asked to imagine 'the future of music', and made some striking prophecies about the roles technology and new media would eventually play. He expanded on the concept of the theremin (as the instrument is now known), looking ahead to the synthesiser and predicting that new electrical instruments would imitate existing timbres and create new ones. He was excited

---

[15] Ibid., 151–2.
[16] Albert Glinsky, *Theremin: Ether Music and Espionage* (Urbana and Chicago: University of Illinois Press, 2005), 27.
[17] From Theremin's interview with Olivia Mattis (Bourges, 1989), http://www.thereminvox.com/article/articleview/18/1/1.html, accessed 24 Apr. 2012.

by the potential of sound amplification, which he imagined would be 'unlimited', and predicted that the telephone would help create mass audiences. His discussion of new possibilities for listeners has proven particularly accurate:

> The development of the telephone will draw the two musical poles further apart: music that influences the masses and music heard in an intimate setting. It is difficult to preserve any sense of intimacy when you realise that thousands or hundreds of thousands are all listening to the same thing at the same time. And it makes complete sense that the masses should be addressed by masses, by huge orchestral and choral collectives. Here we need something broad-brush instead of miniatures [...] Composers will need to take this into account. This is the one pole. The other, the intimate pole, will allow us to hear a nocturne, say, over a private telephone line, without any audience gathered. Or we could let others hear the nocturne unaware [of the mass audience], listening as if it was sung within them. There is a huge difference between listening to an intimate work played by Hofmann in the Hall of Unions[18] or in your own home, where you can give yourself over completely to the mood of the music.[19]

GIMN was eventually absorbed by the Moscow Conservatoire in 1931;[20] but during the NEP period, it played a crucial role in the development of music technology through the work of dreamers and enthusiasts like Theremin, Garbuzov and Arseny Avraamov.

It seems that, in 1921, those who decided to stay to work with the Soviet government had the opportunity to participate in some dream projects. But at the time, the hardships across society made all work a matter of survival. As Kuper said:

> In all likelihood, the only thing that pulsed through everyone's mind was the need to live. And so everything we did, we did in order to preserve our lives.[21]

---

[18] The Polish-American pianist Josef Hofmann performed in Russia almost annually between 1896 and 1913, when the Hall of Unions was still that of the Nobility Assembly.

[19] N. Kochetov, 'Budushcheye muzïki', *Vestnik iskusstv*, nos 3–4 (1922), 8–9.

[20] T. Livanova, 'Iz proshlogo sovetskoy muzïkal'noy nauki (GIMN v Moskve)', *Iz proshlogo sovetskoy muzïkal'noy kul'turï*, ed. T. Livanova, vol. 1 (Moscow: Sovetskiy kompozitor, 1975), 267–335.

[21] Kuper's memoirs, 148.

N. Strel'nikov, '"Yolka" (Mikhaylovskiy teatr)' [*The Christmas Tree* at the Mikhailovsky Theatre], *Zhizn' iskusstva*, nos. 658–60 (21, 23, 25 Jan. 1921), 1.

Vladimir Rebikov's Christmas Tree was his most popular opera, a single-act piece based on Andersen's fairy tale The Little Match Girl *(1900). Rebikov was a representative of the post-*Eugene Onegin *tendency in Russian opera towards smaller-scale psychological drama. One of his operas in this style,* The Abyss *(1907), was based on a novella by Leonid Andreyev, the writer compared to Rebikov by the reviewer. His modernist reputation is based on some adventurous piano pieces, and on his unusual 'melomimes' and 'rhythmodeclamations'. Rebikov died in Yalta shortly before the publication of the review below (different accounts place the date of his death in August, October or December 1920); the reviewer makes no mention of the composer's death, and was quite possibly unaware of it.*

The author of the review, Nikolai Strelnikov (real name Mesenkampf), mocks Rebikov for his aristocratic attire, although Strelnikov himself had belonged to the Tsarist ruling class and was even employed for a time in the Tsar's household. His personal friendships with several important Bolsheviks allowed him to retain high status in the new society. He became the legal advisor to Narkompros and also wrote as chief music critic for the Petrograd daily arts paper Zhizn' iskusstva *(Artistic Life). In the late twenties and thirties, he achieved fame as a composer of Soviet operettas.*

N. Strelnikov
The Christmas Tree at the Mikhailovsky Theatre

There was a time when Rebikov, the composer of this psychological music drama, was honoured as an audacious innovator, a Russian modernist, a bold cutthroat type. But now all these chromatic and dissonant tonal combinations, the augmented [*chrezmerniye*; also meaning 'excessive'] intervals, the illicit progressions, and the whole naïve weaponry designed to overturn the existing order – this merely seems like good behaviour turned inside out!

A man in a top hat with a beaver-fur collar – this is how Rebikov was depicted on the programme booklet for the premiere.

I realise, of course, that basing one's criticisms of artistic creation on [the artist's choice of] headgear is the worst type of criticism. But here's a curious thing: of all the things that were written early on about Leonid Andreyev (a playwright who is extremely fashionable right now at the Academy Drama Theatre), the most appropriate was the review headed by a picture of the tyro writer, author of *Yekaterina Ivanovna*, under his magnificent fur coat [*bekesha*], an image that had been immortalised by a provincial photograph of him.

Although the *bekesha* is not quite the same thing as the top-hat, these [particular] wearers have much in common. This is not only in the fact that both like to don masks expressing a mystical horror for the most ordinary of events, and to convey these horrors in a superficially showy style, using clichés that are naïve and often trivial and tasteless. It is not only because both fill their works with mysteries, abysses, enigmas, fate and curses, and apply extraordinary epithets to domestic objects like coffee-pots or a handkerchiefs. Nor is it only because both have 'the keen-eyed darkness of a silent and mute night' 'in the world of muffled gloomy shadows, over which hangs a severe Fate, like an unknowable eternity'. Both of them have an extraordinary predilection for psychological descriptions of the everyday, and obstinate 'idealist' preaching upon elementary morals. Both have the same streak of mystical anarchism that is neither mysticism nor anarchism, but simply individualist thought that has its sources in something foreign, not their own, and which may even be infinitely alien to themselves.

There is another, more concrete trait common to the work of both: the absence of all movement in action. There is absolutely no dynamism in the unfolding of the plot. And the plot itself does not really unfold, but immediately takes on an ossified form and is conveyed to spectators by mechanically keeping them in the restrictive atmosphere of the same psychological experiences, to the accompaniment of irritating repetitions and a recombination of snatches of phrases and dialectical evasions.

There is an abyss, of course, between Andreyev and Rebikov, both in quality and quantity. Rebikov's talent is a small one, and *The Christmas Tree* is far from being a *Yekaterina Ivanovna*. With Rebikov, our doubts are even stronger: what is the point of all these 'prophetic insights', all these musical-psychological pictures, melo-mime and rhythmic declamation, when all that is revealed is the small world of an intimate lyricist, a sickly-sweet reactionary world on a tiny scale?

I have no wish to deny Rebikov's opera its undoubted virtues: its melodies, its warmth of expression and harmonic refinement. But all of this is still somehow petty and less than fully convincing, failing to justify the artificial coating in which the music is enveloped.

The music of the dances leaves a very good impression. But here, too, it is difficult to banish the treacherous thought that this is just the kind of music enjoyed by the habitués of garden esplanades […].

The fact that *The Christmas Tree* was largely received well I ascribe to the wonderful performance. Rebikov is not a great orchestrator, and the conductor must beware of the underwater reefs that lie beneath his style of orchestration. A great delicacy of touch was needed in the artistry that balanced the different instrumental groups, and which evened out the woodwind-heavy sounds.

This problem was successfully solved by G. Yakobson, whose direction of *The Christmas Tree* demonstrated impressively how much sensitive work had been carried out with the orchestra. […]

M. Kovalenko[22] was scenically and vocally successful, creating a touching and fragile depiction of the freezing girl. […]

The Christmas Tree ran together with Gluck's charming pastoral *The May Queen* [*Cythère assiégée*, as reworked by J. H. Fuchs] […]

---

[22] Mariya Vladimirovna Kovalenko (1873–1950) was a coloratura soprano with a long and distinguished career both in opera and as a recitalist. Between 1908 and 1928, she sang at the Mariinsky, and thereafter at GOTOB and the Bolshoi. She was married to Ivan Ekskuzovich, the head of the Academy Theatres.

Anatoliy, 'Glaza i krïlya: pod vpechatleniyem Skryabinskikh kontsertov v Filarmonii' [Eyes and Wings: under the impression of Scriabin's concerts at the Philharmonia], *Zhizn' iskusstva*, nos. 792–7 (2–7 Aug. 1921), 3.

Anatoly Kankarovich (1885–1956) was a composer of several Symbolist operas, a conductor who had studied with Nikisch, and a music critic. This screed of purple prose was prompted by a Scriabin cycle performed by Emil Kuper at the Petrograd Philharmonia.

Anatoliy Kankarovich

Eyes and Wings: Under the Impression of Scriabin Concerts at the Philharmonia

'Suffering is life', says Remizov in *Fiery Russia*. Art is suffering, I say, and so too does everyone who knows what art is, who carries art within himself.

Joy in art is a climax of suffering, and the reverse too: the climax of suffering is the greatest tension of the human spirit, i.e. joy. These are the two faces of one and the same essence of art. This is why the funeral march from *Götterdämmerung* is the greatest unveiling of the human spirit, revealed through the most extreme unearthly suffering, i.e. through the *joy of suffering*. This is why Beethoven's mournful march from the Third is likewise a climax of *suffering through the joy of existence*. This is why Beethoven, Scriabin, or Vrubel[23] are eternal ...

In art it is not form, not technique, and not even content that is important. The only thing that is important in art is the *approach the artist takes to his creative work*. It is not prettiness, not glitter, and not orchestration or complexity of counterpoint. It is the *thought* with which the creative artist approaches his art – only *that* decides the value of this creativity.

Art and its creation know two true and eternal symbols – Eyes and Wings: Eyes so that you see where to fly, and the Wings to fly there. And only the Eyes and Wings of Art can solve the problems of art and creativity.

This is why Beethoven, Scriabin, and Vrubel are eternal ...

Art without Eyes and Wings, no matter how beautiful, is ultimately of no use to anyone. Because the crux of the matter is not in the prettiness, and not in the form that justifies the content, but in the *seeing* and thus the *knowing* where to *fly*, in the *knowing, feeling,* and *certainty* that the creator of music is not only a composer, but also a *thinker*, an inspired *philosopher of art*, like the eternal Beethoven, and like Scriabin standing before us.

Eyes and *Wings* – those are the Symbols of Art's Creation!

Scriabin's *Ecstasy* and Beethoven's Ninth display the ultimate tensions of the human spirit, and we feel this in the joy of suffering, in the eternal *thought* of

---

[23] Mikhail Alekseyevich Vrubel (1856–1910) was a Russian Symbolist painter. The imagery of this article may have been inspired by some of his paintings.

human strivings, which are hidden in those eternal *Eyes* and those eternal *Wings* of *Art*.

We are gazing into the infinite heights and flying to the space beyond the stars, but before this, the human mind, even a mind of genius like Kant's, finds it can go no further.

Scriabin, Vrubel, Byron, and Wilde – they were the ones who could *see*, who knew how and where to *fly*.

This is why, listening to Scriabin, you see the eyes of Vrubel's creations, and remember Byron's flight of Cain and Lucifer, you feel the wisest and most refined pathology of Wilde's *Salome* – and begin to understand, finally, what Scriabin's *volupté* in the *Divine Poem* is, and start to believe that only through the highest, wisest and most beautiful *Desire* – and the path to it is through *Suffering* – lies the way to the stars, to Eternity, to Divinity.

Eyes and Wings – there is Art's Ultimate Wisdom!

M. Zagorskiy, 'Vpechatleniya' [Impressions], *Teatral'naya Moskva*, nos. 5–6 (11–13 Nov. 1921), 6–7.

The breathless author of the review below was the well-known theatre critic M. B. Zagorsky. A very different account of the same performance by Isadora Duncan was provided by Sabaneyev (note, however, that the memoir from which this is extracted was written some years after his emigration):

> Because she could no longer dance, she attempted nothing beyond a walk from one corner of the stage to the other, carrying a baby in her arms – this, I was told, symbolised the birth of international Communism; the red flag was flown to the sounds of the *Internationale*. The government was probably pleased with this display, but it offered little of aesthetic substance.[24]

Sabaneyev describes only the final part of the performance; perhaps he turned up late, or thought the other parts would not amuse his émigré audience so well. The contrast with Zagorsky's account, in any case, could hardly be greater.

M. Zagorsky
Impressions [On Isadora Duncan]

It's Duncan's night ...
The first encounter after ... when was it?
Ten years ago? Or perhaps 50, 100, 300?
The whole era. A historical mountain ridge ... Empire, republic, constituent assembly, Soviets, an endless chain of wars. The storm. The siege. The retreat. Romanticism. Realism. Two Russias. The mad rush of the Gogolian troika over the bumps of history.
And which of us hasn't changed? And which of us hasn't lived a huge life in these last few fabled years?
And here she is, Isadora Duncan. Also changed. Different. And in her eyes there is a reflection of our dream, and her running is our running, Scythian, crazy. Towards the universal, towards the ultimate.
Tchaikovsky's *Pathétique*. His *Marche Slave*. And the *Internationale*.
The past. The overcoming of the past. And our future.
Yes, this is how it is. Herein lies the remarkable astuteness of this programme and the great fascination of its execution.
May Mr Lunacharsky forgive me, but I can't believe that a universal celebration in the spirit of our times can be built on the basis of Tchaikovsky's *Pathétique*. That is a beautiful fragment of the culture that has fallen away, that is now dead. It can be put on display, but nothing can be built upon it.

[24] L. L. Sabaneyev, *Vospominaniya o Rossii* (Moscow: Klassika–XXI. 2005), 190.

And even in Duncan's interpretation it did not inspire the audience.

But how unanimously thrilled the audience became during the performance of the *Marche Slave*, this apparently ultrapatriotic Tsarist march by the same Tchaikovsky! With its 'God, save the Tsar'!

Why?

Because here, before our eyes, it was shown how the cultural past can be overcome, using its own material.

We have been talking of such an overcoming for three years now.

And *The Government Inspector* is transformed into *Khlestakov*, and *Doctor So-and-So* into *A Communist Whether He Likes it or Not*.[25]

You, the Proletkult activists and the overcomers of the Mastkomdram![26] Go and watch how Isadora Duncan overcomes the *Marche Slave* – in truth and in its entirety.

And you will understand that art can be overcome only by art. But on one condition: if it sees with its eyes wide open –

Our today.

Seen keenly and acutely by our –

Time.

---

[25] The author is satirising the many 'revolutionary' adaptations of traditional repertoire.

[26] Mastkomdram (*Masterskaya Kommunisticheskoy Dramaturgii*), the Workshop for Communist Drama, a theatre where such adaptations (see previous footnote) were staged, together with newly written plays.

1922
Just Like the Old Days?

The introduction of NEP soon swept away the austerity of War Communism. Great quantities of food were suddenly made available in the shops and at the many private stalls, from staple items through to the most extravagant delicacies. There were queues even for items costing upwards of a million roubles. Those who could not hope to buy were glued to the windows. Luxury goods filled the displays at the newly opened department stores bearing fashionable acronyms: GUM and TsUM. The writer Kornei Chukovsky, walking the streets of central Moscow, observed that 'everyone wore the same expression – happiness. Men are made happy by card games, races, wine and women; women with lascivious, drunken faces push their chests against the shop windows on Kuznetsky, where there are silks and diamonds to be seen …'[1] While all this happiness was chiefly the preserve of the newly enriched NEPmen, the rest of society also began to enjoy greater comforts: workers were paid the arrears they were owed, allowing them to experience some of the exuberance of life under NEP. As the student Litvinov noted in his diary, 'people began to work, eat, dress up and multiply'.[2] Music filled the streets: 'they sing and play in their homes, on the boulevards, and above all in the countless cabarets, cafes, corner bars, restaurants, tea rooms, and canteens'.[3] 1 October that year saw the birth of home-grown jazz, at a concert given by Valentin Parnakh's band.

The reprivatisation of previously nationalised enterprises significantly undermined the government's abilities to shape and control intellectual life. First, the bureaucracy had to be cut to half its size, due to the drop in revenue. Second, and crucially, NEP ended the scarcity in paper, enabling private publishing to resume. Under War Communism, censorship had been a simple affair, since Gosizdat had only a trickle of publications to scrutinise. The sudden surge in publishing included a wave of anti-Bolshevik literature, prompting an overhaul of the censorship mechanisms. The Agitation and Propaganda Department of the Party (Agitprop) sought to unify the various existing agencies of censorship, which were now unable to cope in isolation. For example, a collection of essays provocatively entitled *Red Alcohol* (by Matvei Royzman and Vadim Shershenevich)[4] was predictably banned; but the censors had been too slow to act, and the first print run had by then already sold out. The censors now appeared foolish before the public; but not wishing to appear impotent too, they had the authors arrested and charged with criminal offences. In June, a new body, Glavlit, was created, with powers and organisation better suited to the task. Although

---

[1] Vostrïshev, 140.

[2] Vostrïshev, 133.

[3] From the Moscow diary of Nikita Okunev, quoted in Vostrïshev, 133.

[4] Matvey Davidovich Royzman (1898–1973) and Vadim Gabrielevich Shershenevich (1893–1942) were poets, prominent members of the Imaginists group led by Yesenin. Both were able to carve out Soviet careers: Royzman by writing film scenarios, Shershenevich by translating foreign literature.

nominally under the supervision of Narkompros, its staff included members of the GPU and RVSR (Revolutionary Military Council of Russia) who belonged to separate hierarchies. At this point in Soviet history, the official evaluation of literary merit was of little moment, since Glavlit's chief task was to suppress the publication of whatever it regarded as counter-revolutionary material. Beyond this, there was only a vague injunction that 'boulevard' literature should be given no encouragement.[5]

After only a month of its existence, it was already clear that Glavlit could not solve the problem by itself. It was not that Glavlit was insufficiently powerful, but rather that it was all stick and no carrot. The Party leadership, now nervous about the potential threat posed by unruly writers and scholars, decided to take more positive steps to promote whatever seemed worthy in the broad range of writing that was not hostile to the new dispensation, on the principle that would later bear the slogan 'Whoever is not against us is with us'. A special sub-committee of the CC, including both Trotsky and Stalin, attempted to draw together a diverse association of writers and poets around the journal *Krasnaya nov'*. They included old writers (Valery Bryusov, Sergei Gorodetsky, Gorky), 'proletarian' writers, Futurists, Imaginists, the Serapion Brothers, the 'hesitating ones' (Pilnyak and Zoshchenko), and the Smenovekhovtsy (Alexei Tolstoy).[6] This still left a significant minority that was too radically anti-Communist; and for them, Lenin had other plans, as he told Stalin on 16 July:

> [We need] to arrest a few hundred, without giving any reasons: 'Time to leave, gentlemen!' All the writers from the Litterateurs' House [*Dom literatorov*], and from *Thought* [*Mïsl*, a philosophical journal] in Petrograd [...] The purge must be carried out quickly, and no later than by the end of the trial of the SRs ['Socialist Revolutionaries'].[7]

This was the moment when Soviet Russia officially became a one-party state: all rival parties were outlawed at the beginning of August. The key public event signalling the change was the trial of a group of 34 leaders of the Socialist Revolutionary (SR) Party. The SRs had effectively split over the October Revolution, the right wing associated with the ousted Provisional Government, the left wing entering coalition with the Bolsheviks. The left wing itself had split, some entering into open rebellion against the Bolsheviks after the Treaty of Brest-Litovsk, others eventually joining with the Bolsheviks in the renamed Communist Party during the course of the Civil War. The charges ranged from SR participation in the Provisional Government to collaboration with White armies in the Civil War.

---

[5] *Literaturnaya zhizn' Rossii 1920-kh godov: Sobïtiya. Otzïvï sovremennikov. Bibliografiya*, ed. by A. Yu. Galushkin (Moscow: IMLI RAN, 2006), vol. 1, pt 2, 623.

[6] Ibid., 462. The Serapion Brothers (or Serapion Fraternity) was a group that fashioned itself on E. T. A. Hofmann's group *Die Serapionsbrüder*; its leader was Yevgeny Zamyatin. Smenovekhovtsy (from the émigré publication *Smena vekh*, of *Changing Signposts*) was a group of émigré writers who chose to accept the Soviet regime as the inevitable fate of Russia.

[7] Ibid., 469. Dom literatorov was a literary organisation (1918–22) that included Akhmatova, Blok, Sologub, Remizov and others.

There were some acquittals, various prison sentences, and 14 death sentences, subsequently suspended by the government. The trials were greeted with vigorous objections from members of the intelligentsia (including Gorky). Later in August, the expected arrests of the anti-Communist writers took place. Those who agreed to leave the country at their own expense were released to make their departure. Those who refused or who lacked the means, were deported. The numbers were sufficient to warrant a second ship of deportees, and the high concentration of philosophers resulted in these becoming known as 'the philosophers' ships'.[8]

In effect, the government's engagement with artists was narrowed down to a purely political struggle with oppositionist writers. As a result of cuts resulting from NEP, Narkompros was reorganised and lost its department dedicated to the arts; its functions were divided between four other departments: Glavpolitprosvet (Political Education), Glavprofobr (Professional Education), Glavsotsvos (Social Education), and Aktsentr (Academic Centre). Before long, the arts section of Glavpolitprosvet was also closed, and officials admitted that state influence within the arts had been 'reduced to zero'.[9] In political and artistic discourse, the Russian word, *khaltura* (hackwork), thanks to its co-incidental resemblance to the imported word *kul'tura* (culture), was taken up as a label for the commercial artistic produce that flooded the NEP market: 'General All-Russian Khaltura: a definition of the condition of the arts in the RSFSR'.[10]

Low on funds, Narkompros's budget for professional artistic activity now only stretched to the handful of Moscow theatres that it continued to sponsor, including, of course, the Bolshoi. These theatres were granted the status of 'Academy' institutions and they could now add the word to their official titles. The Bolshoi had somehow survived the hardships of the Civil War period, but now its continued existence came under challenge from Lenin as an unnecessary expense; and Lunacharsky found himself battling for the survival of the theatre (which would not have survived without public funding).

Why did Lenin want to remove funds from the Bolshoi at this juncture, in January 1922? A few months earlier, an artistic committee had been forced to back down in the face of the theatre's total resistance to reform. From its repertoire and productions, no one could have guessed that the Revolution had ever occurred, but Lenin was particularly vexed by the fact that the Bolshoi's superior seats were filled once again by the conspicuously wealthy, namely the new NEP entrepreneurs and speculators. As Lenin argued, why should prosperous NEPmen be provided with their entertainments at huge expense to the state? And so, when the Council of Ministers resolved to continue the Bolshoi's funding, Lenin decided his timely intervention was required. On 12 January 1922, he wrote to the members of the Politburo:

---

[8] Among the exiled philosophers were Nikolai Berdyayev, Pitirim Sorokin, Ivan Ilyin, Mikhail Osorgin, Sergei Trubetskoy, Nikolai Lossky, and others.

[9] Lerin, 'Glaviskusstvo. Spetsial'naya beseda dlya 'Zrelishch' s chlenom prezidiuma Tsekrabisa V. K. Vladimirovim', *Zrelishcha*, no. 11 (1922), 19.

[10] 'Nashi zadachi', *Vestnik iksusstv*, no. 1 (Jan. 1922), 1.

Having learnt from Kamenev that the Council of Ministers has unanimously accepted Lunacharsky's utterly outrageous proposal on the preservation of the Bolshoi opera and ballet, I suggest that the Politburo resolve the following:

1) To entrust to the Presidium of the Party Central Committee the revocation of the Council of Ministers' resolution.
2) To leave the opera and ballet with a few dozen *artistes* in Moscow and Petrograd so that their performances (both opera and dance) can pay for themselves,* i.e. to remove the need for high expenditure on sets, etc.
3) From the billions freed up by these economies, to give no less than half towards the elimination of illiteracy and for the establishment of reading rooms.
4) To summon Lunacharsky in order to give the accused a few minutes to say his final words [Lenin's tone is jocular here], and to tell both him and all other ministers that if they put to the vote resolutions such as the one now being revoked by the Central Committee, then stricter measures will have to be enforced by the Central Committee.[11]

* for example through the participation of the opera singers and ballet dancers in all manner of concert presentations, etc.

It is not difficult to see Lenin's point: he had no desire to pull high culture from its pedestal (indeed, he had criticised Proletkult modernists on this count). Instead he sought to reduce the company to its performing members, which would then work as a more mobile troupe able to generate much of its own income rather than depending on a heavy state subsidy. The substantial funds now freed up could then be allocated to the more urgent task of raising the general cultural level of the country (and he refers to the mass illiteracy that was indeed greatly reduced over the following years). The Politburo saw no reason to fight Lenin on the matter, and passed a resolution on the closure of the Bolshoi the same day, although they decided to forgo any showdown with Lunacharsky.[12] As soon as the latter learnt of the resolution, he wrote a long letter to Lenin, complaining both of the procedural 'absurdity', namely that the Party's Central Committee could over-rule the state's Council of Ministers without even troubling to consult them; he further complained that Lenin was badly informed on the issue.[13]

The letter is a showcase for Lunacharsky's shrewdness. In his opening paragraphs, he makes no suggestion that opera and ballet on a grand scale are intrinsically deserving of the state's support, and even when he does eventually broach the matter, he ensures that it remains incidental to the thrust of his

[11] V. I. Lenin, *Sobraniye sochineniy*, vol. 54 (Moscow: Izdatel'stvo politicheskoy literaturï, 1965), 110.

[12] See *Vlast' i khudozhestvennaya intelligentsiya: dokumentï TsK RKP(b) – VKP(b) – VChK – OGPU – NKVD o kul'turnoy politike, 1917–1953*, ed. by A. Artizov and O. Naumov (Moscow: Mezhdunarodnïy fond 'Demokratiya', 1999), 31.

[13] The complete text of the letter can be found in *Vlast' i khudozhestvennaya intelligentsiya*, 31–3.

argument. Instead, Lunacharsky stakes his defence on the cost of closing down the Bolshoi, thereby mounting a direct challenge to the central plank of Lenin's argument, arguing that contrary to the figures that Lenin had accepted, the productions actually paid for themselves. The Bolshoi company was, in itself, effectively self-financing, and the real drain on the state's resources was instead the maintenance of the theatre building. The significance of this fact was not restricted to opera and ballet, since the same building was the regular venue for large official meetings, and so the maintenance costs still had to be met for political rather than artistic reasons. He also cautions that if, despite these arguments, the Bolshoi were still to close as a theatre, it was very likely that the valuables inside would be stolen and dispersed – unless, of course, it was placed under constant guard, but that would be a further expense.

Only when he feels confident that he has won the financial argument, does Lunacharsky finally turn to the Bolshoi's artistic activities. First, the Bolshoi offers international prestige to the state, which takes its foreign guests to the operas and ballets knowing that this will make a good impression on them. Secondly, were the theatre to be closed, the state would need to take care of the resident orchestra, the best in Russia and one of the most important in Europe (presumably Lunacharsky, knowing Lenin's musical tastes, calculated that the future of a symphony orchestra would concern him, even if he was indifferent to the opera company). Then he combines these artistic concerns with socialist principle: the closure of the Bolshoi would mean a loss of jobs for 1,500 people, meaning that many of their families would lose their source of sustenance – this would fit badly with the state's avowed respect for honest labour. And lastly, each night 2,000 people, including 500 workers, would lose the opportunity 'to spend time in a warm, lit building, listening to good music.'[14]

As a result of the letter, a commission was formed to examine the facts behind Lunacharsky's financial arguments, and so the debate was reopened. By the end of the year, Lunacharsky was vindicated, adequate state subsidies were reinstated, and the Bolshoi, together with the former Mariinsky (which had also been threatened with closure), became the two most privileged institutions of the new Soviet state.

The news that the former Imperial Theatres were to be given a new lease of life was not well received by some critics, who had been rather looking forward to 'the death of opera'. As one Petrograd arts journal sarcastically reported:

> The theatre generalissimo Ekskuzovich[15] returned with some joyous news from Moscow: the academic theatres are to stay in place, and the former Mariinsky will on no account be closed 'forcibly' (in Moscow they probably hope that it will close of its own accord).
>
> Thus, instead of an obituary:
>
> At the time when life is seething, when revolutions take place, and classes, outlooks and eras are changing, when the era of capitalism will be supplanted by the era of proletarian culture combined with American super-technology,

[14] Ibid.
[15] See Glossary.

when we may even live to see electrification … on the stages of the opera houses, they will still glorify kings and princes. Igor, Radames and the like will still fight with their cardboard swords, beating their chests and standing on tiptoe for the high notes. Old Larina will still make jam, and poor Tatiana will have to write so many letters …[16]

The operatic time warp was even more perceptible in Moscow, where one of the most talked-about events was the reopening of the Zimin private opera under its pre-Revolutionary management (now entitled 'S. I. Zimin's Free Opera'). Zimin himself, having sat out War Communism as an ordinary employee of his former company, was back in power, confirming the widespread commercial slogan of the time, 'everything just as it was in the old days'. This was certainly the impression given to one critic:

> During the afternoon, the whole troupe gathered for a prayer, while in the evening, a festive performance was given. The auditorium was filled to the brim, there were magnificent gowns, diamonds, and a mood of general excitement. As he took to the conductor's podium, that veteran of the old music, M. M. Ippolitov-Ivanov, was greeted by applause and fanfares from the orchestra.[17]

Another critic was charmed by the 'magnificent' voices, but was lukewarm about the other elements of the production:

> The sets are 'neat', the costumes not bad, the singers stand in their proper places and in a measured, precise way, they press their hands to their chests or shake them vigorously in the air.[18]

The Zimin Opera chose Tchaikovsky's *Mazepa* for its grand reopening on 10 October, and continued with well-tested stories of passion, in the form of Dargomyzhsky's *Rusalka*, *Faust*, *Carmen*, *The Demon*, and *The Tsar's Bride*, adding to these the two grand operas *La Juive* and *Les Huguenots*, which posed a greater challenge to the smaller stage. The hunger for opera in Moscow was such that the company could support two more stages. One of these, at The New Theatre (*Novïy Teatr*), concentrated on classic non-Russian repertoire, including *La Traviata*, *The Barber of Seville*, *La Bohème*, *Rigoletto*, *Manon*; here, the Bolshoi stars Antonina Nezhdanova and Sobinov made regular appearances. Stanislavsky's production of *Eugene Onegin* was a guest feature here, upgraded for the larger stage. The other of these two extra stages, at The Music Drama Theatre, also offered old favourites, such as *Carmen* and *Eugene Onegin*, but showed more ambition in mounting a production of Musorgsky's unfinished comedy, *The Sorochintsy Fair* (completed and edited by Ippolitov-Ivanov).

The symphony orchestras likewise followed public demand. The Gosfil (State Philharmonia) was, in spite of its name, a largely self-supporting, commercial organisation, which sold all seats for its grand opening night. A speech was given

---

[16] G. Krïzhitskiy, 'Vmesto nekrologa', *Muzïka i teatr*, no. 10 (28 Nov. 1922), 3.

[17] Chernomor, 'Opera Zimina', *Zrelishcha*, no. 7 (1922), 21–2.

[18] DODO, 'V opere Zimina', *Zrelishcha*, no. 13 (1922), 17–18.

for the occasion by Boris Krasin, the genial self-proclaimed 'friend of the artists', who had found a perfect position for himself as Gosfil's director. A fantastically weighty programme followed, with Beethoven's Ninth, Scriabin's *Poem of Ecstasy*, one of Rachmaninov's Piano Concertos (with Igumnov as soloist), with further ballast from Taneyev and Ippolitov-Ivanov.[19] Within a week there was another important inaugural concert, this time for the conductorless orchestra, Persimfans (an abbreviated form of First Symphonic Ensemble), a 60-strong group founded by the violin professor Lev Tseitlin, who had been once the leader of Koussevitzky's orchestra, and consisting largely of musicians from the Bolshoi orchestra. Their all-Beethoven programme (the *Eroica, Egmont*, and the Violin Concerto) had been painstakingly rehearsed, and made a great impression on the audience: it was 'like the sound of some mighty chamber ensemble'. Despite the critics' reservations that the interpretation was derived 'mostly from Nikisch', the genuine artistry won the orchestra much acclaim.[20]

Persimfans capitalised on its novelty value in the musical marketplace of the NEP years; but it was, nonetheless, a pioneering venture, a child of revolutionary times. The idea that musical decisions could be taken democratically within a collective of equals cannot be taken quite so seriously as Persimfans claimed – after all, everyone was looking at Tseitlin. But the musicians' level of involvement, and the remarkable amount of work they devoted to each piece, chimed with the communist ideal of free, joyous and conscious labour. Even so, the extreme use of time and resources also harked back to the War Communism years, and Persimfans soon had to struggle to maintain itself in the faster-moving musical life of the NEP dispensation.

Petrograd could also boast of exciting concert music. In December 1922, the renovation of the Philharmonia building was finally completed, greeting the concert-goer with sparkling crystal and luxury rugs. Kuper celebrated the opening of the new building with Mahler's Fifth Symphony, while the second concert was given by Glazunov, the grand old man of Petrograd's concert life. But even these local luminaries were outshone by Oskar Fried, who had the honour of being the first foreign conductor to visit Russia since before the war – he conducted Beethoven's Ninth Symphony and Berlioz's *Symphonie Fantastique*.

The year 1922 brought a new polarisation to Russian society: abundance and urban merriment for some, hunger and strikes for others, while political repression against dissent took place alongside an explosion of popular culture and entertainment. The 'thinkers' might have been sent into exile, but the 'players' remained – and indeed their time was only just beginning. The musical intelligentsia – the composers and critics of high-art music – were now emerging from hibernation. The NEP allowed them to act as themselves, as Europeans of culture and learning, unreconstructed intellectuals with many pre-Revolutionary habits. The government perceived no danger from this quarter, and considered the group worthy of support as representatives of high culture. The desperate scramble for rations was over: at last they began to receive the same privileges

---

[19] L. Sabaneyev, 'Otkrïtiye Gosudarstvennoy Filarmonii', *Teatral'naya Moskva*, no. 26 (7–13 Feb. 1922), 12–13.

[20] Ibid., 5–6 and no. 28 (21–6 Feb. 1922), 14–15.

as scientists, in accordance with their professional standing.[21] Remarkably, out of the jagged landscape of 1922, they could at last see a return to some kind of normality.

---

[21] L. L. Sabaneyev, *Vospominaniya o Rossii* (Moscow: Klassika–XXI, 2005), 192.

L. Sabaneyev, 'Godï revolyutsii v muzïke' [The Revolutionary Years in Music], *Kul'tura i zhizn'*, no. 1 (1 Feb. 1922) 51–5.

Leonid Sabaneyev, once close to Scriabin, was one of the most notable music critics during the early Soviet years Just two days before the publication of this essay, Lunacharsky himself expressed similarly pessimistic thoughts on contemporary Russian music:

> And in music? Literally nothing – a desert. Not a single musical work that would in any way reflect the great multitude of Revolutionary events. And when we witness this, when we hear Little Sir Artist whimpering his protests against these horrid times, we cannot but exclaim, from the depth of our souls: what a bunch of corpses![22]

L. Sabaneyev
The Revolutionary Years in Music

The four years of revolution were years of great plans and of equally great expectations. And as for all the arts, it was commonly held that the revolutionary moment must somehow manage to fertilise music with an unprecedented impulse. As a result, a new revolutionary art would emerge – or at least an art that had never existed before. But then came disappointment. In fact, the revolutionary moment always contains too large a share of purely economic components, which hinder the development of the cultural 'superstructure' to which art belongs, in particular preventing art from leaving the stage of projects and grandiose theories and passing beyond this into artistic practice. For many, this was a surprise; many reproached the artists, accusing them of insufficient sympathy for the Revolution, of insufficient enthusiasm for Revolutionary ideas, of a lack of responsiveness, of being old-fashioned. In fact, this was only the natural consequence of a natural cause.

So what has happened in music during this period? First of all, there has been a great rethinking of pre-Revolutionary values; there has also been a great mixing of opinions and a complete regrouping of musical 'parties'. We have grown up and grown old during this period. These years of war and revolution are not simply 'eight years': they feel like half-a-century or more. We are very old men indeed, rewarded with a whole lifetime's experience, disappointed by things that once exerted a fascination. All that took place five years ago – is this not history and legend already? Is it not a 'faraway past', something contemporary with Ivan Kalita or Guido d'Arezzo?[23] And for us, who survived the years of revolution, who experienced what so few had experienced before us, is it not natural that we

---

[22] Anatoliy Lunacharskiy, 'Gosudarstvo i iskusstvo', *Izvestiya*, no. 252 (29 Jan. 1922), 2.
[23] Ivan Kalita was a fourteenth-century prince of Muscovy. Guido d'Arezzo was an eleventh-century music theorist.

should look at the art of yesterday with very different eyes? Is it not natural that our historical perspective has smoothed out much of the terrain before our eyes, and that what had deceptively seemed great and strong, proved to be otherwise? And finally, is it not natural that the demands we place upon art have changed and that our artistic quests have been transformed?

First of all, one cannot but notice the blurring of boundaries between musical parties and groups. Before the Revolution, we had had two well-defined and largely irreconcilable groups, which could have been characterised roughly as 'modernists' and 'conservatives'. The conservatives were those who stood for the old foundations of art, for art 'before Korsakov' or 'before Wagner'. The age of these foundations may not have been so very great, but it was sufficient. The modernists were all the others, those who sought something different in music, those who strove for a revolutionary 'overthrow' of the old order (although not in the political sense: on the contrary, modernists were political conservatives, and the converse also). They sought out new sounds, new approaches, and new syntheses. For the modernists, who formed a motley and disorderly crew, it was the moment of negation of the musical past that was paramount. They did not concern themselves with the details. This is why the gods of the modernist Olympus included such diverse persons as Debussy, Scriabin, Rebikov, Prokofiev, Strauss, Schoenberg and Roslavets.

Now everything is blurred. From the new historical perspective, some of the modernist gods have proven less than truly 'modernist' – they did not really overturn anything. The conservatives have shifted their position. During these past four years we have 'lost' our 'true' conservatives. Even the most obstinate and dense, who foamed at the mouth while defending their position from the encroachments of modernism, have now became followers of Scriabin and Prokofiev, or at the very least they have accepted them with good grace. But the modernist party has also shifted. Signs of fatigue are showing: sometimes a slowing of the 'leftist' pulse, or sometimes a straightforward shift to a more moderate outlook. Or perhaps they are sated with the very superficial approach to novelty they find in the modernists, perhaps they are tired of chasing after novel devices and are now nostalgic for that inner, essential kind of newness in music.

In this respect, it is interesting to trace the changing attitudes to the brightest star on our modernist firmament, the figure who was once fought over most fiercely by the modernists and conservatives – namely, Scriabin. During these years, our views on Scriabin have undergone substantial change.

First of all, his death was followed with astonishing rapidity by his 'canonisation', and so he was enrolled in the list of musical saints. And saints are always beloved of conservatives. Those elements of continuity with tradition to be found in Scriabin were assiduously drawn out, at the expense of other, revolutionary elements. And this task was easy, since, to be quite frank, Scriabin was really more a conservative than a modernist. A Mozartean simplicity of form, and a schematicism in harmonic construction now came to the foreground. It became apparent that Scriabin's music was based on the same principles as Mozart's, that it develops according to the same laws of continuity. We have got used to his harmonies (one can get used to anything), and they have lost their former sharpness and freshness. And when we got used to them, when those harmonies were dragged into the 'creations' of even second-rate composers, it became clear how simple a fabric Scriabin had woven with his harmonies, even though they had once seemed strange and frightening. His music was woven on the same principles as the music of the past.

And so that aura of innovation that we had previously discerned in Scriabin was now gone. What remains of a composer when the early impression of novel means is destroyed by the passing of time? What remains is 'the inner', the intimate in art, the mystery of creation. What remains is the mystery that Beethoven's primitive harmonies still work in us. It is hard for an artist's contemporaries to judge what this future residue of an art work will be, since their ear, their whole psyche, is enamoured and astonished by impressions of novelty. But we are not those contemporaries any more – we are old men who have by some miracle preserved their lives in this world. And we have got used to it. Not every composer is able to survive this process of historical disrobing. But whoever does will be counted as a genuine saint of art.

I believe that Scriabin's artistic calibre was diminished as a result of this process. He had once seemed to be so much *more* than he proved to be in reality. I am not talking about the brightness and magnificence of his dreams, since they were never realised. Scriabin, as he materialised to us, Scriabin who left us his music (alas, only the music) is not as extraordinary and colossal a genius as even the writer of these lines once believed. He is not even extraordinarily new: Debussy, for example, in his approach to the musical material reveals incomparably more of the true revolutionary, even in his treatment of a harmony, of a sounding moment as a colour unconstrained by any formal logic of succession. Scriabin, it proves, is entirely in thrall to the classical ritual of music (it is too early to say whether this is a good or a bad thing).

Thus, Scriabin was somewhat downgraded during this period, largely at the hands of the same 'modernists' who had hailed him previously. To them, Scriabin became the yesterday of art, while the conservatives now embraced him.

It is another matter whether the today of art has a right to argue with the yesterday. Let Scriabin be placed lower than Beethoven and Wagner, lower even than Liszt and Chopin; let him find a niche beside his 'ideological opponent', Tchaikovsky. But what is truly important, is that no composer of *today* can be put next to him. Today is undoubtedly a workday, while Scriabin's yesterday was a holiday.

I will move on to the fact that revolutionary music is anaemic. Official art can never flourish. Everything significant that was born during those years passed the Revolution by – they are all messages in a bottle from some desert island, which the wind of the revolutionary storm left untouched. Everything remained as it was. Residents of this island grew old, looking from afar at some unprecedented things, but they sing about the old world in the old way. And perhaps we, looking at all this from the vantage point of our experience, see this creative work as a complete anachronism, much as if people were writing Gregorian chant today. There may be values here, but one would not necessarily welcome these values.

Revolution has accustomed us to the cult of all that is grandiose, monumental, and magnificent, all that embraces the whole nation. It has made us forget the compliments, caresses and yearnings of the salon. Perhaps that salon mysticism of Scriabin the theosophist also faded so quickly because, in the terrible storm of revolutionary prose, a new kind of mysticism definitely started to appear, a mysticism that was huge and inexpressibly frightening. While he cannot speak for others, the writer of these lines has a certain nostalgia for grandiose, victorious, and destructive art – art which would engage not merely a select and refined circle under the salon lights, but something broader (although not necessarily the crowd, in the trivial sense of that word).

We have seen much: we have walked past death, famine and constant anxiety; we have learnt and unlearnt to value life. In such moments, toy solutions to world problems seem strange and pitiful. And the shadow of the giant Beethoven, with his heroic and democratic force, became especially close to us, as did Wagner's titanic and elemental force. These two geniuses are alive, while our contemporaries, such as Korsakov, who has become completely desiccated during these years, or Scriabin, who has become too obviously domesticated – they do not suit us at all. But let us see what other composers can offer us.

Not very much. We should discount Prokofiev and Rachmaninov, these two opposites, for they are not developing under the sign of revolution or under the aegis of this country. And Prokofiev still has many elements of sharp modernity. But once again, it is yesterday's modernity. Some have called him a genius already; I would not risk acknowledging this as yet. I can see, however, in spite of my multifarious antipathy to his work, that he undeniably possesses an elemental force (more so than Scriabin); he displays an astonishing energy, a kind of 'pressure' from within, and he displays both courage and, at times, a certain beauty. What is significant about him is that he is merry, quite unlike all our Russian composers. He is full of mischief, he is an eternal scherzo and joke. This is not the 'joyfulness' of Scriabin, which arises from mysticism and through suffering (Prokofiev is not so profound and refined); nor is it the bright, good-spirited, professorial joy of Rimsky-Korsakov that arises from comfort and calm. No, Prokofiev's joy is that of a boy who has broken out into freedom, who thinks that everything is permitted, and who knows that he can achieve much. In our art, there was always a lack of masculinity. Aside from Borodin, we have not had a composer who was a man in spirit. Prokofiev is not yet a man – he is a boy, but he could grow into a man if only psychological content were added to his energy and will.

Rachmaninov is not even the yesterday of art, he is from some day last week. An interesting day, admittedly, but a mournful one. We cannot really deal with him here, for everything he wrote in the last few years was created in an American climate.

The conservative party put forward their own genius – Medtner. His art is old with conviction, and desires to be so. He constructed a Great Wall of China between himself and modernity, which he neither feels nor recognises. He prays to his old eternal gods from the depths of his alienation. And there is something magnificent in his artistic character. If he is not a musical genius, he is still a great personality, a great man. His music at times suffocates me: it has too many notes, it is furnished with too many interesting things, so 'fitted out' that it turns the listener sour.

This art may be quite masculine, and it does not lack a certain grandeur, but it is still not the monumental art that we await. There is too little of the elemental in

Medtner, and this is why he cannot fascinate, although one can develop an interest in him, and having reached that stage, one can receive some elevated impressions and experiences. But we need someone like Wagner – he grabs us and leads us wherever he wants, and his magic is so strong that there is no point in asking whether it is good or bad.

Our modernist camp split during these years. One group moved left, into the Futurist thicket, and is now trying to create art out of dissonances, cutting all ties with the past. These are A. Lourié and Roslavets, our followers of Schoenberg and Stravinsky. The former gives us everything that culture, intellect and artistic taste can give, but without inspiration. His music has invested much in the unexpected, in the gastronomy of dissonance, and in the breaking of laws. And breaking laws is no bad thing? Yes, but not very difficult either. I usually take no pleasure in such music. It is clever, cold and piquant, unmusical and disharmonious. Lourié approaches music not as a musician, but rather as a painter, sometimes overlaying colours, sometimes resorting to line drawing. But his artistic day is still a yesterday, even if he wanted to spend it under the banner of revolution. This is all in the past – Blok, the Symbolists, the refinement and gastronomy of dissonance. He is a son – not quite legitimate – of Debussy and Stravinsky.

As for the art of Roslavets, 'revolutionary in the highest degree', I can only shake my head in sadness. This is not music at all, but merely something that pretends to be music. Roslavets has his own theory of art, in which he states that music does not express feelings, as everyone had hitherto believed, but instead ... thought. And the music itself, like his pitiful aesthetics, borders on illiteracy.

[Alexander] Krein and Gnesin, who are founding a new school of national Jewish music, must be regarded as an interesting phenomenon in our new music. Nationalism in art is also of yesterday, of course, but what is significant here is the fertilisation of art music by Jewish religious ritual. Krein, from the time he set out on this path, has acquired a distinctive physiognomy and his own style; he has become a true composer, and indeed a major one – he has found himself. Gnesin is similar, but with less elemental force and more of the cold reasoning that can be found in all of Rimsky-Korsakov's students. Krein's latest work in this vein (along the lines of a funeral cantata or requiem) shows all the signs of an important musical event.

We must, of course, mention our symphonist, Myaskovsky, although his work stands outside time and especially outside recent events. He, in particular, settled on that desert island and remains oblivious to the Revolution. During these years, his creative powers became stronger and more defined. He is undoubtedly a serious composer of high standing in the lineage of Tchaikovsky and Taneyev, but with leanings towards the emotional and with a contemporary palette. He is the author of five symphonies, which must be taken seriously. But still, he is not the future hero that art awaits.

So what will the future bring? We have lived through a revolutionary grandeur. In the future it will become a heroic legend. And then the creation of this monumental art ought to begin, the art or which we all vaguely dream, but which we cannot realise without a genius who will capture the essence of the moment and express it through sound. No matter how significant all our contemporary composers may be, all of them are children of the past, and of the irretrievable past at that. No matter how much we would like to, we cannot make them composers of today. Revolutionary eras are usually times when geniuses are born but are not yet active. Their activity usually follows a revolutionary era, as if summarising it artistically. Perhaps this is how it will be. All of us have this vague expectation that something has to happen in music. We are all dissatisfied with the present, but we have not yet begun the quest; we dream of grandeur, but have no energy. We have theories and constructions but not a creative genius. From such crepuscular feelings new eras are often born.

Arseniy Avraamov, 'Simfoniya gudkov' [The Symphony of Sirens] and 'Bakinskiy eksperiment' [The Baku Experiment], *Gorn*, no. 9 (1923), 109–10 and 115–16.

These pieces, although published in 1923, are entirely an account of events that took place in 1922, and thus appear in this section. They document a successful performance of Avraamov's Symphony of Sirens in Baku (his subsequent attempt to mount the event in Petrograd failed). This project is often mentioned in the literature as a symbol of its times, but the accompanying descriptions are rarely accurate. Here we reprint the original instructions for the Baku event together with Avraamov's explanation of his purposes.

Arseny Avraamov
The Symphony of Sirens

When the morning sirens roar
Across the workers' districts,
It is not the call of unfreedom
– It is the song of the future.
                                A. Gastev

Of all the arts, music possesses the maximum power for social organisation.

The most ancient myths witness the recognition of this power by humanity from time immemorial.

Orpheus tames the beasts with music.

Joshua destroys the Jericho fortress with trumpets.

Amphion erects magnificent temples from rocks, through the sounds from his lyre: colossal stone structures construct themselves to his music.

Pythagoras hears the 'harmony of the spheres' in the mechanics of the cosmos itself, in the movement of the heavenly bodies.

From myth to history: music and mass song are the inescapable concomitants of mankind's social life at its most solemn moments: festivities, religious and secular rites, collective labour (from barge haulers to soldiers) – none of these can be imagined without music.

The high organisation of collective industrial and cooperative labour in capitalist society ought, it seems, to have created a worthy form of musical embodiment ... it was necessary, however, for October to come before life could be breathed into the idea of a 'symphony of sirens': its realisation had [hitherto] been obstructed by the anarchic tendencies within the very system of [capitalist] production, together with the fear of unity among the workers. Every morning, the chaotic roar was still the roar of 'unfreedom' ...

Revolution came. One night – that unforgettable night – Red Petrograd roared in a thousand-strong choir of sirens and klaxons, and in response, hundreds of lorries, covered with the spikes of protruding rifles, rushed along the little suburban lanes. The Red Guard was flying towards Kornilov's vanguard. How wonderful, and how much it was needed at that terrible moment to draw together the roaring chaos in one will and to replace the alarums with the victorious hymn of the *Internationale*!

The Great October. Across the whole of Russia, the sirens ring out, and the guns thunder – but there is no organising will.

1919. Volga. Nizhny Novgorod. We are seeing off military trains to confront Kolchak in Kazan. The whole squadron roars a farewell until the last cloud of grey smoke disappears from view … at last, we make a first attempt at organisation … It is difficult, there are too many sirens, but still it was possible to discern the contours of the massed forces sounding the *Internationale*.

1922. Baku. The opening of navigation. 26 ships from the oil fleet are departing for Astrakhan. The whole fleet roars, the docks, the factories … It's a grandiose orchestra. Decided: for the fifth anniversary of October, the sounds will come together. And they did.

For the sixth anniversary, we want to see every city that has as much as a dozen steam boilers organise a worthy 'accompaniment' to the October festivities, and here we offer instructions on how to organise a 'symphony of sirens' in different local conditions.

After this successful experiment, it will be less difficult: only initiative and energy will be needed.

[Avraamov then provides detailed instructions for the building of a 'magistral' – a huge instrument consisting of tuned sirens, which will take over the task of sounding the melody, and potentially some basic harmony as well.]

The Baku Experiment

The following was printed in Issue 6 of *The Baku Worker*, and also in *Labour* and *Communist* (in the Türk language):

> *For the Celebration of the Fifth Anniversary of October: Instructions for the 'Symphony of Sirens'*

On the morning of the fifth anniversary, 7 November, by 7 a.m., all the ships of Gokasp, Voenflot and Uzbekokaspiy [fleets], including the small steamboats, are due at the railway pier. Every ship will receive a group of musicians on board, together with a set of instructions; the ship will then take up its allocated place in the area of the customs piers. In front of the signal tower will be the destroyer Worthy, with its 'magistral' steam organ, and the small boats.

By 9 a.m., the whole fleet must be in position.

By this time also, all free steam engines will arrive at the pier (the shunting engines, those from local lines, from armoured trains, and those fresh from repair).

The students of the Fourth Arzamas Courses, the students of the Baku Committee Higher Party School, the TsRK [Central Revolutionary Committee?] workshop students, the students of the Azerbaijani State Conservatoire and the professional musicians must be on the pier by no later than 8:30 a.m.

At 10 a.m., the infantry, artillery, machine guns, armoured cars and automotive transport will take their positions according to the orders issued to the garrison.

By no later than 10:30, the signalmen will take up their positions at the sirens – in the [workers'] districts, at the railway station, and in the docks.

The midday cannon is cancelled.

At the first salvo from the road, the alarum sirens sound from Zykh, White City, Bibi-Eibat and Bayalov [districts of Baku].

At the fifth cannon – the first and second districts of Black City.

At the tenth – the sirens of the Goods Office of the Azerbaijani Oil Company and the docks.

At the fifteenth – the City District. The hydroplanes take off. Bells.

At the eighteenth – the siren of the railway depot and the steam engines in the station (at the same time, the first company of the Fourth Army Commanders' School, led by the assembled brass band playing the *Warsovienne* [revolutionary song], leaves the square for the pier).

The alarum reaches its maximum intensity and is interrupted by the 25th cannon.

Pause.

A triple siren chord. Hurrahs from the pier.

The all-clear from the 'magistral'.

The *Internationale* (four times).

On the second half-verse the assembled brass band enters, together with the automobile choir, playing the *Marseillaise*. During the repeat, the whole choir on the square of the festivities will join in.

At the end of the fourth verse, the students and the infantry return to the square to be greeted there by 'hurrahs'.

After the end – the general solemn chord of all the sirens and klaxons for three minutes, accompanied by bell-ringing.

The all-clear from the 'magistral'.

Ceremonial march.

The artillery, fleet, automotive transport and machine guns receive signals from the conductor's tower. The red and white flag is for the battery, the yellow and blue for the sirens, the four-coloured flag for the machine guns. The red flag is for the solo ships and steam engines, which face the conductor's tower, and also for the automobile choir.

The *Internationale* is repeated twice more during the final procession, following the signals given by the battery.

The heating of the steam boilers is obligatory at every location where there are signal sirens.

All of the above is for direction and strict execution; the governing institutions responsible are: the military authorities, Azerbaijani Oil, Gokasp and the relevant educational institutions.

All performers must have these instructions with them at the time of the performance.

P. Chagin, Chairman of TsOK [TsRK?][24]
Ars. Avraamov, Organiser of the 'Siren Symphony'

---

[24] Pyotr Ivanovich Chagin (originally Bodovkin, 1898–1967), the Party leader of Azerbaijan at the time, was not simply a functionary, but a journalist and editor, and a close friend of Yesenin (Avraamov was himself part of Yesenin's circle of 'Imaginists'). There is little doubt that the success of Avraamov's project was dependent on Chagin's personal support.

1923
The Birth of ASM and RAPM

Accounts of Soviet musical life in the 1920s generally select and locate events within the scheme of a conflict between two factions: namely, ASM (the Association for Contemporary Music) and RAPM (the Russian Association of Proletarian Musicians). We intend to show that many significant events fall outside such a scheme; but the conflict itself certainly deserves attention, and above all in our discussion of 1923, the year that saw the emergence of both groups. The moments of their births were, indeed, connected by a remarkable and symptomatic story that sheds much light on the power struggles of the NEP period, even though its reconstruction is inevitably dependent on an array of fragmentary and partial sources.

To maintain itself and to wield influence, any such association needed a secure financial base, and preferably some degree of support from a well-established state institution. For music, the key institution was the Music Section of the State Publishing House (Muzsektor Gosizdata). From its inception in 1918 up to this point, the head of Muzsektor was Pavel Lamm, a distinguished music scholar and editor of German extraction, and also a close friend of Myaskovsky. From pre-Revolutionary times, the Lamm–Myaskovsky circle had been a pillar of Moscow's musical life, and had attracted the enthusiastic participation of young composers, not least for the opportunity to play through Lamm's own eight-hand arrangements of major new orchestral works. During Lamm's tenure at Muzsektor, Myaskovsky played a leading role in the jury that determined which musical works were passed for publication. The influence of Lamm and Myaskovsky was therefore undiminished after the Revolution, and persisted even through the hardships of the Civil War period. In 1921, Lamm had managed to establish himself in an apartment within the Moscow Conservatoire building, which soon became well known to composers as the venue for their auditions whenever they submitted works for publication. As ever, it was not possible to separate out the private and public aspects of the Lamm–Myaskovsky circle's activities, a situation that was likely to prompt resentment and suspicion from those whose music remained unpublished, as we shall see.

Although neither Lamm nor Myaskovsky were the most visible figures in ASM, they served as its *éminences grises*, and their immediate circle formed the core of ASM. The group's spokesmen were experienced journalists: Vladimir Derzhanovsky in Moscow, who had hoped to revive his pre-Revolutionary music journal since its closure in 1918; Viktor Belyayev in Petrograd, who was Lamm's deputy as Muzsektor's Petrograd representative; and Boris Asafyev, also a resident of Petrograd, a scholar, ideologue and journalist of the highest calibre. The occasion that prompted all these musicians to band together was Derzhanovsky's appointment to Mezhdunarodnaya kniga (abbreviated as Mezhkniga; Books International), an import-export trading company, formed at the beginning of 1923. In his new post, Derzhanovsky was able to cultivate contacts abroad, and to acquire scores of new European music. His ensured that Asafyev and

Myaskovsky were the first to peruse the new acquisitions; their musician friends were then invited to perform them while Asafyev and Belyayev announced them to Soviet audiences through their critical writings. Muzsektor then served as the publishing base for all the composers in the circle, now suitably informed and inspired by these latest Western scores. Their common passion for new music established a network of ventures in performance, publishing and foreign exchanges.

Even so, ASM was traversed by fault-lines:[1] Lamm's relationship with Belyayev, for example, was never better than business-like, and he had no fondness for Derzhanovsky either. When Derzhanovsky brought the critic Sabaneyev into ASM, the Myaskovsky–Lamm circle viewed the new addition as an alien presence. The composer Nikolai Roslavets was no less alien, and often problematic, but potentially too useful to be rejected, thanks to his Party connections and his post in the newly established censorship organisation, Glavrepertkom. Asafyev enjoyed warm relations with Derzhanovsky, but he was tied even more strongly to Myaskovsky and Lamm through gratitude for the lifeline they had thrown him, during the Civil War years, by commissioning a series of brochures: even though these could only be published in very small runs, due to the acute paper shortages, they ensured that Asafyev was always paid at a time when survival was in the balance.[2] By contrast, Asafyev regarded Belyayev as a rival, and avoided direct contact with him.

Although ASM was only formally established at the end of 1923, it was already effectively in existence from the beginning of 1923, and between April and August it even published three issues of the music journal *Towards New Shores of Music* (*K novïm beregam muzïkal'nogo iskusstva*).

Now to the bizarre and tragicomic story that linked ASM and RAPM.[3] In March 1923, Lamm was arrested and confined to Butyrki prison for two months, after which he was released without charge. The circumstances leading to his arrest were as follows. Alexander Krein, a composer who had previously been made welcome at the gatherings of the Lamm–Myaskovsky circle, and who had also been employed under Lamm at Muzsektor, entered into bitter conflict with Lamm over a contract that he considered unfair. The contract in question appears to have been standard, but at any rate, Krein made his complaints widely known, even voicing them in a letter to *Pravda*.[4] At this juncture, he stopped attending

[1] The information on personal relationships comes mostly from O. Lamm, 'Druz'ya Pavla Aleksandrovicha Lamma i uchastniki muzïkal'nïkh vecherov v yego dome (20-ye godï XX veka)', *Iz proshlogo sovetskoy muzïkal'noy kul'turï*, vol. 1 (Moscow: Sovetskiy kompozitor, 1975), 72–103, as well as from the correspondence between ASM members.

[2] See Asafyev's letters to Lamm of 10 June 1921, 12 July 1921, 21 July 1921 and 10 July 1922, all in RGALI, fond 2743 (Lamm), op. 1, ye. kh. 76, ll. 1–12.

[3] This story was brought to light by Svetlana Martïnova who published Olga Lamm's memoirs with commentary and other related documentary materials, see Martïnova, 'Pavel Lamm v tyur'makh i ssïlkakh: Po stranitsam vospominaniy O. P. Lamm', *Trudï Muzeya muzïkal'noy kul'turï: Al'manakh*, vol. 2 (Moscow: Gosudarstvennïy tsentral'nïy muzey muzïkal'noy kul'turï, 2003), 73–120.

[4] B.G., 'Muzizdatel'stvo i kompozitorï', *Pravda*, no. 11 (17 Jan. 1923), 5.

work at Muzsektor, saying that he was resigning. In the absence of a formal letter of resignation, Lamm sacked him. It is unclear whether Krein actually submitted a letter denouncing Lamm to the GPU but he certainly made some drafts of such a letter. It is within the bounds of possibility that he only restated his complaints informally in the presence of someone with GPU connections, but it was at this point that the decisive detail was introduced into the picture. Lamm, if the allegations were true, had made a foolish and reprehensible comment about the poverty of Jewish musical invention at one gathering of the circle. An element of casual anti-Semitism was as much a part of discourse within the Russian intelligentsia as it was among its English counterpart at the time, as continuing controversies over various lines in T. S. Eliot attest, but the situation in Russia was different, since the Bolsheviks, unlike the government of Ramsay MacDonald in England, had declared their intent to eradicate anti-Semitism from Russian society. And so a group of GPU officers demanded entry to Lamm's apartment the next day, arresting Lamm and sealing up his precious music library. The memoirs of his adopted daughter, Olga Lamm, mention that, at the moment of the arrest, a certain David Chernomordikov was present (a fellow member of Muzsektor whose interest in the case we shall soon examine).

Lamm was charged with anti-Semitic speech, the misappropriation of Gosizdat editions for his own library and various other professional misdemeanours. While his friends and associates struggled to contest the charges, Lamm became acquainted with life in a crowded GPU prison, sharing his cell with 25 inmates. He wryly presented his new circumstances as a welcome break from his job as a music publisher:

> Somehow I've managed to rest during this time (I am sleeping a lot and very well). Take, for example, the bimonthly anxiety of how wages are to be paid to the employees. Or the thought that one of the music printing presses might be removed, thus causing the art of music irreparable harm. A million of such meetings, and all without a break for five years. Now here all the cares and responsibilities are suddenly lifted – you can only lie down and gather strength, which is what I'm doing.[5]

While Lamm was 'resting', his domain was falling under new management. Chernomordikov managed to increase his influence within Muzsektor under the new director, Alexander Yurovsky (it appears that he was acting head of Muzsektor in the interim, although it has not been possible to establish this with certainty from the records). The impact of the takeover was summed up by P. I. Kovalyov, a composer who clearly felt underappreciated by the publisher (under either dispensation) and vented his frustrations in a satirical letter to one of his colleagues:

> But what has happened at Muzsektor? All this confusion was used by one Chernomordikov, a Communist. He became head of Muzsektor and decided, like his predecessor, that there wasn't money enough for everyone, although still enough to print out and pay fees exclusively to himself and his friends. But he had no real composers, so he gathered together a band of youngsters

[5] Martïnova, 99.

and dilettantes, set up 'The Union of Proletarian Composers', dispensed with the jury panel, closed down Lamm's journal *Towards New Shores*, and began publication of *Musical Virgin Soil*, or, as Sabaneyev has nicknamed it, *A Musical Stink* [Sabaneyev switched the consonants around, turning *Muzikal'naya nov'* into *Muzikal'naya von'*], and launched an attack against the whole association of composers [i.e. ASM] and against all composers in general, calling them counter-revolutionaries whose composing is 'out of tune with the era', etc. Now Russian composers no longer have the possibility of publication, and the 'Komsomol Ditties' of Ivanov-Buglay [*sic*; Kovalyov means Vasilyev-Buglay] and the like have begun to appear in print.[6]

Kovalyov's colourful report emphasises an important point that is often overlooked by historians: the struggle between ASM and RAPM was not simply an ideological disagreement, but was focused on the very concrete matter of who controlled the State Publishing House's music section. Kovalyov also suggested that Lamm's arrest was engineered specifically to allow power to change hands at this time,[7] but this must be treated with caution in the absence of any direct evidence (as opposed to Kovalyov's interpretation of the events, and the circumstantial evidence of Chernomordikov's appearance at the arrest).

Whether or not there was any such conspiracy, the founders of RAPM dated the birth of their organisation to March 1923, the month of Lamm's arrest.[8] There were three founding members, all employed at the Agitational Section of the State Publishers (Agitotdel). Chernomordikov, whom we have already mentioned, was 54 at the time, and a Bolshevik since 1905. His claim to minor celebrity dated back to 1906, when he became the first Russian publisher of the *Internationale*, supplying his own harmonisation in an edition that included a further nine revolutionary songs. This Bolshevik pioneer of music for revolutionary agitation undeniably possessed the credentials to found a proletarian music organisation. His co-founder, Lev Shulgin, was 33, his Party membership dating back to 1917. He had worked with Red Army choirs and also for Proletkult, leading in 1921 to his appointment as head of Agitotdel, which enabled him to publish many of his own agitational songs. The third co-founder, Alexei Sergeyev, remains an obscure figure; he certainly lacked the reputation of his two colleagues.

Predictably, Muzsektor's new management oversaw a steep increase in the printing of agitational music, while ensuring that the Myaskovsky–Lamm circle lost access to the printing presses. As Myaskovsky complained to the uncomprehending émigré Prokofiev, composers like him were now caught between the rock of NEP market forces and the hard place of the now hostile state publishing house:

> 'Publish and perform!' No, my dear boy, you don't quite understand the situation we're facing. These days, when people only find excitement in their profit margins, and when orchestras would sooner perform without a conductor, I can't even conceive of luxuries like having my music published

[6] P. I. Kovalyov's letter to B. I. Tyuneyev of 31 July 1924, published in ibid., 112–5.
[7] Ibid.
[8] See the document printed below.

or performed, even a tiny symphony like my Seventh. [...] When P. A. Lamm was head of Music Publishing, we were in the habit of ordering parts for every orchestral work that was purchased [...] Unfortunately, there were some misunderstandings, of which you're well aware, and now new music isn't published at all.[9]

The shift of power on the journalistic front only became apparent towards the end of the year, since unlike the office coup, this took time and preparation. Even after its momentous defeat, the Lamm–Myaskovsky side managed to produce three issues of *Towards New Shores* from April to August, as we have seen. By contrast, Chernomordikov's side failed to produce a rival publication until October, when the first issue of *Musical Virgin Soil* finally appeared. The two journals were utterly different. *Towards New Shores* made no attempt at political commentary, focusing on the promotion of modern music, whether Scriabin, Prokofiev or Schoenberg. Vague ruminations predominated, while the house style was devoid of militancy. The title of *Musical Virgin Soil* misleadingly invoked the first heavyweight Soviet literary journal, *Red Virgin Soil*, which in 1921 the Party had intended as a point of convergence for disparate groups of writers to unite on a pro-Soviet platform. *Musical Virgin Soil*, by contrast, was an overtly factional undertaking that set about two main tasks: first, the development of a supposedly Marxist critique of all existing music (this began in Issue 1 with a broadside against Tchaikovsky); the second task was the promotion of 'music for the masses'. The journal's agitational style, like the content, was considered barbaric within the Myaskovsky–Lamm group, but even outside the rival camp, RAPM had difficulty gaining credibility, in spite of its controlling position within Muzsektor.

But while RAPM could take advantage of low-level GPU activity, ASM was able to draw hope from the very top of the political system. While Lenin was fading from active political life as he succumbed to his final illness, many assumed that Trotsky was his most natural successor. In September, just weeks before Trotsky launched his protest against the bureaucratisation of the Party and its inaction in the face of a growing industrial crisis (this led to the creation of the Left Opposition), he issued a succinct essay in *Pravda* under the title 'Party Policy Towards Art', in which he took special pains to reassure the intelligentsia, in the manner of Lunacharsky, rather than the more acerbic and sceptical Lenin:

> In the sphere of the arts, the party should not assume a commanding role. It can and should offer the arts its protection and support, but its governance should only be indirect. The party can and should offer its trust conditionally to those artistic groups that strive to strengthen their links to the Revolution; in this way, the artistic embodiment of the Revolution can be assisted. But whatever the circumstances, the party cannot and will not act as if it were just one more literary circle, merely competing with the others and jostling for position.[10]

---

[9] Letter from Myaskovsky to Prokofiev of 12 Aug. 1923, S. S. Prokof'yev and N. Ya. Myaskovskiy, *Perepiska*, ed. by M. Kozlova et al. (Moscow: Sovetskiy kompozitor, 1977), 167–8.

[10] L. Trotskiy, 'Partiynaya politika v iskusstve', *Pravda*, no. 209 (16 Sept. 1923), 2–3.

Of particular comfort to the Myaskovsky–Lamm circle was Trotsky's insistence that the Party could not be expected to give its endorsement to the Kuznitsa literary group (The Smithy), 'simply because workers are writing for it', since RAPM, in its inaugural statement (see below), explicitly positioned itself as a sister organisation to Kuznitsa. Even as Trotsky's influence was eroded by other factions within the Party leadership, his declaration of a 'broad and flexible policy on art' remained the political consensus for several years. Artists ranging from the conservative to the avant-garde could appeal to this when groups like RAPM and Kuznitsa tried to claim a monopoly on artistic legitimacy.

Musical and theatrical life in 1923 was indeed notable for its great variety, but this was underwritten more by the vagaries of the NEP marketplace than by the Party's 'indirect leadership' or 'broad and flexible policy'. Theatre, as before, led the way in showing that entertainment and experimentation could sit happily together. The Soviet audience had an evident thirst for novelty, which inspired various experimental forms mixing parody, satire, political revue, elements of old-fashioned vaudeville, *bouffonnade*, eccentric farce and the 'grotesque'. Meyerhold's theatre still dominated the headlines in 1923, with its production of *Earth Rampant* (*Zemlya dïbom*), where the stage pretended to be a cinema screen, complete with intertitles and objects from the outside world such as bicycles, motorcycles and even a car. Provocatively, the production also included meetings and rallies with intentionally tedious dialogue, as a further gesture towards everyday life outside the theatre. The press gave a close second place to the extravagant productions of Alexander Tairov's Chamber Theatre. In general, constructivist set design was *de rigueur* in the Soviet theatre of 1923.

The ballet stage was enlivened by Kasyan Goleyzovsky's experimental interpretations, uniting classical pieces with what passed for 'jazz' in a single programme. Lev Lukin, another avant-garde choreographer, sought to bridge the gap between high and low by staging 'erotic dances' to the music of Scriabin, alongside 'eccentric dances' to music by the popular composer Matvei Blanter. MastFor (Masterskaya Foreggera, Nikolai Foregger's Workshop) presented its celebrated *Dance of the Machines*, the first of its three parts featuring more conventional dances such as a tango, a waltz, and a cake walk, while the second offered scenes of city life, with a policeman, women from a typing pool, a circus and a steam engine, and the third finally arrived at the full-blown 'mechanical dances and dances of the machines'. NEP-era Soviet audiences could thus see the familiar urban landscape recycled and served up in the form of a ballet (a startling contrast indeed to the character of Russian ballet under Tsarism and Stalinism alike).

One of the most prominent balletic experiments was an extravagant spectacle performed at the former Mariinsky in March: the *Tantssimfoniya* (Dance Symphony), choreographed by Fyodor Lopukhov to the music of Beethoven's Fourth Symphony, with a loose scenario designed to glorify 'the greatness of creation'. In the first movement, light emerges, followed by life and death; in the second, an 'actively pulsating' male element was contrasted with a passive female element; the Scherzo represented 'the joy of existence' where a pithecanthropus community joined with butterflies and birds in an ecstatic dance; the final *moto perpetuo* was to symbolise 'the unstoppable mechanical striving of all existence'.[11]

The concert format is, of course, centred upon the content of the music, rather than any potentially theatrical elements, but even so, the desire for novelty did prompt concert managers to programme some special attractions for its audiences. Samuil Feinberg undertook to play Bach's Well-Tempered Clavier from memory, and for other recitals, he shared the platform with Goldenweiser and Konstantin Igumnov, who took it in turn to perform Beethoven sonatas. The State Cappella broadened its programmes, giving a concert of Russian folk songs and Soviet 'red songs', one week, and the music of Josquin, Lasso, Gabrieli and Taneyev the next (the second concert was to be performed by candlelight and in costume, but this plan was dropped in the end).

But the main source of novelty was new music itself, although this was generally performed in very small halls and on a non-commercial basis. The Stradivari Quartet gave a series of contemporary music evenings in the Beethoven Hall of the Bolshoi, impressive enough for the Quartet to be given star billing in a series of 'musical exhibitions' organised by Derzhanovsky and held in the small exhibition hall of Mezhkniga. The first set of twelve concerts (by invitation only) was held during a German book fair in September and October 1923, when the quartet played Alfredo Casella's Five Pieces for quartet, Dohnányi's Second Piano Quintet, Kodály's Second Quartet, and Stravinsky's Three Pieces (Shebalin recalled that the audience was greatly amused by the last work). Other chamber music included Bartók (the Sonatina for piano, Romanian Folk Dances for piano and Hungarian Folk Songs),[12] Reger (the Trio for flute, violin and viola and a 'Suite in the Old Style', Szymanowski (the Violin Sonata op. 9, *Myths* for violin and piano, and several song cycles), and Schoenberg (the songs op. 3 and op. 6). The Russians were represented by whole evenings given over to Alexander Tcherepnin, Grechaninov, and Prokofiev, as well as individual works by Myaskovsky, Medtner, Feinberg and Mikhail Gnesin. The Prokofiev evening merits special mention: it established the Jewish Overture as a firm favourite for the public, and also featured the Russian premiere of the Third Piano Concerto (albeit played on two pianos by Igumnov and Mironov).

This unprecedented series of international new-music concerts induced the members of ASM to establish themselves formally as a society at the end of 1923. Due to the creation of ISCM (the International Society for Contemporary Music) the previous year, ASM was now able to provide that international federation with a division in the Soviet Union. The first ISCM festival had already been held in Salzburg and had duly received coverage in *New Shores*, although none of ASM's members had been able to attend. From the beginning, ASM saw Russian culture as a part of European culture and nourished new hopes that the it could bring about the end of the decade-long dearth of new Western music in Russia (beginning from the First World War), which would, in turn, shake Russian

---

[11] *Yezhenedel'nik petrogradskikh gosudarstvennïkh akademicheskikh teatrov*, no. 26 (4 March 1923), 18.

[12] The Bartók 'Romanian Folk Dances for piano' may refer to either Sz. 43 or 56 and the 'Hungarian Folk Songs' to Sz. 71 or possibly the Improvisations, Sz. 74.

composers out of their complacency or weariness. And, indeed, ASM, unlike its ephemeral predecessors, was to play a crucial role in the history of Soviet music, which outlasted the period of its active existence (which ended in 1929, due to external pressures, as we shall see later).

Yet at the very time when Russian composers were to come under the influence of European modernism, Myaskovsky expressed his anxieties over the longer-term prospects:

> I must tell you quite frankly that I now feel my talent has departed and that I've lost the ground under my feet. [...] It is difficult to compose in a way that could be considered useful here, since I'd need to simplify so much that I'd have to take music back to the Garden of Eden, but I'm too far gone from that state of cloudlessness and unclothedness [*beskostyumnost'* – Myaskovsky's coinage]. In a word, I sit between two stools, and of course, in a state of complete impotence.[13]

This, to a large extent, was Myaskovsky's depressive nature speaking, and for several years, he was able to compose as he wished while maintaining his prestige both nationally and internationally. It was only after sustained pressure in 1930 and 1931 that simplification actually became an imperative.

---

[13] Letter from Myaskovsky to Prokofiev of 23 Dec. 1923, *Perepiska*, 179–80.

'O Romanticheskoy "R.S.F.S.R": Beseda s kompozitorom Ya. Polferovïm' [On the Romantic *R.S.F.S.R*: a conversation with the composer Ya. Polferov] *Muzïka i teatr*, no. 32 (13 Aug. 1923), 5–6.

Yakov Polferov, best known as a conductor and musicologist, was also a sometime composer, having studied composition with Rimsky-Korsakov's disciples. Here, he discusses his new work for orchestra, chorus and brass band, whose principal theme is drawn from the initial letters of the Russian Socialist Federative Soviet Republic. Polferov addresses the likely disdain his new work will elicit from many of his fellow musicians, since his theme implies an enthusiasm for the new Russia that goes far beyond the sullen minimal cooperation that was the norm for much of the intelligentsia in the early 20s. Polferov defends both the theme and his relatively conservative musical style, but it is hard to tell where his ironic playfulness ends and his expression of earnest beliefs begin – which was no doubt the author's intention. Unfortunately, we have been able to find no evidence that Polferov's RSFSR Fantasy was ever performed.

On the Romantic *R.F.S.R*:
a conversation with the composer Ya. Polferov

This work, like everything else, has a history, and being a historian first and foremost, I will start with this. About eighteen months ago, in the middle of some banter with the violinist and composer Iosif Akhron,[14] I expressed surprise that the following theme had not been used anywhere: re–sol–fa–sol–re – such a characteristic Russian phrase. [The initial letters spell out R.S.F.S.R.] And then I noticed that my sensitive interlocutor had guessed that there was something more for me in this remark than mere fun. Some conversations on the matter with the composer and conductor S. V. Bershadsky[15] strengthened this line of thinking for me, and five days later I had produced the score of a *Fantasie Pathétique* for an expanded symphony orchestra, brass band and chorus: *R.S.F.S.R* (on the theme re–sol–fa–sol–re). This is its history in superficial terms. But there is another: fourteen changes of power occurred before my own eyes during my four years working in the South; there were 'all kinds of nations' dressed in military uniform, and there she was, my *R.S.F.S.R.*, very poorly dressed, without shoes, dressed in rags, sweating, hungry and tired, represented by a handful of very commonplace ragamuffins, who, time after time, managed to chase away armies of foreign and home-grown pirates in their thousands, with their tanks, cannons and towering

---

[14] Iosif Yulyevich Akhron (also known as Joseph Achron, 1886–1943) was a St Petersburg violinist and composer remembered for his works in the Jewish idiom. He visited Palestine in 1924 and settled afterwards in the USA.

[15] Sergey Vladimirovich Bershadsky (1881–1942), a St Petersburg conductor, composer, and arranger.

ships. Then it occurred to me that there were similar scenes featuring these hungry ragamuffins, not just in my field of vision, but everywhere, on the northern, eastern, and western fronts too, and I was overwhelmed by a feeling of true and genuine romanticism, a quality that can be found in abundance throughout the heroic times of our Revolution.

As a musician, I have been thinking for a long time that we are now once again experiencing a great pull towards romanticism, having left behind a recent fixation on a – pardon the expression – on a mathematical modernism that was very relevant and necessary at the time. [...] We, who have experienced so much, thirst for vivid melodies and intoxicating romantic moods.

Tell me, please, can an artist who witnessed scenes similar to the one above, and who experienced deeply and sincerely all the peripeteia of the revolutionary struggle, nevertheless remain indifferent before this grandiose theme and fail to be fired up by it? Whether I am an artist, I do not know, but the theme did not pass me by: I lived within this struggle, I experienced acutely all its peripeteia, and this is how 'she' was born, my romantic *R.S.F.S.R.* Yes, I know that the great and wise, whose word can mean a patent or a death sentence, will look at me with contempt and ask me in a whisper (for it is, of course, dangerous): 'Romantic'? What about the Che-Ka? What about the GPU? But I reply to them aloud (I've nothing to fear, since I've known eleven White powers): 'And what about the 42-inch guns? The poison gas? The violet rays? And is it better to sing an imperialist anthem in your work dispassionately and rationally, than to glorify proletarian revolution in a romantic delirium?' But we will never reach these questions, because I have already been judged irrevocably. But I still think, perhaps out of a composer's passion for his latest work, that as musicians, they will judge me less severely for the music itself, than they will judge me, before they even hear it, as members of the intelligentsia, because the content of the work is, in their opinion, 'anti-intelligentsia'. [...] But this causes me no upset. I do not want to be placed in the same camp as those who, though inspired by the anthem, can remain indifferent to the intensity hidden beneath [the song] 'We'll go bravely into battle!' – yes, it is primitive on the surface, but it contains endless depths. And if I cannot place myself on the same level with Romain Rolland because my gifts are meagre, my heart and romantic love put me in the same place from which his prophetic incantations emanate.

※ ※ ※ ※ ※

'Assotsiatsiya proletarskikh muzïkantov' [The Association of Proletarian Musicians], *Pravda*, no. 191 (26 Aug. 1923), 6.

This is the first announcement of RAPM's existence (at this stage lacking 'Russian' in its name). Unsurprisingly, RAPM takes as its models the existing writers' groups with a similar 'proletarian' outlook. However, the hope that RAPM musicians would enter into artistic collaboration with these writers never bore fruit.

The Association of Proletarian Musicians (Composers, Teachers, and Performers)

Last March, the Communist musicians of Moscow converged upon the idea that they should form an association.

This is the current situation: we have an isolated musical milieu of an apolitical character, which is estranged from the rhythms of life today and has been unable to will itself to produce revolutionary work; there are the increasingly dissolute concert programmes that have seeped into the workers' clubs; the youth display an ideological instability embracing NEP tastes and populating the cafes and restaurants; there is a complete absence of any methodology that would allow a class-orientated approach to music education (whether in general or specialist schools). All these problems have led to the founding of the association, which will seek, as its principal tasks, to overcome the lack of coordination among the musical forces of revolutionary creation and to arrive at a clear Marxist approach to music.

It will be necessary to submit children's musical literature to a radical revision, because of the lack of pre-school and school-age collections of games and songs, and because of the often debased nature of the musical material that is offered to our future citizens in the kindergartens and schools.

Our musical life is marked by several shortcomings: concert repertoires are in a chaotic state, unified neither on a class basis, nor even on the basis of their artistic content; there is a cavalier attitude to the repertoire of the workers' choirs, military bands and folk ensembles; the lack of popular literature on music history and theory, and on the issue of rhythm in labour processes; finally, the publication of musical works of the past and the present has not been shaped by class-based artistic criteria. These shortcomings should be remedied with the assistance of Communist musicians and others who agree with the Association's main premises.

The Association's founding group has elected a temporary executive bureau consisting of Comrades Chernomordikov, Shulgin and Sergeyev.

This Bureau, with close connections to the Music Section of the State Publishers, is also building connections with Party organs and Politprosvet [political education] institutions in Moscow, and is organising a performing division within the Association to propagandise among the proletariat on behalf of revolutionary musical works and works that are full of dynamism; it is also drawing the Republic's music-theoretical forces within the Association's sphere of influence.

The Executive Bureau of the Association, taking into account the fact that we share our primary goals and proletarian ambitions with the Union of Proletarian Writers and with associations such as 'Young Guard' and 'The Smithy', is considering future collaboration with these groups.[16] As it sets out on its practical work, the Association appeals to all Communist musicians and others drawn to revolutionary art, to unite and to arrive at a clear recognition of their class tasks.

Executive Bureau of Proletarian Musicians
[Contact details for D. A. Chernomordikov,
L. V. Shulgin and A. A. Sergeev follow.]

---

[16] The Union of Proletarian Writers (Soyuz proletarskikh pisateley), 'Young Guard' ('Molodaya gvardiya') and 'The Smithy' ('Kuznitsa') were groups of proletarian writers in existence before the creation of more powerful RAPP (Russian Association of Proletarian Writers).

A. Sergeyev, 'Muzïkal'nïy tupik' [A Musical Cul-de-Sac], *Muzïkal'naya nov'*, no. 1 (20 Oct. 1923), 6–8.

In this, one of RAPM's earliest manifestos, Sergeyev paints a depressing picture of contemporary musical life in terms that can be recognised from Asafyev or Sabaneyev. His prognosis, of course, is quite different, and he advocates a mixture of Proletkult projects (such as the study of labour rhythms and labour songs) with more distinctive RAPM ideas (such as a radical reform of Conservatoire education). Note, however, the respect still paid to Stravinsky and Prokofiev – their denigration was not yet associated with the cause of 'proletarian music'.

A. Sergeyev
A Musical Cul-de-Sac

The present state of music clearly demonstrates that we are in a cul-de-sac, and everyone who retains an organic need for life-affirming art in every area of musical activity must find a way out.

Our musical art, having reached its zenith in Scriabin's emotional and individualist dream, and receiving further light from Stravinsky's creative will and Prokofiev's strength and health, has encountered the greatest of world-historical events – the October Revolution.

Shut up within the confines of individualist dreams of beauty as the salvation of the world, of art as revelation, striving to create an art-religion through the will of a single individual, connected in its past with the ideology of the musical consumer, the bourgeois listener, the art of music suddenly encountered the proletariat entering the world stage. And ... it shut itself up in the laboratory searching after new intonations, continually and worshipfully looking over the shoulder to the West, with its sunset culture, with its experiments in 'quartertones', 'polytonality' and 'atonality', which are so utterly alien to the healthy folk roots from which Russian music grew – the *Ruslan* overture, the Polovtsian Dances, *The Rite of Spring*, *The Scythian Suite*. On the one hand, we have the imminent sixth anniversary of the October Revolution, events brewing in the West, colossal organisational and constructive activity in the USSR, a huge ideological shift and change of position in almost every sphere of the sciences and arts, the founding of the Association of Proletarian Musicians with a clear realisation of music's class nature and with attempts, although still timid, to construct the laws of revolutionary musical creation; on the other hand, there is the almost completely apolitical attitude of the musical milieu, a hermetic confinement to professional exclusivity, an extremely individualistic 'epigonism' in composition, an intolerance towards anything new or unusual, an intolerance towards any attempt to approach contemporary life or cast doubt upon the unshakeability of the past, all of which is already noticeable within the academic milieu. This doubt, we must believe, will lead musical thought towards the imperative of changing its ideological premises, to an involvement of musical creativity in the immediate perception of life, to a communication with modernity, with its rhythms that are both cheerful and class-based.

In concert and opera life, almost everything is ossified.

There are the typical cycles of symphony concerts, which have become *de rigueur* for every season, with a neat play-through of the Beethoven symphonies and a set of Scriabin pieces given by invited foreign conductors, with their admiration for a first-class orchestra that complacently exhausts its old stock of professional mastery, failing to replenish it through constant work on the perfection of technical skills; and there is the motley, indeterminately NEP man constitution of the audience in these concerts, with a return to the old manner of obligatory concert attendance – such things show that there must be a change in orchestral players' routine and indifferent attitude (in terms of ideology) to concert work.

As for concerts in proletarian and Red-Army clubs, we need not press the point.

Everyone knows the attitude of performers to such concerts. These *khalturas*[17] are a means of earning money or a cruel necessity, a duty for professional and Party organisations. The programmes of such *khalturas* present an unbelievable mix of names, from celebrities to female singers of the light genre. The clubs, these centres of proletarian education, due to the weak cultural and political consciousness of the performers and sometimes even the club leaders themselves, have become the seat of anti-musical bacchanalias shameful to the artists' dignity. This debases the educational role of art in the eyes of the proletariat and calls for urgent measures from the institutions of political education to put an end to this variety of 'musical enlightenment', such as, for example, the decision of some clubs to allow only those performers who have a definite class appeal and who recognise of their artistic obligations to the proletariat. In opera, we will probably have to be satisfied for a long time yet with the accidental nature of those rare successful productions that have given some degree of pleasure through good set design and orchestral accompaniment; here we are still dealing with the same comical choruses, helpless *mise-en-scènes*, unshakeable tempi and everything else that has been and for a long time will be a feature of the Academy theatres.

Regarding the compositional and concert/operatic aspects of our musical life, it was to be expected that music criticism, which should serve as a catalyst for shaping the ideological side of our musical present, would clearly point out how today's musical world has ended up in this cul-de-sac of gloom and philistinism.

In reality, however, besides the occasional note on revolutionary festivities, the old-fashioned reviews of concerts and the limp presentations of impractical ideological recipes that have nothing to do with Marxism, we have encountered little in newspapers or journals.

The issues of the musical milieu's ideology, of the Marxist approach to music, of everyday life, the musical and concert life of the clubs, the reports of the worker-correspondents on concerts, the musical tastes and needs of the proletariat, and

---

[17] *Khaltura*, literally hackwork, was also applied at the time to a type of variety concert, which allowed performers to earn some cash on the side. Those who were particularly adept could manage several clubs a night.

thousands more issues of musical life have never been tackled in a broad and practical way by our music critics, given their haphazard approach and their extremely weak ideological understanding.

In the first years of the Revolution, the development of specialist music education and adult education, has been broad but not yet deep; in this, its sixth year, now that the endless and random growth of new educational institutions has been pruned back, it should set out on the path of deep and genuine work according to the tasks issued by existing musical institutions within Glabprofobr, Glavsotsvos, Glavpolitprosvet and Politprosvet of PUR.

Among the other urgent issues in need of a solution is the immense task at the Conservatoire of putting the new curricula into practice, the work on method being undertaken by the subject committees, the creation of new textbooks, the formulation of a class approach to the teaching of music history, which in Conservatoire courses should become the link between political literacy broadly understood and the art of music as such, and finally, the structure of Rabfak, which is defended so stoically by the best sections of the Conservatoire youth and professoriate. Our times demand that the wall of professional exclusivity should be broken down, and we must move away from mythical professional 'secrets' (in pedagogical methods) and into the broad arena of scientifically-based work, in close collaboration with the young, who have such a sincere desire to engage in work in the name of their own art, and who have a degree of enthusiasm that is sometimes alien to the professors.

Taking into account the significance of music in labour education and the near total incompetence displayed by the directors of the kindergartens, orphanages and schools, musicians need to engage in pedagogical issues that they have often ignored in the past.

Creating marching songs and new marches for the Red Army, working out the methodology for music education, constructing concert repertoires for the proletariat that are attached to proletarian anniversaries, studying the rhythm of labour songs and of labour processes – these are the most urgent tasks. They may be very far from the 'pure art' that some still believe in, but we hope that if we approach these 'routine' issues sincerely and work on them honestly, we will in the end find those class-based creative impulses that are so difficult to define theoretically and which so discordantly cut into the essential idealism of the majority [of professional musicians].

The ideological cul-de-sac in which we find ourselves on the sixth year of the Revolution, and which is recognised by the best in the musical milieu, obliges all musicians to create a 'united front' that will draw together all the potential creative forces of the USSR, which will take musical thought out of this hopeless cul-de-sac and bring it to shores of communication that are truly new, and to a shining collaboration with the proletariat at the moment of its greatest struggle for the new life being built on Communist foundations.

1924
ASM in the Ascendant

Lenin's death in January 1924, among other things, led to a new element of Soviet culture that would remain in place until the collapse of the state in 1991. Although Lenin had become increasingly hostile towards Stalin in his final year, the latter became the chief promoter of a cult of personality that endlessly churned out Lenin imagery and slogans, like a magic porridge pot. While appeals to the future continued as before, Soviet citizens were also now expected to look back to Lenin, and measure everything by his example, or rather by that of the sentimental mythology that soon began to accrue. Musicians were quick to offer their tributes. Lenin's supposedly favourite revolutionary song 'Zamuchen tyazhyoloy nevoley' (Exhausted by Harsh Imprisonment) was arranged by Lev Shulgin (one of RAPM's founders) three days after Lenin's death, submitted to the engravers on the same day, then proofread and printed that night; the State Cappella began rehearsing it the next morning so that it would be ready for performance at the funeral.[1] A spate of Lenin pieces followed, largely funereal in character, including Kastalsky's 'At the Coffin', for reciter and piano, but some were cheerful, like Grigory Lobachev's 'The Fighting Lenin Song' (*Boyevaya Leninskaya*) and 'Ilyich Lives' (*Zhiv Il'yich*). Kastalsky wrote his 'Song about Lenin' in the epic folk-song style. Another nascent tradition led in a different direction: on their death, Lenin and other leading Communists after him were commemorated through highbrow concerts with appropriate symphonic repertoire, rather than freshly composed occasional pieces. Lenin's memorial concert at the Bolshoi featured Tchaikovsky's Sixth Symphony, Wagner's Funeral March from *Götterdämmerung*, Strauss's *Tod und Verklärung*, and a Bach aria delivered by ten cellos in unison.

In January, RAPM presented its first concert in the notably unproletarian setting of the sumptuous Blue Room of the former Nobility Assembly (by then, the Dom Soyuzov – Trade Union House). The event consisted of choral works, and fell into three sections: the peasant, the proletarian and the anti-religious. An unsympathetic critic complained about the composers' range of musical styles: first, there was 'a folk-song style – not that of epic, labour songs or round dances, but the gloomy *protyazhnïye* [drawn-out] songs'; second, 'a common European, march-like style, rooted mainly in the *Marseillaise*', third, parodies of the Russian church style; fourth, urban *chastushki* (ditties); fifth, 'a sentimental pseudo-Russian romance style'. 'Were the words taken out', the reviewer remarked, 'we would be bound to attribute this music to the "rightist' camp of composers"'.[2] Much greater outrage was caused by the exhibition of RAPM's comrades-in-arms, AKhRR (the Association of Revolutionary Russia's Artists). The critic Vyacheslav Karatygin (in an essay on Stasov), made the following prescient comment:

---

[1] S.B. [Sergey Bugoslavskiy], 'Muzïkal'no-agitatsionnaya literatura', *Sovetskoye iskusstvo*, no. 2 (1925), 77–9.

[2] Sergei Bugoslavskiy, 'Proletarskiye muzykantï', *Zrelishcha*, no. 69 (Jan. 1924), 7.

Curiously, the latest 'neorealism' of the painters, stepping out onto the stage after all manner of futurisms and suprematisms, will probably turn out to share some kindred features with the realist art of Stasov's period. Who knows, perhaps in the future a revival of 'neostasovian' views on art will be possible? We shall wait and see.[3]

In spite of its efforts, RAPM was left without any institutional base by the end of the year. Returning to the mordant observations of the composer P. I. Kovalyov (whom we encountered in 1923) we can see how this came about:

> [RAPM's tenure at Muzsektor] continued for eight months, and no powers could do anything about it, since Chernomordikov's group hid behind political slogans, with political slander as its method. They were even beyond the reach of Lunacharsky. Yurovsky, the Head of Muzsektor, a charming man himself, was also quite powerless. And so it went on until spring this year [1924]. All this time, however, Roslavets remained vigilant and collected information on every stunt [*plutni*] pulled by Chernomordikov and Co., and since he was a Communist himself, he was eventually able to take Chernomordikov's place. That was in the spring. This development, of course, changed matters for the better, as composers outside the party network now could have their works published, and now everyone has access to Muzsektor. Roslavets behaved as if he had sacrificed himself for the common good, since in his current position, he couldn't publish his own music after the scandalous reigns of Lourié, Lamm and Chernomordikov. We all supported him in his good intentions and told him that he should refrain from publishing his work for at least half a year. He managed to restrain himself for precisely two weeks, and now at all the printing presses, his music is piled up high.[4]

The fact that Roslavets could engage in GPU-style manoeuvring just as successfully as Chernomordikov should not surprise us: his wife Natalya (born Langovaya) had been a prominent member of the GPU since 1918 (a fact that has largely been overlooked), and her brother, Alexander Langovoy, even served as a Soviet spy.[5] Roslavets was a composer of complex and refined post-Scriabin music, making

---

[3] V. Karatïgin, 'Pamyati V. V. Stasova', *Zhizn' iskusstva*, no. 5 (29 Jan. 1924), 10–11.

[4] P. I. Kovalyov's letter to B. I. Tyuneyev of 31 July 1924, published in Svetlana Martïnova, 'Pavel Lamm v tyur'makh i ssïlkakh: Po stranitsam vospominaniy O. P. Lamm', *Trudï Muzeya muzïkal'noy kul'turï: Al'manakh*, vol. 2 (Moscow: Gosudarstvenniy tsentral'niy muzey muzïkal'noy kul'turï, 2003), 112–15.

[5] The status of Natalya Roslavets came to the attention of scholars through the publication of a group portrait photo of senior Chekists, in which she was sitting beside Felix Dzerzhinsky. This photo first appeared in *Vechernyaya Moskva* (19 Dec. 2005): see Felix Berezin, 'Yehscho odno foto iz proshlogo', http://www.vmdaily.ru/article/19135.html, accessed 24 Apr. 2012. Although the existence of this photo has been acknowledged by Marina Lobanova in the Russian edition of her monograph on Roslavets, it has had no significant effect on her portrayal of Roslavets as a pure victim of the Soviet regime. See Marina Lobanova, *Nikolay Roslavets i kul'tura yego vremeni* (St Petersburg: Petroglif, 2011), 83.

him an unlikely recruit to Glavrepertkom. His position as a censor with this body (rooting out songs with monarchist texts and the like) only becomes plausible when we factor in his wife's substantial political influence (she left him at some point after 1927, which was when his troubles began).[6]

Roslavets was appointed to head the Political Department at Muzsektor, and from this advantageous position, he was able to publish a new ASM journal, *Musical Culture* (*Muzïkal'naya kul'tura*). ASM's existing publication, *Contemporary Music* (*Sovremennaya muzïka*), under the editorship of Belyayev and Derzhanovsky, focused mainly on ASM's concert activities. Roslavets (and his wife) thought that this was insufficient, since RAPM had already launched attacks on ASM musicians in the pages of its own journal, *Musical Virgin Soil*. *Musical Culture* accordingly extended ASM's activities into the ideological battleground, defending the organisation's principles and making counter-attacks as it saw fit.

The launch of the new journal was vexed, to say the least. We have a wry account of the problems from Derzhanovsky, in a letter to Myaskovsky that details the organisational complexities and ideological wrangling, and the encounters with the authorities ranging from enthusiastic support to sullen obstruction:

> This morning I went to Muzsektor, buttonholed Rozvalets [a humorous misspelling of Roslavets] and asked him to get a move on with the journal [*Musical Culture*]. It turned out that although he had read all of it himself, he still needed to show the issue to Meshcheryakov [the head of Gosizdat]. I said: OK, but make it snappy. Off he went, holding a copy bearing the solemn inscription: 'Passed for printing. Roslavets'. About an hour later, he barged into my shop on Kuznetsky [Derzhanovsky's Mezhkniga office], and told me this:
>
>   'Well then, I went over to Meshcheryakov, and he says to me:
> – This is all very well, but it seems you haven't been getting along with the communists.
> – Who do you mean? We haven't got any. Sergeyev's just a young candidate, and a lousy one, if you ask me. There's nobody else.
> – What about Shulgin?
> – But he's been purged …
> – ??!
> – There aren't any more; you probably remember there used to be a Chernomordikov, but he's never around now (he only collects his wages), and he's been purged from the party for *shkurnichestvo* [exploiting Party membership for personal advantage].'
>
>   Well, to be brief, my Rozvalets was now getting along famously with Meshcheryakov, who began reading through our little journal 'with pleasure'. He finished 'Our Goals' and said: 'You're right. What the hell are they talking about?' – all that proletarian culture!' [Then he] read Natasha's

---

[6] Yu. N. Kholopov, 'Nikolay Roslavets: Volnuyushchaya stranitsa russkoy muzïki', intr. to N. Roslavets, *Sochineniya dlya fortepiano*, ed. by N. Kopchevskiy (Moscow: Muzïka, 1989), 5–8 (8).

diatribes [the article by Roslavets's wife],[7] and said: 'Good, they're getting what they deserve, those *shkurniki*.' Then he got up, saying: 'Well and good, but we'd best get it passed by Litotdel [Gosizdat's Literature Section] – let's go.' And he led Rozvalets, Marx's loyal servant, to somebody by the name of Usachin. 'Here they are', he said, 'publishing a nice little journal and giving those *shkurniki* a good dressing-down – have a read yourself'. Usachin begged for mercy (or perhaps for Marxy): 'I know nothing about any of this, and my expert advisor [...] isn't here'. But in the end, he decided to go ahead with it, and told Rozvalets to send someone over at around 2 o'clock to pick up the issue.

Nicolas [Roslavets] persuaded me to go, in spite of all my excuses ('I can hardly move, my head's in a fog,' etc.), since he didn't want the issue to fall into enemy hands. I arrived on time, found Cmrd. Usachin and said: 'I need the journal back quickly, so that I can get it to the printers'. But no, he wanted to argue things out. Invectives, diatribes. He talked and talked, and it became clear he'd understood nothing, probably because he was too dim and had a suspicious mind. 'This', he said, 'is all very dubious, and there's definitely a snag somewhere'. What a swine! Then he said: 'let's go and see Cmrd. Ruzer' (the editor-in-chief's assistant).[8] So off we go. Ruzer seemed to be in a great hurry (like all the big cheeses), but at least he offered us a seat, and Usachin launched into his 'report'. 'In the journal', he said, 'we can see a Trotskyite view of art, and apart from that, they're "against the purges", against the communist command system, and they even compare Bolshevik practices with Nicholas I's floggings, just as the White-Guard press has often done ...' I kept making rejoinders and corrections, I emphasised that we are for the purges and not against them, and the 'hurried' Ruzer had to agree in the end that the reference to the beatings was not actually a reference to the Bolsheviks. Nevertheless, he confirmed that it was all a bit dangerous, because Narkompros is mentioned [in the journal], and Narkompros is 'our institution', and that we need to clarify the journal's point of view. I responded that among the head people [on the editorial board] we had Yavorsky, the Chairman of the GUS music section [the State Scholarly Council], and that there are different trends within Narkompros, and that we're not debutantes obliged to defend our views with curtseys – to this he offered to pass the journal to Schmidt for a check, because Schmidt had himself gone through the purge [but was exonerated], and so he knew all about it.[9] All that was left to me was to say my farewells and leave. I ran to Muzsektor, where neither Rozvalets nor Yurovsky were to be found, but I got Roslavets on the phone. He said, 'I don't believe it', that this was all a

---

[7] Natalya Roslavets's article in the first issue of *Musical Culture* was entitled 'Marginalia: Diatribes'. A fragment from this article is reproduced below.

[8] Leonid Ruzer was an old Bolshevik, who had known Lenin personally. He worked in Gosizdat from the moment of its creation in 1919 (see Glossary).

[9] Otto Yulyevich Schmidt (1891–1956), a scientist and Arctic explorer, is mentioned here in his capacity as director of the State Publishers 1921–4 and as a Narkompros official.

lot of rubbish, and 'it would sort itself out'. I demanded that after agreeing things with Yurovsky, he should go to Schmidt. He said: 'it's already too late to do that today. And Yurovsky isn't here, so he can't agree it.' Agniya[10] [the secretary] (who's a total arse) began wailing: 'I knew it, I knew it – I told you that you can't touch "them", and now they'll close the journal down'. I fled. Half an hour later, I found Yurovsky in Agniya's room and reported on how things had unfolded. He listened to me 'diplomatically', making the general comment that 'he had expected all this' but he said that I really shouldn't have gone to the Political Department [Politotdel], where my 'non-Party physiognomy' would have been met with instant distrust. Well, to some extent I agree, but if they all want to sit on their hands, then what can I do about it?![11]

In the end, Derzhanovsky successfully steered the issue through this obstacle course, and two weeks later, Belyayev was able to report:

> *Musical Culture* is coming out at last [... T]he political editors of Gosizdat judged that the content of the first issue was entirely in accord with the current moment, and that the tendency of the journal was Trotskyite.[12]

Perhaps the most substantial journalistic contribution to the polemics of 1924 was made by Asafyev (Igor Glebov) in a set of three essays that covered the most sensitive and topical issues: 'The Crisis of Music', 'The Crisis of Individual Creativity' and 'Composers! Keep up!'[13] Only the first was published in *Music Culture*, since Roslavets found the others too controversial, leaving Derzhanovsky to publish them in *Contemporary Music*. In the three essays, Asafyev questioned composers' state of denial towards the changes taking place all around them and called on them to participate in contemporary life. Unexpectedly, the articles caused great consternation among his closest friends, including Myaskovsky, who now called him an opportunist and likened his writings to those of *Musical Virgin Soil* (the opposing camp). Writing to Lamm, who had also disapproved, Asafyev defended his beliefs unflinchingly, and with some bitterness, insisting on his sincerity:

> Unfortunately, I belong to those writers and composers for whom creative work must reflect life – the whole of it – and this is why I can't move forward until I've solved (and overcome) this or that life problem.[14]

At a meeting of ASM in December 1924, Lamm, Feinberg and Aleksandrov all spoke against the inclusion of political articles in *Contemporary Music*. Myaskovsky tried in vain to find a middle way, suggesting that an exception

---

[10] Agniya Alyavdina was the secretary at Muzsektor Gosizdata.

[11] Letter from Derzhanovsky to Myaskovsky of 17 July 1924, RGALI, fond 2040 (Myaskovsky), op. 1, ye. kh. 114., ll. 9–11.

[12] Letter from Belyayev to Lamm of 31 July 1924, RGALI, fond 2743 (Lamm), op. 1, ye. kh. 84, l. 6.

[13] Igor Glebov, 'Kompozitorï, pospeshite!', *Sovremennaya muzïka*, no. 6 (1924), 145–8.

[14] Letter from Asafyev to Lamm of 10 Dec. 1924, RGALI, fond 2743 (Lamm), op. 1, ye. kh. 76, l. 20v.

could be made for an exceptional writer, and that Asafyev's essays could be published in an appendix. Asafyev, however, only took offence at the idea.[15] While Myaskovsky, Lamm and others felt that Asafyev had taken a step too far towards conformity with the new times, Derzhanovsky, on the contrary, felt he had not gone far enough. In response to Asafyev's tryptich of articles, he concocted a programme of action that would integrate his composer friends with the new world order, making them beneficiaries rather than victims. Pragmatic and even cynical, Derzhanovsky's plan is remarkably close to reality a decade later under Socialist Realism:

> So, all three articles [...] are good. But you're right, you haven't managed to nail 'the main issue', perhaps because it just can't be done at moment – in an article, anyway. If you really want to know (and perhaps you already do), the main issue is *what approach we should take*, and *what we begin with*, and how we can combine the uncombinable; in other words, if musical works are to be attractive both to the street and the salon, then what form should they take, and what emotional colouring should they have? Do you realise (you probably do) that no real composer would settle for anything less? For example, Myaskovsky would love to write a revolutionary cantata, a symphony, an opera or something else in some as-yet-unknown form, except it has to be monumental, and justified in terms of *his* creative path, so that it would be a step forward for him too, albeit a step sideways … Aleksandrov and Shenshin would also agree to that, Feinberg with more difficulty, etc. But each of them has to be given a hint of the form, a text has to be found for them, and a plot, etc. etc. This is a very difficult thing to manage, but we have to start somewhere – and who will do this if not you! As for me, I am ready to aid and abet you. We need to deliver our propaganda both theoretically (through literature) and practically (acting as nanny to composers who are suitable for the purpose). These two aspects must be linked to each other, but in the first [there should] only [be] general lines and hints, while in the second things should be presented in a concrete form. Finally, another very important matter: we need to achieve power and influence in official circles and to push the same line there. And for this, we need to organise ourselves into a 'party', otherwise we'll never attain power. Bearing in mind the nepotism of the Soviet system, it will be very hard to do this, and it's all the more important that we should miss no opportunities. Why don't you exert some pressure on Lunacharsky, since he shows a degree of flexibility? And why don't you hint that only by having power will you be able (and then definitely) to get things moving?[16]

Thinking of how, among other things, he might transform his foot-dragging friend Myaskovsky into a 'revolutionary composer', Derzhanovsky suggests that, through Lunacharsky, it might be possible to obtain a commission for Myaskovsky

---

[15] A report on this meeting is found in Derzhanovsky's letter to Asafyev of 30 Dec. 1924, RGALI, fond 2658 (Asafyev), op. 2, ye. kh. 45, ll. 27–30.

[16] Letter from Derzhanovsky to Asafyev of 5 Dec. 1924, RGALI, fond 2658 (Asafyev), op. 2, ye. kh. 45, l. 5.

to create an opera based on Dostoyevsky's *Idiot*, a project that Myaskovsky himself had considered. This commission could become the basis of a sinecure for Myaskovsky. Derzhanovsky continued:

> [A] 'theatre composer' – and why not? Then, after the success of *The Idiot*, commission a monumental opera from him, perhaps with a revolutionary plot, but something of real value – and then you will have a revolutionary opera. From these large-scale forms, he will move on to the smaller scale, but not the other way round, because all the time there will be a process of reconstruction [*perestroika*] underway, fitting in with other plans, and moving on to other modes [of thinking/ composition], for which *common tones* are needed, as they are for elementary harmonic progressions. Then after Myaskovsky, others will follow.[17]

Although Myaskovsky never actually wrote an opera, Derzhanovsky's prescience is still astonishing, charting the process of reform that composers would have to undergo to fit in with Soviet ways (albeit after NEP had been pushed aside for the First Five-Year Plan). As we shall see, it was a symphony rather than an opera that enabled Myaskovsky to become an establishment Soviet composer. But back in 1924, Myaskovsky would most likely have been outraged if he had been able to read Derzhanovsky's plan.

As Derzhanovsky dreamed on, ASM came to the verge of a split. Not only the Myaskovsky–Lamm circle, but even Roslavets felt that Asafyev had compromised ASM's position and he vowed to never again publish his 'demagogical' essays in *Musical Culture*. But it was too late, and *Musical Culture* itself came to an abrupt end. Derzhanovsky again recorded the events:

> Yurovsky informed Roslavets officially that the journal would be closed down because it's a loss-maker and a source of trouble [...] Roslavets himself was also given to understand that he personally had no future in Muzsektor. They argued, and Roslavets left as if to resign. But [...] he changed his mind on the way [...] thinking that his resignation would mean the victory of Sergeyevshchina, Chernomordovshchina, etc. So instead of resigning, he went to brew up some trouble at the Rabis CC [the Art Workers' Union], where he spoke to Slavinsky [the Chair].[18] As a result, if he's right, we can soon expect an audit of Muzsektor etc. etc. etc, and so there'll be a war against Yurovsky, with Roslavets as its instigator, and all the forces of Rabis as the army.[19]

Derzhanovsky decided it was time to act. He sent Asafyev's controversial articles to Lunacharsky, asking for support. Lunacharsky replied with a brief note stating that he very much welcomed Asafyev and Derzhanovsky's opinions

---

[17] Ibid, l. 6.

[18] Yu. M. Slavinsky was the first Chair of the Central Committee of Rabis, the Arts Workers' Trade Union.

[19] Letter from Derzhanovsky to Asafyev of 16–17 Dec. 1924, RGALI, fond 2658 (Asafyev), op. 1, ye. kh. 542, l. 8.

(although his misspelling of the latter's name suggests the issue was not uppermost in his mind).[20] This was an astute political move on Derzhanovsky's part: a statement of support emanating from the top of Narkompros could be cited in future skirmishes.

ASM went on to secure an institutional affiliation with GAKhN (the State Academy for Scholarship in the Arts), while retaining its ties with Mezhkniga. Its concerts proceeded apace, covering a varied repertoire of Western and Russian music. The first programme was devoted to Hindemith, and consisted of his First Quartet and four of his solo sonatas for string instruments, all performed by what was probably the finest quartet in Russia at the time (with Tsiganov, the Shirinsky brothers and Borisovsky). Then followed a programme of contemporary Russian music, which pieces by Roslavets, Melkikh, Vasilenko, and Dzegelyonok. The next programme was devoted to *Les Six*, and the last two returned to contemporary Russian music, with pieces by Katuar and Polovinkin. The second season opened with a Russian programme of works by Polovinkin and Grigory Krein, the second was devoted to Szymanowski, the third to Sabaneyev, the fourth featured Hindemith (one of the quartets, and *1922*) and Schoenberg (the Second Quartet and *Das Buch der hängenden Gärten*), while the final programme featured Myaskovsky (the Third Piano Sonata), Aleksandrov (various songs), and Feinberg (the Seventh Piano Sonata). Belyayev still found grounds for complaint, writing to Myaskovsky that ASM set its sights too low by ending one season with Polovinkin and then starting the next season with the same composer; in general, he thought ASM should resist local pressures and devote most of its concert time to the best music from the West.[21]

ASM made rapid progress in cultivating Western contacts. In October, Belyayev set out on an official trip to Europe with a view to strengthen musical connections with Europe (offending Asafyev, who thought he should have been sent instead). Belyayev visited Berlin and Vienna, spending time in cafés, where he met up with Paul Pisk, Paul Stefan, and Paul Bekker. He also got to know Schoenberg, and laid the groundwork for future collaboration with Universal Edition.[22] Perhaps most significantly, he managed to organise two concerts of new Russian music in Vienna at the beginning of November.[23] The Viennese public was able to hear chamber works by Grigory Krein, Yevgeny Pavlov, Polovinkin, Sabaneyev, Feinberg, Alexander Gedike, Alexander Shenshin, Alexander Borkhman, Gnesin and Grechaninov – these were mostly the composers of the Myaskovsky–Lamm circle. Feinberg's sonata, according to Pisk, won the warmest reception. In spite of these successes, Belyayev reported that Vienna was not a major centre for new

---

[20] Letter from Lunacharsky to Derzhanovsky of 29 Dec. 1924, copied in Derzhanovsky's letter to Asafyev of 30 Dec. 1924, RGALI, fond 2658 (Asafyev), op. 2, ye. kh. 45, ll. 30–1.

[21] Letter from Belyayev to Myaskovsky of 3 Nov. 1924, RGALI, fond 2040 (Myaskovsky), op. 1, ye. kh. 103, l. 41.

[22] Postcard from Belyayev to Lamm of 10 Oct. 1924, RGALI, fond 2743 (Lamm), op. 1, ye. kh. 84, l. 19.

[23] At the Konzerthaus, 1 and 6 Nov. 1924. Postcard from Belyayev to Lamm of 2 Nov. 1924, ibid., l. 22.

music, and of the other concerts he attended, the best impressions were made by performances of the classical repertoire: 'There is relatively little that's new here, and it's preached by the adepts of a small "sect", just like everywhere else'.[24] But the work of Universal Edition impressed him greatly, and he opened negotiations for a permanent UE contract with Myaskovsky.

It was now clear that Myaskovsky was becoming the most prominent of the Soviet-based composers, both abroad and at home. His Fifth Symphony was performed in Leningrad (as Petrograd has just been renamed), where it was 'received respectfully', according to Asafyev.[25] In Moscow, Golovanov premiered the Sixth, the first major concert work to address the Revolution. *Contemporary Music* ran a series of essays on Myaskovsky. Asafyev contributed, of course, but he now began to feel that he was responding to the promptings of an inner censor:

[My] characterisation of Myaskovsky came across as rather dry: I am worried about writing in my old manner, since that would tempt me to slip into psychologism, metaphysics and mysticism, etc. I feel now that my hands are tied.[26]

On the concert stage, the window on Europe was now wide open, and the musical life of Russia's two capitals was enhanced by the appearance of celebrated performers from abroad: the first arrivals were the conductors Bruno Walter and Oskar Fried (who later became a Soviet citizen), and the pianist Egon Petri. They were soon followed by Joseph Szigeti (who gave the Russian premiere of Prokofiev's First Violin Concerto), Otto Klemperer, and others. On occasion, a lack of organisation led to embarrassments, such as Arthur Schnabel playing Beethoven sonatas in a succession of near-empty concert halls. The return of normal economic activities after the years of war and embargo even led to rumours that Rachmaninov, Stravinsky, and Prokofiev might return.[27]

For the first time since the Revolution, the opera-going public was offered productions of new works. In Moscow, the Zimin Opera presented three such works in its 1923/24 season, but none rose to the challenge of reflecting the changed times (whether the Revolution or European musical modernism). *Rachel's Tears* (*Plach Rakhili*), by the Moscow composer Georgy Dudkevich, was an eclectic affair, drawing particularly from Orientalism. The critic Sergei Bugoslavsky claimed that Dudkevich had mixed arias with *Sprechgesang* and Verdian accompaniments with Wagnerian leitmotives, and had thrown in every Orientalist cliché ever devised. Bugoslavskiy was even more scathing about the dancers, from Inna Chernetskaya's group: apparently, their scanty clothing and Isadora-Duncanisms were expected to compensate for a lack of any properly worked-out choreography.[28]

---

[24] See fn. 20.

[25] Letter from Asafyev to Derzhanovsky of 26 Jan. 1924, GTsMMK, fond 3, ye. kh. 2, no. 731.

[26] Letter from Asafyev to Derzhanovsky of 10 Mar. 1924, GTsMMK, fond 3, ye. kh. 2, no. 734.

[27] 'Okno v Yevropu', *Zhizn' iskusstva*, no. 1 (1 Jan. 1924), 1.

[28] Sergey Bugoslavskiy, 'Opera Zimina: *Plach Rakhili*', *Zrelishcha*, no. 72 (end Jan. 1924), 7.

Prince Serebryaniy (from Dec. 1923 onwards), was by Pyotr Triodin, a part-time composer who was a highly successful medical doctor; the result was not entirely professional, Bugoslavsky tells us, and relied heavily on *style russe* clichés. By all accounts, the best of the three new works was *Trilby*, by Alexander Yurasovsky (he had died of typhoid in 1922, at the age of 32). Bugoslavsky was much better disposed towards this lyrical drama, which was written in the style of Tchaikovsky and his followers, Anton Arensky and Rachmaninov. Lamenting the composer's early death, he thought the work had shown great promise: it was musically attractive and dramatically effective, and also benefitted from good staging and performances (Alexander Pirogov sang as Svengali).[29] Zimin also staged a new operetta by Victor Dolidze, *Keto and Kote*. Aside from these new works, there was also a striking new production of Gounod's *Faust* at the Bolshoi, thanks especially to the creative efforts of the director Vladimir Lossky and set designer Fyodor Fedorovsky.

Leningrad, however, was much more adventurous. In September, the former Mariinsky took the lead as the most progressive opera house by staging *Salome*, the first modern Western opera to play on any Soviet stage (the first fruits of Asafyev's presence on the theatre's Artistic Council). The staging was constructivist, and allied itself with the latest trends design trends in dramatic theatre, with constructions of ladders and platforms in black, illuminated by coloured lights. The public was also impressed by Salome's dance, which was expertly performed by a genuine dancer who discreetly replaced the singer for this scene.[30] As Polovinkin recorded, in a letter to Derzhanovsky:

> Watched *Salome*: the staging is good, and so are the singers – Pavlovskaya is a fine Salome and Yershov is always exciting dramatically,[31] even though he rarely produces a big sound. No one likes the music: it is exhausting and neurasthenic, but I must confess that I listened with mouth – and ears – wide open throughout: the logic of the orchestral writing is amazing, and the composer is always in complete control. Still, the ending is quite revolting and blasphemous: Herod's terror, when he covers his head with a yellow cloth, does not balance out the long kiss bestowed on the head.[32]

Perhaps still more remarkable were the first attempts by major opera and ballet companies to deal with the subject of revolution. Leningrad's second opera house, at this point known as the Akmaliy (The Academy Maly Theatre), produced the first high-profile Soviet adaptation of a classic. In this instance, it was *Tosca* transformed into *The Struggle for the Commune*, with a new scenario and libretto (see review below).

In ballet, the former Mariinsky once again led the way with the first ever revolutionary ballet, Vladimir Deshevov's *Red Whirlwind* (*Krasniy vikhr'*,

---

[29] Sergei Bugoslavskiy, 'Opera Zimina: *Tril'bi*', *Zrelishcha*, no. 76, 3.

[30] K. Yegorov, 'Salomeya Rikharda Shtrausa', *Rabochiy i teatr*, no. 4 (14 Oct. 1924), 13.

[31] See entries on Pavlovskaya and Yershov in the Glossary.

[32] Polovinkin's letter to Derzhanovsky of 6 Sept 1924, 'Perepiska L. A. Polovinkina', ed. by L. Rimskiy in *Iz proshlogo sovetskoy muzikal'noy kul'turi*, vol. 1 (Moscow: Sovetskiy kompozitor, 1975), 176–209, esp. 186.

choreographed by Lopukhov), the premiere timed to coincide with the seventh anniversary of the Revolution. The scenario was an unlikely cocktail of pre-Revolutionary symbolism with both Soviet everyday life and Soviet aspirations: in the Prologue, the symbol of the Cross is rejected in favour of the Star; the 'First Process' (as it was called) features a classical Adagio that represents Socialism; the 'Second Process' includes dances for groups of panhandlers, thieves, hooligans and Red Army soldiers; finally, an Epilogue rounded the work off with the creation of the USSR.[33] The consensus held *Red Whirlwind* to be a failure: the overall conception was considered pretentious, and the Symbolist aspects inappropriate.[34] Deshevov's music, described as a mixture of Stravinsky, Scriabin and Prokofiev, was pale and allegedly lacking in true Revolutionary vigour. The choreography was eclectic, employing classical dance for abstract ideas, with dancers in white costumes for the Revolution (!), and black for Counter-Revolution; the group numbers in the First Process were influenced by Soviet sports parades; the Second Process contained a great deal of mime, peasants depicted with Stanislavskian realism, including imaginary insect bites that needed scratching. The best character dances were found in the attractive divertissements for the street-life groups, leading reviewers to remark on an important point: the disreputable characters (hooligans, drunkards, panhandlers) were presented in the most artistically engaging way – 'such a depiction of the Revolution could be imagined in Paris or New York, rather than on an academy stage in the Soviet Union'.[35] The victory of the Revolution and the First of May procession, by contrast, lacked the requisite heroism and monumentality.[36] The same criticisms resurfaced for later attempts at revolutionary ballet, both abroad, with Prokofiev's *Pas d'acier*, and at home, with Shostakovich's *Golden Age*. But unlike these later works, *Red Whirlwind* also gave the impression that it was a rather slapdash affair, put together in two months in order to have it performed as part of the Anniversary celebrations. Yet for all its shortcomings, it was accepted as the first step on the path towards a Soviet reform of ballet (a reform never to be consummated, since Soviet ballet from Stalin onwards was decidedly conservative).

But while opera and ballet were able to attract attention by making a few Red gestures, RAPM was failing to establish itself as a serious force. And with European music and musicians making great inroads in Soviet musical life, it might have appeared that there was simply no place left for RAPM and the proletarianists. But beneath the surface, they were busy. The stately corridors of Moscow Conservatoire, of all places, were disturbed by the so-called Red Professors' Faction, led by Bryusova. The main point of their manifesto (which we include below) was a protest against the Conservatoire's elitist professionalism. Bryusova, with her pre-Revolutionary background in the 'People's Conservatoire', and her

---

[33] *Rabochiy i teatr*, no. 6 (28 Oct. 1924), 19–20.

[34] 'Krasnyi vikhr'?!', *Rabochiy i teatr*, no. 8 (10 Nov. 1924), 5–8.

[35] St. Volovoy, the workers' correspondent of the Rozhdestvensky Fire Brigade, '... I veterka ne bylo ...' (There wasn't so much as a breeze), *Rabochiy i teatr*, no. 8 (10 Nov. 1924), 6–7.

[36] Yur. Brodersen, 'Obnovleniye-li?' (Was it a renewal?), *Rabochiy i teatr*, no. 8 (10 Nov. 1924), 8.

post-Revolutionary Proletkult experience, clearly had a sincere belief that this unreconstructed institution had to be opened to the masses. She found comrades-in-arms in young activists such as the pianist Nikolai Sherman, and the composer Alexander Weprik, a former student of Myaskovsky's. But their influence reached beyond the younger generation, and they even managed to recruit Kastalsky as a respectable figurehead. Feeling the need to explain his participation to Asafyev, Kastalsky wrote:

> There are enough [pseudo-]revolutionaries trying to elbow in on the deal in Moscow as well (from Sabaneyev onwards), but I, as an old man, don't count myself among them, because from the beginning [i.e. 1917] (or even earlier), I understood the movement away from my own individuality towards its dissolution through contact with the masses. This is something altogether absent in the modernists. [...] Perhaps for this reason, it is not so much that I am 'attaching myself' to them, but rather that 'they' want to attach me to the 'association of proletarian musicians' and to the 'Red professors' (me, a 67-year-old wreck!)[37]

Under pressure from the Red Professors, Goldenweiser felt he had no option but to resign from his post as director of the Conservatoire. There was a rumour that Bryusova would replace him,[38] but her bid failed, and the directorship went to another celebrated pianist, Igumnov, who was not very much different from Goldenweiser in his outlook. The 'breach in the Conservatoire stronghold', as the Red Professors coup attempt was described in the press,[39] was a clear show of strength, but failed to bring about any substantial change.

A few months later, however, the Conservatoire received a greater shock: the expulsion of about a third of its students. One of the expelled was the composer Alexander Mosolov, who was selected (by his own account), simply for being rude to Bryusova,[40] but he was soon reinstated at the request of his teachers.[41] The cause and motive for this 'purge' were complex. The Red Professors' faction had little to do with it, and it would have been found disturbing by some of them at least. In its origins, the 'purge' was a NEP budget-trimming exercise, rather than a political initiative. Even during the NEP period, all higher education was state-funded, and at this juncture, it was decided that the student body had become too bloated, and cuts could be made by expelling the weakest students. That, apparently, was the intention at the top, but some of those who implemented it saw things

---

[37] Letter from Kastalsky to Asafyev of 10 Mar. 1924, RGALI, fond 2658 (Asafyev), op. 1, ye. kh. 581, l. 40.

[38] Letter from Belyayev to Lamm of 6 Aug. 1924, RGALI, fond 2743 (Lamm), op. 1, ye. kh. 84, 8.

[39] 'Bresh' v konservatorskoy tverdïne', *Zhizn' iskusstva*, no. 32 (5 Aug. 1924), 7–8.

[40] 'During the last six years I only lost my temper twice: the first time was with Bryusova [...] and they nearly expelled me from the Conservatoire for that [...]', Letter from Mosolov to Asafyev of 22 Oct. 1927, RGALI, fond 2658 (Asafyev), op. 1, ye. kh. 633.

[41] Ye. S. Vlasova, *1948 god v sovetskoy muzïke: dokumentirovannoye issledovaniye* (Moscow: Klassika – XXI, 2010), 37.

differently. It was considered undesirable to remove all the recently introduced students from families of factory workers and peasants, since they otherwise would have been among the first to go. But this had the potential for turning a financial campaign into a political attack on non working-class students. It was also widely thought that those who supported Trotsky and the Left Opposition made up a disproportionate number of the expelled – a second, and very different political dimension to the campaign.[42] In a strange twist, the official in charge of the expulsions in the conservatories and other arts institutions was Trotsky's sister, Olga Kameneva (wife of the Politburo member Kamenev).[43] Whatever the motives, the Conservatoire was hit harder than most institutions. The campaign, in its results at least, can be seen as part of a longer-term movement towards the proletarianising of higher education and research institutions, creating cadres of 'red professors' and 'red students', who would gradually unpick the old 'bourgeois' fabric of these institutions, removing the need for outside intervention. Kameneva was disappointed to find that the Conservatoire was particularly resilient,[44] and it would later withstand more radical attempts to make it change in the late 1920s and early 1930s.

---

[42] Dmitriy Andreyev, 'Krasnïy student i politika proletarizatsii vïsshey shkolï', publ. in *NLO* (2008), no. 90; http://magazines.russ.ru/nlo/2008/90/an5.html, accessed 21 July 2010.

[43] Vlasova, 36.

[44] O. D. Kameneva, 'O chistke v Moskovskoy konservatorii', *Izvestiya* (1 June 1924), quoted in Vlasova, 36.

A. Sergeyev, 'Potustoronniye' [Those on the Other Side], *Muzikal'naya nov'*, no. 5 (2) (1924), 8–10.

In the spring of 1924, the animosity between RAPM and ASM spilled out onto the printed page. Irritated by the appearance of ASM's journal Contemporary Music *(Sovremennaya muzika), Chernomordikov, one of RAPM's founding members, went on the offensive in the pages of* Musical Virgin Soil *(Muzikal'naya nov'):*

> Despite the fact that ASM falls under the aegis of RAKhN [The Russian Academy of Arts Studies], we very much doubt that its declaration could be adopted as a programme of Narkompros's official organ. We doubt it, because the ideological direction of this Association is incompatible with the ideology and interests of the proletarian state.[45]

In the same issue, Sergeyev, another of the founding members, published a more expansive denunciation of ASM under the title 'Those on the Other Side', from which several extracts are printed below. Sergeyev's polemic drew a wounding response from the pen of the anonymous 'Communist' in the new ASM journal, Musical Culture *(Muzikal'naya kul'tura), which was edited by Roslavets. As only a real Party member would dare to use such a pseudonym, it would not have been difficult to guess that the response was penned by Roslavets's wife Natalya, a Party member and an important official in the secret police, who was conversant with Lenin's arguments against RAPM's position and wielded them effectively on this occasion. Sergeyev never forgot the humiliation, and he retaliated in 1930, bringing Roslavets's career in* Glavrepertkom *to an end.*

A. Sergeyev
Those on the Other Side

[...]

The influence of music is extremely subtle and of the most dangerous kind, because it acts upon the emotional side of the human psyche. At the same time, its creators belong to the most conservative and politically backward milieu. Taking advantage of the timid neutrality displayed by those in charge of Soviet artistic policy, musicians, both 'great and small', quickly took control of the commanding heights in all our musical institutions, from Narkompros through to the specialist music schools. They have become entrenched in their positions. Learning from us, in the Party, they know not to act individually, but as a united group, and setting aside all their debates, personal disagreements and grudges, they have created an unbreachable wall, unbreachable not just by the heretics [non-Party leftists], but

---

[45] D. A. Chernomordikov, 'Tozhe ... internatsional!', *Muzikal'naya nov'*, no. 5 (2) (29 Feb. 1924), 5–8.

even by Communist musicians. If you take a close look at musical life in the capital, you will find the same people everywhere: in the Conservatoire, the Academy of for Scholarship in the Arts, the Bolshoi Theatre, in Narkompros and in the private organisations (the Association of Contemporary Music, The 'Book' Society) – they are all filled with people from 'the other side' [*potustoronniye*].

From their lofty positions (paid positions, albeit for a meagre sum), these musicians issued a series of manifestos (one of their authors, Mr Lourié, who in the years of famine astonishingly published his works on exquisite Bristol paper, has since vanished from the USSR without a trace).[46] A steady stream of these manifestos, and a thousand other projects of no practical value whatsoever, filled with explanations of all kinds of aesthetic experiences and images and with forbidding musical terms, has gone out to the USSR's innumerable MUZOs. Sometimes they brought a wry smile to the faces of musicians working in adult education, sometimes they were glumly filed in a folder with other papers 'from the centre'.

These 'oracles', the former composers of coronation anthems, of church concertos and of mystical and life-negating songs, continue to browbeat our comrades with their specialist music terminology, and continue to yell 'barbarism' and 'illiteracy' every time these young composers (perhaps technically underprepared) attempt to create revolutionary music. And they continue to occupy the commanding heights. The Revolution has passed them by, and their creative work is blind to the greatest causes, to the greatest ideas that humanity has ever known.

[...]

They say (or insinuate, rather) that our composers of revolutionary music are illiterate, but in the end, these composers reflect contemporary life to the best of their ability, even if they sometimes do so in a clumsy and dishevelled way, as I must admit. They learn from their mistakes and organise themselves into an Association of Proletarian Musicians or into the Red Professors Faction at the Conservatoire, and having done so, they advance determinedly towards the times they live in, and towards the class that is struggling hard to build a bright future. What of those who have amassed knowledge, who have given the fruit of their inspiration to the bourgeoisie, and mirrored the ideology of that class? How have these people, who have intimidated us with their greatness, how have they responded to the Great October Revolution?

When the February Revolution came, if I am not mistaken, only A. Grechaninov wrote a timid hymn, to words by Balmont. After the thunder of October, our composers descended into a profound silence. [...]

What of creativity?

Frightened by October, it sought refuge in mysticism or hysterics (Lourié, with his songs on Akhmatova, and other composers, still alive and well, who set the words of Z. Gippius, Merezhkovsky and other writers close to their hearts

---

[46] Sergeyev refers here to 1919 Declaration of the NKP Music Section (translated in the 1919 section of this book), which was co-authored by Lourié. Sergeyev is alluding to the fact that Lourié had failed to return from an authorised trip to Europe in 1921.

and minds).⁴⁷ Cmrd. Trotsky must be right when he says in his *Literature and Revolution* that 'Those who are outside the October perspective, are completely and hopelessly vacuous', and, further: 'They are not creators of life, they do not participate in the creation of its moods and attitudes; they are only belated gatherers of foam [*penkosnimateli*], epigones of cultures that have been created through the blood of other people'.

The Civil War began, the great heroic struggle of the proletariat. How did musicians respond to the great battles fought by the Red Army as it suffered from hunger and cold?

The catalogue of publications of the Narkompros Music Section contains glorifications of Christ, erotic sonnets, tender elegies and 'moaning and groaning' – although not, of course, the moaning of those who broke the circle of generals' bandits in the final bloody assaults.

[...]

All the great artistic achievements of the West, our own intonational quests, the whole sum total of assimilated achievements of past culture that they have worked through and creatively extended – none of these things can vitiate the fact that our musical creators belong to 'the other side', or the fact that they are cut off from the social roots of art. 'We need a stage, a firm, fact-saturated and active outlook and an artistic world-vision to match', says Cmrd. Trotsky, and further: 'Social conditions are first and foremost the conditions of class belonging'. And indeed, outlook and world-vision are very poorly expressed within our musical milieu and by our musical works, which is why our musicians are so otherworldly and lifeless, not excluding those who, in their political quests, failed to adopt the main tone of the Revolution – its severe, active and simple nature.

Cmrd. Lunacharsky, in his article 'The artistic policy of the Soviet state' tells us of a stage when the state clearly has to interfere in the artistic policy of state-sponsored institutions. This need for action is critical on our forgotten musical front. On the one hand, we have the various groups from the other side, who continue to exercise their hegemony over all our musical institutions. On the other hand, we have the calm neutrality of those who direct artistic policy. The two cannot coexist. We need to take a close look at the people entrusted with our music education and appreciation, we need a broad discussion and we need to pay careful attention to the individuals and institutions who are in possession of one of the most powerful means of agitation, in the broadest sense of that word – namely, the art of music.

---

⁴⁷ Zinaida Nikolayevna Gippius (1869–1945) and Dmitry Sergeyevich Merezhkovsky (1865–1941) were Symbolist poets, and Merezhkosky was also a writer and religious philosopher. They were a married couple and emigrated together in 1920. They were close to one of the leaders of the White movement, Boris Savinkov, and this fact further exacerbated their Soviet reputation.

Kommunist, 'Diatribï' [Diatribes], *Muzïkal'naya kul'tura*, no. 1 (July 1924), 54–5.

'Communist'
Diatribes

[...]
After all that Vladimir Ilyich [Lenin] wrote and said about the work of the specialists, about study and about our acquisition of culture, any Communist should be ashamed to issue the kind of appeal we have heard from Cmrd. Sergeyev. We strongly recommend that he should undertake a study of the relevant speeches and articles by Lenin. Take, for example, 'On the work of Narkompros' (*Pravda*, 1921) – we find passages there that hit the mark perfectly, like this one:

> The success of Communists who are active in the area of education for the people (and active in the appropriate institutions), needs to be measured, in the first instance, by how they organise the involvement of specialists: whether they know how to find them, how to use them, and how to establish good collaboration between specialist pedagogues and Communist leaders. If the present abundance of candidates for 'Communist leadership' in Narkompros continues, while at the same time we have nothing on the practical side, a shortage or absence of practical specialists, or the inability to promote them properly, to hear them out and to take their experience into account – in that case, everything will grind to a halt.

Isn't this self-evident? Isn't this the business-like approach? Isn't this the only possible path we can take, given our lack of culture and our poverty?

Instead, moreover, our 'candidates for leadership' feel the need to write such 'diatribes' (to use [Ramsay] MacDonald's expression), with clumsy passages about taking the commanding heights or about an unbreachable wall for 'Communist musicians'. Not that we are inclined to suspect that Cmrd. Sergeyev and his confederates want to put his own people in those commanding positions currently occupied by those from 'the other side'. But still, the passage really has to be interpreted thus: we might be a little bit illiterate, and the art we want to commandeer is all 'incomprehensible theory' to us, but down with all who dare to say (or rather 'insinuate') that we are illiterate, and instead hand over 'the Conservatoire, the Academy for Scholarship in the Arts, the Bolshoi Theatre, Narkompros' to us – everything that is (for now) filled by those from 'the other side'.

But Vladimir Ilyich, as if replying to Sergeyev, writes in the same article:

> In this respect, our slogan must undoubtedly be: let's have less of all that 'leadership', and some more practical work, in other words, less abstract talk and more facts – and facts that have been checked. As for those Communists

who keep talking about 'leadership', but in practice who cannot actually use specialists successfully, and who cannot make any use of the practical experience of hundreds upon hundreds of teachers – such a Communist is good for nothing.

Well, isn't that so, Cmrd. Sergeyev?

[...]

※ ※ ※ ※ ※

'Obrashcheniye gruppï professorov Moskovskoy Gosudarstvennoy Konservatorii'
[A Statement by a Group of Moscow State Conservatoire Professors],
Muzïkal'naya nov', no. 4 (1924), 21–2.

A Statement by a Group of Moscow State Conservatoire Professors

A group of professors of the Moscow Conservatoire has delivered the following statement to the editorial board of this journal:

In the era of the grandiose restructuring of the whole of society, which our Republic is currently experiencing, it is the task of all who consider themselves creators of the new life to work in accordance with this era and to overcome the obstacles on their path.

Many music workers have still not managed to overcome the idea that music has an independent significance (independent of this or that group of people, or class). This idea stems from the notorious principle of 'art for art's sake', whereby musicians tend to see themselves standing outside classes, as 'priests' for this kind of human activity. This outlook, which has its roots in a Romantic era distant from the present day, is hopelessly outmoded and therefore destined to perish; it views conservatoires as institutions placed 'outside time and space', that should strive only to produce the most perfect future 'priests' of this art ('perfect' in the sense of mastering the materials of the art).

Such an ideology is clearly opposed to life's powerful demands, which require that the cultural level of the masses should be raised, and that they should be introduced to the whole range of musical achievement; and such an ideology hinders the process of reconstruction in this sphere.

Aiming to speedily overcome the influence of this ideology, disconnected as it is from life, on the upbringing of professional musicians needed in the present times, and to create at the Moscow State Conservatoire conditions congenial to work that is in step with modernity, a group of Conservatoire professors has emerged that seeks to unite all members of the teaching personnel who are strongly inclined towards the Revolution.

This group sets itself the following tasks:

1. To assist the social and political education of students in every possible way.

2. To construct teaching plans and educational methods according to a productive-professional principle, in order to cultivate socialised musicians, who have fully mastered contemporary knowledge and craft, who are in touch with the needs of the masses and who have an acute perception of these needs.

3. To promote the principle of the proletarianisation of the student contingent.

The group will struggle against:
1. The musical 'priesthood'.
2. The ossified routine of old, traditional, and supposedly sacred educational programmes and methods, which had as its goal the production of 'classless musicians'.
3. The burdening of the Moscow Conservatoire by people who seek music education for their own individualistic purposes, in order to separate themselves from the masses.

The group will strive for:
1. Close contact with student organisations (the [Communist] cell and the Executive Bureau).
2. Links with public and artistic organisations that are ideologically close to it (Glavprofobr [Department for Professional Education], GUS [State Scholarly Council], Vserabis [Union of Art Workers], the Association of Proletarian Musicians, etc.). Aside from its immediate organisational tasks within the walls of the Conservatoire, the group intends to propagate its views through the press, in addition to papers, discussions, lectures, etc. Following the example set in other institutions of higher education, the group will call itself 'The Red Professors' Faction'.

The Provisional Bureau consists of comrades N. Bryusova, N. Sherman and I. Mamayev, who can be contacted with regard to any questions and issues pertaining to the Faction.

Initiating group:
N. Bryusova, A. Weprik, V. Ivanov-Boretsky, A. Kastalsky, I. Dubovsky, I. Mamayev, L. Tseitlin, I. Rabinovich, N. Sherman[48]

---

[48] Iosif Ignatyevich Dubovsky (1892–1969) was a music theorist who was already teaching at Moscow Conservatoire before his graduation, in 1923. The identity of Mamayev is not clear. Isaak Solomonovich Rabinovich (1897–1985), a student of Yavorsky, taught piano method at the Moscow Conservatoire from 1924–70. For others, see Glossary.

N. Malkov, '"Bor'ba za kommunu", ili vzorvavshayasya bomba' [*The Struggle for the Commune, or The Exploded Bomb*], *Zhizn' iskusstva*, no. 40 (30 Sept. 1924), 4–6.

Early Soviet theatre, including opera, thrived on 'revolutionary' adaptations of 'bourgeois' works. These projects have simply been derided and dismissed in most of the literature, so here, for a change, is a fair-minded review by a serious music critic, Nikolai Malkov (1882–1942), who at this point headed the music section of the Leningrad journal Artistic Life *(Zhizn' iskusstva)*.
A contemporary summary of the new libretto ran thus:

> The story takes place in 1871, during the last days of the Paris Commune's heroic struggle with the bourgeois government of Thiers. General Gallifet launches a merciless attack on workers' districts, executing communards by the thousands. We see the steadfast and heroic figures of the workers' leaders, who remain unflinching even in the face of torture or death. One of the principal characters is the Russian Revolutionary Zhanna Dmitrieva, an ardent participant in the events surrounding the Commune. On the other hand, we see the cruel representatives of the officers, bourgeoisie and clergy, full of hatred for the working class. The plot is not based on actual historical facts. The writers have attempted [instead] to suggest the character and atmosphere of the events, in order to draw the spectators into the spirit of those terrible days of proletarian struggle for the commune.[49]

N. Malkov

The Struggle for the Commune, or The Exploded Bomb

Good intentions

In the seventh year of the Revolution, the Academy Opera Houses have decided to start thawing out and take a step towards the modernity born of October. This decision was preceded by fierce attacks and continuous accusations of backwardness, so it was taken under significant pressure.

The policy on opera as a product of bourgeois and aristocratic art allows two possible courses. The more radical of the two is simply to reject traditional opera as an obsolete theatrical form that does not correspond to the demands of the proletarian Revolution regarding artistic creativity. This creativity must find new and broader paths in the stage arts, and it must work out methods of artistic influence that will force open the restrictions of the old theatre, destroying its immobility and imparting the maximum intensity and rapidity to theatrical action. The other course is more moderate and permits compromise. It allows for the

---

[49] 'V bor'be za kommunu', *Rabochiy i teatr*, no. 1 (18 Sept 1924), 28–9.

possibility of renewing old operatic forms by injecting content that is ideologically new.

The Academy Theatres are theatrical museums, carefully preserving the artistic culture of the society that has been swept away by the Revolution. It is well known that nothing is as long-lived as form. The content might be long eroded, but the form has been preserved and lives on like a monument to the past, like the object of a ritualistic cult that has lost its ideological significance. It is natural that out of an instinct for self-preservation, the Academy Theatres, as protective custodians of the old forms, will be more likely to choose the latter, compromising path for arts policy. If we must respond to the appeal of time and cannot postpone a decision any longer, let us try to put our museum valuables to a new purpose, let us attempt to pour new wine into old skins.

This is how good intentions were born, as we were told by N. G. Vinogradov,[50] who spoke solemnly and with great emotion from the stage before the performance began. Vinogradov and Spassky staged the old opera *Tosca* at the Academy Maly Theatre, remodelling it as a revolutionary piece.

An attempt by improper means

If it is granted that we can step onto the path of compromise, that we can try to revolutionise an opera (a very interesting experiment in itself), then it would seem easier to turn to Russian composers, who have survived a great revolution in their own homeland. Whatever they say, the composer plays an important role in an operatic work. But no one has turned to Russian composers.

It turns out that either we have no worthy composers at all (which we rather doubt), or they are all a bunch of counter-revolutionaries and so refused to respond to the Academy Maly Theatre's brave quest.

Most probably, the situation was this: composers, the management of the Academy Theatres decided, may be available, but looking them up is too much bother. So the management took up the old method of appealing to the people, but in a rather original manner, where Vinogradov took upon himself the role of town crier. Imagining, for some reason, that composers would all flock to the premiere, he made his vehement appeal for the creation of revolutionary opera there.

And in the meantime, another compromise was made in the business of revolutionising opera, which is a compromise in its essence. The new operatic production was worked out on the basis of old musical material that had been created more than a quarter century ago and which was saturated in ideological trends that are diametrically opposed to the production's own tasks. It was deemed possible to execute the revolutionary anabiosis of opera through the plot, simply ignoring the music. Such a one-sided and purely literary approach was entirely intentional, as we also heard from the stage [in Vinogradov's speech]. The device of rewriting an operatic text is nothing new. A similarly mechanical procedure was carried out by V. I. Nemirovich-Danchenko in his production of *Carmen* with the

---

[50] Nikolay Glebovich Vinogradov (pseudonym Mamont, 1893–67) was a playwright and theatre director; he worked at the former Mariinsky and directed his own opera and ballet workshop, Mamont (Mammoth). He was involved in various theatrical experiments, including revolutionary festivals with mass participation.

opera studio of the Moscow Art Theatre. And before that, I. M. Lapitsky was active in the field, since he presided over music drama at the time. Vinogradov's work is new only in the fact that he used his predecessors' method for giving a production the revolutionary treatment [whereas his predecessors merely modernised their opera scenarios].

However, it is hard to combine the incompatible. What is *Tosca*, a name that can also be read in Russian? [*toská* in Russian means boredom or gloom]. It is an early work by the celebrated maestro Puccini, with musical material that is careless both in quantity and quality, developed by primitive artistic means through weak impressionistic and decorative brushstrokes. The only virtues of *Tosca*'s music are its dramatic vitality and its closeness to Italian folk melody. But what a huge dose of routine pathos, sentimental lyricism and what blatant reliance on superficial effects! And this is the music that is yoked to a revolutionary plot, which is supposed to have the effect of a bomb blast! This was precisely what Vinogradov told us: 'This production will cause fierce debates. It will be a bomb exploding in the opera house'. But this did not prove to be the case: the Academy Theatre was not bold enough to commit suicide, and there was not much damage from the stage explosion. And fierce arguments are hardly going to follow.

A fine figure of a bastard

A cross-fertilisation of the old artistic culture with the new ideological tendency, *The Struggle for the Commune* does provide some treats with a revolutionary pedigree. The action of the opera is brought 70 years forward, from the Rome of 1800 to Paris of 1871, and is quite masterfully adapted to the framework of the old plot. In its principal situation, it develops according to the landmarks of the former story. And since the old scenario, developed from V. Sardou's drama by the experienced librettist L. Illica, is dramatically effective (albeit with a leaning towards melodrama) and is accompanied by the music that is equally fast-moving, the new revolutionary plot benefits from this expressive power. If Act 1 is rather long and boring, Acts 2 and 3 leave a more powerful impression that would be even stronger if the relationship between the music and the new plot did not approach the norm established in cinema, where any old music will do.

The language is very prosaic and there are many departures from historical truth (the murder of General Gallifet by a female Russian communard), while the revolutionary character, is not, to be frank, embodied in restrained artistic forms, and in many ways the production has the markings of an official agitational spectacle – but despite all these shortcomings, the content itself of the remade opera, which takes us to the heroic era of the Paris Commune struggle, makes the production refreshing and lends it a special interest that chimes with the experiences of [our] revolutionary times (this connection is emphasised by an apotheosis that symbolises the triumph of the ideas of the Commune in the USSR).

Of course, if *The Struggle for the Commune* was an original composition, rather than an appendix to the old work, the plot would have developed in a different direction. It would not have had a preponderance of individual characters over the masses, and the struggle for the commune would not merely have formed a backdrop against which the protagonists' drama was played out. But as it stands, the action unfolds in just this manner. The nature of *Tosca*'s musical and dramatic structure predetermined the concentration of the plot around individual characters, and did not allow the new text to be developed into a heroic tragedy in the grand style, as put forward in Vinogradov's lecture.

The performers' achievements

The staging of the premiere, which was executed meticulously on the whole, also suffered from some shortcomings. The opera's occasional crowd scenes did not come out well. Especially comical was the scene in which the artist Arlène, the communard elected by Versailles, was 'beaten' with little tricolour national flags. Generally speaking, there was no life animating the movements of the crowd. Among the individual performers, Pavlovskaya stood out in the role of Jeanne, owing to her wonderful voice and vivacious acting. Her concluding scene in Act 1 was somewhat routine. Kuklin, in the role of Arlène, showed real temperament and revealed his vocal gifts, much to his benefit. Bolotin, as Gallifet, was impressive on stage, and possesses a sonorous baritone. Sharonov as Pater is not as striking, his appearance turned into caricature by the attachment of oversize ears.[51]

The orchestra was conducted by D. Pokhitonov.[52] The overall precision of the performance was slightly marred by some rhythmic instability. The late entry of the off-stage bells was irksome. In subsequent performances, it is to be hoped that the roughness of the premiere can be smoothed out. The sets were effective in Act 3, and, after the raising of the curtain, the theatre applauded the artist. On the whole, the production was met sympathetically, but there was no particular excitement. Nothing that would make us think of a bomb blast. No – this amounted to nothing more than a fresh breeze.

---

[51] Nikolay Nikanorovich Kuklin (1886–1950), dramatic tenor, sang at the former Mariinsky from 1918–47; Pavel Petrovich Bolotin (1889–1947) was a baritone, who sang at the former Mariinsky and Maly Opera from 1920–47; Vasiliy Semyonovich Sharonov (1867–1929) was a low baritone who was famous for his Wagnerian parts and who also sang in Diaghilev's production of *The Nightingale*, in 1914. For Pavlovskaya, see Glossary.

[52] Daniil Ilyich Pokhitonov (1878–1957) was a conductor at the Mariinsky from 1909–56, and at the Maly Opera from 1918–32.

※ ※ ※ ※ ※

Igor Glebov, 'Kompozitorï, pospeshite!' [Composers! Keep up!], *Sovremennaya muzïka*, no. 6 (1924), 145–8.

This is the third, and most controversial of Boris Asafyev's polemical articles of 1924. His usual pessimistic diagnosis of the present situation in the musical world here gives way to his attempt at a prognosis. As he himself reported to Derzhanovsky, his editor, he wrote the articles in a kind of fever:

> [...] it's as if I've had a revelation: I suddenly understood everything that's happening in music and among musicians, so I'm writing, and speaking, and shouting, and whining, but the main thing is – I'm writing. I'm sending you an essay on the crisis of creativity, a kind of alarm bell. [...]. It seems to me that what I've realised is so simple and natural that it cannot fail to find a response in Moscow [...][53]

The response, however, was negative, even among Asafyev's closest ASM friends (see more on this in the introduction to 1924). In 1931, Asafyev reminisced about this piece as an opportunity squandered, pointing out that the breach was filled by others hostile to ASM (see the introduction to 1931).

Igor Glebov
Composers! Keep up!

For some reason an odd prejudice has arisen: if an appeal rings out for our composers to converge with modernity, it is thought that this necessarily means that we must write music that is base and trivial, music that comes from the street, with the implication that large-scale forms are pointless. There are a number of misunderstandings here, and we must settle these for good, one way or another.

Due to the somewhat aristocratic outlook of the professional musician, music theorists have learnt to enjoy the flowers of folk music, while composers pitch their dwellings on the summits of music. A certain outlook has emerged: folk song is from the past, while now everything that happens outside so-called art music is base and trivial. This gap needs to be filled, otherwise the masses, involved in the work of the state and culture, will pass high-art music by and create music that responds to their needs. Such a turn of events will not only cause Russian musical culture to lag permanently behind contemporary Western culture (which wouldn't be an entirely fatal outcome), but it will also lead to an extremely slow assimilation of past music-cultural heritage and creative experience on the part of the masses. Crucially, it will lead to a similar retardation in the development of auditory perception. Where is the good in this and who benefits? Only the speculators who respond to demand, i.e. the real purveyors of base and vulgar street music.

In order to fill the historical gap between concert hall and street, between

---

[53] Letter from Asafyev to Derzhanovsky of 21 Sept. 1924, GTsMMK, fond 3, ye. kh. 2, no. 750.

creativity within the study and society's need for music, it is not enough to care about fostering general and professional music education and enlightenment – pedagogy alone will not help. We need creative work that is live and intense. We need an artistic atmosphere and a sincere enthusiasm in the place of work-to-commission or trashy pieces that provide a superficial response to demand. All of this is as simple as ABC, and it is only, I repeat, a number of strange misconceptions that prevent composers from seeing this: namely, the ideology of a[n artistic] priesthood, the chains of professionalism and the fear of the street. There are three highly visible obstacles to be surmounted, and we shall start with these.

[Firstly,] the lack of a deeply rooted social-musical life, stemming from the repression of social life in general, has led to the conviction that everything connected to the street is base and vulgar. The street has become a synonym for something repugnant, something good taste should avoid. Remember how Rozanov, comparing the streets of European cities with ours, remarked very aptly that we see the street only as a place for pouring out sewage.[54] Well – is this to be our approach? No, and no again. Parades, rallies, performances, processions, celebrations, appeals and songs, the contemporary crowd, the sum-total of the complex intonations and rhythms of the city, the tempo of movement and street timbres – everything has been transformed and is being transformed day by day. To hear this transformation and to wish to embody it in music, weaving the primary elements of sound into the general fabric of city life – these are the most immediate tasks to be conceived. It would be naive to wait for inspiration in the hope that the spontaneous absorption of everything around might prompt a particular reaction. We should not wait – it would be better to try living in the present and attempt to refract it, perhaps clumsily at first (we won't be able to use harmony textbooks for advice!), but later with true mastery! To achieve this, we need to overcome this tendency to equate the street with all things base, we need to convince ourselves that the street signifies joy and vitality, that it refreshes like a spring, like a source of fresh, limpid, living water.

The second obstacle is the prejudice of taste. Usually we don't perceive the relativity of this concept and don't want to consider the fact that the intellectual and emotional refinement of perception within the limits of professionalism does not guarantee that we have healthy taste under different conditions, which [entail], rather, a change in the very content of artistic criteria. But [we will] only [understand this] if we do not start from the dead deductive premises that it was thus and thus in the Golden Age of music! In this respect, the old masters seem to have displayed greater sensitivity when they adapted the process of shaping the musical fabric to place and time, taking into account why a musical work was created, and for what purpose it was intended. However, this prejudice of taste is closely connected with the third obstacle – with the passion for large-scale forms, especially for the variety of sonata form that tends to concentrate the parts of the cycle within the span of a single movement. In terms of interest, challenge, difficulty, the overcoming of technical conditions and limitations, and working

[54] Vasily Vasilyevich Rozanov (1856–1919) was a Russian religious philosopher, literary critic and journalist.

on form, I think that it is more demanding today to write a small collection of songs than a sonata. Aren't we deluding ourselves when we imagine that it is only in sonata form that inspiration encounters constructive tasks that set it in flight, strengthen its powers, hone it and open up new possibilities? Isn't this just a habit, the comfort of the well-oiled scheme that drives our thinking along the well-trodden paths of the sonata allegro?

The state of the symphony is also rather unfortunate, even when we take into account all of the generalising elements that it contains and the decorative aspects of its composition. The symphony is losing its Aeschylean monumentality: having become more like a Euripidean tragedy, it can arrive, in the end, at complete emotional dissipation (the lyrical drama), or in a state of subjective alienation. Perhaps anticipating this danger, some of Myaskovsky's symphonies reveal a tendency to touch upon objective realities through the use of folk music.

It is my deeply held conviction that opera offers composers the easiest means for breaking out into the society around them, since opera expands the imagination through the extraordinary richness of its action, plot and forms, and at the same time directs it towards the concrete. In addition, opera makes it easier for us to communicate with the people, thanks to the emotional power of the human voice within its dramatic theatrical environment,[i] and there are well known examples of this from the early Venetian opera through to our own Musorgsky. And today the rebirth of opera, after the shining example of contemporary Russian theatre, can provide us with the most valuable results. The composers Polovinkin, Pashchenko and several others have already set out upon this path, namely, the path of monumental opera, instead of satisfying themselves with incidental music for the theatre, where the music is usually just a servant or sometimes a *serva-padrona*, i.e. a servant who is a mistress. The abandonment of opera would effectively be the loss of theatre for music. For composers, this would entail a loss of influence upon the listener through plastic movement [in a genre where] the music, within a huge continuous expanse, embraces all facets of life.

Theatrical forms of another kind (ballet, pantomime and *feérie*) also open up broad possibilities for composers to communicate with the concerns of the contemporary masses. If these were to be transferred to the street and the square in the course of various festivities, perhaps even as separate episodes in the celebrations, then music, an activity that can express and inspire with immediacy, will see the opening of new and broad perspectives, and these will not all take the shape of old-style military marches!

But even outside the theatre, music can, by itself, exchange its customary closed spaces for the free expanses of the external world, without sacrificing any of its artistic qualities. The organising of musical festivities, with performances by choral and even instrumental ensembles, is by no means a utopian pursuit. Where there is a will, there is a way. New forms need to be found for such festivities, but this will make the task all the more interesting. During the long period when musicians have been shut up in professional isolation, confined to the concert hall and salon, they have forgotten about the broader potential of music for bringing people together. I myself have always envied song, which is always able to impress itself on the human psyche with the fullest power – whether in a hut, in the meadow, in the steppe, or in the forest – while the music that is solemnly dubbed 'art', only grows, blossoms and bears fruit in the hothouse. There is a cruel paradox in this.

Even if we leave aside our dreams about festivities, there are still many other opportunities to connect with the masses through live creative work: we need choruses (thankfully there is the hope that where we formerly had a land of songs, we will soon have a choral land); we need songs for a great variety of organisations; we need musical games, and pantomimes on urban subject matter; we need instrumental music as an applied element and also as an active force in its own right for developing a network of free concerts (and what a horror if music pedagogues start to give them 'historical' programmes!), and most crucially, we need a creative will and an understanding of the radical changes that are taking place. Composers, hurry to create music for the sake of the life that has developed around you (be its joy!), and not for the sake of an illusory dream.

[*Note to Glebov's original*]

[i] See my article 'The Social Significance of Opera' in the forthcoming anniversary edition for the centenary of the Bolshoi Theatre (1925).

'VAPM: Ideologicheskaya platforma Vserossiyskoy Assotsiatsii Proletarskikh Muzïkantov' [VAPM: Ideological Platform of the Russian Association of Proletarian Musicians], *Muzikal'naya nov'*, no. 12 (1924), 24–5.

Ideological Platform of the Russian Association of Proletarian Musicians

1. The goal of art is to modify the human psyche through the emotional, subconscious part of the human being.

    Every class imprints its art with its world-vision, its mores.

    Thus, by organising consciousness in a particular way, art is a mighty weapon for disseminating the influence of a particular class.

2. All pre-Revolutionary music, reflecting the general development of the culture of class-based society, developed along two lines that hardly ever crossed: folk music (peasants' songs, factory *chastushki*, concertina, etc) and the music of the landlords and bourgeoisie, which includes all so-called 'written' cultured music.

3. The high level of development of the material-technical culture (whose achievements remained totally in the possession of the ruling classes) led to the flourishing of the musical culture of these classes (complex musical instruments, the special techniques for their production, special music-educational institutions, music publishing, etc) and its widest influence on all the strata and classes of the population, not excluding the proletariat (the distraction of workers from their class interests with the help of music tending towards mysticism, eroticism, pure aestheticism, etc.)

4. The influence of bourgeois culture and art on folk music has recently been much in evidence.

    Taking what is most valuable in folk creativity, and at times feeding its art exclusively on the juices [of folk creativity], the bourgeoisie systematically poisoned the folk song through its debauching influence. As a result of this influence, folk song shows tendencies towards de-classed and degenerate states: sometimes towards the urban romance, at other times towards ecclesiastical-bourgeois aestheticism.

5. However, in the musical heritage of the past, there were periods when music reflected cheerful and heroic moods, especially at the moments of bourgeois revolution and its struggle with the remnants of feudalism, when the bourgeoisie was an agent of economic progress. Such music can serve the proletariat as a healthy musical culture of the past.

6. But the bourgeois music of the latest period (the advent of capitalism in its highest stage of development – financial capitalism) reflected the process of the general self-decay and decline of bourgeois culture. In this period, the bourgeoisie, masking its predatory class interests, proclaimed the slogan of 'art for art's sake' etc, which led to the dominance of form over content and to the impoverishment of content in general.

7. The proletariat, having enacted the Revolution of October 1917, sets its tasks not only in the field of the economical restructuring of society, but also in the field of [society's] social and political re-education. Widening its ideological influence, the proletariat, through the broadest methods of agitation and propagandising is re-educating humanity and leading it towards the new life, towards socialism. One of the most powerful channels of its class influence and self-establishment is art.

8. However, a number of factors – (a) a lengthy period of civil war, (b) urgent economic tasks, (c) the low cultural level of the proletariat, etc. – have prevented the new young class that had just come to power from taking possession of art as the means of its class influence and from bringing forward its own artist/ideologues.

9. This has given the old musicians, ideologues of the bourgeoisie, an opportunity to maintain the decadent trend of bourgeois art even after the October coup, and to impose this upon the proletariat and the proletarian state, passing it off as revolutionary art. The NEP situation greatly benefits this 'cover-up' process.

10. All the so-called 'contemporary' non-proletarian music furthers the development of pre-Revolutionary bourgeois music; in [this music], content is divorced from form and is finally lost; music is classified according to its formal features, and certain aspects of musical form acquire a self-sufficiency and separate themselves into particular trends.

11. The decline of bourgeois musical culture is travelling along the following paths, or musical trends:

    a) the founding of a whole musical work on particular sonorities and their combinations, accompanied by a monotony and poverty in metre and rhythm, which leads to a distortion of musical phrasing and the loss of all dynamism.

    b) a chasing after originality and a fascination with illogical, spasmodic rhythms, which leads to the decline and disappearance of melody, and, among other things, a vocal and operatic crisis in bourgeois music.

    c) a chasing after 'perfect', self-sufficient form, as a result of which creative work degenerates completely, being exchanged for lifeless schematicism.

12. The proletariat, however, achieving great successes in the reconstruction of the economy and financial politics, is gathering and honing its cultural powers for the repulse of petit-bourgeois influences, and is raising the

cultural level of the masses, where a significant growth of initiative and activism is found not only in the fields of politics and the economy, but in the field of culture as well. This growth is assisted by the voluntary and spontaneous proletarian organisations that also constitute evidence of this growth.

13. One such organisation is the Association of Proletarian Musicians. The Association unites those musicians who take an active part in the struggle and construction of the proletarian avant-garde; it has the following goals:
    a) the refining, preparation and cultivation of the soil, and the necessary conditions for the development and growth of proletarian music;
    b) immediate creative work towards the creation of a proletarian musical literature.

14. In order to achieve the first of these goals, RAPM
    a) liaises via the workers' clubs with the proletarian masses, raises their cultural level, and organises, instructs and directs choral, orchestral and other musical groups.
    b) assisting in the uncovering of creative work in the masses of workers and peasants, at the same time organises wide paths for their musical development, and to this end it assists in the proletarianisation of music schools, the organisation of workers' faculties [*rabfaki*] in conservatoires, etc.
    c) works out in detail the following issues through its special departments: the methods of mass and small-group activities in workers' clubs, the issues of special music education, the issues of using the musical heritage of the past, and the creation of new forms of performance. It is also attempting to improve the health of popular music by organising its own choral and orchestral collectives and individual performers.
    d) organises public opinion through the press and the RAPM organ *Musical Virgin Soil* [*Muzïkal'naya nov'*], in which it sheds light on its principal ideas, suggests paths for new musical activities, polemicises with non-proletarian groups of musicians, and analyses and evaluates the emerging musical literature, etc.

15. The work of proletarian musicians [i.e. RAPM] on the creation of proletarian musical literature takes as its starting point the content of the musical work [rather than the form], in opposition to the so-called 'contemporary' musicians.

    As the foundation of their class-based creative work, the proletarian musicians build on the representation of the great heroic struggle of the proletariat for the liberation of humanity, the proletariat's ardent organic hatred of oppression and oppressors, its love of free creative work, and the economic and cultural construction of the proletariat being carried out in the USSR, etc.

The new revolutionary content of the [art of the] proletariat, which thinks in terms of Marxist dialectics, does not embody any of the forms of the above-mentioned bourgeois trends in music, but inevitably entails the construction of a new musical form that is born from content, [and the form] in its turn shapes it [i.e. the content] artistically. We conceive of the interaction between content and form as a dialectical unity. This new [kind of] musical form is being created and will be created by proletarian musicians in the process of their practical creative work, which is inevitably tested against the [intuitions of the] mass proletarian listener.

Music is only proletarian if 'its roots reach down through the masses, uniting their feelings, thought and will, and raising them' to further struggle and construction, and directing their consciousness towards the final goals of the proletariat as builder of a communist society [quotation from Lenin].

1925
Equilibrium

1925 saw both the main trends in Soviet musical life gather momentum, but for the moment, they moved in their own separate spheres without serious conflict, even if this was unavoidable in the long run. One of the two trends was the cosmopolitan opening of Soviet musical culture to new European works and ideas, entailing visits by foreign performers and composers, performances of new Western music, and exploratory trips abroad by members of the Soviet intelligentsia. Here, ASM came to the fore, and its leading members now became known to a wide public. The other trend was the establishment of a self-consciously Soviet repertoire, the structuring of cultural life around the main dates of the revolutionary calendar, and a gradual dilution of Conservatoire elitism. Although RAPM is often considered the equal and opposite reaction to ASM, its role in the second trend was minimal at this point. RAPM had failed to secure any institutional support and after the demise of *Musical Virgin Soil* [*Muzïkal'naya nov'*], it was left without a press outlet. The situation was not the same across all the arts: notably, RAPP, which was RAPM's counterpart for writers, fared much better, acquiring a prominence that caused concern in the upper ranks of the Party. In February, after RAPP's inaugural congress, Bukharin spoke at a CC meeting devoted to literature in order to reinforce the arguments that Trotsky had previously championed: different literary groups and trends should be allowed to compete freely, and proletarian writers, accordingly, were not to be granted any special privileges.[1] Trotsky himself had already been removed from the CC and was gradually being demoted, but these arguments were not uniquely identified with him. Bukharin's plea was given concrete form in the Party resolution of 18 June, which made several important points: although no literature is politically neutral, proletarian artists were not to pursue class struggle with inappropriate vigour, since the struggle at this stage was tending towards 'peaceful organisational work'. The Party would not be pushed into granting exclusive support to any literary group or style and stood against any publishing monopoly. As for 'fellow travellers', the Party called for them to be treated with tact and care, and the 'intermediate ideological forms' that marked their work were legitimate for the time being.[2] There was much here to reassure the intelligentsia, but also a reminder that the current artistic dispensation would not last indefinitely.

The cosmopolitan aspects of musical life in Moscow and Leningrad were on display for all. The appearance of illustrious foreign performers became normal for the two capitals, and many of these performers spent so much time there that

---

[1] N. Bukharin, 'Proletariat i voprosï khudozhestvennoy politiki: Stenogramma rechi, proiznesyonnoy na literaturnom soveshchanii pri TsK v fevrale s.g.', *Voprosï kul'turï pri diktature proletariata* (Moscow and Leningrad: Gosudarstvennoye izdatel'stvo, 1925), 140–52.

[2] 'Postanovleniye Politbyuro TsK RKP(b) 'O politike partii v oblasti khudozhestvennoy literaturï' of 18 June 1925, http://www.sovlit.ru/articles/postanovl_o_politike_partii1925.html, accessed 29 July 2010.

they became integrated into Soviet musical life. The conductors Klemperer and Fritz Stiedry, for example, not only gave orchestral concerts, but also rehearsed and conducted for complete operatic runs, Klemperer with *Salome* and *Carmen* at the former Mariinsky, and Stiedry with *Aida* at the same venue and *Die Entführung aus dem Serail* at the Maly Opera. Through the work of Rosfil, the names of Schnabel, Szigeti, Petri and Hermann Abendroth featured on concert posters as often as the names of local stars, such as the pianists Horowitz and Feinberg, the violinists Naum Blinder and Boris Sibor, and the organist Alexander Gedike.[3]

May saw the year's most prestigious operatic premiere: *Der Ferne Klang* at the former Mariinsky, which opened two days before a rival production at the Berliner Oper.[4] By all accounts, the Leningrad version, directed by Sergei Radlov, with sets by Vladimir Dmitriyev, was very impressive, and Schreker himself came over in October to conduct a performance. He was delighted with the orchestra, which he said 'almost reaches the heights of free improvisation'.[5]

The opera's enthusiasts emphasised the modern aspects of the work:

This is the first truly contemporary operatic spectacle: it reflects contemporary Western life, it is soaked in contemporary psychology and expresses these through an original idiom that melds music and text into a felicitous unity.[6]

Other commentators were quick to point out the ideological dissonance between Soviet life and the stage-world of *Der Ferne Klang*, to which Radlov responded that Soviet citizens could still learn something from it, adding wryly:

No one can claim that the future communist society will be nothing more than 'an institute for political literacy' – the feelings will remain, after all. They may become purer and nobler, but surely love and hate will remain, won't they?!'[7]

The traffic was two-way, and various eminent figures from Russian musical life were sent on business trips abroad. These members of the old musical establishment were now embedded in Soviet musical life, and their material conditions had improved considerably over the previous few years. Emigration, accordingly, lost its attraction, and the authorities no longer had to worry about brain-drain. Belyayev continued touring Europe: he attended a performance of *Wozzeck* in Vienna ('it shakes your whole being'),[8] and the ISCM (International

---

[3] 'Rossiyskaya filarmoniya', *Rabochiy i teatr*, no. 1 (5 Jan. 1925), 5.

[4] P. Konskiy, 'Vpechatleniya opernogo sezona', *Rabochiy i teatr*, no. 23 (7 June 1925), 12.

[5] Frants Shreker, 'Moi vpechatleniya', *Rabochiy i teatr*, no. 42 (20 Oct. 1925), 7.

[6] G. Gur'yev, 'Dal'niy zvon', *Rabochiy i teatr*, no. 20 (17 May 1925), 9.

[7] I. L-skiy, 'Disput o "Dal'nem zvone"', *Rabochiy i teatr*, no. 22 (31 May 1925), 6–7.

[8] 'This is music powerful enough to shake the whole of your being. I am surprised how such extraordinary complexity of construction can be combined with the power of direct emotional communication'. From Belyayev's letter to Myaskovsky of 22 May 1925, fond 2040 (Myaskovsky), op. 1, ye. kh. 103, l. 44v.

Society for Contemporary Music) festival in Prague, where he was filmed and treated to an automobile ride.⁹ Goldenweiser, Yavorsky, and Protopopov all made trips to Europe during the summer.¹⁰ These fully funded trips were a great morale-boosting therapy, but they required considerable effort to organise, as Sergei Popov detailed in one instance after a chance encounter with Feinberg at the Music Publishers: 'Cheerful, looking very well. He got a passport and two visas (Italian and Austrian). Submitted the passport to get a German one. Today the committee for business trips abroad is discussing the issue of financing his trip to Venice'.¹¹ Those who were left behind, on the other hand, were sometimes resentful: Asafyev, for example, complained that Belyayev was a bad choice as a representative of Russia abroad, since he would only pursue personal interests.

Asafiev's complaint was not merely sour grapes. The lucky few granted the privilege to represent Russia in Europe generally took the opportunity to promote their own circle of friends, causing consternation at home when it became too blatant. Thanks to the activities of Belyayev and Feinberg, the March issue of the Vienna journal *Musikblätter des Anbruch* was devoted to Russian composers. But as Alexander Weprik reported to his fellow Red Professor, Bryusova:

> The journal was quite scandalous. If you were to credit what it says, we have four geniuses: Myaskovsky, Aleksandrov, Feinberg and Roslavets – all the rest are rubbish.
>
> There's not a word about the Leningrad composers, but we get a portrait of Belyayev with his pals. In a word, the same old policy of the Association [i.e. ASM]. All this is presented as if it was on Russia's behalf. It's such an outrage that Muzsektor is going to publish a counter-volume [...] Zhilyayev, in his anger, called Belyayev the chairman of the Russian joint-stock company 'International Claque'.¹²

But ASM weathered the criticisms and surged ahead. Belyayev promoted the cause of the Association at Glavnauka, seeking a firmer institutional base.¹³ The concert series continued, including performances of Bartók quartets, chamber works by Malipiero, Casella, Kodaly, Honegger, Ravel, Krenek, Schoenberg, Webern, Paul Pisk and Cyril Scott. The Russian contributions were less spectacular: the second-rank composer Alexander Tcherepnin was supplemented by the third-rank Anatoly Drozdov and by Myaskovsky's students Vasily Shirinsky and Vladimir Kryukov. Myaskovsky himself was well represented: at a time when it was difficult to mount symphonic concerts of new music, he managed to hold

---

⁹ Letter from Belyayev to Lamm of 18 May and postcard of 20 May 1925, RGALI, fond 2743 (Lamm), op. 1, ye. kh. 84, ll. 25 and 27.

¹⁰ Letter from Popov to Lamm of 4 Aug. 1925, RGALI, fond 2743 (Lamm), op. 1, ye. kh. 176, l. 20.

¹¹ Letter from Popov to Lamm of 18 Aug. 1925, ibid., l. 25.

¹² 'Mezhdunarodnaya klaka', a pun on 'Mezhdunarodnaya kniga'. Undated letter from Weprik to Bryusova, RGALI, fond 2444 (Veprik), op. 2, ye. kh. 67, ll. 4–5. Nikolai Zhilyayev worked as an editor for Muzsektor (see Glossary for more details).

¹³ Letter from Popov to Lamm of 9 Aug. 1925, RGALI, fond 2743 (Lamm), op. 1, ye. kh. 176, l. 22.

premieres of his Fourth, Seventh and Eighth Symphonies. While Asafyev, as usual, supplied sympathetic programme notes in *Contemporary Music*, there were signs that his music was not considered to be abreast of the times, perhaps indeed one of the Party Resolution's 'intermediate ideological forms' that would eventually wither away. As the critic Braudo wrote:

> Myaskovsky's line is the extreme intensification of gloomy symphonic emotions reminiscent of Tchaikovsky's Sixth or *The Queen of Spades*. Dark instrumental themes immersed in the hopeless depths of a suffering soul – such is Myaskovsky's favourite imagery. Such music can hardly be considered typical of Russian artistic endeavour today. It is as if these two symphonies [Four and Seven], although separated by five years (1917–22), were frozen in the same note of grief.[14]

Leningrad's composers lagged well behind in promoting their own interests, and they now began to feel that they had somehow missed the boat. Maximilian Shteynberg, for example, enquired of Myaskovsky (perhaps with a hint of sarcasm):

> Would you mind giving me some details about this 'association of composers', which, according to the papers, has successfully fought the propaganda battle for Russian music abroad. Is this a Moscow-only organisation, or is it possible to have 'provincial' branches too? I must say that we are trying not to lag behind either, but we've almost exclusively been promoting foreign music. Now a new series has been announced: four concerts consisting of works that are the *dernier cri* in Western Europe.[15]

The *dernier cri* included Hindemith's Sonatas for Viola and for Cello from op. 11 and the piano Suite '1922', Kodály's Cello Sonata, Honegger's Viola Sonata, and Stravinsky's Piano Rag-Music. Leningrad's own composers weren't completely ignored: audiences heard Vladimir Shcherbachov's Second Piano Sonata, *Vïdumki* (Inventions), and fragments from the Second Symphony, Deshevov's *Bolsheviks*, another incarnation of *Red Whirlwind*, and Pashchenko's Third Symphony. Shteynberg premiered his magnum opus, a 'mysterium' entitled *Heaven and Earth* after Byron, while the prodigy among his students, Dmitry Shostakovich, earned a concert of his compositions, on which Weprik reported:

> Was at Mitya's concert. I think it is too early yet to consider him a real composer. His features haven't yet taken shape. But he's certainly very promising. We'll have to see what he does next.[16]

While all this international music-making was in progress, the 'red' front saw a major regrouping of its forces. In November 1924, RAPM split: Shulgin and Sergeev, the two founding members, left the organisation, and in their wake went the two most productive composers, Dmitry Vasilyev-Buglay and Klimentiy Korchmaryov.

---

[14] Yevg. Braudo, 'Novaya muzïka', *Rabochiy i teatr*, no. 9 (2 Mar. 1925), 11.

[15] Letter from Shteynberg to Myaskovsky of 3 Feb. 1925, RGALI, fond 2040 (Myaskovsky), op. 2, ye. kh. 281, 8.

[16] Letter from Weprik to Bogdanov-Berezovsky of 22 March 1925, RGALI, fond 2444 (Veprik), op. 2, ye. kh. 66, l. 7.

It seems that the exclusionary policies advocated by younger members of RAPM, like Lev Lebedinsky and Sarra Krylova, were too sectarian for Shulgin and Sergeev, who were also established members of Muzsektor's Agitotdel Department, and the version of musical Marxism propagated by *Muzïkal'naya nov'* was too 'vulgarised'.[17] Shulgin's new group sought out a more centrist position, and indeed this was more in keeping with Party policy, not least Bukharin's inclusive approach to fellow travellers. Since, crucially, they had access to music publishing, Shulgin and Sergeyev were perfectly positioned to establish a new organisation with its own journal. The group would go public in the next year, 1926, under the name of ORKiMD (the Association of Revolutionary Composers and Music Workers, sometimes abbreviated to ORK, with 'music workers' omitted), and its journal was entitled *Music and Revolution*. In 1925, the group still organised itself more along the lines of a private circle, but it also served as an informal extension of Agitotdel: the group debated the virtues of the agitational music that Shulgin could publish or reject in his official capacity.

Thanks to the detailed transcripts of the group's meetings, made by Shulgin's wife Elena, we can time-travel to late March/early April of 1925, where Shulgin, Korchmaryov and another regular member, Semyon Klyachko, meet two prospective new recruits, Alexander Davidenko and Boris Shekhter, both composition students at the Conservatoire.[18] Davidenko was studying under Glière at the Conservatoire and under Kastalsky at the Choral Academy, and had recently published a 'revolutionary' piece together with Shulgin, 'Kuznets' (The Smith, 1924), on a text by Igor Severyanin. It is clear that his arrival was eagerly awaited, not least because of all the composers that Shulgin's group could expect to join, Davidenko, son of a seamstress and a telegraph worker, had the strongest claim to a proletarian background. Still, even if he was with the group ideologically, his musical tastes required some reshaping: after Feinberg's Soviet premiere of Prokofiev's Third Piano Concerto (22 March 1925), Davidenko had numbered himself among the composer's most ardent apologists. A few years later, he would become a leading figure on the 'revolutionary music' side – his evening with Shulgin was a watershed for him.

Davidenko duly arrived, with his friend Shekhter (they seemed to be inseparable and later collaborated on an opera), and he was asked to perform his new musical 'poster' (*plakat*) 'Pro Lenina' (About Lenin, on a text by Alexei Kruchenykh). Shulgin and his associates were clearly bemused on discovering that Davidenko had written the piece for solo voice. While they were interested in a personal capacity, they insisted that Davidenko consider his wider audience, arguing that a piano accompaniment was needed to guide listeners through the implicit harmonies of the vocal line. Davidenko was far from convinced. Shulgin

[17] Sergey Bugoslavskiy, 'Proletarskiye muzïkantï', *Zhizn' iskusstva*, no. 15 (14 Apr. 1925), 8.

[18] 'ORKiMD. Protokolï zasedaniy. Fragmentï stenogramm. Avtograf Ye. N. Shulginoy', GTsMMK, fond 474 (Shulgin), ye. kh. 619. Some supporting information for this story is taken from Ye. Krivtsova, 'Iz istorii muzïkal'no-obshchestvennïkh organizatsiy: ORKiMD (1924–1932) (Po materialam arkhiva L. V. Shul'gina)', *Trudï Muzeya muzïkal'noy kul'turï: Al'manakh*, vol. 2 (Moscow: Gosudarstvennïy tsentral'nïy muzey muzïkal'noy kul'turï, 2003), 268–92.

insisted: 'It can be soft, sporadic, off-stage – whatever – but there has to be an accompaniment'. Davidenko was adamant that this would destroy his novel idea of a musical 'conversation', but Shulgin persisted, even hinting that an accompaniment would be a prerequisite for publication. (The published version does indeed include a rather demanding piano part.)

Attention now turned to Shekhter, who played his Piano Sonata. Shulgin and his associates felt that it was irredeemable as 'revolutionary music', and the only immediate reaction recorded on the transcript was that it 'sounds like Scriabin'. Davidenko, coming to his friend's defence said, 'But there is sincerity here'. 'That's not the point', said Shulgin, ' – it can be sincere and still negative'. Shulgin liked to apply this bland 'negative' to modernist music, which he reckoned was on the road to nowhere. Korchmaryov encouraged the two young composers to take a more materialist approach to their work – ultimately, they should see themselves as producers of music for the market. Shulgin was anxious to correct this well-intentioned, but politically clumsy expression: 'The market also demands cocaine and Vertinsky',[19] he reminded Korchmaryov. The point, rather, was that 'you shouldn't be cooped up in your study writing just for yourself'. Having thus dented Shekhter's confidence, Shulgin explained what he thought the sonata's strengths were, but placed them in a broader context: 'I see this as a play of sounds. It's interesting and exciting, but only if heard at the Conservatoire in particular circumstances'. Muzsektor might well be publishing such music by the shedload, Shulgin added, but even so, 'three quarters of it is bound to perish. It'll rot. Nobody needs it'. 'But what about achievement in the area of form?', said Davidenko, 'what about Europe?' Klyachko wasn't impressed: 'We saw this kind of technical achievement at Muzsektor, where they play with their elbows and fists' (possibly referring to the music of Henry Cowell). Davidenko couldn't quite believe that Shulgin could dismiss all modern music as a mere 'play of sounds' or a 'game of chess', and he brought prestigious names to bolster his point: 'what about Myaskovsky, Medtner, and Prokofiev (even if he sometimes plays the fool)?'. Shulgin replied: 'I know Prokofiev personally, and he's the frivolous son of a landlord. He's bold and brave, but he's also wild.' Korchmaryov added that even children's pieces by Prokofiev showed taste and intuitive strengths, and when Prokofiev 'produces leftist music, I believe him. […] Prokofiev isn't Roslavets […] and although it's alien music, he's an honest man. But Roslavets is just hoodwinking the public. At the end of the evening, no consensus had been reached. Davidenko's conclusion was that even if a piece of music is not entirely comprehensible to the listener, it will still have an impact on the listener. Shulgin, on the other hand, insisted that if a piece was to make any worthwhile impact, the listener needed to understand it.

Just a few weeks later, Davidenko was already a celebrated figure in Moscow's musical life. 'About Lenin', the same piece he had presented to Shulgin, had earned him a prize at the Conservatoire. As Lebedinsky later reminisced, Davidenko

---

[19] Alexander Vertinsky (1889–1957) was a popular actor best known in emigration for the 'decadent' style he established in his songs, and also for his stage presence (often presenting himself as a Pierrot figure). He returned to the Soviet Union in 1943, receiving great acclaim both official and popular.

greatly impressed the jury when he appeared on stage, 'looking like a demobilised Red Army soldier', tall, imposing, with a great shock of hair and a powerful bass voice, he sang the piece while walking around the stage and gesticulating.[20] His prize was a scholarship that funded the rest of his Conservatoire course. Naturally enough, this was a great boost to his confidence, and he now felt even less inclined to join Shulgin's group. Instead, he established a group of his own, Prokoll – the Production Collective of Moscow Conservatoire – with Shekhter and Viktor Beliy as his co-founders.[21] The group's industrial-sounding name did nothing to deter an attempt to recruit Davidenko to ASM – clearly, this blue-eyed proletarian and prize-winning student was considered a great catch. Davidenko, however, preferred the independence his own group provided, although for all the criticism he had received from ORKiMD, he kept in close contact with Shulgin, and even appropriated the latter's opinions quite blatantly. It was not long before he was found criticising his friend Shekhter's Second Sonata for its 'psychologism', calling for him to eschew abstraction in favour of a style that would be 'more vivid, decorative and programmatic', a style that would command the immediate attention of listeners.[22]

In the meantime, the musical calendar was increasingly shaped by revolutionary holidays and anniversaries, a feature that came to characterise Soviet culture from the 1930s to the 1980s. The influence of the growing cult of Lenin played a leading role here, far beyond the new anniversary days marking his birth and death. The mythology surrounding him coloured all the other celebrations. In the case of the centenary of the Decembrist uprising, there were pervasive reminders that Lenin had included the event in his landmarks of revolutionary history.

The first anniversary of Lenin's death (21 January) prompted a new wave of Lenin works. Among the most prominent of these was the 'funeral poem' *Vozhd'* (The Leader), staged at the Grand Hall of Moscow Conservatoire. The text was compiled from contemporary poetry; the result was 'quite clever', as reviewers remarked, but at the same time 'rather monotonous'.[23] The text was presented as an ensemble declamation by actors of V. N. Vsevolodsky's State Experimental Theatre, which specialised in this novel art form. The action on stage was performed by students of the Dalcrozian Rhythm Institute;[24] some critics complained that this

[20] L. Lebedinskiy, 'A. Davidenko: Materialï dlya tvorcheskoy biografii', *Sovetskaya muzïka*, no. 4 (1935), 22–37.

[21] The three founder members were later joined by Koval, Chemberdzhi, Levina, Ryauzov, Koposov, Fere, Bruk, and Tarnopolsky.

[22] S. Ryauzov, 'Vospominaniya o Prokolle', *Sovetskaya muzïka*, no. 7 (1949), 54–8, esp. 56.

[23] K.T. and Rabkor [workers' correspondent] S. Gavrilov, 'Traurnaya poema "Vozhd"', *Rabochiy i teatr*, no. 9 (2 Feb. 1925), 7.

[24] Vsevolod Nikolayevich Vsevolodsky (born Gerngross, 1882–1962) was an actor, director and theatre historian. In 1918, he created the Institute of Live Speech (Institut zhivogo slova), and in 1923 an Experimental Theatre, where he attempted to reform the art of declamation. In 1930, he opened an Ethnographic Theatre at the Russian Museum in Leningrad, where folk rituals of various nationalities were staged. Émile Jaques-Dalcroze (1865–1950) was a Swiss composer and educator who developed the 'eurhythmics' method of teaching music, which had already

gave the spectacle a decadent flavour. The sets and lighting effects were much admired, and the audience was able to see the Mausoleum, the factory chimneys in the background and even moving clouds overhead. All present were invited to relive the moment when they heard the news as the time of Lenin's death was projected onto the screen:

> The telegraph wires crackle with mysterious lights: this is how the news of Ilyich's death is transmitted; in the background, a distant snowy plain stretches out, a black railway line visible. [...]
> A choral declamation from the stage:
> 'The sun has grown dim,
> Lenin is dead ...'
> The flags are lowered. The orchestra plays the Funeral March. Everyone rises. All are gripped by this moving, eerie moment.
> But look – a man in a red cloak is rushing through the lines of people: this is the red spectre – the spectre of Communism wandering across Europe among the oppressed.
> The performance ends with the apotheosis of proletarian victory across the globe.[25]

But there was still room for debate over how Lenin should be commemorated. In the case of *Vozhd'*, many were indeed moved, but one reviewer responded sharply, in an essay entitled 'We have no need for mysticism':

> Apparently, this collage of material from the work of different poets, from newspaper articles and slogans is something of a success; [at first] it seems that everything is ours, it's true, it's real, not at all artificial, but then suddenly ... Why the mysticism? Why the symbolism? Why the religious worship of Ilyich? This is an insult to the memory of our leader.[26]

The 'Lenin days' in April (marking the anniversary of his birth) saw the premiere of the first opera to feature a specifically Soviet plot. The Leningrad Maly Opera hosted this pioneering production, a collective work by composers Arseny Gladkovsky and Yevgeny Prussak, entitled *Za krasnïy Petrograd* (For Red Petrograd). The opera enjoyed a long run, continuing through to the November celebrations for the eighth anniversary of the Revolution. The scenario was based on a phase of the Civil War, the Yudenich offensive of 1919, a time that was still fresh in the minds of the audience.

For the November celebrations, the Leningrad composer Pashchenko turned out a large five-act opera *Orlinïy bunt* (The Eagle Revolt). Asafyev claimed to have 'got it passed' as a 'useful *bïtovaya* opera'.[27] Stylistically, the music hardly ventured

---

become popular in Russia before the Revolution. The St Petersburg division of Dalcrozian Institute was founded in 1912, existed until the beginning of the war, and was revived in 1920.

[25] See fn. 22.

[26] Aleksandrov, 'Mistiki nam ne nado', *Rabochiy i teatr*, no. 9 (2 Feb. 1925), 8.

[27] Letter from Asafyev to Derzhanovsky of 13 Oct. 1925, GTsMMK, fond 3 (Derzhanovsky), ye. kh. 2, no. 787. '*Bïtovaya* opera' was opera of everyday life,

beyond Musorgsky and Rimsky-Korsakov, but the work as a whole was found more organically convincing than the other recent offerings:

> This is not a hurried compilation of promising but disconnected scraps of material, as we saw, for example, in the ballet *Red Whirlwind*. Nor is the music moulded to fit ready-made forms in arias and duets, as we saw in the opera *For Red Petrograd*.[28]

The opera's most popular number was a Cossack Dance, as staged by Lopukhov; it was also greatly assisted by the participation of Yershov (as Khlopusha), in one of the last roles of his distinguished career.

Another grand anniversary celebration was the centenary of the Decembrists' uprising, which garnered two operatic offerings. One was Vasily Zolotaryov's *Dekabristï* (The Decembrists), which set a precedent for state encouragement and supervision that became normal in the Stalin years. Zolotaryov was a member of the Myaskovsky–Lamm circle, and the group followed closely the twists and turns of their friend's engagement with the state. As Sergei Popov wrote to Lamm:

> M.M. [Ippolitov-Ivanov] says that the libretto has already been seen by some committee which gave its approval, and copies are now being prepared for five different bodies (Glavrepertkom, Glavpolitprosvet, Glavnauka, TsK Vserabisa, and one other) to be vetted for production; he wants to arrange for the music to be given an audition soon (he himself must already be acquainted with it), and so he's giving the piano score to the Board of Directors. Just imagine, my sister Olya told me yesterday that everyone at the [Bolshoi] theatre is in love with V[asily] A[ndreyevich]'s opera, that it's to everyone's taste, and premiere is already arranged for 6 October. A telegram has been sent to the composer: '*The Decembrists* has been passed. Your presence required. Come with all materials. Expenses paid'.[29]

At this point Zolotaryov had orchestrated only one act, and had to call on the assistance of several fellow musicians. With the rehearsal score in hand, he was rushed to Moscow from his home city of Odessa. As Popov reported further:

> Tonight, at 7 p.m., he will be presenting his opera in the Beethoven Hall. There'll be a good attendance: Lunacharsky hoped to come, and many from Political Censorship and the local Political Education department, together with musicians, conductors (the opera is also intended for a production in Kiev …), and litterateurs whose specialism is the Decembrists. The opera will be performed on the piano by Kramarov, a fine accompanist from the Bolshoi, the male parts will be sung by the composer, and the female parts by a singer of his acquaintance from Odessa.[30]

---

albeit the everyday life of the early seventeenth century in the present case.

[28] B. Valer'yanov, '"Orliniy bunt": ob opere kak takovoy', *Rabochiy i teatr*, no. 46 (17 Nov. 1925), 7.

[29] Letter from Popov to Lamm of 9 Aug. 1925, RGALI, fond 2743 (Lamm), op. 1, ye. kh. 176, l. 21.

[30] Letter from Popov to Lamm of 18 Aug. 1925, ibid., l. 25v.

But there was a problem. Zolotaryov's opera was primarily a lyrical piece, but grand spectacle was what the occasion called for. It was clearly too late to ask the composer for revisions, since the struggle to complete the full score was still in progress; the most stirring passages were reused as an expedient for a crucial new scene, a tableau of the Decembrists' uprising itself, to include the sound of gunfire and soldiers marching.[31] This artistic interference appalled the composer and failed to win the support of the critics. Yuri Shaporin had also declared that he would submit an opera of his own under the same title (although there was an alternative title of *Pauline Gebl*). In the event, he lagged behind Zolotaryov, and only had two scenes ready in time. These were performed nevertheless, at the former Mariinsky as part of the memorial events held on 29 December.[32] Again, Shaporin had conceived of his work in lyrical terms, but in his case, the inevitable interference was much more protracted, extending through the entire Stalin period (evidently, his mistake was the failure to complete the work on schedule). As the years passed, Shaporin had to contend with the demands of Socialist Realism and Russian nationalism before the resulting epic was considered suitable for performance. It had its premiere in 1954.

Even as opera attempted to reflect its Soviet environment, the status of opera in general was contended. Revolutionary content notwithstanding, it was perhaps to be considered another of those 'intermediate ideological forms' to be tolerated for now, in the expectation that it would wither away later. The Bolshoi centenary exposed this ambiguity. On the one hand, there was celebration and displays of state pride in the institution: the soprano Antonina Nezhdanova and the ballerina Ekaterina Geltser both received the title of 'People's Artist'. At the same time, there was unease, to the extent that Lunacharsky still felt it necessary to write an article justifying the Bolshoi's preservation. In the course of his argument, he presented his vision of Soviet opera in the future. To some extent, *Parsifal* was his unacknowledged prototype: he looked forward to the coming of the solemn heroic oratorio, 'a festive act, a people's revolutionary ceremony':

> Of course, this ceremony would best be combined with some sort of plot, an imposing myth reflecting the struggle between our ideas and feelings, but we should only seek out truth of a purely artistic kind. I conceive of the oratorio as an accumulation of orchestral and choral performances, an accumulation of dances in different tempos and in various costumes, all of which would be included in the act. The act can also be presented through elevated verse dialogue (or perhaps in rhythmic prose), which should alternate with arias, anthems, songs and other solo numbers.
>
> It would work best to the extent that it was solemn and free, and close to oratorio, although this would be oratorio with artistic staging, costumes and sets, to create not just an aural, but a visual unity.[33]

---

[31] A. Gozenpud, *Russkiy sovetskiy operniy teatr* (Leningrad: Gosudarstvennoye muzïkal'noye izdatel'stvo, 1963), 142.

[32] B. Gorev, 'Pamyati dekabristov', *Rabochiy i teatr*, no. 1 (5 Jan. 1926), 12.

[33] A. V. Lunacharskiy, 'Pochemu my sokhranyayem Bol'shoy teatr', *Rabochiy i teatr*, no. 6 (9 Feb. 1925), 6–7.

Finally, there was the underside to the celebrations, pointedly revealed in a report from OGPU, the political police:

> We have observed an increase, typically, in anti-Soviet attitudes, and this is particularly noticeable in Moscow, where, for example, we have found several persons in the Bolshoi Academy Theatre alone who have had to be exiled or imprisoned in the camps over the past few months. [...] These incidents, of course, do not indicate that there is any likelihood of counter-revolutionary organisations emerging from anti-Soviet elements in the theatre world, but we must take them into account as a further sign that anti-Soviet attitudes are on the increase among the intelligentsia.[34]

Returning to the opening idea of a temporary equilibrium between opposing ideological trends, we would like to cite a unique concert programme in which the music of both was present. This shows that at this juncture, the two trends were not always seen as completely irreconcilable. The concert in question took place on 2 June in Moscow Conservatoire's Chamber Hall, and was advertised by Mezhkniga as a benefit concert for MOPR,[35] an organisation under the umbrella of Comintern that provided help for revolutionary fighters and their families all over the world. It was this special twofold context of 'international' and 'revolutionary' that prompted the unprecedented mixture of aesthetics. Predictably, the programme opened with the *Internationale*. Part I featured arrangements of folk and revolutionary songs (such as 'The Proletarian Cudgel' and 'The Volga Boatmen'), and pieces with vaguely revolutionary credentials such as Borodin's 'Song of the Dark Forest' and Liszt's 'Lyon' from *Années de Pèlerinage*, together with innocuous Rimsky-Korsakov romances about nightingales and roses. The only genuine Soviet chorus was from an Agitotdel collection, 'Strike with the Hammer' (*Bey molotom*), by Mikhail Lazarev. Part II abruptly switched to typical ASM fare, with Casella's *Ninna-Nanna* and *Valse ridicule* from his *Five Pieces for String Quartet* and Prokofiev's Jewish Overture. After this progressive 'European' interlude, Part III concluded the concert with Russian operatic choruses and the ever-popular Polovtsian Dances. This concert stands as a compendium of Russian musical life in 1925, but such inclusiveness would soon become impossible.

---

[34] From the OGPU report on the intelligentsia of 15 Feb. 1925, quoted in Mikhail Vostrïshev, *Moskva stalinskaya: Bol'shaya illyustrirovannaya letopis'* (Moscow: Algoritm, 2008), 183.

[35] The concert was organised by Derzhanovsky and reflected his own inclusive outlook. (He had hopes that Mezhkniga would not only be importing sheet music from abroad, but also selling Soviet works there, including the mass revolutionary repertoire.) The choir at the concert was directed by Sergei Protopopov (a modernist composer and Yavorsky's partner), who also supplied some of the arrangements of revolutionary songs. As for the reception of this programme, an interesting comment can be found in Derzhanovsky's letter to Prokofiev (received 11 June 1925): 'At the concert for the benefit of MOPR which took place yesterday, much of the audience present had probably heard none of the music prior to this except the *Internationale*. Nevertheless, the Jewish Overture was met with colossal success and demands for an encore [...]' LPA, folder 8, 83.

※ ※ ※ ※ ※

N. Malkov, 'Za Krasnïy Petrograd' [For Red Petrograd], *Zhizn' iskusstva*, no. 18 (5 May 1925), 10–11.

The scenario of For Red Petrograd *was based on one of the campaigns from the Civil War. This is how the plot was summarised in a contemporary account (the meaningful names are translated in brackets):*

> The action takes place during 1919, in Petrograd and Gatchina, at the time of the Yudenich's unsuccessful offensive. Two opposing types are the basis of the whole opera: the worker Ilya Zheleznov [Iron], a steadfast and honest fighter for the ideas of October, and the master Puzanov [Big Belly] – a coward, informer and traitor.
>
> In Zheleznov's basement flat, his elderly mother cooks the dinner on a makeshift stove. Enter Zheleznov and his worker friends Molotov [Hammer] and Sermyagin [Hemp cloth]. Zinovyev's order is read out. The heavy artillery is heard. All, including Zheleznov's son Vasya, leave for the factory, where a rally will be held. At the rally, Zheleznov, Molotov, and Dasha stand on the one side, the master Puzanov and the vacillating Sermyagin on the other. People are signing up for the volunteers' detachment.
>
> At Gatchina, which is occupied by the Whites, in the yard of the commandant's house, White officers are torturing their Red prisoners. The defector Puzanov is also here. A new group of prisoners is brought in, among them Zheleznov and Dasha. Puzanov's witness statement proves fatal for Zheleznov – he is executed.
>
> The Reds attack. The Whites retreat from Gatchina. Puzanov tries to disguise himself, but he is exposed and executed. Apotheosis: the triumph of October, Lenin's behests are reaffirmed.[36]

N. Malkov
For Red Petrograd

Having opened the season with a rehash of Puccini's *Tosca* (renamed *The Struggle for the Commune*), the Academy Maly Opera closes it with a production of an *original* Russian revolutionary opera. This can only be seen as a step forwards, and as a sign of the desire to meet modernity halfway.

Admittedly, the idea of the opera *For Red Petrograd* was born outside the Academy theatres. The moderate success of *The Struggle for the Commune*, the failure of the ballet *Red Whirlwind* (which was not the composer's fault), and an unsuccessful scheme to turn *Les Huguenots* into *The Decembrists*, which did not manage to see the stage – all of this must have disheartened our Academy Opera, and we wouldn't have seen any more opera productions with a revolutionary tilt before the end of the season, were it not for a stroke of good luck.

---

[36] *Rabochiy i teatr*, no. 3 (19 Jan. 1926), 27–8.

So the Academy Theatre was fortunate: somewhere in the depths of the Culture Department of Gubprofsovet [Regional Trade Union Council], a group of people, on the initiative of S. I. Vishnya, had begun work on a plan for an original revolutionary opera, with a view to staging it at the Krasny Theatre. The libretto was written by V. P. Lebedev, the first time he had tried his hand at an opera libretto. Two young composers, A. N. Gladkovsky and Ye. V. Prussak, took it upon themselves to write the music. The celebrated singer N. N. Rozhdestvensky was assigned to direct the production, and he set about the task with vigour.[37]

The Academy Theatres found out about this interesting enterprise and acquired the production for the Maly Theatre, transferring the stage direction to N. V. Petrov.[38] So they would hardly be able to claim that staging *Red Petrograd* was their own initiative.

In the end, it is probably for the better that the new opera made its first appearance on an Academy stage. There, they have an orchestra that is good both in the quality of its musicians and in its ensemble playing. They also have talented and experienced singers, and can stage the opera without having to skimp on the scenery expenses. Still, it must be confessed that this production would have been better suited to the younger and growing Conservatoire Studio.

In any case, despite *Red Petrograd*'s many faults, the production is a watershed in the history of Russian opera during the revolutionary period. The wall has been breached. And it is altogether characteristic [of our times] that it was the Academy Opera itself that wanted to make the breach. This means that the powerful demands of the times can rouse even the sleeping.

And one more characteristic fact: it was two *young Leningrad* composers who volunteered to undertake this task. No musicians of the *previous* generation, who might have been more talented and experienced, would even have contemplated approaching the new revolutionary tasks. Meanwhile, we read and hear so much about music that is 'new' and 'contemporary'! Moscow, which sees itself the centre of contemporary Russian musical thought, even publishes a special journal under the auspices of GAKhN, devoted to propaganda for 'contemporary music', meaning the works of Moscow musicians who have banded together. And yet this publication does not so much as hint at revolutionary modernity in music. The academicians of *Contemporary Music* flee from revolutionary language like a vampire confronted by a crucifix [*kak chert ot ladana*].

And here in Leningrad we have seen the emergence of musicians who

---

[37] S. I. Vishnya was a cultural administrator in the Leningrad Trade Union Council; Vladimir Petrovich Lebedev (1869–1939) was a poet, literary critic and translator who belonged to the Yesenin circle. Nikolay Nikolayevich Rozhdestvensky (1888–1934) was a dramatic tenor equally renowned for his operatic and concert performances. Among his many roles was Oedipus, in the 1928 Russian premiere of Stravinsky's *Oedipus Rex*.

[38] Nikolay Vasilyevich Petrov (1890–1964), was better known as a director of drama rather than opera; he was notable for his introduction of Soviet plays into the repertoire of the Alexandrinsky Drama Theatre in Petrograd/Leningrad. He became a prominent figure in Soviet theatre and was awarded a Stalin Prize in 1948.

have resolved to devote themselves to the service of the Revolution. Nor are Gladkovsky and Prussak (and Deshevov, the composer of *The Red Whirlwind*) the only composers to have come out on the side of the Revolution. We already hear rumours that A. Pashchenko's opera *Pugachyovshchina* (with a text by S. Spassky) is nearing completion.

And so *Red Petrograd* must, in all fairness, be welcomed, not just for the agitational value of the mere fact of its existence, but also for the agitational value of its plot.

The opera's plot is drawn from recent revolutionary events (Yudenich's campaign of 1919). A simple intrigue (none of the opium of love here!) presents the fate of the two main characters: the worker Zheleznov, a steadfast fighter for Red Petrograd, and the master Puzanov, a base traitor, who brings about Zheleznov's death, but who is himself executed once the Reds overcome the Whites.

The action begins in Zheleznov's basement flat, where his elderly mother cooks dinner on a small stove, then moves to the factory (a wonderful set by A. A. Arapov),[39] and to Gatchina, the Whites' camp. A familiar everyday setting, modern everyday dress, and fragments of real life from the recent past that everyone remembers – all this creates a degree of truth that is unusual on the operatic stage and which has a powerful effect on the audience.

This deep connection between the opera's action and real life explains the immediate impact of many scenes on the audience. The reading of an edict on the conscription of workers, the leader's ardent speech at the rally, and many other episodes all excite the listeners and raise their spirits by reminding them of events they have all come through. There was evidence of this in the eager applause that came at the end of Act 1, during the pantomime depicting the victory of the Reds in the Gatchina battle (Act 3), and again after the apotheosis.

It must be admitted, however, that the production's agitational character arises more from the action than from the music, and even then more from the nature of the plot and the various situations than from plot development. The composers probably understood the shortcomings of the libretto, which suffers from longueurs (especially in Acts 2 and 3), and contains some purely operatic conventions (like Zheleznov's aria before the execution). Realising that the text fails to provide adequate material for a robustly structured music drama, the composers of *Red Petrograd* dubbed it a musical and a dramatic chronicle, hoping thereby, it would seem, to pre-empt any criticism of the lack of stage action.

This novelty cannot, of course, lay any claim to artistic significance. Revolutionary opera has yet to find its Glinka. At best, our musical pioneers can be likened to Glinka's predecessor, Cavos.[40] They lack the talent and experience needed to master the plot they chose. Aside from this, the

---

[39] Anatoly Afanasyevich Arapov (1876–1949) was a painter and set designer for theatre and cinema.

[40] Catterino Albertovich Cavos (1775–1840) was an Italian composer who settled in Russia. He is usually considered Glinka's predecessor because of his opera *Ivan Susanin* (1815), which had some influence on Glinka when he composed his own *Life for the Tsar* (1836).

haste in which the task was completed also prevented it from achieving success.

The music of the opera contains hardly any revolutionary elements beyond a few revolutionary tunes scattered around the score (including, of course, the *Internationale*). The lack of uplift and creative inspiration was particularly telling in the apotheosis, which was too official in character.

And yet one cannot say that the two composers were altogether lacking in talent. At any rate, there is no hackwork to be found in the piece. The music fails, quite often, to rise to the high level the situation demands, but it is written conscientiously and with sincerity nonetheless.

It should be said that the composers display a desire to speak in a simple language that would be accessible to the broad masses. In rejecting all the tricks so favoured by our musical gourmets, the composers have demonstrated that they understood their task.

The composers differ from each other in the character of their writing. Gladkovsky is a lyrical composer by nature: he likes songful, rounded melodies. He often shows a predilection for a folk-inspired style, and in this respect shows the influence of Borodin and Rimsky-Korsakov. Prussak has a rather different temperament. His music is characterful rather than primarily melodic. He was successful in creating the winter landscape of Gatchina, and illustrated the Gatchina battle scene well. The character of Puzanov, ignoble and selfish, also came out well. Prussak's writing (encompassing the third and fourth scenes and half of the fifth scene, up to Zheleznov's aria before his death) is more small-scale and mosaic-like; he shows tendencies towards harmonic effects and a declamatory manner, but his vocal lines often find themselves outside the harmonic plan and accordingly lack logic. As orchestrators, neither composer took advantage of the broad orchestral possibilities at their disposal, and they were clearly inexperienced in this area.

As for the staging, it was stylistically in keeping with the realist productions that are typically seen on the Academy stage. It was a conscientiously executed opera premiere, but nothing more.

[Comments on the performances of individual singers omitted.]

The opera was conducted with verve and confidence by S. A. Samosud, who took great care with the ensemble.

On the whole, in spite of all the aforementioned shortcomings, the new production must be considered an essential work of our times. It was awaited with interest by the Leningrad workers, and, to the best of our knowledge, the trade unions have already distributed tickets for a run of performances. The opera will probably feature in the next winter season as well.

V. Blyum, 'Fokstrot – tanets i muzïka' [Foxtrot: The Dance and the Music], *Zhizn' iskusstva*, no. 31 (4 Aug. 1925), 4–5.

This essay demonstrates that the campaign against the foxtrot (and similar dance music) was already in full vigour long before RAPM was able to take the lead. It also sheds some light on the shadowy figure of Vladimir Blyum, the theatre critic and censor, who was able to navigate the murky waters of ideological polemics with a cynical panache. Here, he rejects the dance as bourgeois decadence, but, in an unexpected turn, defends the music.

V. Blyum
Foxtrot: The Dance and the Music

In Soviet Russia, a campaign of persecution has been launched against the foxtrot and all related dance-types, such as the shimmy or the two-step. All 'eccentric' dances are under suspicion, and a hard line of sorts has been taken against them. And rightly so.

The foxtrot is a shameless imitation of the sexual act, and we wouldn't want it to pass its infection on to the workers' clubs, where it would undoubtedly render all cultural-enlightenment work futile.

But every dance, of course, is sexual, including the waltz, which even the chastest spinster would happily dance today. In the ceremonious minuet, the man only brushed against the woman's fingers, standing at a respectful distance, so at the time when the waltz became popular, a century ago, it seemed so dreadfully 'indecent' that the man and the woman should set off in close embrace, whirling round and round, mingling their breath in gasps, and so on. Nevertheless, in spite of the whining of prudes and hypocrites, time has shown that the waltz's sexuality is healthy, because it reveals itself here, so to speak, in artistic abstraction.

The foxtrot's sexuality is quite another matter. Here the 'sensual' surge departs from the traditional, abstract path and fixes its attention on a concrete moment, reconstructing it, so to speak, for its own sake, reducing and debasing the sexuality of dance down to the simplest sexual act. It is well known that the 'refined' bourgeois likes to stoop almost to the level of an amoeba – this is the source of his current great passion for prehistoric cultures and all kinds of exoticism.

Now we are materialists rather than ascetics, and have no desire to throw healthy sexuality overboard, but for the above reasons, we must nevertheless reject the foxtrot resolutely as the rotting fruit of the moribund class's declining culture.

Ah, but it seems we've tripped up over a serious misunderstanding along the way!

Why in the parks, restaurants and canteens, on the stage, and indeed everywhere 'light' music is cultivated, why can we not hear the characteristic *music* of the foxtrot? We'd hardly want to think that someone is banning the mere music of the foxtrot – this would seem too much like a joke! This would surely mean that we are throwing the innocent baby out with the bathwater!

Comrades, let us now come to our senses, and deal with this properly.

What is the music of every dance? It is *pure rhythm*, held together by the simplest, minimal melody. Even if we allow that melody (and harmony) [in general] can contain some qualitative colouring, the extreme simplicity of dance melodies, which completely dissolve in the rhythmic element, naturally excludes the possibility that *they* might possess any definite qualitative significance.

Would anyone seriously consider the melody of a Strauss waltz to be a representation of (healthy) sexuality, the kind that grips a mixed-sex couple of the human species dancing to these sounds? [i.e. are the couple's feelings prompted by the melody itself?] What then, are we to think that the melody of a song like 'Pupsik' [Dolly, a popular song] is definitely sexual? From our everyday experience, we know that this very 'Pupsik', as 'pure rhythm', can serve the broadest range of purposes – German troops, for example, marched along to its rousing strain as they began their occupation of Brussels.

The same goes for the *music* of the foxtrot. Its main element, the rhythm, came from Negro culture. This rhythm (and the simplest melody threaded onto it) is qualitatively indifferent: this rhythm, or one very similar, accompanies the Negros' war dances, their religious hymns, and their erotic orgies, and the Negro mother lulls her black child to sleep to the same rhythm. The *music* of the foxtrot lacks that very specificity that repulses our healthy consciousness in the *dance* of the foxtrot – it can't possibly be so specific, because this music is likewise 'pure rhythm'. There is not even a hint that the rhythm of the sexual act is being imitated here, I trust!

Others will say: no matter, for the bourgeoisie has linked this music to certain shameless body movements; and by means of more or less complex associative reflexes, this music will still stir up a mood of eroticism. But we can feel quite safe on this subject, because we, in removing the *dance* from social life, are breaking the bridge to that chain of reflexes, and the music will acquire its qualitative significance from the circumstances, from the present moment, from the ideological context, etc. The goal colours the means, after all – isn't that so? Imagine that you are walking to the railway station to the merry strains of the 'Electrique' shimmy for the purpose of meeting with a delegation of German workers. Is the quality of your mood going to change ever so slightly? Perhaps, indeed, your mood will be quite noticeably 'lifted'?

And others will retort: but this Negro music has been refracted through the bourgeois prism! Now the proletarian class element is, of course, nowhere to be seen here. But what about all those salon waltzes, polkas, minuets, tarantellas, mazurkas, and so on, that began their lives as folk dances only to become similarly 'refracted'? Yet no one would ever think of eliminating this undoubtedly 'bourgeois' music from the stage, the canteen, or the boulevard.

Devoid of its qualitative significance, dance music still carries in its rhythms an imprint of the era that gave birth to it. The waltz rhythm represents the era of coaches, gentry estates, the countryside after the early nineteenth-century revolutions, and the first confident steps of the bourgeois city. From this point of view, the *music* of the foxtrot, saturated with the rhythms of *modernity*, is, of course, greatly preferable.

Schematically speaking, the foxtrot rhythm, 'tuned' precisely to the rhythms of modern *urbanist* culture, keeps us in the orbit of modern *urbanist* moods, and infuses them with the *dynamic character* typical of modernity.

And this is a very good thing. Because we know that it all depends … The letters 'N-e-g-r-o' are associated for the French bourgeois with restaurants, with tap-dancing, with the Senegalese riflemen who cleared out the 'Boches' so effectively, and with the foxtrot (the dance), etc. For us, the associations are very different: we recall the Comintern, the Guinea plantations, the predatory character of imperialism, the problems of our policy towards the colonised nations, etc.

The same goes for the *music* of the foxtrot. There we hear modernity in all its variety: the intense dynamism of the era, the automobile klaxons, radio, propeller noise, fierce class stratification, rampant speculation, decadence, the ugliness and the good deeds of urbanism, the measured tread of the proletarian battalions and the hum of the Berlin Nacht-Lokal. *What we are going to select for ourselves from all of this*, depends not on the music of the foxtrot, but on the class, ethical, and other colouring of our dominant ideology. And the music (even of the foxtrot) will only amplify the ideological tone that has already been determined.

So there are no reasons to fear that the music of the foxtrot will lead to the 'decay' of our self-consciousness and of the self-consciousness of our working masses; nor will the music cause Soviet citizenry to 'mutate' into the bourgeoisie.

※ ※ ※ ※ ※

Igor' Glebov, 'Tretiy kontsert Sergeya Prokof'yeva' [Sergei Prokofiev's Third Concerto], *Sovremennaya muzika*, no. 10 (1925), 57–63.

This is a preview of Prokofiev's Third Piano Concerto prior to its Russian premiere in March 1925. The work enabled Prokofiev to regain an enthusiastic following in his native land for the first time since the Revolution, and initiated the chain of events that led to his return visit two years later. Asafyev attempts to claim both Prokofiev and his piece for Russia, and hopes that the concerto was the beginning of a trend towards national music that would be consummated in the forthcoming Second Symphony. As it turned out, that abrasive and complex symphony wrong-footed him badly, but in the long term, Asafyev was right. It was only as a national composer that Prokofiev was able to re-establish himself in the USSR after his return in 1935.

Igor Glebov
Sergey Prokofiev's Third Concerto

From the [two-]piano score of the concerto, we can already tell that Prokofiev's extraordinarily rich talent has found its full expression in this work and that it has developed to a stage where the ever-burning ardour of youthful temperament, the bold appeal of the music and that challenging tone of mischievous provocation are all brought together with an emerging maturity and wisdom, when the creative mind seeks a stable foundation for every formal decision, when technical perfection becomes mastery and when the richness of the material is rivalled by the virtuosity of its shaping. Acquaintance with the concerto's orchestral score only confirms its significance: the possibilities that could only be imagined [from the piano score] are indeed realised in distinct and clear contours, in the classical balance of the composition, and here the creative imagination, working at the highest intensity, weaves the simplest elements into a sturdy fabric of unexpected sonorities.

The freshness of the music, the brilliance of the treatment, the ingenuity of the combinations, the inventiveness of all the thematic rapprochements, exchanges, shifts and groupings, and finally, the confident pacing and the determination that can be felt in the presentation of musical thoughts – these are the first things to fascinate us in the concerto and win us over. In the composer's development, such a work is a pivot point that accumulates – after a careful selection – the best things that can be drawn from his past experience. This will serve as a starting point for future evolution, because the organic unity of the whole and its parts, and the rootedness of his habits, that is, the use of characteristically Prokofievian harmonic turns and whimsical ornamental lines, prove that the richness of means and their expressive value have not coincided merely by accident: here, everything is in its place, everything balanced, nothing exaggerated, nothing overbearing, which means that everything has grown naturally from intuitive creative impulses and will develop and mature just as naturally.

As a landmark in the composer's œuvre, Prokofiev's Third Concerto will also take pride of place in Russian music, next to Tchaikovsky's First Concerto, which it resembles to some extent. If I say that they are of equal value, I am not claiming that there is any formal resemblance between models: Prokofiev's consciousness digs deep into the folk-song element but solves the chosen task in an independent manner. The resemblance lies deeper, in the organic fusion with the greatest efforts and achievements of the Russian musical outlook, in the beautiful combination of novel invention with the power of expression, and in the typically Russian inclination to combine formal simplicity with emotional sincerity and immediacy.

The mood of the concerto is largely bright and cheerful. The rhythms are clear and distinct. The perennial contrast we find in Prokofiev's music is present here too (the carefree and unstoppable stream of sound catches on the jagged outcrops of the grotesque episodes). This contrast becomes especially vivid against the backdrop of a severe and astringent, archaically strict diatonicism, of which Prokofiev is the great master. He can be almost crudely schematic in his juxtaposition of diatonic chord layers, simplifying connections between them down to an extreme directness and concision, reaching a perfect expression of the primitive. But next, just a moment later, he manages to replace the 'stamping' vertical harmonic complexes with evasively gliding linear ornamentation, whose whimsical turns should succeed in breaking down and dispersing the dense masses of stable layers. In the Third Concerto, this means of galvanising musical movement is constantly deployed, to the point where even the main theme of the first movement 'jumps out' unexpectedly from the rushing stream, which emerges like a sparkling brooklet following a slowly unfolding folk-like tune, or is hacked out by eight muffled strokes from momentarily torpid sonorities.

However, let us not get carried away by our description of the work's means and devices. It is hard to convey the right impression simply by talking about it. No matter how much we might admire individual details or criticise certain shortcomings, the main point will evade us: namely, that pulsing of life which is spread everywhere, and the blossoming of the joyful composerly thought which is finding the art of expression. Whether in its splendid thematic fabric, in the luminous and tender melancholy of the introductory melody, or in the grotesquely whimsical patterns and Prokofiev's 'barbed wire' that catches the ear (by this I mean the prickly chords that accompany and yet overshadow the melodic line) – everywhere one can perceive a youthful and blossoming creative imagination, thinking that is sparkling and vivid, a life experienced to the full.

Prokofiev's Concerto is a profoundly Russian work, and its essence can only be divined when we throw away the usual textbook standards that have been ingrained in us by West-European musical scholasticism. Form and the structure of the fabric, the functional significance of every element that organises the 'action' in sounds, and even the character of the piano's passagework – everything here is subordinate to the idea of the tonic's undivided rule, the main tone as the centre of movement in every direction, as the point of arrival and departure, as the unified and stable moment. The tonic in this case is not only the closing element that stops the movement. No, its role is also that of an impulse: it arouses and moves. This may sound paradoxical, contrary to the rules of *Tristan*, to the idea that only the avoidance of the tonic can supply an endless melodic intensity; [but in this concerto,] it is the tonic's dominion that engenders a healthy and natural sense of something that is dynamic and mobile, without a hint of anything static or torpid. The cause of this phenomenon is simple: the pull of the bass voice is replaced by the pull of the central line upon all the other sonic elements, and within the central line is the pull of the main focal point. From this line and from this point, as from a *cantus firmus* (but in a dynamic sense), emanate parallel and perpendicular harmonic structures, formations of subvoices [*podgoloski*], ornamental patterns, more-or-less independent contrapuntal material, and, finally, what we might term 'coloratura' – the refined virtuosic passages of the *concertante* part. The foundation of all this is the rather static bass line, which is dominated by folk-style ostinato fifths and tonic-dominant relations.

It is obvious that such a composition is neither specifically polyphonic, nor homophonic/harmonic, nor is it based on the timbral complexes found in impressionist works. Seen from the vantage points offered by any of these systems, the music of the Third Concerto is imperfect. Although this concerto is indubitably *tonal* (it belongs to the glorious group of Prokofiev's sonatas and other pieces in C major), it has nothing in common with scholastic tonal plans that are sometimes contrived before the music itself. Although the concerto is dominated by a mobile structure that is horizontal and linear, it would not satisfy an avid contrapuntalist, because the principle of the subvoices [*podgolosochnost'* from Russian folk heterophony] penetrates almost every part of the composition, preventing the rigorous realisation of any majestically abstract polyphony. As for the colouristic aspect, neither the harmonic complexes that arise from the tonic's diatonic complements, both above and below, nor the instrumentation (economical and practical, very rational but plastically-expressive at the same time), leave any place for the insertion of passages that are colouristic for their own sake.

The texture of the Third Concerto rests on an intuitive premise: melos is the basis of musical dynamism. Not vulgar melody, which is in itself conditioned by the tonic–dominant harmonic formula, but the tense melodic element of song, from which stems the whole of Eastern musical culture – the culture that fed both the Mediterranean coast and the plains of Eastern Europe. Perhaps the time is right for West European music to receive new blood once again, just as it did at the dawn of its history, drawn from the sources where melos springs forth. There is only one of our composers who has long sensed and comprehended the meaning of this ongoing process thanks to his deep artistic insights. From the heights of their greatness, many Russian and European musicians have tended to pass by the 'roughly hewn creations' [*koryavïye zatei*] of the narodnik dreamer – by this, I mean Kastalsky. It always seems that people in general, and musicians especially, are afraid of anything that might broaden their horizons: they proclaim a single system universally perfect, remove any right to existence from the others. This is why people have not known or supported the system of Russian diatonic harmony (in essence not even Russian, but primordially universal) that Kastalsky sought out, and which stemmed from the constructive principles and dynamism of *znamenny* chant and folk song. It is high time to look closer at Kastalsky's achievement. Then we will be able to see that the idea he absorbed appears in the work of many musicians and scholars, among many of those who are seeking a more wholesome alternative that will allow them to leave the dead-end of a highly refined emotionalism and subjectivism.

No matter how complete a European Prokofiev may feel, in his work he is heading (although perhaps instinctively and through thickets of deviations) towards an affirmation of the structural primacy of melos. His stubborn inclination towards the affirmation and glorification of C major as a self-sufficient modal sphere rather than merely one of many keys is indicative of this. It is touching how much care he takes over the sculpting of his melodic relief, and this is characteristic too. But the main point is the originality of his diatonic harmonic language, which typically switches from one harmonic area to another, sometimes without any connecting tones whatsoever, at other times with the aid of special devices akin to portamento or vocal glissando, which can be found in folk singing and playing of instruments. This is why Prokofiev's Third Concerto sounds so unusually clear and free in the Russian manner, even though it has no folk themes, no deliberate stylisation, no folkloric refinements and no attempt to court the fashion for the everyday. This composition, written with sincerity and simplicity, is deeply resonant with modernity. Prokofiev is alien to the West. And if the work is accepted there even so, they will fail to comprehend its essence, but will simply be drawn to it, as they are to Musorgsky's music, as a source of life-giving water.

And, of course, speaking of the purity and clarity of their source, Prokofiev's works, which rest upon diatonicism and melody, are firmer and fresher than Stravinsky's, which are instrumental at heart, and poisoned by a foundationless instrumental chromaticism and by his mechanical and soulless sonic patterns. In this respect, Prokofiev and Stravinsky stand at opposite poles. Stravinsky instinctively feels the danger of instrumentalism and, walking at the edge of the abyss (*L'Histoire du soldat*), unexpectedly climbs a steep slope into the cult of melos: *Les Noces*, an invention of genius, is the result of this strong temptation. Prokofiev, on the contrary, usually allows songfulness to suffuse his instrumentalism, but since he is afraid to lag behind fashionable trends, he sometimes retreats before a terrible enemy – a soulless sarcasm – and, lacking will, creates terrifying images and masks, worthy of Gogol's imagination at the stage when that writer had lost his faith in the value of creativity.

We think that the sunny element will prevail over the phantasms [*navazhdeniya*] of the West in Prokofiev's music, if only his creative consciousness will wake up to the Third Concerto's intuitive revelations. It is remarkable that, from the beginning to the end, the concerto's principal material becomes ever more clearly defined, moving from a folk-like contemplative melody, through running ornamental figurations and the archaically modal main theme, through the fanciful turns of the second subject in the first movement and through the second movement (theme–variations–theme), veiled by chromaticism, to the clear and severe masculine outline of the main theme in the third and final movement, in which for the first time the elements of a symphonic finale, though already to be found dispersed through the compositions of Balakirev, Musorgsky, Borodin and Glazunov, found their complete and most perfect expression (in terms of concision and dynamism). And this is why it would be interesting to get to know Prokofiev's recently completed symphony: will he find a path to what he has been seeking – towards a synthesis, arriving at a Russian symphony, but not of the subjectively emotional type? To the symphony that generalises the aspirations of many diverse and ancient peoples as found in their songs, and which places the result within a structured sonic process, the symphony to which Glinka never found the path, the symphony Balakirev, that exceptionally gifted Russian underachiever, could only dream of.

1926

Guests from the West

In 1926, cultural relations with the Soviet Union were restored. Monteux's visit had been a great success; Szigeti had visited twice, and returned full of enthusiasm. His wife asked me if I would be interested in going there, and I accepted with delight. There were so many contradictory accounts of the Soviet Union that I was fascinated by the prospect of forming my own opinion, and of being the first French composer to restore musical links between the two countries. Wanda then got in touch with the brother of the diplomat Krasin, who took care of the arrangements for my tour, acting as an impresario. He made bookings for me to conduct three concerts in Moscow, and another three in Leningrad. Jean Wiener was to come with me as a [piano] soloist.[1]

Thus wrote Darius Milhaud, one of the first Western composers, and certainly the first modernist, to cross the Soviet frontier, where he was greeted by the banner: 'Workers of the world, welcome'. Milhaud and his wife spent several weeks in Leningrad and Moscow, visiting museums, attending performances at the opera and the Meyerhold Theatre, and concerts given by the conductorless Persimfans orchestra. They were clearly struck not only by the profusion of high culture, but also by the crowds of people in dark overalls filling the auditoriums of Imperial splendour.

When Milhaud describes his meetings with Soviet composers and performers, his tone becomes condescending, even anthropological at times:

Our concert was a great success, the musicians were compliant and quick to understand, and what an amazing audience we had! Such a love for music! In Leningrad, there were a number of musicians banded around the critic Glebov [i.e. Asafyev]. They all had a great desire to hear new French music, and we met up on several occasions. Popov, Kamiensky and Deshevov performed their own compositions for us, and pieces by their fellow composers. Wiener's performance of some syncopated music created a sensation. Kamiensky, 'the gentle giant', who was a fine pianist, had never heard anything like these rhythms, and tried in vain to imitate them! We had a wonderful time with these young men – there was nothing conventional about them, and they were clearly endowed with the poetic spirit.[2]

Writing later with the benefit of hindsight, Milhaud reckoned that he had detected 'a certain quality of greatness' in Shostakovich, 'a young man with dreamy eyes hidden behind enormous spectacles', who had shown Milhaud his First Symphony.

---

[1] Darius Milhaud, *Ma vie heureuse* (Paris: Editions Belfond, 1973), 153.
[2] Ibid., 155. Kamiensky is Aleksandr Danilovich Kamensky, pianist and composer (see Glossary).

But he was evidently more impressed at the time by Vladimir Deshevov, and maintained a correspondence with him after leaving Russia.³

The Russian audience for these Western composers, in turn, could find the new music brow-furrowing – not that the experience was unpleasant, but the point of it all was hard to discern:

> There were grins all round as Wiener gave his pieces an airing. They belonged to the restaurant, especially all the foxtrots. The music was cheery and yet tedious all at once. The public was quite bemused by Stravinsky's sonata 'à la Bach, with wrong notes' [*pod Bakha s fal'shivizmom*].⁴

A perceptive reviewer (possibly Derzhanovsky), elaborated further on this clash of cultures:

> There is a despotism of culture, school and tradition, powerful and severe. The Leningrad audience (and especially the musicians) absorbed contemporary French works only with extraordinary difficulty and intense effort. Here was the music from the far shore, music that had grown from the soil of some very different traditions and habits, and under the winds of musical trends that are quite unfamiliar and alien to us. In this music, perhaps not everything is equally valuable or even convincing, but it is subordinated to a certain logic.
>
> In order to understand and assimilate this music, you would have to be familiar with the everyday life of post-war France, and you would need to have witnessed that monstrous infection that consumed Europe in the guise of a fashion for all things 'Negro' and 'American'.
>
> Darius Milhaud is far from being a superficial composer, in spite of first impressions. His creative psychology is deeply modern, not to mention his technique, which is a wonderful example of polytonal writing with original counterpoint and an original palette of instrumental sonorities. He rushes to fill his fluid forms with timbral and rhythmic ideas and is afraid, it seems, of empty space. Thus sometimes we only have a thin thread of sounds, but the rhythm is pulsing, filling up every instant, and the emptiness sounds in the rests, shaping the form of the work.
>
> In this respect, the works of Jean Wiener are particularly interesting: they are distinguished by a strong and clear rhythmic structure. He deliberately leaves strong beats empty for whole periods, and strongly accents these rests [*sic*]. He has a great variety of asymmetrical rhythms, reminding us that he was the first to welcome jazz and propagandise for it. He touched upon several national dances of the American Negro in his cycle *Blues*. Wiener is weaker in his individual style than his fellow composers; the same can be said for his themes.⁵

---

³ Deshevov's correspondence with Milhaud can be found in Ayna Zhuravlyova, 'Vladimir Deshevov: desyatiletiye poiska', *Sovetskaya muzïka*, no. 2 (1991), 64–75.

⁴ Letter from Anton Dianov to Prokofiev of 10 Apr. 1926 (about the Moscow concerts of 6 and 7 April), LPA, folder 10, 240.

⁵ V.V. 'Muzïka s drugogo berega: Vtoroy kontsert Milo i V'yenera', *Rabochiy i teatr*, no. 14 (6 Apr. 1926), 11.

Alongside Russian musicians, Wiener (with the larger share) and Milhaud took the piano parts in a series of concerts devoted largely to contemporary French music. ASM and Rosfil jointly staged one of these concerts in Moscow on 7 April with the following programme:

Satie, *Morceaux en forme de poire*

Poulenc, *Suite en trois parties*

Wiener, *Trois blues*

Auric, 'Chanson gothique' (from the *Cinq poèmes de Gérard de Nerval*)

Auric, 'Avril'

Poulenc, 'Attributs' (from the *Poèmes de Ronsard*)

Wiener, *Deux blues chantés*

Milhaud, 'Lullaby' and 'Hassidic Song'

Milhaud, No. 2 from *Trois Rag Caprices*

Milhaud, *Saudades do Brazil* for piano

Wiener, *Sonate en trois parties*

Milhaud, *La création du monde* (piano 4 hands)

Milhaud and Wiener enjoyed all the advantages of official supervision, but also the limitations. They had exclusive guides accompanying them everywhere, ensuring their access, smoothing the way and providing information, from their visit to Lenin's tomb down to an evening spent at a 'clandestine night-club' (where a constantly ringing telephone aroused their suspicion). At a specially arranged visit to a school, specially prepared children sang the *Marseillaise* while holding a large portrait of Louise Michel, the famous Communard, as a gesture of Franco-Russian solidarity.[6] The polished cultural diplomacy worked well overall: the Frenchmen were moved by the Russians' quest for a new world and were sad to leave this country of promise for their familiar European world where 'the easy life, and the luxurious shops now seemed out of step with the times'.[7]

Milhaud's visit embodied the two most salient features of the 1925/26 concert season: the abundance of foreign musicians and a growing interest in new music. The Leningrad Philharmonia could boast 70 symphony concerts in a season, 29 of them conducted by foreigners, and 25 recitals, where over half (17) were given by foreign musicians.[8] The lucrative concert market began to attract the attention of Russian émigrés: here the test case was the tenor Dmitry Smirnov, who was allowed to visit, filled the theatres of Moscow and Leningrad, and, after paying 4000 roubles in tax, was still able to leave with a fee that made the trip well worth his while. Not only had he no problems leaving the country, but he was also allowed to take his nephew and niece with him.[9] Next in line stood Prokofiev,

---

[6] Milhaud, 145. Louise Michel (1830–1905), was a celebrated anarchist, who played an important role in the Paris Commune, in propaganda, administration, medical care and combat.

[7] Ibid., 146.

[8] 'Filarmonia v tsifrakh', *Rabochiy i teatr*, no. 10 (9 Mar. 1926), 13.

[9] Letter from Yavorsky to Prokofiev of 7 June 1926, LPA, folder 11, 13.

who was increasingly tempted to capitalise on the growing success of his music in Russia.

Indeed, everything indicated that the time was right for Prokofiev. The Leningrad production of his opera *Love for Three Oranges* had been a success (more on this later), and Prokofiev now displaced Scriabin on the season's concert programmes. There was still room for another Scriabin cycle, including the premiere of the Symphonic Poem in D minor, played from the manuscript, with Lunacharsky's usual pre-concert talks. But the main excitement was to be found elsewhere. Monteux gave the Russian premiere of Prokofiev's *Chout* in a concert performance, together with Honegger's *Pacific 231*, Stravinsky's *Song of the Nightingale* and *The Rite of Spring*. This had a much greater effect on both public and critics. The critic Matias Grinberg, for example, wrote that he wanted a whole month of Prokofiev concerts, so that all of his music to date could be heard.[10] But there was also some grumbling too, as in this letter from the musically conservative Shteynberg to Myaskovsky:

> Did you manage to attend Monteux's concerts? Here [in Leningrad] he played a lot of 'new music' and it was a great success. I was quite impressed with Honegger's *Pacific*, although my impression was not so much musical, but stemmed from my childhood love of steam engines. Prokofiev's *Chout* is witty at times and creates a fine sound, but walking on your hands all the time like this becomes tedious after a while. It is probably much better with stage action. Stravinsky's *Ragtime* is dreadful rubbish (although this wasn't conducted by Monteux).[11]

Stiedry won acclaim for his performances of *The Rite of Spring* in both Moscow and Leningrad – curiously, he yoked it to Mozart's Symphony No. 38 (perhaps to suggest that the Stravinsky was already a classic). He also performed Hindemith's Concerto for Orchestra at the Bolshoi Theatre, placing it alongside Beethoven's Fifth and Wagner's *Meistersinger* overture, while Krenek's Violin Concerto featured in another of his concerts.

Several Russian performers and collectives vied to become the leading new-music ensemble. Persimfans was one, always prepared to invest the necessary time to learn demanding new pieces, such as *Pacific 231*, or Prokofiev concertos. Two Russian conductors, Malko and Vladimir Dranishnikov, were encouraged and advised by Asafyev: Dranishnikov presented Roger-Ducasse's *Orpheus*, Toch's *Chinese Flute*, and Stravinsky's *Ragtime*, and also *Love for Three Oranges* at the opera; Malko presented Krenek's Piano Concerto (with Yudina), Myaskovsky's Seventh Symphony, Schillinger's *The Tread of the East*, and, most famously, Shostakovich's First Symphony. Asafyev's influence was also stamped on the first Russian performance of Stravinsky's *Mavra* (with piano), and the Russian premiere of *Les Noces*, organised and conducted by Mikhail Klimov, which attained a

---

[10] M. Grinberg, 'Vperyod k Prokofievu!', *Rabochiy i teatr*, no. 10 (9 March 1926), 12–13.

[11] Shteynberg's letter to Myaskovsky of 14 Mar. 1926, RGALI, fond 2040 (Myaskovsky), op. 2, ye. kh. 281, 18. The Ragtime was played by Dranishnikov at the Leningrad Philharmonic.

retrospective significance for later commentators, thanks to the participation of Shostakovich, who took one of the piano parts (the other three pianists were Yudina, Isay Renzin and Alla Maslakovets).

Similarly, the Myaskovsky–Lamm circle advised and promoted the conductor Konstantin Saradzhev, who was responsible for many symphonic premieres, and was even sent to Prague to conduct an ASM concert there.[12] His abilities, it seems, fell short of his ambition and enthusiasm. When he was put in charge of the 'Moscow Week' concerts in Leningrad, Malko recalled that Saradzhev 'buried' both Myaskovsky's Sixth and Shebalin's First Symphonies, and the reception of the series was generally very cool, so that Asafyev had to admit that it was a near-failure.[13] Still, the traditional rivalry between the two capitals was likely to have contributed an element of critical *Schadenfreude*, and it was not only the performances under Saradzhev's baton, but also the pieces themselves that failed to please. On hearing Shebalin's First, Glazunov said that 'to write a symphony like this, one need hardly bother to study' (although his dislike for even such mildly modernist works was generally automatic). Knipper's Symphony, included on Asafyev's insistence, and excerpts from Polovinkin's *Telescope* also flopped, and only Aleksandrov's music was received with any warmth. The one work to receive almost universal praise was Prokofiev's Third Piano Concerto, which admittedly fell outside the general theme of the series; Feinberg, as soloist, made the concerto his own, Asafyev reckoned.

But aside from the contingencies of Saradzhev's conducting and some of the works performed, there were particular reasons why Moscow–Leningrad friction should run beyond the level of the usual rivalries at this juncture. A few months prior to the Moscow Week, Leningrad's music circles had suffered a serious split. Asafyev had been immersed in the affairs of ASM in Moscow, and suddenly found that in his home city of Leningrad, the mantle of 'contemporary music' was appropriated by a group with conservative leanings, led by members of Rimsky-Korsakov's family: his son Andrey, a critic, his wife Yuliya Veysberg, a composer, and his son-in-law, Maximilian Shteynberg. They formally declared themselves to be Leningrad ASM, or LASM, and knew they could additionally rely on the support of Glazunov. Asafyev considered the manœuvre illegitimate, and refused to join, instead involving himself in the more 'leftist' activities of the Circle of New Music, together with Dranishnikov and the musicologist Semyon Ginzburg. Shostakovich, as a student of Shteynberg, initially hedged his bets: although he was remote from LASM's conservatism, he agreed that his First Symphony would receive its premiere in one of their concerts. Asafyev could not bring himself to attend, and his relations with the composer were never cordial thereafter. Eventually Shostakovich and many others would desert LASM, but the alternative Circle had no institutional base. In the medium term, the lack of any effective counterpart to Moscow's ASM impeded the promotion of new music in Leningrad (in the long term, of course, neither ASM survived). Since Asafyev had organised the 'Moscow Week', it was bound to be met with suspicion from LASM.

---

[12] *Sovetskoye iskusstvo*, no. 1 (Jan. 1926), 101.

[13] Letter from Asafyev to Derzhanovsky of 15–25 Nov. 1926, GTsMMK, fond 3 (Derzhanovsky), ye. kh. 2, no. 815.

A reciprocal concert of Leningrad music was held in Moscow afterwards, featuring the music of Veysberg and Shteynberg, again under the baton of Saradzhev, with the same dubious results as Asafyev noted.[14]

ASM's chamber concerts still serviced a familiar circle of friends and allies: Myaskovsky, Aleksandrov, Feinberg, Roslavets, Shirinsky, Shaporin, Protopopov, Polovinkin. Viktor Belïy, a member of Prokoll and future RAPMist, contributed to one of the programmes as a conscientious student of Myaskovsky, with a Prelude, a Fugue and his first Piano Sonata. Against the background of these traditionalists, Scriabinists and Myaskovskians, Alexander Mosolov's abrasive ultra-modernist Fourth Piano Sonata stood out, promising a refreshing change in ASM's direction.

Much new music in the ASM vein was played by the Stradivari Quartet, alongside works by Beethoven, Brahms and Glazunov. Quartets from the West by Casella, Hindemith and Milhaud were heard, and both Bartók and Schoenberg were represented by their respective second quartets. Among the contemporary Russian works played this season were Myaskovsky's D-minor Quartet (dating back to 1910), Roslavets's First Quartet, and a quartet by the Scriabinist Dmitri Melkikh.

New music had by now gained a sizeable following, and the venues and concert administrators took notice. Even Rosfil, despised by many in ASM for its purely commercial priorities, now decided it was time to organise orchestral concerts of new music at the Bolshoi. Derzhanovsky, instead of feeling vindicated, was dismayed at the prospect of seeing his influence and prestige diluted. He tried to gain the favour of Yavorsky, who was at this time Lunacharsky's right-hand man for musical affairs. Instead of pulling strings for him, Yavorsky dismissed Derzhanovsky's petitioning (understandably) as mere artistic sectarianism:

> We are talking here about the promotion of a new culture with the assistance of art, and not about the promotion of a little group of people, and we must clear the way for new young musicians, instead of making propaganda for old-timers who like to dabble in a little composing and performing.[15]

On the ballet stage, the creation of new and specifically Soviet repertoire suffered a setback in 1926. Deshevov presented his ballet *Jebella* [*Dzhebella*] for audition, the scenario featuring a liberation struggle by colonials against their English masters. Three forces were represented by the dancers: heroic Soviet sailors, foxtrotting English imperialists, and the colonised peoples of the East. Since imperialism was a popular topic at the time, the prospects for the ballet seemed good, and it was complete through even to the orchestration when the audition was held. Unfortunately for Deshevov, a blander scenario would have been safer, and the ballet never saw the stage, apparently due to some unspecified political mistakes in the libretto by Radlov and

---

[14] Letters from Asafyev to Derzhanovsky of 24 Jan. and 11 Mar. 1926, ibid., nos. 797 and 802.

[15] Letter from Yavorsky to Protopopov of 19 May 1926, publ. in *B. Yavorskiy: Stat'yi, vospominaniya, perepiska*, ed. by I. S. Rabinovich (Moscow: Sovetskiy kompozitor, 1972), 349.

Piotrovsky.¹⁶ As for opera, nothing with a Soviet topic was forthcoming, and the Mariinsky resorted to a new production of *Die Meistersinger* for its 7 November celebrations. The influx of 'the new bourgeoisie' in the theatres explains the Maly's otherwise baffling decision to introduce a new production of D'Albert's *Tiefland* (1903), an extravagant throwback to the heyday of pre-Revolutionary Symbolism. In a similar vein, *Kitezh* was revived at the Mariinsky under Albert Coates. But the Mariinsky's most notable premieres were decidedly modern: Stravinsky's *Pulcinella* and Prokofiev's *Love for Three Oranges*. The latter was particularly groundbreaking, and gave Prokofiev a cult status in the Soviet Union. Milhaud was present to witness the success of *Three Oranges*:

> Among Leningrad composers, there is a true renaissance to be witnessed. An enthusiasm for Prokofiev has now supplanted the remnants of Scriabinism among the members of this youthful school. Prokofiev's influence is significant: I listened to his *Love for Three Oranges* in the Leningrad Opera, and I can vouch for the fact that the famous March has become a true folk tune, destined to enter the annals of a new folk music.¹⁷

Having started with Milhaud's visit, the year ended with a series of concerts given by another international luminary, Alfredo Casella. Unlike Milhaud, Casella did not write much about his first Soviet trip in his memoirs (he covered his second trip of 1935 in much more detail), but his experience was evidently similar to Milhaud's, even if the tone is more dispassionate:

> I was the first Italian musician to go back over there after the Revolution. It was a fascinating trip, and I was received very warmly everywhere I went. The orchestras were not of the first rank, but the audiences seemed to have a real thirst for music and were very enthusiastic. The country was sombre, and looked as if it was inhabited solely by vagrants, since everyone was dressed in such dismal rags. I found some musicians I knew from before the war, and it was a real pleasure to see Glazunov again. [...] Moscow already appeared very much Americanised to me, much less Asiatic than it had been in the times of Nicholas II. Leningrad, on the other hand, was utterly miserable and squalid.
>
> I met Rykov (then President of the Council of People's Commissars, and who would later meet with such a tragic end), Lunacharsky (who was in charge of the arts), and lastly Kameneva, who was Trotsky's sister (and who has also been removed from the scene recently, I believe).
>
> The Artworkers Union [Rabis] held a splendid reception in my honour, during which I was offered honorary membership of the organisation. The next day, a special delegation came to the hotel, and with much 'pomp and circumstance', they presented me with my membership card.¹⁸

Casella's concerts generated much excitement among ASM's members and followers. The emphasis was placed on new Italian music (Casella complained that

---

¹⁶ Zhuravlyova, 69.

¹⁷ Darius Milo, 'Muzykal'naya zhizn' SSSR', *Rabochiy i teatr*, no. 27 (4 July 1926), 11.

¹⁸ Alfredo Casella, *I Segreti della Giara* (Florence: G. C. Sansoni Editore, 1941), 233–4.

Soviet Russia was overrun by Germans), but Casella's idol, Stravinsky, was also present in the programmes:

> 3 December 1926, The Chamber Hall of the Moscow Conservatoire
> Malipiero, Four Atonal Preludes [*sic*, should be 'Autumnal']
> Castelnuovo-Tedesco, *Cypresses*
> Casella, 11 Children's Pieces (performed by the composer)
> Casella, *L'adieu à la vie* par Andre Gide, 2 songs from Tagore
> Stravinsky, Sonata (Casella performing)
> Casella, Concerto for string quartet

In another, orchestral programme (5 Dec. 1926 in Moscow), there was also a concerto by the then little-known Vivaldi, representing the golden past of Italian music – Casella was the leading figure in the Vivaldi revival, only in its early stages at this point. This concerto shared the programme with two neoclassical works inspired by the revival, Vittorio Rieti's concerto for flute, oboe and clarinet with orchestra, and Casella's own Partita for piano and orchestra (Casella played the solo part, badly, according to Asafyev). The concert's international-friendship element took the form of Casella's orchestration of Balakirev's *Islamey*, and the whole programme ended with Casella's orchestral rhapsody *Italia*. Aside from these concerts, Casella's presence was marked by the advance importation of a dozen of his works by Mezhkniga. Even so, his engagement with progressive Russian musicians seems to have been more limited than in Milhaud's case. Asafyev, frank as ever, found him 'conceited, and self-important, with the outlook of the salon'.[19]

Neither Casella nor Milhaud could have as much impact as the news that Prokofiev would soon make his first return visit to Russia since his departure in 1918. Bringing him back, even just for a tour, was a significant coup initiated by Lunacharsky. Back in 1925, Lunacharsky had instructed Yavorsky to send out three identical letters to Prokofiev, Stravinsky, and the pianist Alexander Borovsky. These were not written as warm invitations: opening with a standard bureaucratic flourish: 'In response to your query ...',[20] each letter continued in a headmasterly

[19] Letter from Asafyev to Derzhanovsky of 2 Dec. 1926, GTsMMK, fond 3 (Derzhanovsky), ye. kh. 2, no. 817.

[20] The appearance of the word 'query' here would seem to imply that the exchange was initiated by the three musicians, but this need not have been so. I am grateful to Svetlana Savenko for the observation that this was simply a rhetorical formula, used whether or not any prior query had actually been made (even though the recipient of this phantom query was identified here as Lunacharsky's deputy Pavel Novitsky). What we know for sure is that on 21 July 1925, the Politburo deliberated on and granted Lunacharsky's request that Prokofiev, Stravinsky, and the pianist Alexander Borovsky be allowed to visit the USSR (*Vlast' i khudozhestvennaya intelligentsiya*, 58). Prokofiev had some awareness of these developments: during the preceding months and weeks he had met with several cultural figures from the USSR and discussed various projects. Some of these discussions were quite informal, but the meeting with Boris Krasin had official status. It took place on 24 July, when the favourable Politburo decision has already been taken, although

vein, as if the suspension of three ill-behaved schoolboys was being graciously revoked:

> The Government agrees to your return to Russia. It agrees to give you complete amnesty for any offences that you might have committed previously. Obviously, the Government cannot guarantee your immunity in the event of any future counter-revolutionary behaviour on your part. The possibility of entering and leaving the RSFSR according to your wishes is also fully guaranteed.[21]

The letters passed through Bryusova's hands last before being dispatched, and she decided to append a warmer phrase to Lunacharsky's text:

> I can be sure that the whole musical public of the Soviet Union will sincerely welcome your return.[22]

For Stravinsky, Bryusova's addition was not nearly enough to offset the rest of the letter, and he took the invitation as an insult that merited a sarcastic reply, which he penned in French rather than Russian, for added effect. Prokofiev and Borovsky, however, were much more eager to return, and held negotiations with Yavorsky during one of his trips abroad. The outcome was that they would each make an initial tour in 1927. But it was not long before Prokofiev felt he was being sucked into a bureaucratic mire:

> My negotiations with Russia are still in progress, but I've already been given permission to receive a pass certificate [*prokhodnoye svidetel'stvo*], a document I'll use only during my stay in the USSR – on leaving, I can once again become a subject of Dr Nansen [referring to the League of Nations' Nansen passports for stateless persons]. Persimfans is giving five concerts of my works, and everything would be going very well indeed if it wasn't for the awful squabbling between the various concert organisations. At first, it was the Leningrad Philharmonia that invited me – this is a state organisation. Then Rosfil was resurrected (this is a joint-stock organisation that had been wound down for a while), and I was warned that this joint-stock organisation was going to swallow up the Leningrad Philarmonia,

Prokofiev was not apprised of this. During the meeting, Krasin tried to persuade Prokofiev to accept a commission from TsIK (the Central Executive Committee) to write a Cine-Symphony for official celebrations of the twentieth anniversary of the 1905 revolution; Prokofiev declined the commission, but more importantly, he agreed that he should come to the Soviet Union for a concert tour. It is most likely that Borovsky's name appeared on the list owing to his connection with Prokofiev (he was his classmate and friend) – it could have been mentioned in one of the earlier preliminary discussions with Prokofiev (Lunacharsky, in his instructions to Yavorsky dated 3 August, gives Borovsky's address simply as c/o Prokofiev). Stravinsky, on the other hand, seems to have been completely unaware of the impending invitation.

[21] B. Yavorskiy: *Stat'yi, vospominaniya, perepiska*, 318.
[22] Bryusova's letters to Borovsky, Prokofiev and Stravinsky, RGALI, fond 2009 (Bryusova), op. 2, ye. kh. 4, ll. 1–2.

even though this belonged to the state. Then Glavnauka, a higher-level state institution, sent me a memo saying that I can sign an agreement with no one but Rosfil or Persimfans, and yet privately I was warned that Glavnauka will itself be disbanded some time soon. Can you make the least sense of all this nonsense?[23]

As it happens, we can make some sense of the situation. The business of organising concerts was too prestigious for the Soviet state to leave it entirely to the rigours of the NEP marketplace. Accordingly, state and private bodies were involved alongside each other, and individuals in senior positions were often trying to undercut their rivals. On the surface, the city centres of the two capitals carried an endless succession of star-studded concert posters, but behind this was the confusion that Prokofiev witnessed. But Lunacharsky took personal pride in seeing the capitals enjoy a rich musical life the equal of most major European cities – if Russia was to serve as a beacon for the future, it would hardly do if eminent foreign guests found it culturally backward. He also took trips abroad, as a cultural ambassador, and as Goldenweiser noted after one of these, he looked 'filled-out, in rude health' and 'very pleased with himself'.[24] Bitter power struggles were in progress at the top of the Party – Zinoviev and Kamenev had fallen out with Stalin, and joined forces with Trotsky in a United Opposition, only for all three to find themselves ejected from the Politburo in the autumn. But for Lunacharsky and his ministry, life was good, and the arts flourished.

As far as the average concert-goer was concerned, this was the state of musical life in 1926. Behind the scenes, though, the foundations were being laid for the post-Lunacharskian cultural life that was to emerge at the end of the decade. In spite of its ambitions, RAPM was still only capable of playing a marginal role here. They enjoyed a minor success in securing a publishing deal with Mostorg MONO (the trading section of the Moscow Education Department) for their new journal, *Muzïka i Oktyabr'* [Music and October], but the arrangement proved unstable and the journal folded after only five issues. Shulgin brought out an ORKiMD publication, *Muzïka i revolyutsiya* [Music and Revolution], which was placed on a much more solid footing than its RAPM rival. Although ORKiMD had launched itself on a very thin manifesto, it enjoyed the considerable benefit of Muzsektor's patronage, and Shulgin's astuteness also proved useful. *Music and Revolution* could boast contributions from Bryusova, and Asafyev and Lunacharsky (who provided a vague, almost Symbolist effusion about music and revolution as 'great sisters'). Asafyev's appearance was fitting, since his earlier essay 'Composers! Keep up!', from 1924, had been a major inspiration for Shulgin and ORKiMD.

On the other hand, common goals brought ORKiMD face to face with RAPM at the Glavpolitprosvet conference on 'musical enlightenment' which took place in March 1926. The gathering was not to be a mere talking shop: Robert Pelshe, Head of Glavrepertkom, declared the conference to be a stone thrown into the calm and deep waters of musical life.[25] Shulgin, Sergeyev, and Lebedinsky all spoke on music

---

[23] Letter from Prokofiev to Koussevitzky of 18 Nov. 1926, LPA, folder 46, f. 217.

[24] A. B. Gol'denveyzer, *Dnevnik: tetradi vtoraya-shestaya* (Moscow: Tortuga, 1997), 48.

[25] S. Korev, 'Pervïy kamen', *Sovetskoye iskusstvo*, no. 4 (Apr. 1926), 29–37.

for the masses, and Pelshe himself grappled with the thorny issue of what kind of material should constitute a foundation for new Soviet music, and in particular, for the Soviet mass song. So far, he said, folk song was considered appropriate, on the grounds that this kind of music was familiar to the masses. But this argument was faulty, since familiarity would also have made 'philistine' and 'light-genre' music equally acceptable. Pelshe explained that the Arts Department of Glavpolitprosvet believed the folk-song argument was not properly communist, but a throwback to narodnik attitudes [*muzïkal'noye narodnichestvo*]. Folk music, he said, was the vehicle for an ideology alien to the proletariat, even if it was not as pernicious as 'light-genre' music. Accordingly, there was no need to discourage or suppress folk music, but at the same time, it did not deserve to be promoted as the foundation for the future music of the Soviet Union.

But Pelshe also cautioned against the 'leftist' route, the assimilation of 'the sounds of the city' into music. The result was the chaotic urban symphony, which, he said, represented the negative aspects of modern culture. What, then, was the way forward? Here lay the problem. All Pelshe could suggest was a return to vague Proletkult ideas of developing the 'rhythms of labour' in music.[26] The participants in the conference could speak confidently and concretely about all that they opposed, but they were much vaguer about what should replace the rejected musical genres.

While Politprosvet continued its search for the theoretical base that would allow Soviet mass music to advance, RAPM, ORKiMD, and even Prokoll sought to establish their own national networks of music circles and groups. The 'blonde giant' Davidenko, who only yesterday had admired European modernism, now campaigned in the provinces for a new approach to the art of composition. His experiences were often disheartening, like this visit to the composition faculty of Rostov Music College:

> The atmosphere is one of complete stagnation [*zatkhlyashchaya*] ... The 'creative' lot show off their brand-new ties, their gold teeth, and their shoes of patent leather and suede. They have flings with women in short skirts, and boast about their knowledge of harmony, so on the whole flirting is their major subject, and composition an obligatory discipline studied in order to gain them laurels in the drawing-rooms. Public life [*obshchestvennost'*] is very weak – it's very *mauvais ton*.[27]

Davidenko and his comrades-in-arms were unhappy with Lunacharsky's version of Soviet music culture, with its drawing rooms, new ties and suede shoes. With little or no encouragement from above, they would set out to overturn it from below.

---

[26] Ibid.
[27] Letter from Davidenko to Shekhter and Beliy of 8 Jan. 1926, publ. in *Aleksandr Davidenko: Vospominaniya, stat'yi, materialï*, ed. by N. Martïnov (Leningrad: Muzïka, 1968), 138.

※ ※ ※ ※ ※

Viktor Belyayev, '"Proizvodstvennaya" muzïka (po povodu "Derevenskoy simfonii" Kastal'skogo' ['Production' Music: on Kastalsky's *Village Symphony*], *Zhizn' iskusstva*, no. 1 (5 Jan. 1926), 22–3.

Former church composer Alexander Kastalsky initially worked for the Proletkult and later joined RAPM, where he was the only experienced composer. 'Production music' (proizvodstvennaya muzïka) was a Proletkult term later taken up by RAPM, but usage was too varied or vague to extract a definition. ASM's Belyayev attempts to make sense of the term as best as he can in his critique of Kastalsky's pioneering attempt to construct a large-scale work on Proletkult/RAPM precepts.

This background information, together with the hostile tone of the article, would suggest that Kastalsky and ASM were natural opponents, but this was not in fact the case. On Kastalsky's death, at the end of the year, ASM decided to present a series of memorial concerts, with Asafyev as the prime advocate. Kastalsky was not only a choir director and composer, but also a significant and original thinker on music theory and pedagogy, especially in the area of Russian folk song – here, Asafyev considered him to be his mentor.

Understandably, Asafyev had been upset by the article, and contacted the relevant sub-editor at Artistic Life *to discuss whether it should be published at all, wondering if Belyayev would have adopted such a mocking tone if he had realised that Kastalsky was seriously ill (his terminal decline, as it turned out). The sub-editor disagreed, arguing that the article was an intelligent critique, whatever the tone. Asafyev decided to let the matter rest; aside from his regrets over the article's content, he was still heartened to see that such a prestigious and widely read publication as* Zhizn' iskusstva *should publish the writings of ASM members.*[28]

One strange incident marred the commemorative concerts somewhat. Prior to the Revolution, Kastalsky was well known as the long-time director of the Synodal Choir, and in this capacity, he had written many sacred works. The commemoration would have seemed very lop-sided if this facet of Kastalsky's career was passed over in silence, so several sacred works were included in the programmes of the concerts. Given the circumstances, Glavrepertkom approved the performance of these works, but at a late stage, one of Lunacharsky's deputies, Novitsky, chose to override the official censor's decision.[29]

---

[28] Letter from Asafyev to Derzhanovsky of 28 Dec. 1925, GTsMMK, fond 3 (Derzhanovsky), ye. kh. 2, no. 794.

[29] Letters from Derzhanovsky to Asafyev of 1 Feb. and 3 March 1928, RGALI, fond 2658 (Asafyev), op. 1, ye. kh. 542, ll. 18 and 20.

Viktor Belyayev

'Production' Music: on Kastalsky's *Village Symphony*

Each era has its own style, and we can only depart from one era by taking steps towards a new style. In everything, from clothes to artworks, people cannot but subordinate their inventiveness to the demands of the era's dominant style. And if they fail to do so, adhering instead to the 'old ways', then they create stylistic anachronisms, which are all the more strange, and even ridiculous, the further back into the past they go.

In the age of aeroplanes, the mail coach of the 'good' old days becomes an anachronism. In the age of trams, office blocks and typewriters, it would be strange to see farthingales and crinolines. In the age of steam mills, the psychology of the male and female workers there has changed utterly from the psychology of Romantic-period millers, and so on.

In accordance with these changes of style, or, to be precise, changes in the mode of production, the style of art and music will also change. In this respect, all varieties of good music (i.e. music that fits well with the style of its era) will be production music, and therefore contemporary production music will be nothing other than good contemporary music. This theoretical matter is so clear that it should not require special explanation.

But in practice it is not clear for everyone, and a number of misunderstandings have arisen because of this, such as the most recent example, Kastalsky's *Village Symphony*, which has just been performed in Moscow and which some of our critics declared to be the first example of 'production' symphony music.

So, of what does the 'production nature' of Kastalsky's *Village Symphony* consist? Let us take a look at this work firstly from a purely musical point of view.

In this respect, indeed, we can consider genuine 'production music' to be exclusively the kind of music that not only displays a high level of compositional technique, but that also in some way creates paths that point to the future. The kind of music that remains below the level of our age, in its contrapuntal, harmonic, instrumental, or other aspects, cannot be considered 'production music'. We cannot conceive of contemporary production music being arranged for the orchestra of horns, which dates back to the feudal era; it is equally implausible that contemporary production music could be written with technical means that have long since become obsolete, overtaken by later achievements. Where Kastalsky's symphony is concerned, its ideas and technique take us back to the pre-Glinka period, when Russia's 'enlightened dilettanti' had no conception of symphonism and its foremost attribute, *dynamism*. Listening to Kastalsky's symphony, we can imagine ourselves sitting together with the young Glinka at a concert given by players from an orchestra of serfs, performing potpourris of Russian songs 'arranged for two bassoons and two horns'. Kastalsky's methods for incorporating folk themes in his symphony had already been rejected by the 'New Russian School'. The composers of that era had already worked out methods of treating the folk 'raw material' that cannot be forgotten or ignored today, but only brought to perfection.

From the technical point of view, we should note Kastalsky's weak and outmoded compositional technique in general, his complete inability to master the resources of the modern orchestra, his feeble command of form, his rhythmic monotony and his complete impotence where symphonism is concerned, i.e. in the matter of dynamic and wilful stimuli that could forge a self-sufficient artistic whole.

From the formal point of view, the *Village Symphony* is hybrid in form, combining elements of cantata and symphony in a remarkably ugly manner. Kastalsky has long shown a predilection for hybrid forms. In his 'Brotherly Remembrance' [*Bratskoye pominoveniye*], he sought to unite Russian church *a cappella* singing with Western sacred instrumental music, creating a kind of Russian Requiem. The outcome of that experiment proved to be stillborn. In the first years of the Revolution, Kastalsky tried to 'harmonise' the *Internationale* with the help of Russian counterpoints based on the 'subvoices' [*podgoloski*] of folk song, but the resulting piece is little better than his 'Russian Requiem'. Kastalsky has attempted to at arrive a viable form by crossing symphony with cantata. But such a hybrid is nothing more than an 'unsymphonic symphony', with the addition of a vocal element that is not treated as an equal to the orchestra, but as an unnecessary appendage. Although he is a vocal composer, Kastalsky, in his new symphony, entirely loses sight of the nature of the human voice, and treats the vocal parts of the symphony in an utterly barbaric way, making it quite impossible for them to sound well.

Regarding musical ideology, Kastalsky also demonstrates his bankruptcy. At a time when the composers of bourgeois nations preach the mechanisation of musical creativity and create works that glorify American steam engines (Honegger) or colossal modern factories (Krenek), Kastalsky turns his artistic gaze upon the wooden plough, the scythe, sickle and spinning wheel, thereby glorifying *primitive* agriculture and handicrafts, which we should hardly be glorifying in this age of the radio and the tractor. And Kastalsky's methods are in themselves so impoverished and primitive that they would have been laughed at even by the contemporaries of old J. S. Bach, who provided him with the material that contributed to the musical wit and social ideology of his Peasant Cantata – Kastalsky could never rise to this level. In this cantata, a dialogue between 'young lovers of peasant status', Bach not only provided some wonderful music, but also castigated serfdom, with its landlords (and ladies), its bailiffs, and managers; he even criticised the systems of the court and military recruitment. While Bach had already managed to treat the 'village' theme from the point of view of 'production', Kastalsky, instead giving this theme artistic treatment, provided us with nothing more than a Russian *pseudo-classical symphonic vaudeville on peasant subject matter*. The likes of Kheraskov and Sumarokov are entirely out of step with the times, since they do not fall within the ambit of its style.[30]

If the art of music, like artistic work in general, presupposes a complete mastery of the material, then the *Village Symphony* does not bear the stamp of true art, since it is the material that has the composer in its power here, instead

---

[30] Mikhail Kheraskov (1733–1807) and Alexander Sumarokov (1717–77) were Russian poets whose pre-Pushkin versification generally seemed too antiquated by this date.

of the other way round. Without mastering his material, Kastalsky took the path of least resistance and instead of 'production' music, he gave us an exhibition of feeble amateurishness; instead of musical 'ferroconcrete', he gave us musical wickerwork.

※ ※ ※ ※ ※

'Dvulikiy Yanus' [The Double-Faced Janus], *Muzïka i Oktyabr'*, no. 2 (1926), 21.

This is a mocking preview of the Cappella's performance of Rachmaninov's All-Night Vigil, which took place in February 1926. During the NEP years, it was easier to present religious works before the public, and various individuals and organisations felt they could serve both workers and believers. Kastalsky, for example, felt free to contribute a new sacred piece for 22 protodeacons to a grand celebration held in honour of his fellow church composer Pavel Chesnokov in 1925,[31] while at the same time, he continued to write 'music for the masses'. Although many in the audience would have heard Rachmaninov's Vigil as simply a musical masterwork, there were also believers present who experienced the performance very differently. One of these was the pianist Goldenweiser:

> Although this was nowhere near the level of the Synodal Choir, the singing was still very good. It made an unforgettable impression, especially precious when coarseness, cruelty and the mockery of everything spiritual have triumphed. Art is the highest truth. One cannot lie here. Or one can lie, but then there is no art! And nothing else can help here, which is why 'Marxist' art is not forthcoming – and never will be. But religious art was, is, and shall be. They fear it much as the devil fears the cross, and in this they are absolutely right. It is an incomparably infectious force![32]

The Double-Faced Janus

The autumn of 1925 was such a joy for us!

On Moscow's walls, a poster appeared out of the blue: an extended series of free concerts for *workers* ... Rosfil [the Russian Philharmonia] for workers!

But the outcome wasn't quite what we expected ...

Only the 'serednyaks' [people of middling income] ... Perhaps only 0.5 per cent [of the workers were there] ...

And yet Rosfil sheds no tears!

Because it's been like this since time immemorial: at concerts 'for workers', you can't find a single worker ...

The situation is truly dire!

And no one has tried to make an *honest stab* at solving this puzzle at any point since the beginning of the Revolution.

The best thing would be to make a confession, along these lines:

'We just do not know how we can enlighten the working class! We confess that

---

[31] Mikhail Vostrïshev, *Moskva stalinskaya: Bol'shaya illyustrirovannaya letopis'* (Moscow: Algoritm, 2008), 194.

[32] Diary entry of 13 Feb. 1926, in A. B. Gol'denveyzer, *Dnevnik: tetradi vtoraya-shestaya* (Moscow: Tortuga, 1997), 56.

we do not know what the working class needs ... that we are trying to impose unacceptable things on it! We are happy to step aside and let this be carried out by an organisation that can do a better job!'

Before it announced the [concert] 'series', did Rosfil make any attempt to ask the workers and their organisations what they needed?

Did it research their demands?

But when something is imposed on people against their will – then even free tickets can't save the enterprise, nor justify it.

The worker, even if he had believed [Rosfil] for one moment, would have found his expectations dashed, and would have flown from these 'free' concerts, maybe to the pub, or sometimes even to the church!

But perhaps Rosfil does 'shed a tear', and in its desperation, it's managing to attract new forces, and trying to build a bridge between the workers and music. Well, is it?

The answer to this question is provided by the following poster, from which we can only draw depressing conclusions:

ROSFIL

Rachmaninov – All-Night Vigil

State Cappella

And so, a new 'sacred' task has been set! (on the poster it even says: 'repeat performance').

But, we ask, surely the name of Rosfil has only appeared on this poster through some kind of mistake? [sarcasm]

And what is the purpose of the State Cappella?

Today – to sing of the Revolution?

Tomorrow – the All-Night Vigil?

Somehow, this two-faced nonsense does not sit well with a state institution, *ideologically* speaking.

One position excludes the other.

And the 'historicity' of Rachmaninov's Vigil is extremely dubious; no one is proposing to use it for educational purposes – there would be no reason to do so.

It seems only right, then, to put a question to Rosfil:

– Why did Rosfil make the secular State Cappella sing the 'all-night vigil'?

Or, if that's not the case, then why has *a sacred choir of church singers* been named the 'State Cappella'?

It is clear from the above:

Although Rosfil is an institution belonging to Narkompros [the Ministry of Education], it has a certain commercial streak. But isn't it odd, then, that Rosfil was allowed to take on the functions of Narkomzdrav [The Ministry of Health]? Opium is a prescription medicine in pharmacies ...

Rosfil sells it in unlimited quantities.

In our opinion, Rosfil is doing somebody else's job!
There are limits.
Pornography (as well as religion) also has its own *masterpieces*!!!
So why the preference?
You have to be consistent to the end.
And we have a right to live in hope …
We're waiting for the following poster to appear:

> **Rosfil   Foxtrot**
>
> Ravel. Pokrass. Nikolayevsky. Levin.[33]
>
> Gentlemen in tails, ladies in décolletage.

Editor's note: Something like this does actually exist already (Rosfil's Jazz Band).

---

[33] Dmitry Pokrass, M. Nikolayevsky and Alexander Levin were prolific composers of popular songs (there was also a Miron Levin who composed popular numbers). Ravel's presence in such company is most probably due to his Five O'Clock foxtrot from *L'enfant et les sortilèges*.

Nikolay Mal'ko, 'Dzhaz-band v Moskve' [Jazz-Band in Moscow], *Zhizn' iskusstva*, no. 10 (9 Mar. 1926), 13.

> The conductor Malko was one of the many Russian musicians to attend the performances given by the first authentic jazz band to visit the Soviet Union. In this review, he cannot suppress the fact that he was gawping at the players because of their unfamiliar skin colour, but in the end, the playing won him over completely, and he praises the band sincerely as fellow musicians, rather than patronising them as primitives or exotics.

Nikolai Malko
Jazz-Band in Moscow

Rosfil has brought genuine Jazz-Band music to the USSR.[34] The genuine article, no need for inverted commas, since everything we've had up to now, from Val. Parnakh's effort[35] through to *D.Ye.*, by Meyerhold and the talented Kostomolotsky,[36] was only an experiment in cultivating a foreign plant on our soil. Now the real Negros have arrived, and even though they have become a little Frenchified (the trombonist Withers[37] has been living in Paris for six years, and the others for roughly the same amount of time), their musical culture is so different from the European that that we can regard them as a completely new phenomenon.

The ensemble consists of five musicians: piano, cornet, trombone, (baritone) saxophone and an assortment of percussion. The sixth player, on soprano saxophone, will be arriving soon. The band plays two sets a day, or three during holidays – they're receiving invitations from all around. I had a chance to hear them in Moscow, in the Writers' Club (the former Literary-Artistic Circle), and that was already at night, since it must have been their fifth set [*sic*].

The small basement was filled to the brim, there were many musicians (among them Glière, and the Bolshoi artistes), there was a showing from Rosfil headed by B. B. Krasin, and our French guests Monteux, Astruc, and Gil-Marchex;[38]

---

[34] 'Jazz-Band' here refers to a Russian musical genre of the time, overlapping with, but not identical to 'jazz' in the United States.

[35] Valentin Yakovlevich Parnakh (Parnokh, 1891–1951), was the founder of the first 'eccentric orchestra' or 'jazz band' in Russia, which gave its first concert in 1922. He is also credited with Russifying the word 'jazz' as 'dzhaz'.

[36] Alexander Iosifovich Kostomolotsky (1897–1971), began his career as a drummer in Parnakh's band, and then became an actor and conductor at the Meyerhold Theatre, where he was responsible for the jazz-based score for the play *D. Ye.*

[37] Presumably Frank Withers, a member of Mitchell's Jazz Kings.

[38] Pierre Monteux was a French conductor (see Glossary); Gabriel Astruc (1864–1938) was an important journalist and one-time agent of Diaghilev, was at this time a music-hall producer promoting jazz; Henri Gil-Marchex (1894–1970) was a French composer and pianist, who toured the Soviet Union several times between 1926 and 1935.

Lunacharsky's appearance met with applause. Finally they brought in the percussion, and a mulatto set up the bass drum, snare drums, plates [*plastini*], a cymbal, and metal rods; then the others came out: the pianist with an unbelievably characteristic Negro appearance, the cornettist and the trombonist (both black as well), and the saxophonist, who might have been a mulatto or an Indian, but looked almost white. The first impression was that they were not in the least fatigued and in these conditions (a stuffy room at African temperatures), they went about their business so cheerfully, effortlessly and correctly, that it was as if they'd come here after a good rest. And they do see the point of a good rest: upon their arrival in Moscow, they immediately demanded a holiday, in accordance with the statute (a holiday they wouldn't have had in Paris).

The ensemble performed up to ten pieces, from 'Greetings to Moscow' (their own composition) to songs and dance music. The musical terrain covered by the Negros is not broad, and would not have been of interest for its content alone. But the content wasn't the point – what mattered was how the music was presented. And the performance left the audience truly astonished: there were the acrobatics of the percussionist Paton, the pianist Parvish's remarkable mastery of the keyboard, with his trick of throwing his hands out with a sudden flick of the elbow, the showy use of mutes by the cornettist and the trombonist (they had mutes both of the usual kind, sometimes covered by a kind of rubber bubble, and of a special kind, with a hole that allows the sound to be controlled by the left hand, to produce striking *glissando* effects).

Perhaps some listeners were drawn by these effects, the players' smiles, or their appearance (the elegant dinner jackets throw into relief their characteristic facial features). As for us musicians (I cannot of course speak on behalf of all musicians, since for some of them, Jazz-Band music is something odious, the very term like a swear-word), some of us admire the element of real, genuine play that is present here to an extent that one can only dream of, even in first-class performances. The players are truly *playing*, rather than merely overcoming difficulties. Their tackling of new tempi and new rhythms doesn't come from following a written score, divided up by bar lines and double bar lines; this is play, rather, that is subordinated to the idea of the piece as it freely develops. The ensemble is ideal and doesn't need any visual signals or 'preparatory' moments of unsteadiness or hesitation (which is common with orchestras under a conductor). If we add to this the most phenomenal mastery of the instruments by these musicians, a mastery taken to the very limits of perfection, then it should be permissible to point out the social significance of having such an ensemble in our country, where striving for quality becomes ever more important every minute.

'Pis'mo komsomol'tsev Konservatorii tov. A. V. Lunacharskomu' and 'Otvet tov. A. V. Lunacharskogo' [A Letter from Komsomol members of the Conservatoire to Cmrd A. V. Lunacharsky and Cmrd A. V. Lunacharsky's Response], *Muzïka i Oktyabr'*, nos. 4–5 (1926), 17–18.

This exchange demonstrates that at the height of NEP, when RAPM's influence was negligible, the organisation continued to refine the ideology that would come to play an important role in Soviet music from the 1930s to the 1950s (after RAPM itself had been wound up). Note, in particular, the opposition of 'social realism' (not yet 'socialist realism') and 'the formalist trend'. The Komsomol writers also consider Prokoll to be aligned with their platform. For Lunacharsky, at this juncture, the writers were merely yapping at his ankles, and his rebuttal is condescending and even a little contemptuous. One of the crucial points he makes is his inability to 'furnish workers with musical emotions at the expense of the state' in the economic conditions prevailing under NEP.

A Letter from Komsomol Members in the Conservatoire to Cmrd A. V. Lunacharsky and Cmrd A. V. Lunacharsky's Response

Dear Anatoly Vasilyevich,
Having read your article, 'What We Have Achieved in Our Art', published in the 1 May edition of *Pravda* (no. 100), we will be so bold as to write to you about what we found most striking in your analysis of Soviet musical achievements. The starting point of your article is an epithet that is applicable to the whole of contemporary art: 'an orientation towards social realism, looking back towards classicism'. But your approach to contemporary music ignores this principle. When analyzing the other arts, you pointed out the presence of different trends, the struggle of a moribund formalism (in LEF literature) with revolutionary realism (the painting of OST and AKhRR), but in music, not only did you fail to point out that any such struggle was taking place, but you also took formalism to be the trend that responded to the present times. You count as 'ours' the composers Myaskovsky, Aleksandrov, Shebalin and [A.] Krein. Do these composers, among whom 'the spirit of the nation has been revealed', really respond to the present day? Do they orientate themselves towards social realism? No, they do not. This [formalist] trend has reached a high technical level in form, but in content, it reflects the ideology of the degenerating bourgeoisie.

Aside from this 'contemporary' music (contemporary only in the sense that these composers are still alive), an agitational music also exists. It might not have reached the necessary level yet, but its goals, its reflection of the present time and its genuine orientation towards social realism all guarantee it a great future.

New forces are being born among the representatives of the new organisations:

Kastalsky, Lebedinsky and Lazarev (in RAPM), and Davidenko and Shekhter (in Prokoll), among others.

A final question, on a matter that is not clear to us. You talk about the growing numbers attending concerts, but what kind of audience is this? Do workers attend concerts? Are we striving to bring this about (through programming, introductory lectures, etc)? No, we are not.

These issues are of topical significance and need to be approached and elucidated in depth.

Komsomol members, and students of the Conservatoire:
Loyter. Siver. Kamionskaya, V.M.[39]

Cmrd. Lunacharsky's Response

The letter from Komsomol members in the student body contains some valid points, but there are also many mistakes. We cannot place all the arts on an equal footing, because often they cannot be compared, due to their very nature. What is realism in literature and painting? It is first of all, a language of images taken from immediate reality. If we approached music in the same way and claimed that music had to be realist, it would mean that we wanted the music to approximate various noises. The reality around us is not musical. From the very outset, music stylises it in the most decisive way. Not only is it free of images, but it does not reflect the nature of the sounds that we hear in everyday life. Every attempt to get closer to 'realism' leads to music that is clearly untruthful, and it is in fact the semi-decadent Futurists who have tried to introduce noise orchestras that supposedly bring music closer to life. It is difficult, therefore, to speak of realism in music. Nor is it easy to draw lines that would strictly demarcate one set of class tendencies from another [in music]. Thus, for example, a march created by imperialists can also be put to splendid use by revolutionaries. Olminsky,[40] in one of his articles, writes that 'Even the *Marseillaise* itself can be well received by monarchists so long as the words aren't attached to it'. This is proof of the extent to which music, unlike literature, is ineffable.

What does looking back to the classics mean for literature or painting? It means the reinstatement of a monumental realism and the greater perfection of technique. But what does looking back to the musical classics mean? It means moving closer to a stern and masculine style, which, at its highest point (Beethoven), expresses

---

[39] Note that all three students who signed their names are women – there is something of the spirit of the times in the panache these teenage girls display in taking on the Minister of Education. Elizaveta Loyter (1908–73), then a student at the piano faculty and a Komsomol activist, later became a well known piano accompanist and musicologist. Mirra (Mariya) Siver, also a piano student, became a renowned piano teacher.

[40] Olminsky (real name Aleksandrov), Mikhail (1863–1933). Professional revolutionary, old Bolshevik. After the Revolution, he contributed much to the education of communist cadres. He wrote literary criticism and instigated the chronicling of Party history.

a musical formula for life as it emerged in the new democratic era, when it was still fresh in the time of the Great Revolution – this, however, has nothing to do with any kind of realism. This is why there can be no talk of any struggle between 'moribund formalism' and 'revolutionary realism' in music. We will have to use entirely different terms here.

I cannot call Myaskovsky, Aleksandrov, Shebalin and Krein *our* composers in the sense that they are communist composers or some kind of ideological fellow travellers. I call them 'ours' because they live and work in the USSR. Their surroundings undoubtedly affect their creative work. It is very difficult to translate their works into the language of ideas, because such translation is generally unreliable and unconvincing. But it is still the case that this group of composers, who have remained loyal to their motherland, work in the spirit of the classics, and at the same time express some experiences, if not of the whole country, then of a section of its intelligentsia. Considerable discernment is needed to recognise the distinctive rhythms, vivid and full of the emotional experiences of our time, that are reflected in Myaskovsky's most recent works, or in such a significant work as Melkikh's last quartet, among others.

As for agitational music [*agit-muzika*], this only merits a passing mention in any discussion about purely artistic works, in the same way that a short article on painting cannot deal with agitational woodcuts and posters, etc. These are all very useful things that can reach a highly artistic level (although this is very rare, by the way, in our agit-music), but they only have a tangential relationship to the works that characterise the era, in the same way that an agit-poem is tangential to the history of poetry. An agit-poem that is also highly artistic, or an agitational image that is a true painting both constitute an excellent transitional point, and it is important that we should strive for this. But music has not yet provided us with any such works, so we cannot list them among our achievements. The young people listed by the Komsomol members have not yet achieved anything in art. Most of them are students, and they still have much to learn. It is quite impossible to place them in the ranks of the masters, or to ascribe greatness to them. They are our hope, and perhaps a great hope. We await its fulfilment with excitement.

On the subject of workers and concerts: the Komsomol comrades must know that we cannot set course for any decisive reorganising of the bulk of our spectacles, etc. for workers. On what grounds could we do that? The workers' budget will not permit such institutions to be self-financing, or, to be more precise, it would allow them to do so, but only to a very limited extent. The government does not at present consider it possible to subsidise them, and this determines the economic basis for our theatres and for the self-financing of concerts. Until the time when our salaries are three or four times higher than they are now, and government subsidies are five or six times higher, we cannot implement the policy desired both by myself and by my friends from Komsomol who have written to me. Does this mean that we can't even make a move in this direction? [No, because] *Pravda* has published figures of quite significant theatre attendance among workers, and for this purpose, we have the special distribution of tickets among trade unions and their members at extremely low prices. The same happens with [non-union?] workers.

The low-price concerts organised by Rosfil generate no profits at all (symphony concerts, for example, make losses under all conditions, even with a public paying high prices); despite this, Rosfil has, in the present year, already organised a whole series of first-rate affordable concerts, whose audiences were 75% working class. The programmes were compiled by the leaders of Rosfil with the needs of workers in mind. The excellent attendance figures for these concerts and the stormy ovations they won demonstrate that Rosfil was quite accurate in gauging workers' tastes. If the number of these concerts is not higher, this is again simply because workers do not receive a higher salary. Perhaps we need to improve the other aspects of workers' lives first, before we can start to supply them with musical emotions at the expense of the state. And if we are unable to do this, reproaches from comrades of Komsomol will be of no avail and cannot even be accepted as justified criticisms. For we do as much as we can. I am not saying that discussion of popular concerts, their further development and better organisation is irrelevant today. It *is* relevant, but why? – Because we now have a larger paying public at our concerts, because we receive some profit from them, and, of course, because we do *not* perform the works of Comrades Lazarev, Shekhter et al. there, but instead perform old music, or new music by Prokofiev, Myaskovsky, et al. This has provided us with the means to do something for the popularisation of music. These means will probably increase in the future and must be dedicated to the popularisation of musical works that are closest in spirit to the workers.

The least acceptable aspect of the Komsomol members' letter is that tinge of scorn that marks their attitude to our musical masters, a trait that I have noticed among our youth. 'This is bourgeois', they say, 'this is an expression of a degenerate ideology',' etc. Because music is such an organic entity, built on many centuries of tradition, a break with these traditions would lead to barbarism, to a steep decline. I see it as my duty to warn young people against this tendency. Learn, with attention, love and respect, from our great and major composers, including those who are still alive. Learn from the Myaskovskys and the Kreins, and if you manage to fill their marvellous forms (whose secrets are known to these major artists) with your new rhythms of life, when you can add all the necessary knowledge and skills to the enthusiasm of youth – then we, your older colleagues, will be delighted to acknowledge what you have achieved. But for now, in response to the reproach that music in our country has fallen silent, or to the claim that its tree has been replaced by the grass of agitational music, we can proudly say that the composers who have remained loyal to their motherland during the revolutionary years have not fallen behind European music, and indeed are making a very serious and cultured contribution to it, a redeeming stream of noble music in which a great knowledge of tradition is mixed with a vital creativity.

1927
Celebrations

'Allow me to greet you in the confidence that for the musical world of the RSFSR, this new year will begin under the sign of Prokofiev' – such was the stilted flattery Prokofiev would read over breakfast as the time approached for his first return visit to Soviet Russia.[1] And when he finally arrived there, he received the warmest reception of his life so far, which his diary entries record as quite overwhelming. The more challenging pieces, like the *Chout* suite or the Quintet, were interspersed with lighter and more familiar fare, but the main attraction was the composer himself, tirelessly performing his concertos, sonatas and smaller piano pieces, usually ending with a generous string of encores. He visited Lunacharsky in the Kremlin, turning up in the middle of a soirée – the Minister, who was a particular fan of the *Scythian Suite*, made no secret of his wish that Prokofiev would return permanently. To press the point, he declaimed Mayakovsky's verse appeal to Gorky, which prodded that great friend of the proletarians for preferring balmy Capri to his turbulent homeland. The poem was full of sharp rhymes and sharp critical arrows, lamenting the new dominance of sycophantic literary realism and comparing Gorky to Chaliapin:

Иль жить вам,	Or will you live
Как живет Шаляпин,	As Chaliapin lives
Раздушенными аплодисментами оляпан?	Spattered by perfumed applause?
Вернись	Even if
Теперь	Today
Такой артист	Such an artiste
Назад,	Would return
На русские рублики,	For Russian roubles
Я первый крикну -	I'll be the first to shout:
Обратно катись,	Back you go,
Народный артист республики!	People's Artist of the Republic!

Unlike Gorky or Chaliapin, Prokofiev had never expressed any special love for the proletariat or the Revolution, so no one could regard him as a betrayer, but the reading of Mayakovsky's poem struck him sufficiently that he kept a copy among his papers.[2] But even in the midst of such enthusiasm, he retained a degree of prudence, and preferred not to accept overtly political invitations that might damage his career back in the West. Most prominently, he curtly turned down a commission to contribute a piece to the celebrations for the tenth Anniversary of October. Yurovsky, who had made the offer, was so embarrassed that he sent his secretary out to find Prokofiev, seeking to convince the composer that he had only made the offer because he was obliged

---

[1] Letter from S. Razumovsky (on behalf of the Moscow Association of Playwrights, Writers, and Composers, [MODPIK]) to Prokofiev, LPA, vol. 14, 22–3.

[2] LPA, folder 14, f. 71.

to, and not because he himself was a Communist. Prokofiev was greatly amused.[3]

Constantly fussed over by friends old and new, he soon realised that his visit was a great victory for them, too, a victory for all champions of new music. And he enjoyed a personal vindication, as all his old critics of pre-Revolutionary times, Glazunov at the head of them, had to participate in the daily round of Prokofiev celebrations. Upon his return, he wrote many cheerful reports on his and his wife's behalf:

> We are very pleased with our trip to Essessesseria [USSR]: we were received with affection, the officials were considerate, and in the end we were sorry to leave. In all there were 23 concerts, taking place as far afield as Kharkov, Kiev, and Odessa. [...] I saw the *Oranges* at the Mariinsky, and the staging was very amusing [...] But the Bolshoi is planning to stage them even more lavishly [...][4]

On the day of Prokofiev's departure, his friend Borovsky checked into the same hotel – this was Lunacharsky's other musical returnee of the time (see the Introduction to 1926). Borovsky's tour was also a success and he left with many happy impressions. But not every returning prodigal was met with open arms: Nikolai Medtner, for example, elicited almost no interest. In fairness, he was in direct competition with Prokofiev for his audience, since the two visits coincided, but, as Myaskovsky pointed out, Medtner's music was unlikely to have been received well, even in the best of circumstances:

> He was a complete flop, and now he's outraged. He fails to see that neither fashion nor Prokofiev are to blame, but simply his new compositional style, which is shoddy and banal. I went a second time – just to confirm my impressions – and oh, how dreary it all sounds![5]

Prokofiev's visit gave a boost to the Bolshoi's preparations for *Oranges*, which was now given priority over Glière's ballet *Red Poppy*, in spite of the latter's ideological merits (it was a clear anti-imperialist statement). The great attraction of the *Oranges* production was Isaac Rabinovich's lavish set designs, which Prokofiev had already admired in maquette form. If anything, Rabinovich tried too hard, burdening the production with an excessive number of set changes, and creating an impression of grand and heavy luxury, typical of the Bolshoi but not perhaps not so well suited to Prokofiev's absurdist and mercurial opera (which had its origins in Meyerhold's iconoclastic modernism, after all). The production was at least consistent, and by all accounts, the heaviness of the sets was matched by Golovanov's overwrought performance. But the opera was a novelty for the Moscow public, and the production was a great success.

There were further landmark events for new music soon after Prokofiev's

---

[3] Sergey Prokof'yev, *Dnevnik*, vol. 2 (Paris: sprkfv, 2002), 514.

[4] Letter from Prokofiev to Kusevitskaya of 29 Mar. 1927, LPA, folder 46, f. 222.

[5] Letter from Myaskovsky to Prokofiev of 12 May 1927, publ. in. S. S. Prokofiev and N. Ya. Myaskovskiy, *Perepiska*, ed. by M. Kozlova et al. (Moscow: Sovetskiy kompozitor, 1977).

departure: on the initiative of Asafyev, two new modernist operas were produced in Leningrad. The first of these was Krenek's *Sprung über den Schatten* (premiered on 21 May), which certainly created a stir and yet was widely perceived as a failure, as Malko reported:

> It has been learnt very well (Samosud) – everything is light, flexible and pleasing to the ear. The performers are good, and the staging is interesting. Even so, there are plenty of 'buts'. The public was restive, and the opera was basically a flop. It's a great pity, because the production is of great musical significance. There was thunderous applause after the foxtrot, almost bringing the performance to a halt. At the close of each act, there were a couple of curtain calls, while at the end, there were maybe three, but with little applause, which was partly cowed by the booing. Now it is *Wozzeck*'s turn.[6]

Asafyev himself was jubilant at first, claiming that 'to the surprise of the Directors and everyone else, it is a success – it's *Three Oranges* all over again'.[7] But doubts began to plague him: the critic Strelnikov reported that in the musical circle associated with Universal Edition in Vienna, *Der Sprung* was considered a juvenile trifle, and the serious attention it had received in Russia was wholly inappropriate. Asafyev's opinion was reversed: 'We spent so much effort on this, but we were deceived, and now Europe is laughing at us'.[8]

Asafyev's other operatic project of 1927, the production of *Wozzeck* was another matter, and by general assent was one of the great landmarks of Soviet musical life during the twenties. The effort expended on rehearsals, stretching over six months, was unparalleled. Berg, excited by the prospect, decided to come along to the Russian premiere on his own initiative, and after various predictable difficulties along the way, he sat in the Mariinsky on 12 June for the final dress rehearsal, and the following day for the premiere itself. There was an unofficial reception thrown by the hospitable Shaporin, at which Berg, 'tall, handsome, and looking like Alexander Blok or Oscar Wilde', had little to say, but seemed pleased with the performance.[9] He was more voluble in a letter to Asafyev a year later: '[...] my opera has never been better received than in Leningrad. I'm glad that it remains in the repertoire. With the exception of Berlin, not a single German theatre risked its production, never mind Austria and the Entente countries. From this, Herr Asafyev, you can judge how much you've done for me [...]'[10] But this needs to be put in perspective: after the premiere, *Wozzeck* only clocked up a

---

[6] Letter from Malko to Myaskovsky of 22 May 1927, RGALI, fond 2040 (Myaskovsky), op. 2, ye. kh. 180, l. 33.

[7] Letter from Asafyev to Derzhanovsky of 5 June 1927, GTsMMK, fond 3 (Derzhanovsky), ye. kh. 2, no. 834.

[8] Ibid.

[9] Mikhail Druskin, as quoted in Inna Barsova, *Konturï stoletiya: Iz istorii russkoy muziki XX veka* (St Petersburg: Kompozitor-Sankt Peterburg, 2007), 41. All the information about the *Wozzeck* premiere here comes from Barsova, 34–42.

[10] Letter from Berg to Asafyev of 11 May 1928, publ. in *Materialï k biografii B. Asaf'yeva* (Leningrad: Muzïka, 1981) 136.

further five performances. Still, the enduring fact was that a Soviet opera company had demonstrated that it could master the most demanding of modernist operatic scores, to the extent that even the composer was well pleased.

Gradually gaining in prestige through such activities, Asafyev embarked on a determined struggle against the domination of the Rimsky-Korsakov school at the Leningrad Conservatoire. Shteynberg, the Dean of the Faculty of Scholarship and Composition, found himself increasingly sidelined, losing the control of the musicology department to Asafyev and the composition department to the more 'progressive' Shcherbachov. It was in the composition department where the struggle was most bitter. Shcherbachov sought to implement his new methods of teaching student composers, abandoning the usual progression from harmony to counterpoint to fugue in favour of his own idiosyncratic methods. While Shcherbachov was trying to impress the visiting Prokofiev with his plans (even he found them a little too radical), Shteynberg was in contact with Gnesin, his opposite number in Moscow, lamenting over his loss of control:

> [...] I am asking you to find out gently what the centre's attitude to such a reprisal against the representatives of a different direction in art. If we talk about the slogan 'Art for the masses', then I will be so bold as to say that our school is actually closer to such a slogan than the *derniers cris* of linearism, Asafyevism and the like. If Moscow approves of what is happening here, then I'll have to tender my resignation as soon as possible. No one can claim that I am a reactionary, but I cannot undergo a rebirth in order to teach everything upside down or to take delight in the sound of atonal music.[11]

Shteynberg was ultimately proven correct: only a few years later, the more conservative composers writing in a post-Rimsky-Korsakov idiom would indeed be held up as more accessible to the masses. But their time had not yet come, and for the present, they were relegated to the margins. The atmosphere in LASM deteriorated further, and Asafyev noted the growth of anti-Moscow feelings. Although Prokofiev's visit prompted uniform adulation, it also brought various enmities and jealousies to the surface.

Shteynberg's own star student, Shostakovich, was one of the renegades who had left LASM at the end of the previous year, even though it damaged personal relations between them (his departure prompted an irate phone call from his professor). 'The split from Shteynberg is inevitable',[12] concluded Shostakovich. By this stage, he already knew that his latest works, the uncompromisingly modernist Octet and Piano Sonata had met with Shteynberg's disapproval. Tellingly, both these pieces had been premiered in Moscow. Shostakovich also had a chance to play the Sonata in front of Prokofiev, at a friendly gathering in Shcherbachov's home. Prokofiev's praise was qualified, but even so, he felt that Shostakovich stood out as the most promising of the new composers. Shostakovich, for his part, said

---

[11] Letter from Shteynberg to Gnesin of 12 Dec. 1927, RGALI, fond 2954 (Gnesin), op. 1, ye. kh. 790, l. 18v.

[12] Letter from Shostakovich to Yavorsky of 3 Nov. 1926, publ. in *Dmitriy Shostakovich v pis'makh i dokumentakh*, ed. by I. Bobïkina, M. Yesipova, and M. Rakhmanova (Moscow: Gosudarstvennïy muzey muzïkal'noy kul'turï im. Glinki, 2000), 87.

he was 'entirely smitten by the music and the playing' after one of Prokofiev's recitals.[13]

Just a few months later, Prokofiev was able to read of Shostakovich's great public success with his symphony *To October* (now usually known as the Symphony No. 2) – this was the commission that Prokofiev had summarily rejected, and which was then offered to Shostakovich, who took it up with alacrity. The 20-year-old composer, who had just become a celebrity among Leningrad concertgoers, thanks to his First Symphony, still lacked any funds to ensure the performance of his music, and the commission signalled the prospect of a change for the better, since it promised performance and publication shortly after completion. The commission was issued by Shulgin's Agitational Department at Muzsektor, and the only disadvantage was the stipulation that the work should include a setting of a rather clumsy political text by Alexander Bezïmensky. Shostakovich made no objection to this, and also followed Shulgin's advice that a factory whistle would sit well within the kind of work they hoped to see.[14] At first, his principal motivation was apparently the thought of the foreign trip the commission fee might possibly cover: 'Every day I write four-score pages of "patriotic music" while hearing the call: To Paris! To Paris!',[15] but in the end, he was proud of his new score. It was first performed twice at 'closed' concerts given by the Leningrad Philharmonia, on 5 November at the festive assembly of the Leningrad Union of Education Workers, and the following day at a festive gathering of Glavnauka. A month later, it received a much more prominent performance in a concert given in the famous Hall of Columns, on 4 December, which ASM had been happy to organise.

The story of Shostakovich's *To October* is clear evidence of a changed musical landscape, and the consolidation of musical factions that were formerly at odds with each other. Back in 1924, Myaskovsky and most other ASM members were outraged by Asafyev's and Derzhanovsky's overtures to the Soviet power. Now we find the same Myaskovsky, showing not mere tolerance, but outright enthusiasm as he compares the various works for the tenth Anniversary celebrations of the Revolution. Schillinger's symphonic rhapsody *October*,[16] he liked 'very much – or almost', admiring its orchestration among other things, while finding the quotations of 'vulgar' street songs rather grating. Even then, he is not content to exercise aesthetic judgement alone, but introduces an ideological dimension to his assessment of both Schillinger's and Shostakovich's October pieces:

> [F]rom a certain 'ideological' perspective, the general character of [Schillinger's] work would lead us to conclude that throughout the past decade, poor Schillinger only saw some kind of all-Russian bazaar of the type you will find in Odessa. Compared to this, Shostakovich, in his excellent *To October*, on the one hand appears as a complete dandy, but on the other, he

---

[13] Letter from Shostakovich to Yavorsky of 25 Feb. 1927, ibid., 104.
[14] Letters from Shostakovich to Shulgin of 6 and 26 June 1927, ibid., 170–1.
[15] Letter from Shostakovich to Yavorsky of 12 May 1927, ibid., 113.
[16] This piece was played in another programme, on 21 and 28 Nov. 1927 in Leningrad and also in Moscow (dates unknown).

has actually succeeded in sensing the pulse of the new life. Despite all the mocking gestures (some Milhaud here, some Hindemith there), this work has such balance, freshness of thought, originality and boldness of invention, while at the same time it displays such genuine inner emotion, that all in all, it made the most powerful impression on me – almost astonishingly so.[17]

Apart from Shostakovich's work, the ASM concert included Roslavets's October Cantata, Mosolov's suite from *Steel* and Polovinkin's Prologue (the Schillinger piece mentioned above was performed in a different programme). Mosolov earned a response almost as enthusiastic as Shostakovich had received. His Suite consisted of four movements: an overture, The Factory (now well known under its English title *The Iron Foundry*), The Prison, The Ball, and The Square. The ideologically-minded critic Semyon Korev, although a RAPM member, offered a very positive evaluation of Mosolov's work (this very un-RAPM-like indiscretion eventually caught up with Korev):[18]

The first section is most successful as a depiction. The principal rhythmic-melodic figure, which is very expressive, runs through the entire section, from beginning to end, and creates a vivid musical picture of a factory running at full tilt. But the composer did not limit himself to the creation of a mere 'naturalistic' scene. He goes further and deeper. Without changing his main musical theme, but concentrating intensely on the logic of the gradual build-up, the composer transcends the illustration as he approaches the climax. His mighty melodic-rhythmic figures begin to sound so victorious and uplifting (especially when the brass add their sustained chords over the rhythmic-melodic background) – then this vivid overture, while losing none of its illustrative character, is transformed into a mighty hymn to mechanised labour.

The overture is put together solidly and expressively. It has every reason to become very popular and deserves it. Programmatic works will undoubtedly find their place in the new Soviet music, and the path opened by *The Factory* will lead to further achievements.[19]

Unlike Shostakovich and Mosolov, Roslavets had not developed the same talent for combining his modernism with revolutionary or agitational material (perhaps the Scriabinesque lineage of his modernism simply did not lend itself to the task). His cantata was bound to swing one way or the other, leaving either the 'modernists' or the 'revolutionaries' dissatisfied. As Derzhanovsky had feared, the result was closer to Roslavets's small-scale and simple agitational works. Even Korev, who found the stylistic change largely welcome, expressed some reservations:

---

[17] Letter from Myaskovsky to Asafyev of 17 Jan. 1928, RGALI, fond 2658 (Asafyev), op. 2, ye. kh. 51, l. 2–3.

[18] In a letter to the Editors, Korev had to apologise for his 'erroneous position in his evaluation of … the Association for Contemporary Music'. 'Pis'ma v redaktsiyu', *Proletarskiy muzïkant*, no. 5 (1931), 52.

[19] S. Korev, 'Sovetskaya simfonicheskaya muzïka: yubileynïye Oktyabr'skiye kontsertï', *Sovetskoye iskusstvo*, no. 7 (1927), 48–52, esp. 51–2.

The October Cantata signals a positive and happy stage of Roslavets's career, to some extent, a watershed. The composer approached the cantata with the accumulated achievements of his composerly craft, with all his revolutionary hatred for artistic reaction, routine, church influences, and bourgeois philistinism [*meshchanstvo*]. He brought all these positive traits, all the revolutionary artistic experience of his creative work. But at the same time, Roslavets also went against his own past, and set out along the path of the mass composer. This work does not suffer from the main fault of the composer's earlier music, namely an unjustifiable complexity. The October Cantata is quite immediate and populist. There is no trace of the contrivance that characterises Roslavets's work. On the contrary, in pursuing the 'mass character' of the Cantata, Roslavets perhaps overshot in the other direction – of emotionalism. But the payoff for this exaggeration is the great impact, freshness, and popular appeal of the cantata. Besides, out of all the October musical works this cantata is most fitting for a jubilee: it is solemn without pomposity, and colourfully uplifting without being pretentious.[20]

Polovinkin's 'symphonic movement' [*dvizhenie*], under the non-committal title of *Prologue*, received the least attention and critics suspected that it had nothing to do with the Revolution. They were not entirely correct, since Polovinkin had written the piece in 1925 for an October concert that never took place in the end. Here is a description he had offered in private to Derzhanovsky:

> My head has been populated by dreams about how sound could be structured, and I hope to realise these dreams, at least in part – this would make up the greater part of the task; the other part is the possible realisation of a programme that is somewhat anarchist or SR. The composition is absolutely sincere.[21]

The 'October concert' was undoubtedly the zenith of ASM's concert activities: in the past, it had mounted over a hundred concerts, but the majority of these were smaller affairs – chamber recitals, free-admission or invitation-only events. Now it was able to organise grand symphonic concerts of new music and make a success of them. The October concerts generated an unprecedented critical response for ASM, although Derzhanovsky still complained that the press under-reported them. ASM, it turned out, had managed to provide the tenth Anniversary with its most prominent musical celebrations, besides which the premiere of Prokoll's collective offering, *The Path of October* (Moscow Conservatoire Chamber Hall, 18 December) was a thoroughly small-scale affair, with performances by amateur collectives. As for RAPM, it was nowhere to be seen.

All the above is based on the written accounts of 1927 left by musicians, but we should note that only rarely do these reflect background conditions outside of musical life: everyday hardships, the tightening of state security, and turbulent political events, both internal and external, that were to set a new course for the

---

[20] Ibid., 50.
[21] Letter from Polovinkin to Derzhanovsky of 18 Apr. 1925, 'Perepiska L. A. Polovinkina', ed. by L. Rimskiy, *Iz proshlogo sovetskoy muzikal'noy kul'turï*, vol. 1 (Moscow: Sovetskiy kompozitor, 1975), 176–209, esp. 195.

coming years. Prokofiev's asides on such matters show that his idea of Soviet Russia was largely based on grim accounts published in the émigré press, so he was often pleasantly surprised. Still, he takes it as given that his phone conversations may be monitored and he grasps the significance of one A. S. Tsukker, the only member of Persimfans who didn't play an instrument, a Communist who sincerely rejoiced at the news of the Chinese Revolution that year, and who was able to negotiate preferential rates on some exquisite furs for Prokofiev's wife.[22] Prokofiev was delighted with the general life of comfort he led in Soviet Russia, with the occasional touch of luxury – the émigré press had never suggested that it was possible to eat so well in Moscow, or to sleep on such fine bed linen. His account reassures us that in 1927, the wealthiest layer of Soviet society was again living well. But Prokofiev was not blinkered: he notices, for instance, that while he was able to travel in a well-appointed 'international' carriage, Asafyev had to travel in squalor. He notes also that even his personal intercession was unable to secure the release of a relative who had been arrested on political charges. Even so, his account of his tour is overwhelmingly positive. In an uncharacteristic digression into high politics, Prokofiev mentions that he had expressed a desire to hear a speech that Trotsky was due to make, but that Tsukker raised difficulties and did everything he could to dissuade him. On the day, he describes how he bumped into a crowd of excited Trotsky supporters on the street in central Moscow. For Prokofiev, the outsider, Trotsky is a living legend, whose famous rhetorical powers he wanted to witness for himself. But for Tsukker, Trotsky is already a political leper to be avoided by all but the most reckless.

Glière's greatest popular success came with his musically very modest ballet *The Red Poppy* (premiered in June), but accounts of the music and dancing give us little idea of the production's political resonances: the ballet's enactment of friendship between Soviet sailors and Chinese workers was urgently topical in the wake of a British raid on the Soviet embassy in Beijing in April, an event that had led to the severing of Anglo–Soviet diplomatic relations the following month, prompting a public panic in the Soviet Union that another war was imminent.

One of Shostakovich's letters comments on the murder of Pyotr Voykov, the Russian ambassador to Poland: for Shostakovich this was a personal loss. When Shostakovich had visited Warsaw early in the year, to participate in the Chopin Piano Competition, he had fallen prey to appendicitis, and owed much to the fatherly care that he received from Voykov.[23] Voykov was killed in Warsaw in June 1927, by a White Russian émigré. Goldenweiser, who had no personal interest in

[22] 'Tsukker, as I discovered later, is an active Communist. At one stage, he'd hoped to be a singer, and this accounts for his connection with music. At some point, he fought during the Soviet coup and now is something like the secretary of VTsIK [Central Executive Committee] and thus has direct access to all members of the Government. He is the only member of Persimfans who does not play in the orchestra; his function is to produce programmes, give explanations on the radio during concerts and, of course, to promote various Persimfans business within government'. Sergey Prokof'yev, *Dnevnik*, vol. 2 (Paris: sprkfv, 2002), 462–3, also see 533 and 550. See entry on Tsukker in Glossary.

[23] Letter from Shostakovich to Yavorsky of 12 June 1927, *Dmitriy Shostakovich v pis'makh i dokumentakh*, 116.

the matter, recorded it in his diary as one of a series of causes and symptoms of the worsening political situation:

> The public events are terrible: Voykov has been killed, someone threw a bomb into a Party club in Petersburg, some GPU chief was killed near Minsk [...] Again the executions and arrests have started (two days ago, a list was printed of twenty to be executed). [...] There is a threat of war in the air [...]²⁴

The tenth anniversary of the Revolution, as we saw, drew disparate musical factions together in an enthusiastic unity. Outside the musical world, however, there was anything but unity: 1927 saw the final desperate upsurge in demonstrations and rallies by Trotsky's Oppositionists, before they were cleared off the streets by concerted police attacks, and fragmented through mass arrests. During an attack on one demonstration, Trotsky narrowly escaped death from gunfire directed at his automobile. The same day, Stalin had devised a symbolic death for his defeated rival. He personally supervised the editing of Grigory Aleksandrov's documentary, ensuring that all frames featuring Trotsky were removed. The resulting edit was shown to delegates at a festive assembly in the Bolshoi that evening, with Trotsky and Opposition protest now consigned to oblivion.²⁵ A week later, Trotsky was expelled from the Party and subsequently forced into exile.

All these events – the Chinese Revolution, the Beijing raid, the murder of Voykov, the destruction of the Opposition – may have been absent from most musicians' accounts of the year, but they set in motion a chain of political events that would soon render the musical highlights of 1927 unrepeatable, a distant memory. The country was on shakier ground internationally, with pervasive rumours of war. Internally, the system that came to be known as Stalinism was beginning to take shape. NEP, with all its problems and all its opportunities, was at an end, and harsher times lay ahead.

---

[24] Diary entry of 13 June 1927, A. B. Gol'denveyzer, *Dnevnik: tetradi vtoraya-shestaya* (Moscow: Tortuga, 1997), 154.

[25] Mikhail Vostrïshev, *Moskva stalinskaya: Bol'shaya illyustrirovannaya letopis'* (Moscow: Algoritm, 2008), 239. Grigory Vasilyevich Aleksandrov (1903–83) was one of the most important film-makers of Stalin's time.

※ ※ ※ ※ ※

'"Levïy" flang sovremennoy muzïki' ['The "left" wing of contemporary music', *Muzïka i revolyutsiya*, no. 1 (Jan. 1927), 3–7.

This editorial in Music and Revolution *(Muzïka i revolyutsiya) was most likely written by its editor-in-chief, Shulgin. RAPM was not in a position to publish its own journal at this time, but* Music and Revolution *often offered similar material, including the present article. But while the author here takes a harshly critical stance towards 'contemporary music', the journal also included articles that were neutral, or even sympathetic to it. In effect, the journal was more of a discussion forum than a factional campaigning organ. The article below is a clear attempt to jump onto a political bandwagon, drawing from Bukharin's recent polemics (in particular his 'Angry Notes') castigating the poet Sergei Yesenin, who had committed suicide in 1925 (his funeral had been transformed into a huge public manifestation of grief). It is probable that Bukharin's denunciation of Yeseninshchina was motivated at least in part by political considerations, as a proxy offensive against Trotsky, who had written at length in praise of the poet.*

The author wanted to make a similar condemnation of the modernist atonal composer Mosolov, and compared Mosolov's works to Yesenin's. As it happened, Mosolov did indeed have tendencies towards the same kind of heavy drinking and rowdy behaviour that Yesenin had displayed, but since this only became widely known in the 30s, the author was probably unaware of it, and no such information surfaces in the article. The author's purpose, rather, is to associate Yesenin with Mosolov, and by extension Belyayev and ASM as a whole, inviting the reader to see them all as manifestations of an artistic libertinism that was prominent in the early Soviet years, but which now had to be rejected, on Bukharin's authority. The author tries to persuade his readers that if such artistic amorality is allowed to flourish, it will help to foster a society in which events such as the Chubarov Lane gang rape become commonplace. (See footnote 27 for details of this crime.)

The 'Left' Wing of Contemporary Music

In our times, more than in any other era, when one thing is demolished and another built in its place, every phenomenon must be considered in the light of its social function and meaning.   N. Bukharin

In musical life today, there is a dangerous tendency towards the evaluation of works exclusively on the basis of the talent and mastery they display, or for their striking novelty or individuality. Even the possession of one of these qualities suffices to make a work worthy to sit alongside the great names of the concert stage, or to be preserved for posterity through publication. In this event, no attention is given to the work's content, to its ideological essence, since many still believe that it is impossible to discover the content of, for example, a purely instrumental work that bears neither epigraph nor imaginative title (i.e. lacking any verbal key to help us decipher it). Even so, we often find that even the advocates of the formalist method cannot avoid all mention of content in their analyses, and when they need it, slyly raise the veil of sound [despite their formalist doctrines], throwing light on the meaning and tendencies of the given work. When youthful forces enter the public arena and lay first the first foundation stones of the new culture that is under construction, it is all the more important that we attend to the issue of content in music. We need to discover the *direction* in which these youthful forces *are growing*, to clarify their ideological position and evaluate the social significance of their tendency.

With this in mind, the output classified as 'left wing' by one representative of 'contemporary music' demands our special attention. Here we will take the opportunity to examine this kind of music in depth, through the work of composer A. V. Mosolov, supposedly located 'on the left wing of contemporary Russian composers', according to his supporter, V. M. Belyayev. We have at our disposal Mosolov's vocal works, and these scores grant us direct access to the ideas around which the composer's thoughts circulate. And we also have Belyayev's analyses of Mosolov's instrumental works, which address their content from the viewpoint of a sympathetic critic, and so give us a frank description of the moods reflected by Mosolov.

We have before us the creative output of a composer who is still very young, who started composing only in 1924 (one of 'our cubs', we might say). Let us take, for example, his *Children's Songs* (written for adults). The first begins with the following words (I quote from memory but quite accurately):

> Mummy, mummy, give me a needle, I'll stick it in the cat – why is he sitting in the corner?
> [*Mama, mama, day iglu, ya v kota eyo vsazhu – zachem sidit on v uglu?*]

Another song includes the following phrase:

> I was in such a terrible rush, I had to squash all those flies …
> [*Ya speshil, speshil, speshil, ya vsyo vremya mukh dushil*]

What is this supposed to be? A depiction of children's pointless cruelty? But what is placed in opposition to it? What is the composer's attitude towards it? Certainly, a child may sometimes display the coarse instincts of a prehistoric savage! But this is something we fight against, don't we?! The social conditions of our life here demand that we nurture other psychological traits, some quite different instincts also instilled by nature. But this relishing (what else can we call it?) of the negative traits we find in human nature, and their poeticisation – doesn't this arise from the same kind of mentality that delights in the daring of a *hooligan*, or in moral laxity, or in pointless mischief, in the present case even including an element of the bloodthirsty. Another of the songs begins like this:

> *Oh-ah, oh-ah, oh-ah* [the cry of a child urgently needing to defecate], Granny, come here quick, or there'll be trouble!
> [*A-á, a-á, a-á, babushka, idi syuda skorey, ne to budet beda!*]

This is the coarsest kind of naturalism, which music had never seen before. The poetic depiction of this physical act is the same as Yeseninshchina, which created a poetry of foul language [*matershchina*], of 'dogs', 'bitches', and their explicit physical relationships.[26]

What other themes has the composer chosen? A little later, he returned to everyday life, and once again dwelt on the seamy side of our existence, in his *Newspaper Advertisements*. First he glorifies a product for 'killing rats, mice, and insects', then we have a musical appeal inviting us to 'return a lost dog for a reward', and then a musical advert for a 'callus remedy', and, finally, 'leeches for sale'. And so our composer, for reasons best known to himself, exults in the most sordid aspects of our lives, especially the physical. We have before us a specimen of the human psyche that returns to the narrowness and primitivism of prehistoric interests, placing bodily functions at the centre of its focus. So much, then, for the affirmation of the personal 'I', 'art for art's sake', pure 'inspiration' and the poet's 'holy of holies'! Ultimately, *in our times*, all of this is reduced to the infantile lament of 'Oh-ah, oh-ah!', because those who remain aloof from all that is *socially significant* are left with the naked man and his bodily needs, and ... nothing else! What a pitiful outcome this is, measured against the past achievements of bourgeois culture, which produced some astonishing titans of thought and emotion, artists whose grasp took in the entire world, with expansive horizons and profundity of content! It would be embarrassing to cite those great names in this environment of ideological disintegration.

Where did such works spring from? What nourished them? Let us turn now to Belyayev's analysis of Mosolov's work: he considers these works 'artistically significant' and hopes that the composer 'will continue his work just as intensively and engagingly as he began it'. What does this critic find in Mosolov? What moods? What content? Firstly, we discover that 'psychologism (being engrossed in emotional experiences, more often painful than not)' is highly characteristic of Mosolov. What is the cause of these painful experiences? Reading on, we find that 'the other trait of Mosolov's work is that it is penetrated by the element of the 'nocturne', of 'night music' ... This is a nocturne of the city and its modern tragedy, the *tragedy of loneliness* among people and tragedy of fantasy in reality' (our emphasis). What does this mean? Loneliness in 1924, in the country that has carried out the greatest of revolutions, a country of intense public life, with a general tendency towards collectivism? It is obvious that the composer is so alienated from Soviet reality that he cannot become a part of it, and so he leads the existence of a loner.

This fact is further emphasised by the moods the critic finds in Mosolov's Third Sonata (op. 8): 'the second theme is itself the embodiment of tenderness, which the composer himself seems to disbelieve, *and which he ridicules*' (our emphasis). So, the composer doesn't believe in tenderness, he doesn't credit any tender, beautiful or benevolent feeling. The infection of 'no cherry blossom' has seeped in here too[i] – that is, the reduction of the whole range of psychological phenomena to bare physicality. And it is no accident that the critic discovers in the composer's nature 'a predilection for humour and satire', something that is

---

[26] Here the author tacitly refers to Bukharin's 'Angry Notes': 'in general, Yeseninshchina is a revolting, powdered and brazenly made-up Russian *matershchina*, soaked through with drunkard's tears [...]'.

also expressed in his 'parodies' of 'great composers' compositional styles'; these may be musical portraits, but specifically they are 'portraits *in accordance with the sceptical character of the modern urban outlook, which are somewhat in the manner of a caricature*' (our emphasis). But what kind of satire is this? How can one compare Mosolov with Musorgsky, as Belyayev does? It is entirely proper that we should distinguish between socially significant *satire* and the mere mockery of everyone and everything A satirist castigates, he is outraged, he ridicules the negative aspects of life; holding them up to shame, he also contrasts them with positive phenomena. Mosolov's sceptical mockery of 'tenderness', his disbelief in 'benevolent feelings', his caricaturing of the great composers [...] – this is not satire, but the utter nihilism [*bezveriye*] of a decayed and vacuous spirit, which lacks foundations, knows no principles and holds nothing sacred. This is a product of bourgeois urban culture, generated by bourgeois anarchism – the modern 'superfluous man' who believes in nothing. He has been called back to life, on the one hand, by the decadent thinking of the intelligentsia's more nihilistic members, and on the other, by the impulse towards self-gratification and Mammon-worship that occasionally resurfaces from the depths of the Russian bourgeoisie, squashed, but surviving nonetheless. [...]

So, what publically significant contribution has Mosolov made to our treasury of art? In 1924, his music presented us with faithlessness, mockery and 'funereal moods'; in 1926, it brought us the 'ultra-realism' of the naked man and the lowering of music to the level of a prosaic everyday object. The newspaper advertisements that Mosolov set to music are necessary things, just as the floor cloth is. But the floor cloth doesn't take us beyond the issue of the dirt on the floor. It does not raise us up to a higher level of development, it does not direct our thoughts and feelings to self-perfection, it does not draw our attention to thoughts that are meaningful or significant. [...]

But this is not our only cause for concern. The core of our musical youth is quite healthy and on the right track, cooperating with genuinely progressive revolutionary activists. It works successfully with the masses and produces music that resonates with the revolutionary times we are living in. It is not for solitary individuals like Mosolov to lure it away from its path. We are worried that the ideology of this 'left-wing' direction finds sympathy and support among some representatives of our academic circles. Regrettably, it is not just Belyayev who finds Mosolov's work 'interesting' and 'artistically significant' or bases his evaluation of the composer on novelty and talent alone. He is not the only one to take pleasure in the fact that Mosolov, in his 'children's songs', has turned to '*completely new* themes in our musical literature' (our emphasis). Ah, this pursuit of novelty, which has been so cruelly mocked by Alfredo Casella (himself a representative of contemporary music)! He says: 'Woe to the composer who uses last year's chords in his works of today. He will be told: "This is not the done thing". And the naive young man sets off on a search for ever more absurd, provocative, silly and ugly combinations, all to avoid being seen as "old-fashioned"'.[ii] It is even more dangerous that Belyayev, as a representative of our academicism, should so clearly approve of the 'bold' and 'pictorial' opposition of 'cruel' and physically crude children to 'mamma's boys' and 'well-mannered' children [...]. Unfortunately, he does not follow his thought through to the end, since this would lead him to tell us what such an opposition (favouring the first element), would lead to if it was raised as a slogan for the whole of society. We believe that it leads in a straight line to the terrors of 'Chubarov Lane' and to the cruel physical crudeness of those Chubarov Lane types, those 'fine fellows' who cannot even comprehend why they should have ended up in court.[27] These phenomena, despite their difference of scale, are qualitatively similar – they are of the same order.

We are no less bemused by Belyayev's inability to distinguish 'leftism' from 'progressivism': he says that 'in art, moving to the left means at the same time stepping forward'. The 'infantile disorder of leftism', at least in politics, has long since been exposed by Lenin; he evaluated it as a tendency that is revolutionary in appearance, but deeply reactionary in its essence, and all the more dangerous for hiding behind this revolutionary exterior. By analogy with this pseudo-revolutionary phraseology, we see here on the surface an unusual choice of texts and musical sonorities, while in essence, the composer is openly calling on us to not be ashamed of our bodily functions, which (as Belyayev explains) 'adults treat in the manner of man's nakedness after the Fall' ... Thus, 'leftist' and 'novel' phraseology is combined with a decayed reactionary essence, namely, of physiological and therefore psychological dissipation. And this is called – 'moving forward'? [...]

We thought it necessary to show those who had not yet understood that the tendencies cultivated by the 'left wing' of modern music and its apologists have nothing in common with any real movement forward, but are instead reactionary, harmful and of no use to us. 'What we need', Bukharin says, 'is a literature (and art in general – ed.) of people in good spirits, who are in the middle of life's stream, courageous builders who know life, and who are repelled by rot, mould, grave-digging, tavern tears, dissipation, boasting and playing the fool. The greatest among the bourgeoisie were not like the drunkard of genius (Verlaine), but giants such as Goethe, Hegel and Beethoven, who knew how to *work* like no one else. The greatest proletarian geniuses – Marx, Engels and Lenin – were the greatest toilers, with a great work ethic. The blessed "poor in spirit", holy fools in Christ, the café-chantant 30-minute geniuses – give them a wide berth! Draw closer to the wonderful life that is about to flourish on earth, closer to the masses rebuilding the world!'[iii]

[*Notes to original article*]

i Ionov, 'No Cherry Blossom', *Pravda*, 4 Dec. 1926. [Ionov's essay referred to the controversial eponymous novella by Panteleimon Romanov, which details a girl's state of disillusionment after a thoroughly unromantic and matter-of-fact sexual encounter. The story was supposed to stand for everyday Soviet life.]

ii *Sovremennaya muzïka*, 1926, no. 17–18.

iii N. Bukharin, '"Zlïye zametki"' [Angry Notes], *Pravda*, 12 Jan. 1927.

---

[27] This is a reference to one of the most notorious sexual crimes of the 1920s: a young woman, Lyuba Belyakova, was raped by as many as forty men in Leningrad's Chubarov Lane, and some of the assailants were Komsomol or Party members. During the course of the trial, it emerged that most of the accused and witnesses alike saw little wrong with the rape, and they evidently considered women to be inferior beings. The trial ended in exemplary punishments: instead of serving several years in prison, some of the perpetrators were sentenced to death.

Sadko, '"Krasnïy mak" v Bol'shom teatre' [*The Red Poppy* at the Bolshoi], *Zhizn' iskusstva*, no. 26 (28 June 1927), 4.

> The author of this scathing review is Vladimir Blyum, a fearsome theatre critic at Artistic Life, with a day job as a censor at Glavrepertkom. Blyum's support for artistic radicalism was well known (he supported Meyerhold in his most radical phase), and on many occasions he clashed with Lunacharsky on theatre policy.
>
> Despite the fact that the ballet was panned by the critics on both ideological and aesthetic grounds, it was one of the very few 'revolutionary' pieces to remain in the repertoire. Nor was it imposed from above: it broke all records for popularity with the public. By March 1928, all performances had already been sold out through to the 1930 season.[28]

'Sadko'
The Red Poppy at the Bolshoi

The Bolshoi Theatre's new ballet production, *The Red Poppy*, once again confirms two immutable truths: that new wine can't be poured into old wineskins, and that nowhere have revolutions ever been carried out by the ruling classes.

The 'ruling class' of the ballet world here is a small group representing 'classical' dance, headed by Geltser and Tikhomirov.[29] For some reason or other, they have decided to demonstrate that they have made some kind of 'shift' for the tenth anniversary of October, and have presented the world with an experiment in 'revolutionary' ballet. Let us pay all due respect to their good intentions, with which, as we know, hell is paved ...

As was reported in the press, *The Red Poppy* was created by number of people: the artist Kurilko,[30] the choreographers Lashchilin[31] and Tikhomirov, the composer Glière, and even our prima ballerina, Geltser. Thanks to this 'collective creative work', we were presented with a result of such ideologically muddled and discordant amateurishness, such rampant dilettantism, that even the Bolshoi's stage, which is accustomed to anything, has never witnessed the like.

---

[28] This information comes from a transcript of the meeting on musical theatre organised by Glaviskusstvo, 7–10 March 1928, RGALI, fond 645, op. 1, ye. kh. 332, l. 107.

[29] Ekaterina Vasilyevna Geltser (1876–1962), the first ballerina to receive the title of People's Artist of Russia (1925) and Vasily Dmitriyevich Tikhomirov (1878–1956), head of the Bolshoi ballet troupe, were a married couple of great influence in the ballet world.

[30] Mikhail Ivanovich Kurilko (1880–1969), who studied with Ilya Repin, was a well-established set designer, and the head of design at the Bolshoi (1924–28).

[31] Lev Aleksandrovich Lashchilin (1888–1955) was a dancer and choreographer at the Bolshoi, often serving as an assistant to Tikhomirov.

Strangely enough though, *The Red Poppy* sets out promisingly and positively.

In a Chinese port, the coolie workers are unloading a newly-arrived Soviet steamship. Diagonally across the stage looms the ship's hull (Kurilko has managed this very well), and aboard are young Red Navy sailors, while on the adjacent square, there is a motley crowd, tea houses, etc. There are also English officials, police, and representatives of the Chinese bourgeoisie. Among the last group, one character is either the agent or employer of a great popular actress. During the unloading, as the overseers constantly crack their whips, one of the coolies falls down dead. This causes the coolies to flare up into rebellion. But the Soviet sailors interfere: under the direction of their commander, they organise help for the exhausted coolies, and taking their place, they quickly unload the ship. The people and the female dancer [i.e. the actress] are most impressed. Evening falls, and at this point, the dances of the different nationalities on stage begin. To general delight, the Soviet Red sailors perform their dashing dance at the end to the music of 'The Little Apple' (*Yablochko*).

This act has enjoyed great success, and deservedly so, owing above all to the last scene with the sailors. But it transpires that the official authors of the ballet, the 'ruling class', had very little to do with it. It was the director, Dikiy[32] (who was working at the theatre simultaneously on *Love for Three Oranges*), who had a hand in the sailors' episodes in this act, and the idea of the 'Apple' belongs to him alone.

The 'ruling class' must have decided to show that revolutionary content can conceivably be presented in the forms of classical ballet. An absurd idea, which could only lead to political ambiguity, overall nonsense, and ... the unmitigated boredom and tedium of the second and third acts.

The second act begins with the aforementioned actress falling asleep after smoking opium, and her dreams provide the content of the entire act. Here we have the customary nonsense of old ballet: goddesses and flowers come to life, 'processions' of no one knows who, where or why, 'general' dances, solo and *en masse*, etc. The commander appears for a moment with his people ... This is supposed to mean (according to the published scenario) that while the actress is disturbed by the appearance of the new people and is drawn instinctively to the new truth they have brought with them, her consciousness is nonetheless still in thrall to the old prejudices, traditions, etc. The symbol of this truth is the red poppy, which (rather fleetingly) appears to her in Act 2, and which is presented to her by the Soviet commander in Act 3. But this is what the published scenario tells us. Act 2 ends with the thoroughly confusing and unexpected appearance, at the back of the stage, of a fantastic boat bearing a sail in Kuomintang colours.

In Act 3, irked by the popularity of the Soviet sailors, the English port officials and Chinese bourgeoisie conspire to murder the Red commander. The latter is invited to attend the [English] port governor's ball together with the sailors, and the same actress is supposed to hand him a cup of poisoned tea. But at the crucial moment, she knocks the deadly cup out of the commander's hands. Chaos ensues. The actress receives a fatal wound from a revolver shot. For some reason, the lights

---

[32] Aleksey Denisovich Dikiy (1889–1955) was an actor and a director of both drama and opera. His subsequent career ran from great fame (he played the role of Stalin in several films), to disfavour, including a spell in a labour camp.

go out on stage (all this happens in the English governor's house at the port). The stage is filled with women and children, who all freeze in a deep bow before the dying actress. At last, the actress beckons to a group of children and gives them the red poppy, the gift from the Soviet commander, which she had kept on her breast. With this, she finally dies. Suddenly 'red lances' appear from nowhere, and, to the strains of the *Internationale*, launch the 'revolution' ... Curtain.

What then, in a nutshell, is the political message of this tediously protracted and feeble rubbish? It is, apparently, that modern China (personified here by the actress) is in thrall to old prejudices and will not live to see the Revolution, the liberation of China.

It's an original thought, one which no one has as yet expressed in the debates on the Chinese question. A valuable addition to Trotsky's and Bukharin's speeches at the plenary session of the IKKI [the Executive Committee of the Communist International] ...

Such is the fate of revolution in a ballet realised by the 'ruling class'.

But perhaps, within the framework of classical ballet, something that is at least artistically literate has been created, even if it is of no great value? Alas, everything is feeble, bland and without talent, more like an entertainment at a fairground booth. The climactic point came when four mighty and bare-chested male dancers flew onto the stage wearing little wings on their backs (!) and began waving their arms about; among them was Tikhomirov himself, with legs like pillars and belly bulging, sporting the same wings and sweet smiles ('A pregnant cherub!' – someone behind me could not contain himself).

Geltser performs the principal role of the actress. From the press, we know that she has monopolised it, and there is no understudy for the role in *The Red Poppy*. But this is only a minor problem. What is worse is that the 'ruling class' has constructed the ballet in such a way that there is no other female role that could be entrusted to any dancer of note. Around the central role there is a gap, a desert, a descent into the *corps de ballet* or a group of *coryphées* ... It is clear why this is so. Every ruling class jealously guards its status and evades unfavourable comparison.

Let us be frank: it is difficult for Geltser to dance these days, and her latest roles (in *La Esmeralda* and *The Red Poppy*) are built on gesture and pantomime. Alas, she acts like a cinema actress in a bad film! In *The Red Poppy* her acting is all 'on one note': a frozen expression that tells us she feels lost, and a tedious 'shivering' gesture – look, it's our old friend 'the dying swan', stretched out over several hours and this time representing revolutionary China! Dozens of times, but never with any motivation, she rushes up to the front of the stage and shakes the lamps – all simply so that she can give us another tiresome little 'shiver'.

None of the other roles (all male) are given any kind of interpretation: men in jackets and uniforms simply mill around, not knowing what to do. These roles have also, of course, been taken by the representatives of the 'ruling class'.

The young (male!) dancers were only given microscopic parts, in Act 1 and in part of Act 3. And here, our talented balletic youth (Messerer, Tsaplin and Moiseyev)[33] won a storm of applause on each appearance. Will the domination of

---

[33] Asaf Mikhaylovich Messerer (1903–92) and Igor Alekseyevich Moiseyev (1906–2007) had distinguished careers: Messerer danced leading roles at the

the 'oldies' ever come to an end? How long must we leave young talent marinating, talent that has already grown under *Soviet* conditions?

Staking a production on our balletic youth has already been justified once, in *Iosif*, and even in the classical museum piece *Teolinda*.[34] But this is now the second production organised exclusively by and in the interests of the balletic 'ruling class': after the inane and philistine *Esmeralda*,[35] we are offered the wildest agitprop, created … in a ballerina's boudoir.

Bolshoi until 1955 and also achieved fame as a choreographer; Moiseyev began by choreographing sports parades in the 1930s and founded a pioneering Folk Dance Ensemble in 1937. Viktor Ivanovich Tsaplin (1903–1968) danced at the Bolshoi until 1955 and choreographed dances within operas.

[34] The author refers to the Bolshoi premieres of 1925: Vasilenko's ballet *Iosif prekrasnïy* (Joseph the Handsome) and *Teolinda* (on music by Schubert, 1927), both choreographed by Goleyzovsky, the latter in a neo-classical style.

[35] Cesare Pugni's 1844 ballet *La Esmeralda* (after Hugo) was a staple of the Bolshoi repertoire.

1928
At the Crossroads

1928 was a year of great economic and political turbulence. Trotsky's Opposition had already been destroyed and Trotsky himself expelled from the Party, but far from closing down the Party-wide debates the Oppositionists had demanded, these debates were simply shifted to the upper echelons of the Party. Now Stalin, in a striking about-turn, adopted a policy of rapid industrialisation, which had been the main plank of the Opposition (albeit with very different tactics), while Rykov and Bukharin now found themselves increasingly marginalised on the Party's right wing for trying to sustain the same policies Stalin had so recently endorsed. But what might seem arbitrary, or even perverse on Stalin's part, makes more sense when set alongside events. The country was plunged into a severe economic crisis, through bad luck, it would seem, rather than bad policy: the rumours of impending war, although they had little foundation, prompted fearful peasants to hoard grain instead of selling it on the NEP internal market. Bread now disappeared from the shelves of city shops. This happened at the worst possible moment, since Stalin had just resolved that substantial grain (and oil) exports would earn the Soviet Union much of the foreign currency it needed to import industrial machinery. The resulting conflict made the continuation of NEP an impossibility. Stalin now imposed 'extraordinary measures' to force the peasants to release their grain stocks. To the peasants, this harked back to requisitions of War Communism, but the purpose was different. During the Civil War, it was a measure required to ensure the survival of the urban population and the army, similar to anti-speculation policies pursued by non-Communist governments elsewhere during wartime. But in 1928, it was not so much the survival, but the productivity of the cities that was at stake. And closing the circle, the industrialisation drive was also, to a large extent, prompted by the fear of another war waged against the Soviet Union by hostile powers – no country could hope to win a modern war without an advanced industrial economy. Stalin's 'rightist' opponents instead argued for what they saw as the path of least resistance: they wanted to prevent the collapse of NEP by *importing* grain until the peasantry was persuaded to release its stocks again on the internal market. This, however, meant that the great project of industrialisation would have to be postponed indefinitely, which would, among other things, make the Soviet Union easy prey in case of war (a third course that might have circumvented such a dilemma had been proposed by the now banned and dispersed Left Opposition). The ebb and flow of the debate at the top of the Party brought waves of 'extraordinary measures' followed by relaxations, until Stalin eventually won.

A high-profile show trial, the first since the early twenties, diverted public attention from the government's difficulties, and created scapegoats on whom the economic problems could be blamed. These were the 'saboteurs' and 'wreckers' of the Shakhty trial, highly qualified engineers who were accused of collaborating with the international bourgeoisie. Although Bukharin had been on the losing side of the economic argument, he had no compunction about heightening public paranoia, and in his statement on the trial, published in *Pravda*, we see for the first time how all these events would affect culture. Declaring the present an era of 'violent class struggle', Bukharin addressed cultural issues directly (granted, his concept of 'culture' is broader than ours):

> We have expended much energy in launching the cultural revolution and in creating new, loyal cultural cadres who will construct the socialist economy, and so we shall now steadfastly set about the task of forging the indispensable *armour of socialist culture*, which must surround us like an impenetrable wall, protecting our Party, the Soviets, the trade unions, and the whole of the working class from alien class influences, from bourgeois degeneration, from petit-bourgeois vacillation, and from the dulling of revolutionary vigilance towards the more cultured class enemy.[1]

This 'armour of socialist culture', in spite of Bukharin's description, was not comparable to the descent of the 'Iron Curtain' of later Cold War lore, but it did become increasingly difficult for musicians to defend and promote extensive cultural contacts with the West, not least for the prosaic reason that the Soviet Union now lacked sufficient reserves of hard currency. The import of heavy machinery was now in direct competition with the import of pianists and conductors, making the latter seem extravagant. The old Rosfil organisation had often been criticised for an over-reliance on foreign performers and for the cultural elitism that accompanied this tendency.[2] Rosfil's replacement, Sofil (Soviet Philharmonia), was originally empowered to exercise a monopoly on foreign invitations and to distribute hard currency to a range of smaller musical organisations. But once these hard currency allocations were severely reduced, there was simply not enough to go around. ASM was able to retain its right to invite foreign performers and its hard currency budget was, for the moment, assured.[3]

Surprisingly, thanks to the inertia of the system, concert life continued for some time along the same cosmopolitan lines. The names of Klemperer, Ansermet, Schnabel and Szigeti still adorned the concert posters. Two more modernist Western composers came on tour. Arthur Honegger was regarded by both Myaskovsky and Asafyev as the most serious and significant member of *Les Six*, and he was considered 'very sweet' when they met him in person.[4] Paul Hindemith came on several tours, together with the other three members of his ensemble, the Amar Quartet, and he mesmerised listeners with his performance of his own Sonata for solo viola, during which, it was reported, he seemed to transcend the natural limitations of the instrument.[5]

The previous year's successful production of *Wozzeck* helped to raise the bar for new music, and 1928 saw premieres of several very ambitious orchestral

---

[1] 'Klassovïy protsess' [editorial], *Pravda* (18 May 1928), 1.

[2] S. Korev, 'K organizatsii Sovfila', *Sovetskoye iskusstvo*, no. 4 (1928), 44–7.

[3] Appendix to Derzhanovsky's letter to Prokofiev of 4 Sept. 1928, LPA, folder 18, 316–17.

[4] Letter from Asafyev to Prokofiev of 15 Mar. 1928, LPA, folder 17, 222–4.

[5] Yu. Vaynkop, 'Kvartet Amar-Khindemit', *Zhizn' iskusstva*, no. 1 (3 Jan. 1928), 13.

works: Schoenberg's *Gurre-Lieder*, Myaskovsky's Tenth Symphony (together with his earlier Third and Ninth), and Shcherbachov's Second Symphony. Mosolov maintained a high profile thanks to his ultra-modern Piano Concerto, which deepened the synthesis of expressionist atonality and machine-music that had recently won him acclaim in *The Iron Foundry*. The challenges were sometimes too much for the performers: Myaskovsky's Tenth, in particular, proved to be the undoing of Persimfans. A 'colossal failure', said Derzhanovsky,[6] while Goldenweiser found the playing 'shabby, tedious, talentless and dead',[7] although he felt he could hear beyond the shortcomings of the performance, and detected 'genuine tragedy' in the music.[8]

Prokofiev's Soviet profile took a downturn in 1928. He had arranged a second visit to coincide with a Mariinsky production of *The Gambler*. All was in place for the visit and the opera was already advertised, but the production was shelved, and Prokofiev cancelled his visit as a result. The source of the problems is not entirely clear. Asafyev, grinding his axe, put the blame on conservative elements that he said were now in the ascendant at the theatre. But it is more likely that the demise of the production arose from unfortunate scheduling problems between the composer and Meyerhold the producer. The newly reworked version that Prokofiev had promised took longer than expected, and when it eventually arrived, Meyerhold either could not or would not make himself available. It was a difficult time for him: one of his signature productions, *Woe to Wit*, had come under heavy criticism and for a while, the future of his theatre company hung in the balance. Their project of staging *The Gambler* was still entertained for a few years, both at Mariinsky and the Bolshoi, but in the end, too much time passed, and it eventually became impossible to stage such a work. A production of *Chout* was mounted in Kiev, but this was an annoyance rather than a triumph for the composer, since no permission had been sought, nor any royalties paid. Persimfans, once much admired for their performances of Prokofiev, were now in terminal decline, and although *Steps of Steel* (*Stal'noy skok*)[9] and the Second Symphony were both considered, the orchestra feared another debacle and stuck to safer fare, leaving the field open to others. ASM was anxious that at least one major new work of Prokofiev's should be heard, and they managed to organise the premiere of *Steps of Steel* on 27 May with the conductor Vladimir Savich. The project was rushed, however, and the conductor lacked sufficient time to acquaint himself fully with the demanding score. The whole musical world attended, but, as Prokofiev's aunt bluntly reported, 'no one liked it', and a caustic little review in *Vechernyaya Moskva* followed.[10] On 31 October, Dranishnikov premiered

---

[6] Letter from Derzhanovsky to Prokofiev of 12 Apr. 1928, LPA, folder 17, 303.

[7] Diary entry of 2 Apr. 1928, A. B. Gol'denveyzer, *Dnevnik: tetradi vtoraya-shestaya* (Moscow: Tortuga, 1997), 214.

[8] Ibid.

[9] This ballet is better known under its French title *Le pas d'acier*, but here, in the Soviet context, we will refer to it as *Steps of Steel* which is Prokofiev's own English translation of the title.

[10] Letter from Ye.R. [Yekaterina Rayevskaya] to Prokofiev of 16 June 1928, LPA, vol. 18, 109–12.

Prokofiev's Second Symphony in Leningrad, but this also failed to make the desired impact:

> [T]he symphony's reception (sympathetic on the whole) clearly showed that it was not accessible to the public; this, we believe, should partly be ascribed to its unusual language, which was something new, especially for the avid 'Prokofievians', although it was also due to the performance itself, certainly not short of excitement, but under-rehearsed.[11]

These were still seen as temporary setbacks, however, and new collaborations were planned. Even if Prokofiev did not come to Russia this year, Russia could still come to him, in the shape of Asafyev and Lamm. While the two Soviet musicians were on separate trips to the West, their itineraries converged on Prokofiev's doorstep in Paris. Knowing how much the change of scene meant to them, Prokofiev was at his most hospitable and kept them entertained throughout their stay. One person was missing from the reunion: Myaskovsky, who would have had great difficulty funding such a trip from his own resources, and who was temperamentally ill-equipped to run the bureaucratic obstacle course necessary for gaining the correct papers. Mindful of his role as the propagandist for new Russian music in the West, Prokofiev commended to Diaghilev the three young Soviet composers he had found most promising, namely Shostakovich, Mosolov and Gavriil Popov.[12]

But the most prominent musical event of the year arising from ASM's efforts could hardly be classed as 'contemporary music' – this was the premiere of Musorgsky's original *Boris Godunov* at the Mariinsky, on 16 February. The foundational work on the production was Lamm's painstaking research on Musorgsky's manuscripts. Later, Asafyev prepared the score for performance and organised the staging. Asafyev also led a well-planned press campaign pitching the new *Boris* as an opera whose revolutionary character had been diluted by Rimsky-Korsakov's revisions, but which was now to be revealed in its true colours to the Soviet public. Whatever contribution this line might have made to the success of the production, Lamm considered it to be shameless opportunism, and he argued bitterly with Asafyev behind the scenes:

> Be mindful of the fact that I have never seen Musorgsky label *Boris* as a 'people's music drama' – this is how it was dubbed by Stasov and his associates [in the late 19th century]. But Musorgsky himself didn't say this.[13]

Asafyev, in his influential writing about Boris, tried to emphasise the role of 'the people' in the crowd scenes, but Lamm baulked at this interpretation (admittedly, this might also have arisen from Lamm's own political views, rather than from pure Musorgsky scholarship). He could not find Asafyev's alleged active discontent in the first scene of the Prologue, nor any 'forced' glorification in the Coronation

---

[11] B. Valer'yanov, 'Proizvedeniya Prokof'yeva', *Rabochiy i teatr*, no. 46 (11 Nov. 1928), 4.

[12] Letter from Prokofiev to Diaghilev of 21 Sept. 1928, LPA, folder 16, 231–2.

[13] Letter from Lamm to Asafyev of 13 Jan. 1928, RGALI, fond 2743 (Lamm), op. 1, ye. kh. 42, l. 1.

Scene. He was against assigning any exaggerated dramatic significance to the peasant Mityukha (in the Prologue) or even the Holy Fool, and resented even more any attempt to cast Pimen as a kind of 'political leader' ('he would need to head a party' in that case, said Lamm). His distaste for the Kromy Scene, featuring a popular revolt, led him to prefer the original, 1869 version of *Boris*, although it was largely because of this scene that the opera was guaranteed an honourable place in the repertoire during the coming Stalinist period. Continuing his argument against Asafyev, he said:

> You yourself argue that the second version is less perfect, and I would put it in stronger terms: it spoils the preliminary version, as if Musorgsky was saying: 'You don't understand me, you need an assortment of female roles, superficial effects etc., so here you are – take, eat, and bon appetit!'. And so all kinds of extra numbers appear, Boris's monologue is mutilated, and the Polish scenes are composed. If you want to know my opinion, I would say that if we stage *Boris* precisely in accordance with the preliminary version, then the Kromy scene would spoil it, and might indeed prove quite superfluous, since it introduces something foreign to the main conception. Whatever you do, it will be difficult to avoid turning the scene into a 'night on the Bare Mountain', because the crowd there, unprepared by anything earlier, will suddenly break loose and then only to glorify the 'one saved by God, the one hidden by God'.[14] There is something amiss here, but this is not the time for discussing it, and I cannot reproach you for the 'sociological' approach. This is a tribute to the present time. [...] And still, to call Pimen's tale a 'political agitation' is too much. However, I am not going to talk about politics, because this is a separate matter that we've already discussed many times.[15]

In fact, as Lamm mentions, both he and Asafyev were, in principle, opposed the inclusion of the Polish Scenes, which provided more conventional love music and ballet in the later (1872) version. But here both political considerations and box-office prospects clearly pointed in the other direction, so the scenes were included, albeit with Asafyev's cuts.[16]

Asafyev mitigated some of his most 'opportunistic' formulations,[17] but his line of argument remained unaltered. Disregarding Lamm's response, he reiterated and even heightened his criticisms of the Rimsky-Korsakov version. The closing

---

[14] Lamm here is pointing out the unprepared nature of the people's riot in the Kromy Scene, which breaks away from the original conception of the opera and does not stem from Pushkin. Richard Taruskin investigated this in *Musorgsky*, proposing that Musorgsky was influenced here by the historical works of Kostomarov, as opposed to Karamzin who had influenced Pushkin and the rest of *Boris*. See Richard Taruskin, *Musorgsky Eight Essays and an Epilogue* (Princeton University Press, 1993), 123–200.

[15] See fn. 13 on p. 200, ll. 1–2.

[16] Letter from Lamm to Asafyev of 17 Jan. 1928, RGALI, fond 2743 (Lamm), op. 1, ye. kh. 51, l. 5.

[17] Igor' Glebov, *K vosstanovleniyu Borisa Godunova Musorgskogo* (Moscow: Gosudarstvennoye izdatel'stvo, Muzïkal'nyi otdel, 1928).

peroration in one of his previews, written for the Leningrad *Krasnaya gazeta* (Red Newspaper), was a call to arms:

> It is high time we brought the musical Middle Ages to an end, and musical provincialism with them, for the remnants of a stubborn backwardness survive there, under the banner of preserving Russian cultural traditions.[18]

The 'remnants of a stubborn backwardness' picked up the gauntlet. Glazunov sent in his response, claiming that Rimsky-Korsakov's version was an improvement on the original, and insisted that this was what should be staged. Asafyev, using his connections with the *Krasnaya gazeta*, ensured that Glazunov's text was cut to one column, with his own counter-response printed alongside.[19] Glazunov was outraged, and called for reinforcements. Shteynberg and another composition professor, Alexander Zhitomirsky, had soon sent their own letters of support. Now it was Asafyev who took offence: if Shteynberg was against him, then so, effectively, was LASM. He now played his trump card: the *Boris* he and Lamm were presenting was an opera far better suited to the new times, revealing all its 'revolutionary-narodnik' tendencies. At the same time, he enlisted the public support of the progressive conductors Dranishnikov and Malko, and more strikingly, two Communist officials: the head of the Regional Politprosvet, A. Romanov and best of all, the Old Bolshevik and Party CC member, Alexei Stetsky. There was now little point in the other side continuing the debate. Instead, in a final desperate fling, the heirs of Rimsky-Korsakov sued Lamm and Asafyev for royalties, but unsurprisingly lost the case. The progressives had won this round. Glazunov, the figurehead of the conservative faction, left on a foreign tour from which he never returned. But Asafyev's role as the promoter of a revolutionary Musorgsky also brought him into conflict with his fellow progressives. Musorgsky was also the idol and chief model for the 'proletarian composers', whom Asafyev had now given a great boost – they could now cite his scholarly arguments in support of their own position. As in 1924, Asafyev was again seen by his friends as almost a defector.

It was in 1928 that noisy orchestrated campaigns against musical institutions and individuals began on an unprecedented scale, a trend that continued until 1932, when order was imposed from above. The first of these campaigns, waged against the Bolshoi Theatre, was a confused affair that lacked a clear political purpose. It was partially motivated by a crisis of management that was obvious even to the public. Derzhanovsky, for example, tells us how productions were seriously impaired for a time when the entire horn section walked out; their ensemble passages were rendered by piano or harmonium, and solos transferred to other orchestral instruments.[20] There was also a financial crisis, when a deficit run up

---

[18] Igor' Glebov, 'K novïm beregam', *Krasnaya gazeta* (vecherniy vïpusk), no. 35 (5 Feb. 1928), 4.

[19] See Glazunov's letter to Shaporin of 28 Feb. 1928, publ. in 'Iz perepiski Yu. A. Shaporina (1917–1963)', ed. by R. Rimskaya, *Iz proshlogo sovetskoy muzïkal'noy kul'turï*, vol. 2 (Moscow: Sovetskiy kompozitor, 1976), 55–98, esp. 57.

[20] Letter from Derzhanovsky to Prokofiev of 27 Jan. 1928, LPA, vol. 17, 73–4.

by the opera troupe prompted an audit by the RKI (The Workers' and Peasants' Inspectorate).[21] There were also various problems arising from strained relations between the Bolshoi proper and its 'filial' Experimental Theatre, which was anything but experimental. Finally, there was a sustained personal attack on the Theatre's chief conductor, Golovanov, who was accused of rudeness, favouritism, denying promotion to young singers, and most seriously, anti-Semitism. The last accusation was a more opaque formulation: Golovanov was 'aloof from public opinion' [*chuzhd obchshestvennosti*]. This may have indicated Golovanov's lack of respect not so much for the general public as for the Bolshoi's Party cell.

All these issues, together with the long-standing problem of the Bolshoi's repertoire, were examined by a government committee investigating the claims.[22] The ensuing resolution saw the crisis largely in terms of administrative failure: various specified measures were to be taken not only at the Bolshoi itself, but also at Narkompros, which was held partly responsible for failing to exercise due oversight. But one non-administrative measure was recommended: the removal of Golovanov. On the charge of anti-Semitism, the committee said that it had received no material evidence. But the verdict was effectively 'not proven' rather than 'not guilty'. For the public, the label had already stuck, and Golovanov was greeted by booing when he walked to the podium. He had become a symbol for everything that was non-Soviet and unreformed in the Bolshoi's hermetic culture, and beyond this, for similar traits to be found across a wide swathe of the intelligentsia. The term *golovanovshchina* was coined for use against any individual or institution that was clinging to pre-Revolutionary behaviour.

In this, the year of Stalin's first show trial, it would be natural to assume that the anti-Golovanov campaign was orchestrated from the top. In this case, however, the impetus was from below, involving lower-ranking members of the Bolshoi troupes and spreading out into public discontent. The government committee was only formed in response, to quell the mounting scandal. In February, Stalin decided it was time to speak to the Bolshoi's director, Alexander Burdukov.[23] The outcome was the sacking of Burdukov, while Golovanov was only suspended from his Bolshoi job for one season. As far as the government was concerned, the matter was closed, but the attacks on Golovanov in the press continued. To follow the story through to its end, in January of the following year, the issue had risen all the way up to Politburo level, where it was resolved that the attacks must stop and newspaper editors were instructed not to pursue such campaigns in future (not on their own initiative, at any rate). Stalin, it seems, personally supported Golovanov's return to the theatre. But still the campaign continued, and Golovanov was hounded down to the Conservatoire, where he taught a course. There were two more Politburo sessions with the Bolshoi on the agenda in December 1929, which

---

[21] 'Akad. teatrï pered sudom obshchestvennosti', *Rabochiy i teatr*, no. 24 (10 June 1928), 2–3.

[22] 'Postanovleniye pravitel'stvennoy komissii o Gosudarstvennom Akademicheskom Bol'shom Teatre', *Muzïkal'noye obrazovaniye*, no. 3 (1928), 31–5.

[23] Aleksandr Aleksandrovich Burdukov (1880–1940) was an old Bolshevik, who after the Revolution held appointments in the Red Army and then a series of directorships of educational institutions. He was director of the Bolshoi from 1927–8.

found that the previous order against further persecution of Golovanov had gone unheeded.[24] A few months later, the Bolshoi was transferred under the direct control of TsIK (the Central Executive Committee of the Party). This raised it to the status of an untouchable court institution, which, as we shall see, meant that it was one of the few sectors of musical life that remained off limits for RAPM (an outcome that was by no means incidental for the government).

As for the Bolshoi's repertoire failings, these were criticised vigorously by Platon Kerzhentsev, a former Proletkult activist who had recently been promoted to become deputy head of Agitprop (not a government department, but a high-level Party institution). Kerzhentsev had long been an opponent of Lunacharsky and his preservationist policies for the 'Academy theatres'. Now he was in an excellent position to make his views heard, and took the opportunity to express them in 'The Trouble with Opera', his first article for *Pravda*, which appeared in April.[25] The article lamented the Bolshoi's lack of interest in contemporary opera and ballet, even in Shostakovich, who had already received recognition abroad. The Experimental Theatre, the Bolshoi's second stage, was the obvious venue for daring new pieces, but in practice, it failed to make even token efforts to live up to its name, and was run as a purely commercial operation, showing only the most popular repertoire. On the basis of this article, the champions of new music were delighted, thinking they had found a kindred spirit in the senior ranks of the Party's apparatus. Derzhanovsky posted the article off to Prokofiev, with a brief accompanying note:

> I am attaching an article from *Pravda*, with which I am in complete agreement. This is more 'grist to your mill', since more articles like this one will increase the likelihood that *The Gambler* will be staged.[26]

Derzhanovsky, allowing his enthusiasm to cloud his judgement, even made public statements of solidarity with 'P. Ker-tsev', after the first *Pravda* article was followed by a second, 'More on Opera' (he claimed, perhaps disingenuously, that he did not know the author).[27] But Derzhanovsky had found what he wanted and filtered out the rest. Kerzhentsev had expressed himself clearly enough, and his argument was double-edged. He had indeed said that the Bolshoi's directorate needed to learn more about contemporary Western opera, but he had also insisted that only the those operas that were 'the most acceptable from a social point of view' should be presented to the Soviet public, and not all the 'decadent *Salomes*'. And the Soviet operas and ballets he wanted to see staged in the future would have to be 'close to us in subject matter, and musically cheerful in character, concentrating the will'.[28] This was hardly a description of Shostakovich's *Nose*, at that moment in preparation for production in Leningrad. The quickening

[24] *Vlast' i khudozhestvennaya intelligentsiya*, 747.
[25] P. K-tsev, 'Neblagopoluchiye s operoy', *Pravda*, no. 85 (10 Apr. 1928), 5.
[26] Letter from Derzhanovsky to Prokofiev of 10 Apr. 1928, LPA, folder 17, 295.
[27] P. Ker-tsev, 'Yeshcho ob opere', *Pravda*, no. 104 (6 May 1928), 6 and V. V. Derzhanovskiy, 'Tam, gde chasï – mertvï ...', *Sovremennaya muzika*, no. 31 (May 1928), 160–9.
[28] Ibid.

rate of change in the political landscape was beginning to leave Derzhanovsky disorientated.

With hindsight, we can see Kerzhentsev's intervention as the first sign of a widening gulf between Agitprop and Narkompros that would end with the fall of Lunacharsky. Even so, Narkompros was not standing still, and a harder line in its music policy was emerging. At a Narkompros meeting on music theatre, one Pavel Novitsky showed the way forward (he was soon to head the Theatre and Music Section of Glaviskusstvo, the ministry's new dedicated arts department). Novitsky complained that there still was 'in reality no organ that could issue programmes or ideological artistic directives' and that the ministry could operate 'more than one artistic policy'. He called for a meeting (*partsoveshchaniye*) on music, to be led by Agitprop, whose directives, he hoped, would then have to be adopted by Narkompros.[29] Novitsky's recommendation was accepted, although the meeting did not take place until June 1929, when it did indeed establish the mechanisms for closer Party control over musical affairs.

Meanwhile Lunacharsky, unlike Kerzhentsev, retained an interest in contemporary Western operas that were by no means 'the most acceptable from a social point of view', even contributing his own review of Krenek's *Der Sprung über den Schatten*, which had been performed the previous year with mixed results (we reproduce this review below). It was another Krenek opera, however, that proved the greatest box office success of 1928–29 season: his *Johnny spielt auf*, which played at the Leningrad Maly Opera. Unusually for this theatre, there were several performances of *Johnny* a week, and sometimes even two a day. Other theatres sought to follow this lead: for example, the Stanislavsky studio planned to produce two Kreneks and one Hindemith (*The Heavyweight*, *The Dictator*, and *Hin und Zurück*).

For all the scandal, the Bolshoi Theatre affair was self-contained: it had been propelled from below, and had no real political ramifications. But the second institutional upheaval of the year was very different. This was the Moscow Conservatoire affair, the first significant event in the musical world to reflect the huge political shifts now underway. On 18 November, *Pravda* published an article entitled 'All is not well at the Conservatoire'. The author, effectively anonymous under the initials Z.Z., claimed that the problems emanated from 'right[ist]' professors, and named a *troika* of leading offenders: the pianist Goldenweiser, the conductor Golovanov, and the singer Nazary Raysky (who was also the head of the Conservatoire's management). Z.Z. displayed considerable cynicism in projecting the rift at the top of the Party onto the Conservatoire. To put it bluntly, Goldenweiser was a religious believer, a conservative anti-communist and (it need hardly be added) politically inactive; far from being a right-Communist Bukharinite, he fell off the political map altogether. Stalin had introduced the notion of 'right deviation' to prepare the way for Bukharin's downfall. Still in disagreement with Stalin's new policies of accelerated industrialisation, Bukharin published his own views in *Pravda* on 30 September ('Notes of an Economist'), in a transparent ploy,

---

[29] 'Stenogramma soveshchaniya pri Glaviskusstve po voprosam sovremennogo muzïkal'nogo teatra i estradï i perepiska v svyazi s yego organizatsiyey', RGALI, fond 645 (Glaviskusstvo), op. 1, ye. kh. 332, l. 93.

presenting his views as a criticism of the exiled Trotsky rather than of Stalin. He hoped that his article would open up a Party-wide debate on economics, but Stalin simply fired *Pravda*'s Editorial Board, and the paper now published endless articles on the dangers of right deviationism. Stalin was not simply lashing out in anger: he paced his attack carefully, and at first the articles refrained from naming Bukharin as the chief target. Then during the autumn, Stalin broke up the Moscow Party Committee for its support of Bukharin, wielding the charge of 'right deviationism'. It was only at the end of November that he openly accused Bukharin (already after the Conservatoire article).[30]

The anonymous *Pravda* attack could have emanated from any of several groups and individuals at the Conservatoire. A likely contender was the group around the problematic *pedotdel* or *pedfak*, a Pedagogical Department (Faculty) that had been established in the Conservatoire to offset its professional elitism and overproduction of unemployable virtuosi. In practice, it became a ghetto for weaker musicians who had no prospect of a performing career, and it was disbanded in 1928 on an initiative from Goldenweiser, who suggested that teaching methods should be introduced to the curriculum in the other faculties. This inevitably caused resentments, and Goldenweiser had set himself up as the prime target for any counterattack. Golovanov was a minor player in the Conservatoire, and his inclusion in the alleged rightist troika was another cynical tactic: his name was already tainted, and could blacken the others by association. With '*golovanovshchina*' reawakened, the charges of anti-Semitism were broadened to include Goldenweiser, who was half-Jewish, and utterly bemused by this turn of events. As for Raysky, he was picked mainly for his administrative power, although some personal accusations were also vented: it had been noticed that he sang solos in the church opposite the Conservatoire, and he had allegedly misappropriated Conservatoire funds so that electric lighting could be installed there.[31]

After the first article in *Pravda*, further attacks appeared elsewhere, overturning the lives of the *troika*. Goldenweiser's diary records meetings with various officials, all leading nowhere, and also speaks of his deepening demoralisation:

> Another article today, this time in *Komsomolskaya pravda*, with harsh attacks, some directed against me. Novitsky wrote something similar for *Muzïka i revolyutsiya*. Yurovsky has been trying not to print it for the last four days, but it's probably futile. I don't know whom I could have caused any harm or who could feel compelled to slander me in this way. [...] I feel that a lot of trouble may be coming my way: the loss of my public stature, hardship, housing problems, and the removal of any opportunities to play before the public – in other words, civic death. And all for what?[32]

The Novitsky article that Goldenweiser mentions made it clear to all who were as

---

[30] Vadim Rogovin, *Vlast' i oppozitsii* (Moscow: Tovarishchestvo 'Zhurnal "Teatr"', 1993), 63–7.

[31] 'Rezolyutsiya Ob'yedineniya Revolyutsionnïkh Kompozitorov i Muzïkal'nïkh Deyateley o polozhenii, sozdavshemsya v Moskovskoy Konservatorii', *Muzïka i revolyutsiya*, no. 11 (1928), 33.

[32] Diary entry of 1 Dec. 1928, Gol'denveyzer, 252.

yet unaware that Narkompros (or part of it) was now against the Conservatoire under its current leadership.³³ Novitsky had some colourful terms for his opponents: 'mystics', 'reactionaries', and best of all, 'Black Hundreds'. But this was mere name calling that fell short – in the present circumstances – of accusing the troika of right deviationism. Novitsky, who wielded real power, was being circumspect by comparison with the unscrupulous Z.Z.

After months of meetings that stretched into the following year, the *pedotdel* was reintroduced, Raysky lost his management post to a Communist and, most importantly, the Conservatoire had a new Director imposed, a Communist from outside its own ranks. But Goldenweiser was spared. As evidence of his reformed consciousness, he agreed to teach some *pedotdel* students, who greeted him with hostility and sarcasm, exactly as class enemies ought to be greeted.

---

³³ Pavel Novitskiy, 'Tsitadel' muzïkal'noy khudozhestvennoy reaktsii' *Muzïka i revolyutsiya*, no. 11 (1928), 18–22.

※ ※ ※ ※ ※

A. Lunacharskiy, 'Na "Prïzhke cherez ten"' [At *Der Sprung über den Schatten*], *Krasnaya gazeta (vecherniy vïpusk)*, no. 66 (4 March 1928), 4.

A. Lunacharsky
At *Der Sprung über den Schatten*

In Leningrad, opera is still far ahead of Moscow: this season, there has been nothing new to see in Moscow, while Leningrad has enjoyed many new productions and continues to do so. We hear the excuse that operas borrowed from the West do not lie on the path our cultural construction is taking, but this is absurd, since the old operas that we are content to hear have little connection with our work of cultural construction either! Admittedly, they seem less controversial, because we are used to them, and because their rhythms and content were dictated by the comparatively calm life of past days, which still accords with the inner rhythm of this, our peasant country, where large cities, with their accelerated pace of life, have done little to shake up our nervous system. The Revolution brought about a colossal shift in our country, replacing Oblomov[34] with the image of the quick, energetic and determined Bolshevik. But we should not imagine that we will bring about a corresponding change in mass psychology here without further industrialisation, turning our country from an endless string of villages into the site of industrial production.

There is much that we find repugnant in the urbanisation of Western Europe and America. That is a capitalist, mechanised urbanisation. The future here will be very different. But if we had to choose between the quiet of the country, or the music created in small, cosy German towns, or the music dictated by the bustling streets and squares of today's world capitals, then, in my opinion, we must concede that they all stand at the same distance from our position. This is why we should by no means ignore contemporary European music, and contemporary European opera in particular.

Krenek's opera *Der Sprung über den Schatten*, which I have had the opportunity to hear during my current Leningrad visit, has a plot that does not amount to very much, which is something quite characteristic of contemporary Western culture: it is almost incapable of creating anything of significance. However, even the plot of Krenek's opera contains something positive: *self-mockery*. This opera is an expressionist work, but its expressionism is able to laugh at itself, constructing a self-caricature. If Prokofiev, in his *Three Oranges*, mocks opera in general with great wit and even brilliance, then Krenek, in *Der Sprung*, mocks expressionist

---

[34] Oblomov was the anti-hero of Ivan Goncharov's eponymous novel of 1859. Oblomov was a hopeless underachiever who preferred dreams to action, and he quickly came to stand for the Russian national character (as the author had intended).

opera, again with great wit. The most interesting feature of this opera is not even the music, which is very acute, at times rising to a peak of brilliance (albeit with a few dips and bland spots); the most interesting feature was, rather, the staging at the Academy Maly Theatre.

I have spent quite a lot of time in Europe recently, and I am not surprised that the Berlin conductor Zemlinsky,[35] who was here on tour, was very excited about this production. Indeed, this was probably the most European spectacle among all the productions I have recently seen. In Paris or Berlin, it would have made an astonishing impact. Over there, we only see them taking a few steps towards this kind of production; they have not attained its full realisation, which we can see in the great ball scene of Act 1, or in the finale.

In the best moments of this production, the contemporary European bazaar of merriment (which constitutes a good half of all European life) is portrayed in a highly concentrated manner. It is very hard to convey in words why this is so, but this metallic spectacle, with its lights and reflections, whose movements accompany the dances of people and sounds, is like a magic crystal in which we can see a miniature version of the whole foxtrot-militaristic Europe, rushing headlong towards the next great catastrophe.

This opera is not at all 'ours'. It was born out of European degeneration, and it is a satirical reflection upon itself. But it is useful for our education. And what is most interesting is that when we, with our mighty theatrical culture, take up tasks of a purely European nature, we can solve them even better than Europe itself.

---

[35] The Austrian composer and conductor Alexander von Zemlinsky (1871–1942), a friend of Schoenberg and promoter of his works, was at that time conductor at the Kroll Opera in Berlin.

※ ※ ※ ※ ※

N. Vïgodskiy, '"Put' Oktyabrya"' [*The Path of October*], *Muzïka i revolyutsiya*, no. 11 (1928), 48–50.

The author of this essay, Nikolai Vygodsky, taught organ and non-major piano at the Moscow Conservatoire and like the composers of the project previewed here, he was himself a member of Prokoll (Production Collective). The piece in question did not prove to be viable as a whole (only the two Davidenko choruses became well known), but it is likely to have influenced Prokofiev when he began work on his Cantata for the twentieth Anniversary of October a decade later (in particular, in his use of accordions and 'sound montage', and in general the combination of populism and modernism).

N. Vygodsky
The Path of October

The Path of October, subtitled 'A Musical Action', is the first attempt by the young composers forming the Production Collective at the Scholarship and Composition Faculty of the MGK [Moscow State Conservatoire] to represent through music the revolutionary struggle of 1905, and to mark the most important events of 1917, the Civil War, and our work of socialist construction.[36] This difficult task, which the Collective set for itself, required a special form for its realisation. The most appropriate forms for the artistic embodiment of such a task would be opera or oratorio (i.e. a large-scale work with choir and orchestra, but no stage action). The collective chose oratorio, because their conception was to create a musical work that would not only be accessible to the mass listener, but which could also be performed on amateur stages by music circles. The incorporation of stage action would have made the latter more difficult. So the choice of oratorio should be acknowledged as correct. But this is no ordinary oratorio, like those of a Handel or a Taneyev. For a different era, we have different content, a different grasp of events – all this requires different means. Old, traditional oratorio forms would have been too narrow, and inadequate for *The Path of October*. The original subtitle, 'A Musical Action' [*muzïkal'noye deystvo*], encountered in the history of music for the first time and found after much searching and collective discussion, reflects the novelty of the goals and the form.

The Path of October was conceived for large orchestra with organ, accordion and two choirs (one singing, one reciting). The full score is currently being

---

[36] Nine composers collaborated on this work. For information on Viktor Belïy, Nikolai Chemberdzhi, Alexander Davidenko, Marian Koval, Zara Levina, Sergey Ryauzov, and Boris Shekhter, see Glossary. Genrikh Semyonovich Bruk (1905–1990) was a student of Glière's (graduated in 1930) and went on to be a prolific composer, especially of choral music. Vladimir Moiseyevich Tarnopolsky (1897–1942) was also was a student of Glière's, also graduating in 1930. He died on the Stalingrad front.

prepared by the composers and will soon be published. In this shape, it will be possible to have *The Path of October* performed in large concert halls by highly qualified performing collectives. For now, the 'Action' has been published in a kind of reduced score (for piano, organ or harmonium, trumpet, accordion, and various percussion), and in this shape, all three 'links' [*tri zvena*] can be performed in several of our workers' clubs by music circles. For this kind of performance, the composers have created easier versions of the passages that would be most difficult for amateurs (for example, the third 'link', Nos. 26 and 27). Experience shows that such performances by amateur forces can indeed be carried out: we have heard substantial passages from the 'Action' in [workers'] clubs, and, incidentally, such performances sometimes make a greater artistic impression than academic performances by the Academy cappella.

Let us now look at the main qualities of the 'Action'.

Firstly, let us note the introduction of choral (and solo) rhythmic declamation alongside the participation of a 'singing choir'. This device is not in itself, of course, a very recent invention. We are familiar with rhythmic declamation from the experiments of the 'Reciter's Theatre' [*Teatr chtetsa*]. In recent years, collective declamation has become quite popular in both professional and amateur theatre. But in this 'musical action' the role of the declamation is much broader. To the best of my knowledge, declamation has never been used in such a manner in any musical work prior to *The Path of October*. We already know of cases where solo, non-rhythmic speech has been used (as, for example, in Dargomyzhsky's *Rusalka*, and in operetta the device is used widely). But in *The Path of October*, collective rhythmic declamation is a special colour, which imparts to the entire work the character of an agitational poster [*plakatnost'*], and renders it easier to listen to, offering a diversity of sounds. It is interesting to note the ways in which declamatory moments are used, and how they are combined with purely musical moments. To begin with, we have the use of collective declamation as such, without any musical accompaniment (Link 1, No. 5; Link 2, No. 13). Then, we have collective declamation accompanied by the orchestra, or by the piano in the simplified version (e.g. Nos. 2, 4, the beginning of No. 12). Then, we have the [singing] chorus, collective declamation, and orchestra all combined. In this case, whether one or other element is prevalent, or whether they balance each other is determined by the general conception and meaning of a given passage. An example of such a combination is the second half of No. 12 ('The Storming of the Winter Palace'), one of the climactic points of the work, where all the forces are mobilised: the two choruses, the full orchestra, and the organ. Finally, a very original form of collective declamation is featured in a so-called 'sound montage', by S. Ryauzov. The essence of 'sound montage' lies in the use of unpitched consonants and the simplest onomatopoeic monosyllabic words which are sounded simultaneously as a background. Against this muffled background, rhythmic declamation of the normal kind is heard, accompanied by the small percussion group and at times by the trumpet also. 'Sound montage' is used in the work in various combinations. It could be a combination of slow solo declamation with the 'chorus of pronunciations' [*sic*], a small percussion group and trumpet (No. 17), or a combination of the 'pronunciation chorus' with the snare drum, 'the rhythm of the choir's stamping feet' and two solo reciters (No. 12, 'March'). Here we find a very original intertwining of pure sound effects with a 'double declamation': the first reciter and soprano voices from the choir read two different texts, which will not, of course, be heard properly, but whose main points and general sense will be understood. Finally, a new combination of expressive means is found in No. 20 (a mass song), where a two-part choral song by V. Tarnopolsky is added to the 'sound montage'.

Another interesting peculiarity of this 'action' is the introduction of the accordion. It does not appear very often, and mainly where the story demands the portrayal of a mass movement and where simple folk songs [*chastushka*] are included (as in the middle section and ending of No. 8, 'The street is stirring' [*Ulitsa volnuyetsya*], or in No. 8-bis, 'Mother Russia' [*Kak po matushke Rossii*]).

The introduction of the accordion as a characteristic, picturesque instrument that evokes certain essential associations is an entirely acceptable and indeed desirable innovation, and it is beautifully conceived by the author of the above-mentioned numbers, A. Davidenko. The suitability of the accordion is combined here with a great mastery in the arrangements.

The introduction of the organ is also undoubtedly justified. In part, the role of the organ is to amplify the sound, to make the whole more solid and monumental (e.g. the ending of No. 12, 'The Storming of the Winter Palace' or the ending of the finale, No. 27, which is a kind of 'sonata'). In other places, the organ, thanks to the refinement and variety of its timbral possibilities, lends special colours to the sonority in general (such is the role of the organ in No. 3, 'On the Rails', by Shekhter, and in the reprise of No. 7, 'By the Tenth Milepost' [*Na desyatoy verste*], by Davidenko). Finally, just once in the whole oratorio, the organ is given a completely independent role, in No. 16, Belïy's 'The Twenty-Six'.

The Path of October is a typical child of the Production Collective. It is a collective work in full sense of the word. The essence of the Collective's activities is in their inner creative unity, which can be clearly seen when several of its members' works are analyzed in detail. Their working method itself, auditions of their works, their collective discussions, and so on, all leave a special imprint on the creative identity of individual composers, the members of the collective. But this does not obliterate the original features of each. The make-up of the collective is not at all homogeneous. It comprises both experienced composers whose style and outlook is already established, and the 'young among the young', who are only beginning to study as composers. This is a division according to maturity. On the other hand, within the Production Collective there are 'trends' of its own, which may not be quite definable yet, but are clearly noticeable. All these distinctions, however, do not efface certain common interests and ideals that can be taken as a common denominator, and which make the method of collective creation possible.

Collective creation is revealed in two ways. On the one hand, there is a 'horizontal' separation of authorship, so to speak: each fragment has one definite author. On the other hand, we have an interesting experiment in collective creation between two or more composers. In some cases ('The Storming of the Winter Palace' and the final sonata), where this collective nature is indicated in the score, the 'division of labour' is clearly felt in the style of separate numbers or in the different parts of the same fragment. This is the result of the mutual influence which individual members of the collective exercise upon each other.

This influence is not simply a matter of borrowing or 'stealing', but evidently the manifestation of the fact that this complex of stylistic features is a kind of ideal sought by the individual representatives of a shared artistic trend. Hence there are a number of common devices used in different ways and at different levels of mastery.

The entire 'montage' is viewed by the collective as one whole, united not only by a single dramaturgical conception, but also by the sharing of musical material. This is particularly true of the final sonata, which is rather interesting in terms of its form. A certain heterogeneity of material and style and the all-too-obvious 'seams' between the sections of the sonata can be seen as shortcomings, but it is good, on the other hand, to see the individual 'picturesque thematic moments', which were scattered over the various numbers of the *Path*, now appearing in a developed guise, within a single conception and form. I will not list the themes that found their way into the finale, because the borrowing is quite obvious, and the list would occupy too much space.

At the same time, one needs to remark on the presence of a number of inexpressive 'commonplaces'. One of these is the 'Song of Farewell to Lenin' (*Proshchal'naya-Leninskaya*) by G. Bruk (No. 25), which is, by itself, not a bad mass song, but simply not very original or interesting. M. Koval, a striking individual talent and one of our artistic trailblazers, has also shown here that his work is not always up to the mark. Thus, in his 'Song of the Builders' (No. 23b), Koval has piled up various commonplaces. And yet his 'Factory' and '*Rvaniye-shershaviye*' (No. 10) are fresh and striking. One of *The Path*'s serious faults is an overloading and heterogeneity of style that stems from the participation of too many composers (nine people).

Individual numbers of *The Path* are sometimes superb taken on their own, but this is to the detriment of the whole. The 'seams' I pointed out in the final sonata, reflect the 'seams' in the general conception of the work to some extent.

In general, *The Path of October* is one of the most important contemporary musical works. As a reflection of contemporary revolutionary reality, the work is itself generated by our contemporary strivings.

The creation of *The Path* is one of the first attempts to solve the problem of creating a large-scale musical-dramatic work that is significant in its content, masterful in its execution and also contemporary in the full sense of the word. The attempt made in *The Path of October* may be considered all the more successful because its purely musical virtues are combined with the simplicity that is a requirement of all true art (but which is, in fact, the result of the most complex work of creative thought) – a simplicity that, if not in every detail, then at least on the whole, makes this work accessible, comprehensible, and close to the broad mass of listeners.

I. Sollertinskiy, '"Dzhonni" v Gos. Malom opernom teatre' [*Johnny* at the State Maly Opera House], *Zhizn' iskusstva*, no. 47 (18 Nov. 1928), 14–15.

I. Sollertinsky
Johnny at the State Maly Opera House

In the history of opera, we often encounter a curious phenomenon, namely the kind of composer who proclaims the wisest of truths on the nature of genuinely theatrical operatic texts, but who then does exactly the opposite, writing the most nonsensical and dramatically feeble libretti.

The same would seem to apply to Krenek. We have recently become acquainted with his article on opera libretti, translated in an issue of *Artistic Life*, and we could hardly disagree with his very sober thoughts on the necessity in opera for absolute clarity and logic in the stage action, on the emotional colouring of the situations flowing from the concrete principal subject matter, and so on. And yet this did not prevent *Der Sprung über den Schatten* from gaining the reputation, as far as its story was concerned, of being the most incomprehensible opera ever!

Things are little better with *Johnny*, which has been premiered with noisy and well-deserved success at the Maly Opera House. There is a love intrigue between a composer and a singer, which is conceived with a degree of sentimentality (and this is doubtless the secret behind its sensational success on seventy foreign stages); there is a glacier, to which the composer has recourse in moments of emotional turbulence, and this glacier is characterised in the most grandiose way, in the spirit of the celebrated 'nature theme' from Strauss's *Also Sprach Zarathustra*, and not as a pathological mirage, the fruit of the Composer's narcotic imagination. There is an amoralist, the curly-haired Negro Johnny with his furious temper, who belts out an ideological chorale about the demise of decrepit old Europe and about how jazz will conquer everything under the moon. And there is, finally, an amusing detective story about the theft of a violin, complicated by some not very profound 'sociological' details (the death of the violinist Daniello under the wheels of a train symbolises the death of the old European art, or something like that) and also some Freudian symbolism. All of this is quite petty and somewhat confused.

Let others discuss the musical virtues of Krenek's score, which are undoubted and significant. In terms of the stage action, if we disregard the weakness in the choice of plot and its development, there is much that is deserving of our attention.

Firstly, there is the introduction into the opera libretto of a new kind of material that is borrowed from the life of the modern city: we have automobiles, express trains, overpasses, and so on. Prosaic urban speech is sung, displacing high-minded romantic monologues of dubious taste. Situations that had previously only been acceptable in farce, adventure films or vaudeville, are here paradoxically presented in the lush orchestral garb of opera. All this indisputably speaks of a momentous shift in the operatic culture of our days.

But urbanist attributes are not sufficient in themselves to create a modern musical satire. Krenek's laughter has a double aspect, but it is still rather benign. A theatre that sets itself the goal of pulling Krenek up to the level of social satire is taking the path of greatest resistance. Nevertheless, *Johnny*'s producers, the director N. V. Smolich and the set designer V. V. Dmitriyev,[37] announced that their interpretation of Krenek's opera would do precisely that.

Let us first mention what did not come out well, namely the downgrading [i.e. de-romanticisation] of the love intrigue between Max and Anita, which immediately put the performers of these roles in a false position. Since he could not find any support in the music, where the lyrical cantilenas are generally presented 'seriously', the director enacted this downgrading through purely superficial tricks: the hero sings an agitated aria half-dressed, with collar unbuttoned and no tie; but to bring lyrical heroes down to a lower level should not entail the creation of a parody.

The last act, by contrast, proved to be quite brilliant: its dynamic scenes, as interpreted by the director and designer, make a great contribution towards 'industrialised', or, more precisely, 'technicised' theatre, which is in tune with the whole technological culture of our era. The lights of the locomotive that runs over Daniello, the furious automobile journey through night-time Berlin, the stage actions where the theatre competes successfully with the cinema, the moving walls of the wittily realised structure – all this was fascinating and genuinely new, and allowed us to forgive the visual boredom of the first scenes, the dubious glacier, the European-style grey suits, or the pieces of cloth with moving shadows of figures 'decayed through foxtrot' and all kinds of expressionist visions, familiar in the work of the same Dmitriyev. *Johnny* is an important piece of work for Dmitriyev, and it is more consistent with authorial intentions than *Der Sprung* was – in that production, the monumental structure made of tin would have been better suited to Gordon Craig's *Hamlet*[38] than to Krenek's adultery farce.

Film is used very successfully: an animated film, whose images transform into a close-up of the grimacing Johnny, is a brilliant ending to the show and was rewarded by well-deserved applause. Radio is used a little monotonously: it is heard only on the stage, so that its potential spatial effects remain unused (such as sound emanating from opposite ends of the auditorium), and musicians could raise many objections to its acoustics.

---

[37] Nikolai Vasilyevich Smolich (1888–1968) was a prominent opera director who worked at the Mariinsky, Bolshoi, and the Leningrad Maly (he was director at the last from 1924–30). Vladimir Vladimirovich Dmitriyev (1900–48) was one of the most distinguished set designers of his time, by this stage already famous for his design for the Leningrad production of *Love for Three Oranges*.

[38] The English modernist theatre director Gordon Craig (1872–1966) became renowned for his production of *Hamlet* at the Moscow Art Theatre (1908); one of his innovations was a set consisting of several non-representational moveable screens.

The best acting definitely comes from Freydkov,[39] who sings the title role of Johnny himself. The actor really found himself here: he gives us all the physiological features of a Europeanised Negro, his carriage, predatory springing leaps, even the timbre of the voice, and, if you like, the accent, are all conveyed naturally and with an organic merriment. Johnny is Freydkov's great victory, putting him in the front ranks of performers who sing modern operatic repertoire.

In other cases, as a rule, the dynamics of the stage are not picked up by the actors' movements. This is understandable: in the old repertoire, the operatic actors are used to present an emotion by stretching it out to three or four minutes, while a dramatic actor or especially a film actor would need only seconds.

Olkhovsky[40] cuts a picturesque figure as the violinist Daniello: he embodied the character of that blasé French virtuoso spoiled by his success with the ladies. The good intentions of Kuznetsova as Anita and Balashov as Max[41] were shattered due to the pseudo-parodic interpretation of their roles by the director.

On the whole, for all the shortcomings of the libretto, the far-fetched interpretation of *Johnny* as musical satire, and the production's other faults, we still cannot fail to recognise that the production of *Johnny* is a great step forward in the evolution of Malegot. This already puts down a marker for future modern opera productions. A great amount of work has been done. Of course, the elements of industrial technology introduced here should probably be seen as sketches for future theatrical craft, because much of it is not yet working properly: the walls move very noisily, overpowering the music, while, for the same reason, the aria in the automobile cannot be heard, and so on. Nevertheless, this experiment confirms that the modern opera house can now set new goals, and their grand scale could not have even been imagined even ten years ago.

---

[39] Boris Matveyevich Freydkov (1904–66) was at this point a very young singer (bass), and Johnny was his first major role. He was noted for his all-round appeal – he had the voice, the looks, and the acting ability – and led a successful career at the former Mariinsky (1927–52).

[40] Yevgeny Grigoryevich Olkhovsky (1888–1972) was a lyrical baritone once commended by Rachmaninov. He sang at both the former Mariinsky (until 1931) and the Leningrad Maly Opera (until 1948), and, thanks to his acting and dancing abilities, was also sought after as an operetta singer.

[41] Stepan Vasilyevich Balashov (1883–1966) was a lyrical tenor with an impressive high register (his debut role at the former Mariinsky was the Astrologer in *The Golden Cockerel*). He sang at the Maly Opera throughout the 1920s and 30s. No further information is available on Kuznetsova/Anita.

1929
Velikiy perelom – The Great Turning Point

In Soviet historiography, 1929 is known as the year of the Great Turning Point, but Soviet music histories rarely give the year any special mention because there were no significant Party resolutions that had a direct bearing on musical life. Nevertheless, musicians at the time certainly felt the change, as the following passage in a letter from Boris Asafyev to Alban Berg attests:

> Here, victory belongs to those taking music in a different direction – towards the music of the past and epigonism – and so neither I myself, nor the many other friends of *Wozzeck* will hear it again for a long time![1]

Asafyev's assessment proved correct, and the change in policy did indeed take place (three years hence, Asafyev himself became an unlikely beneficiary). Even at this late stage, RAPM was still unable to take the lead. Of crucial importance was the First All-Russian Conference of Music Workers, held in mid-June. Bringing together over 800 delegates and guests, this musical forum was unprecedented in size, a demonstration of the Soviet leadership's new seriousness in seeking a unified policy on music.

The change of policy did not affect repertoire radically (aside from *Wozzeck*, as we shall see), and new music was still prominent on both the stage and in the concert hall. There was plenty of Stravinsky: Klemperer played *Petrushka* and *Pulcinella*; ASM made forays into the sphere of music theatre by staging *Mavra* (at Tsetetis, the Theatre Institute); *Oedipus Rex* and the Piano Concerto were also given their Soviet premieres Honegger was represented by his orchestral piece *Rugby* and by his opera *Judith*. Prokofiev suffered a setback (discussed below), but his works were still featured in significant concerts: Persimfans gave a successful (if abbreviated) performance of *Steps of Steel*; Ansermet conducted *Chout*; Shostakovich was the soloist in the First Piano Concerto; *Love for Three Oranges*, which had disappeared from the Soviet stage because of the currency crisis, was revived in order to mark Prokofiev's second return visit, in November. There was still some adventurous programming: a series of concerts organised in Leningrad by the Committee for New Music at the State Arts History Academy (GIII) and by the Chamber Music Society, included the music of Berg (the Piano Sonata) and Hindemith, together with some recent Soviet works such as Shostakovich's *Aphorisms*, the premiere of Gavriil Popov's Septet, and Alexei Zhivotov's Nonet (which had to be encored, such was the applause).

ASM, however, was on the way out. The spring of 1929 saw the last sprinkling of ASM concerts, and one of these, unusually, featured works by non-ASM composers Marian Koval and Varvara Gaygerova, who were active in Prokoll and later in RAPM. This came about through the offices of ASM's Myaskovsky, who was Koval's and Gaygerova's composition teacher, but there was also a political significance to their appearance that marked the new turn. Belyayev's review of

---

[1] Letter from Asafyev to Berg of 8 July 1929, RGALI, fond 2658 (Asafyev), op. 1, ye. kh. 454., l. 1v.

the concert addresses this aspect: 'in Koval we apparently have a representative of that young generation in the sphere of Soviet composition, which will, at last, be able to create the true music of the Revolution' (the point holds whether Belyayev wrote the last phrase sincerely or sarcastically).[2] Later in the year, ASM was no longer able to host any more concerts because Narkompros had not seen fit to provide the organisation with further funding. At the same time, Mezhkniga stopped its purchases of new musical scores from abroad (because hard currency reserves were low), as Derzhanovsky lamented on losing his job at that agency.[3] Both ideological and financial factors led to a temporary setback for Prokofiev's Soviet ambitions: his reputation was damaged by RAPM's attacks on *Steps of Steel*, and then his concerts scheduled for the spring were cancelled, again because of the short supply of hard currency (although no doubt RAPM's prior intervention made the decision to cancel much easier).[4]

RAPM was now rapidly gaining in strength alongside kindred artistic groups such as RAPP (in literature) and AkhRR (in the visual arts). After the demise of *Contemporary Music* in the spring of 1929, RAPM became the dominant voice in the musical press (their journal *Proletarian Musician* [*Proletarskiy muzïkant*] began publication in February 1929, on a secure Muzsektor base), and lost no time in attacking its opponents. By this stage, they had effectively taken the driver's seat in Glaviskusstvo's Methods [*metodicheskiy*] Committee. Lebedinsky presented a paper to this committee arguing that guidelines of his choosing should be imposed on the music that could properly be included in concerts for workers; Prokofiev and Stravinsky, among others, he classified as undesirable, since they were, according to him, alien to the working class. The paper raised much controversy but, in the end, it was approved in general terms by Glaviskusstvo.[5] Significantly, the leading composers of Prokoll – Davidenko, Shekhter, Belïy, Koval – joined RAPM early in the year; this was a great boost to RAPM, since it had previously been unable to produce much music to back up its theorising.

New perceptions of RAPM's power on the eve of the Conference can be judged from Myaskovsky's letter to Asafyev of 13 May. Asafyev had been fretting over recent personal attacks he had suffered at the hands of RAPM, and here Myaskovsky tries to reassure his friend:

> My dear Boris Vladimirovich, you forever surprise and even astonish me! Some less-than-civil upstart suffering from clogged bile ducts only has to blabber something about you, and you're immediately thrown into a panic: persecution, *asafyevshchina*, and so on. As if everyone is a Lebedinsky or a Keldysh [...] It all comes down to a particular clique of people who are not very ceremonious, granted, nor are they themselves without sin [i.e. they also have skeletons in the cupboard]; they are not as influential as you

---

[2] V.B-v [Belyayev], "Muzïkal'noye obozreniye: Assotsiatsiya sovremennoy muzïki", *Zhizn' iskusstva*, no. 7 (10 Feb. 1929), 10.

[3] Letter from Derzhanovsky to Prokofiev of 19 Apr. 1929, LPA, folder 20, 286.

[4] Letter from Derzhanovsky to Prokofiev of 2 Feb. 1929, LPA, folder 20, 96.

[5] Minutes of meetings from 7 and 28 Mar., 18 and 25 Apr., and 30 May 1929, RGALI, fond 645 (Glaviskusstvo), op. 1, ye. kh. 333, ll. 27–30, 44–7, 49–51, 54–63, 65–79, 83–92.

imagine. True, Lebedinsky hangs around in Glaviskusstvo, and the fellow is undoubtedly very insolent – but this is plain for others to see, and after the story of the Conservatoire affair did the rounds (the cogs and wheels couldn't remain entirely hidden), the group [that had opposed the Conservatoire's administration] lost its status, particularly in more serious and influential circles. [...]

Argue with them? But with whom exactly, and about what? Can you dispute with the barking of dogs? At best, you would give them a good kick. What can you say in reply to these people, when such writings as these and their constant scoffing is what characterises their behaviour? Had you been very shrewd and declared only the orthodox line – their line – it would still have been to no avail, because they *deliberately* close their ears to anything that doesn't issue from their own swamp. They can only be caught in the act, or subjected to mockery etc., but are you really capable of that? In short, I can't accept all this moaning and groaning from you.[6]

But the situation was volatile, and Myaskovsky failed to guess the direction in which RAPM stocks were moving.

The Conference was called in April, and musical life was now under the scrutiny of the state. The Sixteenth Party Conference had recently appealed for 'socialist competition', and the associated rhetoric was now applied to music in most official statements. Music was described as 'one of the most neglected areas of cultural construction', 'an orphan art', and a victim of 'production anarchy'.[7]

The Conference was preceded by a Party meeting (*partsoveshchaniye*) on music, organised by the Central Committee's Agitprop Department, which sprinkled the rhetoric with a further dash of stridency:

There can be no conceivable further development of musical culture in this country without the establishment of direct connections with our political and economic development. Any other attitude would not only be reactionary, but entirely utopian. This must be firmly grasped by all who have not yet understood it. It is in the nature of the reactionary dreams of pure aesthetes that they can never come true.[8]

It was apparently at the *partsoveshchaniye* that the real decisions were to be taken, directives formulated, and resolutions drafted – the function of the Conference was to promulgate them, while providing a semblance of debate. It is feasible, even, that much was planned prior to the *partsoveshchaniye*, in discussions between Agitprop and the more radical members of Glaviskusstvo. It is very likely that this was Kerzhentsev's coup, his attempt to bring musical affairs under his control at Agitprop instead of leaving them in the hands of Lunacharsky, his old opponent. In the early 1920s, Kerzhentsev (then with Proletkult) once had a polemical exchange with Lunacharsky on the development of Soviet theatre. But now, from his position of power in Agitprop, he was able to mount a sustained attack on Glaviskusstvo as

[6] Letter from Myaskovsky to Asafyev of 13 May 1929, RGALI, fond 2658 (Asafyev), op. 2, ye. kh. 51, l. 15.

[7] 'K sozïvu muzïkal'noy konferentsii', *Zhizn' iskusstva*, no. 17 (21 Apr 1929), 1–2.

[8] 'Muzïka v povestke dnya', *Rabochiy i teatr*, no. 23 (9 June 1929), 1–2.

a whole and Lunacharsky personally, harrying them on the pressing cultural issues of the day, such as the bans on Bulgakov plays and the future of the Meyerhold Theatre, also now hamstrung by bans. Lunacharsky even complained to Stalin that Kerzhentsev hindered Glaviskusstvo's work, and that he had slandered them as 'right deviationists'.[9]

The beneficiaries of Kerzhentsev's new policies were clearly known in advance, as RAPM's members, both old (Lebedinsky, Keldysh) and new (Belïy and Koval), were invited as a representative group, while Sergeyev of ORKiMD was on his own and could do little to defend his organisation. Roslavets was there, too, but only in his official capacity as a representative of Glavrepertkom, so he was unable to defend ASM even if he still wanted to. These were all the composers present, but also present were representatives from the relevant administrative bodies, including Glaviskusstvo and Rabis, the music-workers' union. While all assembled were Party members, they were deeply divided on the issues at stake. The atmosphere was less than cordial.[10]

Kerzhentsev began with a broad statement, and held back from referring to RAPM by name. He lamented the fact that while the Party could appoint directors to any music institution, this did little to assist the creation of 'our forces, our produce, our composers, our conductors'. The fabric of Soviet music culture, he argued, was not yet 'organically' Soviet, or, in the fashionably militarised parlance of the time, the 'commanding heights' still had to be taken (RAPM had been saying much the same in *Musical Virgin Soil* five years earlier). Tempering this part of his argument, he cited the Party Resolution on literature from 1925, which had emphasised the continuing need for reliance on fellow travellers. These 'specialists', he said, were indeed required in the music world, but they should be expected to move gradually over to full Communist ideology.

A more radical statement was unexpectedly made by a freshly appointed deputy head of Glaviskusstvo, Leonid Obolensky. Prior to taking up this new post, Obolensky's entire career (pre- and post-Revolution) had been spent at the Ministry of Finance. Where arts policy was concerned, he was an unknown quantity. He presented a draft resolution, which spoke of the hegemony of proletarian music as if it was current reality. While many of those present wanted to establish this hegemony in the future, Obolensky's wishful thinking was an

---

[9] One major conflict arose over Bulgakov's play *The Days of the Turbins*, which Lunacharsky allowed to reappear on stage after a Glavrepertkom ban had expired. Kerzhentsev attacked Lunacharsky for the decision. As it happens, the *Turbins* did not return merely on Lunacharsky's initiative – he had received a phone call from Stalin, who gave his personal permission. This allowed Lunacharsky to argue (in his letter to Stalin) that Kerzhentsev, in his zeal, was now running counter to the will of the Politburo itself. This letter, of 12 Feb. 1929, is published in *Vlast' i khudozhestvennaya intelligentsiya: dokumentï TsK RKP(b) – VKP(b) – VChK – OGPU – NKVD o kul'turnoy politike, 1917–1953*, ed. by A. Artizov and O. Naumov (Moscow: Mezhdunarodnïy fond 'emokratiya', 1999), 108–9.

[10] The following account of the *partsoveshchaniye* is extracted from its published proceedings, *Puti razvitiya muzïki: Stenograficheskiy otchyot soveshchaniya po voprosam muzïki pri APPO TsK VKP(b)* (Moscow: Gosudarstvennoye izdatel'stvo, Muzïkal'nïy sektor, 1930).

embarrassment to them, and Kerzhentsev expressed his unease. Obolensky also listed the composers who would provide the Soviet Union with its brilliant musical future: Belïy, Koval, Shekhter, Davidenko (all former Prokollists who had recently been absorbed into RAPM).

Whatever side they were on, the delegates could not believe that this draft paper contained the real views of Glaviskusstvo, which Obolensky was supposedly there to represent. Glaviskusstvo, after all, was headed by the Lunacharsky supporter Alexander Sviderksy, as everyone was well aware. It was also very surprising to find that Obolensky, a newcomer and a complete outsider, had suddenly become so embedded in musical life that he was able to choose a faction and effectively act as its mouthpiece. RAPM's Lebedinsky then made a strange move (or so it must have seemed to most of those assembled), somehow conceding on Obolensky's behalf that the draft resolution was not a Glaviskusstvo document at all, but merely a position statement by Obolensky as a Party member (which was not, of course, his remit). But we can reconstruct events to make sense of these puzzles. Lebedinsky would only have been in a position to make this retraction if he knew something about the document already. It was also clear that he expected Obolensky to defer to him, as indeed happened. If we remember that Lebedinsky was noted for 'hanging around Glaviskusstvo' (Myaskovsky's words above), we can see that he would have been in a good position to take an inexperienced and grateful Obolensky under his wing. The draft resolution could well have been his idea, or at least based on all the RAPM propaganda he would have fed to Obolensky. Either Lebedinsky had miscalculated or, more likely, Obolensky had naively failed to realise that his audience would never let him get away with such a transparent trick. But Lebedinsky evidently hoped that he could salvage something from the debacle: 'let us write down and commit to memory the fact that the Party deems it necessary to support [the proletarian groups]'. This attempted sleight of hand only compounded the problem: Obolensky had only pretended to be representing Glaviskusstvo, while Lebedinsky was now effectively claiming that Obolensky spoke for the Party as a whole. A few years earlier, such manipulations could have been torn to shreds by other delegates, but with the political terrain changing so quickly, they could not be sure whether they were being conned by a Svengali and Trilby duo, or whether the pair had been given advance notice of changes in policy that would soon emerge from the shadows.

Obolensky, in his closing speech made two contradictory admissions: first, that the draft resolution had been his 'private initiative', and second, that the document was the product of collective authorship. But the overall message was still a clumsy demand that delegates must support RAPM and the insistence that 'those who are not with us, are against us'. This allowed Kerzhentsev to sound like an angel of moderation in his closing speech. He even had a few kind words for ASM, hoping that the Party would engage in nurturing its 'left wing', that is, the more Communist-friendly members. Looking at the *partsoveshchaniye* from the loftiest perspective, it is possible to see that Obolensky and Lebedinsky were unwittingly serving a larger purpose that was not in accord with their own. Whether this was planned or improvised matters little – the primary factor was who wielded the real power at the meeting. And this was not Obolensky, nor even Lebedinsky, but Kerzhentsev, as later events showed. Delegates left feeling that official support had now been given to RAPM in some nebulous fashion, without the Party actually committing itself in print (Lebedinsky's call for such a commitment was in vain). Looking at the whole period from 1928 to 1931, and broadening our view to all the arts, the Party's behaviour was supportive of the proletarianist organisations in practice, but they enshrined none of this in documentary form. These organisations had become useful to the Party, but that did not mean that interests had fully converged: the Party leadership would subordinate its policy-making powers to no other organisation.

The Conference itself (the First All-Russian Conference of Music Workers) took place on 14–20 June, in Leningrad. Two position papers were presented, by Kerzhentsev and by V. Gorodinsky from the Art-Workers' Union, Rabis (the union's line was similar to Kerzhentsev's). But what of Lunacharsky? He was present too, and gave a two-hour speech that was duly published in abridged form.[11] The archival record of the conference, however, tells a strange and poignant story of Lunacharsky's last shot at influencing musical affairs, in the closing chapter of his long ministerial career.[12] From February 1929, he was already a lame duck, having submitted his resignation letter in protest against class discrimination in favour of proletarians in education.[13]

It was known from the start that Lunacharsky could not stay for the whole conference – he was supposedly extremely busy with other affairs. Moreover, his colleagues at Narkompros had advised him that he would be overstretching himself by attending.[14] He had already endured criticism from various quarters, including Kerzhentsev's latest public trashing of Glaviskusstvo only a few days earlier.[15] From his first words, it was clear how out of touch the Minister was with the ideas and rhetoric of the Cultural Revolution that was underway. Speaking of the unique responsibility that lay on the shoulders of the delegates, he began in an unfortunate way:

> [...] The decisions we take here will be watched attentively by the intelligentsia in Western Europe and America. [...] Essentially, we are taking the first step in determining the social paths along which music will develop for all humanity – we are shouldering a great risk thereby [...].[16]

He explained why he thought this task could not have been undertaken earlier: war, hunger, devastation, a low level of culture. This list was quite sufficient, but he saw

---

[11] A. V. Lunacharskiy, 'Muzïka i sovremennost', *Zhizn' iskusstva*, no. 25 (23 June 1929), 2–3.

[12] The following account of Lunacharsky's speech at the conference is taken from the typescript of the proceedings, RGALI, fond 645 (Glaviskusstvo), op. 1, ye. kh. 336, ll. 53–131.

[13] Sheila Fitzpatrick, 'The Emergence of the Glaviskusstvo. Class war on the Cultural Front, Moscow 1928–1932', *Soviet Studies*, 23/2 (1971), 236–53, esp. 252.

[14] See fn. 12, ll. 101 and 129.

[15] At the Seventh Conference of Arts Workers Kerzhentsev had presented a very critical assessment of Glaviskusstvo's activities, see *Zhizn' iskusstva*, no. 22 (2 June 1929).

[16] See fn. 12, l. 54.

fit to make an unwelcome addition: emigration (his own sore point), 'a draining of resources that has not been compensated for by new cadres'. This point must have been found unsuitable not only for publication, but even for preservation in the transcript, where it was scored through.[17] 'I will not attempt [...] to offer a social theory of the new music that will inevitably be born', Lunacharsky continued, so instead, he rehashed some of the vaguer rhetorical turns of his earlier work, of art as a means to happiness through the heightening of mankind's vital energies – this was also scored through (perhaps through hard-nosed scorn rather than for pressing political reasons).[18] Then, as if he realised that his emphasis on music as pleasure was not the flavour of 1929, he shoehorned in some discussion of 'the colossal sin of formalism' and the problem of 'syncopated music'. Struggling to fit in his own habitual cosmopolitanism with the new isolationist policies, he suggested limply that the task was not to import Western music to the Soviet Union (rejecting both of Krenek's operas as weak), but rather to export Soviet music to the West.[19]

Towards the end of his speech, he addressed what he took to be the two main positions that had emerged from the conference. One he called optimistic: 'music must agitate and reflect the reality of things here'. The other he characterised as sceptical, encapsulating it in the question 'how can music portray a non-payer of agricultural tax?' For himself, he said that music could, at times, simply be neutral, sounding equally appropriate to any text, whether revolutionary or counter-revolutionary. This point provoked most contention in the open discussion that followed. The up-and-coming 'proletarian composer', Beliy, challenged Lunacharsky on the idea that music could ever be neutral. Even when the proletariat takes up existing melodies, Beliy argued, it assimilates them to its own class nature by changing the tempo and mood.[20] It was almost time for Lunacharsky to leave the conference, but he rose eagerly to the challenge. At the last moment, the gloves were off:

LUNACHARSKY The melody of the song 'For Soviet Power' was borrowed from an old Gypsy song, which had been popular among the bourgeoisie. [The proletariat] adopted it, and sings it much more than any of the songs you lot compose under the name 'proletarian music'.

(Laughter).

(FROM THE FLOOR) They sing 'The Brick Factory', too.

LUNACHARSKY Good for them.

(FROM THE FLOOR) No, it's bad for them.

LUNACHARSKY This is where you and I radically part company. There isn't a single person in attendance here who should imagine that he knows what proletarian music is or that he can teach the proletariat. If you really are the representatives of the proletariat, then you will listen out for what the

---

[17] Ibid.
[18] Ibid., ll. 54–6.
[19] Ibid., ll. 83 and 87–8.
[20] Ibid., ll. 122–4.

proletariat likes. And if it sings 'The Brick Factory', then even if that song is of little musical value, it must have something in it that makes it a favourite. You say that it's music 'of the tavern' – but what do you mean by this? That we actually have 'tavern culture' here?

I think not. It seems to me that they are striving for something of their own, something from the peasant life of their origins, perhaps something they heard in their childhood, in the family home. And if you are going to construct some weird and wonderful houses of cards for them, you won't hear the proletariat singing them back to you. No, it will ignore you as a group of fantasists, purveyors of songs they don't understand.[21]

With nothing to lose, Lunacharsky evidently decided to go out fighting. He had the summer to tidy out his desk, and his resignation letter was officially accepted in September, surprising no one.

So who won in the end? RAPM was in no doubt, and published a cheerfully boastful issue of its journal. Kerzhentsev overplayed his hand after the conference, intensifying his conflict with Glaviskusstvo and, in Lunacharsky's absence, with Svidersky, Lunacharsky's deputy. The row became an embarrassment, and reports were made to Stalin. The solution was his preferred tactic of dismissing both sides, and so both the offenders were removed from their positions.[22] Svidersky left at the same time as Lunacharsky, and was given a diplomatic posting to Latvia. Soon afterwards, Kerzhentsev reappeared as director of the Communist Academy. Glaviskusstvo was given a more dependably hard-line director, Fyodor Raskolnikov. His appointment was in October, after Glaviskusstvo's seasonal budget had already been agreed, and as one consequence, RAPM was unable to gain any immediate material benefit from its miraculous elevation.[23] Only in February 1930, after a most thorough purge at Glaviskusstvo, and under another new director, Felix Kon, was RAPM finally able to gain the support it needed to throw its weight around as the Party's favourites in the music world.

One important consequence of the conference was the gradual exclusion of contemporary Western music from the Soviet Union. This was only discernible in retrospect: the issue was not accorded much time at the conference, and delegates were even given tickets for *Johnny spielt auf* at the Maly Opera (and also for a concert performance of *The Nose*). The delegates who mentioned Krenek's opera did so without hostility; at worst, there was a complaint by Gorodinsky, and even this was aimed not so much at *Johnny* itself, but rather at the hype spun around the opera by some enthusiastic Soviet critics:

> When opera-goers rush about from one Western work to another, it is hardly surprising that even a piece as ideologically suspect as Krenek's *Johnny spielt auf* passes for first-class material. But while this is to some extent justified, the position adopted by some of our critics is shameful. Only extreme

---

[21] Ibid., ll. 130–1.

[22] *Vlast' i khudozhestvennaya intelligentsiya*, 115–23 and 748.

[23] S. Korev, 'Glaviskusstvo i rukovodstvo muzykalnoy zhiznyu', *Proletarskiy muzïkant*, no. 3 (1930), 25–30.

zeal can generate the statement that *Johnny* symbolises a rebellious black proletariat.²⁴

Johnny was thus left untouched for the moment, and indeed, thanks to its popularity with Soviet audiences, it continued running throughout 1929, and on many Sundays it was performed both as a matinée and soirée. *Wozzeck*, however, took a very different course: lacking *Johnny*'s popularity, it became the first victim of the drift away from Western culture and away from modernism. The shadow that fell on *Wozzeck* was so dark that even Sollertinsky, the most sympathetic of critics, felt he needed to consign this opera to the past:

> The course taken in the West, which has created a whole epoch in our country's youthful musical culture (we cannot underestimate the influence of Alban Berg's *Wozzeck* on our young composers, for example), does not and cannot figure in our main slogans of today, unlike the situation a few years ago. This does not mean that we should reject Western operas altogether. For example, both the foreign operas that have been included in the forthcoming repertoire of the Leningrad theatres – Brand's *Machinist Hopkins* and Hindemith's *Neues vom Tage* – definitely deserve our attention.²⁵

But even these new Western operas were at best to be regarded as catalysts that would assist Soviet composers in their attempts to produce true Soviet operas. 'Where is Soviet opera?' demanded Gorodinsky and Kerzhentsev, the cultural leaders of the moment. Gorodinsky was utterly scathing in his descriptions of the Sovietised operatic rehashes that had proliferated over the previous decade. He had special scorn for productions of Glinka's thoroughly monarchist opera, *A Life for the Tsar* (in Baku and Odessa), mocking them for their attempts to turn this recalcitrant material into 'a life for the people'; this tellingly distinguishes the First Five Year Plan period from the High Stalinism of the mid-thirties and forties, since the pride of the Soviet operatic repertoire in the latter period was nothing other than a further remake of *A Life for the Tsar* – now given a lavish budget and close official involvement. Gorodinsky regarded *The Red Poppy* and other early attempts at Soviet ballet with similar disdain: he said they were merely standard ballets with a splash of Soviet local colour.²⁶

1929 saw several productions of new operas by Soviet composers, but these turned out to be disappointments. The Bolshoi's Experimental Theatre presented Shishov's *Tupeynïy khudozhnik* (The Wig Maker) after a Russian classic story by Leskov; the critic Dianov conceded that some of the music had potential, but suffered from poor orchestration. The same theatre staged Vasilenko's *Sïn solntsa* (The Sun's Son), but this was judged to be burdened with the tired clichés of exoticism. Leningrad's Grand Opera presented Shtrassenburg's *Taiga*, a work that combined an earnest Soviet plot with Kuchka-style music. Hopes were pinned on works that were still to come: Shostakovich's *Nose* was still only known through

---

²⁴ V. Gorodinskiy, 'O muzïkal'nom teatre', *Zhizn' iskusstva*, no. 27 (7 July 1929), 6–7.

²⁵ I. Sollertinskiy, 'Vozmozhnïye printsipï sovetskoy operï', *Zhizn' iskusstva*, no. 32 (11 Aug. 1929), 3.

²⁶ See fn. 24.

concert performances, and still more promising for Soviet opera, Mosolov and Deshevov had received highly publicised commissions from GOTOB (the new name for the former Mariinsky) to carefully chosen libretti by leading Soviet playwrights. In Soviet ballet, Oransky's *Futbolist* (The Footballer) was being prepared by the Bolshoi. Among productions of standard balletic repertoire, GOTOB's *Nutcracker* stood out for its colourful modernism; the choreographer Lopukhov recast the Act 2 divertissement as an extravaganza mixing music hall, sports and acrobatics.

Soviet opera and ballet were to be devoted to 'the five-year plan, socialist competition, the reconstruction of agriculture, the intensification of class struggle, [...] the grain harvest, the struggle against religion" and other topical themes, but this project remained in the realm of hopes and dreams (until it was not even a desired outcome a few years later).[27] But while this project went unrealised, there were concrete institutional changes that soon began to transform musical life. First, the new desire for centralised Party supervision of the arts resulted in the publication of a new state-wide arts newspaper, *Rabochiy i iskusstvo* (Workers and the Arts, published by Rabis); the same paper has continued in an unbroken line to the present day, undergoing several name changes: *Sovetskoye iskusstvo* (Soviet Art), *Sovetskaya kul'tura* (Soviet Culture), and, finally the post-Communist *Kul'tura* (Culture). During the First Five Year Plan period, it appeared in parallel with the journals of the proletarianist arts organisations, like RAPM's *Proletarian Musician*; beside the fevered rhetoric of the proletarianists, *Workers and the Arts* sounded calm and balanced, the reassuring voice of central power.

And reassurance – even when illusory – was much needed at the time, when employment across the cultural sector had become precarious, every institution being convulsed by endless reorganisation and *chistki* (purges). Glaviskusstvo itself was subjected in the autumn to *orabocheniye*, that is, an injection of new cadres who could claim to have come from a working-class background, sweeping away all the Lunacharskians.[28] The reorganising drive then moved on to GAKhN (the State Academy for Scholarship in the Arts), ASM's parent organisation, which was accused of harbouring reactionary forces in arts historiography, being led by non-Marxists, following formalist methods in its research and displaying idealist tendencies – new cadres were moved in here, too.[29] The State Theatres (which had collectively lost their 'Academy' status in 1927) were also shaken up, and there were reprimands for a broad range of failings: tactless behaviour, careerism, toadying, arrogance, formalism, alcoholism, and anti-Semitism; some employees were expelled from the Party for more serious offences, such as concealing their class origins.[30] The victims of the purge were graded: some got away with a warning, others lost their jobs, yet others could face arrest and criminal conviction.

Moscow Conservatoire's personnel changes had already begun before the Conference, as a result of investigations into the 'rightist' allegations of 1928. Its

[27] P. Kerzhentsev, 'Na novïye puti', *Rabochiy i iskusstvo*, no. 1 (6 Nov. 1929), 1.

[28] 'Reorganizatsiya Glaviskusstva', *Zhizn' iskusstva*, no. 36 (8 Sept. 1929), 14.

[29] 'Korennaya reorganizatsiya GAKhN: Oplot idealisticheskikh sil razrushen. Postanovleniye Kollegii Narkomprosa', *Rabochiy i iskusstvo*, no. 5 (7–13 Dec. 1929), 1.

[30] 'Rezul'tatï chistki', *Rabochiy i teatr*, no. 41 (13 Oct. 1929), 5.

governing board was 'communised', which meant the proportion of Party members was increased. Most prominently, there was a new Communist director, Boleslav Pshibïshevsky, the son of a Polish Symbolist writer, and sometime musicologist. Against all the expectations of the Conservatoire's old guard, Pshibïshevsky made a good first impression: even Goldenweiser found him a 'cultured person', 'gracious in the most refined, Polish way'.[31] Asafyev, however, thought he had managed to scratch below the surface:

> [...] I've been to see your director. I can't read his conscience or inhabit his inner world, but the three hours I spent with him were a pleasant experience: it felt as if I was on a European visit. He was amazed, ostensibly, by my culture, my breadth of knowledge and sensible views, but also bothered by my depressed state. He said that he could speak freely with me, but that he could only 'whisper' the same things to other Moscow Conservatoire professors of music history, etc. [possibly a hint at Ivanov-Boretsky], but that they have hidden themselves well behind red banners and so they are not harangued. [...] But let me tell you the strangest thing: after he acknowledged the philistinism of our shared 'friends', after he cursed the '*chemodanovshchina*',[32] after he agreed with my views on form and content, on music history, etc. etc., – he also cursed the name of Igor Glebov. So I then introduced myself as the very same Igor Glebov. What a scene! It turned out to be that I'd been painted in a beneficial light for him, but his informers forgot to warn him that Prof. B. Asafyev and Igor Glebov are one and the same person. In short, an embarrassment.[33]

But even though he had discovered that the geniality masked a degree of cynicism, Asafyev reckoned that this was hardly the worst the Conservatoire could have faced, and he was still hopeful that their shared culture and intellectualism would make a genuine ally of Pshibïshevsky. But at this time, higher Party functionaries like Pshibïshevsky were generally too busy watching the political weathervane to form solid and sincere relationships with their colleagues.

In the midst of all this upheaval in the arts institutions, 'music workers' now became desperate to understand the extent and import of ideological changes – it could mean the difference between keeping or losing a job in a time of renewed economic hardship. The confusion and panic is apparent in a letter from Asafyev to Prokofiev, written in November while the composer was in Moscow:

> Rask[olnikov, the head of Glaviskusstvo], in his Leningrad speech (on Glaviskusstvo's programme) said that RAPM is the lynchpin [*opora*]. At the same time, he gave special emphasis to the role of Meyerhold's theatre. Of course, Meyerhold is culturally progressive, while RAPM reduces all music to Beethoven and Musorgsky! But leaving aside the oddity of the statement,

---

[31] Diary entry of 7 June 1929, A. B. Gol'denveyzer, *Dnevnik: tetradi vtoraya-shestaya* (Moscow: Tortuga, 1997), 300.

[32] After Sergei Chemodanov, RAPM-serving university professor who supplied a vulgar-Marxist perspective on music.

[33] Letter from Asafyev to Lamm of 1 Oct. 1929 , RGALI, fond 2743 (Lamm), op. 1, ye. kh. 79, 15–16.

> I can see that it places restrictions on what music can and cannot do. I find this disturbing. As for the philosophical part of his speech, this was just the same old dogmatic distinction between content and form. I simply cannot understand how this is supposed to apply to music! It is as if we were to consider an actor's vivid stage gesture a superficial 'technical' device, and perceiving *the very thing* that this gesture expresses as being external form, which means outside that same gesture?! Things are not good for anyone equipped with my views and culture.[34]

ASM members weren't alone in their struggles. The summer events of 1929 effectively destroyed ORKiMD. The newly powerful RAPM had not forgotten or forgiven ORKiMD's 1924 split from RAPM-Mark 1, and still less ORKiMD's powerful position in the intervening years, publishing its eclectic *Muzïka i revolyutsiya* with official backing while RAPM was often unable to issue anything. Back in 1927, in spite of its relatively weak position then, RAPM members had initiated a personal campaign against Shulgin. He was mocked for sharing his editorship of *Music and Revolution* with his wife Elena behind the scenes, and RAPM referred to it as the 'Double-Bed Journal' (*Dvukhspal'nïy zhurnal*).[35] Shulgin ran for protection to Lunacharsky, which helped to keep his position secure, but failed to stifle the criticism. Shulgin was unable to attend the Conference, but Elena wrote to him that although ORKiMD 'had failed organisationally', it 'had won ideologically'. Whatever that meant, the other members of ORKiMD elected to join RAPM in September.

The reason Shulgin missed the conference and the ensuing upheaval deserves comment in itself. He was on assignment to a distant industrial plant. While his colleagues took fright and then caved in under the pressure of cultural revolution, Shulgin discovered for himself that the industrial revolution was a much more stringent creature. He wrote a dismayed report to Elena on his discovery that workers at the plant routinely died of carbon monoxide poisoning. Elena was equally horrified, and replied with the poignant naiveté of an honest Communist of the old school:

> Can they not do something about it, like installing better ventilation? I'm sure they must have made improvements like this elsewhere. Why don't you speak to the engineers, the workers and the managers, and perhaps write to the CC as well? Today hundreds of millions [of roubles] are allocated for the construction and improvement of production, especially in heavy industry. If you could get some results here, that would already be a significant help for the workers. They would feel that the Party and the Soviet power actually cared for them, rather than throwing mere slogans at them. Only attention and care could earn the kind of trust that will help the leadership. [...] By the

---

[34] Letter from Asafyev to Prokofiev of 13 Nov. 1929, LPA, folder 22, 276–7.

[35] See Yelena Krivtsova, 'Iz istorii muzïkal'no-obshchestvennïkh organizatsiy: ORKiMD (1924–1932): Po materialam arkhiva L. V. Shul'ginaʼ, *Trudï Muzeya muzïkal'noy kul'turï: Al'manakh*, vol. 2 (Moscow: Gosudarstvennïy tsentral'nïy muzey muzïkal'noy kul'turï, 2003), 268–90, 274. We have not been able to locate the original article.

way, try to check on the engineers – perhaps there is evidence of wrecking, hidden sabotage or negligence to be found. Seriously, Levik, try to dig around.[36]

In the midst of all the shouting over various reshuffles in the musical world, Elena's letter suddenly brings in another, humbling perspective: the unfathomable sacrifices, the doubts, deceptions and moral dilemmas of Stalin's First Five Year Plan. Engels had once described the grinding hardship and shortened, stunted lives of Manchester's workers during the English Industrial Revolution.[37] This had once lent communism its sense of moral urgency, but it was now just as much a part of the Soviet Union, the supposed workers' state.

---

[36] Letter from Shulgina to Shulgin of 8–10 July 1929, GTsMMK, fond 474 (Shulgin), ye. kh. 190.

[37] Engels's first book was *Die Lage der arbeitenden Klasse in England* (*The Condition of the Working Class in England*, 1845).

※ ※ ※ ※ ※

A. Veprik, 'Tvorchestvo Bartoka i problema fol'klora' [Bartók and the Problem of Folk Music], *Muzïka i revolyutsiya*, no. 6 (1929), 22–6.

This essay by Alexander Weprik (1899–1958) is interesting not merely because it represents a minority 'centrist' position in Soviet musical life of the time (i.e. neither ASM nor RAPM): while on a first reading it may seem dogmatically anti-modernist and anti-jazz (apparently placing it close to the RAPM end of the ideological spectrum), background evidence tells us that Weprik is not striking an ideological pose, but reflecting on his own unique mix of experiences. First, he was among the few figures in Soviet music to have spent several months in Europe meeting the composers he discusses in the essay. But second – and here is the real fascination of the piece – it serves as a latent personal manifesto of Weprik the Jewish composer, even if this cannot be guessed from the text alone.

Weprik was aligned with the 'Red Professors' Faction' of the Moscow Conservatoire, acting as the right hand of the indomitable Nadezhda Bryusova. The great formative experience of his life came in 1927, when he was sent on that lengthy 'business trip' to Europe, to collect useful information on educational methods. From his first day abroad, he experienced a great many cultural shocks: even before he had encountered the new music, he remarked upon the overt sensuality of European high society, so much at odds with Soviet codes of behaviour outside the circles of the NEPmen (the next year, Boris Asafyev found himself equally startled by this aspect of Western society). The following lines from Weprik's letters to Bryusova help to explain his use of Gorky's colourful quotation on the sensual and sexual overtones of jazz, which seems otherwise quite tangential to his discussion of Bartók in the article.

> Poor me, I had to survive a formal banquet over here, and it was simply torture. I can't stand these smoothed-out men in their tails and dinner jackets, or the women, dressed to the nines, yet denuded.[38]
>
> At the start I was simply maddened by that overtly animal element that you can detect here both in the men and the women. It's not love, nor even passion, but simply lust.[39]

Weprik's musical experiences in Europe disturbed him just as much. He went to Europe with the intention to invite Schoenberg himself to a teaching post at the Moscow Conservatoire – he had set out with an open mind and a great interest in European musical developments. But in one of the earliest letters he sent Bryusova from Berlin, it seems that panic was setting in already:

> The music I had to listen to here I simply cannot fathom. I'm not even sure whether it's music at all. Damn it, I write music myself and understand something of this business, but I don't think that anything I managed to listen to over here is music at all. Instead of the contours

---

[38] Letter from Weprik to Bryusova of 15 June 1927, RGALI, fond 2444 (Veprik), op. 2, ye. kh. 68, l. 3.

[39] Letter from Weprik to Bryusova of 16 July 1927, RGALI, fond 2444 (Veprik), op. 2, ye. kh. 68, l. 10v.

of a melody, you get, to my mind, an arbitrary selection of notes of different pitch and duration. I don't feel this to be *convincing*, I don't perceive it as the way things ought to be.[40]

Ten days later, Weprik sends Bryusova another assessment, calmer now, but still more damning:

... the music they write here is revolting, foul. It's such rubbish, that at first I wasn't just frightened, I was simply lost. But now I'm beginning to understand what's going on. For us, music is first of all a revelation: we expect to find a Weltanschauung there, an attitude towards the world. Here, it's very different. They *make* music over here, and that's all. Full stop. Music is seen as the use of timbre or rhythm only as the solution to a structural problem. This is why the most active element, melody, is wholly absent here. That is the principal distinction between contemporary Germany and what we do, all that is dear to us.[41]

After meeting with Schoenberg, whom Weprik even refers to as 'my old love' (his favourites were Gurre-Lieder and Pelleas und Melisande), he is thrown into turmoil:

I was hoping to find out from Schoenberg how he teaches compositional mastery. But where he's concerned, the technical side is inseparably connected with his whole purpose as a composer, and this is *so horrific* that only individual details would be of some use to us. The rest is rubbish nonsense, the devil knows what.[42]

I won't hide from you the fact that Schoenberg made a great impression on me. He is a man of genius. But ... this is the end.[43]

Weprik also gets a chance to observe Hindemith in action, a genial and dedicated teacher who spends unlimited time with his students and even takes them off to the countryside in good weather. He is impressed that Hindemith never allows his students to write music in an abstract manner, but requires that they conceive everything with a particular instrument in mind. If the piece is for bassoon and oboe, Hindemith would 'lug his own bassoon and oboe' into the class, and they would play the piece together. Weprik has nothing but admiration for the high level of technical mastery that Hindemith's students demonstrate, and but he finds nevertheless that they use this technique in the service of 'revolting music'.

The third luminary Weprik visited was Ravel, whom he found totally charming, but relaxed to a fault where his composition teaching was concerned. He did not follow any particular method, but encouraged students simply to rely on their own ear and intuition. Weprik commented admiringly on Ravel's Jewish songs, which he said were an inspiration to younger Jewish

---

[40] See fn. 38.

[41] Letter from Weprik to Bryusova of 26 June 1927, RGALI, fond 2444 (Veprik), op. 2, ye. kh. 68, l. 4.

[42] Letter from Weprik to Bryusova of 22 Sept. 1927, RGALI, fond 2444 (Veprik), op. 2, ye. kh. 68, l. 25v.

[43] Letter from Weprik to Bryusova of 27 Sept. 1927, RGALI, fond 2444 (Veprik), op. 2, ye. kh. 68, l. 27.

composers like him, but Ravel, in reply, only pointed out that the roots of this new Jewish music were to be found in Rimsky-Korsakov and Musorgsky.

Weprik saw the three wise men of European music and came home empty-handed. His trip barely altered the conviction that he had expressed at its very beginning:

> [...] Germany has run out of steam. With Wagner's death, the sunset began. At times, this sunset is blinding (Strauss), but it is still sunset, sunset, sunset.
> A light will come from the East!
> I was a thousand times right when back in Moscow I laid out my thoughts before you, about the sunset of Europe, the dawn of the musical culture of the East, and the role that Jewish music will play in it.[44]

This conviction of Weprik's can be discerned between the lines of his essay on Bartók and folk music, especially when he compiles his list of trans-national figures at the end: four of the five are well known for their representations of Jewishness in their works (the poet Iosif Utkin, 1903–44; the writer Isaac Babel, 1894–1940; the composer Gustav Mahler, and the Soviet composer, Mikhail Gnesin, 1883–1957). The Russian classic, Nikolai Gogol, famous for his Ukrainian motives (and his anti-Semitic passages), is thrown in rather as a decoy. The references to the Russian classical composers, Rimsky-Korsakov, Musorgsky, and Borodin, also seems to point to the Eastern/Western mix that can be found in their works (and perhaps in recognition of their role as distant models for the new Jewish music, following Ravel's pronouncement). It becomes clear that the young Bartók is a perfect model for Weprik himself, in his desire to express his 'progressive nationalism' within the Soviet context. Soviet musicologists have indeed recognised Weprik's leanings towards Bartók in, for example, his Five Little Pieces for Orchestra (first version from 1930).[45]

The essay on Bartók kdoes not directly address Weprik's desire to be both a Soviet and a Jewish national composer, but it became problematic during the course of the Stalin era. In the 1930s, Weprik switched from writing expressly Jewish works (like Songs and Dances of the Ghetto from 1927) to a more generalised Soviet style, and even did a stint in Kirghizstan, co-authoring a Kirghiz national opera. This did not save him, however, from being accused of bourgeois nationalism. He was arrested during Stalin's 'anti-cosmopolitanism' campaign and spent four years in the camps. In Russia, he is known primarily as the author of an orchestration textbook, while in the West his music is better known within the framework of Jewish culture.

---

[44] See fn. 38, l. 3v.
[45] V. Yu. Del'son, 'Veprik', Muzikalnaya entsiklopediya (Moscow: Sovetskaya entsiklopediya), vol. 1, 738.

A. Weprik
Bartók and the Problem of Folk Music

At present, the only kind of music to find success across the whole of Europe is jazz [*dzhaz-band*]. This success is customarily explained by the closeness of jazz to folk music, but it actually arises from very different factors.

Only a few years ago, Europe's most progressive musicians believed in atonality, hoping that it would lead music out of a dead end; now they are putting all their hopes in jazz, which is supposed to make music healthier. It is not hard to see why everything is staked on jazz. Attempts to create a non-emotional music[i] led to a dead end, to the loss any social significance in music: music stopped being infectious, it stopped influencing people. Jazz is the only kind of post-war music that is truly infectious. In this way, jazz becomes a socially significant element: it organises the emotions, and this is the reason for its success.

The aim of jazz, however, is beyond doubt.[ii] One of the ideologues of this movement, Milhaud, conveniently reveals what others have left unsaid. In a discussion of jazz, Milhaud does not forget to mention that it first appeared in Paris, in the *Casino de Paris* (a place of entertainment). This is a very important confession, for it confirms the genetic connection of jazz with the tavern and the brothel. And nevertheless, attempts to explain the success of jazz through its proximity to folk music are very telling. The new objectivity, as the sum-total of the phenomena of non-emotional writing, has long since turned into a set of clichéd constructive devices. This clichéd character led to frightening levels of productivity, to a complete rejection of melody and, in the end, rendered the composer anonymous. Within groups whose members share the same constructive principles, the individual traits of composers have been almost completely obliterated.

The case of jazz is a little different. Jazz fulfils the bourgeois commission for *emotional* music. A return to melody was thus preordained, since melody is the most powerful vehicle for emotion. Perhaps, indeed, there is a certain connection between jazz and Negro folk songs. (This connection, by the way, is denied by a number of music scholars; see Wolfgang Weber's article 'Is Negro music a model for ours?', published in the July 1927 issue of the German journal *Die Musik*). But this is not the point. The point is that every attempt to restore social significance to music leads back to the domination of melody. But we cannot approach this issue in the same way as the bourgeois scholars, who say that jazz is good *because* it is close to folk music, *because* it is emotional.

Emotionality is only a prerequisite for active, socially significant music. Non-emotional music, because it is not accessible to the listener, is devoid of social significance. But within a range of emotions, we have a number of categories on very different levels. This is why we cannot stop once we have merely stated the fact that this or that work exhibits emotionality or has its roots in folk music.

Krenek, in his opera *Johnny*, employs genuine Negro melodies. But what does this tell us? Bartók, in his first period, also used genuine folk songs. Does it mean that these composers are of equal significance? Not at all. It would be a great mistake to lump all folk-related phenomena together on the formal basis of folk-song use alone. We cannot be satisfied by this. We need something else: we need to discover *what emotional category* is cultivated by this or that composer, and what their class nature is. The young Bartók's work relies on folk song to a great extent; his study of peasant music doubtless had a great impact on his work. Bartók himself provides an interesting revelation of his social nature: 'At that time [the 1900s – A.W.] in Hungary there emerged a certain chauvinistic political trend, which also found its reflection in the artistic sphere. In music too, there was a slogan – that we must create something specifically Hungarian. This trend influenced me as well, and turned my attention to the study of our folk music.'

However, the Hungarian national movement was at one time a progressive phenomenon, because despite its national-chauvinist character, it subverted the Dual Monarchy. (A certain analogy may be found between Hungary and India, where the bourgeois nationalist movement is progressive not in itself, but because it helped subvert the British Empire). The young Bartók, through folk music, made contact with a certain social stratum and became a vehicle for its progressive tendencies.

This is why his *Allegro barbaro*, Folk Songs, Peasant Songs, Christmas Songs are so infectious. In the fragment from the *Allegro barbaro* given below [...], as is generally the case in his works of this period, we can discern the sharpness of the melodic line and the intensity of the harmonic language.

Allegro barbaro [Example shortened]

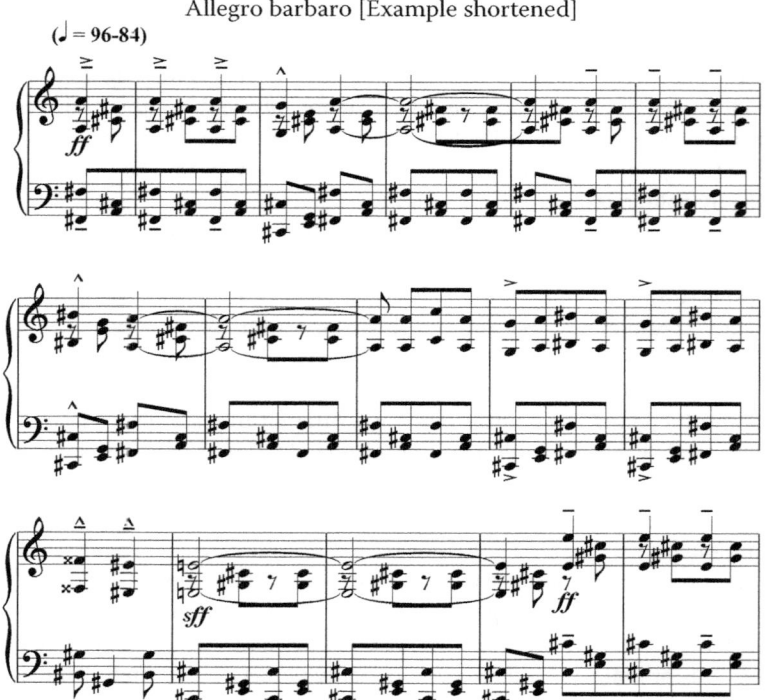

Bartók fully exploits the primary character of melody. In his autobiography, he admits that his melodies led him towards new harmonic possibilities. *It was through his melodies* that he discovered the existence of new modal formations and revealed them through a new diatonicism, having turned away from the ossified major-minor system. This Bartók is close to us, but an analysis of his later works shows that he has changed profoundly. And what is most telling, his former tense melodic lines have been utterly dissolved:

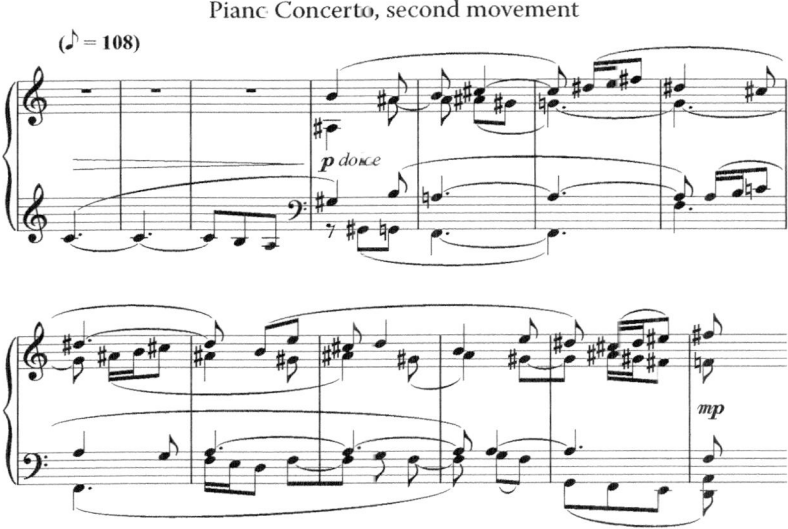

Piano Concerto, second movement

It is clear that this shift is not an accident. Melody is the most powerful means of generating an emotional impact. A rejection of melody always means that music will lose its social significance. Even Bartók's huge talent could not save him. The trajectory of his creative path clearly reflected the historical fate of the class stratum he represented: the work of the *young* Bartók was built on the basis of a historically progressive bourgeois movement, but it would be ridiculous to ascribe the same historically progressive role to the contemporary Hungarian bourgeoisie. Thus, Bartók has shared the fate of his class.

In the West, they still cannot understand our closeness to Beethoven and are sincerely bemused that having brought about such a great revolution, we yet remained so 'conservative' in our music. The attraction to Beethoven, who is chronologically remote from us, was inevitable: he proved to be *closer* than the chronologically close Schoenberg, Hindemith, and Krenek, for Beethoven reflected the young bourgeois class that was revolutionary at the time; he reflected this in his dynamism, his desire to fight and his will to win, while Schoenberg, Hindemith and Krenek reflect the degeneration and death of this class. It is not surprising that they *demand* Beethoven in our clubs.[iii] They demand his music in spite of the fact that no one could call him an ideologue of proletarian revolution. They demand him because the present day has not yet produced works that reflect our era. The heroism and inspiration of a young class is closer to us than the music of a period of degradation and decomposition.

But this does not mean that our revolution has found its composer and that this composer is Beethoven. Out of the whole heritage of Western culture, Beethoven and Wagner are particularly close to us. (I don't mean to say that *all* Beethoven and *all* Wagner are close to us. For example, the Beethoven of *Christus am Ölberge* or the *Missa solemnis*, and Wagner in a number of works, especially *Parsifal*, are undoubtedly alien and adversarial to us). We will definitely create works that resonate with our era. But every work of art grows on its own territorial foundations. As in literature, where the material is the word, the spoken language, and not an arbitrary selection of phonetic formations, the materials of music are likewise not mere arbitrary combinations of individual tones of a certain pitch, but elements of musical speech, which determine the national language of the given author. There exists, of course, a hybrid type that resulted from the crossing of different national lines, as in the cases of Gogol, Babel, Utkin, Mahler or Gnesin. The music of Rimsky-Korsakov, Musorgsky, and Borodin also vividly reveals the crossing of *different national* thematic elements, united by the general ethnographic concept of Russian music. But not a single musical work has yet been created in isolation from the sources of musical speech: no matter how far creative thought might have moved away from folk music, the connection between the two is always present. Only in an era of deepest decline can one observe attempts to make art completely faceless and devoid of ideological significance. Such attempts can be seen in our times. They led to the materials of literature being reduced to a mere arbitrary selection of phonetic formations (as in Dadaism), and the materials of music being reduced to mere arbitrary combinations of individual sounds of a certain pitch (Schoenbergian atonality).

But our era will undoubtedly see the creation of active, emotional music; we will have to turn to melody as the most vivid vehicle for emotional expression. An increase in the importance of melody is always accompanied by a closer relationship with the folk foundation, and the problem of folk music becomes particularly relevant to our era.

[*Notes to Weprik's original*]

i This means the music that does not convey any experiences, feelings, or psychological changes.

ii A brilliant exposé of jazz is provided by Gorky ('On Music for Fat People', *Pravda*, 18 Apr. 1928):

'Wild screams, whistling, thundering, howling, roaring, crackling: inhuman voices rushing in, akin to the neighing of horses, we hear the grunting of a brass pig, the braying of asses, the amorous croaking of a huge frog; all this insulting chaos of deranged sounds is dominated by a rhythm that is hardly intelligible, and after listening to this screaming for a minute or two, you begin to suspect that this is an orchestra of madmen, that they were driven mad through sex, and that the conductor is some human stallion, waving a huge phallus …

[…] This radio in the neighbouring hotel is consoling the world of fat people, the world of predators, transmitting through the air a new foxtrot for them, performed by a Negro orchestra. This is music for fat people. To its rhythms in all the magnificent nightclubs of the 'cultured' countries, fat people, cynically moving their thighs, are simulating the act of a man fertilising a woman, thereby debasing it […]

[...] He, the fat one, does not need a woman as a friend and a human being; she is for him only an amusement, unless she is just as predatory as he is. Nor does he need a woman as a mother, because although he enjoys power, children would place restrictions upon him. And even power is something that he needs only for the foxtrot, and the foxtrot is necessary to him now because Fatty's manhood is lacking. Love is only debauchery for him, and has become more and more a dissipation of the imagination, rather than a riot of dissolute flesh as it was before. In the world of the fat, there is an epidemic of 'homosexual' love. The evolution which the fat are undergoing is nothing but a degeneration [...]'

iii An interesting survey was carried out by Persimfans. See Bergman's article in No. 8 of *Persimfans* for 1927/28.

※ ※ ※ ※ ※

Boris Filippov, '3-ya muzïkal'naya opimpiada v Leningrade' [The Third Musical Olympiad in Leningrad], *Kul'turnaya revolyutsiya*, no. 14 (30 July 1929), 8–10.

This is a description of one of the musical entertainments that was provided for delegates to the All-Union Conference of Music Workers, held in Leningrad. Its impressive scale demonstrates that mass musical work was not abandoned after the demise of Proletkult, but continued within another nationwide structure – the trade unions.

Boris Filippov
The Third Musical Olympiad in Leningrad

The 70,000

The large KIM [Youth Communist International] stadium, located on the shore of the Gulf of Finland, could barely hold the seventy-thousand-strong crowd, which had been streaming to Decembrist Island since early morning.

The character of the festival is clear from the audience that has assembled for this unusual concert-competition. It consists largely of workers who have brought their families along to the musical Olympiad. The atmosphere in the crowd, so extraordinary in size, was reminiscent of some grandiose trip to the country. The sun is scorching ... The listeners settle down informally on the stadium's green lawn, some reading newspapers and magazines while waiting for the concert to begin, others taking their breakfast. Young people have started playing games. The majority, however, sit full of expectation and engage in lively conversations about the programme.

The Olympiad opened [late] at 1:30 p.m. But a delay of just twenty minutes had already unnerved the audience. They had come to the stadium in good time, and this uneasy period of waiting affected the listeners' mood.

Those present were a little puzzled on seeing that the performers' stands were empty. Where were the musicians? They were nowhere to be seen inside the stadium. Doubts began to emerge over the line-up of performers given in the programme. Some were heard saying that the amateur groups, in keeping with the 'customs of the workers' clubs', were going to arrive about an hour and a half late. By one o'clock, the audience had started to express its impatience openly, with loud hand claps and demands for the concert to begin. Few had guessed that the musical army was completely battle-ready, in formation outside the stadium, awaiting only a command from headquarters so it could commence its march.

The Olympiad headquarters is on the balcony running from the choir's benches to the brass band. Everyone has been working frantically since eight o'clock in the morning. An operational plan had been prepared in advance, which anticipated all organisational moments.

The Musical Parade

Listen! Listen! The Third Musical Olympiad of Leningrad Trade Unions is open! On behalf of the Presidium of LOSPS [The Trade Union Council of the Leningrad Region], Comrade Rafail will make an introductory speech.[46]

The fanfares sound their calls, alternating with the mighty roll of 20 drums. Like an echo, the trumpeters respond from their raised platforms. After this exchange, the side gates are thrown wide open and organised columns of musicians come out into the stadium, parading past the tribune for the music-conference delegates. Each column is headed by a group of amateur photographers, organised as a mass outing of the photo-cine-workshop of the Viborg House of Culture of LOSPS. The procession continues in an endless stream for *40 minutes*. The musicians hold their 'production tools' at the ready. At a signal from the tribune, all the instruments are raised aloft, in a kind of salute to the conference delegates. From the delegates' gallery, greetings and applause are heard.

The parade brings a significant theatrical colouring to the festival, strengthening its visual aspect. In future, more attention should be given to the artistic aspect of the amateurs' march. At the Third Musical Olympiad, this attempt to make a colourful carnival of the parade was not altogether a success. A shortage of funds hampered the orderly preparation of the carnival decorations, and the amateur circles themselves did not show enough initiative here.

A Concert of Five Thousand

This impressive concert featured a combined choir of 2,500 singers, a Great-Russian [folk instrument] orchestra of 1,200 players, a brass band of 400 and combined ensembles of *gusli* and accordion players.

Unfortunately, not all the music collectives are equally well suited to open-air performance. In this unusual competition between the choir and different instrumental ensembles, the choir and the brass band have the advantage over the others. The string collectives lose out whenever they leave the confines of their concert halls and enter the acoustically unsuitable conditions of the stadium.

The attempt to use amplification in the stadium did not help. The use of radio technology to amplify the collectives with a weaker sound was, in itself, a correct and valuable idea, but it did not fulfil the hopes that had been invested in it. In the space of a single rehearsal at the stadium, the organisers of the Olympiad had not managed to tune the radio apparatus with enough precision, and had not met the requirements of the large string contingent, which was the most complex broadcast. The choral collective and the brass band sounded much more impressive. The sound from both almost managed to carry across the full extent of the stadium. But the most grandiose impression was made by the performance of the *Internationale*, which was given by the combined forces of all the collectives, with the participation of the entire audience.

---

[46] Cmrd. M. Rafail, Chairman of the Trade Union Council of the Leningrad Region, became a footnote in histories because of his 1930 letter to Stalin questioning the Party's apparent U-turn on collectivisation. Stalin's reply is published in his Collected Works (I. V. Stalin, *Sochineniya*, vol. 12 (Moscow: Gosudarstvennoye izdatel'stvo politicheskoy literatury, 1949), 231–2.

Regarding the artistic side of the programme, we cannot fail to pass comment on the great artistic growth of the Leningrad music collectives. This was manifest in the general orderliness of the performances, where the notion of using several conductors was rejected, since this had previously led to disarray. And the programme itself this time, compared to the programme of the First Olympiad, represents a great step forward. The repertoire of the Third Olympiad comprised pieces of indisputable artistic merit, such as 'Rise, rise you beautiful sun' (*Ti vzoydi, vzoydi, solntse krasnoye*) by Musorgsky, Borodin's 'Song of the Dark Forest' (*Pesnya tyomnogo lesa*) and the chorus and solo from Pashchenko's opera *The Eagle Revolt* (*Oriliniy bunt*). This last piece was performed with a very successful deployment of radio: the amplified performance of the solo part was borne aloft by the powerful choral collective. The brass band gave an excellent performance of a fine work by the composer Yu. Shaporin, his introduction to the drama *The Storming of Perekop*. In all these works, the musical collectives demonstrated high technical abilities. The choir's brilliant performance was undoubtedly assisted by that most talented choral conductor and choir organiser, I. V. Nemtsev.[47] Special mention should be given to one part of the choral programme, which featured small production songs and popular songs, where the entire audience was involved in the singing.

For a fortnight or so prior to the festival, the city had been filled with colourful posters featuring the music and text of a mass production song that reflects the main slogans of today:

Chtob rabota shla ne valko,	If you want the work to go well,
Ne rabotayte s razvalkoy. Dzin'!	Don't work too slowly. Ping!
Vot, k primeru, moy priyatel' –	Here's a friend of mine, for example,
Stal teper' izobretatel'. Raz!	He's become an inventor! One!

And so on. At the same time, on LOSPS radio station, a special team of choral instructors gave lessons in mass singing during factory lunch breaks. The success of this modest song was extraordinary. This was the first attempt to involve the Olympiad audience, to make this entire mass feel that they are performers and active participants in the programme, and it was a complete success.

After the mass concert, special concert platforms were used for performances of the workers' clubs' 'live newspapers', and for a competition involving individual amateur musicians. This music festival of the Leningrad trade unions had an all-union character this time, owing to the presence of the delegates to the All-Union Music Conference, and of groups of visitors who came for the Olympiad from various cities of the Ukraine, the Transcaucasus, etc. The proceedings ended with a mass fête and mass games.

---

[47] Iosif Vasilyevich Nemtsev (1885–1939) studied at the Synodal School and the Court Capella and presumably worked, presumably, with various church choirs (his Soviet-era biographies omit to mention this). After the Revolution, he became active in amateur music making, specialising as a conductor of enormous choirs (Leningrad Musical Olympiads, which started in 1927, were largely his initiative). In the 1937 Olympiad he lined up 30 conductors to direct a choir of a hundred thousand.

Conclusions

The success of Leningrad Musical Olympiads suggests that we ought to take this experiment to other cities of the Union. The Olympiads are irreplaceable in our work with the masses, in order to realise the slogan 'Music to the Masses!' It is essential that we place the issue of an *All-Union Musical Olympiad* on our culture-work agenda. The issue of creating normal conditions for music festivals is no less essential. In particular, there is the need to build a special music stadium that would fulfil at least the basic acoustic requirements.

※ ※ ※ ※ ※

Yuriy Keldïsh, 'Balet "Stal'noy skok" i yego avtor – Prokof'yev', *Proletarskiy muzïkant*, no. 6 (1929), 12–19.

This essay on Prokofiev's Steps of Steel *(the composer's own English rendering of* Le Pas d'Acier*), demonstrates that the quality of RAPM writers has risen substantially, and Yury Keldysh would later become an imperious presence in Soviet musicology. His 'Marxist' analysis may be denunciatory in purpose, but shows a much better understanding of the music and its context than the original RAPM membership had ever demonstrated. The essay, however, was part of an intensive anti-Prokofiev campaign that RAPM had instigated, and even before it was published in November, the Bolshoi had to cancel its planned production of the ballet.*

Back in June, the deputy director of the Bolshoi, Boris Gusman, had written to Prokofiev to tell him that the theatre intended to stage the ballet, and to ask him to accept payment in Soviet currency (hard currency reserves were low, and Prokofiev's second Soviet tour was imminent).[48] *But Prokofiev's fee was the least of Gusman's worries. There was resistance to the ballet's 'undanceable' music, to the extent that even the progressive choreographer Goleyzovsky refused to work on it. There were also political problems: the seamier side of life on the streets of Soviet cities was depicted in the ballet and, while this might have been advantageous for Western productions, it posed an obstacle to a Soviet production, especially in the more restrictive political climate of the First Five-Year Plan period.*[49] *Meyerhold tried to strengthen the case for the project by providing a scenario that would look more edifying on the Soviet stage. Gusman even decided it would be prudent to attend a RAPM meeting, where he presented a report on the Bolshoi's activities, no doubt hoping that a co-operative gesture would deflect criticisms of himself and the ballet.*[50] *Prokofiev had been swaddled in an environment of universal admiration during his first visit, but when he returned in the autumn of 1929, he frequently had to weather strong criticisms by people who thought little of his celebrity status, as in this little pas de deux of mutual disrespect:*

– Why is the finale of the ballet full of machine-like industrial rhythms?

– Because the machine is more beautiful than man.

– Is the factory capitalist, where the workers are slaves, or Soviet, where they are the masters, and if it is Soviet, then when and where did you have the opportunity to study any factory here, since you have been living abroad since 1918 and only came back for the first time in 1927, for just two weeks?

– That is a political question, not a musical one, so I don't intend to answer it.[51]

[48] Letter from Gusman to Prokofiev of 6 June 1929, LPA, folder 21, 15–16.
[49] Letter from Gusman to Prokofiev of 29 Sept. 1929, LPA, folder 22, 110–13.
[50] Letter from Gusman to Prokofiev of 4 Oct. 1929, LPA, folder 22, 135.
[51] As reported by RAPM in D. Gachev, 'O 'Stal'nom skoke' i direktorskom naskoke', *Proletarskiy muzïkant*, no. 6 (1929), 19–23.

In the end, the Bolshoi's Artistic and Political Council gave in to the various pressures, and voted to discontinue work on the planned production of Steps of Steel. A few months later, between productions of the ballet in Cleveland and Chicago, Prokofiev was still smarting: 'the work travels around the world, [while] our good old chauvinists [rusopyati] are still arguing about whether Massine [the choreographer] had visited a capitalist or a proletarian factory'.[52]

Meyerhold was disturbed when his protégé Shostakovich told him that he agreed with Keldysh's hostile remarks on Steps of Steel (in the article below). There was probably an element of provocation or contrariness here, but it is also likely that Shostakovich was quite relieved that his own first ballet would not be overshadowed by Prokofiev's work. Shostakovich reported:

> In the end, [Meyerhold] had to admit that Steps of Steel is not really such a good work, and that he had been defencing it as a counterweight to Davidenko. I said it can't be a counterweight, since Davidenko & Co. haven't written any ballets. 'Don't you worry! They will.' – he replied, wryly.[53]

Yu. Keldysh

The Ballet *Steps of Steel* and its composer, Prokofiev

I

Prokofiev's creative powers took on their shape and grew at a special time in the development of the Russian arts, and the composer's roots were set deep in the ideas and atmosphere of the time. This period, spanning the pre-war and war years, saw the first noisy incursions of Futurism, 'urbanism' and 'machinism' into the Russian arts, counteracting a different set of artistic '-isms', like Symbolism and Impressionism. Back then, these new '-isms' were already being pushed forward under the banner of the struggle against extreme refinement in artistic expression, the concept of the isolated individual, and the over-cultivation of subjective experience; all these were to be set aside in favour of the establishment of a solid and healthy 'objective' art, influenced by machines and aeroplanes, or resurrecting the coarse primitivism of a prehistoric era. For all their diversity, what these trends had in common was a rejection of psychologism, and a foregrounding of the constructive element in art.

In music around 1910, we see the beginning of a reaction against the harmonic over-refinement, highly-strung emotionality and hysterics of Scriabin's musical style, which had previously dominated the scene. Stravinsky spearheaded this reaction. The most penetrating artistic minds were already able to see the inner,

---

[52] Letter from Prokofiev to Gusman of 10 Jan. 1930, LPA, folder 23, 25. Leonide Massine, or Leonid Fyodorovich Myasin (1896–1979), Diaghilev's star dancer and choreographer.

[53] Letter from Shostakovich to Sollertinsky of 10 Feb. 1930, D. D. Shostakovich, *Pis'ma I. I. Sollertinskomu*, ed. by D. I. Sollertinskiy (St Petersburg: Kompozitor, 2006), 53.

or so to speak, dialectical connection between the trends mentioned here, which were superficially contradictory, and yet essentially related. Trying to uncover the roots of Stravinsky's music, V. G. Karatygin wrote:

> The psychological impressionism that is embodied in artistic images takes on different guises, appears in different variants and elaborations, and is sometimes even accompanied by those trends which, strange as it may seem, are directly opposed to impressionism – namely, a tendency towards classical clarity and balance, towards a secondary level of simplicity. In these cases, apparently, the law of psychological contrasts comes into action. The artist, while his art reflects a soul that has been splintered and corroded by neurasthenic impressionism, is fatigued at the same time by all this nervous tension and seeks out an antidote in the knowing return to simplicity.

The causes of this reaction were to be found, of course, at the level of social relations. The intervening period of class battles and then of the war, sobered up the bourgeois intelligentsia to a significant extent, shattering its mystical dreams and directing its thoughts towards the realities of life. Art had to help them set aside the unpleasant thoughts and feelings that were always prompted by close contact with this reality. The less the facts of public life pointed towards hopeful outcomes, the more these demands were placed on art. Some strong and vivid external impulses were needed for this. Impressionist vagueness and transient moods had to give way to a greater clarity of expression and a concentration of formal construction.

Instead of Scriabin's extreme harmonic chromaticism, Stravinsky has clear, primitive diatonicism with schematic rows of parallel intervals. While the contours of individual chords are often lost in the intricate labyrinths of Scriabinesque chromaticism, the basis of Stravinsky's style is the opposite tendency: the most lucid revelation of what might be called *harmonic planes*. The building of more complex harmonies takes place simply by superimposing several such planes, and every complex chord can easily be disassembled into its simple harmonic constituents. But it is precisely because of this mechanical principle of building harmonies that the dynamic line or logical connection between them is broken, and everything is reduced to a purely timbral deployment of the different sound planes and their contrasting juxtapositions. This is why, for example, the dances from the folk scenes in *Petrushka* display more colouristic brilliance than live movement, and this brilliance, stemming from the contrast between vivid individual episodes, is invariably presented in grotesque hues. This is not a naive and natural simplicity, but a 'second-order' simplicity, to use Karatygin's expression, which itself contains an element of the refined aesthete's approach, a delight in rather rough, bright, and often garish colours.

But there is a kind of duality in Stravinsky's own musical style. This can best be seen in *Petrushka* again. By way of contrast to the noisy, motley crowd, there is Petrushka, with his sufferings and his broken heart, expressed through his convulsive rhythms and angular melodies. A wooden doll, a mere puppet, turns out to have feelings too. We have an opposition here: on the one hand, an apparently lifeless puppet jerking mechanically on his strings but capable of refined and complex feelings, and on the other hand we have the living but soulless crowd; this opposition bore a particular social meaning that responded perfectly to the mood of the intelligentsia during the period of reaction following 1905. A complete withdrawal from active social struggle, a forlorn subjectivism, a dissatisfaction with reality – all these were expressed through the passivity of a moribund psyche, embodied by the image of the suffering Harlequin. The bright colours of *Petrushka*'s folk scenes, is thus only a *superficial element* that throws the inner psychological content into relief.

Stravinsky was the first to step forward under the banner of reaction, but he did not manage to bring it to completion. He was hindered by his own ... meaningfulness. Through *Petrushka*, he raised a question, an acute question indeed for the intelligentsia of those years, but one that required an art that could draw them away from their ruminations, dreams and emotions – they had to forget about all those 'eternal questions'. In Stravinsky too, admittedly, there is a superficial brilliance and brightness of colour that decidedly dominates over the ideological content (perhaps owing to the narrowness and poverty of the ideas themselves), but his musical style still contained too large a dose of refined aestheticism. The social and political shifts that had taken place required a more decisive return to the cruel world of physical reality. The nervous, frayed Russian intelligentsia needed the antidote of that 'rough Scythian' who was the embodiment of physical health, with a thick-skinned disposition and a lack of sensitivity towards emotional and aesthetic subtleties alike. Prokofiev was this 'rough Scythian', and his popularity in Russia meant that he soon left Stravinsky far behind in his wake.

Prokofiev was essentially a follower of Stravinsky, but a one-sided and superficial follower, who inherited only some superficial traits from his predecessor. He immediately rejected all ideological content. Stravinsky's 'psychological' *Petrushka* was transformed into a two-dimensional, cartoon-like Buffoon. *The Tale of the Buffoon* [*Chout*] is perhaps Prokofiev's most characteristic work, one that fully reveals the character of his creative powers. The basis of this work (and the basis of Prokofiev's music in general) is not humour, but buffoonery – the desire to provoke a merely *physiological laughter devoid of motivation*. This is achieved by an emphasis on *a deliberate lack of logic in the musical idiom*. Prokofiev often uses the same device of overlaying harmonic planes that we have seen in Stravinsky. But where Stravinsky still strives for some kind of system, even if it is contrived and primitive (like the simultaneous use of the keys of C and F♯ in *Petrushka*),[i] it is often impossible to discern any modal principle at work in Prokofiev. Stravinsky, while following a mechanical principle for generating harmonies, still proceeds from a perception of the sound-complex as a whole, striving for a timbral effect.[ii] In this, we can see an element of impressionism in his practice. In Prokofiev, timbre, the colour of the sounds, is given a subordinate status, while his primary concern is the physiological sensation produced by disharmony and falsity in the structure of musical speech. The basis of his musical style is gimmickry [*tryukizm*], which at times attains a high level of virtuosity in its treatment of the sound material, but does not pass beyond the desire to shock or bemuse the listeners through the abruptness or illogicality of this or that passage. Prokofiev covers up the flat meaninglessness and inertia of his musical thought process with purely superficial and cerebral musical tricks [*Kunststücke*]. The original meaning of this music is entirely contained in the sharpness of various arbitrary harmonic juxtapositions. But this sharpness, this 'prickliness' in our auditory sensations, if it is sustained and unremitting, is transformed into its opposite, and begins to produce a contrary, deadening effect.

We would in no way deny that art has a right to exist even when it does not touch on any deep problems and strives only to cause merriment, a natural release of superfluous vitality. But such art has to stimulate movement and action, toning up our lives, and freeing up our physical and psychological forces. But in Prokofiev, we find the opposite. The complete mechanisation of expression, rhythms and dynamics oppresses and fatigues, impeding the circulation of life forces. Dance, in combination with drama and music, represents the finest means for releasing organic energy, but in Prokofiev, it has degenerated. Is it not typical that the natural free movements of live people in ballet tend to be replaced by the clownish movements of fairground figures? And this is not just a superficial moment. Dull, stereotypical Prokofievian rhythms kill off the dynamism of natural movements with a fateful inevitability, giving them a lifeless, automatic character.

But perhaps this clowning around and buffoon-like grimacing serves as a mask for Prokofiev, covering up his true face? Some of Prokofiev's apologists have tried to portray matters to make it seem that he was fighting outmoded prejudices, caustically and sarcastically mocking the fraudulent conventions of tradition, and overturning them with his scepticism. But a struggle is normally engaged in for the sake of something real, and in destroying one thing we affirm another. Now what is the positive principle Prokofiev can affirm? In the name of what principle does he fight his battles?

We can best uncover this by drawing on the example of a work in which Prokofiev does touch upon immediate live reality. No matter what mask of pseudo- 'objectivity' an artist dons when portraying real life, he inevitably reveals his attitude towards it, his worldview. Over the course of his entire artistic career, Prokofiev has used a social plot only once, in the ballet about Soviet life, *Steps of Steel*, written in 1925 – a decade after *The Tale of the Buffoon*. Naturally, we cannot pass this work by. The very fact that this composer, who left Russia just after the start of the Revolution and who is living abroad today, should write a work on Soviet life, must attract our attention. And our interest is further deepened by the fact that *Steps of Steel* recently provoked fierce debates here. By analysing this work we shall try to establish where Prokofiev's ten-year evolution after the *Buffoon* led him, but we ask the reader to wait until the end of the article for the answer to this question.

II

Steps of Steel was written for production on the stage of the Russian theatre in Paris. One of the creators of this ballet was the owner and head of the theatre himself, Diaghilev, well known in theatrical circles for his productions of Stravinsky's works. He chose as his collaborator the Russian artist Yakulov,[54] who once had

---

[54] Georgiy Bogdanovich Yakulov (1894–1928), an avant-garde artist and designer, was summoned by Diaghilev and travelled from the Soviet Union to Paris to conceive and design the ballet.

close connections with our bohemian literary groups (such as the Imaginists and others), and the composer Prokofiev.

At the audition of *Steps of Steel* in GOTOB [the State Opera and Ballet Theatre], Prokofiev had this to say about the work's conception: "the choreographer was interested in realising new balletic forms based on rhythms and movements of machines, while the artist was interested in new Soviet costumery, and the composer wanted to find musical expression for the new 'spirit of Soviet Russia'.

As far as we can judge from the section titles in the published piano score, the communications from the composer, and the reactions of the foreign press to the Paris production, the content of the ballet can be summarised as follows: In Part I, we are given a series of character types and everyday episodes from the Civil War period. Here we find 'the train with peddlers', 'sellers of sweets and cigarettes', 'a sailor with a bracelet and a female worker', and in the same motley crowd, 'the commissars' and 'the orator.[iii] In Part II, there is 'the transformation of a sailor into a worker', after which we see the portrayal of a factory working at full tilt. It is difficult to discern the unfolding of any story here, and it seems rather more like a pantomime consisting of an introduction ('entry of the participants'), an intermedio ('change of set') and a final episode that repeats the main points of the introduction.

Turning to the music, we note there the same absence of any long build-up or dynamic development. While in Part II a kind of unity is supported by illustrative moments, even if they are purely superficial, Part I is a mere assemblage of independent illustrative episodes. It seems that this is not a failure on the part of the composer, but rather the deliberate realisation of a conception, namely the depiction of a motley, noisy fairground show. The musical characteristics of the individual moments confirm this supposition. The crowd and the individual characters have a definite grotesque character, with the ugly exaggeration of buffoonish caricatured traits so typical of Prokofiev. Such, for example, is the rollicking dance theme that characterises the crowd of peddlers in Part I (Example 1). The device of moving in parallel diatonic triads that we find here is undoubtedly influenced by the fairground scenes in Stravinsky's *Petrushka*. Even the juxtaposition of the keys of C and F♯ is borrowed from that source.

Example 1

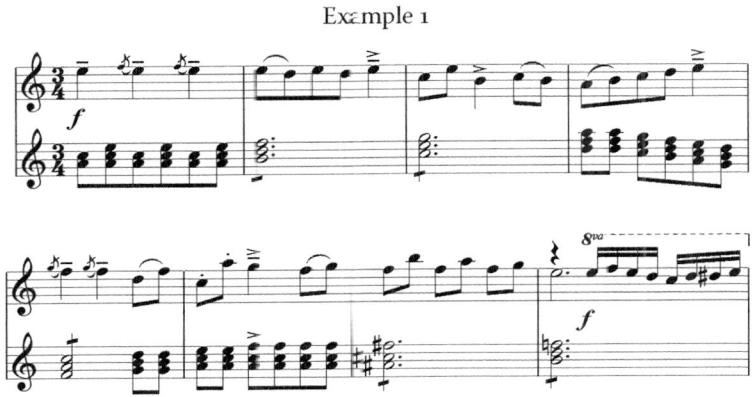

The music accompanying the entry of the Commissars is even more telling (Example 2). Here the effect is based on the comic appearance of people stepping out in a measured way, with assumed self-importance, like wooden puppets. The mechanical character of the rhythm and the sharp angularity of melody, based around a tritone, emphasise this puppet-like character of the movements, while the empty parallel fourths and triplets in the bass are perceived as deliberate barbarisms, once again not 'for real', but feigned. The 'sailor with a bracelet' is no less characteristic of Prokofiev: his rhythmic eccentricities and clamorous melodic ascents (Example 3) might remind us of the jerking movements of a fairground clown.

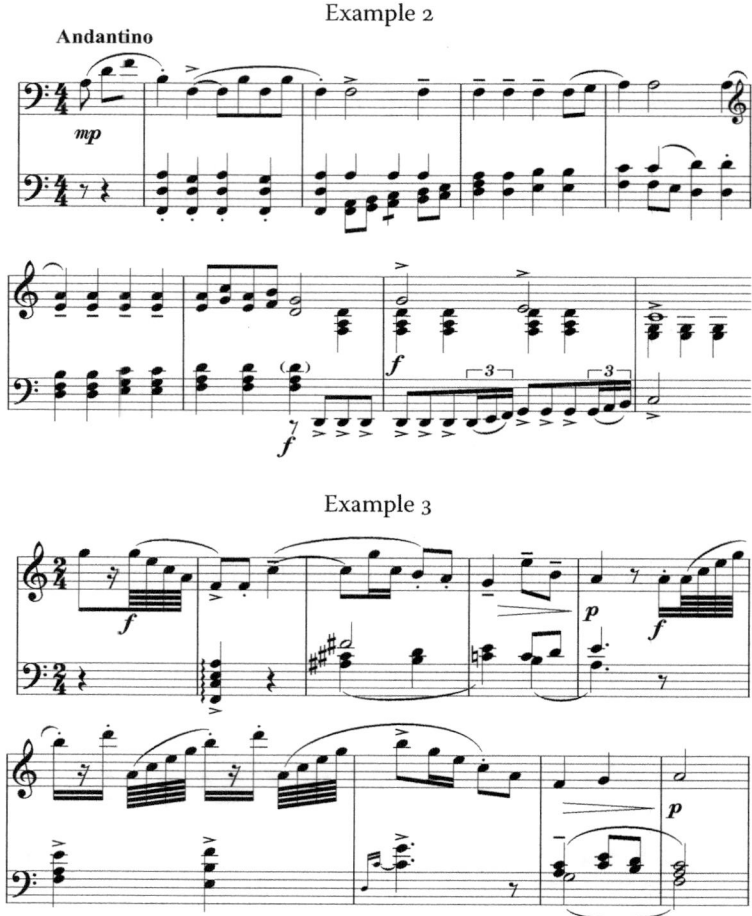

Example 2

Example 3

Do we have to point out how distant these characters and their music are from our conception of that heroic era? Prokofiev does not provide anything to contrast with this clowning about. The entire struggle, its intensity and drama, its richness in great deeds and examples of the highest self-renunciation – all of this must have bypassed his consciousness, and he presents the people who carried the main burden of this struggle through a vulgarised, hostile, philistine refraction. The musical characteristics of *Steps* are all so uniform, so thoroughly imbued with this spirit of buffoonish taunting, that they are sometimes hard to distinguish from one another. To confirm this, we need only give one more example, the orator's theme[iv] (Example 4).

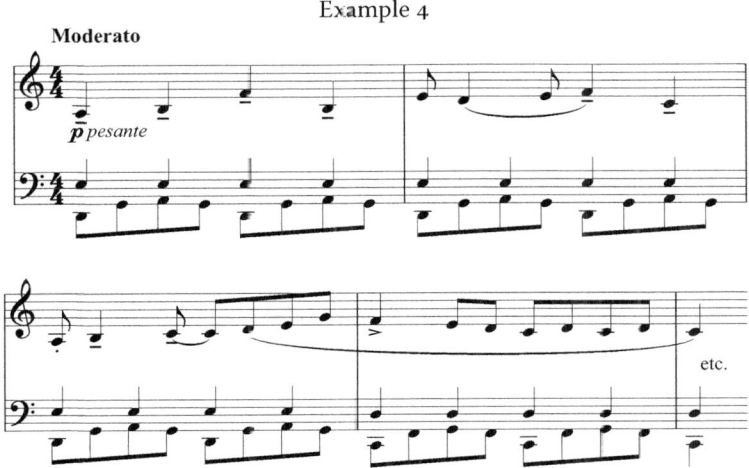

Example 4

One special trait of *Steps of Steel*, which makes it stand out somewhat from Prokofiev's other works, is the extreme *primitivism of the musical vocabulary*. Prokofiev here almost completely renounces complex or remote harmonic combinations; in all the examples we have provided, a pure diatonicism predominates. But this only emphasises the flat schematicism that is the basis of Prokofiev's style. In essence, this element introduces nothing new for Prokofiev. In *The Tale of the Buffoon*, for example, he employs this device when he wishes to highlight utter stupidity and senselessness (as in the buffoonish 'laughter dance' (Example 5). We can perceive a similarity between the device there and its signification in *Steps of Steel*. The bourgeoisie often imagines Soviet Russia to be some backward, half-savage, all-but-idiotic country, and the Bolsheviks inhabiting it are seen as coarse Barbarians with primitive, prehistoric morals, concepts and customs. *Whether willingly or unwittingly – it matters not which – Prokofiev follows this hostile prejudice in the depiction of his Soviet types.*

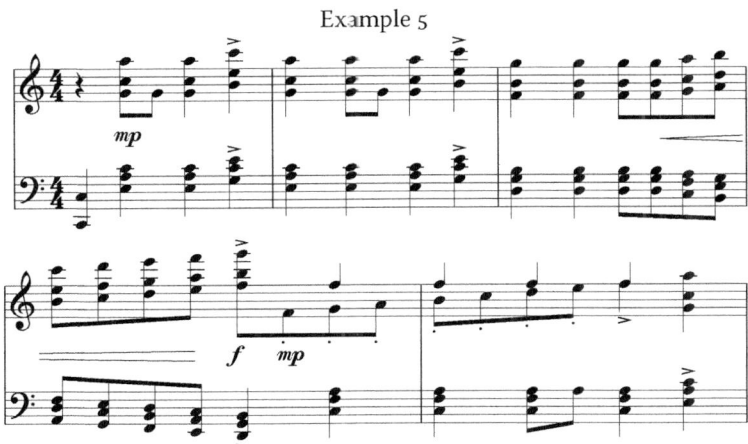

Example 5

The second part of the ballet offers an equally cheerless picture: everything surrenders to the monotonous mechanical motion, giving us a naturalistic impression of a working machine. The mechanical is not just an object of depiction here, but the inner organising force of the music, penetrating all its rhythms, sonorities, and dynamics. It is as if Prokofiev supplied only the music's rhythmic skeleton, striving to wrest complete control of the audience's attention, to hypnotise them through these constant, automated tempi and to divert their own living processes into the riverbed of a similar automaton-like state, devoid of willpower. In the end, these rhythms act as a narcotic, killing consciousness and the vigilance of the will.

The same result is achieved through illogical sound complexes that are again schematic in the extreme. In the episode entitled 'Hammers', Prokofiev, as if striving to create the impression of dull thuds constantly impinging on our consciousness, 'hammers in' just such a complex dissonant chord for many bars, a chord built on two clearly separable harmonic foundations (Example 6). A similar example of harmonic wrongness can be found in the final scene, where it arises from the arbitrary juxtaposition of two chords (Example 7). This device is by no means new for Prokofiev – it is one of his characteristic 'barbarisms'. In a slightly different incarnation one can find a similar passage in *The Tale of the Buffoon*, where the composer tries to 'get on the listener's nerves' through the protracted mechanical repetition of deliberately 'wrong' sonorities (Example 8). The only difference is that in *Steps of Steel* these devices are all raised to the *n*th power, and appear in their pure, or (so to speak) schematic form. The superficial inventiveness which lends most of Prokofiev's works that particular quality of boyish fun betrays him here, and the composer's entire 'kitchen' comes into full view. The mechanical foundations of Prokofiev's work are fully revealed.

Example 6

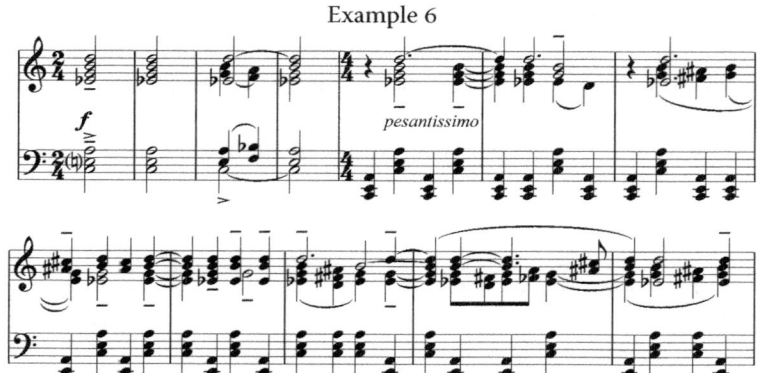

This is why *Steps of Steel* is so surprisingly hard to listen to, so oppressive in its machine rhythms and its unchanging monotony of colour. Some might argue that these machine rhythms contain a certain organising element in themselves. It is easy to see that this argument is empty and groundless. Every manner of organisation implies a conscious subordination of blind elementary forces to the power of its will, while here we see a mechanical, soulless automaton subordinating the human will to itself, depersonalising it and causing it to atrophy.

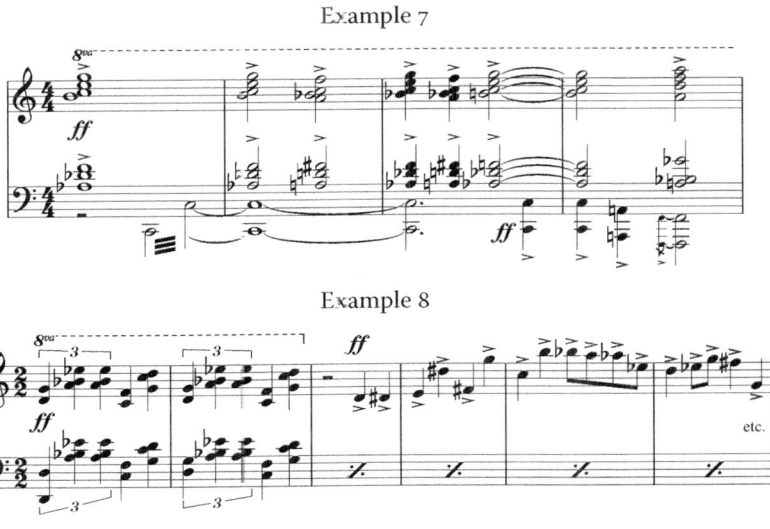

Example 7

Example 8

III

Why didn't *Steps of Steel* come out well, and why does it make such a poor impression? – Because the basis of this ballet is false and far-fetched. The authors of the ballet had a purely bourgeois and philistine approach to the treatment of revolutionary phenomena and people. The commissars, peddlers, and sailors making the revolution – to the middle bourgeois with his limited mind, this is, of course, all quite fascinating, unheard of and exotic. Feeling safe in the West up to a certain point, he can view it as an amusing fairground show. It was no accident that *Steps of Steel* was written in 1925, and not in 1919 or 1920. During the Civil War and the invasion of Russia, the immediate animal fear of the 'Bolshevik monster' was too strong and outweighed all the other feelings of the bourgeoisie, who had not yet recovered from the shocks of the war. 1925 was a year of relative stabilisation for capitalism, a lull at the front in the class war. Thus the bourgeois philistine, who is usually not very forward-looking and who lives only for the present, could allow himself the luxury of laughing at the enemy and joking about him. *Steps of Steel*, in essence, ascends no higher than the level of such feeble philistine jests. Prokofiev's reliance on the sensational has indeed paid off, but the truth and artistic quality of the depiction suffered undoubted losses because of this approach.

It must be said that the music of *Steps of Steel* is no accident in Prokofiev's work. His tendency towards an extreme schematicism, towards primitivism and a bare non-emotional constructivism is characteristic of his latest works, and in this he is doubtless influenced by the 'Zeitgeist'. Stravinsky in France, Hindemith in Germany, and Casella or Malipiero in Italy are the representatives and ideologues of this pure constructivism, and in some cases, the trend has attached itself to certain political tendencies. Thus Casella, in one of his articles, linking the Romantic style with the democratic state based on unlimited personal freedom, says that a firm, 'objective' musical form has to limit the expression of personal feelings, like the main political tendency of our days, which establishes a strong state, and in which the individual must forgo his rights in the service of the common interest. This is an open declaration of fascist ideology. Fascism tries to depersonalise and oppress human individuality, reducing it to the level of a blind tool in the hands of the higher state authority. At this juncture, the bourgeoisie needs to raise up a generation of robust class warriors whose one-sided development leads to the animal deadening of the intellect. This goal is served not only through sport, but also by the kind of music that deadens the human intellect and feelings through its mechanistic soullessness and meaninglessness. This kind of art contains an element of fatalism that paralyzes the active element of the will.

Prokofiev came to this style by a perfectly logical route, because all of its main elements had been typical of him at an earlier stage. But in his latest works, under the influence of social and political events, he reveals these traits in the extreme, leaving no more doubt about the nature of his creativity.

Returning now to the question which we posed earlier, we can decisively say that Prokofiev belongs wholly to the most reactionary trend of bourgeois art, and the one that is most openly hostile to us. We don't know where Prokofiev will rush off to after the failure of *Steps of Steel*. It is hard to say whether he will follow Stravinsky's path and devote himself to stylisations of old music, whether he will wholly immerse himself in 'pure' instrumental music, or whether he will revisit the territory he had already covered in his music. One thing is without doubt: *Steps of Steel* does not promise any creative shift that could fundamentally change our attitude towards Prokofiev.

[*Notes to Keldysh's original*]

i I am talking about the Stravinsky of the *Petrushka* period and to some extent the *Rite of Spring* period too; I am not touching upon the further evolution of his work.

ii In such passages as 'Games of the rival tribes' [*Jeux des Cités Rivales*] in the *Rite of Spring*, where two harmonic planes are clearly differentiated, we are most likely dealing with a special effect.

iii These are all titles of separate episodes in the ballet.

iv During his last visit, Prokofiev, in response to a question, claimed that the orator was presented as a caricature because he had had an anti-Soviet orator in mind. Let the readers judge for themselves whether there is any great difference between this 'anti-Soviet' orator and the 'Soviet' communist commissars.

D. Zhitomirskiy, 'Nos – opera D. Shostakovicha' [*The Nose* – an opera by D. Shostakovich], *Proletarskiy muzikant*, nos. 7–8 (1929), 33–9.

Like Keldysh, Daniil Zhitomirsky was another RAPM member who had begun to flourish as a critic. Both went on to have distinguished careers, but they eventually found themselves on opposing sides: in the forties, Keldysh had become one of Shostakovich's detractors, while Zhitomirsky was one of his most ardent supporters.

In 1929, Shostakovich was clearly one of the most promising of the new generation of Soviet composers, and The Nose, his first opera, became an important talking point in debates over the course that Soviet opera should take. In this review, Zhitomirsky viewed the work as a cul-de-sac, against the contention of Shostakovich's friend Sollertinsky, who claimed that although The Nose could not be regarded as an example of the long-awaited Soviet opera, it was nevertheless a large step in the right direction. Zhitomirsky argued that the work's flaws were primarily a consequence of Shostakovich's predilection for the grotesque, and this probably constituted the first appearance in print of a perennial complaint against Shostakovich (as well as Prokofiev) during the Stalin period.

D. Zhitomirsky
The Nose – an Opera by D. Shostakovich

Among the younger Soviet composers, Dmitry Shostakovich is one of the strongest, a gifted artist, mature in his mastery of composition. In spite of his youth,[i] Shostakovich has already managed to produce several large-scale works (for symphony orchestra and for piano) and a number of smaller pieces distinguished for the remarkable independence of musical thinking behind them. Nevertheless, Shostakovich's artistic path is still not clear. He is not truly attached to any variety of 'contemporaneity' [*sovremennost'*] (neither the European urbanist variety, nor the Russian intelligentsia variety),[ii] but he is still further removed from the opposite pole – that of the proletarians and fellow-travellers.

Shostakovich's endeavours are contradictory: he wrote his symphonic tribute *To October* [the Second Symphony] for the tenth anniversary of the October Revolution – this was a sufficiently serious work that in some manner reflected revolutionary ideas, albeit in the highly abstract mode characteristic of the intelligentsia. At the same time,[iii] however, Shostakovich was composing his *Aphorisms* – the overtly decadent work of an aesthete; and soon after this, he busied himself with a painstaking orchestral arrangement of an ordinary, vulgar foxtrot (the 'Tahiti Trot'), which was performed in several large orchestral concerts together with his [First] symphony and *To October*.

Shostakovich is distinguished for his inexhaustible creative energy: he composes a lot and probably does so with great ease. The most recent large-scale work is his opera *The Nose*. This opera marks a significant turn in his creative path, but undoubtedly it will not be the last. It is necessary to uncover the dangers and blind alleys implicit in this turn.

The Nose takes the plot of the Gogol story of the same name; it consists of three large acts (10 scenes) and involves 78 characters, a choir and a full symphony orchestra.

The very choice of this plot for a large-scale theatrical piece proves the author's alienation from the main tasks facing Soviet theatre. Gogol's *Nose*, of course, contains a number of profoundly drawn and satirical social characterisations. However, unlike his purely realist works (such as *The Government Inspector*, *The Marriage*, *The Dead Souls*) but in keeping with *The Notes of a Madman* and *The Portrait*, the plot of *The Nose* is nothing but a bizarre, semi-delirious fantasy. Gogol himself had probably realised how odd this plot would seem to those of his readers uninitiated in fantastic whimsy, and this is probably why, at the end of his novella, he wrote the following ironic lines (as if pre-empting similar attacks): 'But what is most strange, most incomprehensible, is how authors could pick such plots. I confess that this is totally beyond me ... Firstly, they are of absolutely no use to the Fatherland, and secondly ... but even secondly they are still of no use.'

And indeed, 'it is totally beyond me', what interest or instruction the students, or the metal and textile workers who populate the opera boxes could draw from watching crowds of people rushing across the stage for several hours looking for ... a lost nose. Our theatre demands spectacles that are ideological and socially significant. Gogol's social satire is stuck with its arbitrary and socially pointless plot; and none of the play's brilliance can save a production if the action itself lacks any *meaningful* core. Naturally, the libretto of *The Nose* cannot possess such a core, for the spectator can hardly find interest in the 'mysterious' beginning (the loss of the nose) or in any of the ensuing 'events'. His attention would inevitably be waylaid by details, individual remarks, little scenes, etc., among which there are, it has to be said, a few successful and witty examples. But still, is this not a superfluous luxury, when a huge opera collective has to overcome the difficulties of a very complex score and spend much effort and money on production, simply to provoke a few dubious sniggers?

In his artistic conception of *The Nose*, Shostakovich set himself a very difficult problem: to convey live human speech through musical intonations. Musorgsky set himself the same task 60 years ago in *The Marriage* (also on a Gogol text), which he never finished. But it was hardly accidental that Musorgsky abandoned work on *The Marriage*: in his search for artistic veracity he sensed the fruitlessness of naturalist recitative and the necessity for emotional and psychological generalisation. And indeed, in *Boris Godunov*, he found a generalised *realist* recitative, which tends towards the melodic.

The Nose is written in near-continuous recitative. However, in solving this important artistic problem, Shostakovich chose a path totally different from that of Musorgsky's *realism*. Musorgsky treated *The Marriage* as a social satire: he attempted to uncover the characters' *typical* features, to produce a comic conception resulting from the collision of real human qualities. Shostakovich has a different approach: he works within the sphere of the *grotesque*, and for him the comical is contained in *playing* with *external* tricks.

At one stage, Meyerhold, defending the principles of farce, wrote the following:

> The favoured device of farce is the grotesque. The art of the grotesque is based on the struggle between form and content. The grotesque attempts to make the psychological aspect subservient to decorative problems. This is why in all theatres where the grotesque ruled, the decorative aspect was so significant … Not only were the props, sets and theatre architecture decorative, but so also were mime, bodily movements, gestures and poses of actors. Doesn't the body, its lines, its harmonious movements, sing like sound? When we say 'yes' to this question (which was posed in Blok's 'Unknown Woman'), when in the art of the grotesque, in the struggle between form and content, the former would win, then the soul of the grotesque becomes the soul of the stage.[iv]

Thus, the essence of the formalist spectacle and here of the grotesque (which is a variety of formalism) is reduced to the dominance of self-sufficient structural–compositional moments ('decorative', according to Meyerhold) over the inner, meaningful significance of things. The grotesque style emerged and developed in Russia during the height of reaction and of decadence in art (between 1905 and the beginning of WWI), when the meaningful and thoughtful traditions of the Art Theatre became out of place, and instead the requisite distraction from the problems of a subject-free drama was provided by a sufficiently effect-laden spectacle. It was then that all kinds of half-buffoonish, half-mystical farces appeared: poets in yellow sweaters[55] and other decadence. This bourgeois-aesthete style has not yet run out of energy in Soviet theatre. Thus, for example, Meyerhold's production of *The Government Inspector* essentially constitutes a relapse into his old, decadent ideas. Unfortunately, Shostakovich was seduced by the same principles of the grotesque. I will attempt to show this through several examples.

Gogol's humour has real-life, everyday roots. Not so in Shostakovich – he tries to create a comic effect through a whole system of external devices.

Device No. 1: the illogical accentuation of words and phrases

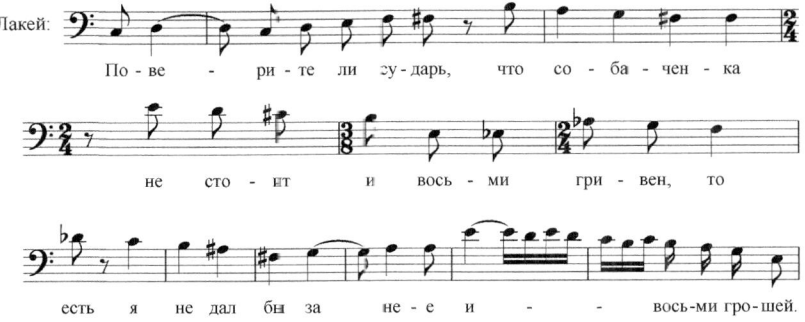

[55] A reference to Mayakovsky, who famously sported a yellow sweater during his Futurist years.

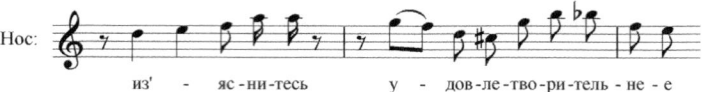

It is entirely obvious that the rhythm here conflicts with the natural pronunciation – by design. Thus, for example, in the first fragment the syncopation inserted into the word *poverite* actually transfers the stress from the [correct] syllable 've' to the syllable 'po'; then, in the same example, at the words *to yest'* the accent is unnaturally transferred to the letter 'ye' [i.e. the Cyrillic letter 'e']. Similar conflicts arise later.

Device No. 2: *fiorituri*, figurations and scales, which are inserted in the middle of a word or a phrase quite artificially and with a contrived strangeness.

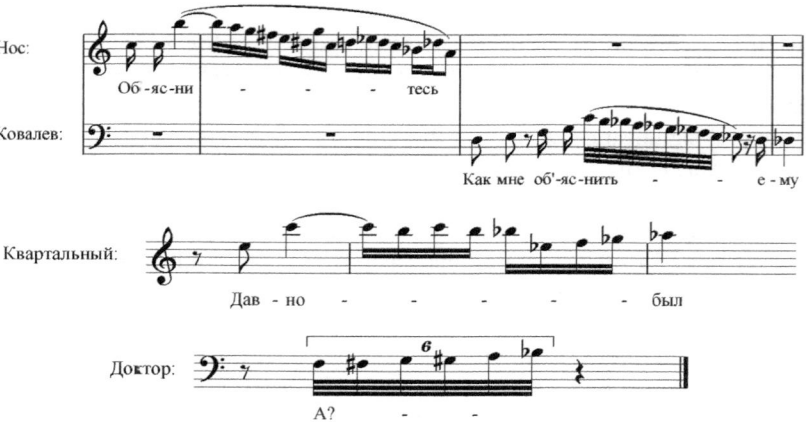

This device, as well as the first one, has unnaturalness as its obvious aim.

Device No. 3: 'back-to-front' harmonisation with deliberately 'grimy' chords. The back-to-front principle is used throughout the opera, but it is especially characteristic of the 'romance' sung by Podtochina's daughter. This sentimental daughter of a staff-officer's widow tells her own fortune with cards, singing a sweet melody to herself. Shostakovich apparently wanted to create a satirical stylisation of a petit-bourgeois romance of the 1830s; he borrowed typical melodic and accompanimental formulae from this style; nevertheless, his satire lay not in the characterisation [of Podtochina's daughter], but largely in the romance's harmonies, which are peppered with sharply contradictory and utterly absurd dissonances in the most inappropriate places.

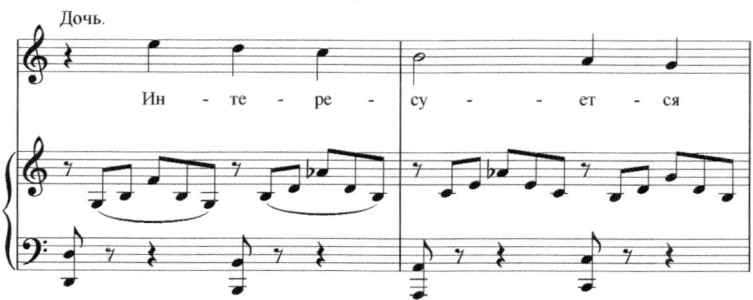

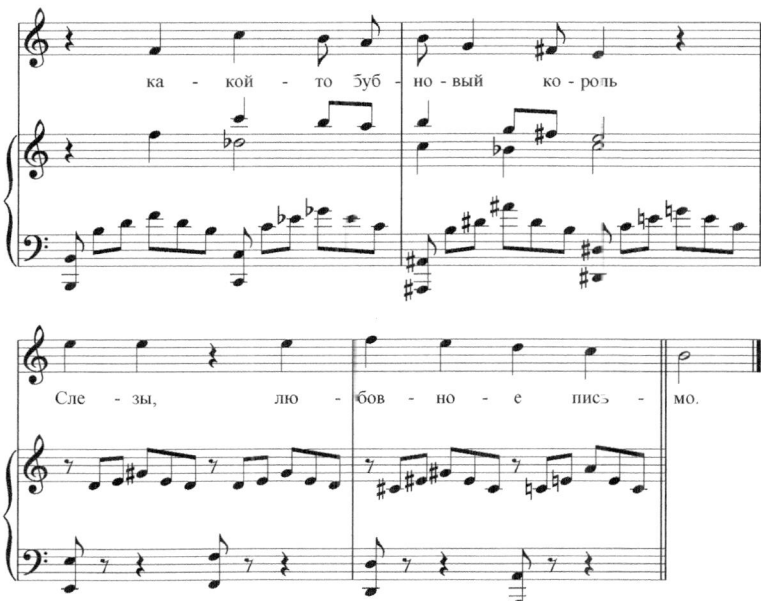

Such stylisations can be found in Stravinsky's *Mavra* as well, although the conception there is a little more natural in spite of the comparable superficiality of this composer's approach. Stravinsky only wanted to convey naturalistically the 'grime' of an amateur performance. Shostakovich, however, uses the kind of dissonances and oddities that one could only conceive of when pulling grimaces and clowning around becomes a special goal. But is this really witty or amusing?

Device No. 4: onomatopoeia in the orchestra. Here you find sneezing, nose-blowing and other physiological sounds. This device, to be fair to Shostakovich, is used very inventively (e.g. the Scene in Kovalyov's bedroom), but these are still only very superficial and naively naturalistic effects, which often go beyond the limits of musical means proper. The devices listed above (especially Nos. 1, 2 and 3) are used by Shostakovich independently of the characters' qualities or the inner meaning of their conversations and actions. Thus, for example, the illogical accentuation which had already made its mark on one of the characters, is used by Shostakovich for other, very different, characters also (this can be seen in Exx. 1, 2, 3, 4, and 5). Therefore, the individual psychological traits of Gogol's types lose their integrity because of these external and completely independent formal devices.

A characteristic example of such formalism is the (superficially) very complex Octet of 'janitors submitting ads to the newspaper'.[v] Gogol's wonderful, sharply satirical text is here sacrificed to this absurd and cumbersome ensemble, in which it would of course be impossible to understand a single word because of the number of voices, while the 'music' is nothing but inarticulate shouts. The conception of this ensemble must have been subordinated to a ready-made formal scheme; this can be guessed not only from the immediate impression it affords, but also from the fact that we find an analogous piece in Shostakovich's *Aphorisms* under the name 'Canon'.

A similar violation of the text is carried out in another place: having found the Nose, Major Kovalyov attempts in vain to stick it back in its proper place, ending in despair; he now writes a threatening letter to Podtochina, the officer's widow, who then sends back a reply – these letters are probably the most brilliantly lacerating passages in Gogol's whole novella. But Shostakovich makes the characters sing both letters *simultaneously*, and in quartet texture (Podtochina and her daughter read Kovalyov's letter together, and at the same time Kovalyov has already received her reply and reads it together with Yarïzhkin).[vi] In this way the text is obviously 'killed off', and it is as impossible to hear and understand it, as was the case in the janitor's octet.[vii]

Thus, in the struggle between 'form and content' in Shostakovich's opera, 'the former triumphed' undoubtedly, and therefore 'the soul of the grotesque became the soul of the stage'. We hardly need to prove the fruitlessness and meaninglessness of the grotesque, for it does not even pretend to be meaningful. But every piece of *grotesquerie*, including *The Nose*, still has an emotional core; this core can be defined as a *grimace*, an ugly and unhealthy one, the face distorted by visceral laughter. In this respect *The Nose* is close to Prokofiev's grotesques (*The Tale of the Buffoon, Love for Three Oranges*, etc.), the only difference being that Prokofiev uses big, coarse brushstrokes, 'hacks away' at hyperbolic grimaces, and 'hews' them; Shostakovich, on the contrary, prefers to concentrate on tiny details, wishing to 'amuse' through a *multitude* of petty grimaces and naughty tricks.

What of the purely musical aspect of *The Nose*? It must be said that Shostakovich did not compromise his compositional mastery here: the opera has a rich variety of timbral, rhythmic and contrapuntal elements. In spite of this, the music as a whole paradoxically gives the impression of a grey, lifeless mass. This is for two principal reasons, I believe. The first is *modal stasis*.[viii] The opera is atonal from the first note to the last (polytonal in places), and the modal foundation here is reduced to various combinations of major sevenths and minor ninths; thus the harmonic language does not develop, and any place in the score (read vertically) can be an opening here, an ending there or a middle somewhere else.

The second reason: *monotonous deliberateness*. The author squanders all his 'tricks' at the beginning of the opera; further on, the musical material does not develop organically, but rather *accumulates* mechanically: there is nothing substantially new after the *Kunststücke* of the first few scenes. It is only natural then, that all these contrivances have already become flat by the middle of the opera, and cannot elicit even a routine level of surprise.

I have provided three excerpts below which I consider most characteristic of the musical content of *The Nose*. The first fragment is taken from the beginning of the opera (Kovalyov's bedroom; noticing the disappearance of his nose, he decides to go to the police and complain); the second fragment is from the middle of the opera (the nose, in the guise of a civil servant, is apprehended by the police; he is beaten up, and as a result, mutates back into his normal form; a police officer wraps the nose in a piece of paper); and finally, a fragment from the last scene (Nevskiy Pospect, people idly walk by).

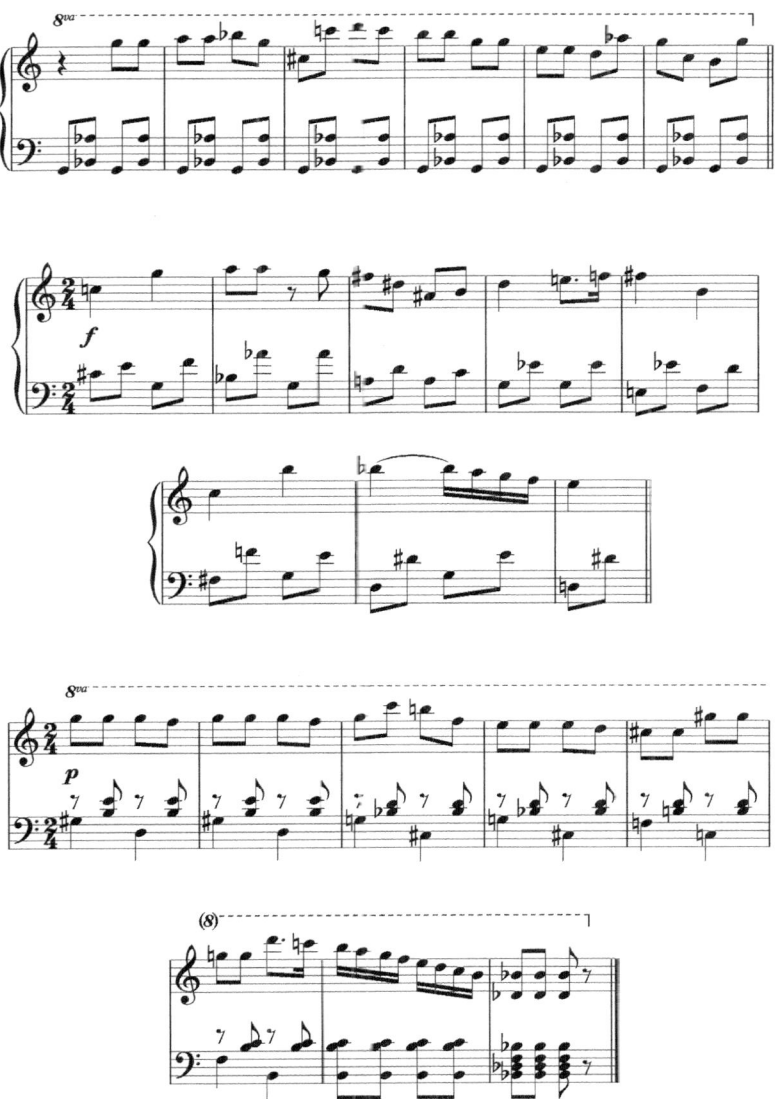

In spite of the complete disparity of the situations on stage, all three fragments have essentially the same content. What is this content? *It is deliberate incongruity.* Thus, for example, *in the first fragment*: the accompaniment is based on a chord containing harsh internal contradictions – g, $b\flat$ and $a\flat$ – and the melody adds to this by rotating around the adjacent notes a, b, and c; *in the second fragment*: when there is a $c\sharp$ in the bass, it is $c\natural$ in the top voice (first bar), while with $b\flat$ in the bass we have a in the top voice (second bar), and so on; a similar picture in the third fragment.

This deliberate incongruity, built into a system, must apparently replace here the true musical humour which was so wonderfully used by Musorgsky in his *Marriage*, 'Rayok', and 'The Seminarist'.

Thus, the false conception of the grotesque underpinning Shostakovich's opera predetermined the falsehood of its musical content.

※ ※ ※ ※ ※

There are several successful and truly witty passages in *The Nose*: for example, the song of Kovalyov's servant, Ivan (Ivan is lying on a sofa in the hall, and having nothing to do, plays the balalaika), or the crowd scene in which the Nose is beaten up ('*Tak yego, tak yego*'). Perhaps the opera will prove stage-worthy and will reveal some more successful moments in live performance. But even in this eventuality, *The Nose* will remain an unwieldy and expensive trifle, just as useless as it is harmless (but in all likelihood it is harmful).

In this opera, Shostakovich has undoubtedly moved away from the mainstream of Soviet art. If he does not recognise the falsity of his path, if he fails to comprehend the live reality that is 'under his nose', his artistic work will unavoidably find itself in a cul-de-sac.

[*Notes to Zhitomirsky's original*]

i Shostakovich was born in 1907 [*sic*].

ii By the former variety I mean the composers who, under the cover of 'leftist' phraseology of the 'newest' 'technological' 'achievements', sneak into their works the decadent music of contemporary Europe (e.g. Deshevov or Mosolov); the latter variety is the last of the 'Mohicans' of the old Russian intelligentsia, the intense psychologist-individualists (e.g. N. Myaskovsky).

iii In 1927.

iv V. Meyerhold, collection of essays 'On Theatre'.

v *The Nose*, scene 5, p. 89.

vi *The Nose*, scene 8, p. 210.

vii For technical reasons, it proved impossible to illustrate the last two examples with musical fragments because of the textural complexity. (Editors of the journal.)

viii In this case, I use the concept of mode figuratively.

1930
RAPM's Glorious Year?

It was the best of times (for RAPM), it was the worst of times (for all others). RAPM started the year by publishing a list of its campaigning successes, couched, as usual, in military terms.

> We have made decisive strikes on the reactionary group of musicians that dominated the most important musical institutions (the concert organisations, the Conservatoire and the opera houses). [...] We destroyed a petit-bourgeois music organisation (ORKiMD) [...] that was standing on an opportunist platform.[1]

They had also delivered a mortal blow against the NEPmen and their 'light genre' music: there was now a ban – so they claimed – on the publishing and performance of this 'musical pornography and opium'.[2] Readers of music journals this year had a choice of either *Proletarian Musician* (*Proletarskiy muzïkant*) or *For Proletarian Music* (*Za proletarskuyu muzïku*). Both allowed readers to keep abreast of RAPM's latest ideas and conquests.

This has been the standard view of the period: RAPM triumphant, having either absorbed or destroyed its rivals. And yet two years later, the organisation no longer existed and many of the defeated musical reactionaries and opportunists were managing very well for themselves. On the surface, RAPM's position looked unassailable, but it was dependent on the Party, which always kept its distance. RAPM never became the Party's music-policy arm, and the same was true of the proletarian organisations in the other arts. Take, for example, a published interview with Glaviskusstvo's new director, Felix Kon, a professional Party official of near-pensionable age (formerly an ethnographer and anthropologist). Kon explained the difficulties in yoking the arts to the grand project of socialist construction. Distinguishing three categories of arts workers, Kon argued that none was up to the job. The old generation was ideologically incompatible, and as far as socialism was concerned, it was needed only so that its knowledge could be 'extracted' from it, for use by the younger generation. The second category was the fellow travellers, some of whom could be brought round to a Marxist perspective, while others were unamenable, privately 'dreaming about growing into a new bourgeoisie'. Kon's third category was the proletarian organisations. On the basis of the claims they made for themselves, Kon might have been expected to embrace them unreservedly, but instead he said that every such group considers its direction infallible and tries to monopolise art, while at the same time, they lack a coherent Marxist perspective on the current transitional period.[3]

---

[1] *Za proletarskuyu muzïku*, no. 1 (1931), 1.

[2] O.T., 'V assotsiatsii proletarskikh muzïkantov', *Za proletarskuyu muzïku*, no. 1 (1931), 8.

[3] 'Navstrechu obshchestvennosti: tekushchiye zadachi Glaviskusstva. Beseda s nachal'nikom Glaviskusstva F.Ya. Kon', *Rabochiy i iskusstvo*, no. 15 (15 Mar. 1930), 1.

These expressions of distrust from the top were common throughout the period when proletarian organisations dominated the arts, a fact that certainly did not pass unnoticed by non-proletarian artists. It is true that RAPM's actions affected every significant musical institution and individual in music at this point. But there is also solid evidence that many of RAPM's victims saw this as a temporary setback, refused to accept RAPM's authority, and either showed defiance, or quietly waited for an improvement or reversal. The minutes of public meetings and letters of the discontent give us a strong sense of the non-proletarians' awareness that real power lay elsewhere. For all RAPM's attempts at intimidation, it failed to instil any widespread fear. It was seen as a scarecrow, not a real menace.

The main battleground was not to be found in venerable professional institutions like the conservatoires, which put up little resistance to the RAPM takeover. Instead, we have to look at organisations that have so far remained on the margins of our narrative. These were the forums for composers affiliated to two copyright agencies, MODPiK (the Moscow Society of Playwrights, Writers and Composers) and Dramsoyuz (the Leningrad counterpart). Why the difference? After all, the staff of large institutions are better placed for concerted resistance than professional societies serving a collection of relatively isolated individuals. But when we look at the different sources of income, the picture becomes clearer. In the institutions, RAPM was able to shake up the administration, but most of the staff could grumble about the situation while continuing to draw a salary. For those, on the other hand, who were dependent on royalties rather than stable salaries, RAPM's activities posed a general threat to their livelihoods. Accordingly, the musicians of MODPiK and Dramsoyuz had to stand their ground.

One battle of the campaign was fought at a Moscow-wide meeting of composers on 20 February, chaired by Glière (a neutral figure, who had participated in none of the factional disputes). Everything began peacefully as members addressed a proposal by Glière to create a union that would include all composers, irrespective of their ideological outlook or the type of music they composed. This, by the way, was not currently desired by the Party, which had no interest in seeing its own interests voted down by majorities in any such broad unions of artists. The basis for the proposed union was to be an existing copyright agency – in the present instance, MODPiK. Curiously, this future union, as described by Glière, very closely prefigured the post-1932 Union of Composers that would eventually play a major role in Soviet musical life – the crucial difference was that the later union was established by the state, not through an independent initiative. Glière envisaged a very centralised union, whose members would subordinate their personal preferences to the regulations passed down from the top. But why should composers submit themselves to such an arrangement voluntarily? There was good reason, as it happens: many composers were tired of trying to guess at the ideological line they should be toeing. Clear guidance from the top would be better than this. Glière expressed the idea pithily:

You play a chord, but no one knows whether it is good or whether it is needed [by the state ...] We need to agree on the kind of works that are needed, and what degree of complexity is proper. We need to address this as the main task over a number of conferences.[4]

The writer Potekhin[5] joined in:

> Soviet and socialist construction in our country is clearly suffering, on the one hand, from a fragmentation of cultural forces, and on the other, the impossibility of proper ideological guidance for them.[6]

The meeting had gone smoothly so far, but now the hostilities surfaced. Belïy, speaking for RAPM, suggested that composers of church and popular music (the latter referred to as 'foxtrot and Gypsy music') should be excluded from the leadership of such a union. If RAPM was as unassailable as its own literature suggested, this provocation should have met with sullen consent. In fact, the 'foxtrotters' themselves confidently mounted a counterattack. Vladimir Messman, the secretary of MODPiK, remarked mockingly that no one could possibly predict 'what tomorrow's policy on foxtrot is going to be' and was supported by peals of laughter from the audience. One of his colleagues, G. Titov, accused RAPM composers themselves of writing workers' songs in foxtrot style, demonstrating his contention very ably by singing an example, again to the great amusement of those present. Instead of forcing its will upon the meeting, RAPM was humiliated.[7]

In the event, a new organisation was indeed created: on 1 April, Vseroskomdram, The All-Union Society of Composers and Dramatists, replaced the existing Moscow and Leningrad copyright agencies. The change was not brought about by the composers and dramatists themselves, however, but by Glaviskusstvo, perhaps wishing to pre-empt independent initiatives. The accounts of the old agencies were examined, and some irregularities were found. Royalties had been collected, for instance, after performances of works whose ownership had passed over to the state. More startling was the revelation that church music led a flourishing, if underground, existence. As one newspaper reported, six priests and eight heirs of church-music composers were still collecting royalty payments.[8]

After Glaviskusstvo's closure of the old agencies, and the embarrassment of the audits, RAPM might have expected Vseroskomdram to be much more pliant. But it was not. The kind of mockery heard at the February meeting was on display again at the First All-Russian Conference of Authors in October, and then again at

---

[4] Transcript of the meeting of Moscow composers on 20 Feb. 1930. RGALI, fond 645 (Glaviskusstvo), op. 1, ye. kh. 340, l. 8.

[5] Presumably this is Yuri Nikolayevich Potekhin (1888–1937), who was on the White side during the Civil War, emigrated, then returned to the USSR as one of the *smenovekhovtsï*. At this point he was a member of the Dramsoyuz Board. He was eventually executed during the Purges.

[6] Transcript of the meeting of Moscow composers on 20 Feb. 1930, RGALI, fond 645 (Glaviskusstvo), op. 1, ye. kh. 340, l. 12.

[7] Ibid., 20 and 37.

[8] 'Chto vskrïto v MODPiKe i Dramsoyuze', *Rabochiy i iskusstvo*, no 27 (15 May 1930), 6.

the December Plenary Session of the Vseroskomdram council. At the December meeting, Belïy chose this time to direct his polemics not only against the foxtrotters, but also against ASM, even though the organisation was now defunct. This time he found himself up against one of the heavyweights of Soviet culture, Meyerhold, who contended that RAPM's own works were merely bourgeois music if their texts were stripped away. He also condemned RAPM's treatment of fellow travellers as outrageous and finished by calling outright for RAPM's disbandment.[9]

Composers could show their courage and laugh when gathered together in one place, and especially when they had such a broad-shouldered defender as Meyerhold. But when victims were singled out and subjected to political slander, RAPM had the upper hand. 1930 put an end to Roslavets's career at Glavrepertkom, when he was denounced as a rightist opportunist and accused of protecting composers of light music, the foxtrotters of the AMA (the Association of Moscow Writers and Composers). The denunciation was penned by Sergeyev, one of the ORKiMD majority absorbed by RAPM. He had disagreements with Roslavets going back several years, but he chose his moment well. And so, Roslavets, for many years a composer of earnest and complex atonal works in a post-Scriabin manner, was brought down because of his alleged support for the foxtrot. This gave the charge a perverse twist, which no doubt delighted Sergeyev. Asafyev expressed his puzzlement to Derzhanovsky:

> What has happened to Roslavets? I can't make head or tail of it. At the conservatoire, I had to sign some piece of paper against all manner of musical nonsense, and for some reason Roslavets's name was mentioned as a 'supporter', or something like that. We do need to fight against vulgarity, but I can't understand what Roslavets had to do with it – he's always been a serious man.[10]

Once Roslavets was 'purged' and demoted, Sergeyev was able to take over his position.[11] As a faint consolation, Roslavets was able to confront his nemesis at a composers' meeting, and recounted the whole long story of their disputes since 1924. The best moment came when Roslavets told all assembled that both he and Sergeyev had belonged to the Socialist Revolutionary Party before they joined the Bolsheviks. Except Roslavets had been a Left SR, and thus a supporter of the October Revolution, while Sergeyev had been a Right SR, and so a counter-revolutionary.[12]

Purges raged at Moscow Conservatoire. The report of the 'purge committee' from August 1930 tells us that the former deputy director Raysky had been

---

[9] 'Novïy Vseroskomdram za rabotoy', *Rabochiy i iskusstvo*, no. 71 (27 Dec. 1930), 2.

[10] Letter from Asafyev to Derzhanovsky of 7 Apr. 1930, GTsMMK, fond 3 (Derzhanovsky), ye. kh. 2, no. 855.

[11] Wofgang Mende, 'Music censorship in the era of NEP and cultural revolution: The case of Nikolay Roslavets', paper presented at the conference *1948 and all That: Soviet Music, Ideology and Power*, 27–8 Nov. 2009, Cambridge, UK.

[12] Transcript of the meeting of Moscow composers on 20 Feb. 1930, RGALI, fond 645 (Glaviskusstvo), op. 1, ye. kh. 340, ll. 103 and 106.

subjected to a 'first-degree purging', being charged with criminal actions. Apparently a variety of financial misdeeds were uncovered: Raysky had made illegitimate sales of grand pianos and had a waste outlet specially plumbed in to his apartment, using funds from the Conservatoire budget (in mitigation, his apartment was actually in the Conservatoire building). The charges also included the ideological offence of oppressing working-class students. The purge, however, had no effect on the Conservatoire, since Raysky was by then already employed as a professor in Tbilisi – self-imposed exile to the south was often the recourse of those wanting to avoid trouble, and Roslavets did likewise, going to Tashkent. Apart from the purging of senior figures, there were scattered sackings of support staff, like the Conservatoire librarian Valentina Alekseyeva, the daughter of a White Army colonel executed in the Civil War, who was accused of cataloguing music in French, 'which could not be understood by proletarian students'.[13] The educational process was also significantly modified: admissions of new students were now to be based much more strongly on class, the new 'Workers' Faculty' (Rabfak) was opened to proletarian students with hardly any musical background, tickets for Conservatoire concerts were now distributed to workers and soldiers, and their programmes were vetted 'in accordance with the views of RAPM'. Myaskovsky considered leaving the Conservatoire at this point, but Pshibïshevsky persuaded him to stay.[14]

Myaskovsky even kept his job at Muzsektor, despite all the changes:

> Muzsektor has been restructured: there is no Editorial Board any more, and everything [...] is now down to personal decisions.[15]

These decisions, Myaskovsky explained, were usually made not just by the director, Yurovsky (who lost his post in September 1930), but in collaboration with his deputy Belïy. He says that Belïy, 'although extreme in his devotion to RAPM, is nonetheless a good musician and really quite an intelligent man'.[16] Belïy, it transpires, managed to preserve a good relationship with his former composition teachers, Myaskovsky and Zhilyayev, and they continued to serve on a Muzgiz committee together with him. This explains some otherwise puzzling items, such as the Muzgiz documents declaring that the works of Roslavets and Shostakovich, now out of favour, should be removed from the catalogue. Among the names on these documents is Myaskovsky's.

Through his Muzgiz connections, Myaskovsky was drawn into a deeper collaboration with the new trends. Viktor Vinogradov, from the agitational-music section, thought that this was a fact worth noting:

> [W]e have managed to establish a set of six shockworkers' brigades of composers. [...] They have signed an agreement on socialist competition

[13] 'Protokolï zasedaniy komissii po chistke apparata Moskovskoy Gosudarstvennoy Konservatorii', RGALI, fond 658 (Moskovskaya Gosudarstvennaya Konservatoriya), op. 6, ye. kh. 121, ll. 15, 27, and 72.

[14] Letter from Myaskovsky to Asafyev of 31 Mar. 1930, RGALI, fond 2658 (Asafyev), op. 1, ye. kh. 641, l. 36v.

[15] Ibid., l. 35.

[16] Ibid.

and are now working well. The *sovremenniki* [former ASM members] are also gradually being drawn in, especially the young ones (Shebalin, Starokadomsky), but even Myaskovsky has written two field marches for brass band.[17]

Indeed, these marches mark a watershed in Myaskovsky's career, the 'pivot chord' of a modulation, to recall Derzhanovsky's prophecies of 1924. Myaskovsky's past military experience had left him well accustomed to military-march idioms, and he reckoned that he could make a competent job of scoring for brass band. The result was a trifle, applied music, not the kind of thing he could show to Prokofiev, but it demonstrated that he was prepared to co-operate with the other side. It was as if Myaskovsky and Asafyev swapped positions. Back in 1924, Asafyev was the 'opportunist', but now, left depressed by RAPM's attacks, he withdrew from the fray, giving up his journalism for the task of orchestrating *Khovanshchina*. It was his hope that he might find his way back to composition, the occupation of his youth. Myaskovsky here tries to raise his spirits with a sarcastic account of recent events:

> A gradual but complete takeover has been carried out at Muzsektor by your enemies, the RAPMovtsï (actually, they are your *friends* – they just have their own way of showing it!), And since, to some degree, this will help satisfy their hunger (in the literal sense of the word), they should by and large quieten down over time, especially since they are becoming obsolete in front of their very eyes. What they are writing now is unimaginable. Now we also have all kinds of competitions for shockworkers' brigades of composers (I was writing my marches also as a shockworker, as a member of a brigade!), and it is here that an obvious mismatch arises between their sluice-gate productivity and the decreasing quality of their work. For some reason, I wasn't invited to the last *pokaz* [a demonstration of new works], but it was truly pitiful – the worst was Davidenko, who has now begun to write pure vulgarities. Koval is still holding on, thanks to his temperament and spontaneity, but he slips up every now and again as well. Belïy is a very gifted and independent-minded musician, but in this context, he's a fish out of water: an emotionalist, a Romantic, delivering a *chastushka* with Tristanesque music. This is no laughing matter – it's tragic. Chemberdzhi is becoming pettier from one work to the next. And so on. In the end, Lunacharsky is right when he says that proletarian music is not yet out of high school. They're all gifted in varying degrees, of course, but they're still *half-educated* schoolboys, in spite of the fact that most of them have graduated from the Conservatoire.[18]

Here, he makes light of the situation, but the issue of whether to collaborate with Soviet power in its current guise weighed heavily on Myaskovsky, as it did on others in his position. On 14 April, Vladimir Mayakovsky, the great poet

---

[17] Letter from V. S. Vinogradov to Shulgin of 29 Apr. 1930 (possibly dated by Shulgin), GTsMMK, fond 474 (Shulgin), ye. kh. 157.

[18] Letter from Myaskovsky to Asafyev of 17 May 1930, RGALI, fond 2658 (Asafyev), op. 2, ye. kh. 51, ll. 38–9.

and enthusiast for the Revolution, took his life. Although rumours about his turbulent personal affairs circulated, many took his suicide as an occasion to examine their own consciences. Myaskovsky discussed the event with Asafyev:

> Oh, how tired I am of all the fuss! Was Mayakovsky right? I don't know. Spiteful gossip has it that if only he could have seen they were going to bury him, he would have held back from shooting himself. It seems that he came to feel a great emptiness inside – [hence his farce,] *The Bathhouse*[19] – and like a 'true Russian', he was naturally in conflict with himself, his conscience troubled. His fate was clear to me already when I met him at Meyerhold's last autumn – the look on his face was too alert and inquisitive, as if he was searching for something.[20]

Asafyev's grim reaction was 'Well done Mayakovsky!'[21] Derzhanovsky, perhaps optimistic as ever, or perhaps fearful for his friend, reproached him:

> Maybe you can say 'well done', but it wasn't done well enough, since it gives people a pretext for taking it all as some kind of aberration resulting from illness, whereas the act probably stands as an accurate assessment of his power and his abilities, or more to the point, his inabilities. [...] With you, it's entirely different: you need to hold your own, while making superficial concessions. [...] If they make an accusation against you, throw the same accusation back in their faces. At the moment, I'm spending all my time yelling about the counter-revolutionary nature and alien class character of RAPM music. This is all the greatest lot of rubbish, but no one can really fathom these things, and the portents are still far from clear.[22]

Myaskovsky, however, advised Asafyev to exercise caution, whatever Derzhanovsky told him:

> On no account should you agree to give a talk about Sergei [Prokofiev]. This will do nothing for you. People argue at cross-purposes. How will you prove that Sergei's music is acceptable because it is good, when they will reply that it's not good because it's not acceptable? [...] Why assume the role of a Don Quixote – as if you haven't suffered enough oppression already? And Derzhanovsky always goes too far when he thinks he has some support; the problem is that he always exaggerates the amount of support he actually has, so whenever he gets into a mess, he drags all his associates down with him.

---

[19] *The Bathhouse* (Banya), a critique of Soviet bureaucracy, flopped in January 1930 in Leningrad, and fared only slightly better at the Meyerhold Theatre (premiered on 16 March). The music was by Shebalin.

[20] Letter from Myaskovsky to Asafyev of 30(?) Apr. 1930 (date on envelope), RGALI, fond 2658 (Asafyev), op. 2, ye. kh. 51, 34.

[21] Letter from Asafyev to Derzhanovsky of 17 Apr. 1930, GTsMMK, fond 3 (Derzhanovsky), ye. kh. 2, no 856.

[22] Letter from Derzhanovsky to Asafyev of 22 Apr. 1930, RGALI, fond 2658 (Asafyev), op. 2, ye. kh. 45, 109.

This isn't a good time for speaking in support of Prokofiev. ... Prokofiev will prevail [in the end anyway] and triumph over them all.[23]

Myaskovsky had good reason to think that Prokofiev was now out of bounds. It was over the potential production of Prokofiev's *Steps of Steel* that the Bolshoi's Board of Directors fell out with its political minders, the Bolshoi's 'artistic-political council'. The council won, the ballet was dropped from the rehearsal schedule, and to press the point home, the Board was disbanded. The theatre was accused of promoting an erroneous policy: the Board had seen contemporary Western works as a stepping-stone to Soviet opera, failing to understand that these works were actually vehicles for damaging bourgeois ideas.[24] The ensuing changes in the administration of the Bolshoi had an immediate effect: Malinovskaya, who returned to the theatre as director, announced in April that

> [T]he planned productions of Shostakovich's *Nose* and Hindemith's *Neues vom Tage* will not go ahead. The contract signed with Meyerhold for the production of *The Nose* has been cancelled. Meyerhold remains in the theatre as artistic consultant.[25]

Although nothing was said about Prokofiev's *Love for Three Oranges*, this opera was also about to fall out of the repertoire. In Leningrad, it had already been withdrawn, an event that led to strained relations between the composer and his Soviet supporters. In their embarrassment, his supporters preferred to mislead Prokofiev rather than admit the real cause of the withdrawal: they claimed the problem was the fault of the publisher, who had supposedly demanded a large hard-currency sum for performance rights. Prokofiev quickly discovered the deception and was outraged. The task to of breaking the truth to him fell to a young musicologist, Mikhail Druskin:

> I share your outrage entirely, and must confirm that the currency issue is only an excuse invented by the directors.
> But the least guilty in this affair are B. V. Asafyev and Vl. Vl. Dranishnikov, who have invested so much effort in making propaganda for new music in Leningrad. Unfortunately, we are powerless to take any action here at present, since the change is the consequence of a new turn in musical politics (and the reasons for this turn are, naturally, to be found deeper, in the fact that the general political situation in the Soviet Union has changed).[26]

Shostakovich soon joined Prokofiev on the blacklist. His 1930 premieres of *The Nose* and the Third Symphony (*First of May*) were the last public performances of new music that was thoroughly modernist before a lengthy RAPM-induced hiatus. By the end of the year, both the symphony and the suite from the *Nose* were struck off the publisher's list, together with a waltz by Johann Strauss – purges could

---

[23] Letter from Myaskovsky to Asafyev of 8 Apr. 1930, RGALI, fond 2658 (Asafyev), op. 2, ye. kh. 51, l. 30.

[24] S. Korev, 'Bor'ba vokrug Bol'shogo teatra', *Sovetskiy teatr*, no. 1 (1930), 7–9.

[25] Ye. K. Malinovskaya, 'V Bol'shom teatre', *Rabochiy i iskusstvo*, no. 21 (15 Apr 1930), 3.

[26] Letter from Druskin to Prokofiev of 28 June 1930, LPA, folder 24, 252.

be eclectic too. Just as Soviet musical modernism was in its last throes, Malko reported from the West that it wasn't much better over there. He reasoned on good materialist lines that in periods of financial crisis, the musical climate turned 'reactionary', since the inclusion of unfamiliar and difficult music in concert programmes was too risky an undertaking.[27]

'Bourgeois' operas were now to disappear, and there was a drive to provide replacement operas on Soviet subject matter, but the results were a disappointment. Indeed, the only properly Soviet opera to receive any positive reviews at all (not just in 1930, but throughout the period covered by this book) was Lev Knipper's *Wind from the North*, based on an episode from the Civil War when 26 Red Army commissars were executed in Baku by the Whites. This was by all accounts a musically interesting and visually gripping production from the Nemirovich-Danchenko Theatre (one of the reviews is provided below). A typical rival effort was Sergei Pototsky's *Proriv* (The Breakthrough), which had a pure agitprop plot coupled with music that amounted to a pastiche of the Kuchka and Tchaikovsky. Knipper's offering, by contrast, was seen as a modern and Westernised work, containing some inspired solutions (in crowd scenes, for example, the stage action was accompanied by orchestra alone, without the need for a conventional chorus).[28]

Various projects that had received much more publicity fared less well. The former Mariinsky's great hope was Deshevov's *Ice and Steel* (*Lyod i stal'*), on a libretto by Boris Lavrenyov, to be premiered on 10 May. The music director, Dranishnikov, confided his thoughts to Prokofiev:

> The music is very odd; it's the first attempt to reflect Soviet realities in music theatre, but there's just one worry: all the negative characters have turned out very colourful and juicy, while the positive ones are too schematic and dry.[29]

The production failed to earn any good reviews, and the Stanislavsky Studio's production the following year fared no better. Matters were much worse, however, for Yavorsky's *Vïshka Oktyabrya* (Watchtower of October), based on a play by Iosif Utkin, and prepared for that year's celebrations of the Revolution anniversary at the Bolshoi. Yavorsky's work was cancelled before it could reach the public. The press claimed that the music of the opera had been considered too refined;[30] Anton Dianov gave a rather different report to Prokofiev:

> [...] it was taken off after the preliminary showing. [...] I heard from the musicians that the work was heavy and difficult to understand, and that

---

[27] Letters from Malko to Myaskovsky of 26 Nov 1930 and 13 Sept. 1931, RGALI, fond 2040 (Myaskovsky), op. 2, ed. ye. khr. 181, ll. 11v and 19.

[28] Georgiy Polyanovskiy, '"Severnïy veter" kak muzïkal'noe proizvedeniye', *Sovetskiy teatr*, no. 5–6 (1930), 19.

[29] Letter from Dranishnikov to Prokofiev of 6 Apr. 1930, LPA, folder 24, 12–13.

[30] M.Z., '"Vïshka Oktyabrya" v Bol'shom teatre', *Rabochiy i iskusstvo*, no. 59 (25 Oct. 1930), 4. The opera's title contains a pun: *vïshka* can mean a derrick or an oil rig as well as a watchtower. (The opera's setting is Azerbaijan.)

the singers were gasping for air. I think the trouble probably arose from the work's hasty genesis, but some deny that.[31]

As for the concert stage, 'there was no season really, just reorganisation'.[32] The switch to Russian currency for the payment of fees sufficed to keep would-be guest musicians away – only the relatively minor conductors Heinz Unger and Johan Ludwig Mowinckel Jr (son of the Norwegian prime-minister) felt it was worth their while playing in the Soviet Union. Persimfans folded, but not entirely for predictable reasons. The first Five Year Plan had been accompanied by a calendar reform (not because of Jacobin zeal, but to enhance productivity). The standard week was replaced variously by five- and six-day units to ensure uninterrupted production (*neprerïvka*), and workers' days of rest were staggered. Persimfans members, who held other jobs, had previously used their days off to rehearse and perform together, but the new system rendered this impossible. The Bolshoi, like other workplaces, implemented the new working week, but the intended increase in productivity led to a reduction in the quality of performances, as the orchestra had to hire extra musicians on an *ad hoc* basis in order to cope with the intensified schedule.

With diminishing prospects for performance and publication, Soviet composers found a refuge in writing incidental music for theatre, where life still went on and fees were still paid. Shebalin managed to earn enough to buy a country dacha from his earnings at the Meyerhold Theatre, and Shostakovich also took on various theatre and film projects. At times, the fee was the only attraction, as with the film *Alone*, which he was commissioned to score. 'The film is shit', he said, 'and so is the music'.[33]

Living standards fell steeply, and survival once again became a real issue. With high inflation, wages were worth only half their 1928 value, there was no food in the shops, and people were forced to rely on their institutional canteens and 'closed distribution points' (*zakrïtïye raspredeliteli*) in order to eat. Meat and eggs were scarce even there. In this situation, job security took precedence over principles whenever a clash arose. Thumbing noses at RAPM was not a priority, and any networking or manœuvring that led to a better position was used without compunction. There would be better days for the musical intelligentsia, but not until the rigours of these years had made them much more amenable to Stalinisation.

---

[31] Letter from Anton Dianov to Prokofiev of 1 Dec. 1930, LPA, folder 25, 346–7.

[32] Letter from Dianov to Prokofiev (received 13 Sept. 1930), LPA, folder 25, 54–9.

[33] Letter from Shostakovich to Sollertinsky or 17 Sept. 1930, D. D. Shostakovich, *Pis'ma I. I. Sollertinskomu*, ed. by D. I. Sollertinskiy (St Petersburg: Kompozitor, 2006), 73.

'Uriel', 'Mozhno li pet' po telefonu? Zametki po povodu "Severnogo vetra"' [Can a phone call be sung? Notes on *The Wind from the North*, *Rabochiy i iskusstvo*, no. 19 (5 Apr. 1930), 2.

Lev Knipper's The Wind from the North *played at the Nemirovich-Danchenko Theatre, where it benefited from a striking and innovative production, and it seems fair to say that it was the first and only successful opera on Soviet subject matter. It is based on a true Civil War story from the Baku Commune, where 26 commissars were executed by the British in September 1918.*

Behind the pseudonym 'Uriel' was the theatre critic and dramatist Osaf Semyonovich Litovsky (1892–1971). In 1932, he became head of Glavrepertkom and played a major role in the official castigation of Bulgakov (Litovsky was satirised as the malicious critic Latunsky in Bulgakov's The Master and Margarita*).*

'Uriel'

Can a Phone Call be Sung? Notes on *The Wind from the North*

The question would seem quite pointless.

Even so, it bothered both critics and the rest of the audience throughout the evening of the premiere, and was the subject of some animated discussions during the intervals.

Geroyan, the central character of Kirshon's play, does indeed direct melodic speech [*naraspev*] into the telephone receiver, but the crux of the matter clearly lay in the disregard for all operatic propriety, allowing the characters of *The Wind from the North* to sing about the most ordinary, everyday and even trite topics ('a decent pair of socks', 'are you not in bed yet?', 'let's have a cup of tea', etc.)

Knipper's work doesn't have any arias or duets, and the singing carries phrases and rejoinders, rather than tedious and absurd rhyming couplets. Singing alternates with speaking, and sometimes the listener doesn't even notice the transition. Only the Ashoug [bard] sings in a frankly operatic manner, but this fits his occupation as a folk singer (he also sings in Kirshon's [otherwise spoken] drama).

However, *The Wind from the North* is not billed as an opera, but as a 'musical show' [*muzikal'nïm predstavleniyem*].

Knipper's 'musical show' can trace its lineage back to its great predecessors, Musorgsky's music dramas (*Boris Godunov* and especially *The Marriage*, where, as is well known, Podkolesin also sings about boots); he is trying to establish a new type of opera based on Soviet material (this is not an ordinary libretto, but [the text of] Kirshon's drama *The City of the Winds* [*Gorod vetrov*] without any special operatic adaptations of the text, and with only very minor cuts and restructuring). Although the attempt is far from perfect, and although the composer has not yet fully liberated himself from old traditions, the result is, for us, something bold and vital, since it is the only work that has taken us any further towards the creation of a Soviet opera genre. The old operatic clichés cannot serve as a vehicle for our new themes. We can and ought to sing about the heroism of the Civil War, industrialisation and collective farms, not through arias, duets, trios and quartets, but in a way that would allow the music to merge organically with the ideas and words of the play, so that it would complement, emphasise and illustrate them, as a necessary component, rather than something self-sufficient imposed on the text.

The language of music can express so much more than the language of drama: for example, the scene of the rally, expanded into a broad tableau filled with music and noise effects, excites us much more than any ordinary crowd scene in a drama. Most significantly, Knipper has a fear of cliché that enables him to arrive at some superb effects. Take, for example, the episode of the underground meeting (with hushed singing of the *Internationale*). It would have been very tempting here to place an elegiac, muted statement of the *Internationale* theme in the orchestra. But the author decided to compose a symphonic illustration that leaves a deep impression, without any agitational element. Or the parade of Scottish Rifles: what a pretext for a swashbuckling military march! But here, too, the composer, opening with the melody of the English colonial song *Tipperary*, increased the gloom of the 'victors' triumph with dry snare-drum rolls and a few intense tragic chords, which had a greater impact than ten marches.

With *The Wind from the North*, it is not at all easy to separate out the music, the text, the acting, the sets, and the production.

This is, essentially, a collective work by several co-authors: Knipper (composer), Kirshon (author of the text), Nemirovich-Danchenko and Baratov (directors), Bron (conductor), Dmitriyev (set designer), together with all the actors, and, of course, the lighting engineer.[34] All the components of the production are tightly knit together, and all the different arts are merged organically rather than technically.

We can only wonder how so many original and memorable scenes were put together on such a cramped and awkward stage, where two different troupes had to co-exist within a very economical and ascetic stage design.

Two Indian sentries, standing with their backs to the audience in one of the wings, perfectly symbolise the place of the execution; the rising gangway in the opposite wing suggests the ship about to depart; the play of light in the Professor's room, and especially the flashes that accompany the rapping at his door, suitably convey a mood of unease; the extremely slowed-down parade scene at 'present arms!' so strikingly emphasises the oppressive triumph of the conquerors.

And, finally, the aptly found finale. If you wish, it is clichéd (the red flag flying in the wind) – just as in *The Break-Up* at the Vakhtangov Theatre, in *The Blockade*

---

[34] Vladimir Mikhaylovich Kirshon (1902–38) was a young playwright, a combatant in the Civil War, a Communist, and a member of RAPP, whose plays appeared to meet all the Party's requirements. Despite this, he was arrested as a Trotskyite and executed during the Purges. Leonid Vasilyevich Baratov (1895–1964), an opera director, went on to enjoy an illustrious career at the Bolshoi and won five Stalin prizes. Onisim Mikhaylovich Bron (1895–1975), a conductor, was at that time in charge of music at the Nemirovich-Danchenko theatre. For Nemirovich-Danchenko and Dmitriyev, see Glossary.

(the march of the military academy students), and in many other revolutionary productions.³⁵

But it acquires an unexpected freshness and exerts a new fascination because of the situation on stage. Immediately after Vartan's words, 'The wind from the North started to blow, but too late', we see a construction with the flag flapping wildly in a furious wind, with a worker standing alongside. The audience is left in no doubt that the north wind has started blowing, and that it is blowing firmly and victoriously. But the spectators, at the back of their minds, also try to work out the direction of the wind from the flag: is it really blowing from the North?

The red flag finishes the opera not as a symbol, nor an apotheosis, but as a necessary part of the action.

The singing and acting were superb. It is here, in this theatre that the players have come closest to the ideal of the 'singing actor'. They have shown that they are not only fine singers capable of mastering a very difficult and unusual musical texture with ease and flair, but also fine dramatic actors (especially Ostroumov as Geroyan, Saratovsky as Vartan and Savelyev as the Ashoug).³⁶ The role of Geroyan is generally performed with power and sincerity by the singer, but if it seems a little too soft at times, this can be traced back partly to the original text (Kirshon's portrayal of Geroyan is rather too elegiac), to the music also, and possibly also by the chosen voice type (irrespective of the artist, the tenor voice always comes across as tender and warm in character). The Menshevik Listikov is humanised far too much, and needlessly so, both in the music and in the acting. He is supposed to be a pitiful, petty, cowardly type in Kirshon, whereas the music tends to elevate him.

But everyone acts and sings very well (and the words are enunciated clearly), and we regret that for reasons of space we cannot list them all.

Neither the directors nor the designer (Dmitriyev) were seduced by Oriental prettiness, nor by equally attractive, but non-figurative abstractions, unlike the MOSPS Theatre.³⁷

This production can boast no *lezghinkas*, no Persian carpets and no luxurious sets. The whole construction looks like an oil rig that narrows upwards and away from us. It is dirty, oily, blackened, made from plain wood, and its severe, non-operatic beauty is in keeping with the Spartan style of the whole production. By turning in various ways, the rig opens up platforms as required for the action.

And, as you leave the auditorium and enter the foyer, you will find yourself in

---

[35] *The Break-Up* (*Razlom*) was a dramatisation of a novel by Boris Lavrenyov, produced at the Vakhtangov Theatre in 1927; *The Blockade* (*Blokada*) was a dramatisation of a novel by Vsevolod Ivanov, produced at the Moscow Art Theatre by Nemirovich-Danchenko (1929).

[36] Sergei Mikhailovich Ostroumov (1888–1943) was a tenor who later sang Sergei in the 1934 Moscow production of Shostakovich's *Lady Macbeth of Mtsensk*. Petr Savvich Saratovsky (1890–1964) was a bass who performed the role of Johnny in Krenek's *Johnny spielt auf*, and later became the director of the Gypsy Theatre 'Romen' (1941–57). Vasily Yakovlevich Savelyev-Damurin (1886–?) was a dramatic tenor who sang Max in the Krenek production.

[37] The MOSPS Theatre (Theatre of the Moscow Regional Soviet of Trade Unions) was the first drama theatre to produce Kirshon's play.

the midst of an exhibition devoted to oil, the precious liquid that drew the English to Baku, 'the city of the winds', and for which they nefariously murdered 26 commissars led by Stepan Shaumyan (Geroyan [in the opera]), who stood firmly as an outpost of Bolshevism on the frontier between the Soviet republic and the colonialist world. It is this heroic story of the 26 commissars that is told in *The Wind from the North*.

N. Mal'ko, 'Pis'mo v redaktsiyu' [Letter to the Editors], *Proletarskiy muzïkant*, no. 6 (1930), 39.

This letter is testimony to the confusion and discord sown by RAPM at the height of its power: Shostakovich and Malko feel compelled to blame each other for the current Tahiti Trot craze, a piece of light dance music disdained by RAPM (better known as 'Tea for Two', by Vincent Youmans, which became a jazz standard). When Malko wrote his letter, he was working in Prague, but was hoping to combine an international career with his work in the Soviet Union, which explains the tenor of this letter. This plan, however, failed, and Malko stayed on in the West.

N. Malko
Letter to the Editors [of *Proletarian Musician*]

I have belatedly received the third issue of *Proletarian Musician*, and see that it contains the composer Shostakovich's response to a questionnaire about 'light genre' music. In his postscript, I read the following lines directed at me:

> I consider it a political error on my part to have given the conductor Malko permission to perform my arrangement of the Tahiti Trot, since this is actually a number from my ballet *The Golden Age*, and if it is performed outside of its proper context (which would demonstrate the composer's attitude to this material), it can create the mistaken impression that I am a proponent of the 'light genre'. Three months ago, I sent word to Malko, who is abroad, telling him that I now withdrew permission.

In order to avoid 'the mistaken impression' that this postscript might create, I find it necessary to make the following statement:

Shostakovich often played this foxtrot on the piano, and he did so very capably. I asked him to orchestrate it, and he carried out the request with enthusiasm. On the manuscript of the score which the author handed over to me, there is the inscription: 'To my dear Nikolai Andreyevich Malko as a sign of my warmest feelings. 27 ix, Leningrad.' This means it was done well before the ballet *The Golden Age* was even conceived. Shostakovich gave me the right to perform this foxtrot, and using his orchestration, I played it in Moscow, Leningrad, Kharkov, Baku, and London. Not on a single occasion has Shostakovich said anything about his 'attitude to the material', or about withdrawing permission. In the summer of 1929, I was told that this foxtrot was played 'almost every other day' in Kiev's Proletarian Gardens.

During my last trip abroad, as it happens, I gave no performances of this work, even though I had never received any withdrawal of permission from the composer. I wrote to him about why it was taken off the programme in Buenos Aires – Shostakovich knew my address there, and I received a number of letters from him [but he did not discuss the matter even then].

My present letter to the Editors arises from the following consideration: the composer Shostakovich, while correcting the 'mistaken impression' about himself, namely that he is a supporter of the 'light genre', transfers this impression onto me in his postscript. This is why I have decided to correct the inaccuracies that crept into the P.S., since 'the composer's attitude to his material' is clearly very relaxed, and might create the wrong impression. This is particularly undesirable with respect to such an important matter as the 'light genre' issue.

As early as 1919, at an 'exposition' of revolutionary musical literature in the city of Vitebsk, I spoke for the first time after the Revolution against those 'compositions' that hid behind a red cover or behind a facade of 'accessibility', but which were, in fact, merely grubby and pernicious printed matter that should be consigned to the wastepaper basket [*makulatura*]. Since that occasion, I have spoken and written about this many times. It is not always easy to find a litmus paper that will immediately produce the correct reaction. The *Proletarian Musician* is right to point out that in our struggle against the 'light genre' we must provide good, but accessible music in opposition to it. A random assemblage of sounds, even if it is very striking and up to date, will never justify itself to a proletarian audience if it is not backed up by sincere feelings and a topical theme.

This is what young composers should try not to forget, when we talk about such important and dangerous phenomena as the pernicious influence of the 'light genre'. It is good that the issue has been raised within a broad framework. In order to put it right, we should not regret the loss of a foxtrot amusingly orchestrated by Shostakovich, even more so because its impact on listeners would hardly change whether it was performed in its 'proper context' or not.

Malko (conductor), Prague.

Addendum from the Editorial Board:

In printing this letter, the Editorial Board notes that both the conductor Malko, who performed the foxtrot many times in various cities, and Shostakovich, who arranged it, are equally responsible for making propaganda in favour of the light-genre through this 'treasure' of the repertoire.

L. Lebedinskiy, 'Nash massovïy muzïkal'nïy bït', *Proletarskiy muzïkant*, nos. 9–10 (1930), 7–30.

This paper, 'Our Mass Music and the Tasks of the Proletarian Music Movement', was presented by RAPM leader Lev Lebedinsky at the Communist Academy's Institute of Literature and Language – the Academy was a special college for communist cadres. A transcript was published in Proletarian Musician. *Here we present only a few fragments from this lengthy and very repetitive speech: we have included a list of songs that Lebedinsky considers genuinely popular with the masses, his classification of mass musical genres, and some passages on RAPM's prime targets: apart from the foxtrot, that RAPM symbol of bourgeois decadence, there is an interesting attack on apparently revolutionary songs that combine political texts with 'Gypsy' and 'chansonette' music. The style of Lebedinsky's analyses was later parodied in anti-RAPM articles by Govorit Moskva (Moscow Speaking), such as 'Under the Proletarian Veil' (see pp. 302–7 below).*

L. Lebedinsky
Our Mass Music [excerpts]

[...] By 'mass music or song' I mean any song, tune, or musical thought that has embedded itself deeply in the masses, influencing its musical tastes and psychology.

[...] Here are about thirty pieces; we can definitely say that these form the backbone or core of the musical life of the masses:

[The best-known Red Army songs:]

'We will bravely go into battle for the power of Soviets' [*Smelo mï v boy poydyom za vlast' sovetov*]

'Red Army' (White Army, Black Baron) [*Krasnaya armiya: Belaya armiya, chyornïy baron*]

The Budyonny March (We are the Red Cavalry) [*Marsh Budyonnogo: My krasnaya kavaleriya*]

'Bravely, comrades, in step' [*Smelo, tovarishchi, v nogu*]

The Warsovienne [*Varshavyanka*]

The Internationale

'The Cudgel' [*Dubinushka*]

'The Sailor' (Hey, sailor, you are so handsome) [*Moryak: Tï, moryak, krasivïy sam soboyu*]

a few of the most popular military marches:

'Under the Double-headed Eagle' [*Pod dvukhglavïm orlom*]

Austrian Military March [*Avstriyskiy voyennïy marsh*]

'Homesickness' [*Toska po rodine*]

'Old Friends' [*Starïye druz'ya*]

[a miscellaneous group of songs:]

'The Send-Off' [*Provodi*]

'Korobochka'

The Dapper Merchant [*Ukhar' kupets*]

'Higher and Higher' [*Vse vïshe i vïshe*] by Khayt

'Successors' [*Smena*], also by Khayt

a few 'Gypsy' romances:

'Little Gypsy' [*Tsïganochka*]

'Crystal Glasses' [*Stakanchiki granyonïye*]

'I'll love when I want to' [*Zakhochu-polyublyu*]

'Hey, coachman, don't rush the horses!' [*Yamshchik, ne goni loshadey*];

a few tunes [unnamed by Lebedinsky] from the most popular operettas (such as *Silva, Gypsy Love, Merry Widow*);

[further miscellaneous songs, including some of a Communist character:]

'They wanted to beat us' (Far-Eastern Song) [*Nas pobit', pobit' khoteli: Dal'nevostochnaya pesnya*] by Davidenko;

'Beyond the seas and mountains' [*Za moryami, za gorami*] by Koval;

'The Brick Factory' [*Kirpichiki*];

'The Communards' Execution' [*Rasstrel kommunarov*];

'On Saturday, on a rainy day' [*Vo subbotu, v den' nenastnïy*];

'Hey, down with it!' [*Nu i doloy!*] by Chemberdzhi;

'Budyonny's Cavalry' [*Konnaya Budyonnogo*] by Davidenko;

a few old urban dances such as the two-step and *Cracovienne* (these dances are often played and sung not only at family celebrations, but also at our demonstrations);

and finally, several foxtrots, imported from the West through the Meyerhold Theatre or our own homegrown foxtrot composers:

'Hallelujah' [imported] by Tsfasman[38]

'Tahiti Trot' [imported] by Fomin,[39] etc.

[...]

---

[38] Aleksandr Naumovich Tsfasman (1906–71) was one of the first propagandists for jazz-band music in the Soviet Union; from 1926 to 1930, he directed the orchestra 'AMA-Jazz', the first to perform jazz-band music on the radio. The piece that was broadcast was the 'Hallelujah' foxtrot referred to here.

[39] Boris Ivanovich Fomin (1900–48) was a composer of popular romances who enjoyed greatest success during the 1920s and then again during WWII. He was the author of the 'Gypsy' romance '*Dorogoy dlinnoyu*' ('Those were the days, my friend').

[Further, Lebedinsky divides mass songs into seven categories, based on the class or social stratum he believes they represent]

1. Songs reflecting the consciousness of a peasantry that is fully tied to patriarchal and primitive forms of agriculture, before sharp [social] differentiation came to the countryside: old folk song.

2. Songs reflecting the consciousness of the trading bourgeoisie, the Russian merchant class, as well as the urban petit bourgeoisie and other city dwellers: so-called 'Gypsy' romances and chansonettes.

3. Songs reflecting the outlook of backward workers, who may have become aware of their condition, but are wholly in thrall to philistine petit-bourgeois influences, and who therefore try to resolve social contradictions through song in a philistine manner: urban 'Cruel romances'.

4. Songs reflecting peasant consciousness during the process of its social differentiation, a peasantry that is already in contact with the city through trade, and which has fallen under the influence of capitalism: pseudo-folk songs.

5. Songs reflecting the consciousness of workers who are being revolutionised, who are rising to struggle against the bourgeois order, in the early period of [the class's] political and cultural growth: old revolutionary songs.

6. Songs and dances of the petit bourgeoisie and other town dwellers, including the petit-bourgeois intelligentsia during the period of monopoly capitalism and the period of the crisis of capitalism: the foxtrot.

7. Songs reflecting the consciousness of workers who are participating in violent struggle against capitalism, overcoming, together with the peasantry, the colossal hardships of the Civil War and reconstruction periods: contemporary proletarian mass song.

[...]

I have retold the history of '*tsïganshchina*' and its evolution for one purpose only: to help bring about the complete uprooting of this genre from our life.

The genre not only flourishes in its pure form, but in collusion with poetry that has likewise prostituted itself, we now find it masquerading as 'songs of the Revolution'.

Someone by the name of Khayt[4C] has an advertising list including pieces of blatant '*tsïganshchina*' ('No more Trysts', 'All Will be Forgotten', [...]), and alongside these, he insolently and cynically lists his own 'Gypsy songs of the Revolution' ('Successors' [*Smena*], 'Higher and Higher', 'The Will of the Collective', etc.). And indeed, there is not and cannot be any difference between the two. Every line from Khayt's 'songs of the Revolution' cries out for the attention of Glavlit and Repertkom [i.e. to be censored]. Here, for example, is the very popular chorus from 'Successors':

---

[40] See Glossary.

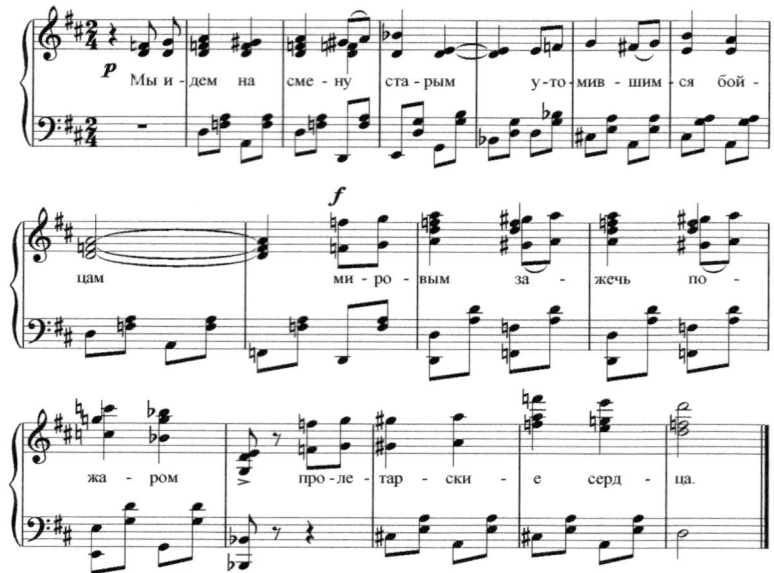

[We are the successors to /The old, fatigued fighters, / We will fire up proletarian hearts / With a worldwide fire.]

[...]

What kind of successors [*smena*] is Khayt singing about? Is it our young, joyful, healthy Komsomol members that he has in mind here, or is it the degenerate dregs and their lustings, who use the Komsomol merely as a cover? [...]

V. Kruchinin[41] is little better: he took the waltz named 'Two little dogs', and presented it as a song named 'The Brick Factory'. He also wrote the famous 'Mine No. 3' (*Shakhta nomer 3*), a revolting piece of '*tsiganshchina*' that has debased the tastes of millions.

Such works are the bloom and perfume that issue from slow degeneration, decomposition and sabotage. In its attempt to draw workers, Komsomol and Party members into the sticky mire of philistinism and debauchery, this music seeks to lull them while assuring them that it speaks of 'Komsomol', 'the ordinary worker', 'the changing of the guard', 'the Revolution', 'the liquidation of illiteracy', and so on. The nadir was reached by one Tikhonova, who composed the following music to an extremely vulgar text by Chuzh-Chuzhenin, 'But my heart draws me into the Party' [*A serdtse-to v partiyu tyanet ...*]:[42]

---

[41] See Glossary.

[42] RAPM was not the first to mock this hilarious example; its title is cited in Mayakovsky's 1927 poem '*Stabilizatsiya bïta*' (The Stabilisation of Life). Chuzh-Chuzhenin was the pseudonym of the poet Nikolay Ivanovich Faleyev (1872–1941), an intriguing character who contributed to satirical journals before the Revolution, served as the deputy minister of agriculture for the Provisional Government, and then, remarkably, served as a member of the Central Executive Committee (VTsIK) in 1918 and the editor-in-chief of the VTsIK bulletin. No further information, however, is currently available to us about the composer Tikhonova.

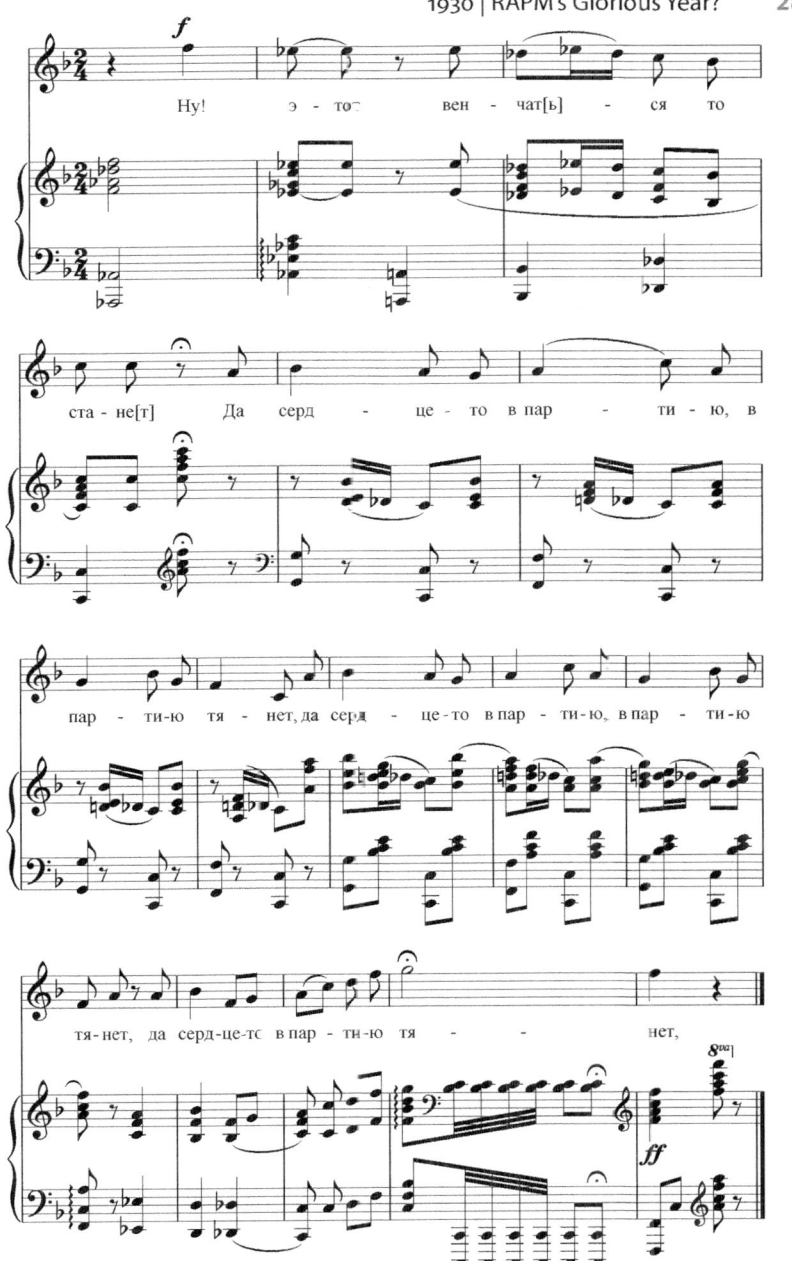

['Now this one will get married in church.' / But my heart draws me to the Party.]

[…]

On the song 'We will go bravely into battle'

We should also adopt a critical stance in relation to the device, formerly common, of grafting a new revolutionary text onto some old popular tune.

Indeed, isn't it depressing to hear 'We will go bravely into battle', as sung by our Red Army soldiers to the tune of the delicate little bourgeois romance 'White acacia'? A certain Poluyanov writes in the *Vechernyaya Moskva* (*Moscow Evening Paper*) that since Red Army soldiers went into battle with this tune, it must therefore be correct for Blyum to speak of music as pure construction, a vessel that can hold any subject matter or ideology.[43] The anti-Marxist views we hear from the likes of Blyum and Poluyanov have become widely known, and we can think of a whole series of speeches that have mounted a fierce defence of 'We will go bravely' against its critics. They usually refer to the fact that our victorious soldiers had sung the tune in battle. Still, we should ask our outraged opponents to consider the possibility that our Red Army soldiers were victorious *despite* the absence of their class culture and their class songs, *despite* the fact that they had to adapt alien art and songs of the enemy [...]

Now the situation is different: we have entered the era of cultural revolution, when proletarian culture will develop and expand, and if we do not eliminate this contradiction [of bourgeois art being used for proletarian purposes] [...] it will retard the development of the working class and the Revolution. It will subvert the hegemony of the working class.

[...]

6. Foxtrot

Category 6 covers the songs and dances of the petty bourgeoisie at the time of capitalism's crash. They reflect the consciousness of the individual who has become slave of capital and of the machine, who has been fully digested by capitalist society, losing not only the ability to protest, but even the ability to think. Understanding how this can be requires a close and highly detailed formal analysis of the foxtrot. As our example, let us take one well-known foxtrot, introduced to the USSR by our homegrown foxtrot composer A. Tsfasman:[44]

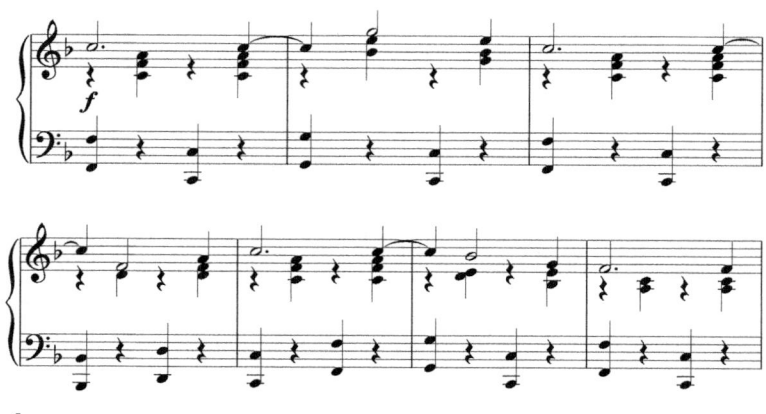

[...]

---

[43] V. I. Blyum, the theatre critic and censor, was involved in musical discussions during these years, and became one of RAPM's primary targets.

[44] See fn. 38.

In this excerpt, it is the bass motion that draws our attention first. In terms of metre, this bass is unchangeable, moving with the precision of a machine, the slow, emotionless oscillation of a pendulum falling on the first and third beats of the bar. Immediately after the appearance of these bass notes [...], middle register notes are enlisted to fall mechanically on the second and fourth beat [...]. Thus, by way of separating the notes of a chord in time (first and second beat) and between registers (low and middle), a continuous machine-like ticking [*perestukivanie*] is represented, an imitation of lifeless mechanical movements.

Against the background of this ticking, measured, emotionless and automatic, we hear in the upper voice an insistent long note, drawn out, deliberately emphasised and accented. It is important to see that these notes of the upper voice do not form a complete melodic contour, since they are not granted the least independence. Above all, they belong inseparably to the measured ticking of the separate parts of the chord, and depend entirely on the movement of the bass. [...]

This brings us to the main point: the changing of the notes (the appearance of motion in the upper voice) takes place in a deliberately automatic way, as if 'a cord is pulled' or 'a button is pressed'. [...]

The foxtrot represents mechanical movement only, and uses every available means to reveal this in its entirety, to expose all the complexity and monstrous force of this movement, hypnotising the listener or dancer, drawing their bodies, movements, ears, consciousness and will into the lifeless rhythm of this machine-like ticking. Clearly, this is just what modern monopoly capitalism needs: the transformation of all humanity, and of the working class in particular, into slaves of the machine and of capitalist society, reducing them to a semi-animal state, dull-witted, obedient, devoid of will and thought. [...]

[In the remainder of the article, Lebedinsky describes the positive examples of mass song by 'proletarian composers', seeing them as the beginnings of a new mass song genre that would reflect the new period of 'socialist reconstruction'.]

1931
RAPM's Fortunes Turning

In the first half of the year, RAPM's domination increased still further, and many of those who had tried to hold out for better times began to succumb. After surviving a purge at the Leningrad Conservatoire, which spared him but resulted in the sacking of his disciple Semyon Ginzburg, Asafyev took a decision:

> Without compunction, I resolve simply to deliver myself into the hands of RAPM, to work solely under their control and according to their instructions (if they accept this, of course). There is no other way out, and alone I won't be able to reform myself, but one needs to live, and above all, I place little trust in Leningrad Conservatoire.[1]

Asafyev's capitulation marked the end of Igor Glebov, the ardently modernist critic and cutting-edge theorist. Asafyev reasoned that RAPM's hegemony was the consequence of his own earlier defeat, when his friends and associates rejected his ideas. RAPM then filled the breach. Here, he rehearses the story in a letter to Derzhanovsky that looks back to lost opportunities in 1924:

> What would be the point in writing any more? Everything has been poisoned. We can put a brave face on it if we like, but RAPM is right. They are right because they did what had to be done. They are taking flak for writing poor music, for self-promotion, for ignorance, etc. etc. But all these shots miss the target. They miss, because all mistakes are forgiven those who have travelled in the right direction. And they succeeded in taking the right direction at the right time. The main point is not whether they are right [in every detail] – it is the cause to which they attached themselves. Remember, my friend, the year 1924 and two of my essays, 'The Crisis of Individual Creativity' and 'Composers, Keep Up!'. I will never forget that only you believed in me, that you alone were courageous enough to print them. You went against everyone. I was astonished at the resistance back then. And now Nikolay Yakovlevich [Myaskovsky], Shebalin and others are doing things 'à la RAPM' (I don't mean it crudely), things that we could all have been doing if only Lamm and Nikolay Yakovlevich and others had realised that I was right, that my instincts had not deceived me. I was so bitter at the time – I retreated, chose a different way and now I've taken a dive. RAPM started using my own weapons against me – and do you imagine they hadn't read those two articles back then? I am convinced they had, and they only pretend otherwise. [...] Now we are beaten.[2]

Myaskovsky had taken the lead in rejecting the proposals of Asafyev's 1924 essays, and yet now he was transforming himself into a prize trophy for RAPM.

---

[1] Letter from Asafyev to Lamm of 13 Mar. 1931, RGALI, fond 2743 (Lamm), op. 1, ye. kh. 80, l. 18v.

[2] Letter from Asafyev to Derzhanovsky of 28 Feb. 1931, GTsMMK, fond 3 (Derzhanovsky), ye. kh. 2, no. 858.

None of this would have been necessary, Asafyev argued, if ASM members had heeded him, and moved in the right direction earlier, making RAPM redundant … perhaps.

It is worth examining the various pressures that led Myaskovsky to succumb. He had faced the customary bullying from parts of RAPM, of course, but there was also the more genial pressure from his own RAPM-aligned students. One matter that could easily be overlooked must have given him pause for thought: he had been listed as an 'old-school composer' by Nikolai Chelyapov (head of GAIS, the State Academy for Scholarship in the Arts) at a discussion of musical fractions that had taken place at the Communist Academy. The meeting had partly defined its term 'old-school composers' in terms of the attitudes displayed by that group, 'attitudes that were clearly hostile to the proletarian, Marxist-Leninist outlook'.[3] Myaskovsky was persuaded (on pragmatic grounds), and in August 1931, he agreed to head a 'new creative association' (*novoye tvorcheskoye ob'yedineniye*) of composers. Apart from the most prominent members (himself, Shebalin, and Dmitry Kabalevsky), the association included the Kryukov brothers (Nikolai and Vladimir), Starokadomsky, Shirinsky, Kochetov and Shenshin. The group declared itself ready to receive help from RAPM and RAPP, while trying simultaneously to insist on their status as composers of serious, large-scale works:

> In its creative work, the association has set itself the goal of creating mass instrumental and vocal works, in small forms (the mass song and Soviet popular music) as well as in large forms (opera and symphony), but regards the creation of the latter as its main task.[4]

The emblematic work for the Myaskovsky group's rapprochement with RAPM was Myaskovsky's own Twelfth Symphony. The archives record the moment when the idea for a symphony on the collectivisation of agriculture entered the head of Marian Koval, one of Myaskovsky's students. Jotting down his own ideas to while the time away during a meeting, Koval passed a note over to his professor:

> N.Ya. [Myaskovsky's initials], what would you think of a topic like this for your symphony?
> Sowing the seed.
> The new people come out to fight nature, not just as individuals, but now as a collective, and their attitude to nature is also different. You could build a symphony on this: from the sufferings of endless toil through to joyful and inspired collective construction. In my view, this is a great topic.[5]

A contract was duly issued by Vseroskomdram, and Myaskovsky set aside other tasks to begin work on the new symphony, as he mentions to Prokofiev:

---

[3] N. Chelyapov, 'Na muzïkal'nom fronte', *Sovetskoye iskusstvo*, no. 6 (7 Feb. 1931), 2.

[4] V. Shebalin, N. Myaskovskiy, Vladimir Kryukov, M. Starokadomskiy, V. Kochetov, N. Kryukov, D. Kabalevskiy, V. Shirinskiy, A. Shenshin, 'Za klassovuyu muzïkal'nuyu kul'turu: ot poputnichestva k soyuznichestvu (obrashcheniye gruppï kompozitorov)', *Sovetskoye iskusstvo*, no. 40 (8 Aug. 1931), 1.

[5] Note from Koval to Myaskovsky, RGALI fond 2040 (Myaskovsky), op. 2, ye. kh. 161, l. 2.

> [...] Regrettably, I am not working on the orchestration of the piece I mentioned to you, the Eleventh Symphony, because I'm very much preoccupied with my search for material that will go into No. 12, which is hanging around my neck with a contract, and that means a directive about the symphony's content as well.[6]

A few months later, he received a much more detailed letter from Koval, where his student entered wholeheartedly into the role of a Myaskovsky's (unofficial) commissar, providing detailed ideological guidance. Myaskovsky was instructed to read from the works of Lenin and Stalin in order to arrive at a 'correct philosophical interpretation' of things. Koval also asked him to consider his 'clarity of language', a political cliché of the day. Turning to specifically musical matters, Koval warns Myaskovsky against two mistaken approaches (the second is a direct reference to Myaskovsky's customary style):

> A superficial, 'light' approach: from a theme along the lines of 'Dubinushka' (The Cudgel) through to some kind of dance. Such a work might even then be rendered interesting through technical brilliance, of course, but it would not amount to a new and significant statement.
>
> An individualistic, 'heavy' approach: some heart-rending themes, gloomy and desperate, turning towards effusive jubilation.

Koval also recommended that solo voice and chorus should feature in some passages, and went so far as to propose texts that Myaskovsky could use for the purpose.[7] Koval had established his political seniority easily enough, but he was mindful that he could go too far in this direction as a conservatoire student in need his professor's good will. Prudently, Koval ended his letter on a more humble note, admitting that his engagement with RAPM had soaked up time that he needed to devote to his postgraduate work:

> I would need to gain mastery over all of the basic wisdom of various compositional techniques in the course of about one-and-a-half years. I can't imagine there is anyone but you that can see me through this task.[8]

Anyone familiar with Myaskovsky's Twelfth Symphony will notice that it does not reflect Koval's advice. It seems that it simply came too late: Koval's letter is dated 6 December 1931, while Myaskovsky finished the piano score of the symphony just six days later.[9] There was no text-setting, no chorus, and surprisingly, not even a programmatic title, so Myaskovsky thought a note of contrition was appropriate:

> Your letter caught me at a time when I was making enormous efforts in my attempt to realise the conception that I had formed in my mind as early as

---

[6] Letter from Myaskovsky to Prokofiev of 15 Nov. 1931, see O. P. Lamm, *Stranitsï tvorcheskoy biografii Myaskovskogo* (Moscow: Sovetskiy kompozitor, 1989), 210.

[7] Letter from Koval to Myaskovsky of 6 Dec. 1931, RGALI, fond 2040 (Myaskovsky), op. 2, ye. kh. 161, ll. 3–4.

[8] Ibid., l. 4.

[9] He notes this date in his diary, see O. P. Lamm, *Stranitsï tvorcheskoy biografii Myaskovskogo* (Moscow: Sovetskiy kompozitor, 1989), 210.

the summer, as a result of your prompting. My searches were a torment to me, and the work consumed and even oppressed me a little. Unfortunately, I must confess that I completely failed to fulfil the task as I myself had wished, and I'm afraid it won't satisfy you either. It seems that I have committed all the mortal sins your letter had warned me against: there is both a superficial 'light approach', and an individualist 'heavy' one, there is no inspiring build-up at the end, and no words at all. But I don't feel that I was mistaken in the direction I chose. I understand the idea of this work in just the same way as you did, namely that the centre of gravity must be in the October Revolution, i.e. in that very moment that must transform the 'idiocy of village life' into something else and from this point, an entirely new historical epoch will begin; what's more, I think that the collectivist transformation of the countryside into a truly socialist sector is the beginning of a new *era* in human life worldwide. Unfortunately, this theme proved to be beyond my powers, and since I don't consider myself a vocal composer, I did not, and could not think organically outside of instrumental music. This was the impetus behind my original conception, that I had to express the theme by purely instrumental means. And I didn't look for any texts. [...] I wrote three separate chapters with a gradual brightening-up towards the end, roughly: the old – the struggle for the new – the new.[10]

By disregarding much of Koval's advice, Myaskovsky acted prudently. Myaskovsky could have ticked off every box on the RAPM wish list and provided them with the symphony they would have written if only they could. But in that case, the symphony might well have gone unperformed. Looking ahead a little, the symphony was in fact premiered after RAPM's disbandment, and in an amusing twist, it became a symbol for the post-RAPM renewal.

Having neutralised ASM's two most prominent members, RAPM was able to concentrate on other campaigns. Flexing their muscles, they attempted to have the popular anthem of the Soviet Air Force scrapped. The offending piece was the '*Aviamarsh*', with music by Yuly Khayt and words by Pavel German.[11] RAPM contended that the Soviet text was a mask of respectability that prevented good Communists from realising that the music was nothing more than a cancan. Despite the numerous letters from factories and military units that RAPM managed to conjure up in support of its denunciatory essays, the campaign failed, and the song lost neither its official endorsement nor its popular appeal.

RAPM had more success with another of its campaigns, against the complete works of Rachmaninov. The composer had, famously, co-signed a letter to the *New York Times* (15 January) protesting at Rabindranath Tagore's recently published eulogy of the Soviet Union; he complained that Tagore had ignored the blood on the Soviet regime's hands. When Rachmaninov's choral symphony, *The Bells* (see review below) was performed at Moscow Conservatoire, RAPM worked itself into

---

[10] Letter from Myaskovsky to Koval of 16 Jan. 1932, repr. in G. Polyanovskiy, *Marian Koval'* (Moscow: Muzïka, 1968), 14–15. I thank Patrick Zuk for providing me with this source.

[11] Pavel Davidovich German (1894–1952) was a poet based in Kiev who wrote many romance texts including 'The Brick Factory'. For Khayt, see Glossary.

a fury. The Conservatoire, thanks to the changes in administration and the student body, joined RAPM in a patriotic gesture against this disloyal son, and banned further performances of Rachmaninov's works, a severe privation for student and professional concert pianists. The ban was only revoked in the 40s, when Rachmaninov raised a substantial sum for the Soviet war effort.

Indeed, it was now hard to recognise Moscow Conservatoire beyond its familiar architecture. It had been given a humiliating new name, the Felix Kon Higher Music School. Innovations in routine and vocabulary changed the character of the institution, although not so profoundly that they couldn't be uprooted over the next few years. The new intake of student composers was organised into 'brigades'. In addition to more conventional classes, brigade members had to bring their compositions regularly to 'production meetings' [*proizvodstvennïye soveshchaniya*], where they fielded criticism from fellow brigade members. Brigades had to engage in 'production practice' [*proizvodstvennaya praktika*] so that they could learn to lead 'the class war on the musical front' – a stirring description of the rather innocuous activity of bringing music to workers' clubs (some of the old Proletkult practices fitted this period, while others would have been roundly denounced).

From reports filed by brigade leaders, some students clearly failed to take their brigade duties seriously. One brigade leader, Popov, reported his brigade member Pirogov as a serious offender. Pirogov had refused to bring his works to production meetings, preferring to write music 'for himself' instead. He considered himself so self-sufficient, indeed, that he saw no need to subscribe to *The Proletarian Musician* or even *For Proletarian Music*. In this, he was evidently mistaken, otherwise he would have known better than to submit orchestrations of foxtrots to his Conservatoire teachers. When he was shown the error of his ways (or the consequences of persisting in them), Pirogov promised that he would reform, but offered some excuses:

> At the beginning of the year, my self-directive [*ustanovka*] was wrong: I came here simply to study, and I wrote music with no particular purpose in mind [...] I was mistaken to see only the academic side of things. My ideology is proletarian in any case. I love music, but there's never any good music to be found at the production meetings. I received a commission from the Aquarium Theatre: the orchestration of some incidental music for a play, and this included some foxtrots.[12] It was honest work that I undertook. I only submitted it for an orchestration assignment.

Bryusova, the most senior person present, repeated Pirogov's self-criticisms, but kindly offered a partial exculpation for the foxtrot debacle:

> Can you be a proletarian composer and think of study alone, without taking the ideological directive into account? Taking the theatre job was acceptable, but it had to be done critically, with some kind of ideological objective.

Her younger colleagues thought this was not enough:

> We need to take a more robust approach. We don't need people like the

---

[12] At the time, the old theatre building in the 'Aquarium' garden, a famous place of entertainment in Moscow, was occupied by the Operetta Theatre.

Pirogov we've seen so far. If he wants to be a Soviet composer, he has to reform himself immediately. He tries to sneak alien music in here under the cover of abstract considerations.

But some advocated leniency: 'Pirogov is still young, and even Myaskovsky is a reformed man now'. The meeting resolved to allow him more time to show a new commitment: he was to change his attitude to composition and public life, bring his pieces to production meetings, start writing mass songs for clubs, and he definitely had to read *The Proletarian Musician* and *For Proletarian Music*. Another composer, Mepurnov,[13] was advised to switch to mass songs instead of writing 'national music in the old manner' and practising his Debussy. 'No one can play an active role in the struggle on the music front when he fills himself with Debussy'.[14] One shudders to think how the struggle on the music front would have been undermined if students still had to practise Rachmaninov for several hours a day.

A fresh breeze was also blowing through Muzgiz (the state music-publishing house), where the Pedagogical Section was taking bold steps to haul its literature into the new times. A piano coursebook, they were saying, should not be thought of as the first step towards the creation of more virtuosos. No indeed, and instead, it must serve to build up a new generation of 'class-directed musician-fighters'. And if it was ever to perform this role, the coursebook had to be 'an ABC of communism in the musical arena'. Accordingly, it should include mass and revolutionary songs, folk songs and, crucially, works by proletarian composers (and fellow travellers close to them). Music of this last category barely existed and Pshibïshevsky chaired meetings to discuss how the gap could best be filled.[15] And so an official appeal was issued. Quite out of character for such a document is its centrepiece, an astonishing rhapsodic anathema that offered catharsis to every Communist piano teacher brought to the brink of despair by the armour-plated tweeness of traditional children's pieces:

To all composers of the USSR,

One of the most acute issues on the front of musical pedagogy is that of children's instrumental literature. This so-called pedagogical literature, which we have inherited from the bourgeoisie, is contaminated by sentimental vulgarity, decadent moods and other anti-artistic material that is hostile to us. We cannot continue feeding Soviet children [...] with all manner of Moorish serenades, doll's romances, autumn songs, evening stars, Gypsy dances, day-dreaming girls, Bayaderes' dances, Spanish caprices, guitars, Grandfather's tales, Mummy's consolations, the deaths of birds and the funerals of birds, sweet dreams, sweet kittens, evening ruminations,

---

[13] Georgy Khristoforovich Mepurnov (1900–57) later became well known as a 'national' composer in the Chechen-Ingush Republic. It is not known what happened to his lesser-known classmates.

[14] 'Protokol otkrïtogo sobraniya profbyuro NKF (nauchno-kompozitorskogo fakulteta)', 22 May 1931, GTsMMK, fond 30 (Davidenko), ye. kh. 150, 1–7.

[15] 'Protokolï zasedaniy Konsul'tatsionnoy kommissii', RGALI, fond 653 (Muzgiz), op. 15, ye. kh. 265.

autumn winds, songs of piety, the thoughts of teenage girls, good schoolmarks, Gretchen-waltzes, forget-me-nots, anything 'from the good old days', sweetie-pies subjected to questioning,[16] ghost stories, ghosts by the hearth, nocturnes, idylls, barcarolles, pastorals, lullabies, prayers, elegies, songs without words. And so on. [...]

The State Music Publishers appeal to all composers of the USSR to close the breach on this front and to shoulder the duty to provide our children and Pioneers with Soviet pieces of high quality. [...]

The ideology expressed in the pieces (the themes, the style) must to be close to the proletarian outlook and should contain no passages of modernism, bourgeois education, etc. [...][17]

In the long term, Soviet composers did indeed take the task seriously, and produced a wealth of more robust and innovative music for children. In the West today, Kabalevsky's contribution to this project is still well known (he had already begun writing children's pieces a few years before the appeal). A Muzgiz committee member, I. S. Rabinovich,[18] presented a draft of the topics that should be covered by a new children's piano course for the 8–12 age group: life in the Pioneers, socialist construction, revolutionary struggle and celebrations, the Red Army, anti-religious material, and others. How composers could convey all of this was another matter. Pshibïshevsky attempted a similar draft for an adult learners' course. He did not want the target to be the eventual creation of an elite of virtuoso pianists, but hoped such a course would produce large numbers of teachers capable of bringing music to the wider population. This, again, drew from the democratic, Proletkult component of RAPM thought. But Pshibïshevsky lost his enthusiasm in the course of committee discussions. A simple query about whether there would be a different coursebook for a professional stream led to an intractable dispute over the desirability of universal vs professional musicianship.[19]

Even while RAPM was at the peak of its power, there were still areas where RAPM had little influence, such as the Radio Committee and the Bolshoi Theatre. And instead of moving towards official endorsement, senior Party members kept their distance, and liked to refer to RAPM by the vaguely patronising euphemism 'our musical youth'. And since RAPM was not the Party, neither could mockery of RAPM be construed as mockery of the Party – which was sufficient licence for many. The most prominent instance of this mockery carried the issue well beyond the confines of the musical world. Meyerhold was the culprit again. His production of *The Final Battle*, a play by Vsevolod Vishnevsky, was premiered on 7 February 1931.[20] This was a fantasy piece about the final battle between the socialist and capitalist worlds, but it often merged with the form of the topical

---

[16] The Russian here is 'lyubimchikami na doprose' (!).

[17] See fn. 15, ll. 35–6. 'Modernism' here is *sovremennichestvo* (contemporaneity), which refers specifically to ASM's name.

[18] Isaak Solomonovich Rabinovich (1897–1985), a student of Yavorsky, taught piano method at the Moscow Conservatoire from 1924 to 1970.

[19] See fn. 15, l. 37.

[20] The title is quotation from the Russian version of the *Internationale*: 'This is our final decisive battle'.

political review. Among the topical references was a casual insult aimed at RAPM. The insult hit home, and RAPM made its anger known by publishing its debate on the matter. This is how Lebedinsky addressed his RAPM comrades:

> [Lebedinsky]: [The characters in the play] don't know how to get rid of some balding conductor, but finally they say, 'Let's send him over to the Association of Proletarian Musicians'. Then there was a moment of silence. Some philistines began to clap: they hate RAPM because it takes their foxtrots and chansonettes away from them. At that moment, quietly, so that almost no one will be able to hear it, they add the words, 'to put him at their mercy'.
>
> From the floor: No, it wasn't like that; they said 'put him at RAPM's mercy' straight away.
>
> [Lebedinsky]: When I was at the public preview, it happened as I said. Perhaps they've changed it since, but it's not much of a change. The most important thing in this phrase, in this little joke, is that some old conductor, a clown, is sent to RAPM – to be put at their mercy or to become a member, it does not matter – the philistines applaud. The addition 'at their mercy' is for the simpletons at Glavrepertkom, because if they just said 'let's send him to RAPM', no one would let that insolent mockery of a proletarian organisation pass, since everyone knows that there are no reactionary old hack-conductors here.
>
> From the floor: Still, I think it was quite subtle.
>
> [Lebedinsky]: In my opinion, it was crude and it was not funny [...].[21]

This was wishful thinking on Lebedinsky's part. To persuade himself that the censor, Glavrepertkom, would have deleted the 'insolent mockery of a proletarian organisation', he had to assign an exaggerated significance to the timing of a throwaway line. It is hardly likely that Glavrepertkom would have been bothered either way.

Since his scuffle with RAPM in December of the previous year, Meyerhold encountered them again when they attacked the use of 'foxtrot' music in his production of *D.S.Ye.* (Give us a Soviet Europe!).[22] The reference to RAPM was most likely a last-minute addition prompted by this incident, since there is nothing else of the sort in Vishnevsky's play. From the exchange with Lebedinsky, the audience members who clearly enjoyed it even included at least one RAPM member.

Meyerhold could bring amusement to those waiting for RAPM's demise, but it was only Stalin who could bring deliverance. The astute noticed that Stalin's address of 23 June 1931, 'New Conditions – New Tasks', given to a meeting of economic managers, had consequences for culture, even though it was ostensibly

---

[21] 'Posledniy reshitel'nïy' (doklad L. Lebedinskogo), *Za proletarskuyu muzïku*, no. 5 (March 1931), 7–12.

[22] D.Zh., 'D.S.Ye. ili "agitprop" fokstrota v teatre im. Meyerkhol'da', *Za proletarskuyu muzïku*, no. 1 (1931), 16–18.

about industry. This hinged on the fact that the 'intelligentsia' extended from culture narrowly defined through to the sciences and engineering – whatever applied to the latter generally carried across to the rest of the intelligentsia. In his speech, Stalin declared that the majority of the Soviet intelligentsia was now turning towards Soviet power. In the cultural sphere, this statement was taken as a clear signal that it was now time to recognise the contribution made by fellow travellers. Even if this was not yet obvious to the fellow-travelling composers themselves (such as Myaskovsky, who could well serve an illustration of Stalin's statement), RAPM's fall was now only a matter of time. It could try to adapt to the new shift in policy, but it was clearly not the vehicle that could carry it through.

A daring attack was mounted on RAPM soon after the speech, by the remnants of ASM hidden away in the committee of the Narkompros Radio Section. Derzhanovsky had found a refuge there after the demise of Mezhkniga, and he was joined by the friendly theatre critic Vladimir Blyum, who was still trying to push forward a modified ASM-type agenda in 1931. While the speech might have given them an extra degree of confidence, they were likely to have mounted the attack in any case. They found a supporter in their senior colleague N. I. Smirnov, who was editor-in-chief of Soviet radio's print journal *Moscow Speaking* (*Govorit Moskva*), but also the head of the Radio Section, and a deputy to Bubnov, Lunacharsky's replacement at Narkompros. Mounting direct criticisms of RAPM ideology would have been a futile gesture at this point. Instead, Derzhanovsky, Blyum and at least one other person, hiding behind pseudonyms, tried to show that even RAPM's own music had bourgeois roots and ought to be condemned by the standards of RAPM ideology. In successive issues of *Moscow Speaking* from the late August onwards, they published this material with impunity for a while. As Shekhter complained to Davidenko, *Moscow Speaking* 'has indeed begun to speak – in a voice that is becoming ever more insolent'.[23] The opponents of RAPM, of course, were delighted with the *Moscow Speaking* articles, which raised their morale greatly. The outcome of this story must wait, however, until two further events have been discussed.

In the wake of these publications, non-RAPM composers and dramatists were able to pull off a major victory. Leading non-RAPM members of Vseroskomdram met with the RAPP leaders Alexander Afinogenov and Leopold Averbakh – that is, with the most prestigious figures in the entire proletarian culture movement. It was agreed that the meeting should be held without the presence or knowledge of RAPM. Afinogenov and Averbakh were more interested in hearing out the Vseroskomdram complaints in peace and without interruptions than including their musical sister organisation. Now it was not just Meyerhold who spoke out, but also the composers Mikhail Gnesin, Gavriil Popov, Levon Atovmyan, and also Shebalin, even though he was already within Myaskovsky's RAPM-friendly grouping. Afinogenov and Averbakh listened benignly and even showed some solidarity with the composers, drawing a line between RAPP on the one hand, which had already reformed itself after a spate of self-criticism, and RAPM on

[23] Letter from Shekhter to Davidenko (undated; most likely Sept. or Oct. 1931), GTsMMK, fond 30 (Davidenko), ye. kh. 112, 1–2.

the other, which had continued in disregard of Stalin's June speech. Without the support of the much more weighty and influential RAPP, RAPM was now in danger of isolation.

At the same time,[24] the Narkompros Collegium, chaired by the Minister Andrey Bubnov, published a resolution on the former Moscow Conservatoire. The effects of Stalin's June speech were now widespread, and the Collegium harshly criticised the drop in professional standards of music education and pledged a sharp turn in favour of the neglected academic aspects of the institution's work:

> The Narkompros Collegium notes that the desire to apply Marxist-Leninist methodology to specific music disciplines has led to some mistakes in the work of this institution: at times musical technique and the importance of critically assimilating the heritage of the past were both underappreciated, while the Marxist understanding of music's class nature was at times vulgarised to the detriment of any deep study of facts. [... A] decisive struggle [has to be conducted] against 'leftist' deviations in the general area of musical education and its methods, in particular against the underappreciation and neglect of systematic theoretical study, which should be run in accordance with firm study plans and specialist preparation in this sphere of artistic culture.[25]

Lamm was delighted, and looked forward to future vindications:

> The atmosphere is thickening on the musical front, and the rumble of approaching thunder can be heard every now and again. It's my opinion that RAPM will be pulled down from the commanding heights very soon and will take the place it deserves.[26]

Now came news of setbacks for the opponents of RAPM. There was a reorganisation of Soviet radio, which was removed from Narkompros on 20 September and given a ministry of its own. Smirnov was no longer in charge, and *Moscow Speaking* was handed over to Felix Kon, the head of Glaviskusstvo and donor of the Conservatoire's new name. The 21 September issue of *Moscow Speaking* was released as normal, with the most aggressive attack yet on RAPM. This was to prove the last of the attacks, and indeed the last issue of the journal, as Kon took charge. By 7 October, the new administration had worked its way round to Derzhanovsky, Blyum and their collaborators, who were sacked for their anti-RAPM antics.[27] Shostakovich's letters to Sollertinsky cover the ensuing events in detail. Shostakovich, when all still seemed well, had sent an anti-RAPM letter to *Moscow Speaking*, and was now fearful of the consequences:

---

[24] The exact date of the meeting is uncertain, but it is referred to in a letter from Lamm to Asafyev of 7 Oct. 1931, RGALI, fond 2743 (Lamm), op. 1, ye. kh. 42, l. 14v.

[25] As quoted at the December meeting of Vseroskomdram, transcript in Gnesin's archive, RGALI, fond 2954 (Gnesin), op. 1, ye. kh. 139, l. 115.

[26] Letter from Lamm to Asafyev of 7 Oct. 1931. See fn. 24.

[27] Letters from Shostakovich to Sollertinsky of 7 and 14 Oct. 1931, D. D. Shostakovich, *Pis'ma I. I. Sollertinskomu*, ed. by D. I. Sollertinskiy (St Petersburg: Kompozitor, 2006), 87 and 90.

With the blessing of that old fart Felix ... [words omitted in published source], they'll add a footnote to my unpublished letter. I'm already reading it in my head: 'The journal *Moscow Speaking* was a centre for hostile-class dregs under the old management. Ivanchikov,[28] Shostakovich and the like all took delight in pouring dirt over Beliy's work of genius 'Proletarians of All Lands, Unite'. Woe is me, they can measure me up for a coffin now. [...] I never thought all the commotion over *Moscow Speaking* would end so badly for me. It looked as if they'd eased up on my persecution a little. Now it will start all over again.[29]

On top of this, it turned out that a transcript of the closed Vseroskomdram/RAPP meeting had immediately been leaked to RAPM. As we saw, Shebalin had spoken out against RAPM at the meeting while RAPM still considered him to be one of their own fellow travellers. Now that the leak had exposed him, he could not continue to hedge his bets. The changes at the radio did not augur well for him, and he decided it was in his best interests to make his humble apologies to RAPM. At a December meeting of Vseroskomdram, Beliy triumphantly read out Shebalin's recantation. This was news to the other side, which reacted with dismay. Atovmyan stated before all assembled that Shebalin and the other members of the Myaskovsky grouping were a pack of hypocrites. Shostakovich expressed his feelings in a letter to Shebalin, written at the very end of 1931:

> Happy New Year, dear defector [*perevooruzhenets*] [...] It is not with pleasure but with indignation that I'm rereading your speech of repentance that received applause [from RAPM]. [...] To all those who hold the art of music dear, or, specifically, to their best representatives, among whom I count you and also myself (forgive my conceitedness), I would recommend that they cultivate the strongest self-criticism when they are amongst themselves (in the company of those best representatives). But on no account should they criticise each other in the presence of rogues, know-nothings and demagogues.[30]

While the musical world saw a swing of the pendulum back towards the proletarian side, the complaints against RAPM were making their rounds within the bureaucracy, which increased the pressure on them to reform in line with the new policies. Feeling the heat, RAPM had begun its first round of self-criticism as far back as the beginning of October.[31] These events continued into the winter, following the model that RAPP had already established months earlier. In November, there was a critical discussion centred around Davidenko's piece 'Hoisting the Wagon' (*Pod'yom vagona*), where Shebalin was a participant, invited

---

[28] Ivanchikov was one of the pseudonyms of V. I. Blyum.

[29] Letter from Shostakovich to Sollertinsky of 14 Oct. 1931, ibid., 90.

[30] Letter from Shostakovich to Shebalin of 29 Dec. 1931, RGALI, fond 2012 (Shebalin), op. 1, ye. kh. 188, l. 3v. Quoted in Ye. S. Vlasova, *1948 god v sovetskoy muzïke: dokumentirovannoye issledovaniye* (Moscow: Klassika – XXI, 2010), 121.

[31] 'Samokritika na fronte proletarskoy muzïki. Nuzhna massovaya oboronnaya pesnya. Pervïy vecher konkretnoy kritiki v RAPM', *Sovetskoye iskusstvo*, no. 53 (13 Oct. 1931), 1.

as a friend of RAPM. The proceedings were published for all to read and some to gloat. At the plenary session held in the same month, it was Koval's turn to self-flagellate, 'mercilessly uncovering' his own 'mistakes and deviations'.

After all the drama of the last quarter of 1931, nothing was quite settled yet, but musical life was not suspended to await the outcome. Vseroskomdram realised two new practical initiatives that were advantageous to its members. With hindsight, we can see that these were important precursors of musical life under the Socialist Realist dispensation that established itself over the following couple of years. One of the initiatives was the issuing of contracts to composers, often retrospectively, so that they then appeared to be composing in line with official demands. By the end of 1931, 22 composers had received Vseroskomdram contracts, among them Myaskovsky, for his already completed 'Collective Farm Symphony', Alexander Krein, for 'a large work depicting the victories of the general Party line at different stages', and Anatoly Aleksandrov, for an opera about the new Kazakhstan.[32] The other new initiative was a series of concerts of Soviet music, which excluded RAPM and was instead centred on 'fellow travellers' (in the broadest sense). For the previous two years, concerts of new Soviet music had been practically non-existent, and this new development caused much excitement. Its realisation was only possible because one musical institution still remained outside RAPM's grasp – the Bolshoi Theatre. The director Malinovskaya and the music director Kubatsky looked favourably on Vseroskomdram's proposals and programming, and the first concert (featuring Myaskovsky's Sinfonietta, Shebalin's Second Symphony and Kabalevsky's Piano Concerto) took place in the main auditorium of the Bolshoi in December 1931.

Two or three years earlier, a programme like this would not have drawn much attention, but on this occasion the whole 'artistic beau monde' turned up.[33] It is true that people were starved of symphony concerts, which were almost extinct by that stage, having been replaced by all kinds of medleys. But there was more to it: the whole of Moscow's artistic intelligentsia was following the dramatic encounters between RAPM and Vseroskomdram (to which RAPM members still nominally belonged). Notably, the composers featured in the programme weren't just any composers – there were the ones who, pledging allegiance to RAPM, were understood to be doing this only hypocritically. Now they offered their works in serious symphonic genres, with no trace of Soviet-style titles. RAPM refused to submit any pieces, but some of their members attended. On the night, the auditorium thus contained both RAPM and foxtrotters, who could respectively glare and smirk across at each other. The struggle 'on the music front' was running out of options. 'We live in interesting times', as Shostakovich remarked.[34]

---

[32] Kl. Korchmaryov, 'Kontraktatsiya kompozitorov', *Sovetskoye iskusstvo*, no. 60 (25 Nov. 1931), 4.

[33] Memoirs of Levon Atovmyan (unpublished typescript), 31. I am grateful to Simon Morrison for allowing me to use this source.

[34] Letter from Shostakovich to Sollertinsky of 13 Dec. 1930, D. D. Shostakovich, *Pis'ma I. I. Sollertinskomu*, ed. by D. I. Sollertinskiy (St Petersburg: Kompozitor, 2006), 99.

'Kiyevskaya gazeta o balete Shostakovicha' [A Kiev Newspaper on Shostakovich's Ballet], *Proletarskiy muzïkant*, no. 1 (1931), 46.

While RAPM grumbled about Shostakovich from time to time, the composer managed to avoid provoking any attacks that could have damaged his career. But he was less circumspect with UAPM, the Ukrainian counterpart. On holiday in the south, he evidently felt he was free to follow his inclinations, since he was far enough away from the hub of musical and political life. Here, he confesses to (or boasts of) a misdemeanour in a letter to Sollertinsky, written from Odessa in September 1931:

Another vivid impression of Odessa comes from my conversation with a member of UAPM's Odessa branch. She was a very attractive and feisty Ukrainian woman. [...] Yesterday morning, she phoned me and suggested that we have a chat. At once, I could feel my facial muscles settling into that old 'self-satisfied' expression. [...] Picture then my dismay when I realised that she had only come to turn me into a composer of mass songs. 'Just think about it', said she, 'All of us from the local UAPM heard your ballet [*The Golden Age*] and we found it highly decadent ... light genre ... contemporary music ...' – such were the words pouring from, hmm, that delightful little mouth of hers. I listened in admiration. My inner dude came to life: 'What's all this about then? Isn't life beautiful?', said I, taking her in my arms and trying to plant a kiss on her. At that instant, I received a vigorous slap to the face, and with the parting shot 'For *Proletarian Music* is going to hear about all this!', she left the room.[35]

But perhaps she kept it to herself, since RAPM's organs carried no reports of scandalous behaviour in Odessa. The Golden Age, the ballet she referred to in Shostakovich's company, was due to have a run in Odessa, but it was cancelled after the dress rehearsal (this occurred before Shostakovich's visit). The ballet had met with better luck in Kiev, where it enjoyed a run beginning in January 1931, and this is the subject of the article below. While some of Shostakovich's work won grudging admiration from RAPM, it must be said that The Golden Age *emphatically did not fall into this category, as the report makes clear.*

A Kiev Newspaper on Shostakovich's Ballet [*The Golden Age*]

Kiev Opera House has mounted a production of Shostakovich's ballet *Zolota doba* (*The Golden Age*). *The Kiev Proletarian* newspaper gives its impressions of the production in the 6 November issue:

---

[35] Letter from Shostakovich to Sollertinsky of 27 Sept. 1931, D. D. Shostakovich, *Pis'ma I. I. Sollertinskomu*, ed. by D. I. Sollertinskiy (St Petersburg: Kompozitor, 2006), 79–80.

Not only a deep disappointment, but also a decisive condemnation of the production – this was the main view among the audience at the show.

After explaining the ballet's plot, the newspaper evaluates it thus:

An almost complete absence of dramatic action, a lack of any contrasting elements and a weak characterisation of the Soviet team, which symbolises the Soviet Union – all of this makes the scenario colourless, limp and lifeless, and it does not provoke the requisite emotions from the audience, such as disgust at the degenerate character of the Western bourgeoisie, or the realisation of the power of the proletarian state and its joyful belief in the future.

As for the music of *The Golden Age*, the newspaper writes as follows:

Listening to the music of *The Golden Age*, we don't know which should surprise us more: the composer's mastery in illustrating expressively dramatic events that are insignificant, or the music's ideological meaninglessness on the whole, over the course of hundreds of pages in the score. We have some musical 'puns' and interesting musical 'witticisms', but the principal matter – deep and clear content – is lacking.

Musical 'gourmets' of all shades will be delighted by music of this kind, like lovers of mature cheese with worms. But the bemused proletarian masses will laugh at best, and more likely be outraged that instead of healthy musical food they are served 'gourmet' dishes that can only induce nausea despite all the chefs' artistry and all their squandered talent.

The paper's conclusion is expressed in the very title of the article: 'The ballet *The Golden Age* is of no use to the worker audience'.

On 23 February, *The Kiev Proletarian* returns to the production once again. The paper now speaks still more decisively in favour of removing Shostakovich's ballet from the repertoire:

The ballet *The Golden Age*, as the coarsest amalgam of sickening foxtrots and other decadent dances, should not be tolerated on the academy stage at all. The production's extremely common and vulgar baggage all outrages the worker audience. The Soviet football team is shown dancing among the debauched regulars of a cabaret, which yet again emphasises the plot's ideological poverty. The worker audience is correct in saying that a Soviet sports organisation has no place among the erotic debaucheries of the unbridled bourgeoisie. Shostakovich's music, which has no inner weight despite its technical intricacy, and which has been specially devised for lovers of spicy dishes, cannot serve as the motive for producing a ballet revue that is naive and false throughout and lacks any passable logic in its plot. It is obvious how much ideological harm such works can cause.

※ ※ ※ ※ ※

N. Vïgodskiy, 'Nebesnaya 'idilliya' ili fashizm v popovskoy ryase' [Heavenly 'Idyll', or Fascism in Priestly Garb], *Proletarskiy muzïkant*, no. 2 (1931), 27–8.

Even in the 1930/31 season, RAPM could not fully control the concert repertoire, and when something untoward slipped through, RAPM's critics launched broadsides at the offending musicians and venue management. While the political insults were often of a predictable and scattershot nature, there were sometimes more specific insinuations, such as the invocation of no less than three current show trials in the closing paragraph of the present review: namely, the Industrial Party trial, the Menshevik trial, and the 'Peasant Labour Party' trial (an attack on advocates of agrarian co-operatives). If the reviewer hoped to associate the organisers of this concert with such 'enemy class forces', nothing came of it – RAPM lacked the influence to have its broadsides translated into action at high levels of state.

The combination of Rachmaninov, Balmont and Poe in The Bells *ticked many boxes in the RAPM book of anathemas, which are duly rehearsed here. Even so, Rachmaninov is attacked on ideological rather than specifically musical grounds, which cannot be said of the vigorous denigration of Holst that follows. The writer attempts to demolish the composer both as a bourgeois ideologist and as an artist. Holst is reduced to a simpering hypocrite retailing a contradictory mix of patriotism, pacifism and mysticism, while the music is presented as mawkish kitsch. Although he had much earlier been a member of William Morris's revolutionary Hammersmith Socialist Society, Holst had left himself open to such mockery in the twenties by reworking a section of the 'Jupiter' movement of his* Planets *Suite to fit the text of a patriotic/religious kitsch poem 'I Vow to Thee My Country'. The resulting hymn soon received official sanction through its use in British Armistice Day ceremonies.*

N. Vygodsky
Heavenly 'Idyll', or Fascism in Priestly Garb

(Concerts given by Albert Coates, 5 and 6 March 1931)

The programme for these concerts consisted of two large-scale works, Rachmaninov's *Bells* and Holst's *Planets*. Their subject matter, which faces 'heavenwards', must prompt some misgivings. These are only heightened when you see that the composer is Rachmaninov, and the poet Balmont, those demigods of the decadent pre-Revolutionary intelligentsia of the bourgeois salons, now turned White émigrés; and that the other composer is Holst, that glorifier of the contemporary imperialist bourgeoisie of Europe and America; and then finally, we have a favourite of fashionable audiences in Europe, the former conductor of the former Mariinsky Theatre, Mr Coates, who left Russia in 1917.

These misgivings mount further when you look at the public, redolent with the priesthood and the Okhotny Ryad [i.e. NEPmen traders];[36] the concerts are aimed

---

[36] Okhotny Ryad, a large market in the centre of Moscow, near the Kremlin walls.

at such people, and they pack out the Grand Hall, applauding wildly. The ovations, of course, are addressed jointly to the conductor, the works and the composers, and also, we would imagine, to the institution that decided to organise a Lenten liturgy, namely the Bolshoi Academy Theatre.

Let us look at the programme in more detail.

Rachmaninov's *Bells*. The work is pessimistic throughout. Its leading idea is the rejection of life and action and the expectation, indeed the desire for death, death as a blind elementary force of universal annihilation. Here are some excerpts from Balmont's text (after Edgar Allan Poe)

> They [the bells] say
> That the days of delusion
> Will be followed by rebirth
>
> And now there is no salvation for us
> Flame and conflagration is everywhere
> Fear and outrage is everywhere.
>
> A black figure stands over there,
> Laughs and rumbles,
> And crones, drones, drones,
> He leans towards the bell tower,
> The swinging bell rocks,
> The droning turns to tears,
> Moaning in the silent air
> And slowly announces the deathly peace.

The musical setting is entirely in harmony with the mood of the poem. It is gloomy and pessimistic. The poem is pervaded with a cold and deathly horror. For twenty minutes, we are faced with hysterical screams, the pompous pathos of an individualist who stands aloof from society, and the affectations of a decadent aesthete. For the listener, the music is intoxicating: it clouds the consciousness and weakens the will. And all of this is accompanied by church bells. Just where are we supposed to be? Is this a funeral service, a black mass, a spiritualist séance or a sacred concert? Where does all this horror and the mysticism spring from?

It must be said that *The Bells* is quite characteristic of Rachmaninov's broad artistic direction. It was written before the war (in July 1913), and is a kind of 'pinnacle' in the composer's œuvre.

Rachmaninov is quite close to the writer Leonid Andreyev[37] in his artistic personality. Extreme individualism, psychological instability, a lack of will power, interminable pessimism, separation from life, a lack of belief in the forces of man and society, gloomy mysticism, an apologia for death and darkness – these are the main themes in the creative work of both artists. The source of their work is in the pre-war mood found among some circles of the Russian bourgeois intelligentsia.

The October Revolution drew a sharp line through the Russian bourgeois and petit-bourgeois intelligentsia, dividing it largely into two camps: the fellow travellers of the working class, and the enemies of the working class. In the White

---

[37] See Glossary.

émigré camp we find such 'pillars' of the past as Rachmaninov and Balmont, the creators of the work performed a few days ago in Moscow, at the Felix Kon Higher School [the Conservatoire].

Holst, *The Planets*. This symphony is conceived along different lines from *The Bells*. Its unusual title speaks of its programmatic nature. The symphony consists of seven numbers, each of them portraying one of the planets (Mars is the bringer of war, Venus the bringer of peace, Neptune symbolises the mystery and silence of the spheres, etc.). Earth is missing from the planets, yet this fact does not at all prevent the symphony from being very 'earthly'.

[The vision of] a departure for heaven is a variety of mysticism that represents the 'spiritual' side of international priestly skulduggery. Holst's *Planets* is a deeply political work. It is even more a political document than it is a work of art, since artistically it contains nothing but an impoverished and meaningless eclecticism, a stew of every style, covered up with the superficial pomp of its supposedly 'brilliant' orchestration (which is, in fact, superficial and inexpressive).

Holst's symphony is a typical reflection and promotion of modern imperialism, both open and veiled ('diplomacy', that is). The first piece depicts war ('Mars, the god of War'). This is not the first time music has turned to the theme of war, but artists of different classes and eras interpret war in different ways. Holst, as an ideologist of modern imperialism, approaches war as sport, in a naturalistic manner.

'Capitalism needs to quicken the pace, to increase the readiness for battle. The bourgeoisie does that, for example, through its extensive development of such an "abstract" sphere as sport. When we have to fight, we will be better soldiers and better at smashing heads. For what purpose, however? For the glory of the bourgeoisie.' [quoting Lunacharsky] i

Mars is followed by Venus, 'the bringer of peace'. Here Holst dons the pacifist cloak of modern imperialism.

The most tender effusions of the solo violin in its high register, and the sweet chords of harp and celeste make this movement so sickly-sweet, so slobberingly sentimental, enveloping us in such a cloud of incense, that Henderson himself would feel a pang of envy.[38]

Indeed, such music is much needed by the imperialists of the world. What could be better: to demonstrate your military might first, to instil fear by threatening horrors of a future war, and five minutes later to declare all this an illusion and declare peace among all the peoples.

As it progresses, the work, like all modern bourgeois symphonies, represents all the aspects of its class. On the one hand, we see youth and merriment (Jupiter), on the other, old age and death (Saturn).

How does one represent the youth and merriment of a class that is destined to die? Here jazz music is inevitably trundled out, irreplaceable for this purpose, with its rigid mechanical rhythms.

---

[38] Arthur Henderson, British Foreign Secretary at the time. Henderson attempted to reduce political tensions in Europe, and re-established diplomatic relations with the Soviet Union. Henderson gave his full support to the League of Nations by arguing for international arbitration, demilitarisation and collective security.

Old age and death are represented in a different way. The bourgeoisie has now found 'stability' and all its tears are spent. Today there is no time for weeping: it is time to prepare for the great battles ahead. This is why the bourgeois composer must draw from old melodies in order to express mourning. In these movements, Holst paraphrases the composers of the older generation as an epigone of the tritest order.

The entire symphony is built, on the one hand, upon a juxtaposition of belligerent imperialism, crude militarism, and fascism, and on the other, upon an unctuous and hypocritical social-fascist pacifism.[39] The whole affair concludes on decadently mystical notes of deathly hallucinations.

Mounting such a programme during 'Lent' and concurrently with the trial of the Menshevik saboteurs,[40] reinforces the political character of these concerts as a manifestation of enemy class forces. This is brought out especially by the fact that Rachmaninov's 'bells' are used as a musical symbol of the priestly and Black-Hundreds reaction in Chayanov's book[41] (see Yaroslavsky's article 'Chayanov's dreams and Soviet actuality', which was published in *Pravda* during the Industrial Party trial, on 18 October last year).[42] The responsibility for this reactionary manifestation must rest with the organisers of the concerts: the artistic directors of the Bolshoi Academy Theatre.

[*Note to Vygodsky's original*]

i A. V. Lunacharskiy, 'Sotsial'nïye istoki muzikal'nogo iskusstva', *Proletarskiy muzïkant*, no. 4, 1929. [A. Lunacharsky, 'Social Origins of Music', *Proletarian Musician*, no. 4, 1929].

---

[39] 'Social fascism' was an official pejorative term used in the Soviet Union in the late twenties and thirties and applied to social-democratic parties that refused to support the Communist International (the Comintern). The accusation was that such parties functioned as the enemies of proletarian revolution, and thus fulfilled the same function as fascist parties, however different their rhetoric might have been. The term disappeared in the mid-thirties, with the onset of the 'popular front' phase of Comintern policy.

[40] The prosecution of 'Menshevik wreckers' in February–March 1931 was a show trial of members of another 'party', and was entirely a fabrication of the Soviet GPU. It was connected to Soviet foreign policy at the time: during the trial, the anti-Comintern Second International (of social-democratic parties) was accused of plotting a renewed invasion of the Soviet Union.

[41] Aleksandr Vasilyevich Chayanov (1888–1937), Soviet agrarian economist and rural sociologist, a proponent of small-scale agricultural cooperation in distinction to large collective farms. During collectivisation, Chayanov's views were attacked by Stalin, and in 1930 he was arrested, tried and sent to a labour camp where he was finally executed in 1937. The book mentioned here is *The Journey of My Brother Alexei to the Land of Peasant Utopia* (1920).

[42] The Industrial Party Trial, a show trial of eminent Soviet scientists and economists that took place at the end of 1930. The defendants were accused of attempting to wreck the Soviet economy and of plotting to stage a coup against the Soviet government.

※ ※ ※ ※ ※

Tertset, 'Pod proletarskoy vual'yu' [Under a Proletarian Veil], *Govorit Moskva*, nos. 26–7 (21 Sept. 1931), 12–14.

This was possibly the last major blast against RAPM during the height of its dominance, and it came from the Soviet Radio journal, Moscow Speaking, *which published a series of these articles from late August to late September. The journal was run by the Radio Committee, then within Narkompros, and one of the very few institutions connected with music that remained free of RAPM control. The pseudonym suggests collective authorship, most likely including Derzhanovsky and Blyum. A year earlier, Derzhanovsky, writing to Asafyev, gave a perfect description of the method used in this essay:*

> If you are accused of something, accuse your accusers of the same thing. These days, I spend all my time shouting about the counter-revolutionary nature and alien class character of RAPM music.[43]

After patronising RAPM as students with much still to learn, the essay does indeed analyse RAPM's own music in the best RAPM manner, and finds it wanting. The heavy and earnest prose style, overburdened with worthy political clichés, is a RAPM pastiche, adding to the mockery.

The essay was illustrated with two cartoons, one portraying Davidenko as a priest pronouncing an anathema on 'the critics', the other representing Koval's song, 'The Wings of the Soviets' as a prostitute sitting on a toy-sized aeroplane (the significance of this will become clear during the course of the article).

'Terzetto'
Under a Proletarian Veil

In the pages of its journals, *The Proletarian Musician* and *For Proletarian Music*, the Association of Proletarian Musicians has claimed from time to time that it is awaiting constructive and friendly criticism of works by proletarian composers. Curiously, though, RAPM can't abide criticism. Because all hell broke loose the moment *Moscow Speaking* printed a handful of comments written by critics who hadn't already sworn an oath of loyalty to *The Proletarian Musician*. [...] RAPM's intolerance in this instance is entirely characteristic.

Since RAPM seeks to lead all creative musical work in the USSR, it has an obligation to treat its own work with the greatest seriousness, particularly when they assess [their] new pieces, which surely ought to be representative of our socialist era's creative style.

This seriousness is all the more important for the creators of proletarian music, because their music, through Soviet radio broadcasting, travels beyond the borders of our country to proletarians of other lands, where it must bring true

---

[43] Letter from Derzhanovsky to Asafyev of 22 Apr. 1930, RGALI, fond 2658, op. 2, ye. kh. 45, l. 109.

edification and cement the links between proletarians across the world. It is clear that proletarian music ought to justify its name and evoke a response in proletarian hearts, while at the same time, it must eclipse – yes, eclipse – all the works of the capitalist era, the bourgeois exemplars left to us by the great musicians of the past.

This, of course, is too much to ask – a demand that we can't yet address to the 'proletarian' musicians, for they are only beginning to work; they must learn and look for direction. So we need to consider them as nothing more than students, who may have creative energy, but should not be boasting of their talents; they should settle down to some honest and conscientious work, as befits any student.

In practice, however, we see something entirely different. On the one hand, RAPM members prefer to borrow their [musical] themes from other composers, largely from those whom they brand as 'fascists', 'reactionaries', etc., while on the other hand, they mount vigorous attacks on all those who defend other composers, all those who have not risen up through RAPM's ranks, and all those who dare to compose original music. [… M]usicians who are not steadfast enough are then driven to behave like cowardly philistines and reject all other types of music in order to promote the work of proletarian musicians exclusively.

This is the method used by RAPM and their comrades-in-arms, and it leads to the most unabashed stifling of self-criticism.[44]

In the meantime, the 'proletarian composers' themselves are strongly influenced by the style (the devices and textures) of contemporary bourgeois musicians, especially the decadents Stravinsky, Prokofiev, Scriabin, and the reactionaries Medtner and Rachmaninov. [...] At times the themes they borrow from each other are the same themes they have already borrowed from 'bourgeois' musicians.

Let us compare, for example, Beliy's song 'The virtuous deed' [*Delo doblesti*] and Davidenko's 'The Smith' [*Kuznets*]. Their themes are near identical, and the difference [between the two songs] arises from the fact that the introduction to Davidenko's *Smith* was written under the influence of the counter-revolutionary composer Rachmaninov.

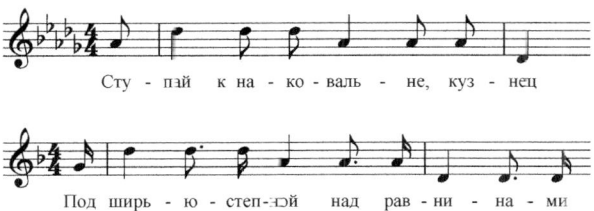

Сту - пай к на - ко - валь - не, куз - нец

Под ширь - ю - степ-ной над рав - ни - на - ми

Let us focus now on Davidenko, who seems to be the most prolific of the younger composers. He is especially susceptible to the influence of bourgeois musicians, both of the past and the present. In the 'Ballad of Bread and Swords' [*Ballada o khlebe i mechakh*] on a text by Utkin, we cannot fail to see the influence of late-period Scriabin and also of Medtner at the same time. It should also be noted that the 'world of kings' is portrayed much more successfully than 'our world', probably because the proletarian musicians could find models for the former in bourgeois music, but no ready-made sources for 'our world'. [...]

---

[44] This was a serious political shortcoming for any proletarian cultural organisation in the atmosphere of late 1931.

The same approach is taken in Davidenko's 'Mother', whose first bars are closely related to Rimsky-Korsakov's *Snow Maiden*, while the harmonisation of the whole song is in the spirit of Ravel. The past must have a significant hold over Davidenko, because in his 'Song of Industrialisation', on the theme of shockworkers, the words 'Hey you, press that lever harder' are sung, but at the same time, the music provides us with the pealing of bells, almost Rachmaninov-like – despite the fact that the theorists of proletarian music justifiedly protest against the performance of that composer's works. [...]

Davidenko has more teachers than his comrades-in-arms; he is more flexible and unabashed. He doesn't disdain to use Prokofiev in the introduction to his 'Shockworking Pioneer Song' [*Udarnaya pionerskaya*], nor the Romantic Mendelssohn – the latter's 'Hunting Song' provided the style for Davidenko's sentimental 'Workers' May' [*Rabochiy may*], to words by Tretyakov. Davidenko's romantic moods tend to slip into the decadent minor key, as in 'The Workers' Palace' [*Rabochiy dvorets*]. Decadence and degeneration reach the level of a brilliant effect in his song 'A Letter' on a text by Utkin – it is hardly surprising that [the Gypsy-romance singer] Tamara Tsereteli herself included it in her repertoire![45]

But here is what surprises us. Whenever the author tries to show his own face, writing independently, without borrowings from the material of 'bourgeois' composers, it is a face that turns out to be sour and grey, which will never inspire [in the proletarian listener] any desire to work. But when the foreign hand of some important master begins to guide the composer's scratchy scrawl, then something like a musical work emerges. An example of this appears in the latest of Davidenko's works, which appeared in Issue 12 of the journal *For Proletarian Music*. He calls this piece 'A Dance of Defence' [*Tanets oboroni*]. However, this very dance was written by Stravinsky some time ago, in the ballet *Petrushka*, where it was entitled 'The Dance of the Coachmen'.

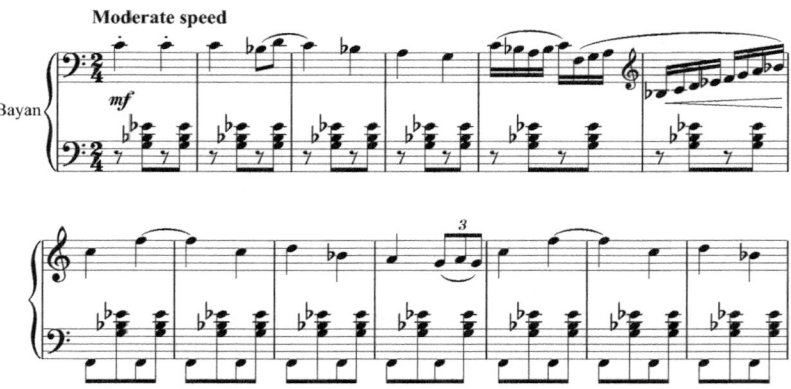

---

[45] Tamara Semyonovna Tsereteli (1900–68) was a celebrated performer of Russian and Gypsy romances who had admirers in the Kremlin.

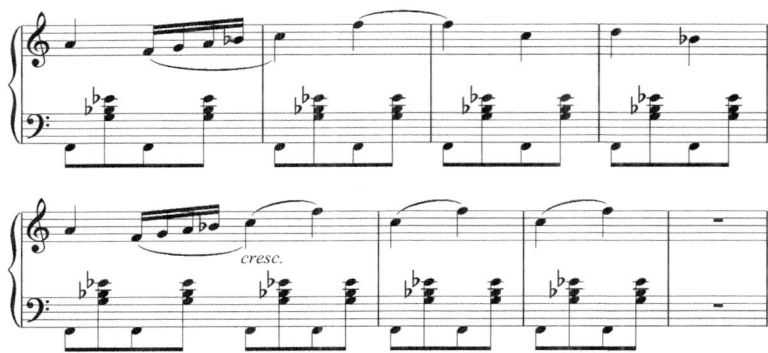

And this is how it goes on up to the *mezzo forte*, at which point the singing starts, instantly revealing nothing more than the useless scrawl of a student lacking in creative discipline.

And here is Stravinsky's Dance of the Coachmen:

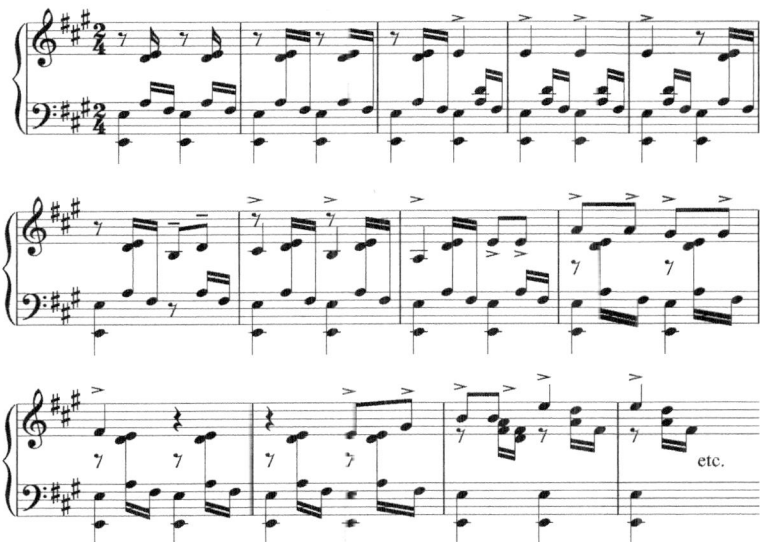

In this dance Stravinsky masterfully conveys the image of plumped-up servants, grown fat, self-satisfied and debauched, the landlord's little favourites, who know how to please their masters and multiply their wealth. This Stravinsky dance has the stink of kulak Black Hundreds. [...]

Can it possibly be true that any musical work whatsoever becomes proletarian merely because a 'proletarian' composer has added his signature? We have a name for this kind of creative work, don't we? And for these attitudes too. This is dyed-in-the-wool, unbridled right opportunism – as with Stravinsky's coachmen, or maybe even something stronger still? Perhaps Davidenko wants to give us an example of, so to speak 'the peaceful integration of kulaks into socialism'?[46] [...]

An old student song with the words 'Fill your glasses fuller' [*Naley, naley*

---

[46] This was a phrase of Bukharin's that Stalin liked to use mockingly.

bokalï polney] serves the prolific Davidenko as material for no less than three of his highly prized works: 'Be alert, comrade' [*Glyadi, tovarishch, v oba*], 'The Song of the Atheist Komsomols' [*Bezbozhnaya Komsomol'skaya*] and 'The Workers' May' [*Robochiy May*].Presenting listeners with the same tune in three hopelessly arranged variants goes beyond all honesty and good conscience, but the composer is not embarrassed. The single foundation for these three proletarian works is a song glorifying wine – this tells us how seriously the proletarian musicians take the great tasks they have set for themselves. [...]

Given his lack of creative imagination, Davidenko is of course absolutely right to study the models of musical masters. But he displays a strange liking for romanticism's decadent representatives, for dubious songs glorifying wine, and especially for the work of contemporary composers who have been branded 'fascists' by the same Association of Proletarian Musicians. There is something here to give us pause for thought. [...]

While Davidenko is unusually prolific, Marian Koval has been recognised as the most talented, thoughtful and serious of them. But his famed 'Urchin' [*Besprizorniy*] and 'The wind is rapping at the window' [*Za oknom stuchitsya veter*] hardly provide evidence of any originality or colour in the young composer's work.

'The Urchin', in particular, is not simply a decadent piece, but it further emphasises the sickliness of the urchin, who is essentially a lumpen proletarian with a depressive pathological mentality; his disorganised behaviour insistently recalls the ugliness of the old [pre-Revolutionary] life because he got used to it, absorbed it. This song is oppressive for listeners.

Such a taste for decadence is typical of the promising Koval. 'The wind is rapping at the window' and 'In Siberia' have the character of gloomy lamentations, the latter in the spirit of a sentimental German song. His 'Komsomol Girl' [*Komsomolka*] is distinguished by a pseudo-authenticity, a pretence at an ethnographic colour (in brackets, it is noted that the subject is drawn 'from the life of the Votyaks'). The intention in 'A Persian Carpet' is to convey a similar ethnographic exoticism, and the song is obviously composed in the style of Miron Yakobson.[47]

To convey the rhythmical movements of a 'Weaver Girl' [*Tkachikha-chelnochikha*], Koval managed to find nothing better than a foxtrot syncopation, pretending that his music reflects industrialisation. This kind of 'creativity' reaches its peak in Koval's lamenting, hysterical minor-key song 'The Wings of the Soviets' [*Kril'ya Sovetov*], which is quite bemusing on a first encounter. The words speak of the uplift, flight, the beauty of effort and achievement, but in the music there is nothing but a heart-rending melancholy. What is going on here?! When we listen more closely, however, the text changes by itself [in our minds] to fit the music, and we begin to hear the well-known tavern song 'Marusya poisoned herself' [*Marusya otravilas'*] (!). [...]

How can we summarise the 'proletarian' musicians' output? The majority of their works are unoriginal, small pieces of two or three pages, helpless and pitiful. They haven't moved on to anything beyond this. They don't have sufficient strength

---

[47] A composer of popular songs before the revolution, famous for his Tricolour march, which was used by the Whites during the Civil War.

or knowledge to write an opera. 'Proletarian musicians' limit themselves to the writing of songs that are collages of ready-mades, taken largely from reactionaries such as Stravinsky, Prokofiev, Medtner and Rachmaninov.

Their slogan of the inseparability of word and music is not realised in any of their works; on the contrary, we observe an obstinate separation of word from music.

Finally, the 'novelty' of the music usually amounts to nothing more than the revival of vulgar, outdated melodies in arrangements that are much worse than the originals.

The 'proletarian' artists have no face or style of their own. What they do have, however, is the ability to promote themselves noisily, including [through] the harassment and real persecution of all those who are dissatisfied with their work and who refuse to accept their output […]

The Association is essentially the administrative centre for all musical creation in the USSR. It sends circular letters into every corner of our country, and instructs us – telling us what the correct attitude is and what line is to be taken towards all other music, all 'other' music being 'bourgeois'. Administrative measures are its true weapon.

[…] Their music, which they dare call 'proletarian', is decadent through and through, bland, boring, unjustifiable on any political or artistic grounds, and on the grounds of vocal technique, it is equivalent to sabotage, as it makes singers force their voices, thus inflicting damage. This is the music of the past, with a depressing and unhealthy effect; it has nothing to do with the proletariat.

※ ※ ※ ※ ※

Kl. Korchmaryov, 'Muzïka k fil'me "Odna"' [Music for the film *Alone*], *Sovetskoye iskusstvo*, no. 58 (15 Nov. 1931), 4.

This is a notably fair-minded review for this intemperate period, and the author, the former ORKiMD composer Klimenty Korchmaryov, makes a conscientious attempt to restrict himself to constructive criticism, instead of making the blanket condemnations and political insinuations typical of the time. The review shows a lively interest in the technological problems of sound movies, and gives a vivid description of the problems that still had to be surmounted. The film Alone, *directed by Grigory Kozintsev and Leonid Trauberg (who represented the group FEKS, the Factory of Eccentric Actors),*[48] *follows the character of a young female teacher who is sent to a remote Altai village, where she tries to overcome her sense of distance from local life. The film was much criticised, particularly for its pessimism, but the role of Shostakovich's music received more favourable coverage. The critic Boris Alpers wrote:*

> The film is constructed on musical lines, as a kind of cine-oratorio. Its action is accompanied by symphonic music almost throughout, which plays the role of a psychological commentator on dramatic situations. One moment it rushes to the screen in an orchestral whirlwind, at another, it switches to the singing of an invisible choir and soloists.[49]

For Alpers, however, the dominant role of the music stemmed more from the 'fear of spoken word' and the technical difficulties this posed, than from any positive desire to promote 'cine-oratorios'.

Kl. Korchmaryov
Music for the Film *Alone*

Alone is a silent movie to which sound was added later. This is why it has all the shortcomings of silent cinema: lots of intertitles, scenes with actors posed before the camera (but not the microphone) in a drawn-out and static manner, and so on. All these devices are necessarily at odds with the sound that was added later. The music in this film is used not as an acoustic illustration of what is happening on screen, but as an independent element that indicates what the attitude of the authors is to the screen action. In many places, the music is given a symbolic role (for example, when the heroine dreams her way through two whole reels about achieving individual bourgeois happiness, the music constantly imitates the

---

[48] The film-makers Grigory Mikhaylovich Kozintsev (1905–73) and Leonid Zakharovich Trauberg (1902–90), collaborated on several films from the 1920s to the 1940s. Shostakovich wrote several film scores for them, as well as for Kozintsev alone.

[49] B. Alpers, 'Oshibka "Feksov": otkrïvayem diskussiyu ob "Odnoy"', *Sovetskoye iskusstvo*, no. 54 (18 Oct. 1931), 4.

barrel organ, or resembles a bourgeois polka). Although [in general] such musical symbolism is entirely admissible in films where the sound is added later, in *Alone* it does not fit in with the naturalistic recording of noises and other onomatopoeia (an alarm clock ringing, the noise of typewriters, etc.). All this shifts the function of sound towards illustration and realism, and lowers the overall level of the work. Onomatopoeia, which was recorded simultaneously with the picture, is not always properly synchronised, with frustrating results (especially where the words fail to coincide with the lip movements).

Dmitry Shostakovich's music creates a two-fold impression. It has many valuable moments, saturated with emotion and technically impeccable. The round dance on the snow is particularly impressive, where the guerrilla song 'From the midday sky' is used. But Shostakovich's rich orchestral colours, his principal virtue, are bleached out when they are heard in sound cinema, and the music suffers badly because of this.

The uneven quality of the music also significantly damages the impression. Alongside some very successful episodes, we have the impoverished atonal meanderings of lonely instruments, and this takes up more than half of the sound track. The composer must have tried to fill out the time required by the size of the film.

There is one gratifying aspect of Shostakovich's work, namely the move away from atonal chaos [*sumbur*] borrowed from the most negative models offered by the bourgeois West, and towards lucid harmonic and melodic structures. Of course, this Soviet composer's path does not point back to these decadent Western models, but rather to full textures that ought to be comprehensible to the masses.

Shostakovich needs to consider cutting down on the number of works he creates for the market. The phenomenally large quantity of works he writes in every imaginable form (ballets, sound films, music hall plays, music for TRAM [Workers' Youth Theatre], symphonic pieces, etc.), does not guarantee quality. As a result, good ideas often perish, because they have not been given enough thought and were poorly realised by the composer.

Our system of sound recording is much improved in comparison with the first attempts. But it remains far from perfect. At times, the sound of the orchestra is conveyed very well and even the timbres come close to reality, but in other places the same sonorities sound outrageously dirty. The timbres of the flute and the oboe suffer most of all. The strings do not come across well, and the percussion sounds awful. Aside from this, the 'sound effects' are often more like 'sound defects', because they simply fail to resemble the sounds they are supposed to represent. Perhaps this is the result of a certain carelessness in the handling of the apparatus. We will need to increase the pace of progress here.

※ ※ ※ ※ ※

A. Davidenko, 'Kak ya rabotal nad pesney "Nas pobit', pobit' khoteli"' [How I worked on the song 'They wanted to beat us'], *Za proletarskuyu muziku*, no. 11 (1931), 11–14.

Davidenko begins his description of his working methods by expressing some worthy pedagogical sentiments: no longer will composers act as a closed guild, fencing its working methods behind a smokescreen of elitist mystification. Unfortunately, the details that follow are embarrassingly minute and trivial, as if every last whim that supposedly entered Davidenko's mind contained a precious insight for budding proletarian composers. The reception of the essay provides a good illustration of its times. On the one hand, it was loudly mocked in anti-RAPM circles for its pretensions. On the other, it was taken very seriously by RAPM composers at Moscow Conservatoire (renamed at the time as the Felix Kon Higher Music School), where they tried to impose it on composition classes, much to the dismay of the established professoriate. Whatever the value of the essay though, the song under discussion was a great hit for Davidenko.

A. Davidenko
How I worked on the song 'They Wanted to Beat Us'

Proletarian artists shouldn't follow the example of the bourgeois masters in art and hold back their 'inventors' secrets'. On the contrary, proletarian artists should share their creative experience as widely as possible, assisting the emergence of new artists from the working class and the working peasantry, and helping with their development and growth. The purpose of this essay is to share the experience of my work on a mass song, starting from the emergence of its musical image and ending with the technical polish.

The most vivid experience is linked to my work on the song 'They wanted to beat us, to beat us'.

This song has become popular not only among the broad masses across the Soviet Union, but also, according to recent news, in foreign countries.

It's hardly a secret that composers select their texts slowly and torturously. There are very few good texts for mass songs. The best examples were produced by Demyan Bedny,[50] and composers of mass songs have been following his work very closely, always awaiting new song texts from him.

It should be easy, then, to imagine my delight when I came across Demyan's text 'They wanted to beat us, to beat us', which had been published in *Pravda*. A better example of a Red-Army marching song would be hard to find. I think that after the song 'When my mother was seeing me off' ['*Provodi*'], this text should be considered one of the best in the song literature of our times, in the power and clarity of its imagery and its infectious emotionality.

---

[50] See Glossary.

I remember how I was riding on a tram and suddenly began to think up a musical rendition of this text, trying *to bring to mind a vivid picture of Red-Army divisions marching to this song*. It was clear to me that because the text was based on a phrase from a folk tune, I should look for a musical solution in the active assimilation of folk material. So, after a few hours of wandering the streets, thinking about the musical image, and humming to myself, the following tune for the chorus came to me, and this established itself very clearly in my mind:

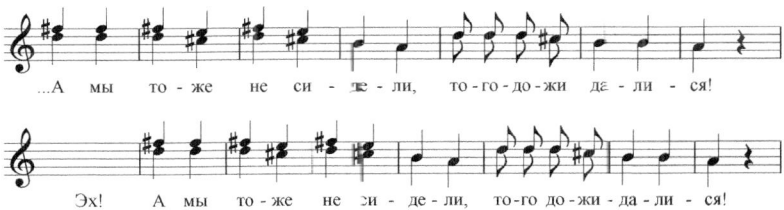

[The complete lyric for this refrain is: 'They wanted to beat us / They tried to beat us, / But hey, we weren't going to / Sit around and wait for that.]

I didn't have anything for the 'Ekh!', but that hardly mattered. It's easy to find a transition, and the main thing was that the overall shape of the chorus had already been sketched out. But the hardest part still lay ahead of me – I had no beginning, no active impetus for the melody to lead into the chorus that I have already hit upon.

After considering five or six musical images,[51] each of which proved unsatisfactory because of its schematic or artificial character, I chose the following version:

Version 1:

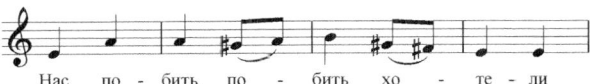

This version, which is based on the right kind of active musical thought, had to be honed down to produce the vivid melodic image that I thought was needed to fit the text's robust opening.

In the chosen version, there were still some aspects that undermined and softened the robustness of the musical image. The melody was too soft! What's the problem? Let's think about it.

After repeating this version several times, I convinced myself that the G♯ in the second and third bars gives the melody that softness which, in my opinion, is superfluous. Changing these notes, I arrived at the following version:

---

[51] We render the Russian idiom *muzikal'nïy obraz* literally as 'musical image' instead of using a more familiar English phrase such as 'musical idea' or 'musical figure', because the word 'image' is of significance in the present context. Lenin's notes on aesthetics took the arts to be, in various ways, reflections of reality, and the phrase 'musical image' was later taken up by Soviet writers on music to suggest that melodic patterns also somehow reflected reality.

Version 2:

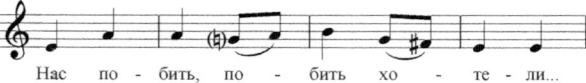

That's better! But another thing occurs to me: the song starts off rather well, but then suddenly in the third bar the melody gets stuck on the note B, as if it has tripped up, and falls down. It sounds like it has taken fright and fallen. Not good! I would need to make the retreat smoother, more organised, so that then I could rise again more robustly and reposition myself at the top [of the melodic line].

Version 3:

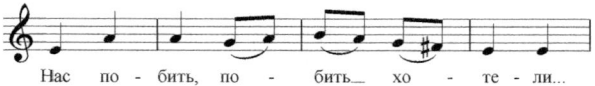

Yes! I've got an organised, gradual retreat to my prepared positions. All is correct. Let's go on. But something is still not quite right!

I check once again, listen carefully and think. I find that the second crotchet of the second bar weakens the vividness of the melody's descent in the third bar, as if anticipating it, unduly. I remove this melodic gesture, replace it with something more drastic and come up with the following version:

Version 4

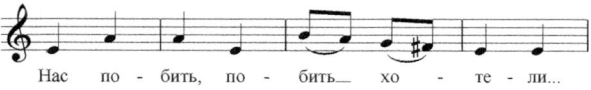

That's better already! But don't you feel, I ask myself, that you've got too many Es in this phrase, don't you feel that this note is like a cable preventing the melody from leaving its moorings? How could I loosen it a little?

Version 5:

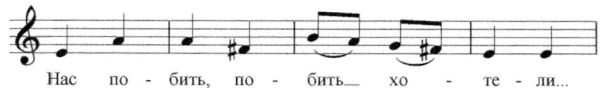

Something at the beginning still doesn't satisfy me. The leap of a fourth here can give the impression of an incorrect grammatical [sic] stress: '*nas pόbit*', and then there is still that E at the start, anticipating the end of the phrase, where the same note appears, and sounding as if it only starts on the second attempt, after climbing up a step. This goes against my whole approach. Let's get rid of that E! And then after some more work:

Version 6:

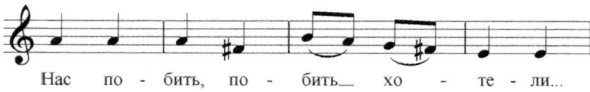

Now everything seems fine, aside from the ending. This seems to be taking a lie down. It fudges the robust beginning of the song. Let's make it more active, let's pull it up onto its feet!

Version 7:

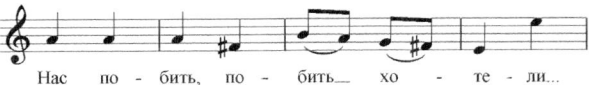

Taking into account now the range that would be comfortable for mass singing, I shift the song down by a tone and, after adding a rest at the end for breathing, I arrive at the final version:

Version 8:

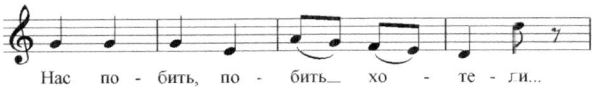

I won't demonstrate in detail the rest of the working process for the melodic contours and the form of this mass song. I will only point out that the phrase in the chorus '*togo dozhidalisya*' became the starting point for a phrase in the verse '*Nas pobit, pïtalisya*', the only difference being that the melodic line in the verse goes up, rising towards the climax (the highest point) of the chorus.

For comparison, I've supplied the original version of the song. Comrades will be able to trace how the final, published version differs from the first version.

Original version:

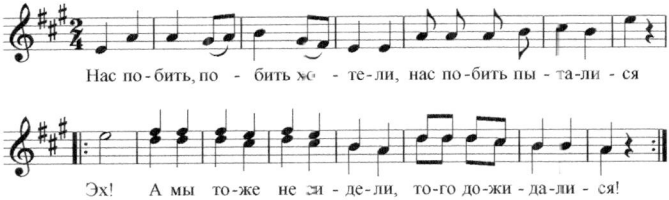

I think that in order to create a mass proletarian song, two conditions are required, among others: a clear vision of the image and the goal of the mass song, and correct use of the old culture (critically assimilated), together with the experience of proletarian composers.

Without the first, one cannot even create the necessary basis for the mass song, while the second will help composers to realise their ideas and convey them to the masses.

I would ask the comrades working on mass songs and the music activists introducing new proletarian songs to the masses to send me their comments on this essay, mentioning both its shortcomings and positive aspects.

The question of sharing creative experiences in the sphere of music is now on the agenda for the first time, and it can be solved correctly by forging a practical connection between the composer and the creative proletarian youth, with the music activists among workers and with the broad proletarian musical public.

I think that responses from different parts of the country will allow me to return to this topic once more on the pages of this journal.

1932
The Rules Change

'How did it happen that the whole of RAPM was left standing alone, while everyone else turned to Comrade Stalin for protection?'[1] This was the question thrown at members of RAPM, who had been called to attend a special closed session of the Narkompros Collegium on 26 February 1932. What brought RAPM to this point was the so-called 'Gnesin affair', when a fight with Vseroskomdram peaked in an open and bitter confrontation with one man who would not retreat – the composer and Conservatoire professor Mikhail Gnesin. A man of strong views, Gnesin retained his independence and refrained from aligning himself with any group during the 1920s. In 1928, for example, we find him opposing Goldenweiser and taking the side of Pedfak (he became its Dean). But later he fought against Rabfak, which had caused a lowering of standards that dismayed him. During the previous year, he had been involved in several highly publicised events. The first was a discussion of his own music at a Conservatoire 'production meeting', where he made an unguarded comment:

> [I] once had the opportunity to play my part in the life of a particular peasant who is now a well-known writer, Chapygin.[2] I could hold him in great affection, I could assist him in his work, learn from him and also teach him some things, but I have always felt that next to him I am a complex man, that my thoughts and feelings were more complex, and his were simpler.[3]

The Proletarian Musician soon published a report on the meeting under the title 'I am a complex man', portraying him as a profoundly alien and reactionary representative of bourgeois intelligentsia.[4] Gnesin became a favourite RAPM target.

But Gnesin did not flinch, and played an active part in the criticisms of RAPM at both the October and December meetings of Vseroskomdram. He spoke his mind as freely as before, and some of his words found their way into a denunciation RAPM sent to Narkompros. The Narkompros official Mikhail Arkadyev preserved the passage, adding his emphasis to the most offending phrase:

> I am not entirely sure that I can put my complete trust in Marxist criticism. It is absolutely right that Marxist criticism, more than any other kind of

---

[1] Arkadyev's letter to Selitsky (Stalin's Secretariat), RGALI, f. 645 (Glaviskusstvo), op. 1, ye. kh. 352, ll. 51–2. There is no date on this copy of the letter, but the content locates it in early 1932, and most probably in February.

[2] Aleksey Pavlovich Chapygin (1870–1937) was by that stage already the author of a large novel about Stepan Razin and of many other smaller works.

[3] Transcript of Gnesin's answers to questions on 24 Mar. 1931, 'Vïstupleniya na zasedaniyakh v Moskovskoy konservatorii …', RGALI, fond 2954 (Gnesin), op. 1, ye. kh. 139, ll. 6–7.

[4] '"Ya slozhnïy chelovek" … M. F. Gnesin o sebe i okruzhayushchey ego deystvitel'nosti', *Proletarskiy muzïkant*, no. 8 (1931), 22–8.

criticism, can take upon itself the task of predicting the future. But even so, the failure of a prediction is always possible, especially in the present world, and when the method has not yet been perfected – when completely different things are thrown into the same pile. We don't need to look at the musical world – TAKE PHILOSOPHY, WHICH CHANGES EVERY YEAR. What is now considered Marxist will become non-Marxist next year. Thus, changes are possible. What is now in tune with [the present directives] may become out-of-tune in a year's time. I accept that Marxist criticism, compared to other branches of critical thought, establishes a better basis for looking at a work as a whole and trying to crystallise its class essence. Nevertheless, a lot of mistakes are still being made.[5]

RAPM, reassured that Gnesin would be an easy target, began a full-scale persecution against him, putting his professorship at stake. Among the weak points they uncovered was his advocacy of Jewish national music, which, he thought, should evolve along the same lines as Russian music under the Kuchka, giving RAPM a pretext for adding 'bourgeois nationalism' to Gnesin's list of offences. (The Kuchka's official prestige under Socialist Realism was nowhere to be seen in 1932.) At this point, Gnesin decided he had nothing to lose by writing a letter to Stalin, putting his career on the line and asking for a wise judgement:

> If I am not right, then let me be 'persecuted', for I must have deserved it. But if the truth is on my side in any of these matters, then significant changes need to be made in the way music is run.[6]

Gnesin gave Stalin a lengthy and frank description of the current situation in the musical world. He spoke about concert life:

> I maintain that under the influence of erroneous, baseless and clichéd characteristics worked out in the RAPM laboratory, almost the entire repertoire disappeared from the programmes of concert institutions and schools everywhere in the country during the past two years. Every performer, on returning from a concert tour, tells us that in one town he couldn't play Bach, a church composer, in another Chopin, a salon musician, and in a third – Schumann, as a bourgeois romantic [...]

He spoke about the Muzgiz and its plans for a new literature of piano instruction:

> To insist that studies in octaves or trills are to be written on Soviet topics is to open the way towards blatant opportunism and to discredit any class criterion in art. The students will laugh when they find studies in 'broken octaves' or 'double thirds' appearing under pretentious titles like 'A shockworker of the Sormovo factory at labour' or 'Removing the Veil from Uzbek women'.

---

[5] RGALI, f. 2954 (Gnesin), op. 1, ye. kh. 139, l. 167. The letter was first published in Yekaterina Vlasova in '"Venera Milosskaya" i printsipï 1789 goda', *Sovetskaya muzïka* (1993), no. 3, 178–85.

[6] Ibid.

Finally, he spoke about the teaching of composition, which mattered most to him:

> In response to a suggestion I had made – that students should work through preparatory technical sketches before tackling 'production' assignments – my graduate student Cmrd. Davidenko claimed that 'by raising the question of quality, you slow down the pace of production'. [...] Later [this was twisted, and] I was directly accused of protesting against Stalin's pace in the study of composers because of my political tendencies.

Gnesin's letter to Stalin, and a further letter from 36 professors in support of Gnesin's position, prompted the Soviet leader to take an interest in the matter, as is clear from a letter sent by Arkadyev, a member of the Narkompros Collegium, to Selitsky of Stalin's Secretariat:[7] Stalin, through his Secretariat, had evidently demanded that Narkompros clarify its position regarding the dispute.[8] Arkadyev's response throws much light on Narkompros's attitudes during the final struggles that preceded RAPM's final disbandment. Arkadyev reports that Gnesin, in 1931, had given several speeches at meetings held by Vseroskomdram; in these speeches, 'together with some correct observations of the situation on the music front, there were several incorrect statements that were even to some extent reactionary'. Arkadyev quotes these contested statements at length, placing the most troubling phrases in upper-case letters, so that his letter looks like a denunciation of Gnesin at first glance (see Arkadyev quoting Gnesin above).

Turning to Gnesin's most recent Vseroskomdram speech, given in December 1931, Arkadyev emphasises that the source of Gnesin's criticisms of RAPM was 'not from our positions'. But here the direction of his report changes, and he castigates RAPM for its reaction to the speech, a reaction that he says was 'on no account correct politically'. This had taken the form of a review in *Proletarian Musician* that condemned Gnesin,[9] and Arkadyev argues that it failed to address the current alignment of forces among musicians, with the result that the majority of Soviet composers were repulsed by RAPM's behaviour, and felt obliged to support Gnesin. The ending of Arkadyev's letter is quite surprising, and would indicate that the imminent demise of the proletarianist organisations had already been discussed at the most senior levels:

> Regarding Gnesin, no administrative measures have been imposed. An attempt by the leftist elements among the teachers and students of the Moscow Conservatoire to remove him from the professorial ranks was rebuffed just in time, and decisively. At present, Gnesin is composing a large symphonic work for the fifteenth anniversary of October, commissioned by Muzgiz. The Arts and Literature Department [of Narkompros] has made Professor Gnesin a member of its Musical Council and intends to deploy him in its work.

---

[7] Viktor Nikolayevich Selitsky (1885–1936) was a professional revolutionary, an old Bolshevik, worked for OGPU from 1923 to 1936 and was at this point a secretary in Stalin's Secretariat.

[8] See. fn. 1.

[9] D. Zhitomirskiy, '"Povest' o rïzhem Motele" Mikhaila Gnesina', *Proletarskiy muzïkant*, no. 10 (1931), 27–31, 140.

As for the general matter of RAPM's leftist deviations in musical politics, and also the particular matter of the fellow travellers' cadres, Narkompos has made its opinions clear through Comrade Epshteyn's speech at the All-Union Congress of Rabis.[10]

Comrade Epshteyn roundly criticised RAPM for its mistakes, and suggested that such leftist deviations only help reactionary elements on the music front.

[...] In order to correct RAPM's line, we are announcing that there will be a special closed session on 26 February 1932, and this must finally liquidate all the leftist tendencies that have surfaced in the treatment of Gnesin and other fellow-travelling composers.[11]

Did RAPM members sense that defeat was in the air? Let us hear a voice from the other side in the form of a striking letter written by Davidenko (signing off as 'Shura') to his comrades-in-arms, Zara Levina (Zaryushka) and Nikolai Chemberdzhi (Kolyushka). A married couple, Zaryushka and Kolyushka were far away from the din of the capital cities, on a RAPM assignment to the Stalingrad Tractor Plant. Establishing a RAPM cell there wasn't easy: they had to fight foxtrot-loving cultural activists and also encountered workers who sang Davidenko's hit 'They wanted to beat us' to a distorted and vulgar tune.[12] Davidenko, in this letter, is trying to raise their morale with some fighting talk, but he cannot hide his worries about criticism from the Party. From his letter we get a different perspective on the events of late 1931 and early 1932:

My dear Kolyushka and Zaryushka!

You haven't written for a long time, you bastards, but I'll willingly forgive you because of your business and especially your creative work. Judging from your letter and the materials you sent, you are managing to get things done, and some of them rather well. I think when you were leaving you hardly expected to find nothing but roses and rivers of milk and honey there, and the contradictions that have arisen in the course of your work were probably not unexpected. The question is, how to get rid of them? The crux of the matter is tactics and the correct line. I could smell from between the lines of your letter that you've got more than enough fire and heat, and therefore there is a danger of 'deviations'. You have to be firmer, but at the same time more careful. Not administrative means, but education. Flexibility, and yet at the same time a principled position. We've all got to learn some of this from Lyovka [Lev Lebedinsky]. So first – no deviations. Second, you have to find support from the youth, especially in the Komsomol. To be in contact always, and to work together. It is most important to gain authority there. And then to spread tentacles into all the other organisations. More statements in the local press, but with lively, concrete examples from

[10] M. S. Epshteyn was at that time head of Glavsotsvos (see Glossary entry for Epshteyn).

[11] See. fn. 1, l. 52.

[12] Chemberdzhi's letter to Davidenko of 2 Feb. 1932 and Levina's letter to Davidenko, n.d., GTsMMK, fond 30 (Davidenko), ye. kh. 109 and 89.

everyday musical life. [...] More life and spirit, keeping in mind the worker activists. As for your creative work, I think you will just have to plan it out and collect material, even without starting to shape it. Try to immerse yourself in your surroundings. Get to know the shock workers and spend more time with them at the meetings, but perhaps also over a bottle of beer (I ask you not to take this in a vulgar way). What really worries me – please forgive my frankness – are your clothes. Your clothing should let you blend in with your milieu, but the clothes you actually wear still display something of the petit-bourgeois influences that you still haven't overcome. Wear some kind of overalls, or something like that. The same goes for the food. Guzzle away in their canteen and lead the agitation for proletarian music there. I am very glad that you have brought your work to such a high temperature – let it be the same in your compositions. As a trace of your presence, you would need to leave behind at least a circle of RAPM friends. Are you doing anything in this direction? Vit'ka [Victor Belïy], Keldysh and I have been to Leningrad for the Vseroskomdram conference. There we smashed Rafalovich's face in. Organised a team of fellow travellers (Ryazanov, Yudin, Tyulin, and others), two youth brigades (Dzerzhinsky, Chicherina, and others),[13] held a production meeting at the Leningrad Conservatoire, drank all the beer in Leningrad and ate up all the pasties. In Moscow, the Vseroskomdram composers' concerts have started. Boredom and tedium. Everything shabby, scruffy and smelly has crawled out into the light once again. Again the public is full of mothballed old ladies, respectable-looking balding old men, chewed-over young ladies and NEPmen from the Okhotny market, Khayt and Kruchinin presiding.[14] Atomyan [sic] runs around and licks everyone's a***. Gnesin wrote a letter to Stalin's secretariat. The old man is in trouble now. 'Ah – ah – ah! Oh my God!' [*Oy-oy-oy – bozhe moy!*].[15] Psha [Pshibïshevskiy] is thinking of fleeing the VMSh. The cell isn't letting him do that. Bor'ka [Boris Shekhter] and I have taken our leave of the VMSh until ... the fifteenth anniversary. Agreed that with Rashnovskaya

---

[13] Vasily Yevgenyevich Rafalovich (1900–77) was a Leningrad theatre historian, and a member of the Leningrad Repertory Committee. He served as one of RAPM's critics (elsewhere he is mentioned by Belïy as a right opportunist, together with Ledogorov and Atovmyan). Pyotr Borisovich Ryazanov (1899–1932), was a Leningrad composer and musicologist, who at the time lectured on folk music in the Conservatoire. Mikhail Alekseyevich Yudin (1893–1948), composer, also taught at the Leningrad Conservatoire at that point, as was Yuriy Nikolayevich Tyulin (1893–1978), music theorist and composer. Ivan Ivanovich Dzerzhinsky (1909–78), would reach his early peak of fame as a composer for the opera *And Quiet Flows the Don* (*Tikhiy Don*), which was commended by Stalin in 1936. Sofya Nikolayevna Chicherina (1904–83), who was a niece of the famous G. V. Chicherin (the Soviet foreign minister in the 1920s) was then at the beginning of her career as a composer. She went on to write several symphonies.

[14] Yuli Khayt and Valentin Kruchinin were prolific composers of popular music (see Glossary).

[15] A reference to Gnesin's Jewishness.

and Litinsky[16] (he is now head of Composition). How do you like that? Isn't it great? I pushed Litinsky into a corner by saying that if he hasn't reformed by the fifteenth anniversary, we'll kill him! He got scared: 'I'm always with the Association', and so on. But we know him well – we need to be on our guard. [...]

With fighting RAPM greetings, (write to me),

Shura[17]

Davidenko was not present at the Narkompros meeting of 26 February, but Lebedinsky and Belïy both came – they were regarded by friends as the most politically astute members. Narkompros was represented by Epshteyn, Arkadyev and Gorodinsky, and the Conservatoire by Pshibïshevsky. From an imperfect and partial transcript of the meeting, the Narkompros representatives felt no need to mince their words and bluntly accused RAPM of alienating the majority of musicians.[18] Pshibïshevsky was also attacked, for allowing RAPM, whose members were 'extremely weak in technique', to take charge of the Conservatoire composition department, 'where a high level of technique is needed, rather than political literacy alone'. In the wake of this meeting, Pshibïshevsky was replaced by Stanislav Shatsky as head of the Conservatoire.

It is not clear how widely Stalin's reaction to Gnesin's letter was already known, but his recourse to the Party Secretary was seen by others as the way forward. In March, Stalin's Secretariat received another cry for help, this time from the composer Mosolov. Like Gnesin, Mosolov could also point to the fact that RAPM had labelled him a 'class enemy'. Similarly, he called for broader changes in musical life rather than for personal protection alone. But unlike Gnesin, Mosolov played the card of his success abroad, which was in such stark contrast with his persecution at home, a situation more common among Soviet writers rather than composers:

> I am neither published nor performed, I feel myself to be persecuted and entirely disenfranchised musician. I don't know what to do, but I can't work in such conditions.[19]

Mosolov told the story of his opera *The Dam* (about the construction of a power station), which lost its chance of being produced at the former Mariinsky because of an under-rehearsed audition of Act 1. He also told the story of his great

---

[16] Genrikh Ilyich Litinsky was a young Moscow composer (graduating from the Conservatoire in 1928), who was promoted to Head of the Conservatoire's Composition Department during the wave of RAPM-inspired reorganisations. No information on Rashnovskaya has been found.

[17] Letter from Davidenko to Chemberdzhi and Levina, undated, RGALI, f. 2315 (Chemberdzhi), op. 1, ye. kh. 32, ll. 1–4; fragments published in *Aleksandr Davidenko: Vospominaniya, stat'yi, materialï*, ed. by N. Martïnov (Leningrad: Muzïka, 1968).

[18] Transcript of the meeting with Comr. Epshteyn, RGALI, fond 645 (Glaviskusstvo), op. 1, ye. kh. 352, ll. 39–41.

[19] 'Iz neopublikovannogo arkhiva A. V. Mosolova', ed. by I. Barsova, *Sovetskaya muzïka* (1989), no. 7, 80–92.

success, *The Iron Foundry*, which had subsequently been banned from reprinting by Muzgiz. Still worse, when Universal Edition had persisted in its requests for the score and parts, Muzgiz threatened to destroy the engraved plates. RAPM should be told to desist, begged Mosolov, or, failing that, let me go abroad.

It seems improbable that Mosolov's letter could have played a major role in the final destruction of RAPM, but the timing suggested exactly this to musical Moscow. On 16 April, Derzhanovsky reported on this state of affairs to Prokofiev:

> Since my return to Moscow, some events of extraordinary import have unfolded here, events that are capable of restoring Soviet musical life to its normal and fruitful ways of functioning. Mosolov couldn't bear any more of the shameless and idiotic persecution he'd received from the RAPMites (whom you know very well), and so he wrote a letter to the General Secretary of the Party CC [i.e. Stalin]; the final paragraph, which I confess I had a hand in, spoke of the outrageous state of the musical front in general and of the RAPM's role as saboteurs. Mosolov's letter, which demonstrated the composers' trust in the Party, was accepted with extraordinary and benevolent attention. RAPM has now been crushed, their poisonous *Proletarian Musician* has been taken away from them, and the members will probably be removed from all responsible positions in concert, pedagogical and publishing departments. A new course has been boldly outlined in musical politics, and we, the Soviet musicians who have long striven to shift from fellow-travelling over to a union [with the Party] [*ot poputnichestva k soyuznichestvu*] – we are finally seeing the necessary conditions put in place for the essential reforms, in the spirit of Marxism-Leninism.[20]

(Derzhanovsky used the standard Soviet rhetoric of the day, as if Prokofiev was already a Soviet composer who likewise wanted to reform himself in the Marxist-Leninist spirit.)

It was comforting for Mosolov, Gnesin, or even Derzhanovsky to think that their influence had brought RAPM down. For that matter, it is comforting to the musicological mind today. But we must be realistic: the same outcome would have been seen even if every musician had kept silent. The development of musical events was only a modest parallel stream to the development of literary events, in which Stalin took personal interest (and even literary policy was partly determined by economic policy and major political events).

This is not the place to describe that parallel evolution of Soviet literary life, but we will jump in at the point we have already reached with music – the spring of 1932. By this stage, Stalin had received dozens of writers' complaints about RAPP's behaviour and its internal conflicts. By the time Gorky wrote to Stalin from Sorrento that 'the endless arguments and fights between different RAPP groups are, in my opinion, very harmful' (24 March);[21] the Politburo had already created

---

[20] Letter from Derzhanovsky to Prokofiev of 16 Apr. 1932, LPA, folder 29, f. 390.

[21] Gorky's letter to Stalin of 24 Mar. 1932, publ. in *Vlast' i khudozhestvennaya intelligentsiya: dokumentï TsK RKP(b) – VKP(b) – VChK – OGPU – NKVD o kul'turnoy politike, 1917–1953*, ed. by A. Artizov and O. Naumov (Moscow: Mezhdunarocnïy fond 'Demokratiya', 1999), 169.

a committee to deal with the issue, consisting of Stalin, Molotov, Kaganovich and two others.[22] It is not clear just how well briefed Gorky was, although he might well have received information on this subject after Stalin's lengthy meeting with Gorky's personal secretary P. P. Kryuchkov, which had taken place on 27 March.[23] In any case, the actual Politburo Resolution disbanding all the proletarian organisations was nicely timed for Gorky's return (25 April), so that he could start building the new Union of Soviet Writers with a clean slate. What the musicians who wrote to Stalin managed to achieve, without doubt, was the specific reference to RAPM by name in the Resolution (not every affected organisation was named). Even this needs to be kept in perspective, since the name was insufficiently known for it to be spelt correctly: it was abolished under the more sonorous acronym of 'RAMP'. At any rate, this elevated the stature of music in the Soviet cultural landscape while greatly diminishing the luckless members of RAMP.

As the momentous shift was about to be made public, composers received invitations to a two-day meeting with Bubnov, the Head of Narkompros (23 and 25 April). The whistleblowers Mosolov and Gnesin, together with Shebalin, represented Moscow; Shostakovich, Popov and Shteynberg were among the Leningrad delegation. The meeting began before the publication of the Resolution that would disband RAPM, but the direction of the flow was clear, so composers held nothing back in their complaints against RAPM, and the officials broadly concurred. Shatsky, the newly-appointed director of Moscow Conservatoire, placed some of the blame on the Conservatoire professors, who, according to him, had let Davidenko and other RAPMites occupy professorial positions, by 'retreating from the field without struggle'. The RAPM composers, Lebedinsky, Beliy, Davidenko, Keldysh, and Chemberdzhi, were given a chance to confess to their wrongdoings and declare that they would mend their ways, but they continued regardless, evidently imagining that their disputes with Narkompros could run on indefinitely. The second day of the meeting took place after the Resolution, and was devoted to the planning of musical life in the future, including the prospect of a specialised music journal that would represent Soviet composers as a united body (*Sovetskaya muzïka* started coming out in 1933).

By the end of May, the foundations of a new Composers' Union were laid; in Moscow the City Committee (*Gorkom*) of Composers was elected, which included the anti-RAPM activist Atovmyan, the centrist Glière, some composers of the Myaskovsky circle such as Gedike, Aleksandrov and Shebalin, but also representatives of the other side such as Vasilyev-Buglay and Shekhter – the RAPMites only lost their organisation, not their careers.[24] During the summer, the formation of the Union of Soviet Composers was declared (although it failed to hold Soviet-wide meetings until as late as 1948). The Board of the Moscow Regional Branch was headed by Arkadyev (with Goldenweiser as his deputy and Gorodinsky as Secretary) and included Myaskovsky, together with many of

---

[22] The committee was created on 8 March and also included Postïshev and Stetsky. See *Vlast' i khudozhestvennaya intelligentsiya*, 168.

[23] Arkadiy Vaksberg, *Gibel' burevestnika. M. Gor'kiy: posledniye dvadtsat' let* (Moscow: Terra–Sport, 1999), 265–6.

[24] 'Vïborï gorkoma kompozitorov', *Sovetskoye iskusstvo*, no. 24 (27 May 1932), 1.

his close associates, such as Aleksandrov, Feinberg, Shebalin, and Gedike; again, ex-RAPMites like Shekhter, Beliy, and Pshibïshevsky were able to join. It was, however, remarked in the press, that RAPM members still appeared unrepentant, even after they had belatedly declared their own disbandment at the end of June.[25]

In a speech to the directors of arts colleges, Arkadyev claimed that RAPM had distorted the Party line, and as soon as the Party found out about these distortions, they were corrected (the claim of temporary ignorance was a common gambit for all levels of officialdom, up to Stalin himself):

> Only very recently, we discovered that such popular revolutionary songs as 'For Soviet Power' (*Za vlast' Sovetov*), the Budyonny March, 'The Red Banner' (*Krasnoye znamya*), 'The Young Guard' (*Molodaya gvardiya*) and various others had apparently been banned from performance. We asked the relevant Soviet organs and found that they had never issued any such instructions; nevertheless, in the schools and colleges these songs went unperformed. After an investigation, it transpired that the ban on these songs was actually the outcome of administrative measures and agitation by RAPM activists. The same story emerged in the case of the ban on Mosolov's symphony *Zavod* [The Iron Foundry]. Mosolov's *Zavod* had never been banned by anyone, and yet we have information that in many places its performance was forbidden. Later, when we investigated the matter, it transpired that here again, the RAPM organisations had interfered.

Arkadyev continued setting out the (new) Party line by declaring that RAPM's canonisation of Beethoven and Musorgsky, and their 'elimination' of Chopin and Tchaikovsky were both to be opposed. He mocked RAPM's style of 'Marxist' music criticism, which made critics 'attempt to determine which musical phrase exemplified dialectical materialism, which revealed the face of class enemy, etc.'.[26]

Another reversal of musical politics was the treatment of opera, which was not merely rehabilitated, but placed in a position of central prestige. In this vein, Arkadyev complained in another paper that RAPM's theory of the 'withering away of opera' had (obviously enough) hindered the development of this genre in the Soviet Union. Noting that very few Soviet operas had been published, he pointed out that 'even such an undoubtedly interesting opera as Shostakovich's *Nose* remained unpublished by Muzgiz'. He declared that the foremost task was to encourage and facilitate the production of new Soviet operas, but also mentioned that existing Soviet operatic repertoire should be broadened to include works by Wagner, Mozart and Gluck.[27] This policy shift created a very benign environment for the premiere of Shostakovich's *Lady Macbeth of Mtsensk*, which

[25] 'Sozdan soyuz sovetskikh kompozitorov', *Sovetskoye iskusstvo*, no. 30 (3 July 1932), 1.

[26] 'O reshenii TsK o khudozhestvennom obrazovanii (Stenogramma vïstupleniya zav. Sektorom iskusstv Narkomprosa t. Arkad'yeva na konferentsii direktorov khudozhestvennykh tekhnikumov RSFSR)', *Sovetskoye iskusstvo*, no. 25 (3 June 1932), 1.

[27] 'Ob opernom teatre (doklad sektora iskusstv Kollegii Narkomprosa o sostoyanii opernogo i baletnogo iskusstva v strane)', *Sovetskoye iskusstvo*, no. 48 (21 Oct. 1932), 1.

was now brought to the stage with the speed of shock-workers. Rehearsals at the Nemirovich-Danchenko Music Theatre even began well before the last act was completed, and Shostakovich's semi-public demonstration of the opera on the piano was a great success and created much expectation.[28]

The most important piece for the fifteenth-anniversary celebrations proved to be Asafyev's ballet *The Flames of Paris*. Asafyev now reinvented himself as a ballet composer, drawing upon his early experience as a répétiteur and staff composer for the Mariinsky ballet. Official acclaim for *The Flames* ran so high that Asafyev was for a while touted as the next artistic director of the Bolshoi (although the appointment never took place).[29]

And so by the end of 1932, Soviet musical life had been shifted onto Socialist Realist tracks, and, officially at least, it remained there for the next 60 years. The musical canon of Socialist Realism at this point already contained a symphony, Myaskovsky's Twelfth, and a ballet, Asafyev's *Flames of Paris*. An opera, Shostakovich's *Lady Macbeth*, was expected to join them soon (and so it did for a short time). The foundations of an all-embracing Composers' Union were established, and the first edition of its publication, the journal *Sovetskaya muzïka*, was in press. Musicians knew their art would be supervised along ideological lines, but still expected a degree of artistic freedom, suggested by slogans such as 'the multi-faceted character of art' or 'broad and free competition between different styles and genres'.[30] Most importantly, they expected to be treated with respect by the state in return for their willing participation in the construction of a new musical life.

The terms of this new contract between the state and artistic intelligentsia were drawn in an atmosphere of peace and goodwill on both sides (even most of the former RAPM members, however disgruntled, were given the opportunity to participate). It was clear that the previous few years had thoroughly Sovietised the formerly reluctant intelligentsia. Yet for many Russian émigrés too, working in the USSR now seemed like an attractive prospect, especially in comparison with crisis-stricken Western Europe, and several wrote to Prokofiev to canvas his opinion on the matter or even to solicit his help. In a letter from one of these exchanges, written at the end of 1932, Prokofiev sums up his thoughts on the year's events in the Soviet Union:

> It's hard for me to voice my opinion on such an important issue, but I must say that the attitude to scientists and artists of every trend has significantly improved of late, while the interest of the masses in both words and sounds is extraordinary. As for me, I'll be very happy to travel to the USSR again in the spring.[31]

---

[28] Letter from Anton Dianov to Prokofiev of 16 Oct. 1932, LPA, folder 31, ff. 176–7; see also the reviews published below.

[29] Letter from Prokofiev to Malko of 11 Dec. 1932, LPA, folder 32, f. 49.

[30] 'Istoricheskaya konferentsiya', *Sovetskoye iskusstvo*, no. 27 (15 June 1932), 1.

[31] Letter from Prokofiev to D. N. Krachkovsky (dated end of 1932 from content), LPA, folder 32, f. 48.

※ ※ ※ ※ ※

'O perestroyke literaturno-khudozhestvennïkh organizatsiy. Rezolyutsiya TsK VKP(b) ot 23 aprelya 1932 goda' [On the restructuring of literary and artistic organisations. Resolution of the Central Committee of the VKP(b) of 23 Apr. 1932]. *Sovetskoye iskusstvo*, no. 20 (27 Apr. 1932), 1.

No decree or resolution in the first decade and a half after the Revolution wrought such an immediate and momentous change on the art world as this document from 1932. The disbandment of all proletarianist organisations ended the period of their domination, but it certainly did not signal a return to the status quo ante: the era of rivalry between motley artistic factions was also consigned to the past. Prior to the resolution, artistic unions were freely formed, but often had little power; the resolution declared that a single official union would be created for each of the arts and all professional artists were to join. At the same time, the aesthetic doctrine of Socialist Realism was being honed by the intellectual elite, to become the only aesthetic outlook available to the members of the new artistic Unions.

On the Restructuring of Literary and Artistic Organisations

Resolution of the Central Committee of the VKP(b) of 23 April 1932

The Central Committee notes that during recent years, on the basis of significant successes in socialist construction, literature and the arts have enjoyed a great burst of growth, in quality as well as in quantity. Several years ago, when the influence of alien elements was obvious in literature, being especially vigorous in the early NEP years, and when the cadres of proletarian literature were still weak, the Party took every step to help create and strengthen special proletarian organisations in the sphere of literature and art, in order to strengthen the positions of proletarian writers and art workers.

At present, while the cadres of proletarian literature and the arts have had time to grow, and while new writers and artists have come forward from the plants, factories, and collective farms, the limits of the existing literary and artistic proletarian organisations (VOAPP,[32] RAPP, RAMP [*sic*, i.e. RAPM], and others) are becoming too narrow and are impeding the serious development of artistic work. This creates a danger, namely that while these organisations have been the means for the utmost mobilisation of Soviet writers and artists in the tasks required by socialist construction, they could change into a means for cultivating group insularity, separation from the political goals of today and from important groups of writers and artists who are sympathetic to socialist construction.

Accordingly, this necessitates the restructuring of the literary and artistic

---

[32] VOAPP was the organisation uniting RAPP with all the other associations of proletarian writers, together with The Smithy.

organisations, and the widening of the base of their activities. On this basis, the Central Committee resolves:

1) To liquidate the association of proletarian writers (VOAPP, RAPP);
2) To unite all writers who support the platform of Soviet power and who strive to participate in socialist construction into a single union of Soviet writers, with a Communist fraction inside it;
3) To effect equivalent changes in other arts;
4) to entrust the Organising Bureau [Orgbyuro] with the task of working out measures for the implementation of this resolution.

'Na muzïkal'nom fronte' [On the Music Front], *Sovetskoye iskusstvo*, no. 20 (27 Apr. 1932), 1.

This Sovetskoye iskusstvo *editorial was printed together with the Resolution above.*

On the Music Front

The situation on the music front, especially in its creative sector [i.e. RAPM composers], cannot be considered satisfactory. If nothing is done to counteract certain facts that we have observed, this could hinder the further development of musical culture and its genuine reorientation towards the goals of socialist construction.

We are, of course, far from being like those pessimists of little faith, who are inclined to believe that musical composition is in a critical, if not hopeless situation. There is no basis for such a mood or for such talk.

A number of concerts showcasing the output of Soviet composers, organised by the Philharmonia and the Bolshoi theatre, demonstrate the high standard of our musicians and composers.

The quantity and quality of our composers is such that if they continue improving, and if they reject formalism, constructivism and the like, we shall soon have works that exceed in their mastery. It is clear that this should be accompanied by great efforts among the fellow travellers towards their ideological rearmament, and towards the task of reflecting socialist construction in our country through specifically musical means.

In this respect, it must be stated that we see a significant shift towards reform among the fellow travellers. By way of proof, it suffices to point to the latest works of the most outstanding composers, such as Myaskovsky, Shostakovich, Shebalin and others.

However, all is not well on the music front. To this day, we have not created the conditions that would stimulate the fellow travellers' reforms and help them switch to the subject matter of our times.

We need to admit that Soviet organisations have paid insufficient attention to the issue of providing guidance for the creative musical associations. Hence a series of mistakes and incorrect directives on the music front. Hence also the paradoxical situation in which RAPM, an organisation that has not yet gathered sufficient creative strength [i.e. whose composers are too weak], found itself in a position of leadership on the music front.

Hence the mistakes made by RAPM: although it correctly raised some basic political questions about the class character of music, it should have immersed itself in study simultaneously, to assimilate the technique and attain the mastery essential for its creative forces, but instead it awarded itself the role of mentor, to issue instructions to the fellow travellers.

A creative organisation can become a leader only when it manages to create great works, at a high level of mastery and written from the Marxist-Leninist perspective.

RAPM has not managed to create such works so far.

Instead of ensuring that its creative forces sat down to study and work, some representatives of RAPM indulged in self-advertising, and attempted to present the relatively weak works of its composers (like Davidenko's *Pod otkos*) as models for genuine proletarian works.

Such directives, from individual leaders representing RAPM, only confused the situation on the music front; and the elements of conceit, which were present when they criticised some fellow travellers, the lack of the necessary tact, and, at times, the incorrect approach to them (pasting on labels instead of making substantive criticisms) did not assist the ideological reform of the fellow travellers, but only aggravated relationships between the creative groups.

This situation demands decisive administrative measures, which would remove all the obstacles that hinder and complicate creative work. The Resolution of the Central Committee on the restructuring of the literary and artistic organisations has put an end to the insularity of creative organisations (RAPM) that have paid scant attention to work with fellow travellers, and then did so only by giving orders.

Proletarian musicians need to reform their work in such a way that when they enter into separate creative groups within the union, they can actively assist in the fellow travellers' reform, not by knocking them unconscious, as in the past, but by means of friendly criticism and help towards the assimilation of Marxist-Leninist doctrine in music.

※ ※ ※ ※ ※

D. Kabalevskiy, 'Simfoniya bor'bï: o 12-y simfonii N. Ya. Myaskovskogo' [Symphony of Struggle: On Myaskovsky's Twelfth Symphony], *Sovetskoye iskusstvo*, no. 27 (15 June 1932), 3.

Kabalevsky, the writer of this review, was one of Myaskovsky's most prominent former students, but he proved much more politically astute than his teacher. This review performed a useful service for Myaskovsky, by supplying the musical public (and officials) with a programme for his new symphony, his Twelfth, dubbed the 'Collective Farm Symphony'. Myaskovsky had failed to claim the political capital this would have earned him, and did not publicise the programme, although rumours of its existence had circulated in advance of the premiere; Kabalevsky now made good the omission. The variety of music criticism that appears here focuses on the 'content' of a purely instrumental work, but stops short of the 'vulgar' or forced descriptive writing sometimes produced by less sophisticated members of RAPM. Kabalevsky's approach here anticipated the norm for Socialist Realist critical writing.

D. Kabalevsky
Symphony of Struggle:
On Myaskovsky's Twelfth Symphony

Myaskovsky's Twelfth Symphony, performed in the latest concert at the USSR Bolshoi Theatre, attracted much attention and won the interest of the wider musical public. This interest can be explained not only by the fact that it was the premiere of a new symphony by the most important Soviet symphonist, but also because a large number of printed and oral sources made it known that the symphony was programmatic, being entitled 'The Collective Farm Symphony'. The programme was not publicised at the premiere, however, and this created much confusion in the evaluation of the work, leading to various arbitrary interpretations.

The programme of the Twelfth Symphony emerged well before its composition – it was not something imposed from the outside. The symphony's concept is the socialist reconstruction of the countryside. Three phases are given in succession: the tsarist countryside, with unbearable forced labour that oppressed the people, then the struggle for the new socialist countryside – for collective labour – and finally a song of the new life, of joyful liberated labour, a song of socialism. This programme unfolds successively in the symphony's three movements. But it would be more correct to define the symphony not as a tale of the countryside as a whole, but as the tale of man who grows and changes together with the countryside, its everyday life and its struggles, to attain the new way of life. The listener is presented with the various stages in this struggle, with all their contradictions, falls and ascents.

The first movement of the symphony paints a picture of the old, pre-revolutionary countryside. This movement is structured with utmost architectonic clarity. The music develops towards the centre of the movement and then follows a 'mirror reflection' pattern, repeating all the phases of that development in reverse order and bringing us in the end to an almost exact restatement of the first bars of the symphony.

The symphony begins with a theme of the 'shepherd's pipe' variety, vividly depicting the Russian country landscape with its gloominess, melancholy and despair. Against the background of this melancholy picture, a person appears on the scene, a worker of the old countryside, oppressed and exhausted by his hard labour. This second phase develops, brightening up somewhat, and then follows the middle episode of the first movement – a folk dance. Uncertain at first, it becomes increasingly expansive, but never turns into real, healthy merry-making; there is no cheeriness, the dance moves within fixed limits, and this inebriated merriment replaces the main gloomy and oppressed mood for only a short time. The latter reappears and, gradually contracting and decreasing in its movement, takes us back to the introductory passage with the same 'shepherd's pipe' theme. This theme also fades away gradually; thus ends the first movement of the symphony.

The rounded, closed character of this movement gives us an impression of great constraint and hopelessness. Severe themes in a folk style are developed in a restrained manner, and even the middle section cannot break away from the general severity; they suggest a vivid picture of the old Russian countryside, but mainly of the external aspect, the landscape. This picture is even somewhat idealised: the rounded and soft themes, the character of their presentation and development, and, lastly, the rounded character of the whole movement – none of these sufficiently expose the contradictions of the phenomenon depicted, and we hardly see any of the negative aspects of the old countryside. We don't see enough of the aspects that had to be fought. In the foreground, and subordinating everything else to itself, is the image of one person against the background of the landscape – a person who is psychologically depressed, in low spirits. This conception, which is basically correct, is not fully completed. This is the first of the symphony's contradictions.

The second movement begins with a bugle call to attention. The struggle begins. The main theme, dark and unstable, is opposed by a second, 'Samoyed' theme, which is much brighter and more stable, but very primitive and static in its structure. Further on, a new and energetic melody appears. This theme, as if organising the struggle, penetrates not only the second movement of the symphony, but its finale as well, unifying them thematically. In the middle episode of the second movement (the development section), we find these themes submitted to intensive development, leading to a great build-up. The bugle call again, and the recapitulation repeats all the stages of the struggle in a condensed form (from the exposition), but does not lead to the high point that had been reached earlier. The bugle call, repeated once again, closes the second movement of the symphony.

In this movement we see the struggle of the conception: the idea cannot be fitted into a scheme; and the scheme doesn't allow the idea to develop fully and restrains the entire conception of the movement. In its dramatic intensity and dynamic saturation, this movement leaves the ordinary scherzo far behind. However, we find the same essentially rounded and closed character as we did in the first movement. The 'sonata scheme' undoubtedly dominates over the development of the conception. This is the symphony's second contradiction.

At last, the finale. A victorious song, the song of a new socialist countryside – such is the conception of this movement. The first theme, of a victorious, jubilant character, is followed by a second that is much softer and attains a soaring lyricism. But the struggle is not yet over: a theme from the first movement reappears, showing that the old has not yet been overcome completely; this is followed by the finale theme, which leads this time to the formation of something qualitatively new: a mass song and mass dance, which have grown from the first finale theme. The symphony ends with a quick, lively dance. Here the scheme is overcome, subordinated to the logical development of the idea.

What conclusions can be drawn from this brief, schematic overview? There can be no doubting that Myaskovsky's Twelfth Symphony is one of the most important events in our musical life over the past few years. The very fact that such a great master has made the transfer to Soviet subject matter is very significant in itself. This subject matter was nevertheless approached from an individualistic outlook, which follows naturally enough from the deeply individualistic direction of his earlier works. Yet this does not diminish the interest and significance of the symphony, and neither do the contradictions noted earlier. The new content has inevitably led to a new approach to expressive means: a clarity and distinctness of melodic outlines and harmony, transparency and lucidity in the orchestral writing – these qualities, which were hinted at in Myaskovsky's recent work, find their full expression in the Twelfth.

Turning briefly to the performance of the symphony, it is necessary to point out that Coates, who was conducting, must have failed to grasp the symphony's content. An emphasis on individual moments that were superficially beautiful and showy, which generally characterises Coates as a conductor, was of little help in revealing the composer's conception. Thus the entire second movement was directed towards to the enjoyment of individual sonorities, and the dance, which was played as a simple scherzo, lost its dynamism, drive and tension. The finale was too sweetly lyrical, with the emphasis once again on individual moments of colourful orchestration. And so the premiere of the Twelfth Symphony did not, on the whole, allow us an opportunity to hear it performed in a correct manner.

'"Ledi Makbet Mtsentskogo uyezda". Novaya opera Dmitriya Shostakovicha' [*Lady Macbeth of the Mtsensk District*, a new opera by Dmitriy Shostakovich], *Sovetskoye iskusstvo*, no. 47 (16 Oct. 1932), 3, including D. Shostakovich, 'Tragediya-satira' [A Tragedy-Satire] and M. Grinberg, 'Opera i kompozitor' [Opera and the Composer].

The following two pieces appeared together, taking up an unprecedentedly large amount of space for a preview of a work that was not yet finished. This indicates Shostakovich's uniquely high status even at this early juncture, and also the great burden of expectation placed on his second opera. Lady Macbeth *was premiered in 1934, almost simultaneously, by both the Maly Opera in Leningrad and the Nemirovich-Danchenko Theatre in Moscow, and it ran for two years to great acclaim. This phase in the opera's life was brought to a close by the notorious denunciatory article in* Pravda, *'Chaos instead of Music' (28 January 1936), which followed in the wake of Stalin's attendance at a performance of the opera.*

D. Shostakovich
A Tragedy-Satire
[*Lady Macbeth of the Mtsensk District*]

I have been working on *Lady Macbeth* for about two and a half years. It is part of a trilogy I conceived, which is devoted to the position of Russian women in different eras. The plot of *Lady Macbeth of the Mtsensk District* is borrowed from Leskov's novella of the same name. This novella is striking for its exceptional vividness and intensity. I think it is one of the finest for its very truthful and tragic portrayal of the fate of a talented, intelligent and outstanding woman, who is being stifled by the nightmarish conditions of pre-Revolutionary Russia. In his anniversary speech, Maxim Gorky said: 'We need to study. We need to find out about our country, about its past, its present and its future'. And Leskov's novella corresponds to Gorky's demand better than anything else. For the composer, *Lady Macbeth* is quite literally a treasure. The vividly drawn characters and the dramatic conflicts I found altogether gripping. The libretto was developed by A. G. Preys, the young Leningrad playwright, together with me. It is almost entirely built upon Leskov, except for Act 3, which, for greater social weight, diverges slightly from Leskov. A scene in the police department has been introduced, while the murder of Yekaterina Lvovna's nephew has been taken out.

I have interpreted the plot in a tragic aspect. I would say that *Lady Macbeth* can be called a tragic-satirical opera. In spite of the fact that Yekaterina Lvovna is the murderer of her husband and her father-in-law, I still sympathise with her. I tried to paint her everyday surroundings in a dark and satirical manner. By 'satirical' I don't mean anything 'amusing' or 'scoffing'. On the contrary, I tried to create in *Lady Macbeth* a satire that lays things bare, that rips off the masks and makes you loathe the dreadful lawless oppression [*proizvol*] and harassments of merchant life.

Lady Macbeth's musical material is very different from that of my previous operatic work, *The Nose*. It is my deep conviction that opera is about singing. And all the vocal parts in *Lady Macbeth* are singable, and cantilena-like. The orchestra, in some moments of high emotion, becomes very weighty. I have also introduced a military band and various additional instruments. So far, I have written three acts; there should be four altogether. I am expecting to finish it in about three or four months' time.

M. Grinberg

The Opera and the Composer
[*Lady Macbeth of the Mtsensk District*]

Four deaths ... three murders and one suicide. Passionate love scenes ... A sumptuous wedding feast – a heart-rending plot that is unashamedly operatic. For all its apparent clichés, however, *Lady Macbeth* is a challenge to every kind of operatic tradition, a rejection of all that is trivial and pompous in opera – it is a work of exceptional brilliance and boldness, a work of great and mature mastery. Such is Shostakovich's *Lady Macbeth*.

For his opera's plot, Shostakovich drew upon the wonderful novella by Leskov that tells of a merchant's wife, Yekaterina Lvovna, who falls in love with a steward, and who goes on to poison her father-in-law and then murder her husband for love. But Shostakovich does not want to follow the well-trodden path of the ordinary opera libretto. Being a truly contemporary Soviet composer, he filters all his thoughts through social categories and relations. Behind the personal drama of individuals he sees a social drama of the period: Yekaterina Lvovna's tragedy is understood by Shostakovich as the inevitable consequence of social conflicts under Nicholas I. In *Lady Macbeth*, many of the scenes and characterisations, and certain musical passages all provide a graphic and strongly social representation of the period. Such are the scenes of Sergei's flogging, the carousing of the stewards, the wedding, the scene of the police. These scenes are of great interest, for in them we see for the first time a successful operatic attempt to 'expose the past'; Shostakovich does not attempt to offer us a kind of lyrical sadness over this past in the manner of *Eugene Onegin*, nor does he idealise the life of the people, which was certainly a characteristic of the Kuchkists, but instead he gives us authentic, real life in all its hopelessness, oppression and savagery under Nicholas's regime. And in this respect, all the aforementioned scenes (which haven't yet been brought to completion) represent something new in opera.

A love intrigue dominates *Lady Macbeth*, but it is interesting to see how the composer approaches it musically. *Lady Macbeth* knows nothing of erotic refinements and supersensual ecstasies. But what it does offer us, wherever the plot demands it, is a vivid representation of a deliberately coarse and openly animalistic love.

Speaking of the novel in *Lady Macbeth*, one needs to mention musical characterisation – the composer's approach to the musical portrayal of his characters musically. These characterisations are very laconic, distinctive and graphic. Take Yekaterina Lvovna: how masterfully those plaintive intonations, taken at a slower pace, convey her longing and her thirst for affection! And throughout the three acts, with all the changes, in the most dramatically acute moments, her speech does not lose its character of drawn-out and intense songfulness. Or take Sergei, a steward 'touched' by culture. Shostakovich uses an original, novel device to expose this character. When Sergei is in Yekaterina Lvovna's room at night, he tries to make a good impression and tells her of his longing, yet at this moment in the orchestra a snide, vulgar polka appears, which is revealingly merry. Or [take] Boris Timofeyevich, Yekaterina Lvovna's father-in-law. In the pre-dawn twilight, he is wandering around the house, and wouldn't resist the temptation to make a pass at his daughter-in-law. He can't sleep – he is remembering his past. And here, in the midst of completely calm and contemplative music, a rollicking, insolent, provincial mazurka breaks out in the orchestra. The effect is totally astonishing. It is notable that the music of Boris Timofeyevich had already contained some distant hint of the mazurka rhythm. It is as if Shostakovich is trying to provide dynamic development for the character. There is something natural and organic about it. At times, individual passages in *Lady Macbeth* give an impression of musical mischief-making; but even behind the musical pranks, one can perceive an intelligent mastery.

Lady Macbeth represents a new phase in Shostakovich's œuvre. But the best of the 'old' Shostakovich – his elemental power, his artistic temperament, his wilful strength and cool-burning passion – all this can still be detected in the music of *Lady Macbeth*. And, as usual, we find the striking power of his mastery, the clear structural organisation, the iron logic and rhythmic discipline, which holds back the surging, overwhelming energy. The flogging scene, the wonderful love scenes, the scene of Yekaterina Lvovna's argument with her husband, the wedding and the arrest scene – in these we recognise the 'old' Shostakovich, the traits of his [Symphony] *To October* or the *May* Symphony. At the same time, there are many new traits in the music of *Lady Macbeth*. Above all, a lyricism and warmth have appeared in Shostakovich. His First Symphony contained elements of lyricism, but then, starting with *October*, which was a turning point in his creative development, this lyrical current was completely submerged for a time. His spiky musical language lost its songful elements. Now Shostakovich himself says that opera is about singing, and in many passages Shostakovich offers expressive musical lyricism, not to mention the fact that all the parts are very cantilena-like. This is especially the case in his portrayal of the protagonist, Yekaterina Lvovna. In some places her lyricism is stylised: Shostakovich masterfully, and with apparent irony, imitates the style of Russian dilettanti of the eighteenth century [sic; actually early nineteenth century], such as Gurilyov and Varlamov. His melodies characterising 'the lady' contain hidden elements from Russian folk song and from the Gurilyov-Varlamov type of salon song [*romans*]. But this is not the cool stylisation of a gourmet, nor the aestheticised grotesque of Stravinsky's *Mavra*. In Shostakovich, the grotesque is softened by a current of genuine live feeling. For example, we find a little masterpiece in a song such as the surprisingly simple and expressive, 'The foal runs after the filly'. In the intonational curves of this song, in its unexpectedly fresh and acutely novel harmonies, we can sometimes hear distant echoes of

Prokofiev (we may recall the lyrical theme from the second movement of his Third Piano Concerto). But the point is that as with every authentic, genuine creation, we can find various influences in Shostakovich, but they are always transcended; we always perceive something uniquely Shostakovichean – his own creative style. Shostakovich's music also possesses a calm and deeply contemplative strain: the majestic and profound musical entr'acte between Scenes 4 and 5 comes across exactly in the manner of Bach. The beginning of Act 2, the night scene (Scene 5) and Yekaterina Lvovna's dream – all these are wonderful pages in the 'new' Shostakovich. I am listing individual passages that are particularly notable, but we can recall more exciting episodes – it would be hard to list them all. The whole of Act 2, Yekaterina Lvovna's scene in Act 1, the song of the 'seedy lout', the wedding, a portrayal of revolting drunken carousing in Act 3 – all these are most wonderful and memorable musical fragments.

Shostakovich has himself remarked on the novel devices he introduces in his orchestration. His orchestral textures can, at times, swell to a huge but dense sound. Some moments in the score deserve special mention. In Aksinya's Act 1 conversation with Sergei, a lonely bassoon is given an exceptionally expressive melody. Musicians will take delight in this fresh device much as Rimsky-Korsakov [*sic*; should be Tchaikovsky] once delighted us with the scene of Herman's letter reading (in the barracks) in *The Queen of Spades*, which is accompanied by a similarly lonely melody in the bass clarinet. With a single stroke, Shostakovich knows how to create characteristic motives that are laconic, vivid and witty. For example, he employs an octave jump in the bassoon to characterise Boris Timofeyevich, placing the image of a stupid and conceited old man immediately before us.

I would also like to mention the use of the alto flute against trombones at the beginning of Act 2, and the trombone solo against harps at the end of Act 2, and much else.

These are only first impressions, brief jottings on the new work. *Lady Macbeth* has not yet been completed. Only three of the four acts have been written. Much still needs to 'settle down' in the opera. There are some undoubted longueurs, and some weak and even unsuccessful passages. In our opinion, the scene with the ghost is unnecessary, and the priest's characteristic motive is not vivid enough.

When the opera is finished, the form will be more lucid, but even now it is quite beyond doubt that we have before us an outstanding work. The appearance of *Lady Macbeth* on our operatic stage is a milestone, for it is absolutely clear that, while the reform of our dramatic theatre is dependent on the development of Soviet dramaturgy, this can be also applied to opera. Only the emergence of new works, novel in content and in form, can help to overcome the stagnation of our operatic theatre.

※ ※ ※ ※ ※

Igor' Glebov (B. Asaf'yev), 'Muzïka "tretyego sosloviya"' [Music of the 'Third Estate'], *Sovetskoye iskusstvo*, no. 48 (21 Oct. 1932), 3.

> *At this point in Asafyev's transformation from musicologist to composer, he is quite modest about the value of his work, which he still sees in musicological terms: based on his research from primary sources (procured from Paris with the help of Prokofiev), he says that he has assembled a 'historical novel in music'. Again, as a musicologist, he summons his own 'intonation theory' to his aid ('intonations' were melodic idioms that carried social meaning). Asafyev gives his theory a Marxist slant, saying that in any given era, some of these idioms have 'progressive' associations, while others are 'decadent'. Some of his composer colleagues saw the resulting work as a mere compilation rather than a composition proper, but its great public and official success nevertheless launched Asafyev on his new career as a composer.*

Igor Glebov

Music of the 'Third Estate'
[On the Ballet *The Flames of Paris*]

The music of the ballet *The Flames of Paris* is partly a montage of material from our musico-historical heritage, largely from the era of the Great French Revolution, and partly a composition in the character and style of this material. My main aim was to draw from the music of the past those 'utterances' that are close to us, that resonate with us, and transfer them to the present day, using the means of contemporary technique. I looked at this music through the eyes of an historian: I was not so much interested in the individual achievements of this or that composer, but rather in the musical creation of a great era in all the richness of its content, both as a *historical document* and as live, passionate, and persuasive emotional speech, which conveys heroic uplift, great sorrow or the stormy joy of people's jubilation. I worked on this task not only as a dramatic composer, but also as an historical and theoretical musicologist, and as a writer, without avoiding the methods of the contemporary historical novel. This is why, in addition to composing music on the basis of what I had assimilated from the musical speech (or, more correctly, the musical language) of the Great French Revolution, I also quoted, paraphrased and developed the great amount of material I had in my hands, behaving in such cases as a historical writer, but without ever ceasing to be a musician. I repeat: I was composing a musico-historical novel, paraphrasing musico-historical documents in contemporary [i.e. French Revolutionary] instrumental language as far as I have understood it and assimilated it. Of course, I emphasised and dynamically expanded the musical documents, but where there are quotations, I did not change the character of the music. I tried not to interfere with the melodies or the main principles of voice-leading, since I saw them as essential stylistic indicators. But I juxtaposed pieces of material and orchestrated them in such a way that the content of the music would be revealed through a symphonically continuous development across the entire ballet, and in clear images, saturated by the ideological and emotional influence of our own reality. I put to one side my interests in musical archaeology and the classifications of the museum. And yet, because my 'musical narrative', through quotations and paraphrases, represents all that is most typical of the music of the French 'third estate' at the apex of its revolutionary struggle, the ballet is also a kind of illustrated musical anthology.

I now dare to speak generally and not only for myself: we have known little of the music of the Great French Revolution. When it was approached from a formal, aesthetic perspective, when one paid attention only to individual, named achievements and looked for original and autonomous conceptions, it seemed that the music heard in their theatres, salons and cafes, on their squares, boulevards and streets, on their battlefields, and at their mass festivities, rallies and so on, was all rather slight and unworthy of the majestic uplift of that era. But one needed only, by means of lengthy and careful explorations of musical creation as an ideological and emotional speech complex, to reveal in all its manifestations the deep and complicated contradictions dictated by the class war of the period; one needed only, as a result of this, to discover the clear traits and tendencies of the musical creation of the 'third estate' (I was greatly helped here by the 'documents' of eighteenth-century French music theatre), and then to compare these results with absolutist feudal music – and completely different evaluations emerged, a different understanding, a different interpretation of the musical events and phenomena of that time. There is no space here to talk about all of my work and its consequences for Soviet musicology in the prospects it offers for the combining of theory and practice. I will only say that the melodic content and the rhythms, partly transformed from 'feudal material' rooted in everyday life, partly created and nurtured anew by the revolutionary *petit bourgeoisie* of France, contain all of the best things (that were 'fireproof', and free of 'decadence') that nourished nineteenth-century European music. The music of the Great French Revolution contains the preconditions both for Beethoven's heroism and also for the 'furious' Romanticism: the Romanticism that later presented the Revolution its unpaid credit notes, its unfulfilled promises – in the creative quest of Berlioz, for example – and tried to carry out the behest of the music of revolutionary struggle and festivities in a changed world, among the 'business people of the bourgeoisie'.

It is amazing how deeply rooted Beethoven was in the music of the Revolution, and how many valuable melodic ideas and images were suggested to him by the songs and theatre music of Revolutionary Paris. It is amazing how the events of the Revolution broke the psychology of composers who had previously served the feudal lords, and how, together with the French language, both everyday and literary, emotional speech (i.e. music) also changed and was filled with new content. I won't list the names of composers whose material I borrowed. I have already mentioned that my work was not concerned with individual pieces, and any work that interested me I considered a valuable musical representation of the content of the epoch. But I have to remember at least Grétry, who has been only one-sidedly appreciated, while a careful analysis of his 'responses' to revolutionary ideals demands that conventional views of his work should undergo expansion and a radical change.³³ The same can be said about Méhul, Gossec, Lesueur and Cherubini.³⁴

The plot of *The Flames of Paris* is based on the march of a Marseille detachment to Paris and the events connected with the taking of Tuileries (10 August 1892) and the revolutionary dissolution of the feudal regime. The ballet is structured through its episodes as an emotional and symphonic build-up to a climax that represents the explosion of the people's fury in the taking of the Tuileries (end of Act 3). A release from this intensity follows in the scenes of mass festivities in Act 4, which have been conceived in essence as the finale of a heroic symphony; the finale has a tragic prologue – Gossec's famous funeral march – which, in the present theatrical context accompanies the funeral of those who fell in the Revolution. The first act of the ballet is a kind of dramatic exposition of events in the French provinces (among the peasantry and petit bourgeoisie), and it is concentrated in the area around Marseille at the time of revolutionary enthusiasm: I have not used the 'Marseillaise' as an anthem, but rather as a mass song, which the crowd takes up at the moment when the Marseille detachment is formed. The Prologue before Act 1 depicts the morals of the feudal landlords and the punishing treatment meted out to the peasants. The second act of the ballet portrays the 'old regime' (in the Versailles counter-revolutionary coup). In the music, I do not present the 'old regime' through a sentimental pastoral topic or through affected salon songs; I present it, rather, as an aristocratic monarchy doomed to perish, but still armed and dangerous. To symbolise this, I use musical material from Lully, who was a vivid representative of French absolutism, as well as some feudal 'relics' from Gluck.³⁵ But everything in Gluck that was accepted by the Revolution, I have transferred to the corresponding moments of revolutionary enthusiasm. The main colouring of Act 2 is severe and dark, even funereal and requiem-like; it is a kind of 'funeral mass for the old regime', hence the significant role given to the organ, which accompanies both the dances and the climax of the conspiracy, marked by an anthem for the King (at the arrival of Louis XVI). If Act 2 is like a symphonic andante, then Act 3, the central act, is conceived as an expansive dramatic scherzo. It is brimful of crowd dance scenes. Its main content is the build-up of the people's anger and their revolutionary enthusiasm, leading to the march on the Tuileries, which is accompanied by the singing of the *Ça ira*; the taking of the palace leads

---

[33] André Ernest Modeste Grétry (1741–1813) was best known for his operas. He enjoyed equal favour from the old regime, the Revolutionary government, and Napoleon.

[34] Etienne Nicolas Méhul (1763–1817) enjoyed great operatic renown in the 1790s, when also wrote many revolutionary songs and choruses, one of which became the national anthem under Napoleon. François-Joseph Gossec (1734–1829) is remembered for several large-scale works he wrote to celebrate the Revolution. Jean-François Lesueur (or Le Sueur, 1760–1837) came to fame through the operas he produced in revolutionary Paris. Luigi Cherubini (1760–1842), an Italian who settled in Paris, also won fame with his operas in the 1790s, and wrote many patriotic pieces, especially for Napoleon.

[35] Jean-Baptiste de Lully (1632–87) was an Italian-born French composer at the court of Louis XIV. Christoph Willibald Ritter von Gluck (1714–87) was a Bavarian-born opera composer who had particular success in Paris during the 1770s.

to the ultimate jubilation of the people, set to music that anticipates the 'victory symphony' of Beethoven's *Egmont*. The central mass dance of Act 3 had developed the melodies of the *Carmagnole* and other characteristic songs that reverberated in the streets of Revolutionary Paris. A response to these wrathful songs is to be found in the songs of joy in the ballet's closing scene, which is a final mass dance in the form of a rondo–contredanse.

※ ※ ※ ※ ※

Vl. Derzhanovskiy, 'V vagone (Sergey Prokof'yev: K priyezdu v Sovetskiy Soyuz)' [In the Carriage (Sergei Prokofiev: Marking his Arrival in the Soviet Union)], *Sovetskoye iskusstvo*, no. 54 (27 Nov. 1932), 2.

During these years, Derzhanovsky was Prokofiev's regular correspondent and played an active role in facilitating and organising the composer's visits to Russia and performances of his works there. It is worth noting that not only Derzhanovsky, but also Prokofiev have acquired a fluent command of Sovietese, hence the ponderous talk of 'socialist construction', 'the new life', 'the new people' and 'mighty movements' among artists dedicated to fulfilment of the latest Party resolution. This is no longer the vocabulary of the disbanded RAPM, but the vocabulary of the state which both men hoped would provide them with a good living (in Prokofiev's case, an exceptionally good living). At this juncture, such talk was therefore neither ironic, nor reflective of the private outlook of either individual – it was merely normal public speech for the early-Stalin period, before the old utopian rhetoric gave way to Russian nationalism.

Vl. Derzhanovsky

In the Carriage (Sergei Prokofiev: Marking His Arrival in the Soviet Union)

After the Warsaw express arrived at the platform in Negoreloye station, V. Ya. Shebalin and I, sent by the City Composers' Committee to meet Sergei Prokofiev, were almost immediately approached by the senior border guard, who politely, but curtly enquired:

– Sergei Prokofiev?

To our affirmative reply there followed another clipped response:

– Arrived.

45 minutes later, we were aboard the Vladivostok express flying towards Moscow.

– It is a great joy for me to be coming back home to the Soviet land, says the composer.

Prokofiev, who follows the Soviet press closely and who corresponds regularly with his friends in Moscow and Leningrad, is very well informed about the mighty movement that has gripped all Soviet composers and the goal of which is to realise the 23 April Resolution of the Party Central Committee. Prokofiev remarks on the necessity for complete and comprehensive support for young composers, without differentiating between creative groups.

The conversation moves on to Prokofiev's own works.

– And what are your own creative plans?

– Well, at the moment, you know, Western subject matter repels me. Somehow, it seems superfluous – it has an air of indifference about it, something you might want to call formalism or whatever. In Paris last summer, I met [the playwright] Afinogenov, whose clear-sightedness I appreciated and who promised to provide me with a plot. He even offered to write a comedy drawn from life in the froth of the Parisian bourgeoisie. But that kind of play would be negative, or subversive. For myself, though, I find Soviet subjects more attractive. What I'm looking for is a robust and solid plot drawn from Soviet life – I'm really hoping to find one. I'm striving to produce a work that would be constructive and cheerful, something that would represent the new life, something that would portray those who are building our era – the new people. Afinogenov has some very interesting ideas in this area. But it looks as if he's saving them for his next play. Still, we haven't finished discussing the matter. Some friends have also drawn my attention to several other interesting subjects, and my next stage-work, of course, will be based on the subject matter of our [socialist] construction. Last year, the latest foreign production of *Steps of Steel* took place in New York. In their largest theatre, the Metropolitan, they took care over the presentation of the ballet – with red curtains, and hammer and sickle emblems. The ballet was received with interest and quite calmly [i.e. without political controversy]. Of course, here [in New York] there could have been some swings of the political pendulum. I would particularly like to conduct this piece myself during my Moscow concerts, in order to try to convince people that it resonates with the new life. I managed to construct the newly compiled concert suite in such a way that the gradual build-up is preserved in the last part ('The Factory'); in the ballet, this alternates with dips in the momentum that were motivated by the stage action, but during a concert performance these would weaken the effect.

The last brief questions concern Prokofiev's professorship at the Moscow Conservatoire.

– As for my work at Moscow Conservatoire, I'm ready to begin in the spring. The delay, it seems, has been caused by the fact that the higher department, the *Meisterschule*, as the Germans would call it, has not yet been formed. It's unlikely that I'd take on the burden of lecturing. I'll probably teach a course on practical composition.

This brings our conversation with Prokofiev to a close.

Key to Acronyms and Institutional Names

Agitotdel (Muzizdata). Agitatsionnïy otdel (Gosudarstvennogo Muzïkal'nogo Izdatel'stva). Department of agitational music of the State Publishing House.

Agitprop. In general, stands for 'agitation and propaganda'. When capitalised, refers specifically to the department of the Party Central Committee responsible for agitation, propaganda, and press (see **APPO**).

AKhRR (Assotsiatsiya Khudozhnikov Revolyutsionnoy Rossii). The Association of Artists of Revolutionary Russia, 1922–32 (from 1928 named AKhR). A counterpart of RAPP and RAPM in the fine arts, which promoted realist aesthetics in painting, although unlike RAPM, its aesthetic placed much greater emphasis on professionalism.

APPO (Otdel agitatsii, propagandï i pechati TsK VKP(b)). A department of the Party Central Committee responsible for agitation, propaganda and press. This name was used in the years 1928 to 1929.

ASM (Assotsiatsiya sovremennoy muzïki). The Association for Contemporary Music (1923–32, active 1923–29). An organisation of composers and musicologists that promoted close links with progressive Western composers. During its active life, it ran a concert series each year, and published the journal *Sovremennaya muzïka* (Contemporary music).

Cheka (ChK, or VChK, (Vserossiyskaya) Chrezvïchaynaya Komissiya po bor'be s kontrrevolyutsiyey i sabotazhem). The (All-Russian) Extraordinary Commission for Combating Counter-Revolution and Sabotage (1917–22). The earliest Soviet state security organisation, replaced in 1922 by the GPU.

Comintern (The Communist International). A world-wide organisation of Communist and related parties, created with the aim of assisting foreign communist parties in spreading the Revolution, but later serving to subordinate communist parties to the changing requirements of Stalin's foreign policy. Also known as the Third International (1919–43).

GaKhN (Gosudarstvennaya akademiya khudozhestvennïkh nauk). State Academy for Arts Studies, 1921–30. Initially, from 1921 to 1925, it bore the name RAKhN.

Glaviskusstvo (Glavnoye upravleniye po delam khudozhestvennoy literaturï i iskusstva), 1928–30, Moscow. Formed in September 1928 for the ideological governance of art within Narkompros. In September 1929, it was transformed into an inter-ministerial body (*Sovet po delam khudozhestvennoy literaturï i iskusstva*), which consisted of a Chair, two Deputies, the subordinate Chair of Glavrepertkom and a Collegium comprising 44 members. It was disbanded in May 1930, its functions given to the Arts Sector of the Ministry of Education (*Sektor iskusstv Narkomata Prosveshcheniya*).

Glavlit (Glavnoye upravleniye po delam literaturï i izdatel'stv). Central Administration for Literature and Publishing. A censorship body within Narkompros (1922–45), later a separate organisation under the Council of Ministers.

Glavnauka (Glavnoye upravleniye nauchnïmi, nauchno-khudozhestvennïmi i muzeynïmi uchrezhdeniyami). Central Administration for Science, Arts-Scholarship, and Museum Institutions, a Narkompros department, 1921–30.

Glavpolitprosvet (Glavnïy politiko-prosvetitel'nïy komitet). Central Committee for Political Education. A Narkompros committee (1920–30) responsible for agitation and propaganda, it had its own Arts section.

Glavprofobr (Glavnoye upravleniye professional'nogo obrazovaniya). Central Administration for Professional Education. A Narkompros department (1920–30) responsible for higher education.

Glavrepertkom (Glavnïy repertuarnïy komitet, or later Glavnïy komitet po kontrolyu za zrelishchami i repertuarom). Central Repertory Committee, or later Central Committee for Control of [Public] Spectacles and Repertory. A censorship body (1923–34) within Narkompros, part of Glavlit.

Glavsotsvos (Glavnoye upravleniye sotsialnogo vospitaniya i politekhnicheskogo obrazovaniya detey). Central Administration for Social Upbringing and Technical Education of Children. A Narkompros department (1921–30) responsible for children's education.

GPU (Gosudarstvennoye politicheskoye upravleniye). State Political Directorate, 1922–34 (from 1923 the abbreviation OGPU is used, with 'Obyedinyonnoye' (joint) added to the name). A body overseen by the Internal Affairs Ministry (NKVD) and which replaced the Cheka.

GUS (Gosudarstvennïy uchyonïy sovet). State Scholarly Council (1919–33), a body within Narkompros responsible for scholarship, with an Arts section alongside three other sections. In 1928, its function of overseeing the arts was transferred to Glaviskusstvo.

Komsomol (Kommunisticheskiy Soyuz Molodyozhi). The Young Communist League, a youth organisation founded in 1922, considered to be the junior wing of the Communist Party.

LASM (Leningradskaya Assotsiatsiya Sovremennoy Muzïki). The Leningrad Association for Contemporary Music (1926–32). It acted independently of the Moscow-based ASM, although the two organisations pursued similar goals.

LEF (Levïy front iskusstv). The Left Front of the Arts, an artistic association (1922–8), mostly of former Futurists, it was led by the poet Vladimir Mayakovsky.

LOSPS (Leningradskiy oblastnoy sovet professional'nïkh soyuzov). Leningrad Regional Council of Trade Unions.

Mezhkniga (Mezhdunarodnaya kniga). 'Books International', an export and import trade organisation, from 1923–30 a joint-stock company, later a state trade body.

MODPiK (Moskovskoye obshchestvo dramaticheskikh pisateley i kompozitorov). Moscow Society of Dramatic Writers and Composers, a copyright agency, 1926–9.

MOPR (Mezhdunarodnoye obshchestvo pomoshchi bortsam revolyutsii). International Society for Aid to Revolutionary Fighters (1922–40). An international charity formed by Comintern for supporting persecuted revolutionaries, it operated in as many as 70 countries.

Muzgiz (Gosudarstvennoye Muzïkal'noe Izdatel'stvo). State Music Publishers, successor to Muzsektor Gosizdata

MUZO (Muzïkal'nïy Otdel). The Music Section of Narkompros, 1918–22.

Muzsektor (Gosizdata). The Music Section (of the State Publishing House), 1921–30, later under the name Muzgiz. Was formed on the basis of the nationalised Jurgenson Music Publishing House in 1918, originally as a subdivision of MUZO.

Narkompros (Narodnïy Komissariat Prosveshcheniya). People's Commissariat of Enlightenment. The Soviet Ministry of Arts, Sciences and Education (1917–46). After 1946, it was subject to several phases of reorganisation and changes of name.

NEP (Novaya ekonomicheskaya politika). The New Economic Policy introduced in 1921, which signalled a return to some forms of capitalist economy, mainly on the level of small- and medium-scale private enterprise. The abbreviation is also used to refer more broadly to the period 1921 to 1928. **NEPmen** were the nouveaux-riches who rose under NEP.

OGPU. See **GPU**.

ORKiMD (Obyedineniye Revolyutsionnïkh Kompozitorov i Muzïkal'nïkh Deyateley). Association of Revolutionary Composers and Music Workers (1925–9). Its nucleus was a group that split from RAPM in 1924, with a view to foster the creation of agitational music on a broader and less strident ideological platform. Most of its members joined or rejoined RAPM in 1929, under pressure.

OST (Obshchestvo Khudozhnikov-Stankovistov). Society of Easel Painters. An association of artists (1925–31) led by David Shterenberg, that tackled Soviet themes in a range of styles that were both modernist and representational.

Pedotdel/Pedfak (Pedadogicheskiy otdel/fakul'tet). The Pedagogical Department of Moscow Conservatoire, which was created in 1921, and later promoted to faculty status. The purpose of its creation was to give vocational training appropriate to instrumentalists who would pursue a career in teaching rather than become virtuoso soloists. Seen by many professors as a ghetto for weaker students, often with a 'proletarian' background, it became a perennial bone of contention. Eventually it was reorganised into a Pedagogical Practice Division that still exists today.

Persimfans (Pervïy simfonicheskiy ansambl'). First Symphonic Ensemble, a conductorless orchestra, 1922–32.

Politprosvet of PUR (Politiko-prosvetitel'nïy otdel Politicheskogo Upravleniya RVSR). Department of political education of the Red Army's Political Administration, 1921–2, subsequently known under a series of other names.

Prokoll (Proizvodstvennïy kollektiv studentov-kompozitorov Moskovskoy Konservatorii). The Production Collective of Moscow Conservatoire Composition Students. A student organisation that promoted collective work on Soviet-orientated pieces. Its members joined RAPM in 1929.

Proletkult (Proletarskiye kul'turno-prosvetitel'nïye organizatsii). Proletarian Cultural and Enlightenment Organisations. A mass movement for the development of distinctively proletarian culture, spearheaded by Alexander Bogdanov, it was formed as a web of circles, studios and clubs devoted to music, drama, literature, etc. An active force from 1917 to 1922, nominally continuing until 1932.

Rabis or Vserabis ((Vse)rossiyskiy Professional'nïy Soyuz Rabotnikov Iskusstv). (All) Russian Trade Union of Arts Workers.

RaKhN. See GAKhN.

RAPM (also APM or VAPM; (Vse)Rossiyskaya Assotsiatsiya Proletarskikh Muzïkantov). Russian Association of Proletarian Musicians, 1923–32. This was an organisation of musicians who sought for an alternative to the elite music culture of the opera houses and concert halls. It was active from 1923 to 1924, then lost its sources of funding between 1925 and 1928, but thereafter won increasing (if always qualified) Party support and became especially powerful from 1929 to 1932, until the moment of its dissolution by government decree.

RAPP (Rossiyskaya Assotsiatsiya Proletarskikh Pisateley). Russian Association of Proletarian Writers, 1925–32.

Rosfil (Rossiyskaya Filarmoniya). 'Russian Philharmonia', one of the first Soviet concert agencies (1922–7), and predecessor of the current Moscow Philharmonia.

RSFSR (Rossiyskaya Sovetskaya Federativnaya Sotsialisticheskaya Respublika). Russian Soviet Federative Socialist Republic. The name was adopted in 1918; in 1922, the RSFSR was joined by other republics to form the Soviet Union.

TsIK (Tsentral'nïy Ispolnitel'nïy Komitet). Central Executive Committee, the supreme organ of state power between Congresses of Soviets, 1922–38.

TsK (Tsentral'nïy Komitet). Central Committee (of the Party).

VChK. See Cheka.

VKP(b) (Vserossiyskaya Kommunisticheskaya Partiya (bol'shevikov)). All-Russian Communist Party (Bolsheviks). The name used by the Communist Party from 1925 to 1952.

VMSh (Vïsshaya Muzïkal'naya Shkola (imeni Feliksa Kona)). The (Felix Kon) Higher Music School, the name given to the Moscow Conservatoire in the period 1931 to 1932.

Vseroskomdram (Vserossiyskoye Obshchestvo Dramaturgov i Kompozitorov). All-Union Society of Playwrights and Composers, 1930–33. It was primarily responsible for the publication and performance rights of its members, but was also drawn into the ideological battles of the time.

Glossary of Names

Russian surnames are given here in their customary English spellings (as in the main text). Where there is a substantial difference between the customary form and the correct transliteration of a given name, the transliteration is added in square brackets; where there is only a trivial difference (e.g. '-sky' instead of '-skiy'), only the customary form is given. First names and patronymics are given in transliteration only (e.g. Aleksandr rather than Alexander).

Abendroth, Hermann (1883–1956). German conductor. He toured the USSR in 1925, 1927 and 1928.

Afinogenov, Aleksandr Nikolayevich (1904–41). Playwright. A Party member since 1922, he was a leading figure in RAPP by the early 1930s. His plays cover some of the more painful aspects of Soviet society, as in *Fear* (1931) and *Lies* (1933), which overstepped the boundaries of the politically acceptable (the former had to be revised, the latter was banned). During the years 1936–7, Afinogenov was denounced, and then expelled from both the Party and the Union of Writers, but he was rehabilitated in 1938. He died in an air raid during the war.

Akhmatova (born Gorenko), **Anna Andreyevna** (1889–1966). Poet. Before the Revolution, she belonged to the Acmeist movement, and she became one of the most prominent figures of the Russian 'Silver Age'. From the late 1920s, little of her work was published, and she became an obscurity in the Soviet literary world. She was romantically linked to Lourié just before his emigration.

Aleksandrov, Anatoliy Nikolayevich (1888–1982). Composer, pianist and teacher. He studied under Taneyev and belonged to Myaskovsky's circle.

Andreyev, Leonid Nikolayevich (1871–1919). Writer. He was widely known from 1901 as an author of highly charged short stories. He was generally associated with Symbolism, but some of his work places him among the Russian Expressionists.

Ansermet, Ernest Alexandre (1883–1969). Swiss conductor. As a conductor for Diaghilev's *Ballets Russes*, he premiered Prokofiev's *Chout* and several important works by Stravinsky.

Arens, Lev Yevgen'yevich (1890–1967). Biologist and Futurist poet. Punin invited him to work for Narkompros, where he was a Secretary of the Collegium.

Arensky, Anton Stepanovich (1861–1906). Composer. He studied under Rimsky-Korsakov in St Petersburg, but became a professor at Moscow Conservatoire and is usually associated with the Muscovite Tchaikovskian school of composition.

Arkadyev, Mikhail Pavlovich (1896–1937). Diplomat and cultural official. During the years 1929–32, he was a member of the Narkompros Collegium, with responsibility for the arts. He worked later as director of the Moscow Art Theatre. He was arrested and executed in 1937.

Arkhangelsky, Aleksandr Andreyevich (1846–1924). Russian choral conductor and composer of church music. From 1880, he toured with his own mixed choir.

Asafyev, Boris Vladimirovich (wrote under the pseudonym Igor Glebov; 1884–1949). Soviet musicologist and composer. The creator of musical 'intonation' theory, he was a leading figure in ASM during the 1920s, but under pressure from RAPM, he switched to the composition of pastiche ballets and operas. When he resumed his career as an essayist and critic, in the 1940s, his outlook had changed dramatically to a conservative nationalism, in keeping with Soviet rhetoric of the period.

Atovmyan, Levon Tadevosovich (1901–73). A composer by training, he became an important figure in Soviet musical life, first as Secretary of the Composers' Section of Vseroskomdram (1929–33), and later as the Director of Muzfond, The Union of Composers' financial body (1939–48).

Auric, Georges (1899–1983). French composer. He studied under d'Indy, and in 1920 became a member of the Cocteau-inspired grouping, *Les six*. In later life, he was best known as a composer of film music, creating scores for both French and Hollywood productions.

Averbakh, Leopol'd Leonidovich (1903–39). Leader of RAPP from 1926 to 1932, and Editor-in-Chief of the RAPP journal *On Guard for Literature* (*Na literaturnom postu*). He was arrested and executed during the purges because he was the brother-in-law of the denounced NKVD chief Genrikh Yagoda.

Avraamov, Arseniy Mikhaylovich (1886–1944). Russian composer, music theorist and folk-song collector. In the 1920s and early 1930s he experimented with tuning systems, invented technology for improving the synchronisation of films with their sound tracks, and organised a spectacular avant-garde event, the Symphony of Sirens (*Simfoniya gudkov*, 1922).

Babel, Isaak Emmanuilovich (1894–1940). Journalist and writer. He is most famed for his edgy and witty tales of the Civil War and the Jewish ghetto. His affair with the wife of the NKVD chief Yezhov is likely to have sealed his fate, and he fell victim to the Purges.

Bakaleynikov, Vladimir Romanovich (1885–1953). Celebrated violist and conductor; member of the Stradivari Quartet. His career as a conductor began while he was still in Soviet Russia. After his emigration, in 1927, he established himself in the USA where he became principal conductor of the Pittsburgh Symphony Orchestra (and teacher of Lorin Maazel).

Balmont, Konstantin Dmitriyevich (1867–1948). Symbolist poet. He emigrated twice, first because of the defeat of the 1905 revolution, and second (in 1920) because of the success of the Bolshevik Revolution. He was associated with various musical circles, and many Russian composers (including Rachmaninov and Prokofiev) set his poetry to music.

Baltrušaitis, Jurgis (1873–1944). Symbolist poet, who wrote in both Lithuanian and Russian. From 1920 to 1939, he was (independent) Lithuania's ambassador to the Soviet Union.

Bartók, Béla (1881–1945). Hungarian composer and ethnomusicologist who combined modernism with folk-song influence. He gave concert tours in Russia and Ukraine during the 1920s. Fleeing the Nazis, he emigrated to the USA in 1940.

Bedny, Dem'yan (Yefim Alekseyevich Pridvorov) (1883–1945). Poet. The son of a peasant, and a Party member since 1912, Bedny was ideally placed to become the Soviet poet laureate. He was close to Lenin, had his topical satirical verses published in *Pravda*, and was even allocated an apartment within the Kremlin. Under Stalin, he could no longer count on official favour, and he was denounced on several occasions, leading to the loss of both his apartment and his Party membership. He returned to favour during the War years.

Beethoven, Ludwig van (1770–1824). German composer. He was one of the few classics regarded as ideologically unimpeachable in the early Soviet Union, since his music was regarded as an artistic embodiment of the ideals of the French Revolution.

Bekker, Paul (1882–1937). An influential German music critic, he championed new music and highlighted sociological aspects of the art. He emigrated to the USA in 1934.

Belïy, Viktor Arkad'yevich (1904–83). Composer, student of Myaskovsky, and member of Prokoll and RAPM. He wrote several popular mass songs such as 'Orlyonok' ('The Eaglet', 1936).

Bely, Andrey (Boris Nikolayevich Bugayev) (1880–1934). Symbolist poet and prose writer, particularly celebrated for his novel *Petersburg*. After the Revolution, he worked for Proletkult together with other symbolists; while most of his friends emigrated, he chose to stay in the USSR. By the time of his death, he had fallen into obscurity.

Belyayev, Viktor Mikhaylovich (1888–1968). Musicologist, a leading member of ASM. Best known for his ethnomusicological work on the Caucasus and Central Asia.

Berg, Alban (1885–1935). Austrian composer. A pupil of Schoenberg, he achieved major success with his opera *Wozzeck*, which had its premiere in 1925 in Berlin. In 1927 this complex, atonal opera was produced in Leningrad after a six-month rehearsal period. Berg's operatic aesthetic made a particularly deep impression on the young Shostakovich.

Bezïmensky, Aleksandr Il'yich (1898–1973). Poet. A Party member since 1916, he became famous in the 1920s as a 'Komsomol poet', glorifying the new Soviet life. From 1923 to 1926, he was a member of RAPP.

Blanter, Matvey Isaakovich (1903–90). Composer. He was a 'foxtrot composer' in the 1920s, and successfully moved over to the light-music style of the Stalin period. He is particularly remembered for his song *Katyusha*, which achieved record popularity during World War II (a Soviet rocket launcher was even named after the song).

Blinder, Naum Samoylovich (1889–1965). Violinist. He studied under Pyotr Stolyarsky in Odessa and Adolf Brodsky in Manchester. In 1928, he emigrated from the USSR and settled in the USA, enjoying an international career, and acquiring several distinguished students, including Isaac Stern.

Blok, Aleksandr Aleksandrovich (1880–1921). Celebrated lyric poet, associated mainly with the Russian Symbolist movement. He surprised many by co-operating with the Soviet authorities, writing *The Twelve* as a kind of defence of the Revolution. By 1921, Blok was seriously ill, and hoped to receive medical attention abroad; he died while waiting for permission to leave Russia.

Blyum, Vladimir Ivanovich (1877–1941). Influential theatre critic. He was widely published before the Revolution. After the Revolution, his Party membership assisted him in finding posts as a cultural official, in which capacity he edited journals and worked for the censorship body, Glavrepertkom. He continued to write critical articles on theatre and music (especially on light music) and regularly published these in *Zhizn' iskusstva* (Artistic Life), as well as in *Pravda* and *Izvestiya*. During 1929 and 1930, he acted as a spokesman for the virtually defunct ASM, which earned him vilification from RAPM.

Bogdanov, Aleksandr Aleksandrovich (1873–1928). Revolutionary, philosopher and polymath. Lenin saw him as a rival for leadership of the Bolsheviks in the wake of the failed 1905 revolution, and heavily criticised his philosophical work *Empiriomonism*. He was one of the founders of Proletkult, and after Lenin's attack on that body in 1920, he left the organisation, and also lost his seat on the Party Central Committee. His experiments in medical rejuvenation lead to his death during an elective blood transfusion.

Borisovsky, Vadim Vasil'yevich (1900–72). Celebrated Russian violist, and a founder member of the Beethoven Quartet (1922–64).

Borkhman, Aleksandr Adol'fovich (1872–1940). Composer. A medical doctor by profession, he studied composition under Gliére and Grechaninov. He enjoyed a brief period of fame with his symphonic poem *Kuzum* (after Tagore) in 1925.

Borovsky, Aleksandr Kirillovich (1889–1968). Pianist. He studied with Yesipova at St Petersburg Conservatoire (where his friendship with his fellow student, Prokofiev, began). He emigrated, basing himself in Paris, and established an international career for himself. For the decade from 1927, he gave annual concert tours in Soviet Russia. In 1940, he moved to the USA.

Brand, Max (1896–1980). Austrian composer. He achieved his greatest success in Weimar Germany, with his opera *Machinist Hopkins*, which addressed contemporary concerns over urbanisation and industrialisation. The opera was premiered in 1929 in Duisburg and was also given a Soviet production in Kharkov, Ukraine (by Nikolai Foregger). He fled from the Nazis in 1938, and spent most of his life in the USA, where became a pioneer of electronic music.

Braudo, Yevgeniy Maksimovich (Moiseyevich) (1882–1939). Musicologist and music critic. Born in Riga, he studied with Reger, Riemann and Kretschmar, and became professor at the Russian Institute of the Arts in Petrograd. His many publications included a *General History of Music* (1922). During the 1920s, he was also a music critic for *Pravda*.

Bruni, Lev Aleksandrovich (1894–1948). Painter. His style was described as Futurist and Constructivist before he took a more conservative turn in the 1930s.

Bryusov, Valeriy Yakovlevich (1873–1924). Symbolist poet, brother of the musicologist Nadezhda Bryusova. His open support for the Bolshevik government lost him the support of many in his literary circle. He took up a post in Narkompros.

Bryusova, Nadezhda Yakovlevna (1881–1951). Musicologist, sister of the poet Valeriy Bryusov. A dedicated educator, she worked for the Moscow People's Conservatoire prior to the Revolution. Together with her mentor, Boleslav Yavorsky, she joined the Red Professors group in 1924. She participated in RAPM, and occupied a number of posts in music administration.

Bubnov, Andrey Sergeyevich (1883–1940). Professional revolutionary. Although he had never completed his higher education, he was appointed in 1929 as Commissar for Enlightenment, replacing Lunacharsky. He was arrested in 1937, and eventually executed.

Buglay. See **Vasilyev-Buglay.**

Bukharin, Nikolay Ivanovich (1888–1938). A professional revolutionary, he rose to the top of the Soviet hierarchy. He was a member of the Politburo and the editor of *Pravda*. He has been identified as the main author of the 1925 Party resolution on literature. During the years 1928–29, he stood in opposition to Stalin's plans of rapid industrialisation, and was expelled from the Politburo. He was executed after a show trial in 1938.

Bulgakov, Mikhail Afanas'yevich (1891–1940). Novelist and playwright. Although his novel *The Master and Margarita* posthumously earned him international fame, he was better known for his stageworks during his lifetime. His dramas *The Days of the Turbins* and *Flight* proved controversial, and his career was marred by the banning of his work and other restrictions.

Casella, Alfredo (1883–1947). Italian composer, most famous for his ballet *La Giara* (1924). Following in the footsteps of Stravinsky, he developed a neoclassical style. He visited Russia both before and after the Revolution, and wrote about his visits in his memoirs.

Castelnuovo-Tedesco, Mario (1895–1968). Italian composer, best known for his guitar music. Much of his music was banned under Mussolini. He emigrated to the USA and wrote film scores for Hollywood.

Chaliapin (Shalyapin)**, Fyodor Ivanovich** (1873–1938). Operatic bass. His early career was spent in the Mamontov Private Opera. He continued his career at the Bolshoi and Mariinsky. After the Revolution, he was one of the leading cultural figures sympathetic to the Bolsheviks; he participated in the running of the Bolshoi and directed opera productions there. One of his trips abroad, however, in 1922, became his emigration. Chaliapin's most famous role was Boris Godunov, which he sang in the famous Diaghilev production in Paris.

Chelyapov, Nikolay Ivanovich (1889–1941). A professor of law, he taught in various Soviet educational institutions for Party functionaries, such as the Communist Academy. Owing to his musical interests (he had studied piano) he held a brief appointment as Editor-in-Chief of *Music and Revolution*, to replace its politically discredited founder Shulgin, and then headed the Music Department of GAIS (State Academy for Scholarship in the Arts). In 1932, he was chosen as Chairman of the first Union of Composers, and he edited its journal *Soviet Music* from 1933 to 1937.

Chemberdzhi, Nikolay Karpovich (1903–48). Composer, student of Anatoly Aleksandrov, he became a member of Prokoll (the Production Collective of the Moscow Conservatoire), and then of RAPM. Later, he occupied senior positions in the Union of Composers.

Chemodanov, Sergey Mikhaylovich (1888–1942). He wrote and lectured on history and music history in many educational institutions, with a particular interest in music's sociological aspects and the development of a Marxist critique of music.

Cherepnin. See **Tcherepnin.**

Chernetskaya, Inna Samoylovna (1894–?). Dancer and choreographer. She studied with Isadora Duncan's sister and at the Dalcroze studio; under their influence, she opened a school of 'synthetic dance' in Moscow in 1914. After the Revolution, the studio was supported by Lunacharsky (with whom Chernetskaya had an affair).

Chernomordikov, David Aaronovich (1869–1947). A graduate of the St Petersburg Conservatoire who participated in the 1905 revolution, he wrote a number of workers' songs and marches and made arrangements of popular revolutionary songs (the *Internationale* was first published in Russia in the shape of his 1906 version). In 1908, he helped found the Jewish Music Society and was elected its first chairman. After the Revolution, he held posts in Narkompros, in the State Music Publishers, and in 1923 became a founder member of RAPM.

Chukovsky, Korney Ivanovich (Nikolay Vasil'yevich Korneychukov) (1882–1969). Poet. Although established as an essayist and translator of English literature, he later found his vocation in writing verses for children, and in this capacity became a celebrated Soviet poet.

Coates, Albert (1882–1953). English conductor. The son of an English businessman in Russia, he studied both in Russia (with Rimsky-Korsakov) and in Europe, and for five years was chief conductor of the Mariinsky Imperial Opera. He was appointed President of the Soviet Opera Houses, but serious illness drove him abroad in 1919, after which he became chief conductor at of the London Symphony Orchestra. He returned to the Soviet Union on three occasions for concert tours.

Cowell, Henry (1897–1965). American experimental composer. His writing for piano was innovative and influential, and he pioneered devices such as tone-clusters and the scraping of the strings inside the piano. He visited the Soviet Union in 1929.

D'Albert, Eugen (Eugène) **Francis Charles** (1864–1932). Pianist and composer. Born in Scotland and educated in Britain, he immigrated to Germany and studied with Liszt, becoming a virtuoso pianist with an international career.

He composed 21 operas, the most popular of these being *Tiefland* (The Lowlands).

Davidenko, Aleksandr Aleksandrovich (1899–1934). Composer, founder and head of Prokoll (the Production Collective of the Moscow Conservatoire), and subsequently a prominent member of RAPM.

Derzhanovsky, Vladimir Vladimirovich (1881–1942). Music critic, founder of the Evenings of Contemporary Music in 1909 (together with his wife, singer Yelena Koposova-Derzhanovskaya, 1877–1942, and the conductor Konstantin Saradzhev, 1877–1944). He edited the journal *Music* (*Muzïka*, 1910–16). He became one of the founders of ASM and one of the editors of its journal, *Sovremennaya muzïka* (*Contemporary Music*, 1924–28).

Deshevov, Vladimir Mikhaylovich (1889–1955). Composer. He graduated from the Petersburg Conservatoire in 1914. After serving in the army and teaching in the provinces, he returned to Petrograd in 1922 and became one of the city's most colourful modernist composers. He was one of the first composers to tackle Soviet themes, in his ballet *The Red Whirlwind* (1924) and other works. His challenging opera on a Civil-War plot, *Ice and Steel* (1929), was criticised and withdrawn before the premiere. His prominence waned thereafter, and in later years he concentrated on film scores and incidental music for the theatre.

Diaghilev (Dyagilev)**, Sergey Pavlovich** (1872–1929). Impresario. He founded an association of artists 'Mir iskusstva' (The World of Art), and organised exhibitions of Russian art at home and in Paris. He extended his activities in Paris to the to concerts and opera productions, finally establishing the celebrated *Ballets Russes* (1909–29). Although an impresario rather than an artist himself, he was one of the most influential figures in the development of modern art, choreography and music. Among Russian composers, Stravinsky and Prokofiev particularly benefited from his patronage.

Dianov, Anton Mikhaylovich (1882–1939). Composer and music critic, one of Prokofiev's correspondents.

Dmitriyev, Vladimir Vladimirovich (1900–1948). Distinguished theatre designer. In the 1920s he worked for Meyerhold's theatre and opera houses. He designed the sets for Prokofiev's *Love for Three Oranges* (1926) and Musorgsky's *Boris Godunov* (1928). His later career was spent largely in drama, in particular for MKhAT (Moscow Art Theatre).

Dobroveyn, Isay Aleksandrovich (1891–1953). Pianist and conductor. He was the pianist who famously gave a private performance of Beethoven's *Appassionata* for Lenin. He emigrated in 1923 and became a Norwegian citizen.

Dohnányi, Ernst von (Ernő) (1877–1960). Hungarian composer and conductor. He held teaching posts in Berlin and Budapest, and later emigrated to the USA.

Dolidze, Viktor Isidorovich (1890–1933). Georgian composer, author of the first Georgian comic opera (or operetta) *Keto and Kote*.

Dranishnikov, Vladimir Aleksandrovich (1893–1939). Conductor. He studied conducting under Nikolay Tcherepnin (where he was Prokofiev's classmate), and in 1918 began conducting at the Mariinsky. During his tenure as chief conductor there, from 1925 to 1936, he sought to change the repertoire, introducing contemporary and rarely staged operas.

Drozdov, Anatoliy Nikolayevich (1883–1950). Music critic. He graduated as a pianist, taught piano and composed. During the 1920s he became active as a music critic, writing for *Music and Revolution*.

Druskin, Mikhail Semyonovich (1905–91). Musicologist. He studied piano under Schnabel and musicology under Asafyev, eventually choosing a musicological career. He became a professor of musicology at the Leningrad Conservatoire in 1947.

Dudkevich, Georgiy Nikolayevich (1887–1978). Composer. The best known of his works was the opera *Rachel's Tears* (*Plach Rakhili*, 1924). He also performed as a pianist and conductor. From 1932 to 1962, he was chief sound engineer at the Moscow Recording House.

Duncan, Isadora (1877–1927). American dancer. She achieved celebrity after her move to Europe in 1899, and became a highly influential reformer of dance. Her growing interest in communism brought her to the Soviet Union from 1922 to 1924 where she set up one of her several dance schools. This time was also marked by a brief and unhappy marriage to the poet Sergei Yesenin.

Dzegelyonok, Aleksandr Mikhaylovich (1891–1969). Composer, mainly of music for military band.

Dzerzhinsky (Dzierżyński)**, Feliks Edmundovich** (1877–1926). Marxist revolutionary in Poland; he led the Polish Social-Democratic Party. His determined agitational activities earned him many years of imprisonment and exile. Early in 1917, he joined the Bolsheviks and, owing to his reputation as a courageous revolutionary, he rose to become a member of the Central Committee within months. After the Revolution, he was appointed as head of VChK, the secret police, and became notorious as the organiser of its 'red terror' activities.

Ehrenburg (Erenburg)**, Il'ya Grigoryevich** (1891–1967). Journalist and novelist. He played an active role in the 1905 revolution, then fled into exile to Paris. In 1917, he returned to Russia, but his dissatisfaction with the Bolshevik government led him to return to Europe, settling in Berlin and Paris. Even so, he began working as a propagandist for the Soviet Union while still abroad, and moved back permanently in the 1930s. He courted controversy, negotiating the boundaries of the acceptable and moving in and out of favour with the authorities. His novel *The Thaw* lent its name to the period of liberalisation under Khrushchev.

Ekskuzovich, Ivan Vasil'yevich (1882–1942). Architect and opera administrator. Although he was trained as an architect, he gravitated towards the operatic world, and from 1917 became head of the Petrograd Academy Theatres (the former Imperial Theatres), extending his duties later to the Moscow Academy Theatres. Having worked closely with Lunacharsky, he left his post in 1928 upon the latter's demotion. After 1928, he created architectural designs for several opera houses on Soviet territory.

Epshteyn, Moisey Solomonovich (1890–1938). Soviet administrator. He was head of Glavsotsvos in 1928, then became Deputy to Bubnov, the new Commissar for Enlightenment, in 1929. He was executed in 1938, during Stalin's purges.

Fedorovsky, Fyodor Fyodorovich (1883–1955). Artist and designer. He became one of the most prominent Soviet set designers, winning five Stalin Prizes and many other accolades. He served as head designer for performances at the Bolshoi, and was also responsible for decorating the theatre when it was used for Party meetings. He was the designer of the stars on the Kremlin towers.

Feinberg (Feynberg)**, Samuil Yevgen'yevich** (1890–1962). Pianist and composer, professor of the Moscow Conservatoire from 1922 to 1962.

Fere, Vladimir Georgiyevich (1902–71). Composer. A student of Myaskovsky, he went on to write a series of Kirghiz national operas in collaboration with Vladimir Vlasov and the local musician Abdylas Maldybayev.

Fitelberg, Grzegorz (1879–1953). Polish conductor and composer. From 1914 to 1921 he lived in Russia, serving as an operatic and symphonic conductor in St Petersburg/Petrograd.

Foregger (Foregger von Greifenturn)**, Nikolay Mikhaylovich** (1892–1939). Theatre director, set designer and choreographer. Stemming from a noble Austrian family that had settled in Russia, from 1920 to 1924, he led MastFor (*Masterskaya Foreggera*, or Foregger's workshop), which staged groundbreaking shows of a satirical and grotesque nature, winning particular renown for his *Dances of Machines* (1922). After a fire, the theatre was dissolved, and Foregger went to work in the provinces, mainly in opera. After his aesthetic trend lost favour with the authorities, he drifted into obscurity.

Fried, Oskar (1871–1941). German conductor, best known as an advocate for Mahler's works. He first toured Russia in 1905, became the first foreign performer to tour the Soviet Union (1922), and in 1934, and on fleeing the Nazis, he settled in Tbilisi, eventually acquiring Soviet citizenship.

Gabrieli, Andrea (1532/3–85) and **Giovanni** (*c.* 1555–1612). Venetian composers (uncle and nephew), both organists at St Mark's cathedral and pioneers of polychoral writing.

Garbuzov, Nikolay Aleksandrovich (1880–1955). Music theorist and acoustician, one of the founders of the State Institute of Music Studies (GIMN, 1921–31), of which he was also the director. After GIMN was absorbed by Moscow Conservatoire, he continued his pioneering research into music perception in the Acoustics Laboratory there.

Gaygerova, Varvara Andrianovna (1903–44). Pianist and composer. A student of Myaskovsky's, her compositions from the 1930s onwards largely drew from folk themes of different Soviet nationalities.

Gedike, Aleksandr Fyodorovich (1877–1957). Composer, pianist and organist. He served as a professor of Moscow Conservatoire, and his many piano pieces for learners remain in use internationally.

Geltser, Yekaterina Vasil'yevna (1876–1962). Dancer. Most of her career was spent on the stage of the Bolshoi Theatre in Moscow (1898–1935). She was one of the earliest recipients of the title 'People's Artist' (1925). She was married to the choreographer Vasily Tikhomirov.

Ginzburg, Semyon L'vovich (1901–78). Musicologist. A student of Asafyev's, in the 1920s he was a frequent contributor to the various publications initiated by Asafyev and ASM. From the 1930s, most of his research was devoted to the folk music of the different Soviet nationalities.

Gladkovsky, Arseniy Pavlovich (1894–1945). Composer. After graduating as a mathematician, he studied composition at Petrograd/Leningrad Conservatoire, graduating in 1924. He came to prominence in 1925 as the composer of the first opera on Soviet subject matter, *For Red Petrograd*, 1925 (the compositional task was shared with Yevgeny Prussak). Later he taught composition and chaired the Leningrad Union of Composers from 1932–40.

Glazunov, Aleksandr Konstantinovich (1865–1936). Composer. He studied under Rimsky-Korsakov and is regarded as the leading representative of the Rimsky-Korsakov school. He became the director of St Petersburg Conservatoire in the wake of the 1905 revolution, and remained in this post until 1928, when he failed to return from a European concert tour.

Glebov, Igor. See **Asafyev.**

Glière, Reyngol'd Moritsevich (Reinhold Ernst) (1874/5–1956). Composer. He studied composition under Ippolitov-Ivanov, and he is normally considered to be a representative of the Rimsky-Korsakov school. Early in his career, he became Prokofiev's composition teacher. With his unabashedly conservative style, he enjoyed considerable recognition in the USSR, winning three Stalin Prizes. From 1938 to 1948, he was head of the Composers' Union.

Glinka, Mikhail Ivanovich (1804–57). Composer. He has the status of founding father of Russian national music, based above all on his two operas, *A Life for the Tsar* and *Ruslan and Lyudmila*.

Gnesin, Mikhail Fabianovich (1883–1957). Composer. Studied under Rimsky-Korsakov and Lyadov at St Petersburg Conservatoire. Served as a professor at Moscow Conservatoire (1925–36), and later at Leningrad Conservatoire and the Gnesin Institute.

Gogol, Nikolay Vasil'yevich (1809–52). Novelist and dramatist. Author of many satirical prose works and plays, often with Hoffmann-esque supernatural elements.

Goldenweiser (Gol'denveyzer), **Aleksandr Borisovich** (1875–1961). Pianist. In spite of his conservative outlook and religious views, he remained a professor at Moscow Conservatoire from 1906 to 1961.

Goleyzovsky, Kas'yan Yaroslavich (1892–1970). Dancer and choreographer. He received a broad education, showing proficiency in languages, painting, music, and sports. He danced at the Bolshoi from 1909 to 1918, and from 1916 began to choreograph short ballets and individual concert numbers for various private theatres and for his own Moscow Chamber Ballet company, winning renown for his unusual ideas and innovations. His Soviet career was chequered, but he enjoyed a late return to fame in the 1960s.

Golovanov, Nikolay Semyonovich (1891–1953). Conductor. He began his career as a choral conductor with the Synodal choir, and from 1915 worked at the Bolshoi Theatre (from 1919 to 1928 and 1930 to 1936 as conductor, and from 1948 to 1953 as head conductor). He was married to the soprano Antonina Nezhdanova.

Gorbachev, Mikhail Sergeyevich (b. 1931). Soviet politician, General Secretary of the Communist Party from 1985–91. His foreign policy initiatives helped to bring about the downfall of Eastern Bloc regimes, while his internal political reforms effectively served as a transition to the dissolution of the Soviet Union (a goal he disavowed). The recipient of many international awards (including the Nobel Prize in 1990), he has continued to be active as a speaker and writer on the international political scene.

Gorky, Maksim (pen-name of Aleksey Maksimovich Peshkov) (1868–1936). He became a popular writer at the turn of the twentieth century, acquiring fame for his socially conscious portrayal of the dispossessed. Unhappy with the forcefulness of Bolshevik rule in the aftermath of the Revolution, he spent most of the 1920s abroad. In 1932 he returned to the USSR, and played a key role in establishing the aesthetic doctrine of Socialist Realism.

Gorodetsky, Sergey Mitrofanovich (1884–1967). Poet. Prior to the Revolution, he was known for his Symbolist work, but he later dedicated most of his time to translations and opera libretti, famously creating the Soviet version of Glinka's opera *A Life for the Tsar* (*Ivan Susanin*, 1939).

Gorodinsky, Viktor Markovich (1902–59). Soviet musicologist. He rose through the administrative ranks to become head of the arts section of the Communist Party Central Committee (1935–7).

Gorsky, Aleksandr Alekseyevich (1871–1924). Ballet dancer and choreographer, he studied in St Petersburg, then from 1902 became a choreographer at the Bolshoi in Moscow, where he remained until his death. Gorsky's choreographical innovations, breaking many of the classical conventions, were one of the influences on Diaghilev's practices.

Grechaninov, Aleksandr Tikhonovich (1864–1956). Composer. He was best known for his operas (particularly the nationalist *Dobrinya Nikitich*, 1901, and the symbolist *Sister Beatrice*, 1910), and for his church music. He emigrated in 1925.

Grinberg, Matias Markovich (also used the name Sokolsky) (1896–1977). Pianist and musicologist. He occupied various posts in Soviet music administration.

Gusman, Boris Yevseyevich (1892–1944). Music and theatre critic and arts administrator. Although a violinist by training, he rose through the ranks to become head of repertoire and deputy director of the Bolshoi Theatre in 1929–30. From 1933, he worked for Soviet radio, then served as a member of the Committee for Arts Affairs (*Komitet po delam iskusstv*).

Hindemith, Paul (1895–1963). German composer, violist and violinist. In the 1920s, he achieved international fame for his compositions in a neoclassical style mixed with expressionism and popular dance music. In 1921 he founded the Amar Quartet in which he served as violist; the quartet toured extensively in Europe and the Soviet Union. His music fell into disfavour under the Nazis, and in 1938 he emigrated, first to Switzerland and then to the United States.

Holst, Gustav Theodore (1874–1934). English composer. He wrote several operas (some of them based on Sanskrit texts), but achieved fame as the composer of *The Planets*, a symphonic suite inspired by his interest in astrology. Holst's adaptation of the theme of the 'Jupiter' movement to fit the words of a patriotic and religious text 'I vow to thee my country', was first performed in 1925 and used thereafter in official British Armistice Day ceremonies.

Honegger, Arthur (1892–1955). French composer of Swiss extraction, a member of *Les six*. His oratorio *King David* (1921) first brought him to public attention, but this was overshadowed by his machine-age symphonic poem *Pacific 231*, portraying a high-speed steam engine.

Horowitz (Gorovits), **Vladimir Samoylovich** (1903–89). Pianist. A graduate of the Kiev Conservatoire, he toured extensively during the early 1920s. In 1925 he went to study with Artur Schnabel, but did not return to the Soviet Union, rejecting an invitation to represent the Ukrainian Soviet Republic at the 1927 Chopin Competition. He settled in the US, and visited Russia again only in 1986, at the end of his illustrious career.

Igumnov, Konstantin Nikolayevich (1873–1948). Pianist and piano teacher. He graduated from Moscow Conservatoire in 1894, then gave recitals (mainly in Moscow) and taught at the Conservatoire. From 1924 to 1928, he served as the director of the Conservatoire.

Ippolitov-Ivanov (born Ivanov), **Mikhail Mikhaylovich** (1859–1935). Composer and conductor. He studied under Rimsky-Korsakov at St Petersburg Conservatoire, graduating in 1882. In 1893, he was appointed as a professor of composition at Moscow Conservatoire, and from 1906 to 1922 served as director. As a conductor, he worked for the Mamontov and Zimin Private Opera Houses, and later at the Bolshoi. As a composer, he carried the Orientalist strand of the Russian national style into the Soviet era, working with different folk materials.

Ivanov, Vyacheslav Ivanovich (1866–1949). Poet. Before the Revolution, he was a prominent member of the Symbolist movement, hosting the celebrated 'Tower' artistic salon. After the Revolution, he also worked in the Theatre Department of Narkompros. He travelled abroad in 1924, with Lunacharsky's permission, and never returned, settling in Italy.

Ivanov-Boretsky, Mikhail Vladimirovich (1874–1936). Musicologist. A law graduate, he studied composition with Rimsky-Korsakov and music history in Italy. He was appointed as a professor at the Moscow Conservatoire in 1922, founding the musicology department. Among his works are important publications of music-historical sources.

Josquin des Prez (*c*. 1450/55–1521). French composer of polyphonic choral music.

Jurgenson, Boris Petrovich (1868–1935). Music publisher. He inherited the firm from his father Pyotr Jurgenson, a friend of Tchaikovsky's. He owned the company until its nationalisation in 1918, after which he was employed as the company's manager.

Kabalevsky, Dmitriy Borisovich (1904–87). Composer. He studied composition under Myaskovsky and piano under Goldenweiser. He became one of the most prominent Soviet composers and achieved international fame through his music for children.

Kaganovich, Lazar' Moiseyevich (1893–1991). Soviet party functionary. A shoemaker by trade, he took part in revolutionary protests in Ukraine. During the 1920s, he worked his way to the highest ranks of the Party, and became a close associate of Stalin. His fraudulent management of the vote at the 1934 Party Congress prevented Stalin from being replaced by Kirov. He held senior positions until the late 1950s.

Kamenev (born Rosenfeld)**, Lev Borisovich** (1883–1936). Old Bolshevik, member of the Central Committee from 1907. Together with Zinoviev, he voted against the armed uprising in October 1917, hoping to achieve power by electoral means. Despite this, he became a member of the Politburo in 1919. In the years 1925–27 he led the so-called 'new opposition' against Stalin. His official standing fluctuated until his arrest in 1934; he was executed two years later.

Kameneva, Ol'ga Davidovna (1883–1941). Trotsky's sister and Kamenev's first wife, she was placed in charge of theatres by Narkompros after the Revolution. Her hard-line stance led to her removal from the post in 1920, after which she occupied several other official positions. In the wake of Kamenev's trial, she and her two children were also arrested and later executed.

Kamensky, Aleksandr Danilovich (1900–52). Pianist and composer. As a pianist, he studied with Leonid Nikolayev (he was a classmate of Shostakovich), and as a composer under Shcherbachov and Yavorsky. In the 1920s, he was much in demand for premieres of both Russian and Western new music.

Kamensky, Vasiliy Vasil'yevich (1884–1961). Futurist poet. Together with Mayakovsky, he was a member of LEF (the artistic 'left front').

Kankarovich, Anatoliy Isayevich (1885–1956). Composer, conductor, and musicologist. As a composer, he studied under Rimsky-Korsakov and Liadov, as a conductor under Nikolay Tcherepnin. He conducted at the Zimin Opera House from 1914 to 1918, at the Leningrad Philharmonia from 1926 to 1928. From 1922 to 1924, he served as an emissary of MUZO.

Karatygin (Karatïgin)**, Vyacheslav Gavrilovich** (1875–1925). Music critic. A keen advocate of Scriabin, Prokofiev, and Stravinsky, he was a professor at the Petrograd Conservatoire from 1919 onwards.

Kastalsky, Aleksandr Dmitriyevich (1856–1926). Choral conductor, composer, and musicologist. From 1910 he was director of the Synodal School, which in 1918 became the People's Choral Academy. He wrote influential studies of Russian 'folk harmony'.

Katuar, Georgiy L'vovich (1861–1926). Composer and music theorist from a Russified French family. From 1919, he taught composition at the Moscow Conservatoire.

Keldysh (Keldïsh)**, Yuriy Vsevolodovich** (1907–95). Musicologist. A member of RAPM from 1926 to its demise in 1932, he went on to have a distinguished career as a scholar of Russian music.

Kerensky, Aleksandr Fyodorovich (1881–1970). A barrister by training, he became a deputy of the State Duma, where he earned a reputation as a brilliant orator for leftist factions. After the February Revolution of 1917, he was appointed first as Justice Minister, then as an Army and Navy Minister, and from July as a prime-minister of the Provisional Government, where his reputation as a leftist served to cover for the continuation of the war, the lack of land reform and the postponement of elections. After he was ousted from power by the October Revolution, he fled first to the south, then to France, and eventually settled in the USA.

Kerzhentsev, Platon Mikhaylovich (1881–1940). Soviet functionary, principally in the arts. A professional revolutionary, he spent much of his early life in exile and emigration. After 1917, returned to Russia and occupied positions in Narkompros, Narkomindel (Ministry of Foreign Affairs), also serving as a diplomat and newspaper editor. From 1928 to 1930, he was deputy of the Central Committee's Agitprop Department, and from 1933 to 1936, Head of the Radio Committee. From 1936 to 1938, his career reached its apex as he served as head of the Committee for Arts Affairs.

Khayt, Yuliy (Il'ya) **Abramovich** (1897–1966). Composer. After flourishing as a composer of light music in the NEP period of the 1920s, he switched to mass songs and brass band marches. His main claim to fame is the song '*Vsyo vïshe*' ('Ever Higher') which, despite being a target of RAPM criticism, was in 1933 proclaimed the official anthem of the USSR air force.

Khlebnikov, Velimir (Viktor Vladimirovich, 1885–1922). Futurist poet. He was one of the most important experimental poets of the time and is also remembered for his utopian ideas: one of them was to create a global government of 317 best people (Chairmen of the Globe). Khlebnikov himself was one, and invited Lourié to become another.

Klemperer, Otto (1885–1973). German conductor. He was a friend and protégé of Mahler, and went on to hold positions in a number of German opera houses. As a symphonic conductor, he toured Europe and the Soviet Union. He emigrated to the USA in 1933, but after the war returned to Europe.

Klimov, Mikhail Georgiyevich (1881–1937). Choral conductor. He studied at the Synodal School and St Petersburg Conservatoire (composition under Rimsky-Korsakov, conducting under Nikolay Tcherepnin). He began his career at the Imperial Court Cappella in 1904, and from 1917 to 1930 served as its director, presiding over the Cappella's secularisation after the October Revolution. From 1925 to 1927, he was also director of the Leningrad Philharmonia.

Knipper, Lev Konstantinovich (1898–1974). Composer. He studied at Moscow Conservatoire under Glière. In the 1920s, he was a member of ASM, and in 1930 wrote the opera *Wind from the North* (*Severnïy veter*) which was the first artistically successful opera on Soviet subject matter. His main claim to fame, however, is his mass song '*Polyushko-pole*' (internationally known as 'Meadowland'). There has been much exploration of Knipper's colourful and puzzling biography. Born into a Russified German family, he was a nephew of Olga Knipper-Chekhova, Chekhov's wife. His sister, Olga Chekhova, emigrated to Germany and became a famous film actress, a favourite of Hitler's. It has been widely suggested that both Lev and Olga served as spies for the Soviet government.

Kochetov, Nikolay Razumnikovich (1864–1925). Music critic, conductor and composer. He taught at the Moscow Synodal School and its Soviet successor, the Choral Academy. He was the composer of one of the earliest choruses on Soviet subject-matter ('*Gimn-marsh*'). He is not to be confused with his son Vadim (1898–1951), also a Soviet composer.

Kochetov, Vadim Nikolayevich (1898–1951). Composer. He studied composition with Vasilenko and Anatoly Aleksandrov, and made his mark in particular on music for children.

Kodály, Zoltán (1882–1967). Hungarian composer, ethnomusicologist, and pedagogue. Together with Béla Bartók, he forged an idiom that was both nationalist and modernist, winning widespread recognition with his Psalmus Hungaricus (1923). Today he is better known for his pioneering 'Kodály Method' in music education.

Kolchak, Aleksandr Vasil'yevich (1874–1920). Vice-Admiral in Tsarist Navy, counter-revolutionary dictator of eastern Russia during the Civil War. He was removed from his command in the wake of the February Revolution. After the October Revolution was persuaded by the British to launch a counter-revolutionary offensive. In Siberia, he became dictator when the anti-Bolshevik Government in Omsk was overthrown by its more right-wing elements, sparking a revolt that ended with mass executions ordered by Kolchak, driving the anti-Bolshevik remnant of the Socialist Revolutionaries to amalgamate their forces with the Red Army. His brutality in restoring the Tsarist *status quo ante* led to large-scale rebellions in the territory he ruled, causing his military campaign at the front to crumble. He was captured, tried and executed.

Komissarzhevsky, Fyodor Fyodorovich (1882–1954). Theatre director, brother of the celebrated actress Vera Komissarzhevskaya. He originally worked in drama, then also in opera, where he was famous for his experimental productions. In 1919, he emigrated and developed a successful international career.

Kon, Feliks Yakovlevich (1864–1941). A Polish revolutionary, he spent much of his early adulthood in Siberian exile, where he conducted anthropological research, and in European emigration. He returned in 1917, and was appointed to a number of political and editorial posts in Ukraine and Russia. In 1930 to 1931, he was appointed head of Glaviskusstvo and its successor, Narkompros's Arts Sector. During the same period, Moscow Conservatoire was given his name in its full title.

Koposov, Aleksey Pavlovich (1902–67). Composer. He studied under Mikhail Gnesin at Moscow Conservatoire, graduating in 1931. He wrote many choral songs and arrangements.

Korchmaryov, Klimentiy Arkadyevich (1899–1958). Composer. He studied at Odessa Conservatoire, then moved to Moscow in 1923, where he joined ORKiMD. Known for his prolific output and blandly conservative style, he was the composer of the opera *Ivan-soldat* (*Ivan the Soldier*) which was staged at the Bolshoi in 1927, much to the consternation of ASM composers.

Korev, Semyon (Simon) **Isaakovich** (1900–53). Musicologist. From 1925 to 1932, he was a member of RAPM, and from 1931 to 1932, served as deputy director of the Moscow Philharmonia. The dissolution of RAPM did not harm his career in music administration, and he went on to occupy important posts in radio and concert organisations.

Kornilov, Lavr Georgiyevich (1870–1918). General in Tsarist Army, counter-revolutionary military leader. In a move to quell dissent among right-wing military leaders, the Provisional Government made him Commander-in-Chief of the Russian Army in July 1917, but he nevertheless led a coup attempt in August 1917, marching his troops towards Petrograd. The Provisional Government was able to survive only by calling upon forces loyal to the Petrograd Soviet. After the October Revolution, he became leader on the Southern Front of the White forces in the Civil War. Boasting that 'the greater the terror, the greater our victories', his campaign lasted only from December 1917 to April 1918 before his army fell to the much larger forces of the Red Army. He died in battle while attempting to besiege the Soviet regional capital.

Koussevitzky (Kusevitskiy)**, Sergey Aleksandrovich** (1874–1951). Celebrated conductor and double-bass player. He emigrated in the early 1920s, after which he continued to lead a successful career as a conductor in the USA.

Koval (real name Kovalyov)**, Marian Viktorovich** (1907–71). Composer. He studied under Gnesin and Myaskovsky at Moscow Conservatoire. He was a member of Prokoll and then RAPM. He won a Stalin Prize in 1943 for his opera *Yemelyan Pugachov*, and after the Party Resolution of 1948 against formalism in music, he was promoted to the top ranks of the Union of Composers' administration, and appointed Editor-in-Chief of the journal *Sovetskaya muzïka*. He published his own hostile account of Shostakovich's entire career in the pages of the journal.

Krasin, Boris Borisovich (1884–1936). Prominent revolutionary and Soviet functionary, brother of Leonid Krasin. He studied music theory and composition, collected folk songs in remote regions of Russia and Mongolia, and participated in the revolutionary movement. After 1917 he became a Soviet cultural official, holding positions in Proletkult, MUZO, and other bodies. From 1921 to 1926, he was Managing Director of the Russian Philharmonia (Rosfil).

Krasin, Leonid Borisovich (1870–1926). Revolutionary and diplomat, brother of Boris Krasin. He left the Bolsheviks and abandoned political activities after conflict with Lenin in 1908. During exile in Berlin, he worked for the company Siemens-Schuckert and became director of its Moscow branch. In 1918 he re-joined the Bolsheviks after some hesitation, and later participated in a number of important peace and trade negotiations including the Brest-Litovsk peace treaty. He held senior diplomatic posts in Paris and London.

Krein (Kreyn)**, Aleksandr Abramovich** (1883–1951). Composer, brother of Grigoriy Krein. Before the Revolution he taught at the People's Conservatoire. From 1918 to 1927 he worked in Narkompros and at the State Music Publishers. He was one of the first composers to write systematically on Soviet subject-matter. Another significant part of his work employed Jewish plots and musical material.

Krein (Kreyn)**, Grigoriy Abramovich** (1879–1955). Composer, brother of Alexander Krein and father of the composer Yulian Krein. From 1926 to 1934, he lived abroad. A significant part of his work employs Jewish plots and musical material.

Krenek, Ernst (1900–91). Austrian composer. His greatest success was the opera *Jonny spielt auf* (1926), a work on contemporary subject matter and containing jazz-influenced music. The same opera earned him a place on the list of 'degenerate' composers during the Nazi period, and in 1938 he emigrated to the USA.

Kruchenykh (Kruchyonïkh)**, Aleksey Yeliseyevich** (1886–1968). Futurist poet. He is credited with the invention of *zaum*, or 'transrational' poetry based on combinations of sounds for their own sake. He had to abandon poetry at the beginning of the 1930s, and his output thereafter consisted of critical and scholarly work only.

Kruchinin, Valentin Yakovlevich (1892–1970). Popular composer. He wrote many popular songs in the 1920s. His career survived RAPM attacks, and he went on to become a prolific composer of Soviet mass songs and operettas.

Krupskaya, Nadezhda Konstantinovna (1869–1939). Revolutionary and Soviet politician; married to Lenin. She met Lenin in 1894 in a Marxist circle, and thereafter participated in his revolutionary activities. After the Revolution, she was given a leading role in Soviet education and, in particular, the communist education of children. In 1920 she was appointed Chair of Glavpolitprosvet, in 1927 became a member of the Central Committee, and in 1929 was appointed Deputy Minister of Education. In the 1930s, she was demoted, but did not succumb to Stalin's purges.

Krylova, Sarra Alekseyevna (1894–1988). Singer and music critic, wife of Lev Lebedinsky and member of RAPM.

Kryukov, Nikolay Nikolayevich (1906–61). Film composer; brother of Vladimir Kryukov. In 1950 he created a new score for Eisenstein's *Battleship Potemkin*.

Kryukov, Vladimir Nikolayevich (1902–60). Composer; brother of Nikolay Kryukov. He studied with Myaskovsky and is best known for his operas *The Stationmaster* (1940) and *Dmitry Donskoy* (1947).

Kryzhanovsky, Ivan Ivanovich (1867–1924). Doctor of medicine who worked with Pavlov, he was also a composer, a student of Rimsky-Korsakov. He published works on biological and physiological aspects of music and musical performance. He was Myaskovsky's music-theory teacher and is the dedicatee of that composer's First Symphony.

Kubatsky, Viktor L'vovich (1891–1970). Cellist in the Bolshoi Theatre orchestra. He took initiative in nationalising valuable musical instruments which had been in private hands. Founded the Stradivari Quartet, in which he and his colleagues played these expropriated instruments (1920–30). He took part in the administration of the Bolshoi Theatre during Elena Malinovskaya's periods of directorship (in the early 1920s and early 1930s).

The Kuchka (The Five, The Mighty Handful, '*Moguchaya kuchka*'). A group of composers whose members came together in the 1860s under the leadership of the fine-arts critic Vladimir Stasov and composer Mily Balakirev. The four other composers were Modest Musorgsky, Nikolai Rimsky-Korsakov, Alexander Borodin and César Cui. For at least a decade, they espoused common ideas of musical nationalism. Even after their work and opinions began to diverge, the image of the group as a united musical party was preserved in Stasov's journalism reinforced by younger students and followers of the Kuchka, such as Glazunov and Lyapunov. The Kuchka's nationalism and professed folk inspiration were discussed critically during the 1920s, but were largely endorsed again during the Stalin period, and they were established as a model for Soviet composers on these terms.

Kuper, Emil' Albertovich (1877–1960). Conductor. He worked from 1910 to 1919 at the Bolshoi Theatre and from 1908 conducted the concerts of the Russian Music Society. After working with Diaghilev on the *Saisons Russes*, he served as chief conductor of the former Mariinsky from 1919 to 1924. He emigrated in 1924, and went on to lead a distinguished international career.

Kustodiev (Kustodiyev)**, Boris Mikhaylovich** (1878–1927). Painter and set designer. He produced highly colourful and theatrical paintings, including a famous portrait of Chaliapin. In 1922, he joined AkhRR.

Kuzmin, Mikhail Alekseyevich (1872–1936). Poet. Close to Symbolist circles, he acquired notoriety because of his open references to homosexuality. He created musical accompaniments for many his poems and performed them as melodeclamations. After the Revolution, he turned to translation.

Lamm, Pavel Aleksandrovich (1882–1951). Music scholar. He restored many original scores, including Musorgsky's *Boris Godunov*. For most of his life, he ran a celebrated music circle at his apartment, where many orchestral works played in piano eight-hands arrangements by Lamm himself. A lifelong friend of Myaskovsky, in later life he became Prokofiev's assistant, orchestrating his music from short score.

Lapitsky, Iosif Mikhaylovich (1876–1944). Opera director. After working for the Solodovnikov Opera House (1903–6) and the Bolshoi (1906–8), he founded his own company, the Theatre Of Music Drama in St Petersburg, which allowed him to explore more innovative approaches to opera production. The theatre did not survive the hardships of the Civil War and was closed in 1919.

Lasso, Orlando di (Orlandus Lassus) (1530/32–94). Renaissance composer of choral music.

Lavrenyov (born Sergeyev)**, Boris Andreyevich** (1891–1959). Poet and dramatist. Before the Revolution, he wrote Futurist poetry. On the outbreak of the Civil War, he fought in the Red Army, and became commander of an armoured train. His play *Break* (1927) became one of the first canonical works of Socialist Realism, and he went on to win two Stalin Prizes.

Lebedev-Polyansky (Lebedev)**, Pavel Ivanovich** (1881/2–1948). A professional revolutionary, he became Chairman of the Proletkult Council in 1917. In 1921, after Proletkult's loss of autonomy, he was appointed to head the newly-created censorship organ, Glavlit. He also wrote literary criticism and edited encyclopaedias.

Lebedinsky, Lev Nikolayevich (1904–92). Musicologist. A member of the Communist Party from 1919, he became a founding member of RAPM and a leader of the organisation.

Lentulov, Aristarkh Vasil'yevich (1882–1943). Avant-garde artist. A member of the 'Jack of Diamonds' group, he is best known for his colourful cubist-inspired paintings and for his theatrical designs.

Leskov, Nikolay Semyonovich (1831–95). Journalist and writer. He was renowned for his unusual use of language, including many archaic and dialect words, and for his striking and intensely dramatic plots. His 1864 novella, *Lady Macbeth of the Mtsensk District*, was the basis for Shostakovich's opera of the same name.

Levina, Zara Aleksandrovna (1906–76). Composer. She studied under Glière and Myaskovsky, graduating from Moscow Conservatoire in 1932. Together with her husband, Nikolay Chemberdzhi, she was a member of RAPM. Her work lay mainly in art song and chamber music.

Litinsky, Genrikh Il'yich (1901–85). Composer. He studied under Glière at Moscow Conservatoire, and upon his graduation was appointed to teach composition and theory there. In 1932 he became head of the conservatoire's Composition Department. He contributed to the development of music in the Yakut Autonomous Republic (now Sakha), becoming the first Yakut 'national' composer.

Litolff, Henry Charles (1818–91). Pianist and composer. His symphonic works for orchestra with piano obbligato (his 'concertos symphoniques'), which he performed himself, won him much renown during his lifetime, and he was also a prolific operatic composer. His work is now largely forgotten, and he is better known as the founder of the Litolff Edition publishing house. He was born in England but moved to continental Europe after an elopement.

Lobachev (Lobachyov), **Grigoriy Grigor'yevich** (1888–1953). Choral conductor and composer. He composed some of the earliest choruses on Soviet themes, and is seen as one of the creators of the 'mass song'. He was active in Proletkult, and was associated with ORKiMD.

Lopukhov, Fyodor Vasil'yevich (1886–1973). Dancer and choreographer. He danced at the Mariinsky and Bolshoi before the Revolution, and in 1922 became chief choreographer at the former Mariinsky, staging both classical ballets and modern works by Stravinsky and Shostakovich.

Lossky, Vladimir Apollonovich (1874–1946). Operatic bass and opera director. After a career in opera and operetta, he began work as a director in 1909, and in the 1920s worked at the Bolshoi Theatre, producing both the classics and early Soviet operas.

Lourié, Artur Sergeyevich (Arthur Vincent) (1892–1966). Composer, head of MUZO from 1918 to 1921. He emigrated in 1921, settling in the USA.

Lukin (born Saks), **Lev Ivanovich** (1892–1961). Choreographer. He was renowned for his experimental stagings of short ballets and concert numbers. From 1920 to 1924, he led his own company, the Free Ballet Studio.

Lunacharsky, Anatoliy Vasil'yevich (1875–1933). First Soviet minister for the arts, sciences and education. He studied philosophy under Richard Avenarius at Zürich University. A member of the Russian Social-Democratic Party from 1898, he became an active revolutionary, siding with Lenin's Bolsheviks. One of the principal targets of Lenin's philosophical polemic against 'Empiriocriticism', he joined the leftist group 'Forward' in 1909. In 1917, however, he rejoined the Bolsheviks and after the October Revolution became Minister for Enlightenment. Simultaneously with his political activities, he maintained a literary career as a playwright and critic. He was removed from his ministerial position in 1929, where he was seen as a potential obstacle to a policy shift towards tighter control of the arts. He was demoted, and served as a senior Soviet diplomat until the time of his death, four years later.

Lyapunov, Sergey Mikhaylovich (1859–1924). Composer. He studied under Taneyev, but his principal artistic influence was Mily Balakirev. He taught at the St Petersburg/Petrograd Conservatoire from 1910 to 1923, then emigrated to Paris.

Lysenko, Trofim Denisovich (1898–1976). Agronomist. A proponent of Lamarckism (the heritability of acquired characteristics), he won Stalin's patronage and was placed in charge of the whole of Soviet agriculture. After Stalin's death, Lysenko's influence waned, and his methods were officially discredited by the 1960s, when he was blamed for the destruction of Soviet genetics.

MacDonald, Ramsay (1866–1937). British Prime Minister (1924, 1931–5). Labour Party leader who headed Britain's first Labour Government, which was brought down after only nine months, due to the scandal created by a faked letter supposedly from Zinoviev, which cast MacDonald most implausibly as an agent of 'Leninism' in Britain. He later left Labour, joining forces with the Conservative Party to head a National Government.

Mahler, Gustav (1860–1911). Austrian composer of nine expansive symphonies, and one of the leading conductors of his time. His style bridges late Romanticism and Expressionism. He won a significant following in the Soviet Union during the 1920s among ASM musicians, and exerted a lasting influence on Shostakovich.

Malinovskaya, Yelena Konstantinovna (1870–1942). Theatrical administrator. A Bolshevik, she was wife of the architect and fellow Bolshevik P. P. Malinovsky. Before the Revolution she was involved in the popular theatre movement; after the Revolution she worked in the Narkompros department responsible for state theatres. She was director of the Bolshoi Theatre from 1920 to 1924 and from 1930 to 1935.

Malipiero, Gian Francesco (1882–1973). Italian composer. He came to prominence after his move to Paris in the 1920s, where he associated with Alfredo Casella and came under Stravinsky's influence. Casella helped to bring his works to the attention of Russian audiences on his tour of the Soviet Union in 1926. His career under Mussolini was chequered, and he developed an anti-Germanic Italian nationalist style that eventually moved towards atonality. He was also notable for his work on the Complete Edition of Monteverdi's works.

Malko (Mal'ko)**, Nikolay Andreyevich** (1863–1961). Conductor. A student of Nikolay Tcherepnin, he became a prominent conductor in Soviet Russia during the 1920s, remembered particularly for his premiere of Shostakovich's First Symphony in 1926. From 1929 he went to work abroad, at first hoping to establish an international career without having to emigrate. After finding various posts in Europe, he moved to the USA on the outbreak of war, and ended his career in Australia.

Malkov, Nikolay Petrovich (1882–1942). Music critic. A law graduate, he was a musical autodidact. He began publishing his critical articles in 1912. In the 1920s, he headed the Music Section of the Petrograd/Leningrad journal *Zhizn' iskusstva* (Artistic Life).

Mandelshtam, Osip Emil'yevich (1891–1938). Poet and essayist, originally a Symbolist, later an Acmeist. In 1933 he penned an acerbic anti-Stalin poem which someone forwarded to the authorities. He was arrested in 1934, and died in a labour camp from typhoid fever.

Mayakovsky, Vladimir Vladimirovich (1893–1930). Poet. He began his career as a Futurist, and after the Revolution enthusiastically worked for the Soviet government (although Lenin, for one, did not appreciate his efforts). He was the organiser of LEF (The Left Front in literature and arts). His suicide in 1930 was widely considered an act of political despair, but he was posthumously given the status of leading Soviet poet a few years later.

Medtner (Metner)**, Nikolay Karlovich** (1879–1951). Composer and pianist. He served as a professor of the Moscow Conservatoire until 1921, when he emigrated, eventually settling in England. As a composer of conservative bent, principally of solo piano music and songs for voice and piano, he worked in the shadow of Rachmaninov. In 1927, he returned to the Soviet Union for a concert tour, which met with little success (it coincided with Prokofiev's much more high-profile tour).

Melkikh, Dmitriy Mikheyevich (1885–1943). Composer, student of Yavorsky.

Meshcheryakov, Nikolay Leonidovich (1865–1942). He was the first head of Glavlit, the censorship body.

Messman, Vladimir L'vovich (1898–1972). Composer and musicologist. A student of Ippolitov-Ivanov, he was a military band leader during the Civil War. In 1922, he published the journal *Muzika*, and from 1926 to 1928 he chaired the Composers' Section of MoDPiK. He was best known thereafter for his military marches and film scores.

Meychik, Mark Naumovich (1880–1950). Pianist, who after the Revolution held many positions in arts administration.

Meyerhold (Meyerkhol'd)**, Vsevolod Emil'yevich** (born Karl Kasimir Theodor Meyerhold) (1874–1940). Actor and theatre director. Born to a German-Russian family, he converted to Orthodoxy and took the name Vsevolod. He began his career as an actor at the famous Moscow Art Theatre, and during the 1910s, he participated in various experimental productions, developing his own, non-realist style of theatre. In 1918, he joined the Bolshevik party, and in 1922, as NEP began, he opened his own theatre, which continued to be the most prominent representative of the Soviet avant-garde, stirring up controversy until Meyerhold's arrest in 1939.

Milhaud, Darius (1892–1974). French composer, member of the group *Les six*. He visited the Soviet Union for a concert tour in 1927.

Miturich, Pyotr Vasil'yevich (1887–1956). Artist and theorist of art. In the 1910s and early 1920s, he was close to the Futurists. He painted the best-known portrait of Lourié.

Mogilevsky, Aleksandr Yakovlevich (1885–1955), first violin of the Stradivari Quartet, in 1920–21. Emigrating in 1922, he eventually settled in Tokyo, where he was a great influence on the playing and teaching of the violin in Japan.

Molotov, Vyacheslav Mikhaylovich (1890–1986). Old Bolshevik, he came to occupy some of the top positions in Soviet government and was one of Stalin's closest associates. During his tenure as Foreign Minister, he put his name to the pact of non-aggression between the Soviet Union and Nazi Germany.

Monteux, Pierre (1875–1964). French conductor. He came to public attention through conducting for Diaghilev's *Saisons russes*, including the premieres of Stravinsky's *Petrushka* and *The Rite of Spring*, and Debussy's *Jeux*. His subsequent career was divided between the USA and Europe: he was at different times chief conductor of the Boston Symphony and London Symphony orchestras. He visited the Soviet Union in 1926 for a highly successful concert tour, performing several major modernist works, including the Russian premiere of Prokofiev's *Chout*.

Mosolov, Aleksandr Vasil'yevich (1900–73). Composer. He worked for the post-October Revolutionary Government before joining the Red Army during the Civil War. A leading figure in ASM during the 1920s, he wrote uncompromisingly modernist music, drawing from Expressionism, machine-age styles, and from Central Asian traditional music. Unlike most of his fellow composers, he never recovered as an artist from the imposed conservatism of Socialist Realism.

Myaskovsky, Nikolay Yakovlevich (1881–1950). Composer and teacher, patriarch of the Soviet compositional school. Exceptionally prolific, he wrote 27 symphonies, 13 quartets and many other instrumental and vocal works. He played a leading role in ASM, but took steps towards a rapprochement with RAPM at the height of its power. His Twelfth Symphony 'The Collective Farm', became an early model for symphonic writing under Socialist Realism. He suffered a loss of prestige in 1948, and died before this was reversed.

Nebolsin, Vasiliy Vasil'yevich (1898–1958). Conductor for the Bolshoi Theatre and the Moscow Philharmonia.

Nemirovich-Danchenko, Vladimir Ivanovich (1858–1943). Theatre director, critic, and dramatist. Together with Stanislavsky, he founded the Moscow Art Theatre (1898) and later headed its 'Music Studio' (an operatic troupe), which competed with Stanislavsky's Opera Studio at the Bolshoi (in 1941 the two were amalgamated in the Stanislavsky and Nemirovich-Danchenko Music Theatre).

Nezhdanova, Antonina Vasil'yevna (1873–1950). Operatic soprano. She sang at the Bolshoi for 30 years, taking many leading roles. She was married to the conductor Nikolay Golovanov.

Nikisch, Arthur (1855–1922) Hungarian conductor. He held posts with the Leipzig *Gewandhaus* and Berlin Philharmonic for most of his career, but also conducted the Vienna, London, and Boston symphony orchestras. He was one of the first conductors to have his work preserved in audio recordings.

Novitsky, Pavel Ivanovich (1888–1971). Critic, scholar of drama, and arts administrator. He headed the Arts Section of Glavnauka (1925–6), and then the Theatre and Music Section of Glaviskusstvo (1928–9), continuing a successful administrative career well into the 1940s.

Obolensky, Leonid Leonidovich (1873–1930). Soviet politician. His higher education was musical, and he studied under Rimsky-Korsakov. In 1917, he left the Mensheviks to join the Bolsheviks. After the Revolution, he was appointed to senior positions in the Finance Ministry, and also served as a diplomat during the 1920s (he was the Soviet representative in Poland from 1923 to 1924). In 1929, he was a short-lived head of Glaviskusstvo, and in the last year of his life, he was appointed director of the Hermitage Museum.

Oransky, Viktor Aleksandrovich (born Gershov) (1899–1953). Composer. He wrote the ballet *Futbolist* (*The Footballer*) and much other music for the stage, including several operettas and children's operas.

Parnakh, Valentin Yakovlevich (real name Parnokh) (1891–1951). Poet, translator, dancer and musician. He lived in Europe during the pre-Revolutionary years, researching medieval Jewish poetry in Spain and performing at Dadaist meetings in Paris, among other activities. In 1922, he returned to Russia, along with a full set of instruments for jazz. He soon established Russia's first jazz band, introducing the music to Russian culture several years before the first American jazz musicians arrived. He is also responsible for the Russianised word '*dzhaz*'. He worked for the Meyerhold theatre, incorporating jazz into its incidental music.

Pashchenko, Andrey Filippovich (1883–1972). Composer and conductor. He studied under Shteynberg at St Petersburg Conservatoire, and began conducting from 1919. He was prolific, writing 17 operas and 16 symphonies, but is particularly remembered as the composer of one of the earliest Soviet operas, *Orliniy bunt* (*The Eagle Revolt*, 1925).

Pavlovskaya (Orlova), **Valentina Konstantinovna** (1884/1888–1947). Operatic soprano. She sang leading roles at the former Mariinsky from 1924 to 1947. She was the first Russian Salomé.

Pelshe (Karklis), **Robert Andreyevich** (1880–1955). Revolutionary activist, diplomat and cultural administrator. A Party member since 1898, he participated in the 1905 revolution in Latvia, fled to Paris, then participated in the 1917 Bolshevik Revolution in Moscow. After the Revolution, his career spanned diplomatic posts and cultural administration. From 1925 to 1926, he was Chairman of Glavrepertkom, and later became the editor of the arts paper *Sovetskoye iskusstvo*.

Petri, Egon (1881–1962). Pianist. He was a disciple and friend of Busoni. Born in Germany to parents from The Netherlands, he lived in Switzerland, Poland, and eventually the United States. In 1923, he became the first foreign soloist to play in the Soviet Union.

Piotrovsky, Adrian Ivanovich (1898–1938). Philologist and translator of ancient texts. He was Director of the State Institute of Arts History (GIII) from 1925. He was active on the cultural scene as a supporter of modernist theatre and cinema. His reluctance to adjust to the new dispensation in the 1930s eventually led to his arrest and execution.

Pisk, Paul Amadeus (1893–1990). Austrian composer and musicologist. He studied with Schreker and Schoenberg, and was one of the founding members of the International Society for Contemporary Music (ISCM).

Pokrovsky, Mikhail Nikolayevich (1868–1932). An old Bolshevik and eminent Marxist historian, he was Deputy Minister of Education from 1918 to 1932.

Poletaev, Evgeniy Alekseyevich (1885–1937). Philologist and translator. He was recruited to work for Narkompros alongside Lourié and Punin. In 1918, he and Punin co-authored the brochure *Against Civilisation*, which called for a shift of emphasis in policy towards the encouragement of culture produced by the masses; this polemic was published with a foreword by Lunacharsky.

Polferov, Yakov Yakovlevich (1891–1966). Composer and conductor. He studied at St Petersburg Conservatoire in 1908–11, then at Odessa Conservatoire. During the early 1920s, he earned his living as a conductor at various opera houses in Petrograd and the provinces, and he edited a weekly Petrograd theatrical journal. In 1924, he moved to Kharkov where he worked as a musicologist and administrator.

Polovinkin, Leonid Andreyevich (1894–1949). Composer, particularly known for his theatre and children's music. He was active in ASM.

Popov, Gavriil Nikolayevich (1904–72). Soviet composer. His modernist Septet (1927) and his ambitious Symphony No. 1 (1928–35) held out the (unfulfilled) promise that he might become a composer the equal of Shostakovich. Among Soviet audiences, his best-known music was the film score for *Chapayev*.

Popov, Sergey Sergeyevich (1887–1937). Music scholar, who held positions in the Radio Committee, at the Bolshoi Theatre and at the State Music Publishers. He was a member of the Lamm–Myaskovsky circle. He was arrested and executed in 1937 (although his relatives were later given 1942 as the year of his death).

Pototsky, Sergey Ivanovich (1883–1958). Composer. He studied at Moscow Conservatoire under Taneyev and Vasilenko. He composed four operas, but is best remembered for the first, *Proriv* (*The Breakthrough*, 1930), which was one of the earliest to tackle Soviet subject matter.

Poulenc, Francis Jean Marcel (1899–1963). French composer, member of the group *Les six*. Wiener and Milhaud helped to publicise his music for Russian audiences during their concert tours of 1926.

Preys, Aleksandr Germanovich (1905–42). Opera librettist. He collaborated with Shostakovich on his operas *The Nose* and *Lady Macbeth of Mtsensk*.

Prokofiev, Sergey Sergeyevich (1891–1953). Composer and pianist. A graduate of St Petersburg Conservatoire, he left Russia in 1918 with Lunacharsky's reluctant acceptance, but after his triumphant Russian tour of 1927, he gradually spent increasing amounts of time there, until he returned permanently in 1936. With Shostakovich, he occupied a privileged position as one of the Soviet Union's most eminent artists. His status suffered a reversal in 1948.

Protopopov, Sergey Vladimirovich (1893–1954). Composer. He graduated in 1921 from Yavorsky's class at the Kiev Conservatoire. In the 1920s, he was one of ASM's composers, his works following Yavorsky's theory of 'modal rhythm'. He lived with Yavorsky as his partner.

Pshibïshevsky, Boleslav Stanislavovich (Bolesław Przybyszewski) (1892–1937). Musician and revolutionary. Son of the Polish Symbolist writer Stanisław Przybyszewski, he moved to Russia after the Revolution and joined the Party. From 1929 to 1931 he was Director of the Moscow Conservatoire. In the 1930s, he wrote a Marxist monograph on Beethoven. He served three years in labour camps for homosexuality after Stalin reversed earlier Soviet laws. Like many other non-Russians, he was arrested and executed on charges of espionage.

Puccini, Giacomo (1858–1924). Italian composer, whose operas *La Bohème*, *Tosca*, and *Madama Butterfly* have been among the most popular items in the operatic repertoire since the time of their composition.

Punin, Nikolay Nikolayevich (1888–1953). Art historian. He championed the artistic avant-garde, and in 1918 was appointed by Lunacharsky to head the Fine Arts section of Narkompros. He was later given charge of the Russian Museum and the Hermitage Museum in Petrograd. He was arrested several times: in 1921, in the 1930s (released owing to Akhmatova's petition on his behalf), and finally in 1949. He died in a labour camp.

Putin, Vladimir Vladimirovich (b. 1952). President of the Russian Federation 2000–2008, and again 2012–. Prime Minister 2008–12.

Rabinovich, Isaak Moiseyevich (1894–1961). Artist and set designer. In addition to his theatrical work, he received commissions for the Moscow Metro and for the (unrealised) Palace of Soviets.

Rachmaninov (Rakhmaninov, Rachmaninoff), **Sergey Vasil'yevich** (1883–1943). Pianist and composer. In the 1910s, he was the most prestigious composer in Russia, but he emigrated in 1918 and developed an international career as a pianist, based in the USA. His relations with the Soviet Union became strained after he co-authored an anti-Soviet letter to the New York Times in 1931, and his works were removed from the repertoire. Relations were repaired during the Second World War, when Rachmaninov raised substantial sums for the Soviet war effort through benefit concerts; his works reappeared thereafter.

Radek, Karl Berngardovich (real name Karol Sobelsohn) (1885–1939). A professional revolutionary in Germany and Poland, he became an important figure in the international Communist movement. While a member of the Central Committee from 1919 to 1924, he was close to Trotsky. He was arrested and murdered in prison during the Purges.

Radlov, Sergey Ernestovich (1892–1958). Theatre director. He was a member of the Meyerhold studio before the Revolution and in the 1920s became one of the most prominent drama and opera directors in Leningrad. He became a prisoner of war during the Second World War, and like many returnees, he was sent to a prison camp, and released only in 1953, following Stalin's death.

Raskolnikov (Ilyin)**, Fyodor Fyodorovich** (1892–1939). A Bolshevik from 1910, he served on the editorial board of the pre-Revolutionary *Pravda*. After the February Revolution he became deputy chairman of the Kronstadt Soviet. He famously read out the Bolshevik statement against the Constituent Assembly, after which the Bolsheviks walked out. During the Civil War, he served as a fleet commander and then Deputy Minister of the Navy. After the War, he served as a diplomat, but his ambitions as a writer brought him closer to positions in the literary and cultural bureaucracy. He became Chairman of Glavrepertkom in 1928, then head of Glaviskusstvo, where he took a harder line than his predecessor Sviderskiy. Held a series of diplomatic positions in the 1930s, but was recalled to the Soviet Union in 1938. He failed to return, and instead published an 'open letter to Stalin'. He fell from a window to his death in 1939, most likely by the hand of an assassin.

Ravel, Maurice (1875–1937). French composer. His early career was marked by scandals over his failure to win a major composition prize, ending in the replacement of the conservative director of Paris Conservatoire with Ravel's mentor, Gabriel Fauré. initially cultivated a progressive and complex style of his own, but was later influenced by neo-classicism and jazz, taking on George Gershwin as a pupil.

Raysky, Nazariy Grigor'yevich (real name Kapitonov) (1876–1958). Operatic tenor and chamber singer. From 1921 to 1929, he was Deputy Director (*prorektor*) of Moscow Conservatoire.

Rebikov, Vladimir Ivanovich (1866–1920). Composer. He studied music privately and from the start of his career cultivated the reputation of a modernist and decadent. In his piano music, he experimented with non-triadic harmony and different modes. Under the influence of Symbolism, he also attempted to combine music with other arts in his 'rhythmodeclamations', 'melomimics' and 'meloplastics'. In his opera *The Christmas Tree*, his most popular work, he demonstrated that he could also compose ably in a post-Tchaikovskian style.

Remizov, Aleksey Mikhaylovich (1877–1957). Writer. He won renown as the author of several strikingly unusual Symbolist novels and dramas. He left Russia in 1921, and eventually settled in Paris.

Renzin, Isay Mikhaylovich (1903–69). Pianist. He studied together with Shostakovich in Nikolayev's class at Petrograd Conservatoire. He remained a friend of Shostakovich, and also performed many of his works.

Rieti, Vittorio (1898–1964). Italian composer. He wrote the ballet *Barabau* for Diaghilev (1925).

Rimsky-Korsakov, Andrey Nikolayevich (1878–1940). Music critic and scholar, son of Nikolay Rimsky-Korsakov. He became chief librarian of the Manuscript Department at the Leningrad Public Library. He undertook significant work on his father's archive and published his biography.

Roger-Ducasse, Jean (1873–1954). French composer. He was a pupil and friend of Fauré.

Roslavets, Natal'ya Alekseyevna (born Langovaya) (1888–1957). Bolshevik, senior secret police officer. She was the first wife of Nikolay Roslavets. A journalist with a higher education, she joined the Bolshevik party in 1918 (previously she had been an SR, then a left SR after the split). From 1918 she was in the Moscow secret police (MChK), where she achieved a high position (department head and member of the Collegium). Her brother Alexander Langovoy (1895–1964) was a high-ranking spy for the Soviet government.

Roslavets, Nikolay Andreyevich (1881–1944). Composer. As a post-Scriabin modernist, he was a leading composer and polemicist for ASM. He was an enthusiastic supporter of the Revolution and condemned RAPM for its 'pseudo-proletarian' outlook. He abandoned his modernism in 1930. He worked in Uzbekistan, and after his return to Moscow he was once again able to work in administrative positions.

Ryauzov, Sergey Nikolayevich (1905–83). Composer. Studied under Glière at Moscow Conservatoire, graduating in 1930. During his Conservatoire years, he was a member of Prokoll. He made a career of writing music on folk themes of different Soviet nationalities.

Rykov, Aleksey Ivanovich (1881–1938). Professional revolutionary and Old Bolshevik. He replaced Lenin as head of the Soviet government (1924–30). Demoted by Stalin, he was eventually arrested and executed as a Trotskyite.

Sabaneyev, Leonid Leonidovich (1881–1968). Music critic and mathematician. He is best remembered as a music critic and friend of Scriabin, and wrote a memoir on that composer. He combined his musical activities with his career as a professor of mathematics. He stayed in Russia until 1926, then emigrated to Paris.

Samosud, Samuil Abramovich (1884–1964). Conductor. He came to prominence in the 1920s in Leningrad as music director the Maly Opera, and served as chief conductor of the Bolshoi from 1936 to 1943. He is particularly remembered for his promotion of Soviet operas.

Saradzhev (Saradzhian), **Konstantin Solomonovich** (1877–1954). Conductor. A student of Nikisch, he was close to ASM in the 1920s and conducted some important premieres of new Russian works. In 1935, he moved to Armenia.

Satie, Erik (Éric Alfred Leslie) (1866–1925). French composer. While lacking the sophistication of his contemporaries, Ravel and Debussy, his eccentric and innovative music eventually emerged from the margins to exert a strong influence on *Les Six*, in the next generation of composers. His ballet *Parade*, a Diaghilev production, was a *succès de scandale* in the 1920s.

Schillinger (Shillinger), **Iosif Moiseyevich** (1895–1943). Composer, graduate of the Petrograd Conservatoire, he was one of the most notable Leningrad composers in the 1920s. He emigrated to the USA in 1928, where he explored his music-theoretical ideas further, and taught composition (Gershwin was among his students).

Schnabel, Artur (1882–1951). Austrian pianist. Best known for his performances of Beethoven and Schubert. He was one of the first foreign soloists to tour Soviet Russia.

Schoenberg, Arnold (1874–1951). Austrian composer. Founder of the 'Second Viennese School', who pioneered twelve-tone method of composition. In 1933, he fled the Nazis and settled in the USA.

Schreker, Franz (1878–1934). Austrian composer and conductor. He is best remembered for his 1910 opera *Der Ferne Klang*, which received its Russian premiere in the 1920s.

Scott, Cyril (1879–1970). English composer and poet. He is best known for his orchestral pieces in a late-Romantic style.

Scriabin, Aleksandr Nikolayevich (1871/2–1915). Composer and pianist. He graduated from Moscow Conservatoire together with Rachmaninov. His earlier piano works were Chopinesque, but he developed a highly innovative harmonic style of his own that eventually broke with tonality. Creating ever more ambitious works (such as *Prometheus*, for piano, orchestra, choir and coloured light), he dreamed of composing *Mysterium*, a work intended as a perfect synthesis of the arts that would transform humanity. He was influenced by the mystical ideas of Helena Blavatsky.

Sergeyev, Aleksey Alekseyevich (1899–1958). Choral conductor. Although he was a product of the Synodal School in Tsarist times, he became one of the founder members of RAPM and the editor of its journal, *Musical Virgin Soil*. After the early split in RAPM, he became a founder member of ORKiMD. After 1932, he worked with children's choirs.

Severyanin, Igor' (Lotaryov, Igor' Vasil'yevich, 1887–1941). Poet. He is best known as a quintessential Silver Age poet, highly refined in his style and use of imagery. He declared himself an Ego-Futurist. In 1918, he emigrated to Estonia (which became Soviet territory in the last year of his life).

Shaporin, Yuriy Aleksandrovich (1887–1966). Composer, conductor and arts administrator. He studied at St Petersburg/Petrograd Conservatoire under Nikolay Sokolov (composition) and Nikolay Tcherepnin (conducting), graduating in 1918. In the 1920s he served as musical director in the Leningrad Bolshoi and Alexandrinsky drama theatres, and wrote much music for theatrical productions over this period. His *chef d'œuvre* was his opera *The Decembrists*, which he worked on from the mid-1920s, but which only received its premiere at the Bolshoi in 1953

Shatsky, Stanislav Teofilovich (1878–1934). Educationalist, disciple of Tolstoy, organiser of an experimental labour school-colony (1911). After the Revolution, he worked for Narkompros. He was director of Moscow Conservatoire from 1932 to 1934.

Shcherbachov (Shcherbachyov, Shcherbachev)**, Vladimir Vladimirovich** (1889–1952). Composer. A graduate of Petrograd Conservatoire and from 1921 professor of composition there, he became the leader of the 'progressive' camp, basing his teaching on the music of contemporary Western composers.

Shebalin, Vissarion Yakovlevich (1902–63). Soviet composer. A member of ASM in the 1920s, he later became director of Moscow Conservatoire (1942–8), but was condemned for his 'formalism' in 1948.

Shekhter, Boris Semyonovich (1900–61). Composer. A student of Myaskovsky, he was a member of Prokoll and then RAPM. He collaborated with Davidenko on an opera (*The Year 1905*), which he completed after Davidenko's death.

Shenshin, Aleksandr Alekseyevich (1890–1944). Composer and conductor. He was best known for his chamber works and for his theatre music.

Sherman, Nikolay (Noy) **Samoylovich** (1896–?). Pianist. He taught at Moscow Conservatoire from 1922, became one of the Red Professors and then a member of RAPM. He went on to occupy important administrative positions (including his work on the Committee for Arts Affairs in 1936–9), and took revenge on former ASM rivals in 1948 by sending a lengthy denunciation to the Party CC (mentioning ASM by name even though the organisation had effectively ceased to exist nearly two decades earlier).

Shirinsky, Vasiliy Petrovich (1901–65). Violinist and composer. He studied composition with Myaskovsky and completed a number of works that were performed in the 1920s, but is better remembered as the second violinist in the celebrated Beethoven Quartet (his brother Sergei was a cellist there) and as the dedicatee of Shostakovich's Quartet No. 11.

Shishov, Ivan Petrovich (1888–1947). Composer, teacher, and critic. He studied composition with Koreshchenko, Kastalsky, and Kalinnikov. From 1925 to 1941, he taught a course on melody at the Moscow Conservatoire. He came to prominence with the production of his first opera, *The Wig Maker* (1929), after Leskov.

Shostakovich, Dmitriy Dmitriyevich (1906–75). Composer. Studied composition under Shteynberg at Petrograd Conservatoire, graduating in 1925, with his First Symphony submitted as his graduation piece. A protégé first of the Conservatoire's director, Glazunov, and later of Marshal Tukhachevsky, his post-graduation style moved into acerbic modernism (First Piano Sonata, 1926) and avant-gardism (Second Symphony 1927, *The Nose* 1928), before his interests in Mahler and neo-classicism contributed to the evolution of his mature style. His use of Soviet texts and his employment at a workers' theatre company, TRAM, prevented him from becoming a major target for RAPM attacks (although they declared *The Nose* to be 'formalist'). After the advent of Socialist Realism, he, along with Prokofiev, was allowed greater latitude than other composers, although he was subjected to discipline in the form of denunciations in 1936 and 1948.

Shterenberg, David Petrovich (1881–1948). Painter. He lived in Paris from 1906, taking part in many avant-garde exhibitions and moving from one style to another. After the Revolution, he returned to Russia and took active part in the organisation of Soviet artistic life.

Shteynberg, Maximilian Oseyevich (1883–1946). Soviet composer. Shostakovich's principal composition teacher.

Shtrassenburg, Stanislav Kazimirovich (1893–1937). Composer. He wrote the music for the 1927 anniversary celebrations of the Revolution at the Maly Opera, *Dvadtsat' pyatoye* (*The Twenty-Fifth*) and the opera *Taiga* (1929). He left the public eye thereafter, working at the Polish House of Culture in Leningrad. He fell victim to Stalin's show trials.

Shulgin (Shul'gin), **Lev Vladimirovich** (1890–1968). Composer. A graduate of the St Petersburg Conservatoire, he joined the Party in 1917 and served as a music instructor in both Proletkult and the Red Army. From 1921 to 1933, he headed the agitprop department of the State Music Publishing House. In 1923, he was a founding member of RAPM, but he later split from RAPM to found ORKiMD. From 1926- to 1928 he edited the journal *Music and Revolution*. Choral songs comprise a major part of his œuvre.

Sibor, Boris Osipovich (1880–1961). Violinist. A student of Leopold Auer, he served as a Professor at the Moscow Conservatoire from 1923.

Siloti (Ziloti), **Aleksandr Il'yich** (1863–1945). Pianist and conductor. A student of Liszt and one of Rachmaninov's teachers. He also had a distinguished career as a conductor, establishing his own concert series in St Petersburg (the Siloti Concerts). In 1922, he emigrated to the USA.

Smirnov, Dmitriy Alekseyevich (1882–1944). Operatic tenor. He made his Bolshoi debut in 1904 and Mariinsky in 1907. He left Russia in 1920, but in 1926, he was one of the first émigrés to return for a concert tour.

Sobinov, Leonid Vital'yevich (1872–1934). Operatic tenor. After his debut in 1897, he developed a flourishing international career. He served as Director of the Bolshoi Theatre during two periods of crisis for the institution, from 1917 to 1918, and again in 1921. He continued to sing until 1933, and was particularly associated with the role of Lohengrin.

Sofronitsky, Vladimir Vladimirovich (1901–61). Pianist. He was a pupil of Nikolayev (a classmate of Shostakovich and Yudina) at the Leningrad Conservatoire, and soon rose to national fame, best known for his interpretations of Scriabin and the Romantic repertoire. He gave concerts during the Leningrad siege, and was the first pianist to be awarded a Stalin Prize.

Sollertinsky, Ivan Ivanovich (1902–44). Musicologist. A notable polymath, he gave pre-concert lectures at the Leningrad Philharmonia in the 1920s (he later became its Director) and published music criticism. He was one of Shostakovich's closest friends.

Sologub (born Teternikov), **Fyodor Kuz'mich** (1863–1927). Writer and poet. He was variously described as a Symbolist or Decadent. While he did not welcome the October Revolution, he engaged with the Bolsheviks as a leading member of the Union of Arts Workers, campaigning to extend the freedom of speech.

Somov, Konstantin Andreyevich (1869–1939). Artist. A member of the *Mir iskusstva* group, he left Russia in 1923.

Spassky, Sergey Dmitriyevich (1898–1956). Writer and critic. As a poet, he was part of the Futurist movement and was a friend of Mayakovsky. From 1924, he served on the Artistic Council of the Academy Theatres and wrote several opera librettos, including the adaptation of Puccini's *Tosca* as *The Struggle for the Commune* and the libretto for Pashchenko's *The Eagle Revolt*.

Stanislavsky, Konstantin Sergeyevich (1863–1938). Actor and theatre director. He was a founder of the Moscow Art Theatre (together with Nemirovich-Danchenko, 1898), and proponent of naturalistic acting, in connection with which he created the celebrated 'system' or 'method' used worldwide in drama schools.

Starokadomsky, Mikhail Leonidovich (1901–54). Organist and composer. A student of Myaskovsky, and a fellow member of ASM.

Stasov, Vladimir Vladimirovich (1824–1906). Music and art critic. He was the ideologist of the Kuchka composers and a keen supporter of realist trends in painting and sculpture.

Stefan (Stefan Grünfeldt)**, Paul** (1879–1943). Austrian music critic and scholar. He was a pupil of Schoenberg's, and the co-founder of ISCM (International Society for Contemporary Music). He emigrated to the USA in 1938.

Stetsky, Aleksey Ivanovich (1896–1938). Soviet politician. A Party member since 1915, he was appointed to a number of important positions in the Party bureaucracy, from 1926 to 1930 in the Leningrad Region, and from 1930 to 1938 in the Central Committee (heading the Agitprop Department for a time). He initially supported Bukharin, but later switched his loyalties to Stalin, which did not prevent his arrest and execution in 1938.

Stiedry, Fritz (1863–1968). Austrian conductor. A protégé of Mahler, he held the post of principal conductor at Kassel and Berlin. He left Germany in 1933, accepting a post with the Leningrad Philharmonic. In 1937, he moved to the USA.

Strauss, Johann, Jr. (1825–99). Austrian composer of waltzes and operettas.

Strauss, Richard Georg (1864–1949). German composer of Late Romantic and Expressionist music.

Stravinsky, Igor' Fyodorovich (1882–1971). Composer. A student of Rimsky-Korsakov, he won international fame for his early Diaghilev ballets: *The Firebird* (1910), *Petrushka* (1911), and *The Rite of Spring* (1913). He had already settled in Europe prior to the Revolution, and did not visit the Soviet Union until 1962, in a much publicised visit that reversed the Stalin-period ban on his music.

Strelnikov (Strel'nikov)**, Nikolay Mikhaylovich** (1888–1939). Composer and music critic, best remembered for his operettas.

Sverdlov, Yakov Mikhaylovich (1885–1919). Professional revolutionary and Soviet politician. He was a close ally of Lenin and a member of the Central Committee. The circumstances of his death were kept secret; scholars suggest that he died after being struck on the head with a heavy object during one of his factory visits – possibly assassination.

Svidersky, Aleksey Ivanovich (1878–1933). A Social Democrat/Bolshevik from 1899, professional revolutionary and Soviet politician. After the Revolution, he held a variety of government posts (including Deputy Minister of Agriculture). From 1928 to 1929, he was a member of the Narkompros Collegium and the head of Glaviskusstvo.

Szigeti, Joseph (József) (1892–1973). Hungarian violinist. He gave the Russian premiere of Prokofiev's First Violin Concerto.

Szymanowski, Karol Maciej (1882–1937). Polish composer and pianist.

Tairov (born Kornblit)**, Aleksandr Yakovlevich** (1885–1950). Actor and theatre director. In 1914, he established the Tairov Chamber Theatre together with his wife, Alisa Koonen, and mounted many experimental productions. The theatre survived into the Stalinist period, but was eventually shut down by order in 1949.

Taneyev (Taneev)**, Sergey Ivanovich** (1856–1915). Pianist, composer and music theorist. A pupil and friend of Tchaikovsky. He is the composer of the operatic epic *Oresteia*, and of a range of cantatas, symphonies, and chamber music. For many years he taught at the Moscow Conservatoire, with Rachmaninov and Scriabin among his students. His mathematised theoretical work on counterpoint was also of major importance.

Tatlin, Vladimir Yevgrafovich (1885–1953). Artist and designer. A leading figure in the Futurist and Constructivist movements, he is best remembered for various utopian architectural projects, such as the Monument to the Third International (the Tatlin Tower).

Tcherepnin (Cherepnin)**, Aleksandr Nikolayevich** (1899–1977). Pianist and composer, son of Nikolay Tcherepnin. He emigrated with his parents to Paris in 1921, where he graduated from the Conservatoire. He enjoyed some renown as a composer in Paris, then spent several years working in China and Japan, playing a significant role in the assimilation of Western art music in both countries. From 1948, he lived in the USA.

Tcherepnin (Cherepnin)**, Nikolay Nikolayevich** (1873–1945). Composer and conductor, father of Aleksandr Tcherepnin. Studied composition under Rimsky-Korsakov, and taught conducting at the St Petersburg Conservatoire (Prokofiev was among his students). His career took off when Diaghilev invited him to conduct his first season in Paris, which included a production of his ballets, *La pavillon d'Armide* and *Narcisse*. Fleeing the revolutionary upheavals, he moved to the quieter Tbilisi, where he was Director of the Conservatoire until it fell to the Red Army in 1921, after which he emigrated to Paris together with his composer son, Aleksandr.

Theremin (Termen)**, Lev Sergeyevich** (1896–1993). Physicist, engineer and musician. He was the inventor of the first electric instrument, the theremin (*termenvoks*). He graduated as a cellist from St Petersburg Conservatoire.

Toch, Ernst (1887–1964). Austrian composer. He was considered one of the leading modernists during the 1920s.

Triodin, Pyotr Nikolayevich (1887–1950). Composer. He was a student of Glazunov and the composer of the operas *Prince Serebryaniy* (1923, Zimin Opera), and *Stepan Razin* (1925, the Bolshoi).

Trotsky (born Bronshteyn)**, Lev Davidovich** (1879–1940). Professional revolutionary, Marxist theorist, Soviet military leader and politician. He was elected to lead the St Petersburg/Petrograd Soviet in both 1905 and 1917. Although he joined the Bolsheviks only in the summer of 1917, he quickly became second only to Lenin in the Party. He was in charge of the uprising in Petrograd, and as commander-in-chief of the Red Army, played a crucial role in the Civil War victory. In opposition to Stalin, he led a popular Left Opposition movement, and then joined with Zinoviev in a United Opposition. During the late 1920s, he was successively removed from his military positions, expelled from the Politburo and then the Party and exiled. He was finally assassinated in Mexico by a Soviet agent in 1940.

Tseitlin (Tseytlin)**, Lev Moiseyevich** (1881–1952). Violinist. A pupil of Auer, he was the leader of Koussevitzky's orchestra from 1908 to 1917. In 1922, he founded Persimfans, the first conductorless orchestra, which continued until 1932.

Tsïganov, Dmitriy Mikhaylovich (1903–1992). Violinist. He was a founder member of the Beethoven Quartet, which he led for more than 50 years (1923–77).

Tsukker (Sakharov)**, Arnol'd Solomonovich** (1897–1960). Music critic. He was member of the Persimfans Artistic Council, and its administrator and chronicler.

Unger, Heinz (Heinrich) (1895–1965). German conductor. A champion of Mahler and other new music, he was based in Berlin. Beginning in 1924, he undertook thirteen concert tours of Russia, and was under contract with the Leningrad Radio Orchestra for annual six-month seasons. He wrote a book of memoirs *Hammer, Sickle and Baton*.

Utkin, Iosif Pavlovich (1903–1944). Poet and journalist. Although he was initially promoted as a 'Komsomol poet', he won acclaim for a work in a highly original style, his *Tale of Red-Haired Motele* (1925), about life in a provincial Jewish town, noted by its original style. He fought at the front during World War II and worked as a war journalist, meeting his death in a plane crash.

Vasilenko Sergey Nikiforovich (1872–1956). Composer and conductor. He studied composition under Ippolitov-Ivanov. He conducted at the Mamontov Private Opera in 1903 to 1905, then became Professor of orchestration and composition at the Moscow Conservatoire. His compositions were stylistically conservative, and he apparently had little trouble conforming to the demands of Socialist Realism. He co-wrote the first Uzbek opera, *Buran* (1938).

Vasilyev-Buglay (Buglai)**, Dmitro** (Dmitriy) **Stepanovich** (1888–1956). Composer and choral conductor. He fought in the Red Army during Civil War. He worked principally in the genre of the choral mass song, and is best known for his romances and popular songs on texts by Mayakovsky and Yesenin. In the 1920s, he was a member of ORKiMD.

Veprik. See **Weprik**.

Veysberg, Yuliya Lazarevna (1879/80–1942). Composer. Daughter-in-law of Rimsky-Korsakov. One of her best-known works is the cantata *The Twelve* (1928), based on Blok's famous revolutionary poem.

Vinogradov, Viktor Sergeyevich (1899–1996). Musicologist and arts administrator. He joined the Party in 1921, while still a student at Moscow Conservatoire, and was a co-founder and the first head of Rabfak (the Workers' Faculty). He also organised the Sunday Conservatoire for workers and the society 'Music to the masses' (*Muzïka – massam*). He was Editor-in-Chief of the state music publishing house, and worked for the censorship bodies Glavlit and Glavrepertkom.

Vishnevsky, Vsevolod Vital'yevich (1900–51). Writer and playwright. He fought in the Civil War, and wrote several plays on the subject of revolutionary battles, which contributed to the canon of Socialist Realism.

Vivaldi, Antonio (1678–1741). Venetian composer and violinist. He composed operas and sacred vocal works, but is best known for his violin concertos. His music fell into obscurity until the early twentieth century, when its revival was assisted by the rediscovery of many scores previously thought lost, and by the scholarly work of the composer Alfredo Casella.

Voykov, Pyotr Lazarevich (1888–1927). Professional revolutionary and Soviet politician. Originally a Menshevik, joined the Bolsheviks in 1917 and was sent to Ekaterinburg. He took part in preparations for the execution of Tsar's family and in the sale abroad of the Tsar's hoard of treasures. From 1924, he was Soviet Ambassador to Poland, where he was murdered in 1927 by a Russian émigré.

Vygodsky, Nikolay Yakovlevich (1900–39). Organist and pianist. He studied piano at Tbilisi Conservatoire, and then organ in Moscow under Gedike. From 1924 he taught organ, non-major piano and score-reading at Moscow Conservatoire. He was a member of Prokoll and then RAPM.

Walter, Bruno (1876–1962). German conductor. He worked with Mahler at Hamburg Opera, then took up positions in Riga, Berlin, Munich, New York. In the 1920s, he toured Russia. He emigrated to the USA in 1939.

Webern, Anton (1883–1945). Austrian composer. He was a student and follower of Schoenberg, member of the Second Viennese School.

Weprik (Veprik)**, Aleksandr Moiseyevich** (1899–1958). Composer. He was a student of Myaskovsky. As a young teacher at Moscow Conservatoire (from 1923), he was one of the activists seeking to proletarianise and Sovietise the institution. In 1927, he was sent on a trip to Europe, during which he met Schoenberg, Ravel, Hindemith and Honegger. As a composer, he was primarily interested in the development of a Jewish idiom. In 1950 he was arrested as a 'Jewish nationalist' and spent some time in the GULAG before the mass releases following Stalin's death.

Wiener, Jean (1896–1982). French pianist and composer. He was close to Satie and the composers of *Les Six*, especially Milhaud. From 1925 to 1937, he performed as part of a piano duet in a music hall, playing classical music, contemporary dance and jazz. He composed numerous film scores.

Yavorsky, Boleslav Leopol'dovich (1877–1942). Musicologist, composer, and pianist. He was Professor at Kiev Conservatoire from 1916, and in 1922 was invited by Lunacharsky to Moscow, where he played important roles in the Ministry of Education and taught at the Conservatoire. His opera on a Soviet subject, *Vishka Oktyabrya*, was a failure. He is better remembered as an important music theorist, and particularly for his theory of 'modal rhythm'. He lived with Sergey Protopopov, as his partner.

Yeltsin, Boris Nikolayevich (1931–2007). Soviet and post-Soviet politician. Wielding great influence as Mayor of Moscow at the time of the break-up of the Soviet Union, he became the first President (1991–9) of the post-Soviet Russian Federation. His privatisation policies, concentrating wealth in the hands of a few 'oligarchs' while impoverishing much of the population, were forced through by the abrogation of the constitution and the shelling of the Russian Parliament. He suddenly relinquished power at the beginning of 2000, with almost no remaining support inside Russia, but with the reputation of a democratic reformer in the Western media.

Yershov, Ivan Vasil'yevich (1867–1943). Operatic tenor. He sang at the Mariinsky from 1895 to 1929, and was best known for his Wagnerian roles.

Yesenin (Esenin), Sergey Aleksandrovich (1895–1925). Poet. He led the literary group the imaginists. His death by suicide was met with a huge outpouring of grief.

Yudenich, Nikolay Nikolayevich (1862–1933). Tsarist Russian soldier. As a general, he led campaigns during the First World War; after the Revolution, he became one of the main leaders of anti-Revolutionary forces.

Yudina, Mariya Veniaminovna (1899–1970). Pianist. A graduate of the St Petersburg/Petrograd Conservatoire. She suffered persecution for her uncompromising behaviour towards the authorities and for her public espousal of Russian Orthodoxy.

Yurasovsky, Aleksandr Ivanovich (1890–1922). Composer and music administrator. He was best known for his opera *Trilby*. He served as head of the Glavpolitprosvet Music Section (February 1921 until late 1921), and as such, was in charge of music selection for mass festivals. In 1921, his song *Serp i molot* (*Hammer and Sickle*, about fighting hunger) won a competition and was published by Muzgiz.

Yurovsky, Aleksandr Naumovich (1882–1952). Pianist, musicologist and music administrator. From the 1920s to the 1940s, he served as Editor-in-Chief of the state music publisher (Muzsektor Gosizdata/Muzgiz).

Zamyatin, Yevgeniy Ivanovich (1884–1937). Writer. He often criticised Bolshevik policies from an independent socialist perspective. His anti-utopian novel, *We*, caused a scandal, not least because it was published abroad in 1929 (which was seen as an anti-Soviet gesture). Now ostracised, Zamyatin wrote a letter to Stalin asking for permission to emigrate. He was allowed to do so, and settled in Paris.

Zhilyayev, Nikolay Sergeyevich (1881–1938). Music critic, editor and educator. He was a friend of Scriabin, and the editor of various works by that composer. He was also a prominent teacher at the Moscow Conservatoire (1926–30 and 1933–7). He was arrested and executed during the purges, not for his musical ideas, but for his connections with Marshal Tukhachevsky.

Zhitomirsky, Aleksandr Matveyevich (1881–1937). Composer. He studied with Rimsky-Korsakov and Glazunov, and from 1919 taught at the Petrograd/Leningrad Conservatoire.

Zhitomirsky, Daniel' Vladimirovich (1906–92). Composer and musicologist. A graduate of Moscow Conservatoire, he joined RAPM. After RAPM's demise, he shed the group's ideas and led a long and distinguished career as a musicologist.

Zhivotov, Aleksey Semyonovich (1904–64). Composer. He was a student of Shcherbachov. In the 1920s he was famous as a young modernist, particularly for his Fragments for Nonet (1929) and a vocal-symphonic cycle *The West* (1932).

Zimin, Sergey Ivanovich (1875–1942). Founder and owner of a private opera house (Zimin Opera) in Moscow in 1904, which became Moscow's second opera after the Bolshoi. After the Revolution he stayed on at his opera house as one of the Directors, then in the years 1921–24 became the owner again. From 1924, he also worked at the second stage of the Bolshoi as a consultant.

Zinoviev (Zinov'yev), **Grigoriy Yevseyevich** (born Radomïslsky) (1883–1936). Professional revolutionary and Soviet politician. He returned from exile in April 1917 and opposed Lenin on the issue of an armed uprising. Nevertheless, after the October Revolution he occupied important positions and became a member of the Politburo. Demoted for his opposition to Stalin, he was eventually arrested, tried and executed.

Zolotaryov, Vasiliy Andreyevich (1873–1964). Composer. He studied with Rimsky-Korsakov and Lyadov at the St Petersburg Conservatoire. He came to prominence with his opera *The Decembrists* (1925).

Zoshchenko, Mikhail Mikhaylovich (1895–1958). Writer. He began publishing his work in 1922 as a member of the Serapion Brothers group. He is best known for his short stories satirising various aspects of Soviet life, often at the boundaries of acceptability. He was able to continue in his career nevertheless, but came under severe criticism in 1946 for his autobiographical novel and had to relinquish his profession until after Stalin's death in 1953.

Bibliography

Archives

GTsMMK   The Glinka Museum of Musical Culture, Moscow
LPA   The London Prokofiev Archive, London
RGALI   The Russian State Archive for Literature and Art, Moscow

Russian Periodicals

Artist-muzïkant
Betkhovenskiy byulleten'
Biryuch Petrogradskikh gosudarstvennïkh teatrov
Byulleten' Vserossiyskoy Muzïkal'noy Konferentsii
Gorn
Iskusstvo (Teatr. Muzyka. Zhivopis'. Skul'ptura)
Izvestiya
K novïm beregam muzïkal'nogo iskusstva
Krasnaya gazeta
Kul'tura i zhizn'
Kul'turnaya revolyutsiya
Lad
Muzïka
Muzïka i bït
Muzïka i Oktyabr'
Muzïka i revolyutsiya
Muzïka i teatr
Muzïkal'naya kul'tura
Muzïkal'naya nov'
Muzïkal'noye obrazovaniye
Novaya muzïka
Novïy zritel'
Persimfans
Petrogradskiye kurantï
Pravda
Proletarskiy muzïkant
Rabochiy i iskusstvo (1929–30); from 1931 *Sovetskoye iskusstvo*
Rabochiy zritel'
Sovetskaya filarmoniya (Byulleten')
Sovetskiy teatr
Sovetskoye iskusstvo (from 1926)
Sovremennaya muzïka
Teatr
Teatral'nïyi kur'yer
Teatral'nyi listok
Teatr i iskusstvo
Teatr i muzïka
Vechernyaya Moskva
Vestnik iskusstv
Vestnik teatra i zrelishch
Za proletarskuyu muzïku
Zhizn' iskusstva
Zrelishcha

Books (including document collections) and articles

Apetyan, Zaruya Apetovna, ed. *Nikolay Karlovich Metner: Pis'ma*. Moscow: Sovetskiy kompozitor, 1973.

Artizov, A. A., and Naumov, eds. O. *Vlast' i khudozhestvennaya intelligentsiya: dokumentï TsK RKP(b) – VKP(b) – VChK – OGPU – NKVD o kul'turnoy politike, 1917–1953*. Moscow: Mezhdunarodnïy fond 'Demokratiya', 1999.

Aymermakher, Karl et al., eds. *Institutï upravleniya kul'turoy v period stanovleniya: 1917–1930-ye gg. Partiynoye rukovodstvo; gosudarstvennïye organï upravleniya. Skhemï*. Moscow: ROSSPEN, 2004.

Barenboym, L. A. et al., eds. *Iz istorii sovetskogo muzïkal'nogo obrazovaniya: sbornik materialov i dokumentov, 1917–1927*. Leningrad: Muzïka, 1969.

Barsova, Inna Alekseyevna. *Konturï stoletiya: Iz istorii russkoy muzïki XX veka*. St Petersburg: Kompozitor, 2007.

——. 'Sostoyalsya li v Sovetskom Soyuze "kinodinamicheskiy simfonizm"?: Tvorchestvo Iosifa Shillingera 1920-kh godov'. In *Naslediye: Russkaya muzïka – mirovaya kul'tura*, vol. 1, ed. by Ye. S. Vlasova and Ye. G. Sorokina, 335–54. Moscow: Nauchno-izdatel'skiy tsentr 'Moskovskaya konservatoriya', 2009.

——, ed. 'Iz neopublikovannogo arkhiva A. V. Mosolova'. *Sovetskaya muzïka* (1989), no. 7, pp. 80–92.

Bernandt, G. B., Yampol'skiy, I. M., and Kiselyova, T. Ye, eds. *Kto pisal o muzïke: bio-bibliograficheskiy slovar' muzïkal'nïkh kritikov i lits, pisavshikh o muzïke v dorevolyutsionnoy Rossii*, in 4 vols. (Moscow: Sovetskiy kompozitor, 1971–89).

Blok, V. M., and Polenova, Ye. A., eds. *Anatoliy Nikolayevich Aleksandrov: Stranitsï zhizni i tvorchestva*. Moscow: Sovetskiy kompozitor, 1990.

Bobïkina, I. A., Yesipova, M. V., Rakhmanova, M. P., eds. *Dmitriy Shostakovich v pis'makh i dokumentakh*. Moscow: Gosudarstvennïy tsentral'nïy muzey muzïkal'noy kul'turï im. M. I. Glinki, 2000.

Bobrik, O. *Venskoye izdatel'stvo Universal Edition i sovetskiye muzïkantï: istoriya sotrudnichestva v 1923–1945 godakh*. Dissertatsiya na soiskaniye uchenoy stepeni kandidata iskusstvovedeniya. Moscow, 2007.

Bobrik, O., ed. 'V. Belyayev. Dnevnik poyezdki v Venu (oktyabr'- noyabr' 1924)'. *Muzïkal'naya akademiya* (1999), no. 3, 167–79, and no. 4, 227–33.

Brooks, Jeffrey. *Thank You, Comrade Stalin!: Soviet Public Culture from Revolution to Cold War*. Princeton: Princeton University Press, 2001.

Brown, Edward J. *The Proletarian Episode in Russian Literature, 1928–1932*. New York: Octagon Books, 1971.

Bruk, M. 'Iz proshlogo sovetskoy muzïki. Pedfak Moskovskoy Konservatorii 1920-kh godov'. In *Iz proshlogo i nastoyashchego sovremennoy otechesvennoy muzïki*, Issue 4, ed. by Ye. Dolinskaya and M. Sokolova, 7–24. Moscow: Moskovskaya konservatoriya, 1991.

Bryusova, N. 'Massovaya muzïkal'no-prosvetitel'naya rabota v pervïye godï posle Oktyabrya (iz vospominaniy)'. *Sovetskaya muzïka* (1947), no. 6, 46–65.

Burbank, Jane. *Intelligentsia and Revolution: Russian Views of Bolshevism, 1917–1922*. New York and Oxford: Oxford University Press, 1986.

Clark, Katerina. 'The "Quiet Revolution" in Soviet Intellectual Life'. In *Russia in the Era of NEP: Explorations in Soviet Society and Culture*, ed. by Sheila Fitzpatrick, Alexander Rabinowitch, and Richard Stites, 210–30. Bloomington and Indianapolis: Indiana University Press, 1991.

Clark, Katerina, and Dobrenko, Evgeny, with Artizov, Andrei and Naumov, Oleg, eds. *Soviet Culture and Power: A History in Documents, 1917–1953*. New Haven and London: Yale University Press, 2007.

David-Fox, Michael. *Revolution of the Mind: Higher Learning among the Bolsheviks, 1918–1929*. Cornell: Cornell University Press, 1997.

Dreyden, Simon. *V zritel'nom zale – Vladimir Il'yich*. Moscow: Iskusstvo, 1986.

Druskin, Mikhail. *Ocherki, stat'yi, zametki*. Leningrad: Sovetskiy kompozitor, 1987.

Edmunds, Neil. *The Soviet Proletarian Music Movement*. Bern: Peter Lang, 2000.

Ferenc, Anna. 'Reclaiming Roslavets: The Troubled Life of a Russian Modernist'. *Tempo* (new ser.) 3(1992), 6–9.

Fitzpatrick, Sheila. 'A. V. Lunacharsky: Recent Soviet Interpretations and Republications', *Europe-Asia Studies*, 18:3 (1967), 267–89.

——. 'Ascribing Class: The Construction of Social Identity in Soviet Russia'. *Journal of Modern History* 65:4 (1993), 745–70.

——. *The Commissariat for Enlightenment: Soviet Organisation of Education and the Arts under Lunacharsky, October 1917–1921*. Cambridge: Cambridge University Press, 1970.

——. *The Cultural Front: Power and Culture in Revolutionary Russia*. Ithaca and London: Cornell University Press, 1992.

——. 'Culture and Politics under Stalin: A Reappraisal'. *Slavic Review* 35:2 (1976), 211–31.

——. *Education and Social Mobility in the Soviet Union, 1921–1934*. Cambridge: Cambridge University Press, 1979.

——. 'The Emergence of Glaviskusstvo. Class War on the Cultural Front, Moscow 1928–29'. *Soviet Studies* 23:2 (1971), 236–53.

——. 'The "Soft" Line on Culture and Its Enemies: Soviet Cultural Policy, 1922–27'. *Slavic Review* 33:2 (1974), 267–87.

——, ed. *Cultural Revolution in Russia, 1928–1931*. Bloomington: Indiana University Press, 1978.

Fitzpatrick, Sheila, Rabinowitch, Alexander and Stites, Richard, eds. *Russia in the Era of NEP: Explorations in Soviet Society and Culture*. Bloomington: Indiana University Press, 1991.

Fox, Michael S. 'Glavlit, Censorship, and the Problem of Party Policy in Cultural Affairs, 1922–28'. *Soviet Studies* 44:6 (1992), 1045–68.

Froud, Nina and Hanley, James, eds. *Chaliapin: An Autobiography as told to Maxim Gorky*. London: Macdonald, 1967.

Galushkin, A. Yu., ed. *Literaturnaya zhizn' Rossii 1920-kh godov: Sobïtiya. Otzïvï sovremennikov. Bibliografiya*, vol. 1, parts 1 and 2. Moscow: IMLI RAN, 2006.

Gaydamovich, T. A. *Lev Knipper. Godï zhizni*. Moscow: Izdatel'skiy dom 'Kompozitor', 2005.

Glinsky, Albert. *Theremin: Ether Music and Espionage*. Urbana and Chicago: University of Illinois Press, 2000.

Gojowy, Detlef. *Arthur Lourié und der russische Futurismus*. Laaber: Laaber-Verlag, 1993.

———. 'Half-Time for Nikolai Roslavets (1881–1944): A Non-Love Story with a Post-Romantic Composer'. In *Russian and Soviet Music: Essays for Boris Schwartz*, ed. by Malcolm H. Brown, 211–20. Ann Arbor: UMI Research Press, 1984.

Gol'denveyzer, A. B. *Dnevnik: tetradi vtoraya-shestaya*. Moscow: Tortuga, 1997.

Goyovi, Detlef. *Novaya sovetskaya muzïka 20-kh godov*. Trans. and ed. by Natal'ya Vlasova. Moscow: Izdatel'skiy Dom 'Kompozitor', 2006.

Gozenpud, Abram Akimovich. *Russkiy sovetskiy operniy teatr (1917–1941): ocherk istorii*. Leningrad: Gosudarstvennoye muzïkal'noye izdatel'stvo, 1963.

Groys, Boris. 'The Birth of Socialist Realism from the Spirit of the Avant-Garde'. In *The Culture of the Stalin Period*, ed. by Hans Günther. New York: St Martin's Press, 1990.

Gusin, I. L. 'Sovetskoye muzïkal'noye gosudarstvennoye stroitel'stvo'. In *V pervïye godï sovetskogo muzïkal'nogo stroitel'stva*, ed. by V. Bogdanov-Berezovskiy and I. Gusin, 62–157. Leningrad: Sovetskiy kompozitor, 1959.

Haas, David. *Leningrad's Modernists: Studies in Composition and Musical Thought, 1917–1932*. New York: Peter Lang, 1998.

Hakobian, Levon. *Music of the Soviet Age, 1917–1987*. Stockholm: Melos Music Literature, 1998.

Hatch, John. 'The Formation of Working Class Cultural Institutions during NEP: The Workers' Club Movement in Moscow, 1921–1923'. *Carl Beck Papers in Russian and East European Studies* 806 (1990).

———. 'Hangouts and Hangovers: State, Class, and Culture in Moscow's Workers' Club Movement, 1925–28'. *Russian Review* 53 (1994): 97–117.

———. 'The Politics of Mass Culture: Workers, Communists, and Proletkul't in the Development of Worker's Clubs, 1921–25'. *Russian History/Histoire Russe* 13 (1986), 119–48.

Holter, Howard R. 'The Legacy of Lunacharsky and Artistic Freedom in the USSR', *Slavic Review* 29:2 (June 1970), 262–82.

Ivanov-Boretskiy, D. 'Deyatel'nost' AK MUZO Narkomprosa – nachal'naya stranitsa sovetskogo muzïkoznaniya (Iz arkhiva M. V. Ivanova-Boretskogo)'. In *Iz proshlogo sovetskoy muzïkal'noy kul'turï*, ed. by T. N. Livanova, vol. 2, 263–85. Moscow: Sovetskiy kompozitor, 1976), 263–85.

Jacobson, Jon. *When the Soviet Union Entered World Politics*. Berkeley, Los Angeles and Oxford: University of California Press, 1994.

Jelagin, Juri. *Taming of the Arts*. Trans. by Nicholas Wreden. New York: E. P. Dutton, 1951.

Kagarlitsky, Boris. *The Thinking Reed: Intellectuals and the Soviet State from 1917 to the Present*. Trans. by Brian Pearce. London: Verso, 1988.

Keldïsh, Yu. V., et al., eds. *Muzïkal'naya entsiklopediya*, vols. 1–6. Moscow: Sovetskaya entsiklopediya, 1973–82.

Kelly, Catriona, and Shepherd, David, eds. *Constructing Russian Culture in the Age of Revolution: 1881–1940*. Oxford: Oxford University Press, 1998.

———. *Russian Cultural Studies: An Introduction*. Oxford: Oxford University Press, 1998.

Kemp-Welch, A. '"New Economic Policy in Culture" and Its Enemies'. *Journal of Contemporary History* 13:3 (1978), 449–65.

——. *Stalin and the Literary Intelligentsia, 1928–1939*. New York: St Martin's Press, 1991.

Kenez, Peter. *Birth of the Propaganda State: Soviet Methods of Mass Mobilization, 1917–1928*. Cambridge: Cambridge University Press, 1985.

Kiaer, Christina, and Naiman, Eric, eds. *Everyday Life in Early Soviet Russia*. Bloomington and Indianapolis: Indiana University Press, 2006.

Kirschenbaum, Lisa A. *Small Comrades: Revolutionizing Childhood in Soviet Russia, 1917–1932*. Bloomington: Indiana University Press, 1989.

Komarov, Aleksandr. '"Prirozhdyonnïy archivist": ocherk biografii S. S. Popova'. In *Trudï Gosudarstvennogo tsentral'nogo muzeya muzïkal'noy kul'turï im. M. I. Glinki: Al'manakh*, ed. by M. P. Rakhmanova, vol. 3, 769–800. Moscow: Deka-VS, 2007.

Konecny, Peter. 'Chaos on Campus: The 1924 Student *Proverka* in Leningrad'. *Europe-Asia Studies* 46:4 (1994), 617–35.

Korobova, Tat'yana. 'Prokoll v stat'yakh i vospominaniyakh D. V. Zhitomirskogo'. In *Naslediye: Russkaya muzïka – mirovaya kul'tura*, vol. 1, ed. by Ye. S. Vlasova and Ye. G. Sorokina, 569–77. Moscow: Nauchno-izdatel'skiy tsentr 'Moskovskaya konservatoriya', 2009.

Kotlyarov, Yu. and Garmash, V., eds. *Letopis' zhizni i tvorchestva F. I. Shalyapina*, vol. 2. Leningrad: Muzïka, 1985.

Koval'skiy, K. 'B. B. Krasin'. *Sovetskaya muzïka* (1936), no. 7, 105–7.

Kozlova, M., ed. 'Pis'ma S. S. Prokof'yeva – B. V. Asaf'yevu (1920–1944)'. In *Iz proshlogo sovetskoy muzïkal'noy kul'turï*, ed. by T. N. Livanova, vol. 2, 4–54. Moscow: Sovetskiy kompozitor, 1976.

——. et al., eds. *S. S. Prokofiev and N. Ya. Myaskovskiy: Perepiska*. Moscow: Sovetskiy kompozitor, 1977.

Krasavina, L. 'Prokoll i muzïkal'naya zhizn' 20-kh godov'. In *Iz proshlogo i nastoyashchego sovremennoy otechesvennoy muzïki*, Issue 2, ed. by Ye. Dolinskaya and M. Sokolova, 24–35. Moscow: Moskovskaya konservatoriya, 1991.

Krasovitskaya, T. Yu., and Nenarokov, A. P. 'Protokolï Kollegii Narkomprosa RSFSR kak istoricheskiy istochnik'. In *Sovetskaya kul'tura: 70 let razvitiya*, ed. by B. B. Piotrovskiy, 353–62. Moscow: Nauka, 1987.

Krebs, Stanley Dale. *Soviet Composers and the Development of Soviet Music*. New York: W. W. Norton, 1970.

Krivtsova, Yelena. 'Iz istorii muzïkal'no-obshchestvennïkh organizatsiy: ORKiMD (1924–1932): Po materialam arkhiva L. V. Shul'gina'. In *Trudï Gosudarstvennogo tsentral'nogo muzeya muzïkal'noy kul'turï im. M. I. Glinki: Al'manakh*, ed. by M. P. Rakhmanova, vol. 2, 268–90. Moscow: Gosudarstvennïy tsentral'nïy muzey muzïkal'noy kul'turï imeni M. I. Glinki, 2003.

Kryukov, A. N., ed. *Materialï k biografii Asafyeva*. Leningrad: Muzïka, 1981.

Lamm, O. 'Druz'ya Pavla Aleksandrovicha Lamma i uchastniki muzïkal'nïkh vecherov v yego dome (20-ye godï XX veka)', In *Iz proshlogo sovetskoy muzïkal'noy kul'turï*, ed. by T. N. Livanova, vol. 1, 72–103. Moscow: Sovetskiy kompozitor, 1975.
——. 'Pervïye godï rabotï Gosudarstvennogo muzïkal'nogo izdatel'stva'. In *Sovetskaya muzïkal'naya kultura: istoriya, traditsii, sovremennnost'*, ed. by D. G. Daragan, 190–206. Moscow: Muzïka, 1980.
——, ed. 'Perepiska B. V. Asaf'yeva s P. A. Lammom'. In *Iz proshlogo sovetskoy muzïkal'noy kul'turï*, ed. by T. N. Livanova, vol. 1, 104–41. Moscow: Sovetskiy kompozitor, 1975.
Lebedinskiy, L. 'A. Davidenko: Materialï dlya tvorcheskoy biografii'. *Sovetskaya muzïka* (1935), no. 4, pp. 22–37.
——, ed. *V. A. Belïy: Ocherk zhizni i tvorchestva, stat'yi, vospominaniya, materialï*. Moscow: Sovetskiy kompozitor, 1987.
Lenin, V. I. *O literature i iskusstve*, ed. by N. I. Krutikova. Moscow: Khudozhestvennaya literatura, 1979.
Leonova, M. 'Aleksandr Ivanovich Yurasovskiy: ocherk zhizni i tvorchestva'. In *Iz proshlogo sovetskoy muzïkal'noy kul'turï*, ed. by T. N. Livanova, vol. 2, 213–46. Moscow: Sovetskiy kompozitor, 1976.
——. *Dmitriy Pokrass*. Moscow: Sovetskiy kompozitor, 1981.
Levaya, Tamara. 'K izucheniyu kompozitorskogo naslediya 1920-kh godov: A. N. Skryabin i ASM'. In *Naslediye: Russkaya muzïka – mirovaya kul'tura*, vol. 1, ed. by Ye. S. Vlasova and Ye. G. Sorokina, 327–34. Moscow: Nauchno-izdatel'skiy tsentr 'Moskovskaya konservatoriya', 2009.
Likhacheva, I., ed. *S. Ye. Feynberg: Pianist, kompozitor, issledovatel'*. Moscow: Sovetskiy kompozitor, 1984.
Livanova, T. 'Iz proshlogo sovetskoy muzïkal'noy nauki (GIMN v Moskve)'. In *Iz proshlogo sovetskoy muzïkal'noy kul'turï*, vol. 1, ed. by T. N. Livanova, 267–335. Moscow: Sovetskiy kompozitor, 1975.
Lobanova, Marina. *Nikolay Roslavets i kul'tura yego vremeni*. St Petersburg: Petroglif, 2011.
Lokshin, D. L. *S. Vasil'yev-Buglay*. Moscow: Sovetskiy kompozitor, 1958.
Lourié, Arthur. *Sergei Koussevitzky and His Epoch*. New York, 1931. Reprint: New York: AMS Press, 1971.
MacFadyen, David. *Songs for Fat People: Affect, Emotion, and Celebrity in the Russian Popular Song*. Montreal: McGill-Queens University Press, 2002.
Maksimenkov, Leonid. *Sumbur vmesto muzïki: Stalinskaya kul'turnaya revolyutsiya, 1936–1938*. Moscow: Yuridicheskaya kniga, 1997.
Malko, Nikolai. *A Certain Art*. New York: W. Morrow, 1966.
Malko, Nikolai., Gessen, Ya., and Kristi, P., eds. *Desyat' let simfonicheskoy muzïki, 1917–1927*. Leningrad: Gosudarstvennaya akademicheskaya filarmoniya, 1928.
Mally, Lynn. *Culture of the Future: The Proletkult Movement in Revolutionary Russia*. Berkeley and Los Angeles: University of California Press, 1990.
——. *Revolutionary Arts: Amateur Theater and the Soviet State*. Ithaca: Cornell University Press, 2000.
Martïnov, N., ed. *Aleksandr Davidenko: Vospominaniya, stat'yi, materialï*. Leningrad: Muzïka, 1968.

Martïnova, Svetlana. 'Pavel Lamm v tyur'makh i ssïlkakh: Po stranitsam vospominaniy O. P. Lamm'. In *Trudï Gosudarstvennogo tsentral'nogo muzeya muzïkal'noy kul'turï im. M. I. Glinki. Al'manakh*, ed. by M. P. Rakhmanova, vol. 2, 73–120. Moscow: Gosudarstvennïy tsentral'nïy muzey muzïkal'noy kul'turï, 2003.

Mazayev, Anatoliy Il'yich. *Iskusstvo i bol'shevizm, 1920–1930: Problemno-tematicheskiye ocherki i portretï*. Moscow: KomKniga, 2007.

Meshko, N. K., ed. *A. V. Mosolov: Stat'yi i vospominaniya*. Moscow: Sovetskiy kompozitor, 1986.

Mikkonen, Simo. *Music and Power in the Soviet 1930s: A History of Composers' Bureaucracy*. Lewiston, NY: Edwin Mellen Press, 2009.

Nelson, Amy. *Music for the Revolution: Musicians and Power in Early Soviet Russia*. University Park, PA: The Pennsylvania State University Press, 2004.

Nest'yev, I. V. 'Iz istorii russkogo muzïkal'nogo avangarda'. *Sovetskaya muzïka* (1991), no. 1, 75–87.

O'Connor, Timothy Edward. *The Politics of Soviet Culture: Anatolii Lunacharskii*. UMI Research Press, 1983.

Ol'khovskiy, Andrey. *Music under the Soviets: The Agony of an Art*. Westport, Conn.: Greenwood, 1975 [1955].

Ossovskiy, A. V., ed. *Leningradskaya filarmoniya*. Leningrad: Leningradskaya filarmoniya, 1934–35.

Paisov, Yuriy Ivanovich. *Aleksandr Grechaninov: zhizn' i tvorchestvo*. Moscow: Izdatel'skiy dom 'Kompozitor', 2004.

Pinegina, L. A. *Sovetskiy rabochiy klass i khudozhestvennaya kul'tura, 1917–1932*. Moscow: Izdatel'stvo Moskovskogo universiteta, 1984.

Piyashev, N. F., ed. *Lunacharsky? –– Net, on Antonov!: dokumental'noye povestvovaniye o zhizni i deyatel'nosti A. V. Lunacharskogo*. Moscow: GNTS RF 'Niopik', 1998.

Polyanovskiy, G. *Marian Koval'*. Moscow: Muzïka, 1968.

Ponyatovskiy, S. S. *Persimfans – orkestr bez dirizhera*. Moscow: Muzïka, 2003.

Prokofiev, Oleg, ed. *Sergei Prokofiev: Soviet Diary 1927 and Other Writings*. London and Boston: Faber and Faber, 1991.

Prokof'yev, Sergey. *Dnevnik*, 2 vols. Paris: sprkfv, 2002.

Puti razvitiya muzïki: Stenograficheskiy otchyot soveshchaniya po voprosam muzïki pri APPO TsK VKP(b). Moscow: Gosudarstvennoye izdatel'stvo. Muzïkal'nïy sektor, 1930.

Rabinovich, I. S., ed. *B. Yavorskiy: Stat'yi, vospominaniya, perepiska*. Moscow: Sovetskiy kompozitor, 1972.

Read, Christopher. *Culture and Power in Revolutionary Russia: The Intelligentsia and the Transition from Tsarism to Communism*. New York: St Martin's Press, 1990.

Richmond, Steven. '"The Conditions of the Contemporary": The Censors and Censoring of Soviet Theatre, 1923–1927'. *Russian History* 27 (2000), 1–56.

Rimskaya, R., ed. 'Iz perepiski Yu. A. Shaporina (1917–1963)'. In *Iz proshlogo sovetskoy muzïkal'noy kul'turï*, ed. by T. N. Livanova, vol. 2, 55–98. Moscow: Sovetskiy kompozitor, 1976.

Rimskiy, L., ed. 'Perepiska L. A. Polovinkina'. In *Iz proshlogo sovetskoy muzïkal'noy kul'turï*, ed. by T. N. Livanova, vol. 1, 176–209. Moscow: Sovetskiy kompozitor, 1975.
Rothstein, Robert A. 'Popular Song in the NEP Era'. In *Russia in the Era of NEP*, ed. Sheila Fitzpatcick et al. Bloomington: Indiana University Press, 1991.
——. 'The Quiet Rehabilitation of the Brick Factory: Early Soviet Popular Music and Its Critics'. *Slavic Review* 39:3 (Sept. 1980), 373–88.
Rumyantsev, Sergey. *Ars Novïy ili Dela i priklyucheniya bezustal'nogo kazaka Arseniya Avraamova*. Moscow: OOO 'Deka-VS', 2007.
Ryauzov, Sergey. 'Vospominaniya o Prokolle'. *Sovetskaya muzïka* (1949), no. 7, 54–8.
Sabaneyev, Leonid. *Muzïka posle Oktyabrya*. Moscow: Rabotnik prosvescheniya, 1926.
Savenko, Svetlana. '"Gosudarstvennoye muzïkal'noye stroitel'stvo": lozungi i real'nost' 1917–1920 godov (k istorii voprosa)'. In *Naslediye: Russkaya muzïka – mirovaya kul'tura*, vol. 1, ed. by Ye. S. Vlasova and Sorokina, Ye. G., 311–26. Moscow: Nauchno-izdatel'skiy tsentr 'Moskovskaya konservatoriya', 2009.
Schwarz, Boris. *Music and Musical Life in Soviet Russia, 1917–1970*. London: Barrie and Jenkins, 1976.
Shalyapin, F. *Maska i dusha: moi sorok let na teatre*. Moscow: V/O 'Soyuzteatr', 1989.
Shcherbakova, Mariya. 'Avtograf S. S. Prokofyeva v arkhive S. E. i A. D. Radlovïkh: Iz istorii postanovki operï "Lyubov' k tryom apel'sinam" na stsene b. Mariinskogo teatra v 1926 godu'. In *Naslediye: Russkaya muzïka – mirovaya kul'tura*, vol. 1, ed. by Ye. S. Vlasova and Ye. G. Sorokina, 357–69. Moscow: Nauchno-izdatel'skiy tsentr 'Moskovskaya konservatoriya', 2009.
Shostakovich, D. D. *Pis'ma I. I. Sollertinskomu*, ed. by D. I. Sollertinskiy. St Petersburg: Kompozitor, 2006.
Sigeykina, Yelena, ed. 'Novoye v epistolyarii A. T. Grechaninova. Pis'ma A. T. Grechaninova k V. A. Lammu'. In: *Trudï Gosudarstvennogo tsentral'nogo muzeya muzïkal'noy kul'turï im. M. I. Glinki: Al'manakh*, ed. by M. P. Rakhmanova, vol. 3, 79–150. Moscow: Deka-VS, 2007.
Slonimskaya, R., and Kryukov, A., eds. *V. V. Shcherbachyov: Stat'yi, materialï, pis'ma*. Leningrad: Sovetskiy kompozitor, 1985.
Starr, S. Frederick. *Red and Hot: The Fate of Jazz in the Soviet Union*. New York: Oxford University Press, 1983.
Stepanova, Svetlana Romanovna, ed. *Muzïkal'naya zhizn' Moskvï v pervïye gody posle Oktyabrya*. Moscow: Sovetskiy kompozitor, 1972.
Stites, Richard. *Revolutionary Dreams: Utopian Vision and Experimental Life in the Russian Revolution*. Oxford: Oxford University Press, 1989.
——. *Russian Popular Culture: Entertainment and Society since 1900*. Cambridge: Cambridge University Press, 1992.
Tarakanov, M. *Sergey Prokof'yev, 1891–1953*. Moscow: Sovetskiy kompozitor, 1991.
Taruskin, Richard. *Defining Russia Musically: Historical and Hermeneutical Essays*. Princeton: Princeton University Press, 1997.
Thorpe, Richard G. 'The Academic Theatres and the Fate of Soviet Artistic Pluralism, 1919–1928'. *Slavic Review* 51:3 (Autumn 1992), 389–410.

Tolstoy, Vladimir, Bibikova, Irina and Cook, Catherine, eds. *Street Art of the Revolution: Festivals and Celebrations in Russia, 1918–33*. New York: Vendome Press, 1990.
Tolz, Vera. *Russian Academicians and the Revolution: Combining Professionalism and Politics*. New York: St Martin's Press, 1997.
Unger, Heinz. *Hammer, Sickle and Baton: The Soviet Memoirs of a Musician*. London: The Cresset Press, 1939.
Vaynkop, Yu. 'Muzïkal'naya kul'tura Leningrada'. In *V perviye godï sovetskogo muzïkal'nogo stroitel'stva*, ed. by V. Bogdanov-Berezovskiy and I. Gusin, 16–61. Leningrad: Sovetskiy kompozitor, 1959.
Veprik, A. 'Vstrechi s Khindemitom, Shyonbergom i Ravelem'. *Sovetskaya muzïka*, (1962), no. 12, 110–17.
Vlasova, Yekaterina. '"Venera Milosskaya" i psintsipï 1789 goda'. *Muzïkal'naya akademiya* (1993), no. 2, 154–60, and no. 3, 178–85.
——. *1948 god v sovetskoy muzïke: dokumentirovannoye issledovaniye*. Moscow: Klassika – XXI, 2010.
Vlasova, Natalya. 'A. Shyonberg v Rossii: iz istorii vospriyatiya'. In *Naslediye: Russkaya muzïka – mirovaya kul'tura*, vol. 1, ed. by Ye. S. Vlasova and Ye. G. Sorokina, 56–94. Moscow: Nauchno-izdatel'skiy tsentr Moskovskaya konservatoriya, 2009.
Volkov, Solomon. 'Dmitri Shostakovitch and "Tea for Two"'. *Musical Quarterly* 64 (1978), 223–9.
von Geldern, James. *Bolshevik Festivals, 1917–1920*. Berkeley and Los Angeles: University of California Press, 1993.
von Geldern, James, and Stites, Richard, eds. *Mass Culture in Soviet Russia: Tales, Poems, Songs, Movies, Plays, and Folklore, 1917–1953*. Bloomington: Indiana University Press, 1995.
Vorob'yov, Igor'. *Russkiy avangard i tvorchestvo Aleksandra Mosolova 1920-kh – 1930-kh godov*. St Petersburg: Sankt-Peterburgskaya konservatoriya, 2001.
Vostrïshev, Mikhail, ed. *Moskva stalinskaya: Bol'shaya illyustrirovannaya letopis'*. Moscow: Algoritm, 2008.
Walker, Barbara. 'Kruzhok culture: The Meaning of Patronage in the Early Soviet Literary World'. *Contemporary European History* 11:1 (2002), 107–23.
Yeroshkin, N. P., ed. *Vïsshiye organï gosudarstvennoy vlasti i organï tsentral'nogo upravleniya RSFSR (1917–57 gg.). Spravochnik*. Moscow: Tsentral'nïy gosudarstvennïy arkhiv RSFSR, 1971.
Youngblood, Denise J. *Movies for the Masses: Popular Cinema and Soviet Society in the 1920s*. Cambridge: Cambridge University Press, 1992.
Zakharova, Ol'ga, ed. 'Nikolay Golovanov. Iz "Zapisok"'. In *Trudï Gosudarstvennogo tsentral'nogo muzeya muzïkal'noy kul'turï im. M. I. Glinki: Al'manakh*, ed. by M. P. Rakhmanova, vol. 3, 353–90. Moscow: Deka-VS, 2007.
Zarubin, V. I. *Bol'shoy teatr: Pervïye postanovki oper na russkoy stsene, 1825–1993*. Moscow: Ellis Lak, 1994.
Zhitomirskiy, D. V., Kisun'ko, V. G., and Korabel'nikova, L. Z., eds. *A. V. Lunacharskiy o muzïke i muzïkal'nom teatre: stat'yi, rechi, pis'ma, dokumentï*, vol. 1. Moscow: Muzïka, 1981.

Index

Abendroth, Hermann, 133, 345
Adam, Adolphe, 40
   Le Corsaire, 40
Afinogenov, Aleksandr, 292, 340, 345
Agitotdel (Agitational Section/Department of the State Publishing House), xvi, 88, 136, 142, 183, 341
Agitprop (the Agitation and Propaganda Department of the Party CC), xviii, 44, 67, 204–5, 219, 341, 358, 375
Akhmatova, Anna, 68n, 114, 345, 369
Akhron, Iosif, 93&n
AKhRR (AKhR), 100, 175, 218, 341
Aleksandrov, Anatoliy, 26, 104–5, 107, 134, 159–61, 175, 295, 321–2, 345, 350, 359
Aleksandrov, Grigoriy, 187&n
Alpers, Boris, 308
Alyavdina, Agniya, 104&n
AMA, 264, 278n
Amar Quartet, 198, 355
Andersen, Hans Christian, 61
Andreyev, Leonid, 61–2, 299, 345
   The Abyss (*Bezdna*), 61
   Yekaterina Ivanovna, 61–2
Ansermet, Ernest, 198, 217, 345
APM, *see* RAPM
Arapov, Anatoliy, 145
Arens, Lev, 8, 345
Arensky, Anton, 109, 345
Arkadyev, Mikhail, 314, 316, 319, 321–2, 345
Arkhangelsky, Aleksandr, 24, 346
Asafyev (Glebov), Boris, xi, xiv, xvi–xx, xxvii, 18, 27, 31, 40–1, 85–6, 97, 104–11, 124, 134, 139, 150, 155, 158–60, 162, 164, 166, 181–3, 184n, 186, 198–202, 217–19, 227, 228n, 230, 264–8, 284–5, 293, 302, 323, 335, 346, 352, 354
   The Flames of Paris, xxvii, 323, 335–8
ASM, xv–xvii, xxiv, xxvi, 26, 85–9, 91–2, 100, 102, 104, 106–7, 113, 124, 132, 134, 138, 142, 157, 159–61, 166, 183–5, 188, 198–200, 217–18, 220–1, 226, 228, 230, 264, 266, 285, 287, 290n, 292, 341–2, 346–8, 351, 354, 358–9, 364, 366, 368–9, 371, 373, 375
Astruc, Gabriel, 173&n
Atovmyan, Levon, 292, 294, 295n, 318, 321, 346
Auber, Daniel, 9
   La Muette de Portici (*Fenella*), 9
Auric, Georges, 157, 346
   'Avril', 157
   'Chanson gothique' from *Cinque poèmes de Gérard de Nerval*, 157
Averbakh, Leopol'd, 292, 346

Avraamov, Arseniy, xxiii, 60, 81–4 (84n), 346
   Symphony of Sirens (*Simfoniya gudkov*), xxiii, 81–4

Babel, Isaak, 232, 236, 346
Bach, Johann Sebastian, 25, 91, 100, 156, 168, 315, 334
   'Peasant' Cantata, 163
   Well-Tempered Clavier, 91
Bakaleynikov, Vladimir, 8, 346
Balakirev, Milly, 153–4, 162, 362, 364
   Islamey, 162
Balashov, Stepan, 216&n
Balmont, Konstantin, 27, 38, 114, 298–300, 346
Baltrušaitis, Jurgis, 26, 38, 346
Bankovsky (Ban'kovskiy), Grigoriy, 32–3
Baratov, Leonid, 272&n
Barbusse, Henri, 50
Barsova, Inna, x
Bartók, Béla, 91&n, 134, 160, 230, 232–5, 347, 359
   Allegro barbaro, 234
   Sonatina for piano, 91
   Romanian Folk Dances for piano, 91
   Hungarian Folk Songs, 91
   Quartets, 134
Bedny, Dem'yan, 42, 310, 347
Beethoven, Ludwig van, xv, 9, 34–5, 38, 41, 59, 63, 73, 76–7, 89–91, 98, 108, 158, 160, 176, 192, 227, 235–6, 322, 336, 338, 347, 351, 369, 372
   Christus am Ölberge, 236
   Egmont, 73, 338
   Fidelio, 9
   Missa solemnis, 236
   Piano sonatas, 91, 108
   Symphony No. 3, *Eroica*, 38, 73
   Symphony No. 4, 92
   Symphony No. 5, 160
   Symphony No. 9, xv, 9, 35–6, 40, 61, 65, 75
   Violin Concerto, 73
Beethoven Hall, 42, 91, 140
Beethoven Quartet, 348, 373, 377
Bekker, Paul, 107, 347
Belïy, Viktor, 138, 160, 165n, 210n, 212, 218, 219–21, 223, 263–6, 294, 303, 318–19 (318n), 321–2, 347
   Prelude, 160
   Fugue, 160
   Piano Sonata, 160
   'The Twenty-Six' ('26'), 212

Bely, Andrey, 39, 55, 347
Belyayev, Mitrofan, 20
Belyayev, Viktor, 20n, 24, 27, 41–2, 56,
    85–7, 102, 104, 107, 111n, 133, 166–7,
    188–92, 217–18, 347
Benois (Benua), Albert, 41&n
Benois (Benua), Aleksandr, 41n, 48–9
    (48n)
Berdyayev, Nikolay, 69n
Berg, Alban, xxvi, 133, 181, 198, 217, 225, 347
    Piano Sonata, 217
    Wozzeck, xxvi, 133, 181&n, 198, 217, 225,
    347
Berlioz, Hector, 24, 73, 336
    Grande Symphonie funèbre et triomphale,
    24
    Symphonie fantastique, 73
Bershadsky, Sergey, 93&n
Bezïmensky, Aleksandr, 183, 347
Bizet, Georges, 2, 234, 72, 121, 133
    L'Arlésienne, 2
    Carmen, 2, 24, 72, 121, 133
Blanter, Matvei, 90, 347
Blinder, Naum, 133, 347–8
Blok, Aleksandr, xxi, xxiii, 29&n, 34, 54&n,
    68n, 79, 180, 255, 348, 378
    'The Unknown Woman', 255
    The Twelve, xxi, 54, 348, 378
Blyum, Vladimir (Sadko, Ivanchikov), 147,
    193, 282&n, 292–3, 294n, 302, 348
Bobrik, Olesya, x
Bogdanov, Aleksandr, 9–10, 43, 344, 348
Bolotin, Pavel, 123&n
Bolshoi Theatre, xvii, xxiii, xxvii, 4–5, 7,
    25, 34, 39–41, 50, 55, 69–73, 91, 100, 109,
    114, 116, 127, 140–51, 158, 160, 173, 180,
    187, 193, 195n, 199, 202–5, 215n, 225–6,
    242–3, 268–70, 272n, 290, 295, 299, 301,
    323, 326, 328, 349, 353–6, 359, 361–4,
    366–8, 371–2, 374, 377, 380
Borisovsky, Vadim, 107, 348
Borkhman, Aleksandr, 107, 348
Borodin, Aleksandr, 39, 78, 142, 146, 153,
    232, 236, 240
    Prince Igor, 39; Polovtsian Dances, 142
    'Song of the Dark Forest' ('*Pesnya
    tyomnogo lesa*'), 142, 240
Borovsky, Aleksandr, 25, 162–3 (162n), 180,
    348
Brahms, Johannes, 160
Brand, Max, 225, 348
    Machinist Hopkins, 225
Braudo, Yevgeniy, 11, 135, 348
'Brick Factory, The' ('*Kirpichiki*'), 223–4,
    278, 280, 287n
Bron, Onisim, 272&n

Bruk, Genrikh, 138n, 210n, 213
    'Song of Farewell to Lenin'
    (*Proshchal'naya-Leninskaya*), 213
Bruni, Lev, 6, 349
Bryusov, Valeriy, 34, 68, 349
Bryusova, Nadezhda, 6, 10, 23, 42, 58,
    110–11 (111n), 119, 134, 163–4, 230–1, 288,
    349
Bubnov, Andrey, xxvi, 292–3, 321, 349, 353
Bugoslavsky, Sergey, 108–9
Bukharin, Nikolay, xxv, xxvi, 45, 132, 136,
    188, 192&n, 193, 197–8, 205–6, 305n, 349,
    375
    'Angry Notes' (*Zlïye zametki*), 188, 192n
    '*Klassovïy protsess*', 197–8
    'Notes of an Economist', 207
Bulgakov, Mikhail, 55, 220&n, 271, 349
Burdukov, Aleksandr, 203&n
Byron, George Gordon, 64, 135

Ça ira, 24, 337
Carmagnole, 24, 338
Casella, Alfredo, 91, 133, 142, 160–2, 191,
    251, 349, 364, 378
    5 Pieces for String Quartet, 91, 142
    11 Children's Pieces, 162
    L'adieu à la vie, 162
    Concerto for String Quartet, 162
    Italia, 162
    Partita, 162
Castelnuovo-Tedesco, Mario, 162, 349
    Cypresses, 162
Cavos, Catterino, 145&n
Central Committee/CC (of the Party), viii,
    xxiv, xxvi, 43n, 68, 70n, 132, 202, 219,
    228, 320, 324–5, 327, 339, 341–2, 344,
    348, 352, 355, 357–8, 361, 370, 373, 375
Chagin, Pyotr, 84&n
Chaliapin, Fyodor, 1, 8, 24–5, 39–40, 50, 52,
    54, 179, 349, 362
Chapygin, Aleksey, 314&n
Chayanov, Aleksandr, 301&n
Cheka (VChK), 7–8, 341–2, 352, 371
Chelyapov, Nikolay, 284, 349–50
Chemberdzhi, Nikolay, 138n, 210n, 266,
    278, 317, 319n, 321, 350, 363
    'Hey, down with it!' ('*Nu i doloy*'), 278
Chemodanov, Sergey, 227, 350
Chernetskaya, Inna, 108, 350
Chernomordikov, David, 87–8, 95–6,
    101–2, 113, 350
Cherubini, Luigi, 337&n
Chesnokov, Pavel, 170
Chicherina, Sof'ya, 318&n
Chopin, Fryderyk, 77, 186, 315, 322, 356,
    372
Chukovsky, Korney, 67, 350

church music/composers, 7, 100, 114, 166, 168, 170–1, 185, 206, 240n, 263, 299, 315, 346, 355
Chuzh-Chuzhenin (Nikolay Faleyev), 280&n
Coates, Albert, 161, 298, 330, 350
Comintern, xxii–xxv, 39, 50, 142, 149, 301n, 341–3
Communist Academy, 284–5, 349
conference: First All-Russian Conference of Music Workers of 1929, xxvi, 217–19, 222, 226, 228, 238–40
Contemporary Music (*Sovremennaya muzika*), 102, 104, 108, 113, 135, 218, 341, 351
Court Cappella/State Cappella/Petrograd Choral Academy xxii, 7, 91, 100, 170–2, 358
Cowell, Henry, 137, 350
Craig, Gordon, 215&n

D'Albert, Eugen, 161, 350–1
Tiefland, 161
Dalcroze, Émile, *see* Jaques-Dalcroze, Émile
Dargomyzhsky, Aleksandr, 72, 211
Rusalka, 72, 211
Davidenko, Aleksandr, x–xi, xix, 136–8, 165, 176, 210&n, 212, 218, 221, 243, 266, 277–8, 292, 294, 302–6, 310–13, 316–17, 319, 321, 327, 351, 373
'About Lenin' ('*Pro Lenina*'), 136–7
'Ballad of Bread and Swords' ('*Ballada o khlebe i mechakh*'), 303
'Be Alert, Comrade' ('*Glyadi, tovarishch, v oba*'), 305
'By the Tenth Milepost' ('*Na desyatoy verste*'), 212
'Budyonny's Cavalry' ('*Konnaya Budyonnogo*'), 278
'A Dance of Defence' ('*Tanets oboroni*'), 304
'Hoisting the Wagon' ('*Podyom vagona*'), 294
'A Letter' ('*Pis'mo*'), 304
'Mother' ('*Mat'*'), 303
'Mother Russia' ('*Kak po matushke Rossii*'), 212
'*Pod otkos*', 327
Shockworking Pioneer Song (*Udarnaya pionerskaya*), 304
Song of Industrialisation, 304
'Song of the Atheist Komsomols' (*Bezbozhnaya komsomol'skaya*), 306
'The Smith' ('*Kuznets*'), 136, 303
'The Street is Stirring' ('*Ulitsa volnuyetsya*'), 212

Davidenko, Aleksandr, *continued*
'They Wanted to Beat Us' ('*Nas pobit', pobit' khoteli*'), 277–8, 310–13
'Workers' May' ('*Rabochiy may*'), 306
'Workers' Palace' ('*Rabochiy dvorets*'), 306
Debussy, Claude, 6, 26, 76–7, 79, 289, 366, 371
Delibes, Léo, 39
Lakmé, 39
Derzhanovsky, Vladimir, xi, xiv, xvi, xviii–xix, 18, 85–6, 91, 102–7, 109, 124, 139n, 142n, 156, 159n, 160, 162, 166n, 181n, 183–5, 198n, 199, 202, 204–5, 218, 264, 266–7, 284, 292–3, 302, 320, 339, 351
Deshevov, Vladimir, xxiv, 109–10, 135, 140, 145, 155–6, 160, 226, 260n, 269, 351
Ice and Steel (*Lyod i stal'*), 269
Red Whirlwind (*Krasnïy vikhr'*), xxiv, 109–10, 135, 140, 143, 145
Bolsheviks, 135
Jebella, 160
Diaghilev, Sergey, 46, 47n, 49n, 123n, 173n, 200, 243n, 246&n, 345n, 349n, 351, 355, 362, 366, 371, 375–6
Dianov, Anton, 26, 32, 156n, 225, 269, 270n, 323n, 351
Dikiy, Aleksey, 192&n
Dmitriyev, Vladimir, 131, 213&n, 270–1, 351
Dobroveyn, Isay, 41, 351
Dohnányi, Ernst von, 91, 351
Piano Quintet No. 2, 91
Dolidze, Viktor, 109, 351
Keto and Kote, 109
Dostoyevsky, Fyodor, 106
Idiot, 106
Dramsoyuz, 262, 263n
Dranishnikov, Vladimir, 158–9, 199, 202, 268–9 (269n), 351–2
Drozdov, Anatoliy, 134, 352
Druskin, Mikhail, 268, 352
'*Dubinushka*'/'*Proletarskaya dubinushka*' (The (Proletarian) Cudgel)), 52, 142, 277, 286
Dubovsky, Iosif, 119&n
Dudkevich, Georgiy, 108, 352
Rachel's Tears (*Plach Rakhili*), 108
Duncan, Isadora, xxiii, 65–6, 108, 349, 352
Dzegelyonok, Aleksandr, 26&n, 107, 352
Dzerzhinsky, Feliks, 101n, 352
Dzerzhinsky, Ivan, 318&n

Edmunds, Neil, x
Ehrenburg (Erenburg), Il'ya, 55, 352
Eisenstein, Sergey, xxv, 361
Battleship Potemkin, xxv, 361
Ekskuzovich, Ivan, 71, 352
Eliot, T. S., 87

Engels, Friedrich, 192, 229&n
Epshteyn, Moisey, 317&n, 319, 353
Experimental Theatre, the (Bolshoi's second stage), 202, 204, 225

Fascism (used as a label), 252, 298, 301, 303, 306
Fedorovsky, Fyodor, 109, 353
Feinberg, Samuil, 91, 104–5, 107, 133–4, 136, 159–61, 322, 353
   Piano Sonata No. 3, 107
Fere, Vladimir, 138n, 353
Fitelberg, Grzegorz, 23, 41, 353
Fitzpatrick, Sheila, x
Five Year Plan, xii, xvii, xxvi–xxvii, 106, 225–6, 229, 242, 270
Fokine (Fokin), Michel (Mikhail), 47&n
folk songs/folk music/folk style, 16–17, 27n, 29, 47–8, 91, 95, 97, 100, 122, 124, 126, 128, 138n, 142, 146, 148, 151–3, 161, 164–8, 196n, 212, 230, 232–4, 236, 239, 244–5, 271, 279, 289, 311, 318n, 329, 333, 346–7, 353–4, 356–7, 360, 362, 371
foxtrot (and composers of foxtrots), xvii, 147–9, 156, 160, 172, 181, 209, 215, 236–7, 253, 263–4, 275–9, 282–3, 288, 291, 295, 297, 306, 317, 347
Fomin, Boris, 278&n
For Proletarian Music (Za proletarskuyu muzïku), 261, 288–9, 291, 296, 302
Foregger, Nikolay, 90, 348, 353
   Dance of the Machines (Tanets mashin), 90
Freud, Sigmund, 214
Freydkov, Boris, 216&n
Fried, Oskar, xxiv, 72, 108, 353
Frunze, Mikhail, xxv
Futurism, xiv, 6, 21, 44–5, 56–7, 68, 79, 101, 176, 243, 255n, 342, 345, 349, 357–8, 361, 362, 365–6, 372, 375, 376

Gabrieli, Andrea and Giovanni, 91, 353
GAKhN/RAKhN/GAIS (the State/Russian Academy for Scholarship in the Arts), 107, 113–14, 116, 144, 226, 285, 341, 350
Gallifet, Gaston, 120, 122–3
Garbuzov, Nikolay, 59–60, 353
Gastev, Aleksey, 33&n, 81
Gaygerova, Varvara, 217, 353
Gedike, Aleksandr, 26, 107, 133, 321–3, 353, 378
Geltser, Yekaterina, 141, 193&n, 195, 353–4
German, Pavel, 287&n
GIII, 59, 217, 368
Gil-Marchex, Henri, 173&n
GIMN, 59–61, 353
Ginzburg, Semyon, 159, 284, 354

Gippius, Zinaida, 114, 115n
Gladkovsky, Arseniy, xxv, 139–40, 143–6, 354
   For Red Petrograd, xxv, 139–40, 143–6, 354
Glaviskusstvo, xxvi–xxvii, 193n, 205, 218–22, 224, 24–7, 261, 263, 293, 341–2, 359, 367, 370, 376
Glavlit, xxiii, 67–8, 279, 341–2, 363, 365, 378
Glavnauka, 134, 140, 164, 183, 342, 367
Glavpolitprosvet, 37, 56, 57n, 69, 99, 140, 164–5, 342, 361, 379
Glavprofobr, 58, 69, 99, 119, 342
Glavrepertkom, xxiv, 86, 101, 113, 140, 164, 166, 193, 220&n, 264, 271, 279, 291, 341–2, 348, 368, 370, 378
Glavsotsvos, 69, 99, 316n, 342, 353
Glazunov, Aleksandr, 8–9, 20n, 26n, 40–1, 59, 73, 153, 159–61, 180, 202, 354, 362, 373, 377, 380
   Raymonda, 40
   Stepan Razin, 9
Glebov, Igor' (pseudonym), see Asafyev, Boris
Glière, Reyngol'd, xii, xx, xxvi, 136, 173, 180, 186, 193–5, 210n, 225, 262, 321, 348, 354, 358, 363, 371
   The Red Poppy, xxvi, 180, 186, 193–5, 225
Glinka, Mikhail, 19, 25, 39–40, 59, 97, 145&n, 154, 167, 225, 354–5
   A Life for the Tsar, 40, 153n, 225, 354–5
   Ruslan and Lyudmila, 25, 39, 97, 354
   'Skylark' ('Zhavoronok'), 59
Gluck, Christoph Willibald, 62, 322, 337&n
   The May Queen/Cythère assiégée (Koroleva maya), 62
Gnesin, Mikhail, xvii, 79, 91, 107, 182, 232, 236, 292, 293n, 314–21, 354, 359–60
Gogol, Nikolay, xxvii, 65, 153, 232, 236, 254–5, 257–8, 354
Gojowy, Detlef, x
Goldenweiser (Gol'denveyzer), Aleksandr, xxiv, 1, 11–12, 26, 91, 111, 134, 164, 170, 186, 199, 205–7, 227, 314, 321, 354, 357
Goleyzovsky, Kas'yan, 90, 196n, 242, 354
Golovanov, Nikolay, 25–6, 39, 108, 180, 203, 205–6, 355, 367
Gorbachev, Mikhail, 2, 355
Gorky, Maksim, xxiii, 6, 55, 68–9, 179, 230, 236n, 320–1, 331, 355
Gorodetsky, Sergey, 68, 355
Gorodinsky, Viktor, 222, 224–5, 319, 321, 355
Gorsky, Aleksandr, 55, 355
GosBOT, 24, 225
Gosfil, 57, 72–3

Gosizdat, 67, 85, 87, 102, 103n, 104
Gossec, François-Joseph, 337&n
Gounod, Charles, 25, 39, 72, 109
  Faust (*Margarita*), 39, 72, 109
  Romeo and Juliet, 25
Govorit Moskva, see *Moscow Speaking*
GPU/OGPU, 68, 87, 89, 94, 101, 142&n, 187, 301n, 316n, 341–2, 373
Grechaninov, Aleksandr, xxv, 25, 91, 107, 114, 348, 355
  Domestic Liturgy (*Demestvennaya liturgiya*), 25
  Hymn to the February Revolution, 114
Grétry, André, 336, 337n
Grinberg, Matias, 158, 331–2, 355
Guido d'Arezzo, 75&n
Gurilyov, Aleksandr, 333
GUS, 58, 103, 119, 342
Gusman, Boris, 242, 243n, 355
'gypsy music'/*Tsïganshchina*, xxi, 10, 15, 223, 263, 277–9, 289, 304&n

Hakobian, Levon, x
Halévy, Fromental, 72
  La Juive, 72
Hammer, Armand, 55
Handel, Georg Frideric, 210
Hegel, Georg Wilhelm Friedrich, 192
Henderson, Arthur, 300&n
Hindemith, Paul, 107, 135, 158, 160, 184, 198, 205, 217, 225, 231, 235, 251, 265, 355–6, 378
  1922, 107, 135
  Concerto for Orchestra, 158
  Hin und Zurück, 205
  Neues vom Tage, 225, 268
  Quartet No. 1, 107
  Solo sonatas for string instruments, 107
  Sonata for solo viola, 198
  Sonatas for Viola and for Cello from op. 11, 135
Hoffmann, E. T. A., 68n
Hofmann, Josef, 60&n
Holst, Gustav, 298, 300–1, 356
  The Planets, 298, 300–1, 356
Honegger, Arthur, 134–5, 158, 168, 198, 217, 356, 378
  Judith, 217
  Pacific 233, 158, 356
  Rugby, 217
  Sonata for viola and piano, 135
Hoover, Herbert, 55
Horowitz, Vladimir, 133, 356
Hugo, Victor, 196n
Humperdink, Engelbert, xiii
  Hansel and Gretel, xiii
Huxley, Aldous, ix

Igumnov, Konstantin, 73, 91, 111, 356
Illica, Luigi, 122
Ilyin, Ivan, 69n
Imaginists, 42, 67n, 68, 83n, 247, 379
Internationale, 16, 24, 26, 38, 40, 53, 65, 82–3, 88, 142&n, 146, 148, 168, 195, 239, 272, 277, 290n, 350
Ippolitov-Ivanov, Mikhail, 72–3, 140, 354, 356, 365, 377
ISCM (International Society for Contemporary Music), 91, 133–4, 368, 375
Ivanov, Vsevolod, 273n
Ivanov, Vyacheslav, 26, 34, 39, 356
Ivanov-Boretsky, Mikhail, 119, 227, 356

Jaques-Dalcroze, Émile, 138&n, 350
jazz(-band), 66, 90, 156, 172–4, 230, 233, 236, 277–8, 301, 361, 367, 370, 379
Jewish idiom in music, 79, 87, 93n, 142, 230–2, 315, 350, 361, 378
Josquin des Prez, 91, 356
Jurgenson, Boris, 23, 353, 356

Kabalevsky, Dmitriy, 285, 290, 295, 328, 357
  Piano Concerto, 295
Kaganovich, Lazar', 321, 357
Kalinin, Mikhail, 52–3 (52n)
Kalita, Ivan, 75&n
Kálmán, Emmerich, 25
  Der Kleine König/*Mateo*/*Revolyutsionerka*, 25
Kamenev, Lev, xxiv–xxv, 70, 112, 164, 357
Kameneva, Ol'ga, 112, 161, 357
Kamensky (Kamiensky), Aleksandr, 155&n, 357
Kamensky, Vasiliy, 27, 357
Kamionskaya, 176
Kankarovich, Anatoliy, 59, 63, 357
Kant, Immanuel, 64
Karatygin (Karatïgin), Vyacheslav, 100, 244, 357
Karpilovsky, 8
Karsavina, Tamara, 50&n
Kashperova-Levshina, Ye., 26
Kastalsky, Aleksandr, 7, 26–7, 38, 55, 100, 111, 119, 136, 152, 165–70, 176, 357
  'At the Coffin' ('*U groba*'), 100
  Brotherly Remembrance (*Bratskoye pominoveniye*), 166
  Festivals of the People (*Narodnïye prazdnovaniya*), 27
  Internationale (arrangement), 26, 38
  'Song about Lenin' ('*Pesnya pro Lenina*'), 100
  Sten'ka Razin, 27

Kastalsky, Aleksandr, *continued*
  To Our Brothers Abroad ('*K zarubezhnïm brat'yam*'), 55
  Village Symphony, 166–9
Katuar, Georgiy, 107, 357
Keldysh (Keldïsh), Yuriy, 218, 220, 242–3, 252–3, 318, 321, 357
Kerensky, Aleksandr, 40, 45, 50, 358
Kerzhentsev, Platon, xviii, 204–5, 219–21 (220n), 222n, 224–5, 358
Khayt, Yuliy, 278–80, 287&n, 318&n, 358
Kheraskov, Mikhail, 168&n
Khlebnikov, Velimir, 6, 358
Kirillov, Vladimir, 32–3 (33n)
Kirshon, Vladimir, 271–3 (272n)
Klemperer, Otto, 108, 133, 198, 217, 358
Klimov, Mikhail, 158, 358
Klyachko, Semyon, 136–7
Knipper, Lev, 159, 269, 271–2, 358–9
  Symphony, 159
  The Wind from the North (*Severnïy veter*), 269, 271–3, 358
Kochetov, Nikolay, 10, 59, 359
  March-Hymn (*Gimn-marsh*), 10
Kochetov, Vadim, 285, 359
Kodály, Zoltán, 91, 134–5, 359
  Quartet No. 2, 91
  Cello Sonata, 135
Kolchak, Aleksandr, xxii, 82, 359
Komissarzhevsky, Fyodor, 25, 39, 359
Kon, Feliks, xxvii, 224, 261, 288, 293, 300, 310, 344, 359
Koposov, Aleksey, 138n, 359
Koposova-Derzhanovskaya, Yelena, 350
Korchmaryov, Klimentiy, 135–7, 308, 359
Korev, Semyon, 184&n, 360
Kornilov, Lavr, 82, 360
Kostomolotsky, Aleksandr, 173&n
Koussevitzky, Sergey, 25, 37–8, 73, 164n, 360, 377
  Concerto for Double Bass, 25
Koval, Marian, xix, 138n, 210n, 213, 217–18, 220–1, 266, 278, 285–7, 295, 302, 306, 360
  'Beyond the seas and mountains' ('*Za moryami, za goramï*'), 278, 285–6
  'The Factory' ('*Zavod*'), 213
  'In Siberia' ('*V Sibiri*'), 306
  'The Komsomol Girl,' ('*Komsomolka*'), 306
  '*Rvanïye-shershavïye*', 213
  'The Song of the Builders' (*Pesnya stroiteley*), 213
  'Urchin' ('*Besprizornïy*'), 306
  'Weaver Girl' ('*Tkachikha-chelnochikha*'), 306

Koval, Marian, *continued*
  'The Wind is Rapping at the Window' ('*Za oknom stuchitsya veter*'), 306
  'The Wings of the Soviets' ('*Krïlya Sovetov*'), 306
Kovalenko, Mariya, 62&n
Kovalyov, P. I., 87–8, 101
Kozintsev, Grigoriy, 308&n
Kramarov, 140
Krasin, Boris, 10, 15, 57–8, 73, 155, 162n, 173, 360
Krasin, Leonid, 57, 155, 360
Krein, Aleksandr, 26, 79, 86–7, 175, 177–8, 295, 360–1
Krein, Grigoriy, 26, 107, 361
Krenek, Ernst, xxv, 134, 158, 168, 181, 205, 208, 214–15, 223–4, 233, 235, 273n, 361
  The Dictator, 205
  The Heavyweight, 205
  Johnny spielt auf, 181, 205, 214–16, 224–5, 233
  Piano Concerto, 158
  Der Sprung über den Schatten, xxv, 181, 205, 208, 214–15
  Violin Concerto, 158
Kruchenykh, Aleksey, 136, 361
Kruchinin, Valentin, 282, 318&n, 356, 361
Krupskaya, Nadezhda, xxiv, 5, 56n, 361
Krylova, Sarra, 136, 361
Kryzhanovsky, Ivan, 41, 361
Kryuchkov, P. P., 321
Kryukov, Nikolay, 284, 361
Kryukov, Vladimir, 134, 284, 361
Kubatsky, Viktor, xiii, 7–8, 295, 361
Kuchka, the, xvi, 225, 269, 315, 332, 362, 375
Kuklin, Nikolay, 123&n
Kuper, Emil', 5, 8–9, 22, 58–60, 63, 73, 362
Kurilko, Mikhail, 193–4 (193n)
Kustodiev, Boris, 40, 362
Kuzmin, Mikhail, 55, 362
Kuznetsova, Mariya, 216&n

Lamm, Ol'ga, 87
Lamm, Pavel, xiii, 26, 28n, 42n, 56n, 85–90, 101, 104–7, 111n, 134n, 140, 159, 200–2, 227n, 284, 293, 362, 368
Langovaya, Natal'ya, *see* Roslavets, Natal'ya
Langovoy, Aleksandr, 101, 371
Lapitsky, Iosif, 39, 122, 362
Lashchilin, Lev, 193&n
LASM, 159, 182, 202, 342
Lasso, Orlando di, 91, 362
Lavrenyov, Boris, 269, 273n, 362
Lazarev, Mikhail, 142, 176, 178
  'Strike with the Hammer' ('*Bey molotom*'), 142

Lebedev, Vladimir, 144&n
Lebedev-Polyansky, Pavel, 10, 362–3
Lebedinsky, Lev, 136–7, 164, 176, 218–22, 277–83, 291, 317, 319, 321, 361–3
LEF, 175, 342, 357, 365
Left Opposition/United Opposition, xxiv, xxvi, 50, 89, 111, 164, 187, 197, 377
Lenin, Vladimir, xiv, xxi, xxiii–xxiv, 2–3, 6, 9–10, 41–5, 57–9, 68–70, 89, 100, 103n, 116, 131, 136–9, 192, 213, 286, 348, 350–1, 354, 356–8, 364–5, 372–4, 376, 379–80
Leningrad/Petrograd/St Petersburg Conservatoire, xxi, 7, 20, 56, 182, 264, 284, 318, 311n, 348, 350–1, 353, 355, 357–8, 362, 365, 367–70, 372, 376–7
Lentulov, Aristarkh, 9, 363
Leontyev, Leonid, 46–9 (47n)
Leskov, Nikolay, 225, 331–2, 363
Lesueur, Jean-François, 337&n
Levin, Aleksandr, 172&n
Levina, Zara, 138n, 210n, 317&n, 319n, 363
Levinson, Andrey, 46
'light genre', 98, 165, 261, 275–6, 296
Liszt, Franz, 77, 142, 350, 374
'Lyon' from *Années de Pèlerinage*, 142
Litinsky, Genrikh, 319&n, 363
Litolff, Henry Charles, 40, 363
Robespierre, 40
Litovsky, Osaf, 271
Litvinov, 67
Lobachev, Grigoriy, 100, 363
'The Fighting Lenin Song' (*Boyevaya Leninskaya*), 100
'Ilyich Lives' ('*Zhiv Il'yich*'), 100
Lobanova, Marina, x, 101n
Lopukhov, Fyodor, 90, 110, 140, 226, 363
Dances in *For Red Petrograd*, 140
Red Whirlwind (*Krasnïy vikhr'*), 109–10
The Nutcracker, 226
Dance Symphony (*Tantssimfoniya*), 90
LOSPS, 239–40, 342
Lossky, Nikolay, 69n
Lossky, Vladimir, 109, 363
Lourié, Artur, xii, xxi, 5–8, 26–7, 29, 31, 38, 41, 57, 79, 101, 114&n, 345, 358, 363, 368
Forms in the Air, 6
Our March (*Nash Marsh*), 6–8
Loyter, Elizaveta, 176&n
Lukin, Lev, 90, 364
Lully, Jean-Baptiste de, 337&n
Lunacharsky, Anatoliy, xii, xvi–xviii, xxiii, xxvi, 2–8, 10–11, 23–4, 38–9, 41, 43–4, 54–8, 65, 69–71, 75, 89, 101, 105–6, 115, 140–1, 158, 160–6, 174–6, 179–80, 193, 204–5, 208, 219–24, 226, 228, 266, 292, 300, 349, 350, 352, 356, 364, 369, 379
Lyapunov, Sergey, 59, 364

Lysenko, Trofim, 44, 364
Lyukom, Yelena, 50&n

MacDonald, Ramsay, 87, 116, 364
Mahler, Gustav, 73, 232, 236, 353, 358, 364, 373, 375, 377–8
Symphony No. 5, 73
Maksimenkov, Leonid, xviii
Malevich, Kazimir, xii
Malinovskaya, Yelena, 5, 268, 295, 361, 364
Malinovsky, Pavel, 5, 364
Malipiero, Gian Francesco, 134, 162, 251, 364–5
Autumnal Preludes (*Preludi autunnali*), 162
Malko, Nikolay, 59, 158–9, 173, 181, 202, 269, 275–6, 323n, 355
Malkov, Nikolay, 120, 143, 365
Maly, the (Mikhailovsky Theatre, The Maly Opera, Akmalïy, Academy Maly Theatre, Malegot), 2, 61, 109, 121–3 (123n), 133, 139, 143–6, 161, 205, 208–9, 214–16, 224, 331, 371, 374
Mamayev, I., 119&n
Mandelshtam, Osip, ix, 365
Mariinsky, the (or the former Mariinsky, GOTOB), xxiv–xxvi, 2, 4, 9, 23–4, 40, 47n, 49n, 50–1, 71, 90, 109, 121n, 123n, 133, 141, 161, 180–1, 199–200, 215n, 226, 247, 269, 298, 319, 323, 349–51, 354, 360, 362–3, 367, 374, 379
Marseillaise, 33, 40, 83, 100, 157, 176, 337
Marx, Karl, 6, 32, 192
Maslakovets, Alla, 159
Massenet, Jules, 72
Manon, 72
Massine (Myasin), Leonide, 243&n
Mastkomdram (Workshop for Communist Dramaturgy), 66&n
Mayakovsky, Vladimir, xxi–xxii, xxvii, 6–7, 9, 57, 179, 255n, 266–7, 280n, 342, 357, 365, 375, 377
150,000,000, xxii, 57
The Bathhouse, 267
'Letter from the writer Vladimir Vladimirovich Mayakovsky to the writer Alexei Maksimovich Gorky', 179
Mystery Bouffe, xxi, 9, 57
'*Stabilizatsiya bïta*', 280
Medtner, Nikolay, xxiii, 26, 78–9, 91, 137, 180, 303, 307, 365
Méhul, Étienne, 337&n
Melkikh, Dmitriy, 107, 160, 177, 365
Quartet, 160
Mendelssohn, Felix, 304
Mepurnov, Georgy, 289&n
Merezhkovsky, Dmitriy, 114, 115n

Meshcheryakov, Nikolay, 102, 365
Messerer, Asaf, 195&n
Messman, Vladimir, 263, 365
Meychik, Mark, 26, 365
Meyerbeer, Giacomo, 72, 143
  Les Huguenots/The Decembrists, 72, 143
Meyerhold, Vsevolod, xii, xvii, xxi, xxvii, 6, 9, 57, 90, 173, 180, 193, 199, 220, 227, 242–3, 255, 264, 268, 270, 278, 290–2, 351, 365–7, 370
  Earth Rampant (Zemlya dïbom), 90
  The Final Battle (Posledniy reshitelnïy), 290
  Give us Europe, Give us a Soviet Europe (D.Ye./D.S.Ye.), 173, 291
  The Government Inspector, xxvi, 255
  Mystery-Bouffe, xxi, 9, 57
  Woe to Wit, 199
Mezhkniga (Mezhdunarodnaya kniga), xxiv, 85, 91, 102, 142, 162, 218, 292, 342
Michel, Louise, 157&n
Milhaud, Darius, 155–7, 160–2, 184, 233, 366, 369, 378
  'Lullaby' and 'Hassidic Song' from op. 86, 157
  Trois Rag Caprices, 157
  Saudades do Brazil, 157
  La création du monde, 157
Mikhailovsky Theatre, *see* Maly
Miller, A., 26
Mironov, 90
Miturich, Pyotr, 6, 366
modernism (musical), xix, 26, 61, 76–7, 79, 89, 91–2, 94, 97, 108, 110–11, 137, 142n, 159–60, 165, 181–2, 184, 188, 198, 210, 225, 230, 268–9, 284, 290, 346, 350, 358, 364, 366, 369, 371, 374, 377
MODPiK, 262–3, 365
Mogilevsky, Aleksandr, 366
Moiseyev, Igor', 195&n
Molotov, Vyacheslav, 321, 366
Monteux, Pierre, 155, 158, 173, 366
MOPR, 142&n, 343
Moscow Conservatoire/Felix Kon Higher Music School, xv, xvii, xxi, xxiv, xxvi–xxvii, 7, 26, 41, 58, 60, 85, 99, 110–12, 114, 116, 118–19, 136–8, 142, 144, 162, 175–6, 185, 203, 205–7, 210, 219, 226–7, 230, 261, 264–6, 286–8, 290n, 293, 300, 310, 314, 316, 319, 321, 340, 343–5, 350–1, 353–4, 356–60, 363, 365, 368–74, 376–8, 380
Moscow Speaking (Govorit Moskva), 277, 292–4, 302
Mosolov, Aleksandr, xxvii, 111, 160, 184, 188–91, 199–200, 226, 260n, 319–21, 366

Mosolov, Aleksandr, *continued*
  Three Children's Scenes, 188
  The Dam (Plotina), 319
  Four Newspaper Advertisements, 190
  Piano Concerto, 199
  Piano Sonata No. 4, 160
  Suite from the ballet *Steel*, 184; *The Iron Foundry*, 184, 198, 320, 322
Mowinckel, Johan Ludwig, 270
Mozart, Wolfgang Amadeus, 8, 76, 133, 158, 322
  Die Entführung aus dem Serail, 133
  Requiem, 8
  Symphony No. 38, 158
Music and October (Muzïka i Oktyabr'), 164
Music and Revolution (Muzïka i revolyutsiya), 136, 164, 188, 206, 228, 352, 360, 374
Music Drama Theatre *(Teatr muzïkal'noy drami)*, 39, 72, 362
Musical Culture (Muzïkal'naya kul'tura), 102–4, 106
Musical Virgin Soil (Muzïkal'naya nov'), 88–9, 102, 104, 113, 130, 132, 220
Musorgsky, Modest, 12, 72, 126, 140, 153, 191, 200–2, 227, 232, 236, 240, 254, 259, 266, 271, 322, 351, 362
  Boris Godunov, xvii, xxvi, 13, 39, 200–2, 254, 271, 351, 362
  Khovanshchina, 266
  The Marriage, 254, 259, 271
  'Rayok', 259
  'The Seminarist', 259
  'Rise, rise, you beautiful sun' ('Tï vzoydi, vzoydi, solntse krasnoye'), 240
  Sorotchinsy Fair, 72
Muzïkal'naya kul'tura, *see* Musical Culture
Muzïkal'naya nov', *see* Musical Virgin Soil
MUZO (The Music Section of Narkompros), xxi, xxiii, 5, 7, 18, 23–4, 26–7, 29–31, 37–8, 41, 57–8, 113–14, 343, 347, 357, 360, 363
Muzsektor Gosizdata (the Music Section of the State Publishing House, Muzgiz), xv, xvii, 85–9, 95, 101–3 (103n), 106, 134, 136–7, 164, 183, 218, 265–6, 289–90, 315, 320, 322, 343, 379
Myaskovsky, Nikolay, xi–xiii, xvi, xviii–xx, xxiv, xxvii, 24n, 26–7, 41, 42n, 56n, 79, 85–6, 88–92, 102, 104–8, 110, 126, 133n, 134–5, 137, 140, 158–60, 175, 177–8, 180, 181n, 183, 184n, 199–200, 217–19, 221, 260, 265–9, 284–7, 289, 292–5, 321, 323, 326, 328, 330, 345, 347, 353, 357, 360–3, 366, 368, 373, 375, 378

Myaskovsky, Nikolay, *continued*
  Cello Sonata, 41
  Idiot (operatic project), 105
  Marches, 266
  Piano Sonata No. 3, 160
  Quartet in D minor, 160
  Symphony No. 1, 362
  Symphony No. 3, 198
  Symphony No. 4, 135
  Symphony No. 5, 42, 108
  Symphony No. 6, xxiv, 108, 159
  Symphony No. 7, 89, 135, 158
  Symphony No. 8, 135
  Symphony No. 9, 198
  Symphony No. 10, 199
  Symphony No. 11, 286
  Symphony No. 12, xix, xxvii, 285–7, 295, 328–30

Nansen, Fridtjof, 163
Napoleon, 337n
Napravnik, Eduard, xiii
  Dubrovsky, xiii
Narkompros, xiii, xviii, xxii–xxiii, 2, 5, 7, 9–10, 18, 23, 26, 29–31, 34, 37, 44, 54, 56, 61, 68–9, 103, 106, 113–16, 171, 203–5, 207, 218, 222, 292–3, 302, 314, 316, 319, 321, 341–3, 345, 349–50, 356–60, 363, 367, 370, 376
Nebolsin, Vasiliy, 26&n, 366
Nelson, Amy, x
Nemirovich-Danchenko, Vladimir, 121, 269, 271–2, 273n, 323, 331, 366–7, 375
Nemirovich-Danchenko Music Theatre, 269, 271–2, 323, 331, 367
Nemtsev, Iosif, 240&n
NEP (New Economic Policy), xii–xvii, xxiii, xxvi, 40, 44, 55–7, 59–60, 67, 69, 73, 85, 88, 90, 95, 98, 105–6, 111, 129, 164, 170, 175, 187, 197, 230, 261, 264n, 298, 318, 324, 343, 358, 366
Nezhdanova, Antonina, 72, 141, 354, 367
Nicholas I, 103, 332
Nicholas II, 10, 161
Nietzsche, Friedrich, 35
Nijinsky, Vaslav, 48&n
Nikisch, Arthur, 63, 73, 367, 371
Nikolayevsky, M., 172&n
Novitsky, Pavel, 162n, 166, 205–7, 367

Obolensky, Leonid, 220–1, 367
OGPU, *see* GPU
Olkhovsky, Yevgeniy, 216&n
Olminsky, Mikhail, 176&n
Olympiad, Third Musical, 238–40
operetta, 25, 61, 108, 211, 216, 278, 288n, 351, 360, 362, 365, 372, 373

Oransky, Viktor, 226, 367
  The Footballer (*Futbolist*), 226, 367
ORKiMD/ORK, xvii–xix, 45, 136, 138, 164–5, 220, 228, 261, 264, 308, 343, 359, 363, 372, 374, 377
Osorgin, Mikhail, 69n
OST, 175, 343
Ostroumov, Sergey, 273&n
Ozolin, Yan (Ozoliņš, Jānis), 32–3 (32n)
  'In memory of Karl Marx' ('*Pamyati Karla Marksa*'), 32
  'The First of May' ('*Pervoye maya*'), 32
  'The Workers' Palace' ('*Rabochiy dvorets*'), 32

Pakelman, 8
Paris Commune, xv, 38, 119–22, 143, 157n
Parnakh, Valentin, 67, 173&n, 367
Partsoveshchaniye, 205, 219, 220n, 221
party resolutions
  1925 Party Resolution on Literature, xxv, 132, 135, 220, 349
  1932 Party Resolution on the Restructuring of Literary and Artistic Organizations, xix, xxvii, 321, 324–7, 339
Parvish, 174
Pashchenko, Andrey, 126, 135, 139–40, 145, 240, 367
  The Eagle Revolt (*Orliniy bunt*/ *Pugachyovshchina*), 139, 145, 240, 367
  Symphony No. 3, 135
Pastukhov, V. L., 31
Paton, 174
Pavlov, Evgeny, 26&n, 107
Pavlovskaya, Valentina, 109, 123, 367
pedotdel/pedfak, 206–7, 314, 343
Pelshe, Robert, 164–5, 367–8
Persimfans, xiv, xxiii, 73, 155, 158, 163–4, 186, 199, 217, 237, 270, 343, 377
Petlikov, 6
Petri, Egon, 108, 133, 368
Petrograd/Leningrad Philharmonic/ Philharmonia, xiii–xiv, xxiii–xxiv, 56, 58–9, 63, 73, 157, 163, 183, 357–8, 374–5
Petrov, N., 13
Petrov, N. V., 144&n
Pilnyak, Boris, 68
Piotrovsky, Adrian, 161, 368
Pirogov, Aleksandr, 109
Pirogov (student composer), 288–9
Pisk, Paul Amadeus, 107, 134, 368
Pletnev, Valerian, 44
Poe, Edgar Allan, 298–9
Pokhitonov, Daniil, 123&n
Pokrass, Dmitriy, 172&n
Pokrovsky, Mikhail, 57, 368

Poletaev, Evgeniy, 6, 368
Polferov, Yakov, 93–4, 368
  R.S.F.S.R., 93–4
Politburo, xxv–vii, 44, 69–70, 111, 162n, 164, 203, 220n, 320–1, 349, 357, 377, 380
Polovinkin, Leonid, 107, 109, 126, 159–60, 184–5, 368
  The Prologue, 184–5
  The Telescope, 159
Poluyanov, 282
Pomorsky, Aleksandr, 32, 33n
Popov, Gavriil, 155, 200, 217, 292, 321, 368
  Septet, 217
Popov, Sergey, 27, 28n, 42, 134, 140, 368
Potekhin, Yuriy, 263&n
Pototsky, Sergey, 269, 368
  Proriv, 269
Poulenc, Francis, 157, 369
  'Attributs' from 5 *Poèmes de Ronsard*, 157
  Suite en trois parties (Suite for Piano), 157
Pravda, xxvi–vii, 11, 44–5, 56n, 57, 86, 89, 95, 116, 175, 177, 192, 198, 204–6, 236, 301, 310, 331, 347–9, 370
Preys, Aleksandr, 331, 369
Prokofiev, Sergey, xi, xiii, xix–xxi, xxv, 25, 76, 78, 88–9, 91, 92n, 97, 108, 110, 136–7, 142&n, 150–4, 156n, 157–9, 161–3, 178–80, 182–3, 186, 193, 198n, 200, 202n, 204, 208, 210, 217–18, 227, 228n, 242–3, 245–53, 258, 266–9, 270n, 285, 286n, 303–4, 307, 320, 323, 334–5, 339–40, 345–6, 351, 354, 357, 362, 365–6, 369, 373, 376
  Cantata for the Twentieth Anniversary of October, 210
  Chout (*The Tale of the Buffoon*), 158, 179, 199, 217, 245–6, 258, 345, 366
  The Gambler, 199, 204
  Jewish Overture, 91, 142&n
  Love for Three Oranges, xxv, 158, 161, 180–1, 194, 208, 215n, 217, 258, 268, 351
  Piano Concerto No. 1, 217
  Piano Concerto No. 3, 91, 136, 150–4, 159, 334
  Piano Sonata No. 2, 25–6
  Piano Sonata No. 3, 25–6
  Quintet, 179
  Scythian Suite, 97, 179
  Steps of Steel/*Pas d'acier* (*Stal'noy skok*), 110, 199, 217–18, 242–3, 246–52, 268, 340
  Symphony No. 2, 150, 200
  Violin Concerto No. 1, 108, 376
  Visions fugitives, 26
  Sarcasms, 26
Prokofieva, Lina, 180, 186

Prokoll, xxvi, 138, 160, 165, 175–6, 185, 210, 217–18, 221, 344, 347, 350–1, 360, 371, 373, 378
The Path of October, xxvi, 185, 210–12
Proletarian Musician (*Proletarskiy muzïkant*), 218, 226, 261, 275–6, 288–9, 301–2, 314, 316, 320
Proletkult, xiii–xiv, xxi–xxii, 9–11, 15–17, 29, 32–3, 37, 42–5, 57–8, 66, 70, 88, 97, 111, 165–6, 204, 219, 238, 288, 290, 344, 347–8, 360, 362–3, 374
Protopopov, Sergey, 58, 134, 142n, 160, 369n, 379
Prussak, Yevgeniy, xxv, 139–40, 143–6, 354
  For Red Petrograd, xxv, 139–40, 143–6
Pshibïshevsky, Boleslav, 227, 265, 289–90, 318–19, 322, 369
Puccini, Giacomo, 109, 120–3, 143, 369
  La bohème, 39, 72, 369
  Tosca (*The Struggle for the Commune*), 109, 120–3, 143, 369
Pudovkin, Vsevolod, xxvi
Pugni, Cesare, 195, 196n
  La Esmeralda, 195
Punin, Nikolay, 5–6, 345, 368–9
PUR, 99, 343
Pushkin, Aleksandr, 13, 201n
Putin, Vladimir, 2, 369

Rabfak, 99, 130, 265, 314, 378
Rabinovich, Isaak Moiseyevich, 180, 369
Rabinovich, I. S., 119&n, 290&n
Rabis/Vserabis, xiii, 106, 119, 140, 161, 220, 222, 226, 317, 344
Rachmaninov, Sergey, xiii, xxi, 73, 78, 109, 170–1, 216n, 287–9, 298–300, 303–4, 307, 346, 365, 369, 372, 374, 376
  All-Night Vigil, 170–1
  The Bells, 287, 298–300
Radek, Karl, 38, 370
Radio Committee, 290, 292–4, 302, 358, 368
Radlov, Sergey, 133, 160, 370
Rafail, M., 239&n
Rafalovich, Vasiliy, 318&n
RAKhN, *see* GAKhN
RAPM (APM, VAPM), xii–xiii, xv–xix, xxiv, xxvii, 15, 45, 85–91, 95, 97, 99–102, 110, 113, 119, 127–32, 135–6, 147, 160, 164–6, 175–6, 184–5, 188, 204, 217–24, 226–8, 230, 242, 253, 261–70, 275, 277, 279–99, 301–3, 305, 307, 309–11, 313–24, 326–8, 339, 341, 343, 344, 346–51, 357–8, 360–1, 363, 366, 371–4, 378, 380
RAPP, xxvii, 96n, 132, 218, 272n, 285, 292–4, 320, 324&n, 325, 341, 344–7
Rashnovskaya, 318, 319n

Raskolnikov, Fyodor, xxvi, 224, 227, 370
Ravel, Maurice, 134, 172&n, 231–2, 304, 370–1, 378
Raysky, Nazariy, 205–7, 264–5, 370
Rebikov, Vladimir, xxii, 61–3, 76, 370
  The Abyss (*Bezdna*), 61
  The Christmas Tree (*Yolka*), 61–2
Red Professors Faction, xxiv, 110–12, 114, 118–19, 134, 230, 349, 373
Redepenning, Dorothea, x
Reger, Max, 91, 348
  Trio for Flute, Violin and Viola, 91
  Suite in the Old Style, 91
Remizov, Aleksey, 55, 63, 68n, 368
  Fiery Russia (*Ognennaya Rossiya*), 63
Renzin, Isay, 159, 370
Rieti, Vittorio, 162, 371
  Concerto for flute, oboe and clarinet, 162
Rimsky-Korsakov, Andrey, 159, 371
Rimsky-Korsakov, Nikolay, xvii 9, 20n, 24. 31n, 39, 75, 78–9, 93, 140, 142 146, 159, 161, 182, 200–2, 232, 236, 304, 334, 345, 350, 354, 356–8, 361–2, 367, 371, 376, 378, 380
  Boris Godunov (revision of Musorgsky's opera), 200–2
  The Golden Cockerel, 9, 39, 216
  Kashchei the Immortal, 24
  The Maid of Pskov, 9, 24
  Sadko, 25, 39–40
  The Snow Maiden, 304
  The Tale of Tsar Saltan, 39
  The Tale of the Invisible City of Kitezh, 161
  The Tsar's Bride, 25, 39, 72
Roger-Ducasse, Jean, 158, 371
  Orpheus, 158
Rolland, Romain, 94
Romanov, A., 202
Romanov, Panteleymon, 192
Rosfil, 133, 157, 160, 163–4, 170–2, 178, 198, 344, 360
Roslavets, Natal'ya/'Communist', 101–2, 113, 116–17, 264, 371
Roslavets, Nikolay, xv, 26, 76, 79, 86, 101–3 106–7, 113, 134, 137, 160, 184–5, 220, 264–5, 371
  Quartet No. 1, 160
  October, 184–5
Rossini, Gioachino, 39, 72
  The Barber of Seville, 39, 72
Royzman, Matvey, 67&n
  Red Alcohol (*Krasnïy alkogol'*), 67
Rozhdestvensky, Nikolay, 144&n
Rubinstein, Anton: *The Demon*, 39, 72
Ruzer, Leonid, 103&n
RVSR, 68, 343
Ryauzov, Sergey, 138n, 210n, 211, 371

Ryazanov, Pyotr, 318&n
Rykov, Aleksey, 161, 197, 371

Sabaneyev, Leonid, 37, 57, 65, 75, 86, 88, 97, 107, 111, 371
'Sadko', *see* Blyum, Vladimir
Saint-Saëns, Camille, 25
  Samson and Dalila, 25
Samosud, Samuil, 146, 181, 371
Saradzhev, Konstantin, 159–60, 351, 371
Saratovsky, Pyotr, 273&n
Sardou, Victorien, 122
Satie, Erik, 157, 371, 378
  Trois morceaux en forme de poire, 157
Savelyev-Damurin, Vasiliy, 273&n
Savenko, Svetlana, x, 162n
Savich, Vladimir, 199
Savinkov, Boris, 115n
Schillinger, Iosif, 158, 183–4, 371
  October, 183–4
  The Tread of the East (*Postup' Vostoka*), 158
Schmidt, Otto, 103–4 (103n)
Schnabel, Artur, 108, 133, 198, 352, 356, 372
Schoenberg, Arnold, 76, 79, 89, 91, 107, 134, 160, 199, 209n, 230–1, 235–6, 347, 368, 372, 375, 378
  6 Songs, op. 3, 91
  8 Songs, op. 6, 91
  Das Buch der Hängenden Gärten, 107
  Gurre-Lieder, 199, 231
  Quartet No. 2, 107
  Pelleas und Melisande, 231
Schreker, Franz, xxv, 133, 368, 372
  Der Ferne Klang, xxv, 133, 372
Schubert, Franz, 196n, 372
Schumann, Robert, 315
Scott, Cyril, 134, 372
Scriabin, Aleksandr, 9, 26, 34–5, 38, 63–4, 73–8, 89–90, 97–8, 101, 110, 137, 158, 160–1, 184, 243–4, 264, 303, 357, 371–2, 374, 376, 380
  The Mysterium, 36, 372
  Preparatory Act, 36
  Prometheus, 9, 35, 372
  Piano Sonata No. 3, 26
  Piano Sonata No. 5, 26
  Piano Sonata No. 9, 26
  Piano Sonata No. 10, 26
  Poem of Ecstasy, 63, 73
  Symphonic Poem in D minor, 158
Selitsky, Viktor, 314n, 316&n
Serapion Brothers, the, 68&n
Serge (Serzh, Kibalchich), Victor, 50
Sergeyev, Aleksey, 88, 95–7, 102, 106, 113, 114n, 136, 164, 220, 264, 372

Serov, Aleksandr, 24, 40
 The Power of the Fiend, 24, 40
Severyanin, Igor', 136, 372
Shakhty Trial, the, xxvi, 197
Shaporin, Yuriy, 141, 160, 181, 202n, 240, 372
 The Decembrists/Pauline Gebl, 141
 The Storming of Perekop (*Shturm Perekopa*), 240
Shaposhnikov, Adrian, 26&n
Sharonov, Vasiliy, 123&n
Shatsky, Stanislav, 319, 321, 372
Shaumyan, Stepan, 274
Shcherbachov (Shcherbachyov), Vladimir, 59, 135, 182, 199, 357, 373, 380
 Piano Sonata No. 2, 135
 Symphony No. 2, 135, 199
 Vïdumki, 135
Shebalin, Vissarion, 91, 159, 175, 177, 266, 267n, 270, 284, 292, 295, 321–2, 326, 339, 373
 Symphony No. 1, 159
 Symphony No. 2, 295
Shekhter, Boris, 136–8, 165n, 176, 178, 210n, 212, 218, 221, 292, 318, 321–2, 373
 'On the Rails' (*'Na rel'sakh'*), 212
 Piano Sonata No. 1, 137
 Piano Sonata No. 2, 138
Shenshin, Aleksandr, 105, 107, 285, 373
Sherman, Nikolay, 111, 119, 373
Shershenevich, Vadim, 67&n
 Red Alcohol (*Krasnïy alkogol'*), 67
Shirinsky, Sergey, 107, 371
Shirinsky, Vasiliy, 107, 134, 160, 285, 373
Shishov, Ivan, 225, 373
 The Wig Maker (*Tupeynïy khudozhnik*), 225
Shostakovich, Dmitriy, xi, xvi, xviii–xix, xxv–xvi, 32, 110, 135, 155, 158–9, 182–4, 186, 200, 204, 217, 224–5, 243, 253–60, 265, 268, 270, 273n, 275–6, 293–7, 308–9, 321–3, 326, 331–4, 347, 357, 360, 363–5, 368, 373–4
 Aphorisms, 217, 253, 257
 Alone (*Odna*), 270, 308–9
 Lady Macbeth of the Mtsensk District, xviii–xix, 273n, 322–3, 331–4, 363, 369
 The Golden Age, 110, 275, 296–7
 The Nose, xix, 204, 224–5, 253–60, 268, 322, 332, 369, 373
 Piano Concerto No. 1, 217
 Piano Sonata No. 1, 181
 Symphony No. 1, xxv, 155, 158, 183, 253
 Symphony No. 2 ('To October'), xvi, xxvi, 32, 183–4, 253, 333
 Symphony No. 3 ('First of May'), 268, 333

Shostakovich, Dmitriy, *continued*
 'Tahiti Trot', 253, 275, 278
 Two pieces for string octet, 181
Shterenberg, David, 6, 343, 373
Shteynberg, Maksimilian, 135, 158–60, 182, 202, 321, 367, 373–4
 Heaven and Earth (*Nebo i zemlya*), 135
Shtrassenburg, Stanislav, 225, 374
 Taiga, 225
Shulgin, Lev, xi, xvi, 88, 95–6, 100, 102, 135–8, 164, 183, 188, 228–9, 266n, 350, 374
Shulgina, Yelena, 136, 228–9
Sibor, Boris, 133, 374
Siloti, Aleksandr, 4, 374
Siver, Mirra, 176&n
Six, Les, 107, 198, 346, 355, 366, 369, 371, 378
Slavinsky, Yu. M., 106&n
Smirnov, Dmitriy, 157, 374
Smirnov, N. I., 292–3
Smithy, the (*Kuznitsa*), 90, 96&n, 324n
Smolich, Nikolay, 215&n
Sobinov, Leonid, 5, 72, 374
Socialist Realism, ix, xvi, 104, 141, 175, 315, 323–4, 328, 355, 362, 366, 373, 377–8, 384
Sofil, 198
Sofronitsky, Vladimir, 59, 374
Sollertinsky, Ivan, 214, 225, 243n, 253, 270, 293, 294n, 374
Sologub, Fyodor, 11n, 39, 68n, 374
Somov, Konstantin, 41, 374
Sorokin, Pitirim, 69n
Sovetskaya muzïka, 321, 323, 360
Spassky, Sergey, 121&n, 145, 375
SRs (Socialist Revolutionaries), xxi, 10, 68, 185, 264, 371
Stalin, Joseph, xvii–xviii, xxiii–xxv, xxvii, 37, 45, 50, 68, 90, 100, 110, 140–1, 164, 187, 194n, 197, 201, 203, 205, 220&n, 224–5, 229, 232, 239n, 253, 272n, 286, 291–3, 301n, 305n, 314–22, 331, 339, 341, 347, 349, 353–4, 357, 360–2, 364–6, 369–72, 375–80
Stanislavsky, Konstantin, 25, 72, 110, 205, 366–7, 375
Stanislavsky Studio, 25, 205, 269, 365
Starokadomsky, Mikhail, 266, 285, 375
Stasov, Vladimir, xvi, 100–1, 200, 375
State Collection of Musical Instruments, xiii, xxii, 3, 7–8
Stefan, Paul, 107, 375
Stetsky, Aleksey, 202, 321n, 375
Stiedry, Fritz, 133, 158, 375
Stites, Richard, xiv
Stockhausen, Karlheinz, 6

Stradivari Quartet, xiii, 8, 41, 91, 160, 346, 361, 366
Strauss, Johann, Jr., 148, 268, 375
Strauss, Richard, 41, 76, 100, 214, 232, 367, 375
  Also sprach Zarathustra, 214
  Salomé, xxiv, 109, 133, 204, 367
  Tod und Verklärung, 100
Stravinsky, Igor', xiii, xxii, xxv, 8, 31n, 40, 46–9, 79, 91, 97, 108, 110, 135, 153, 156, 158, 161–3 (162n), 217–18, 243–7, 251–2, 257, 303–5, 307, 333, 345, 349, 351, 357, 363–4, 366, 375
  Firebird Suite, 8
  L'histoire du soldat, 153
  Mavra, 158, 217, 257, 333
  The Nightingale, 31n, 123n
  Les Noces, 153, 158
  Oedipus Rex, 144n, 217
  Petrushka, xxii, 40, 46–9, 217, 244–5, 247, 254n, 302–5, 364, 375
  Piano Rag-Music, 135
  Piano Concerto, 217
  Piano Sonata, 156, 162
  Pulcinella, 161, 217
  Ragtime, 158
  The Rite of Spring, 97, 158, 252, 364, 375
  The Song of the Nightingale, 158
  Three Pieces for String Quartet, 91
Strelnikov, Nikolay, 61, 181, 375
Sumarokov, Aleksandr, 168&n
Sverdlov, Yakov, 26, 375–6
Svidersky, Aleksey, 221, 224, 370, 376
Synodal School/Choral Academy/Choir xxii, 7, 26, 136, 166, 170, 240n, 355, 357–9, 372
Szigeti, Joseph, 108, 133, 155, 198, 376
Szymanowski, Karol, 91, 107, 376
  Violin Sonata, op. 9, 91
  Myths, 91
  Songs, 91

Tagore, Rabindranath, 162, 287, 348
Tairov, Aleksandr, 90, 376
Taneyev, Sergey, 25, 73, 79, 91, 210, 345, 364, 368, 376
  Oresteia, 25
Tarnopolsky, Vladimir, 138n, 210n, 212
Tatlin, Vladimir, 6, 376
Tchaikovsky, Pyotr, 39–40, 65–6, 72, 77, 79, 89, 100, 109, 135, 151, 226, 269, 322, 332, 334, 356, 356
  Eugene Onegin, 39, 61, 72, 332
  Marche Slave, 65–6
  Mazepa, 72
  The Nutcracker, 226
  Piano Concerto No. 1, 151

Tchaikovsky, Pyotr, *continued*
  The Queen of Spades, xiii, 25, 39, 135, 334
  Swan Lake, 40
  Symphony No. 6, *Pathétique*, 65, 100, 135
Tcherepnin, Aleksandr, 91, 134, 376
Tcherepnin, Nikolay, 8, 349, 351, 357–8, 363, 370, 376
Termen, Lev, *see* Theremin, Lev
Theremin, Lev, xxiii, 59–60, 376
Tikhomirov, Vasiliy, 193&n, 195, 354
Tikhonova, 280&n
Toch, Ernst, 158, 376
  Chinese Flute, 158
Tolstoy, Aleksey, 68
Tolstoy, Leo, 12, 372
Towards New Shores of Music (K novïm beregam muzïkal'nogo iskusstva), xxiv, 86, 88–9, 91
TRAM, 309, 371
Trauberg, Leonid, 308&n
Tretyakov, Sergey, 304
Triodin, Pyotr, 109, 377
  Prince Serebryany (Knyaz' Serebryanïy), 109
Trotsky, Lev, xxiv–xxvi, 68, 89–90, 103–4, 112, 115, 132, 161, 164, 186–8, 195, 197, 205, 272n, 357, 370–1, 377
  Literature and Revolution, 115
Trubetskoy, Sergey, 69n
Tseitlin, Lev, 73, 119, 377
Tsereteli, Tamara, 304&n
Tsetetis, 217
Tsfasman, Aleksandr, 278&n, 282
Tsïganov, Dmitriy, 107, 377
TsIK (VTsIK), 163n. 186n, 203&n, 344
Tsïperovich, Grigoriy, 21&n
Tsukker, Arnold, 186&n, 377
Tyulin, Yuriy, 318&n

UAPM, 296
Unger, Heinz, 270, 377
Union of Composers, xix–xx, 262, 321, 323, 346, 350, 354, 360
Universal Edition, 108, 181, 320
Usachin, 103
Utkin, Iosif, 232, 236, 269, 303–4, 377

VAPM, *see* RAPM
Varlamov, Aleksandr, 333
Varunts, Viktor, x
Vasilenko, Sergey, 107, 196, 225, 359, 368, 377
  Iosif Prekrasnïy, 196
  Son of the Sun (Sïn solntsa), 225
Vasilyev-Buglay, Dmitro, 88, 135, 321, 377
Vaulin, A. P., 31
VChK, *see* Cheka

Veprik, Aleksandr, *see* Weprik, Aleksandr
Verdi, Giuseppe, 1–2, 25, 39, 72, 108, 133
  Aida, 25, 39, 133
  Don Carlos, 1–2
  Rigoletto, 72
  La Traviata, 25, 72
Verlaine, Paul, 192
Vertinsky, Aleksandr, 137
Vertov, Dziga, xxvi
Veysberg, Yulia, 159–60, 378
Vinogradov, Nikolay (Mamont), 121–2 (121n)
Vinogradov, Viktor, 265, 266n, 378
Vishnevsky, Vsevolod, 290–1, 378
Vishnya, S. I., 144&n
Vivaldi, Antonio, 162, 378
Vlasova, Ekaterina, x
VOAPP, 324–5 (324n)
Voroshilov, Kliment, xxv
Voykov, Pyotr, 186–7, 378
Vrubel, Mikhail, 63–4 (63n)
Vseroskomdram, 263–4, 285, 292, 294–5, 314, 316, 318, 344, 346
Vsevolodsky, Vsevolod, 138&n
Vygodsky, Nikolay, 210, 298, 301, 378

Wagner, Richard, 23–5, 34–6, 39, 63, 75, 77–9, 100, 108, 123n, 141, 151, 158, 161, 232, 236, 322, 374, 379
  Lohengrin, 5, 39, 374
  Die Meistersinger, 24, 158, 161
  Parsifal, 141, 236
  The Ring of the Nibelungs, 36; *Götterdämmerung*, 63, 100; *Die Walküre*, xiii, 22, 25, 34
  Tannhäuser, 24
  Tristan und Isolde, 151, 266
Walter, Bruno, 108, 378
War Communism, xiii, 59, 67, 72–3, 197
Weber, Wolfgang, 233
Webern, Anton, 134, 375
Weprik (Veprik), Aleksandr, 111, 119, 134–5, 230–3, 236, 378
  Five Little Pieces for Orchestra, 232
  Songs and Dances of the Ghetto, 232
Wiener, Jean, 155–7, 367, 378–9
  Deux blues chantés, 157
  Trois blues, 157
  Sonate en trois parties, 157

Wilde, Oscar, 64, 181
  Salomé, 64
Withers, Frank, 173&n

Yakobson, G., 62
Yakobson, Miron 306
Yakovlev, Yakov, 44
Yakulov, Georgiy, 246&n
Yaroslavsky, 301
Yasinsky, Ieronim, 32, 33n
Yavorsky, Boleslav, 58, 103, 119n, 134, 142n, 157n, 160, 162–3 (163n), 182n, 186n, 269–70, 290n, 349, 357, 368, 369, 379
  Vishka Oktyabrya, 269–70, 379
Yeltsin, Boris, 2, 379
Yershov, Ivan, 59, 109, 140, 379
Yesenin, Sergey, 26n, 33&n, 42, 67n, 84n, 188–9 (189n), 352, 377, 379
Yudenich, Nikolay, xxii, 24, 139, 143, 145, 379
Yudin, Mikhail, 318&n
Yudina, Mariya, 59, 158–9, 379
Youmans, Vincent, 275
Yurasovsky, Aleksandr, 108, 379
  Trilby, 108, 376
Yurovsky, Aleksandr, 87, 101, 103–4, 106, 179, 206, 265, 379

Zagorsky, M. B., 65
Zamyatin, Yevgeniy, 68n, 379
Zemlinsky, Alexander von, 209&n
Zhilyayev, Nikolay, 134&n, 265, 380
Zhitomirsky, Aleksandr, 202, 380
Zhitomirsky, Daniel', 253, 260, 380
Zhivotov, Aleksey, 217, 380
  Nonet, 217
Zhizn' iskusstva, 18, 61, 120, 166, 193, 214, 348, 365
Zimin, Sergey, 22, 72, 109, 380
Zimin Opera (former Zimin Opera, Malaya Opera), 9, 23, 25, 39, 72, 109, 356–7, 377
Zinoviev, Grigoriy, xxiv–xxvi, 7, 45, 50–1, 164, 357, 364, 377, 380
Zolotaryov, Vasiliy, 140–1, 380
  The Decembrists, 140–1, 380
Zorin, Sergey, 51&n
Zoshchenko, Mikhail, 68, 380